MASTERS OF ART

LEONARDO DA VINCI

Artist, inventor and scientist of the Renaissance

FRANCESCA ROMEI

ILLUSTRATED BY

SERGIO, AND ANDREA RICCIARDI

PETER BEDRICK BOOKS
NTC/Contemporary Publishing Group
NEW YORK

DoGi

Produced by
Donati-Giudici Associati, Florence
Text
Francesca Romei
Illustrations
Sergio
Andrea Ricciardi
Editorial coordination
Francesco Fiorentino
Art direction and design
Oliviero Ciriaci
Research
Francesca Donati
Editing
Enza Fontana
Pagination
Monica Macchiaioli
Desktop publishing
Ugo Micheli
English translation
Simon Knight
Editor, English-language edition
Ruth Nason
Typesetting
Ken Alston – A.J. Latham Ltd.

This edition published
in the United States in 2000
by Peter Bedrick Books
A division of NTC/Contemporary
Publishing Group, Inc.
4255 West Touhy Avenue
Lincolnwood (Chicago)
Illinois 60712-1975 U.S.A.

ISBN: 0-87226-640-0

Photolitho:
Venanzoni DTP, Firenze

Printed in Italy in 2000
by *Eurolitho*
Cesano Boscone, Milano

◆ HOW THE INFORMATION IS PRESENTED

ILLUSTRATED PAGES

Every double-page spread is devoted to a particular theme. The main illustration is a faithful reconstruction of a given environment, or represents a significant incident or event.

The text at the top of the left-hand page interprets this illustration. The text in italics gives a chronological account of developments in Leonardo's life. The other material (photographs, paintings, drawings, artefacts) enlarges on the central theme.

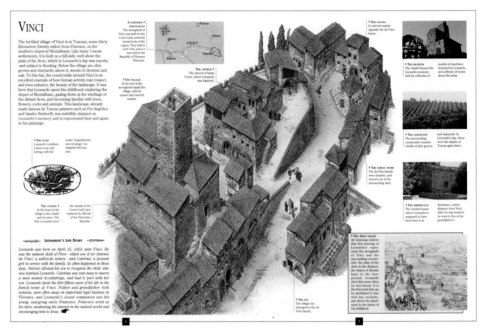

PAGES DEVOTED TO WORKS OF ART

Some pages focus on the great works of art created by Leonardo. They include background information about the painting, in the left-hand column; a description of the work, at the top; a detailed

analysis of certain aspects of the work; an explanation of its significance and the technical problems involved, in italics; and comparisons with works by other artists, which highlight the historical context and the originality of Leonardo's approach to the subject.

CONTENTS

CONTEMPORARIES

Born in Tuscany in the mid-fifteenth century, Leonardo da Vinci excelled in painting, sculpture, music, mathematics, engineering and architecture. In the wealthy and cultured city of Florence he was apprenticed to one of the outstanding artists of the time, Andrea del Verrocchio. During his life he came into contact with some of the key figures of European politics: Lorenzo the Magnificent, ruler of Florence; Ludovico il Moro, lord of Milan; the Pope; and two kings of France. Of the artists and scientists of the Renaissance, Leonardo was the one who best summed up the new culture. He represents a new understanding of the world, and of man's capacity to penetrate the mysteries of nature and the human mind.

✦ **LEONARDO'S FATHER AND MOTHER**
His father, ser Piero di Antonio, was a well-known notary; his mother, Caterina, was a peasant girl in service with the family.

✦ **FILIPPO BRUNELLESCHI**
(1377-1446)
The greatest Florentine architect of the Renaissance.

MASACCIO ✦
(1401-1428)
Tuscan painter, the first artist to use perspective systematically.

SANDRO BOTTICELLI ✦
(1445-1510)
Florentine painter. Like Leonardo, he trained in Verrocchio's workshop.

MICHELANGELO ✦ **BUONARROTI**
(1475-1564)
Sculptor, painter, architect and poet. A great Italian artist.

DONATO BRAMANTE ✦
(1444-1514)
Architect and painter. With Leonardo, he served Ludovico il Moro, lord of Milan.

✦ **ZOROASTRO**
Skilled in mechanics, and metal work, he made models for Leonardo's designs.

✦ **LEONARDO**
Often portrayed with a long beard, Leonardo was described by his contemporaries as outstandingly good-looking.

✦ **ANDREA DEL VERROCCHIO** (1435-1488) Goldsmith, sculptor and painter. Leonardo was trained in his workshop.

✦ **LUCA PACIOLI**
(1445-1514)
Franciscan friar and man of science. He knew Leonardo in Milan, and awakened his interest in mathematics.

FRANCESCO MELZI ✦
(1493-1570)
Leonardo's favorite pupil. He followed his master to France and, on his death, inherited his manuscripts and paintings.

♦ **Niccolò Machiavelli**
Writer, philosopher and political theorist. He was secretary to the Florentine Republic after the fall of the Medicis.

♦ **Piero Soderini**
Head of the Florentine Republic. He commissioned important works from Leonardo.

♦ **Isabella d'Este**
Marchioness of Mantua. Leonardo drew her portrait in 1499.

♦ **Louis XII**
King of France from 1498 to 1515. He conquered Lombardy in 1499 and commissioned several works of art from Leonardo.

♦ **Raffaello Sanzio (Raphael)** (1483-1520)
Painter and architect. With Leonardo and Michelangelo, he is considered the greatest Italian artist of the period.

♦ **Ludovico il Moro**
Ruler of Milan. In 1482 he invited Leonardo to live at his court.

♦ **Cecilia Gallerani**
Ludovico il Moro's mistress and a key figure at the Sforza court. She protected Leonardo, and he painted a famous portrait of her.

Charles of Amboise ♦
Governor of Milan in the early years of the sixteenth century. Leonardo planned a palace for him in Milan, but it was never built.

♦ **Lorenzo the Magnificent**
Head of the Medici family. He ruled the city of Florence during a period of great cultural and artistic brilliance.

♦ **Francis I**
He succeeded Louis XII as king of France. In 1517 he invited Leonardo to France, and gave him a splendid manor house to live in.

VINCI

The fortified village of Vinci is in Tuscany, some thirty kilometres (twenty miles) from Florence, on the southern slopes of Montalbano. Like many Tuscan settlements, it is built on a hill-side, well above the plain of the Arno, which in Leonardo's day was marshy and subject to flooding. Below the village are olive groves and vineyards; above it, woods of chestnut and oak. To this day, the countryside around Vinci is an excellent example of how human activity may respect, and even enhance, the beauty of the landscape. It was here that Leonardo spent his childhood: exploring the slopes of Montalbano, gazing down at the windings of the distant Arno, and becoming familiar with trees, flowers, rocks and animals. This landscape, already made famous by Tuscan painters such as Fra Angelico and Sandro Botticelli, was indelibly stamped on Leonardo's memory and is represented time and again in his paintings.

♦ A FORTIFIED STRONGHOLD
The stronghold of Vinci was built by the Conti Guidi, powerful feudal lords of the region. They held it until 1254, when it was sold to the Republic of Florence (Firenze).

THE CHURCH ♦
The church of Santa Croce, where Leonardo was baptized.

♦ THE VILLAGE
At the foot of the stronghold stands the village, with its square and covered market.

♦ THE PLOW
Leonardo's emblem: a plow in an oval setting, with the motto "impedimento non mi piega" (no obstacle will stop me).

THE CITADEL ♦
At the heart of the village is the citadel and its tower. The first occupants were the vassals of the Conti Guidi, later replaced by officials of the Florentine Republic.

LEONARDO'S LIFE STORY

Leonardo was born on April 15, 1452, near Vinci. He was the natural child of Piero - eldest son of ser Antonio da Vinci, a well-to-do notary - and Caterina, a peasant girl in service with the family. As often happened in those days, Antonio allowed his son to recognize the child, who was baptized Leonardo. Caterina was sent away to marry a man named Accattabriga, and had to part with her son. Leonardo spent the first fifteen years of his life in the family home at Vinci. Father and grandfather, both notaries, were often away on important legal business in Florence, and Leonardo's closest companion was his young, easy-going uncle Francesco. Francesco acted as his tutor, awakening his interest in the natural world and encouraging him to draw. ☞

✦ THE LOGGIA
A covered market opposite the da Vinci home.

✦ THE MUSEUM
The citadel houses the Leonardo museum, with its collection of models of machines invented by Leonardo, and a library of books about the artist.

✦ THE LANDSCAPE
The surrounding countryside consists chiefly of olive groves and vineyards. In Leonardo's day, these were the staples of Tuscan agriculture.

✦ THE FAMILY HOME
The da Vinci family were notaries, and owned a lot of the surrounding land.

✦ THE BIRTHPLACE
The modest house where Leonardo is supposed to have been born is at Anchiano, a short distance from Vinci. After he was weaned, he went to live at his grandfather's.

✦ THE ARNO VALLEY
Art historians believe that this drawing of Leonardo's represents the stronghold of Vinci and the surrounding countryside: the plain of the Arno in the distance, the slopes of Montalbano in the foreground. Leonardo drew this scene when he was twenty. It is the first work that can be attributed to him with any certainty, and shows his attachment to the places of his childhood.

✦ THE INN
The village inn belonged to the da Vinci family.

FLORENCE

Florence, as Leonardo first experienced it in 1467, was one of the major centers of European culture. Although the Black Death, in the middle of the fourteenth century, had halved the city's population and arrested its growth, Florence had reacted energetically to become one of the world's main places of business and trade. During the fifteenth century, the city enjoyed a long spell of political stability, which led to an extraordinary flowering of the arts. Florence was the cradle of Humanism and the Renaissance. By the time Leonardo arrived on the scene, the first fruits of this revolution were clearly visible. The great families, led by the Medicis, had abandoned their austere medieval houses in favor of elegant new residences. They built churches, convents and hospitals, and enriched the city with works of art. To complete their cathedral, the Florentines commissioned a dome of extraordinary daring. Florence was not governed by tyrants like many of its neighbors. The patronage which transformed the face of the city was dispensed by a ruling class of bankers and merchants.

♦ THE CITY
This view of Florence, drawn some time between 1471 and 1482, helps us to reconstruct the city as it would have looked in Leonardo's day.

☞ *In 1467 Piero da Vinci's career dictated that he settle in Florence and marry a woman of his own social class. Leonardo accompanied him. With his father and young stepmother, he lived in a house near the Piazza della Signoria. Piero served the government as a notary, took part in politics, and turned his attention to his son's education. Leonardo had lessons in music, grammar and geometry. He was a ready pupil, with a curious, restless temperament. The story goes that, having quickly mastered the abacus, an ancient instrument for making calculations, he confused his teacher with a string of searching questions. He was particularly gifted in music and excelled in playing the lyre. The new interests did not dampen his enthusiasm for drawing, which remained his dominant passion.* ☞

A PROJECT ♦ NEVER FULFILLED
Ground plan of a grandiose palace designed by Lorenzo de' Medici and Giuliano da Sangallo, but never built.

SANTISSIMA ♦ ANNUNZIATA
A church built by Michelozzo from 1444. The raised loggia (1447) was designed by Alberti.

OSPEDALE DEGLI ♦ INNOCENTI
A hospital built by Filippo Brunelleschi in 1419 to care for abandoned children.

CONVENT OF ♦ SAN MARCO
Built by Michelozzo in 1436-44 for Cosimo il Vecchio. In 1438-46 Fra Angelico adorned the cells, cloister and chapter room with fresco paintings.

PALAZZO MEDICI ♦
Cosimo il Vecchio commissioned the Medici residence, which was built by Michelozzo, 1444-59.

SAN LORENZO ♦
One of Florence's oldest churches, remodeled for the Medicis by Brunelleschi in 1442.

PALAZZO STROZZI ♦
Building of this residence for Palla Strozzi was begun by Benedetto da Maiano in 1489 and completed by Simone del Pollaiuolo, who designed the cornice and inner courtyard.

SANTA MARIA NOVELLA ♦
This church houses Masaccio's *Trinità*, 1427. The façade was built by Leon Battista Alberti in 1470.

PALAZZO RUCELLAI ♦
The palace was built in the years 1447 to 1451. Leon Battista Alberti designed the façade.

THE CITY WALLS ♦
Built between 1287 and 1321 to accommodate the city's growing population, which then numbered some 100,000 inhabitants.

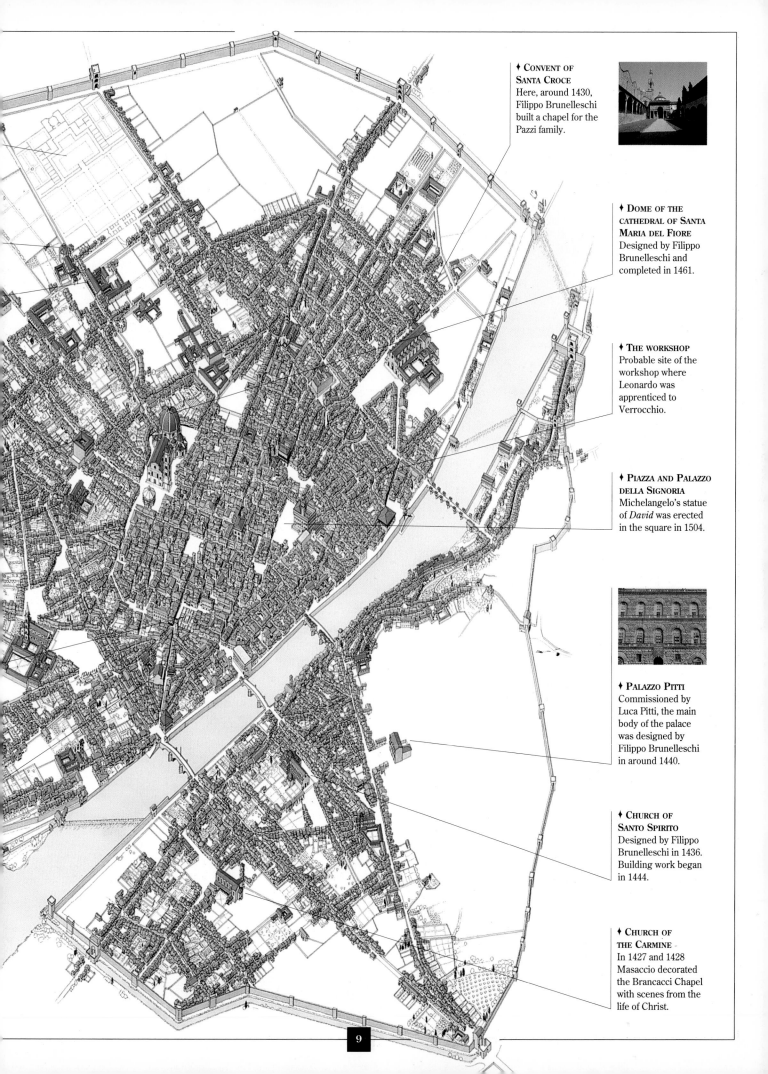

✦ **CONVENT OF SANTA CROCE**
Here, around 1430, Filippo Brunelleschi built a chapel for the Pazzi family.

✦ **DOME OF THE CATHEDRAL OF SANTA MARIA DEL FIORE**
Designed by Filippo Brunelleschi and completed in 1461.

✦ **THE WORKSHOP**
Probable site of the workshop where Leonardo was apprenticed to Verrocchio.

✦ **PIAZZA AND PALAZZO DELLA SIGNORIA**
Michelangelo's statue of *David* was erected in the square in 1504.

✦ **PALAZZO PITTI**
Commissioned by Luca Pitti, the main body of the palace was designed by Filippo Brunelleschi in around 1440.

✦ **CHURCH OF SANTO SPIRITO**
Designed by Filippo Brunelleschi in 1436. Building work began in 1444.

✦ **CHURCH OF THE CARMINE**
In 1427 and 1428 Masaccio decorated the Brancacci Chapel with scenes from the life of Christ.

THE RENAISSANCE

Renaissance means "new birth." The idea of a new beginning based on classical Greek and Roman art, and direct observation of the natural world, was embraced by many fifteenth-century artists and men of letters. The civilization born in Florence and the prosperous Low Countries (Flanders) in the early years of the fifteenth century was to influence all areas of human activity: the organization of society, economics, art and science. The main features of Renaissance painting and sculpture are a desire to investigate and represent the real world - evident in the works of great Tuscan artists such as Masaccio and Donatello, or Flemish masters like Van Eyck - and a systematic study of Greek and Roman models. In architecture, whose greatest exponent was Filippo Brunelleschi, we find a new reliance on reason, which made it possible to solve complex problems of building technique. In philosophy and science, for the first time in history, humankind came to be regarded as the center of the universe.

✦ TWO CRUCIFIXES
Sometime between 1410 and 1415, Brunelleschi carved a wooden crucifix for the church of Santa Maria Novella (above). Christ is depicted with a composed expression and a body of classical perfection. The light caresses the polished surfaces, creating a soft, hazy effect and emphasizing the harmonious proportions. At around the same time, Donatello also carved a crucifix, which can be seen in the church of Santa Croce. His is a tortured Christ, face pinched and body racked with pain. In this case, the natural lighting heightens the intensity of the figure, striking the awkwardly angled planes and creating violent contrasts of light and shade. Donatello was harshly criticized for having "crucified a peasant."

BRUNELLESCHI ✦
In 1430 Filippo Brunelleschi built the Pazzi Chapel in the cloister of Santa Croce, Florence. It is considered one of his masterpieces.

ALBERTI ✦
In 1452 Leon Battista Alberti wrote a treatise on architecture. Though not published until a century later, it had an enormous influence on the new Renaissance style of building.

PAOLO UCCELLO ✦
Between 1456 and 1460 the Florentine artist Paolo Uccello painted three large canvases on the subject of the victory of Florence over Siena in the battle of San Romano in 1432.

✦ NANNI DI BANCO
Four Crowned Saints, for the Florentine church of Orsanmichele. With Brunelleschi and Ghiberti, Nanni di Banco is one of the pioneering figures in Renaissance sculpture.

✦ THE SACRIFICE OF ISAAC
In 1401 a competition was held for relief sculptures to adorn one of the doors of the baptistery in Florence. Among the candidates were the young sculptors Lorenzo Ghiberti and Filippo Brunelleschi. Brunelleschi's trial panel (below left) was considered too revolutionary: he had arranged his figures freely, with parts projecting outside the confines of the frame. Ghiberti, whose entry is shown above, was more traditional and ordered in his approach. It was he who won the commission.

☛ *In Florence, the workshops of goldsmiths, painters and sculptors were on every street. The churches were adorned with major works of art, and it was not unusual to come across an artist intent on a new commission. Leonardo was a young man of insatiable curiosity: he would visit the craftsmen's workshops, and enthuse over the new works of art he saw being created. He also took an interest in the machinery and tools used by architects and artists. On visits to the surrounding countryside and gardens, he made drawings of plants, birds and insects to improve his powers of observation. His father, meanwhile, pursued a successful career in law, and would have liked Leonardo to follow in his footsteps. But Leonardo was beginning to show signs of strong leanings in a quite different direction.* ☛

MASACCIO ✦
In 1427 and 1428 Masaccio decorated the Brancacci Chapel in the Florentine church of the Carmine. In his fresco of the *Tribute Money*, he used perspective and the interplay of light and shade to create a new, more realistic sense of space. The window of the chapel is to the right of his mural, and Masaccio painted the scene as if the light were falling from the same direction. The picture, therefore, appears to be a continuation of the real environment.

✦ FACES
In the intensity of facial expression depicted by Masaccio, we sense moral depth and a heroic view of human destiny. His characters belong to a human-centered universe.

DONATELLO ✦
Feast of Herod, executed in 1427 for the baptismal font of San Giovanni in Siena. The bronze panel combines a "schiacciato," or "flattened," low-relief technique with the use of scientific linear perspective, to give a sense of depth.

✦ HUGO VAN DER GOES
A triptych painted by Hugo van der Goes for the Florentine banker Tommaso Portinari arrived in Florence in 1483, and was displayed in the church of Sant'Egidio. These flowers are from the foreground of the central panel of the triptych which represents the *Adoration of the Shepherds.* The Flemish painters showed great interest in the natural world and paid minute attention to detail.

✦ VAN EYCK
Giovanni Arnolfini and his wife was executed in 1434 by the Flemish painter Jan van Eyck (1390-1441). His work was much admired in Italy, where his use of perspective gave further impetus to the revolution begun by Masaccio. It used to be said that Van Eyck invented oil paint, which enabled him to achieve novel effects in depicting light and atmosphere.

PERSPECTIVE

Linear perspective was the great innovation of Renaissance painting. Using precise mathematical principles, artists discovered how to represent a three-dimensional view as perceived in reality, even though they were working on a flat, two-dimensional surface. Objects and figures were positioned in the picture space, so that it seemed to recede towards a single central vanishing point. At the unveiling of Masaccio's fresco of the *Trinity* in the Florentine church of Santa Maria Novella, the on-lookers could hardly believe their eyes: it was as if the painter had really carved out a chapel in the wall and placed his figures at different distances, such was the illusion of space he had created. The inventor of perspective may well have been Brunelleschi, but it was Leon Battista Alberti who first dealt with the subject systematically, in a treatise he wrote in 1435. Another artist, Piero della Francesca, developed the technique further, publishing a treatise on the subject in 1478. Leonardo later wrote a contribution of his own, but the manuscript has been lost.

MASACCIO'S GENIUS ♦
In 1427 Masaccio painted a fresco of the *Trinity* for the church of Santa Maria Novella, using a perspective technique developed by Brunelleschi. In the setting of a chapel, he depicted Christ Crucified, with God the Father and the dove of the Holy Spirit behind, and St John and the Virgin Mary on either side. Mary points to Christ, while looking out of the picture space towards the observer. Outside, Masaccio depicted the donors, who appear to be worshipping in the body of the church.
The *Trinity* was a new departure in Florentine painting. Unlike their medieval counterparts, who did not attempt to portray religious subjects in a real setting, Renaissance artists sought to create the illusion of space and depth. The faithful could then feel involved in the scenes before them.

PERSPECTIVE ♦ PAINTED
The illusion of depth is evident in this detail from Piero della Francesca's painting of the *Annunciation*. By foreshortening the columns, he has given the church a sense of space and volume.

AND IN REALITY ♦
Photograph of a side aisle, church of Santo Spirito, Florence. Comparison with the painted scene on the left reveals strong similarities. Painters often practiced perspective techniques by drawing architectural features.

♦ THE MEDIEVAL VIEW
In the Middle Ages painters did sometimes make use of perspective, but their methods were unscientific. Their approach gave them the freedom to represent the various stages of a story in one and the same picture, or to depict people and things large or small, according to their importance. In his fresco of *St Francis expelling the devils from Arezzo*, Giotto shows us the inside and outside of the town, devils bigger than houses, and the saint almost as tall as the apse of the basilica on his left.

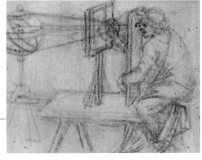

✦ **THE ILLUSION OF PERSPECTIVE**
To enjoy the perspective effect to the full, the observer must stand at a certain distance from Masaccio's fresco.

This then gives the impression of looking into a real chapel, with the figures arranged - some inside, some outside - as shown in this diagram.

✦ **THE RENAISSANCE ARTISTS' VIEW**
Renaissance artists represented three-dimensional space as it is perceived in reality. In this painting of the *Baptism of Christ*, by Piero della Francesca (c. 1410/20-92), all lines converge on the central figure. The landscape behind him has been precisely constructed to create an illusion of depth, with objects apparently receding into the distance. All parts of the painting have a geometrical simplicity and are shown smaller, the further they are from the scene in the foreground.

☛   *Ser Piero da Vinci, who had meanwhile been appointed to the prestigious post of procurator to the convent of the Santissima Annunziata, finally had to admit defeat: his son was not cut out to be a lawyer. His artistic leanings were too strong. The vocation that had been stirred to life during Leonardo's care-free early years in the countryside around Vinci blossomed in the first period he spent in Florence. There, in the church of Santa Croce, he admired the frescoes Giotto had painted just over a century before; at Santa Maria Novella and in the church of the Carmine, he could wonder at Masaccio's murals, only a few decades old. There were great opportunities for a young man aspiring to be an artist. Antonio del Pollaiuolo, a famous sculptor and painter, and Andrea del Cione, nicknamed Verrocchio, were the leading masters of the day, and an apprenticeship in their workshops was highly sought after. Ser Piero was attracted by the reputation of Verrocchio's workshop, where, it was said, there was opportunity to master many different techniques and be involved in important commissions.* ☛

Verrocchio's Workshop

Traditionally, artists' workshops in fifteenth-century Florence produced a wide range of artifacts: paintings of religious and secular subjects, sculptures in terracotta, marble and bronze, decorated objects for use in the home, gold and silverware, painted banners and coats of arms, death masks, and designs and prototypes of machinery for peaceful and military purposes. Andrea del Verrocchio was outstanding in all these pursuits, and his workshop attracted the most talented young men. Some of the greatest artists of the century trained with him: Pietro Vannucci, known as Perugino, Lorenzo di Credi and Sandro Botticelli, who served for some years as Verrocchio's assistant, after an initial period with the painter Filippo Lippi. Following a long-standing Florentine tradition, drawing was given special attention, with the emphasis on accuracy.

♦ NUDE STUDY
A preparatory drawing by Verrocchio for an intended statue.

♦ DEATH MASKS
Verrocchio was highly skilled in taking impressions of the faces of dead people, using a mixture of plaster and warm water. His skill was much in demand. The white images were often copied in marble or cast in bronze.

♦ THE COPPER BALL
As an engineer, Verrocchio had been commissioned to construct an enormous gilded copper ball to adorn the dome of the cathedral.

PIERO DA VINCI ♦ AND VERROCCHIO
Piero da Vinci showed Verrocchio drawings that Leonardo had been doing almost in secret. "Leave your son with me," Verrocchio is supposed to have said. "We'll make something of him."

♦ A YOUNG TEACHER
Born in 1435, Verrocchio was little more than thirty years old when Leonardo entered his workshop.

✦ A DRAPERY STUDY BY LEONARDO
So that pupils in the workshop could practice drawing drapery, a piece of fabric was arranged on an appropriate support, then impregnated with glue to fix the contours. Leonardo made this study in 1478.

✦ LORENZO DI CREDI
A portrait of the painter Perugino by his pupil, Lorenzo di Credi.

BOTTICELLI ✦
A drawing by Botticelli, who was also one of Verrocchio's pupils.

✦ MASTER AND PUPIL
This head is from a workshop study for a painting of *Venus and Cupid*. Verrocchio and his young apprentice Leonardo worked on it together.

✦ DRAWING
For figures and faces, live models were used; the folds of clothing, which required days of patient and painstaking work, were drawn from dummies.

✦ PAINTS
One of the first tasks of the apprentices: grinding pigments.

☞ *In 1469 Leonardo was apprenticed to Verrocchio, a famous goldsmith, sculptor, painter and engineer. His workshop consisted of several rooms. The main room was used for metal work, carving and modeling statues, and drawing; the others for preparing the materials needed for the various activities. Normally, an apprentice would enter the workshop at the age of twelve. He would begin by learning the humblest tasks: sweeping up, and grinding and mixing paints. Leonardo was already seventeen, and sufficiently mature to turn his hand to drawing. Under Verrocchio's guidance, he learned the techniques of line drawing and shading in silver point, how to make rapid ink sketches, the secrets of perspective, and how to bring a portrait to life.* ☞

PAINTING

At the time of Leonardo's apprenticeship, the main characteristic of Florentine painting was a concern for outline. Subtle, distinctly-drawn contours were used to make the figures stand out from the surrounding space, and emphasize anatomical details and the folds of clothing. But some painters - Domenico Veneziano and Piero della Francesca, in Florence, and particularly the artists of the powerful and magnificent city of Venice - were experimenting with different techniques. They based their compositions on the juxtaposition or contrast of colors. Michelangelo, who was about twenty years younger than Leonardo, summed up the situation with a characteristic touch of irony: "God is always even-handed: to the Florentines he gave drawing; to the Venetians, color." From the very start of his career, when he was asked to help paint the *Baptism of Christ*, Leonardo adopted a highly individual way of blending his colors, to create a clear, limpid atmosphere.

BOTTICELLI'S USE ✦ OF OUTLINE
A detail from Sandro Botticelli's *Birth of Venus*, painted in 1482. The various areas of different colors are separated by clearly defined lines.

BELLINI'S USE ✦ OF COLOR
In this *Pietà* by the Venetian Giovanni Bellini (1432-1516), the outlines of the figures are less distinct, their contours suggested by delicate gradations of color.

✦ THE BAPTISM OF CHRIST
The work was painted between 1472 and 1475 for the cloister of the church of San Salvi, in Florence. Leonardo's contribution was the angel on the left and the landscape to the left of the standing Christ.

✦ UNDER VERROCCHIO'S WATCHFUL EYE
The apprentice at work. According to tradition, Leonardo's extraordinary ability was the cause of his master giving up painting.

LEFT-HANDED ✦
Leonardo was left-handed. Here, he puts the final touches to the angel's head, using a support to steady his hand.

☛ *As ser Piero had been informed, Verrocchio's workshop was asked to carry out important commissions. The* Baptism of Christ *is a good example. As was customary, the master's best pupils were also engaged on the work. Leonardo was given the task of executing the head of one of the angels, and the landscape behind them: a valley with a river running through it. According to legend, Leonardo painted the angel on the left so perfectly that Verrocchio decided to give up painting, breaking his paint-brush in a gesture of surrender before the superior skill of his young pupil. In fact, it was Verrocchio's training that led Leonardo to strive for formal perfection in his rendering of figures and landscapes. The perfect combination of subjects and natural setting is the hallmark of his later, mature works.* ☛

◆ THE ANGEL
Leonardo probably
only did the painting.
The figure would
have been drawn by
Verrocchio.

THE LANDSCAPE ◆
The landscape of
rocks and running
water depicted by
Leonardo on this first
occasion was to
remain a constant
feature of his work.

◆ TEMPERA
In tempera painting
the pigments are
diluted with water
and egg yolk, and dry
very quickly. The
artist makes
corrections over the
original layer of paint.

◆ OIL
In oil painting
the pigments are
diluted with raw
linseed oil.
The paint dries
more slowly, and
the composition
can therefore be
reworked over
a period of several
days.

◆ MIXED TECHNIQUE
At around this time,
oil painting was
introduced into Italy
by Flemish painters,
and the new
technique gradually
replaced the old
tradition of tempera
painting. The
transition is apparent
in Leonardo's
Annunciation: he
painted the angel and
the landscape in oils;
the rest of the
composition in
tempera.

THE ANNUNCIATION

♦ THE WORK
Oil and tempera on wooden panel, 98 x 217 cm (39 x 85 inches). Uffizi Gallery, Florence. The painting stayed at the monastery of San Bartolomeo until 1867, when it was transferred to the Uffizi Gallery. The marble sarcophagus

The Archangel Gabriel, sent to Nazareth, greeted Joseph's intended bride with the words: "Do not be afraid, Mary, for God has been gracious to you: you shall conceive and bear a son, and you shall give him the name Jesus." This is St Luke's account of the Annunciation, and he adds that Mary drew back, deeply troubled. Leonardo's painting of this famous scene, for the monks of San Bartolomeo at Monteoliveto, was his first independent commission. He used a number of traditional symbols, as in earlier paintings of the subject: the lily in the angel's hand is a sign of purity and chastity; the grass and flowers typify spring-time; the book lying open on the lectern recalls Isaiah's prophecy that a virgin would conceive and bring forth a son.

♦ BOTTICELLI
Botticelli, who worked on this *Annunciation* during the same period, around 1470, sets his figures in an open gallery, with a low wall cutting off the more distant view. The trees above the wall are reminiscent of those in Leonardo's painting.

was inspired by Verrocchio's decoration of Piero de' Medici's tomb in San Lorenzo, and the influence of another famous painter and sculptor of the period, Antonio del Pollaiuolo, can also be detected. This suggests a very early date for the work, between 1470 and 1471. Leonardo may even have completed this *Annunciation* before he painted the angel in Verrocchio's *Baptism of Christ*.

Having made a number of preparatory drawings to fix the positions and gestures of the figures, the details of the landscape and the architectural setting, Leonardo began to organize the surface of his panel. He sub-divided the picture space into several equal parts, creating a framework in which to arrange the various elements of the composition. As we study this Annunciation, *we become aware that*

Leonardo chose a very regular arrangement. The empty areas of landscape in the background alternate with the figures in the foreground, giving his work the rhythm and balance of a phrase of music. The hand of the angel raised in blessing corresponds to the Virgin's defensive gesture of surprise.

♦ ANOTHER ANNUNCIATION
Strong similarities between the panel in the Uffizi and the small *Annunciation* (below), now in the Louvre, suggest that the latter was also painted by Leonardo as a young man. It formed part of the predella for the *Madonna di Piazza*, a work commissioned from Verrocchio but actually painted by Lorenzo di Credi for the Cathedral in Pistoia.

Some errors show in
Leonardo's
perspective layout:
one arm appears
bigger than the other,
and there is an
awkwardness in the
way the right arm
rests on the lectern.

**✦ SPILLING OUT
OF THE PICTURE**
The angel's garment
is cut off by the left-
hand edge of the
picture, which seems
to spill out of its
frame. In this way,
Leonardo created an
illusion of continuity
between the picture
and its real setting.

FILIPPO LIPPI ✦
A Florentine painter
active in the first half
of the fifteenth
century, Filippo Lippi
worked on this
Annunciation in the
years 1437 to 1440 for
the church of San
Lorenzo, where it can
still be seen. The
architectural setting,
with a foreshortened
view of an internal
courtyard in the
background, shows
an interest in
perspective that is
typical of Florentine
painting of the
period.

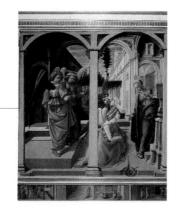

**✦ A GEOMETRICAL
COMPOSITION**
Leonardo arranged
his painting on
geometrical lines.
The straight lines
of the wall and
building give the
design strength.
The four pine trees,
set at regular
intervals serve to
divide the picture
space into equal
rectangles; and the
figures, which
occupy their own
triangular areas,
create a series of five
triangles across the
picture.

**✦ DOMENICO
VENEZIANO**
Domenico Veneziano
was born in Venice
and came to Florence
around 1439. One of
his assistants was
Piero della Francesca.
In this *Annunciation*,
painted for the
Florentine church of
Santa Lucia dei
Magnoli, the two
slender figures in a
simple setting
emphasize the
miraculous nature of
the event.

MACHINES

Until quite recently it was thought that the many drawings of construction-site machinery contained in Leonardo's notebooks were purely the fruit of his teeming imagination: designs for futuristic devices unrelated to the technology of his own time. We now know that many of the machines he drew had in fact been built, particularly by Brunelleschi, and that Leonardo watched them at work on the cathedral building site in Florence. From the twelfth century, when Gothic architecture developed and flourished, cathedral building sites were the great centers of technical achievement, rather like modern-day satellite launch pads. On these sites, architects, carpenters, engineers, blacksmiths and mechanics from all over Europe met and exchanged knowledge and experience. They planned and built amazing machines, now long forgotten. We have Leonardo to thank for keeping a record of some of these machines. His drawings are so accurate that it has been possible to reconstruct them.

✦ THE DOME
Brunelleschi began building the cathedral dome in 1420. At his death, in 1446, only the lantern remained unfinished. Twenty-five years later Verrocchio's great copper sphere was fixed in place.

✦ A MASTERPIECE OF ENGINEERING
The dome was to be so huge, that Brunelleschi had to devise innovative internal scaffolding to support it. There are in fact, an inner and an outer dome, making a double shell held together by the eight massive vertical ribs.

✦ CONES
Each loyer of bricks is like part of a "cone". Because each layer is inclined toward a different point on the central axis, the "cones" fit together, each one into the next.

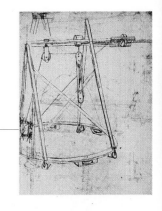

A SKETCH ✦
Sketch of the swivel crane, made by Leonardo while the copper sphere was being positioned.

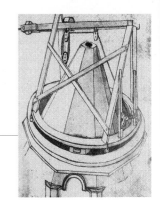

BUONACCORSO ✦ GHIBERTI
Another drawing of the swivel crane, by Buonaccorso Ghiberti, an engineer and contemporary of Leonardo.

✦ INSIDE THE DOME
A drawing of the crane as it would have stood inside the dome.

A MODEL ✦
A wooden model of the giant crane, based on Leonardo's drawings.

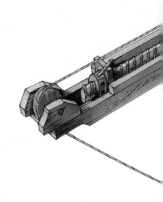

THE BIG CRANE ✦
For raising loads from the base of the dome to the platform, Filippo Brunelleschi had designed a huge jib crane, similar to those used on modern building sites. Below right is a wooden model of the crane.

👉 *As a child, Leonardo had learned to observe the natural world. Verrocchio introduced him to the world of machines and technology. In his workshop Leonardo watched the building of the great copper sphere that was to crown the dome of the cathedral, but what particularly fascinated him were the enormous engines designed to lift and maneuver this heavy object safely. On May 27, 1471, when the sphere was eventually fixed in place, Leonardo was there taking notes. Throughout his life, in his search to understand how things worked, Leonardo made notes and drawings on subjects from anatomy and botany to astronomy and mechanics. Over three thousand pages of his notebooks have been preserved. Leonardo was left-handed and wrote in an unusual way: from right to left, with the letters the wrong way round. This is known as mirror writing. The way to decipher it is to hold his pages of notes in front of a mirror.* 👉

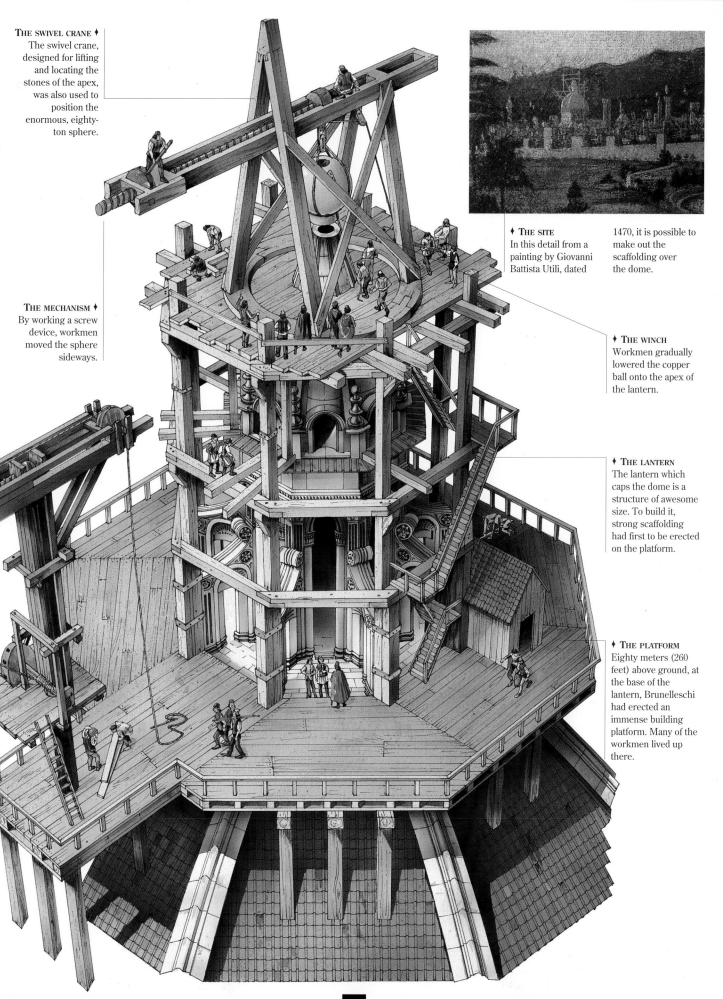

THE SWIVEL CRANE ✦
The swivel crane, designed for lifting and locating the stones of the apex, was also used to position the enormous, eighty-ton sphere.

THE MECHANISM ✦
By working a screw device, workmen moved the sphere sideways.

✦ THE SITE
In this detail from a painting by Giovanni Battista Utili, dated 1470, it is possible to make out the scaffolding over the dome.

✦ THE WINCH
Workmen gradually lowered the copper ball onto the apex of the lantern.

✦ THE LANTERN
The lantern which caps the dome is a structure of awesome size. To build it, strong scaffolding had first to be erected on the platform.

✦ THE PLATFORM
Eighty meters (260 feet) above ground, at the base of the lantern, Brunelleschi had erected an immense building platform. Many of the workmen lived up there.

BRONZE CASTING

In the Middle Ages there was no attempt to cast large bronze statues of the kind made by the Greeks and Romans. However, the technique of bronze casting was still used in the making of bells. Master bell-founders had kept the tradition alive, and in the fourteenth century their knowledge was put to use in the casting of cannon. When Florentine sculptors such as Ghiberti and Donatello turned their hand to large bronze statues, the experience of the bell-founders was invaluable. Verrocchio, too, drew on their skills, and eventually became famous throughout Italy for his ability in casting bronze. In his workshop he set up a full-scale foundry, and there Leonardo learned the rudiments of the technique.

♦ DAVID
A bronze statue cast by Verrocchio around 1465.

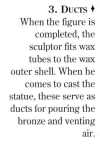

3. DUCTS ♦
When the figure is completed, the sculptor fits wax tubes to the wax outer shell. When he comes to cast the statue, these serve as ducts for pouring the bronze and venting air.

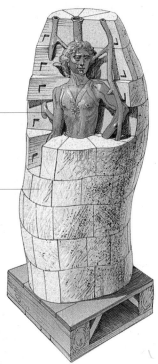

♦ 4. THE MOLD ♦
The sculptor then makes a heat-resistant plaster mold - a sort of "negative" of the statue. This outer casing is tightly held together with strong iron bands.

♦ 1. THE MODEL
The first stage in the "lost wax" process of bronze casting: the sculptor makes a clay model.

♦ 2. THE COPY
The sculptor then makes a copy of the model, building up a shell of wax over a metal framework. The thickness of the wax determines the final thickness of the bronze.

♦ WINGED "PUTTO"
This bronze sculpture, by Verrocchio, can be seen in the courtyard of the Palazzo Vecchio, Florence.

☞ *In 1472 Leonardo was enrolled in the Corporation of St Luke - the painters' guild - but continued his training with Verrocchio. His master was best known as a sculptor, accomplished in all techniques. Leonardo learned from him that art is first and foremost an intellectual activity. He was encouraged to make a careful and systematic study of a subject he intended to reproduce in painting or sculpture. He learned that to sculpt a convincing figure, it was first necessary to make models. Following Verrocchio's instructions, he spent a lot of time modeling the faces of children. The complicated procedures of bronze casting fascinated him. He began to acquire the technical concepts that awakened his interest in science. In 1476, at the age of twenty-four, Leonardo left Verrocchio's workshop. But when his former master received a commission to make a great equestrian monument, Leonardo was quick to offer his assistance.* ☞

♦ DOUBTING THOMAS
A bronze group from the artist's later years, completed by Verrocchio in 1483.

8. REMOVING THE ♦ PLASTER
When the bronze has cooled, workmen break off the plaster mold with hammer and chisel. The unfinished statue emerges, the ducts now consisting of solid bronze.

9. FINISHING ♦
The ducts are now sawn off and the sculptor can put the finishing touches to his work: trimming off excess metal, correcting any mistakes, engraving decorative features, and finally polishing the statue.

♦ 5. MELTING THE WAX
The mold is heated in a special oven, until all the wax melts and runs out. This creates the empty space that will be filled by the molten bronze.

♦ THE RISKS
Casting was a difficult and dangerous operation: difficult, because any change in the temperature or weather might make the process go wrong; dangerous, because any moisture in the mold could cause an explosion.

6. CASTING ♦
From the furnace, molten bronze is poured into the mold through a funnel-shaped opening.

7. BURYING THE ♦ MOLD
The mold is buried, to prevent the heat of the molten bronze causing it to explode.

♦ LIFTING
The mold is lifted and maneuvered using a winch and strong tackle.

♦ THE ANVIL
The metal bands used for holding the mold together are forged on the anvil.

THE EQUESTRIAN MONUMENT

Renowned for his skills as a sculptor and caster of bronze, in 1476 Verrocchio received a most desirable commission from the republic of Venice: to fashion an equestrian monument to the soldier of fortune Bartolomeo Colleoni. It was to be a statue of exceptional size, no less than four meters (13 feet) high. Since Roman times, only Donatello had dared undertake so difficult a task. The project galvanized the whole workshop. Verrocchio's team had to make dozens of preliminary drawings, prepare models of various sizes on which to study the problems they would encounter in the actual casting, and show the client what the monument would eventually look like. From the small-scale models, they would progress to a full-sized one, make from it a gigantic mold, and finally cast the statue. Leonardo's involvement in the project led him to want to produce an equestrian monument of his own. And many years later the ruler of Milan asked him to cast a horse seven meters (23 feet) high.

STUDY ✦
Leonardo made this sketch sometime between 1508 and 1511.

👉 *Leonardo's first major paintings - the* Annunciation *or his panel painting of the* Adoration of the Magi *- took up only part of his time. When he was not busy, he would visit the fascinating laboratory of Tommaso Masini, nicknamed Zoroastro, a craftsman skilled in foundry work and mechanical and hydraulic engineering. Leonardo designed bridges, hydraulic devices and military machines; Zoroastro would faithfully reproduce them as scale models. Concerns on the part of Leonardo's father that his son lacked application were soon laid to rest by Leonardo's diligence and enthusiasm in studying the anatomy of the horse. At this time, Leonardo produced a host of drawings of horses' heads, hocks and manes. His immediate intention was to help Verrocchio with his monument, but gradually he began to nurture an ambition that stayed with him for the rest of his life: to design and cast a huge equestrian monument of his own.* 👉

THE CAGE FOR ✦ THE STATUE
A second cage was built, double the size of the original. Inside this cage the full-sized statue was modeled. To achieve the correct dimensions, rods were again used to measure the distances between statue and cage.

✦WORKING OUTSIDE
The statue was to be installed in an open square. To gauge the effect of natural light, it had to be worked on out of doors.

THE CAGE FOR ✦ THE MODEL
The model was installed in a cage. Thin rods were inserted through holes in the woodwork, as a way of measuring the distance between the cage and the various parts of the model.

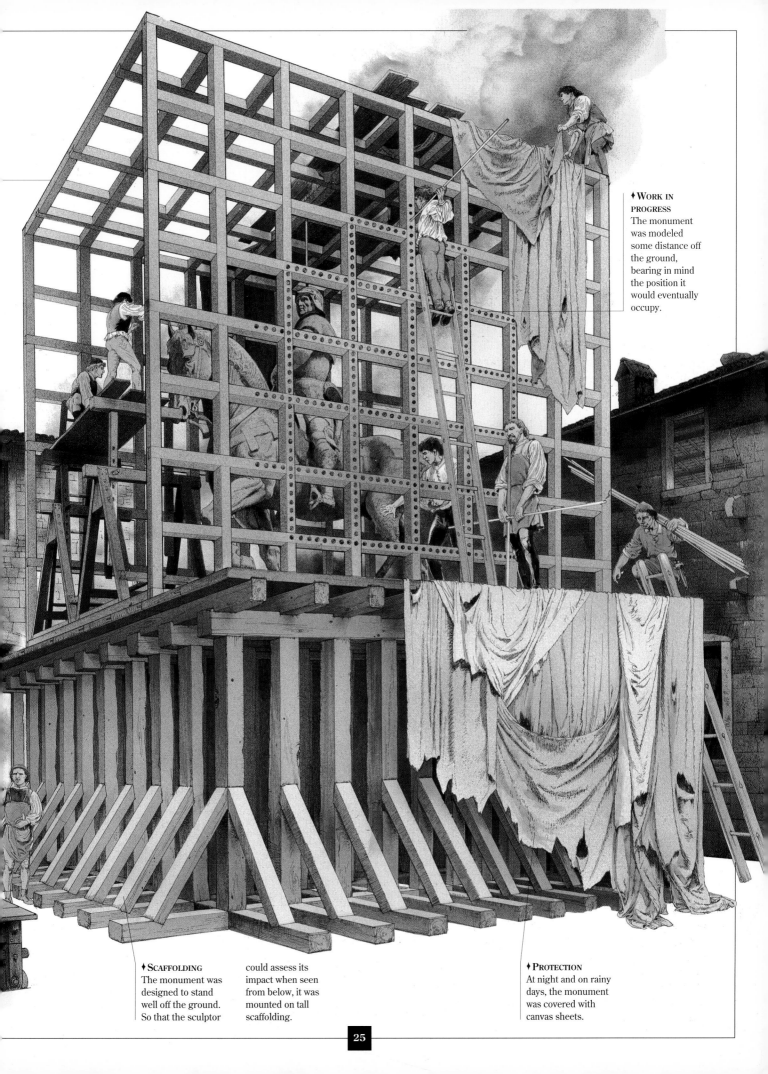

♦ **SCAFFOLDING**
The monument was designed to stand well off the ground. So that the sculptor could assess its impact when seen from below, it was mounted on tall scaffolding.

♦ **PROTECTION**
At night and on rainy days, the monument was covered with canvas sheets.

ADORATION OF THE MAGI

According to the gospels, shepherds were sent by a heavenly host of angels to worship the infant Jesus; they were followed by astrologers from the East, who had been guided by a star. Departing from tradition, Leonardo depicted the scene in quite a different way. His composition shows a great crowd arranged in a semi-circle around the Virgin and Child, while horsemen fight among the ruins in the background.

THE WORK
Antimony yellow with green earth, bistre and white lead, 246 x 243 cm (8 x 8 feet). Uffizi Gallery, Florence. In 1481 the monks of San Donato a Scopeto commissioned Leonardo to paint an altar-piece of the *Adoration of the Magi*. The work was to be completed in two and a half years, but Leonardo did not meet the deadline and, on his departure for Milan, the painting remained unfinished. Fifteen years later, the monks gave up and commissioned another version of the scene by Filippino Lippi. Above and below are three

preparatory drawings for Leonardo's painting. Executed towards the end of his first stay in Florence, the work was experimental in composition and technique. It belonged to the Medici collections in the early seventeenth century, but was already at the Uffizi in 1670, though not exhibited until 1794.

Leonardo's technique is easy to analyze in this picture, because he left it unfinished. We can make out the stages of his work, from the bare outlines of the Virgin to the more or less completed figure on the right. Leonardo drew the scene with a brush and green earth. In modeling the figures, he used bistre for the darker areas and let the underpainting show through for the lighter tones. After painting the foreground in brown, he returned to the figures, using blacks and touches of white.

♦ IMPROVISATION
Leonardo did not follow a set pattern but allowed his creative genius free rein. It is unusual to find in a painting the immediacy of expression characteristic of drawing.

✦ ALMOST FINISHED
These figures, first modeled in chiaroscuro (light and shade), then given added contrast with black and highlights of white, lack only the final touches of color.

BOTTICELLI ✦
In his *Adoration of the Magi* of 1480 - Uffizi Gallery, Florence - Botticelli arranged his subjects on either side of the picture so that the eye is drawn in to the center.

✦ A PREPARATORY DRAWING
In a grandiose setting of classical ruins, horsemen and warriors engage in battle. They symbolize human conflict, in opposition to the reign of peace brought by the infant Christ. The roof supported by the ruins probably symbolizes the Church arising out of the chaos of the pagan world. This feature was not carried over into the final painting.

✦ CONTRAST
The emphasis on dark colors makes the lighter tones stand out all the more clearly, and this produces a three-dimensional quality. Here, Leonardo comes close to the light-and-shade effects of sculpture.

FILIPPINO LIPPI ✦
Completed in 1496 in place of Leonardo's painting, Filippino Lippi's *Adoration* - Uffizi Gallery, Florence - is composed on similar lines, but lacks the complexity of Leonardo's work.

THE MEDICIS

Fifteenth-century Italy was a mosaic of petty kingdoms, principalities, dominions and city-states, often in conflict with one another. Some, like Naples and Milan, were ruled by kings or dukes. Others had a republican form of government, for instance Venice, Siena and Genoa. Florence was also nominally a republic, but in fact the city was dominated by a rich and powerful family of bankers: the Medicis. They rarely held public office, but from their palace pulled strings to direct the affairs of the state. When they gave advice, it was treated as an order, and they ensured that the levers of power were controlled by people they could trust. In 1469 Lorenzo de' Medici became head of the family. His abilities as a statesman and his love of the arts earned him the nickname of "the Magnificent." In politics he displayed intelligence and caution. Knowing that Florence could not compete with stronger states on the battlefield, he sought to maintain peace: forming alliances, lending money and making gifts. He cultivated close relations with artists. As well as sponsoring works of art to beautify the city, Lorenzo used artists as instruments of diplomacy, effectively lending them to the rulers of other cities in exchange for political favors.

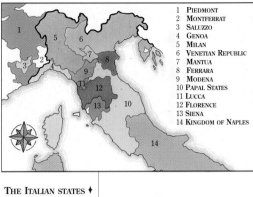

THE ITALIAN STATES ✦
In the second half of the fifteenth century, Italy was divided into many petty states.

1	PIEDMONT
2	MONTFERRAT
3	SALUZZO
4	GENOA
5	MILAN
6	VENETIAN REPUBLIC
7	MANTUA
8	FERRARA
9	MODENA
10	PAPAL STATES
11	LUCCA
12	FLORENCE
13	SIENA
14	KINGDOM OF NAPLES

✦ THE MEDICIS
The Medicis were a family of rich country landowners, who subsequently moved to Florence. They engaged in trade and soon became involved in banking. Having acquired great wealth, they began to be influential in the political life of the city. They became dominant in the time of Cosimo il Vecchio, Lorenzo's grandfather. It was Cosimo, rather than Lorenzo, who commissioned many of Florence's magnificent new buildings: the church of San Lorenzo, the convent of San Marco, and the Palazzo Medici-Riccardi itself. The Medicis were to dominate the city for centuries. The last member of the dynasty, Gian Gastone, died without heir in the eighteenth century.

FRESCOES ✦
At the heart of the Medici residence, the chapel was richly decorated by Benozzo Gozzoli in 1459. His frescoes glorified the Medicis, including portraits of the founder and other members of the dynasty.

THE PALAZZO ✦
The Medici residence in via Larga was designed and built in the years 1444 to 1459 by the architect Michelozzo.

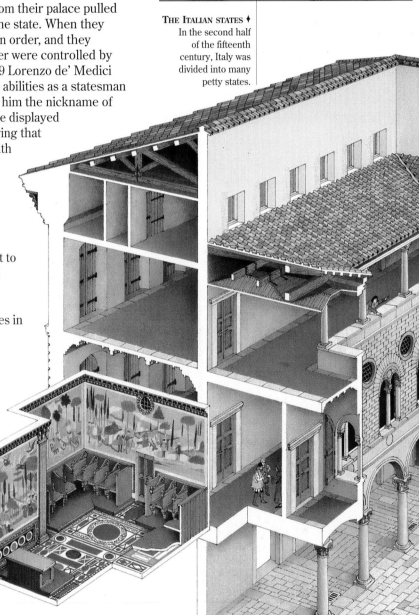

THE COURTYARD ✦
The palace was built around an open courtyard, its elegant loggia supported on classical columns.

♦ A Medici party
This miniature by Apollonio di Giovanni, painted in 1460, shows a party in the garden of the Palazzo Medici-Riccardi.

As one of Verrocchio's brightest pupils, and the son of an influential supporter of the Medici family, Leonardo did not long escape the attention of Lorenzo the Magnificent. He was a frequent visitor at the Medici residence in via Larga, where he met artists, poets and scholars, and he carried out restoration work on sculptures in the Medici gardens near the piazza San Marco. At the same time he continued to paint. Then an unexpected turn of events gave him the opportunity to leave Florence and move to the rich and powerful city of Milan. Lorenzo had been promising the lords of Milan - the Sforza family - that he would send a Florentine artist to cast an impressive equestrian monument to the memory of Francesco Sforza, soldier of fortune and founder of the dynasty. The choice fell on Leonardo. Leaving the Adoration of the Magi unfinished, Leonardo set out for Milan.

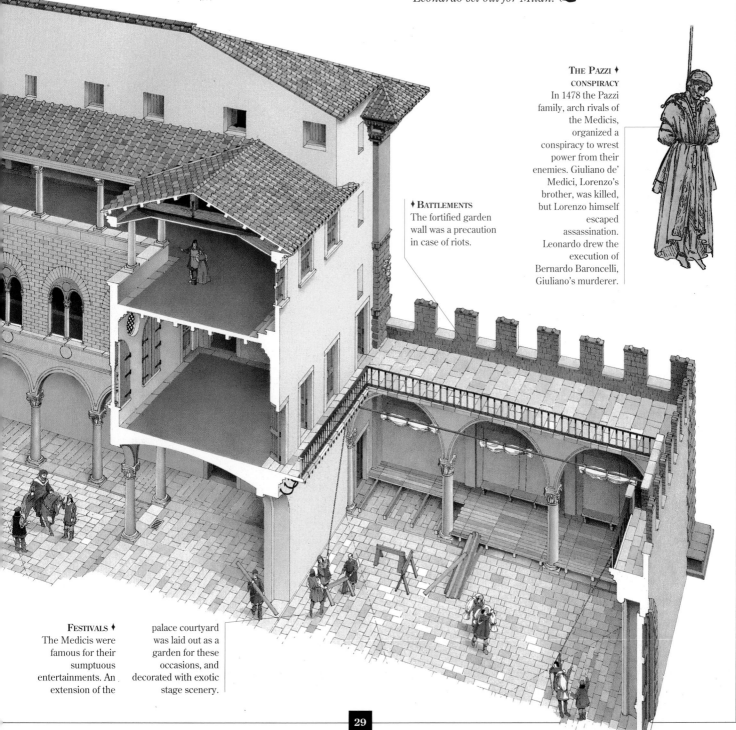

THE PAZZI ♦
CONSPIRACY
In 1478 the Pazzi family, arch rivals of the Medicis, organized a conspiracy to wrest power from their enemies. Giuliano de' Medici, Lorenzo's brother, was killed, but Lorenzo himself escaped assassination. Leonardo drew the execution of Bernardo Baroncelli, Giuliano's murderer.

♦ BATTLEMENTS
The fortified garden wall was a precaution in case of riots.

FESTIVALS ♦
The Medicis were famous for their sumptuous entertainments. An extension of the palace courtyard was laid out as a garden for these occasions, and decorated with exotic stage scenery.

MILAN

When Leonardo entered the service of Ludovico Sforza, he was thirty years old. Milan was a very different place from Florence. Ludovico, known as "Il Moro" (the Moor), was an absolute ruler and lived in an immense fortress, a city within the city. His power rested on a large army, equipped with the most modern weapons available. Milan was famous throughout Europe for the production of armaments, and there were foundries and metal-working shops in every street. The Milanese were open to new ideas: silk-worm culture had recently been established, and textile businesses were prospering thanks to the invention of advanced new weaving looms. Farmers were just beginning to experiment with growing rice, and irrigation canals were being dug in the surrounding countryside. Because of Ludovico's insatiable thirst for prestige, Milan offered great opportunities to artists and men of science. The seventeen years Leonardo spent there were a time of growth, during which he was fully engaged on many works and projects.

♦ CANALS
The dense network of canals around Milan was used for transporting goods and raw materials from the region of the Italian lakes and the River Po. For the construction of the castle, timber was brought from the Alps, bricks from the surrounding countryside, and cement from Lake Maggiore.

♦ CECILIA GALLERANI
The mistress of Ludovico il Moro. She took a special interest in Leonardo.

♦ FRANCESCO DI GIORGIO MARTINI
A great architect and engineer, with whom Leonardo became friends. He gave Leonardo a precious manuscript containing drawings of machines and architectural projects.

♦ LA ROCCHETTA
The Rocchetta courtyard, like the Duke's courtyard, was built to the orders of Galeazzo Maria Visconti.

♦ BLANCHE OF SAVOY TOWER
The stronghold in which Ludovico il Moro imprisoned his sister-in-law.

♦ THE CASTLE
The first part of the castle was built in 1368 under Duke Galeazzo Visconti. It incorporated part of the city wall.

♦ THE SFORZAS
On the death of Filippo Maria Visconti in 1447, the people of Milan rose up and proclaimed a republic. The castle was partially destroyed. In 1450 Francesco Sforza seized the dukedom of Milan and began an ambitious program of rebuilding and extending the fortress. This work was continued by his successors: Galeazzo Maria Sforza and Ludovico il Moro. They engaged some of the greatest contemporary architects: Filarete, Bramante, and Leonardo.

THE MODEL ♦
In 1493, to mark the marriage of Maria Sforza, the clay model of Leonardo's horse was exhibited in the center of the "great court."

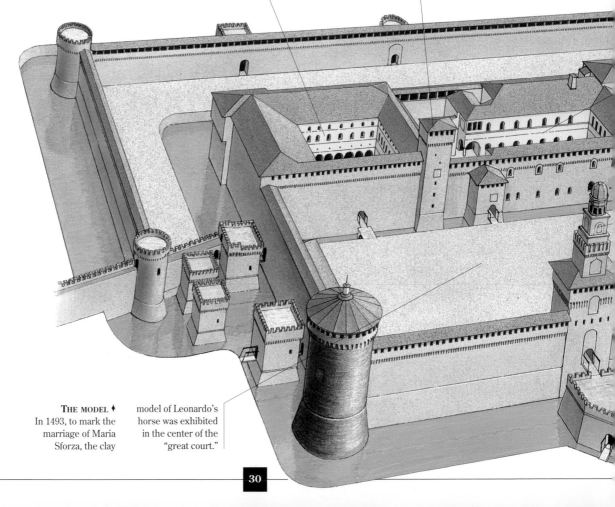

♦ A COMPARISON
Leonardo's horse (4) would have towered over: 1) the Roman statue of *Marcus Aurelius*, 4.30 meters (14 feet) high; 2) Donatello's *Gatta-melata* in Padua, 3.20 meters (10.5 feet); 3) Verrocchio's *Colleoni* in Venice, 4 meters (13 feet); 5) Girardon's *Louis XIV* in Paris, 6.82 meters (22 feet).

♦ THE MONUMENT
Leonardo had come to Milan to create an equestrian monument in memory of Duke Francesco, founder of the Sforza dynasty. He worked on the project for some ten years. His plans were daring: the monument would be larger than any existing work of its kind. The horse alone would stand six

meters (19 feet 8 inches) high. Having made preliminary drawings and produced a number of proposals, he got as far as building a life-sized model of the horse, which was displayed in the great court of the castle. He studied possible methods of casting the statue, and designed colossal engines for moving

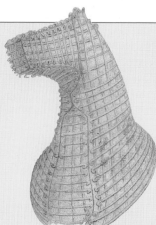

the model and the planned bronze horse. He devised a system for boxing the mold and, helped by his mathematician friend Luca Pacioli, calculated how much bronze would be required. However, when French troops captured Milan in 1499, they destroyed the model, viewing it as a symbol of Sforza ambition.

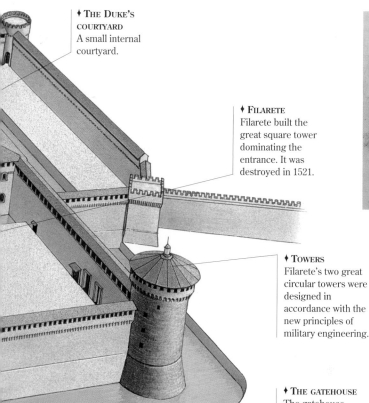

♦ THE DUKE'S COURTYARD
A small internal courtyard.

♦ FILARETE
Filarete built the great square tower dominating the entrance. It was destroyed in 1521.

♦ TOWERS
Filarete's two great circular towers were designed in accordance with the new principles of military engineering.

♦ THE GATEHOUSE
The gatehouse protects the entrance to the castle. This is where the equestrian monument was intended to stand.

♦ CELEBRATIONS
Leonardo played many roles at the Milanese court: painter, sculptor, military and hydraulic engineer, architect, and even master of ceremonies. Contemporaries praised his organization of festivities, and some of his drawings for the costumes have survived.

☞ *Having studied the anatomy of the horse so thoroughly under Verrocchio, Leonardo was impatient to create an equestrian monument of his own. But the first call on his services was as a musician. Lorenzo had asked for Leonardo's beautiful silver lyre, and sent it to Ludovico together with its maker and player. In the spring of 1482 Leonardo addressed a letter of introduction to his new patron, listing his skills in mechanics, hydraulics and military engineering, as well as painting and sculpture, in which he claimed to be second to none. Ludovico's curiosity was aroused by an artist who dared deal on equal terms with the lord of Milan. He therefore sent for him, to see if he was really a madman with an inflated idea of himself, or a true creative genius.* ☜

THE VIRGIN OF THE ROCKS

The story goes that, while Mary and Joseph were fleeing to Egypt with Jesus to save him from the anger of King Herod, they found refuge in a cave in the Sinai desert. There occurred a miraculous first meeting between Jesus and John the Baptist, whom Leonardo depicts as little more than babies. St John is portrayed as kneeling to receive the blessing of his cousin. This little-known episode from the life of Christ is not related in the gospels, but in later - apocryphal - books, to which the Church ascribed a lesser status.

♦ THE PAINTING
Oil on wooden panel, 199 x 122 cm (6.5 x 4 feet). Louvre, Paris. In 1483 the Brotherhood of the Immaculate Conception commissioned Leonardo to paint an altar-piece for their chapel in the church of San Francesco Grande in Milan. The work was to be flanked by two other panels and a number of painted bas-reliefs by Ambrogio and

Evangelista De Predis. Above and below are preparatory drawings for the work which was painted between 1483 and 1486. It seems never to have occupied its intended position, but found its way eventually to the Louvre. Instead, the altar was graced with a second version of the subject, which Leonardo finished around 1507. This is now in the National Gallery, London.

THE SECOND VERSION ♦
Completed ten years after the first *Virgin of the Rocks*, the London painting shows the same scene, although the figures are proportionally larger. The only difference is that the angel in this version is not shown pointing to St John.

As the diagram above illustrates, there are two different light sources in this picture. Leonardo observed that light is present, in different degrees, in all parts of the atmosphere. Because a single light source creates over-sharp contrasts, and Leonardo wished to achieve a softer "sfumato" *effect, he imagined the main source of light as being in front of his subjects, with a second, weaker source in the background. "Sfumato" means blending one color area subtly into the next.*

AN EXPERT IN ♦ BOTANY
Fascinated since childhood by the wonders of the natural world, Leonardo studied plant species with the enthusiasm of a botanist.

♦ TRANSPARENT EFFECTS
Leonardo achieved transparent effects of great delicacy by applying thin coats of boiled walnut oil. The light appears to penetrate gradually into the depths of the painting.

SHADOW ♦
Leonardo studied optical phenomena. He observed that whereas darkness is a total absence of light, shade results from a diminishing of the light source.

♦ HANDS
Gestures are vital in conveying the meaning of this silent scene. The angel is pointing to St John, whose hands are joined in prayer in recognition of Jesus, the appointed Redeemer. The Christ child in turn blesses the prophet who is to herald his coming. The Virgin extends her hand in a gesture of protection.

♦ THE ROCKS
In his *Treatise on Painting*, Leonardo stated that the arid, rugged summits of mountains should be represented with "small, stunted vegetation" and roots emerging from the dry earth. Towards the valley, the plant life should gradually become more luxuriant.

PLANT LIFE ♦
The iris in the left foreground, and all the other flowers and plants represented in the painting, are drawn from nature.

ARCHITECTURE

The principles of the new building style that Brunelleschi and Alberti had pioneered in Florence were spreading to other Italian cities. In Milan, Ludovico invited forward-looking architects to undertake the major task of transforming an old medieval city into an ideal modern metropolis. Between 1460 and 1465 Antonio Averulino, nicknamed Filarete, built the Ospedale Maggiore, a prototype of later European hospitals. In 1473 Lazzaro Palazzi built the first isolation hospital. Donato Bramante, Francesco di Giorgio and Antonio Amadeo designed churches, convents, town houses, and chapels. The fashion for symmetrical buildings with a central plan - a classical idea taken up by Brunelleschi - also caught on in Milan. Meanwhile, engineers were engaged to construct a dense network of inland waterways. This was the climate in which Leonardo embarked on a series of architectural studies, none of which was ever realized. His most ambitious project anticipates many of the principles of modern town planning.

✦ SANTA MARIA PRESSO SANTO SATIRO
This church was one of Bramante's first achievements in Milan (1483).

✦ BRAMANTE
Bramante already enjoyed great prestige when he arrived in Milan in 1480. He dedicated a poem on Roman architecture to Leonardo.

✦ L'OSPEDALE MAGGIORE
Milan's new hospital was designed by the architect Antonio Averulino, nicknamed Filarete (1400-1469). The grandiose and orderly lay-out of the building was much admired by Leonardo.

✦ A NEW RESIDENTIAL AREA
Leonardo drew plans for rebuilding the old heart of Milan. A severe outbreak of plague had revealed the terrible lack of hygiene in the area. Leonardo was the first to insist on proper sanitation.

✦ A RATIONAL VIEW
In Leonardo's day many of the cities of northern Italy were served by a network of canals, most of which have now disappeared. Milan had much in common with Venice, Amsterdam or Bruges. Leonardo came from Tuscany, a region poor in water resources, and he was fascinated by the busy canals, the boats laden with merchandise, and the way the buildings were mirrored in the water. He realized that water could be utilized in a more rational way: for transport, hygiene, and to enhance the urban environment.

✦ ARCADES
Pedestrian streets were protected from the rain by arcades.

RAISED ROADWAYS ✦
Leonardo made a separation between pedestrian areas and roads intended to carry traffic.

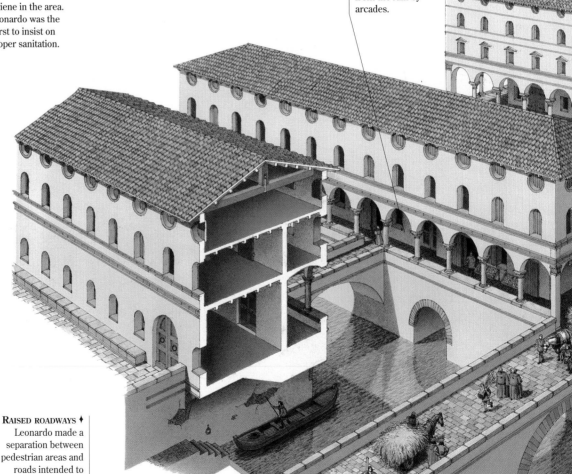

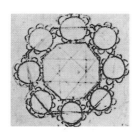

♦ BUILDING TO A CENTRAL PLAN

Renaissance architects were fascinated by geometry, and saw buildings as skilful combinations of geometrical shapes. The most perfect were the square and the circle, the cube and the sphere. They therefore devoted special attention to centrally-planned buildings which would fit into a circle or a square. Leonardo showed a great deal of interest in the new developments. He drew up plans for a number of symmetrical churches, but unfortunately they were never built.

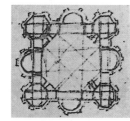

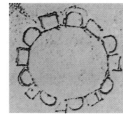

Ludovico granted Leonardo an annual allowance of five hundred ducats. While waiting to build the promised war machines and the gigantic equestrian monument, the artist painted such major works as the Virgin of the Rocks *and a portrait of Cecilia Gallerani, entitled* Lady with an Ermine. *But Leonardo's mind was particularly stimulated by the enthusiasm for architecture that had taken hold of the city. He knew and worked with such great architects as Bramante and Francesco di Giorgio. There had been much discussion of what would constitute a suitable dome for Milan's cathedral, and Leonardo, too, submitted a project. With scientific rigor he elaborated plans for enlarging Milan, and designed a canal network linking two rivers. Even an outbreak of the plague did not distract him from his many research projects. On the contrary, it gave him the opportunity to work undisturbed.*

♦ BUILDINGS

The buildings were designed on several levels, with access to waterways, roads and pedestrian walkways.

♦ THE CATHEDRAL

Leonardo produced some brilliant studies of how a dome might be added to Milan cathedral.

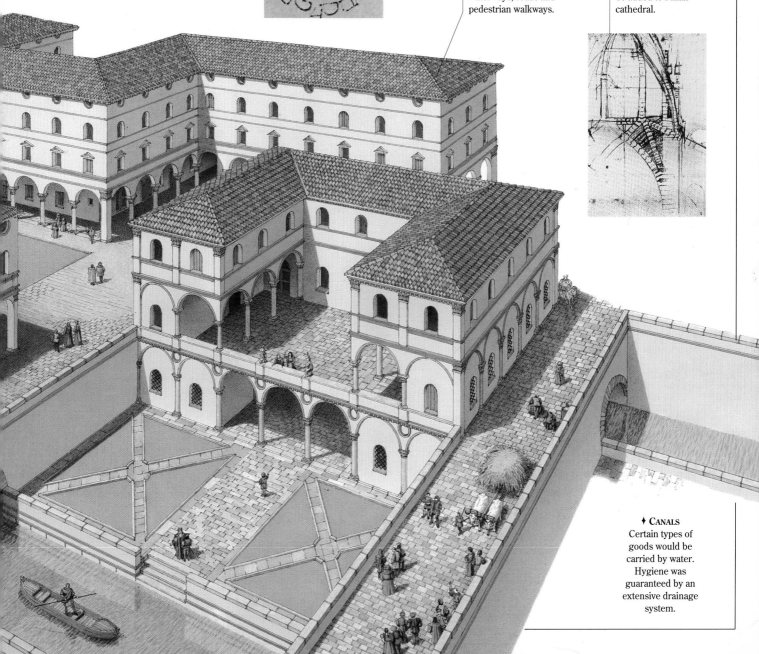

♦ CANALS

Certain types of goods would be carried by water. Hygiene was guaranteed by an extensive drainage system.

ANATOMY

Even before 1400 Italian painters and sculptors had made careful studies of the human body so as to reproduce it faithfully in their art. During the Renaissance a growing concern for realism involved artists in more detailed and painstaking anatomical research. They wanted to understand and represent the movement of the limbs, muscles under stress, and facial expressions. To further their understanding, many dissected dead bodies, first in secret, then more openly. Leonardo was no exception. However, his drawings reveal that he took a scientific, as well as a purely artistic, interest in the subject. His studies of the muscles, nervous and vascular systems, and of the skeleton are fine examples of what we would call scientific drawing. Thirty or forty years later, Andreas Vesalius (1514-1564), a Flemish anatomist and surgeon, published magnificent illustrations of the human skeleton, which mark the real beginning of modern anatomy.

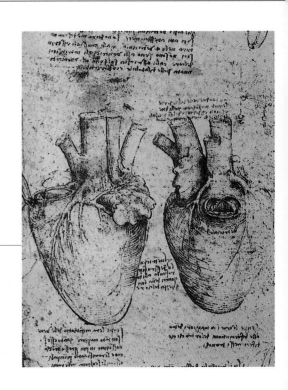

THE HEART ✦
Leonardo's annotated diagrams of the cardiac muscle (right). The anatomical characteristics are well defined, though Leonardo had not fully understood how the heart works. At the top left of this page is the famous diagram showing the proportions of the human body, which Leonardo took from the Roman architect Vitruvius.

✦ **DISSECTION**
To gain the precise understanding of the human body which his drawings show, Leonardo carried out as many as thirty dissections.

✦ **THE HEAD**
These three drawings by Leonardo show the skull,

a cross-section of the head, and the structure of the neck.

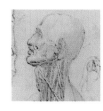

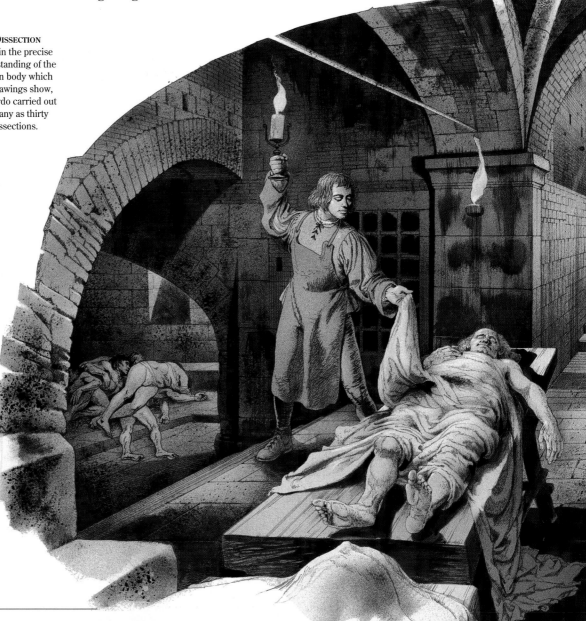

THE THORAX ✦
This drawing of the thoracic and abdominal organs was made around 1512, when Leonardo was studying with the Paduan scientist Della Torre. The kidneys and urinary system are accurately reproduced, the result of direct observation of dissected bodies.

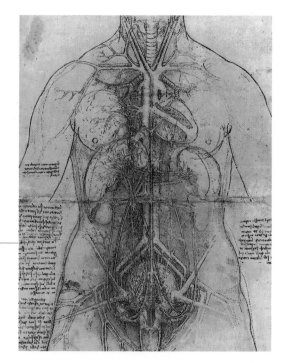

☞ *The years went by, but still Leonardo had not begun casting the horse, for which Lorenzo the Magnificent had first sent him to Milan. Ludovico occasionally reproved him, and complained of the delay to the Florentine ambassador. Leonardo's response was to re-immerse himself in his studies but, being a perfectionist, he often changed his mind and began all over again. In 1489 Ludovico asked Lorenzo to send two master foundrymen to begin work on the monument. Meanwhile Leonardo continued to create the scenery for court entertainments. In 1490 he built elaborate stage sets for the marriage of Gian Galeazzo Sforza to Isabella of Aragon, representing paradise and seven orbiting planets. Another distraction was Leonardo's growing interest in the study of anatomy. Originally motivated by an artistic impulse, he soon became involved in scientific classification, driven by his insatiable curiosity. His drawings are natural and realistic, even when he depicts anatomical features of his own invention.* ☞

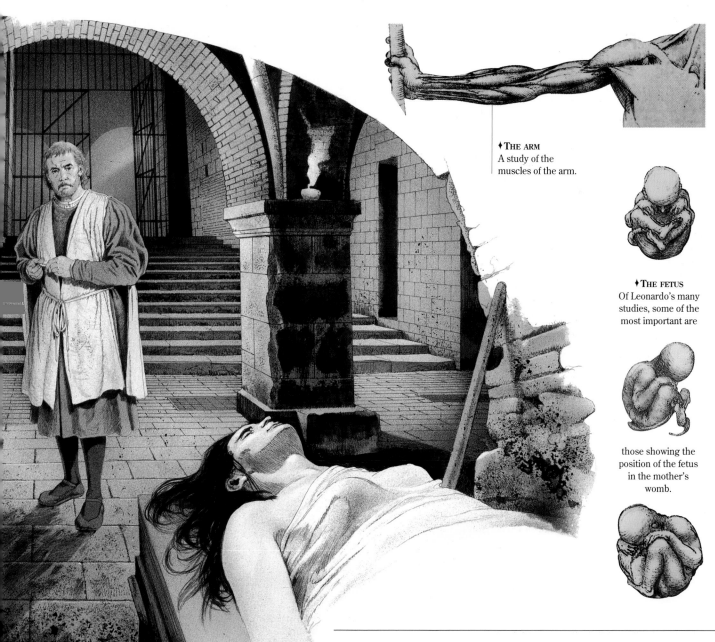

✦ THE ARM
A study of the muscles of the arm.

✦ THE FETUS
Of Leonardo's many studies, some of the most important are those showing the position of the fetus in the mother's womb.

PORTRAITS

Leonardo painted many portraits of women, including
the best-known *Mona Lisa* (left); but only one of a
man. Whereas artists before him had portrayed
women in the abstract, representing an ideal of beauty,
Leonardo endowed them with personality, force of
character, and social status. He managed to combine a
spirited physical description with considerable
psychological insight. As in a modern puzzle, he
sometimes included symbols - objects, plants or
animals - suggesting the name of his subject and
alluding to her moral qualities.

*Ginevra de' Benci, sister of
an astronomer friend of
Leonardo's, was married at
the age of seventeen. Her
portrait (above), painted
in 1474 for the occasion,
reveals a pale young
woman with adolescent
features, gazing sadly into
the distance. The juniper
bush in the background
symbolizes the chastity of a
young bride. The Italian
word for juniper, "ginepro",
also suggests her name.
On the reverse of the
portrait is an emblem, as
shown top right.*

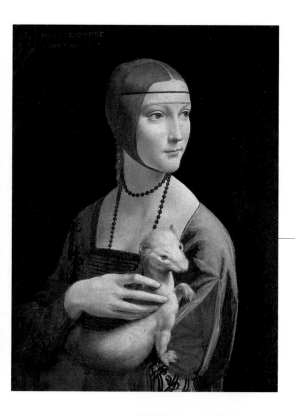

LA BELLE ♦ FERRONNIÈRE
The subject's gaze is directed slightly above and to the right of the observer, creating the impression of an ambiguous, evasive personality.

♦ CECILIA GALLERANI
Ludovico's mistress, a woman of wit and beauty, who for many years shone at the Milanese court. The severe hair-style emphasizes the perfection of her face and striking eyes. The white ermine she holds is a symbol of purity; its name in Greek suggests her name.

PORTRAIT OF A MUSICIAN ♦
Leonardo's only male portrait. Although the clothing and hand holding the musical score were left unfinished, the face is highly expressive.

♦ LADY WITH PEARLS
The rigid profile and rather fixed expression are quite unlike the other portraits. Though long thought to be by Leonardo, this is now recognized as a painting of the Bolognese school.

ISABELLA D'ESTE ♦
The head of the Marchioness of Mantua is seen in profile, while the bust remains rigidly turned towards the viewer, suggesting an important person with a strong personality. Although she insisted for years, Leonardo never fulfilled her request for a portrait of herself to hang in her study. The bust and hands of this portrait are reminiscent of the *Mona Lisa*.

♦ LA SCAPIGLIATA
(Lady with Hair Undone). This splendid face, a study for the angel in the *Virgin of the Rocks*, or possibly a sketch for the long-awaited portrait of Isabella d'Este, expresses youthful melancholy and reflection.

MATHEMATICS

In 1453, when the Ottoman Turks conquered Constantinople, many Byzantine scholars sought refuge in Italy, taking with them precious Greek manuscripts. These included treatises on geometry. At the same time the German Johannes Gutenberg was perfecting the technique of printing with moveable type (originally a Chinese invention), so making books more widely available. These two developments are closely related to the spread of mathematical knowledge. Another factor was the great voyages of discovery. Sailors needed accurate nautical charts, precise tables for predicting their position, and better ways of making astronomical calculations. Sophisticated accounting systems were developed as trade flourished. Artists also made a contribution to science, with the invention of perspective. At this time mathematicians played an important role in the spread of algebra and geometry. An influential figure was Luca Pacioli. Leonardo is said to have drawn the polygons for Pacioli's *De divina proportione*, a treatise on geometry.

♦ **REGIOMONTANUS**
Johann Müller of Königsberg, known as Regiomontanus (1436-1476), was the most accomplished mathematician of his time. He studied in Leipzig and Vienna, and in Rome learned Greek, in order to read the classical texts on mathematics.

♦ **NEW UNDERSTANDING**
The spread of scientific knowledge continued throughout the fifteenth century. New mathematical symbols were devised, some of which can be seen on the left of this print of 1491.

♦ **LUCA PACIOLI**
A Franciscan monk, Pacioli lived from 1445 to 1514. In 1487 he published his *Summa de aritmetica e geometria*, a popular work which greatly influenced his contemporaries. He was on friendly terms with Leonardo, teaching him the geometry of Euclid and Archimedes.

♦ **MOVEABLE TYPE**
The technique of printing with moveable type was perfected by Johannes Gutenberg in 1439. Invented by the Chinese three centuries earlier, the moveable characters were first made of terracotta or wood. Gutenberg had the brilliant idea of casting them in lead, which meant they could be made in far greater quantities and much reduced in size. This made printing quicker and cheaper.

THE GOLDEN SECTION ♦
Luca Pacioli published a work entitled *De divina proportione*. It was concerned with polygons and solids, and the proportional relationship later referred to as the golden section. The book was illustrated by Leonardo.

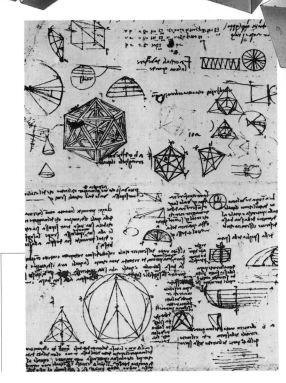

♦ **POLYGONS**
A page from Leonardo's notebook devoted to geometrical shapes. It contains a study for one of the polygons he drew for Luca Pacioli's *De divine proportione*.

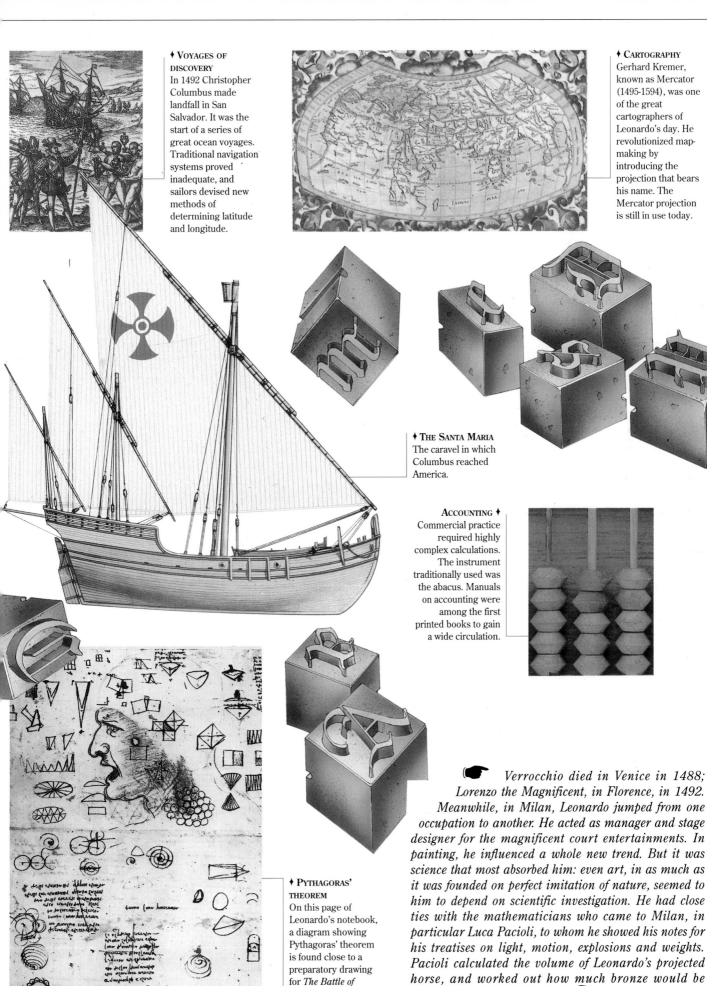

♦ **VOYAGES OF DISCOVERY**
In 1492 Christopher Columbus made landfall in San Salvador. It was the start of a series of great ocean voyages. Traditional navigation systems proved inadequate, and sailors devised new methods of determining latitude and longitude.

♦ **CARTOGRAPHY**
Gerhard Kremer, known as Mercator (1495-1594), was one of the great cartographers of Leonardo's day. He revolutionized map-making by introducing the projection that bears his name. The Mercator projection is still in use today.

♦ **THE SANTA MARIA**
The caravel in which Columbus reached America.

ACCOUNTING ♦
Commercial practice required highly complex calculations. The instrument traditionally used was the abacus. Manuals on accounting were among the first printed books to gain a wide circulation.

♦ **PYTHAGORAS' THEOREM**
On this page of Leonardo's notebook, a diagram showing Pythagoras' theorem is found close to a preparatory drawing for *The Battle of Anghiari*.

☞ *Verrocchio died in Venice in 1488; Lorenzo the Magnificent, in Florence, in 1492. Meanwhile, in Milan, Leonardo jumped from one occupation to another. He acted as manager and stage designer for the magnificent court entertainments. In painting, he influenced a whole new trend. But it was science that most absorbed him: even art, in as much as it was founded on perfect imitation of nature, seemed to him to depend on scientific investigation. He had close ties with the mathematicians who came to Milan, in particular Luca Pacioli, to whom he showed his notes for his treatises on light, motion, explosions and weights. Pacioli calculated the volume of Leonardo's projected horse, and worked out how much bronze would be needed to cast the monument.* ☞

THE LAST SUPPER

♦ THE WORK
Tempera and oil on a plaster wall, 460 x 880 cm (15 x 29 feet). Santa Maria delle Grazie, Milan. Painted towards the end of Leonardo's first stay in Milan, between 1495 and

This is the dramatic moment in the gospels when Christ, meeting with his disciples to celebrate the Jewish Passover, announces that one of them will betray him. Leonardo depicted the scene in a novel way. Instead of choosing the moment in which the identity of the traitor is revealed, he focuses on the reactions and gestures of the apostles as they question the Master: "Is it I, Lord?" Jesus sits impassive, while his disciples, all potential traitors, look questioningly at one another to protest their innocence.

♦ GROTESQUES
Another aspect of Leonardo's interest in facial expressions is apparent in his grotesque portraits.

1498, the *Last Supper* was commissioned by Ludovico il Moro. It was done on the end wall of the monastery refectory, facing a representation of the *Crucifixion*. For technical reasons, the *Last Supper* soon began to deteriorate. It has been restored, retouched and repainted many times, but without great success. Recently it underwent delicate treatment to remove earlier over-paintings.

Why did the artist choose this particular moment for his painting of the Last Supper? Leonardo was a keen student of physiognomy, the science which seeks to establish a person's character from his or her features and facial expression. He observed that every emotion has its corresponding reaction or gesture, which differs with the age and character of the person concerned. By choosing this moment of self-questioning, Leonardo

was able to record varying reactions to a single stimulus. For instance, a preparatory drawing for the figure of James is shown top left. "Men's gestures are as varied as the thoughts running through their minds," Leonardo wrote. Observing the apostles, dramatically arranged in groups of three, we experience something of what they felt on the evening when Christ announced his supreme sacrifice.

♦ THE FIRST IDEA
Leonardo's intention to depict the moment at which Jesus announced his betrayal is evident in this preliminary drawing.

♦ **ANDREA DEL CASTAGNO**
Painted in 1450 for the refectory of Santa Apollonia in Florence, Andrea del Castagno's *Last Supper* shows Judas Iscariot isolated on the near side of the table. Judas was traditionally shown from behind, separate from the other eleven, often reaching his hand into the dish with Jesus.

♦ **MATTHEW**
Arms outstretched towards Jesus, Matthew addresses the two disciples at the end of the table. His face wears an expression of incredulity and desperation.

PHILIP ♦
The gesture Leonardo used here was traditional: Philip draws his hands in to his chest, as in Ghirlandaio's painting.

♦ **ANDREW**
His hands raised, palms towards the viewer, the apostle seems to be warding off something disagreeable.

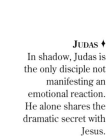

JUDAS ♦
In shadow, Judas is the only disciple not manifesting an emotional reaction. He alone shares the dramatic secret with Jesus.

GHIRLANDAIO ♦
Domenico Ghirlandaio painted this version of the *Last Supper* for the Florentine convent of Ognissanti in 1480. As in the painting by Andrea del Castagno, the apostles are seated in a row on the far side of the table with Jesus, while Judas sits alone, opposite the man he is to betray.

VIEWING THE PAINTING

Throughout the Middle Ages the Last Supper was depicted as one part of the full cycle of Christ's passion, usually beginning with his entry into Jerusalem and ending with the entombment. Not until later, during the fifteenth century, was it chosen as an independent subject. It then became an important theme for paintings which were to cover a whole wall of a monastery refectory: the room where the monks met to eat their meals. The inner meaning of the Last Supper was lived on a daily basis by the monks and their prior. Like Jesus and the apostles, they sought to practice divine teaching by studying and conforming to the holy scriptures.

♦ **THE EFFECTS OF BOMBING**
This was the state of the refectory after a bombing raid in August 1943. The protective curtain prevented flying debris from causing irreparable damage.

♦ **TECHNIQUE**
Always dissatisfied with his achievements, Leonardo took a very long time over his works, which is why so many are unfinished. If he had painted his mural of the Last Supper using the traditional fresco technique, he would have had to work very quickly: covering the area of plaster prepared for him each day while it was still damp. Because he knew he would want to rework parts of his painting, Leonardo adopted the technique of applying a mixture of oil and tempera over two layers of plaster. He could not have predicted that these materials would succumb to the attacks of pollution and humidity. During Leonardo's own lifetime an irreversible process of deterioration set in. The colors now are dull and neutral, but originally they were probably vivid and luminous. Study drawings for Jesus and Judas (below) are shown.

If the spectator views the painting of the Last Supper *from a standpoint four meters (13 feet) off the ground (which was the height at which Leonardo worked), the scene appears to be an extension of the real architecture of the refectory. The vanishing point in fact coincides with Christ's head, the central feature of the composition (see the illustration on page 45). The remarkable thing is that the same sense of continuity between real space and picture space is also commmunicated to spectators at ground level. How did Leonardo achieve this effect? The diagram above shows that Leonardo constructed a kind of stage set. He "tipped" his painting towards the refectory to reveal the top of the table, and "forced" the perspective to increase the illusion of depth. For additional realism, he made it appear that the light was falling from the right, as if from the refectory's own windows.*

STILL LIFE ♦
The objects on the table are painted with the care normally devoted to a still life.

♦ **A THEATRICAL EFFECT**
The ideal standpoint from which to view the *Last Supper* is the place occupied by the prior at meal-times. Here, the spectator receives the full benefit of Leonardo's double perspective effect: the architecture in the painting appears as a continuation of the real refectory building; and the figure of Christ seems to offer the bread and wine from the picture to the real spectators outside.

WAR

Defensive systems were all-important in the Middle Ages. The heavy armor worn by horsemen offered protection against swords and arrows, and castle walls would resist the longest siege. In the fifteenth century the rules of war were revolutionized by the development of fire-arms: mounted knights and crossbowmen were replaced by soldiers with handguns and artillerymen, and the balance swung in favor of attack. In centers producing weapons, such as Milan, armor, swords, lances and halberds took second place to arquebus and cannon. Military architecture, too, underwent a transformation, and new defensive systems were developed. Walls became lower and thicker; towers were built with rounded contours to deflect cannon balls; fortifications were designed so that attackers could be kept constantly under fire.

✦ WAR: COLLECTIVE MADNESS
Leonardo described war as "bestial madness," but made many sketches for new military machines. In this he was not unlike some modern scientists who, while hating war, helped to manufacture the atomic bomb.

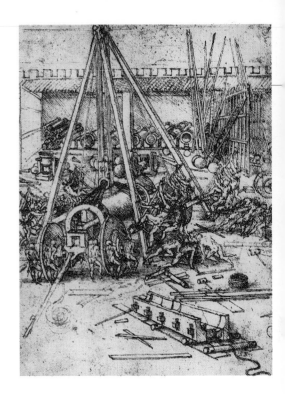

✦ THE TRANSFORMATION OF DEFENSIVE SYSTEMS

✦ 13TH CENTURY

Tall tower with battlements ✦

Battlements ✦

Machicolations ✦

Curtain wall ✦

Talus ✦

No ditch ✦

✦ 14TH CENTURY

Truncated tower to ✦ minimize exposure to artillery fire

Curtain wall backed ✦ with earth

Communicating ✦ trench in advance of curtain wall

Dry ditch ✦

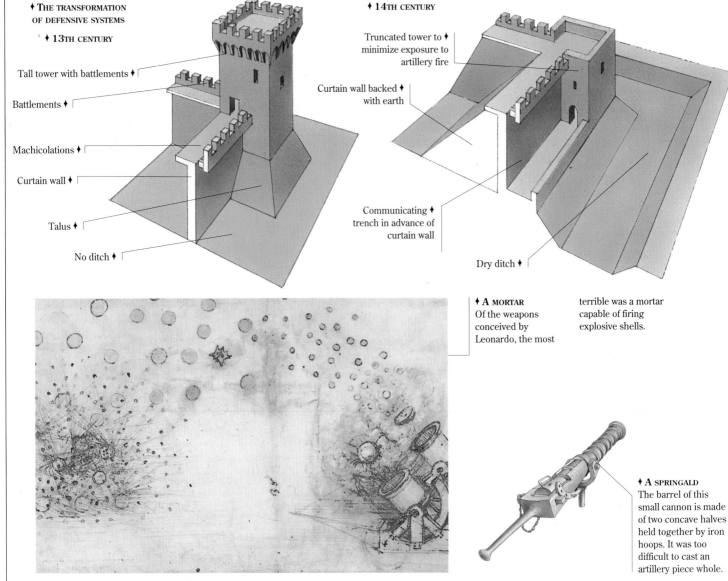

✦ A MORTAR
Of the weapons conceived by Leonardo, the most terrible was a mortar capable of firing explosive shells.

✦ A SPRINGALD
The barrel of this small cannon is made of two concave halves held together by iron hoops. It was too difficult to cast an artillery piece whole.

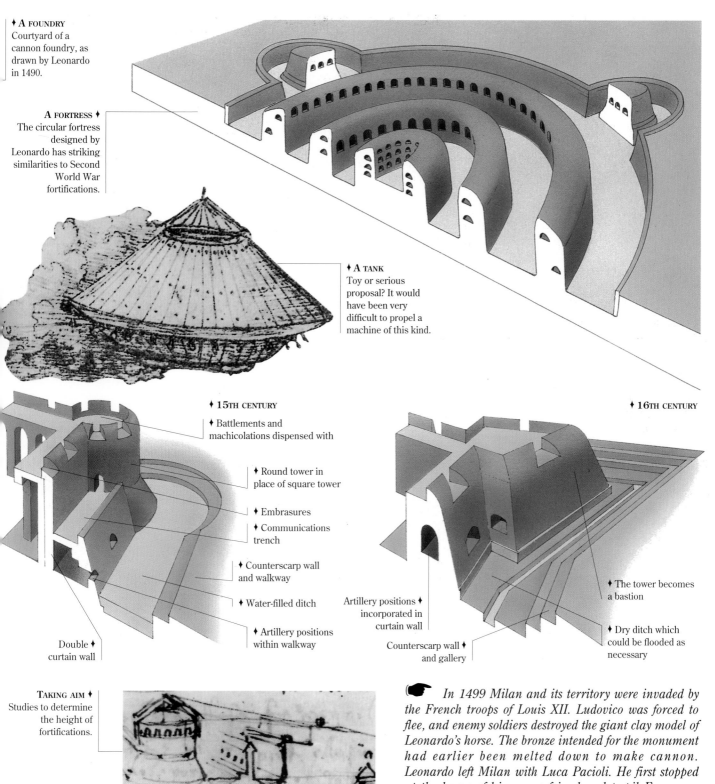

↞ A FOUNDRY
Courtyard of a cannon foundry, as drawn by Leonardo in 1490.

A FORTRESS ↟
The circular fortress designed by Leonardo has striking similarities to Second World War fortifications.

↟ A TANK
Toy or serious proposal? It would have been very difficult to propel a machine of this kind.

↟ 15TH CENTURY

↟ Battlements and machicolations dispensed with

↟ Round tower in place of square tower

↟ Embrasures

↟ Communications trench

↟ Counterscarp wall and walkway

↟ Water-filled ditch

↟ Artillery positions within walkway

Double ↟ curtain wall

↟ 16TH CENTURY

↟ The tower becomes a bastion

↟ Dry ditch which could be flooded as necessary

Artillery positions ↟ incorporated in curtain wall

Counterscarp wall ↟ and gallery

TAKING AIM ↟
Studies to determine the height of fortifications.

↟ A MACHINE GUN
The barrels are arranged in a fan to obtain a machine-gun effect.

☛   *In 1499 Milan and its territory were invaded by the French troops of Louis XII. Ludovico was forced to flee, and enemy soldiers destroyed the giant clay model of Leonardo's horse. The bronze intended for the monument had earlier been melted down to make cannon. Leonardo left Milan with Luca Pacioli. He first stopped at the home of his young friend and pupil Francesco Melzi at Vaprio. He then moved on to Mantua, where he made a charcoal drawing of Isabella d'Este. Fearing the arrival of the French, she urged Leonardo to depart, but later regretted her decision and in vain begged the artist to return. Leonardo went on to Venice and finally, in April 1500, returned to Florence. Since 1494, when the Medicis had been expelled, the city had experienced a period of republican government. Leonardo was offered hospitality in the Servite convent of the Santissima Annunziata. There he displayed a sketch for a painting of the* Virgin and Child with St Anne, *which greatly impressed the Florentines.* ☚

RIVALRY WITH MICHELANGELO

of state, in 1502. In those years the city was shaken by a Dominican monk, Girolamo Savonarola, who preached extreme puritanism. In 1498, Savonarola fell and was burned alive in the Piazza della Signoria. But the republic was short-lived, and soon the Medicis returned to power.

In 1497 the republican government of Florence enlarged the ancient seat of government – known as the Palazzo Vecchio – by adding a council chamber capable of seating five hundred. Following the expulsion of the Medicis, the Florentine authorities, mindful of their prestige, commissioned many works of painting, sculpture and intarsia (mosaic woodwork). To decorate the walls of the new chamber, they chose the most famous contemporary artists: Leonardo and Michelangelo, who were fierce rivals. Their task was to depict two famous victories won by Florentine armies. Unfortunately, little survives of their efforts. Michelangelo drew the cartoons for his *Battle of Cascina*, but they have since been lost. For his painting, the *Battle of Anghiari*, Leonardo wanted to revive a mural technique used by the Romans: encaustic. The results were disappointing. The colors ran, spoiling the whole work.

♦ **ENCAUSTIC**
Encaustic, developed around the fourth century BC, was the most widespread painting technique in the classical world. The pigments were mixed with hot wax before being applied. Leonardo hoped to achieve a high-gloss effect. Unfortunately, he misinterpreted the instructions he had found in ancient texts. When he used braziers to heat the wall, the colors merged and ran.

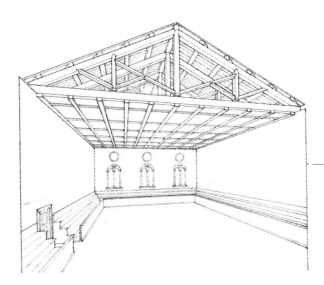

♦ **THE COUNCIL CHAMBER**
The council chamber as it appeared at the time. Leonardo was allocated the right-hand wall for the *Battle of Anghiari*.

♦ **THE COUNCIL CHAMBER TODAY**
Despite recent investigations, no trace of Leonardo's work has been found.

☞ *In 1502 Leonardo left Florence again and entered the service of Cesare Borgia, an ambitious military commander protected by his father, pope Alexander VI. With Cesare, Leonardo spent two years in the field, engaged on fortifications in the area between Urbino and the Adriatic coast. On his return to Florence, in 1503, he began his most famous painting, the* Mona Lisa. *There was sad news in 1504: his father had died, aged eighty, and Leonardo subsequently experienced great difficulty in obtaining his share of the inheritance. Meanwhile, he had to take up the challenge with Michelangelo. The cartoons for the* Battle of Anghiari *were to be completed by February 1505. He worked in the great council chamber, using the long-forgotten encaustic technique, but the results were disappointing and, embittered by his failure, Leonardo gave up the attempt.* ☞

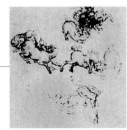

PRELIMINARY ✦ DRAWINGS
We can get some idea of Leonardo's intentions for the *Battle of Anghiari*, from the fine drawings that survive. The heads of the warriors and rearing horses belong to the central scene of the painting, a ferocious struggle for the standard between Florentine and Milanese horsemen. The battle was fought in 1440, near the town of Arezzo.

✦ A FAMOUS COPY
The Flemish painter Peter Paul Rubens (1577-1640) made a copy of the central scene of Leonardo's *Battle of Anghiari*.

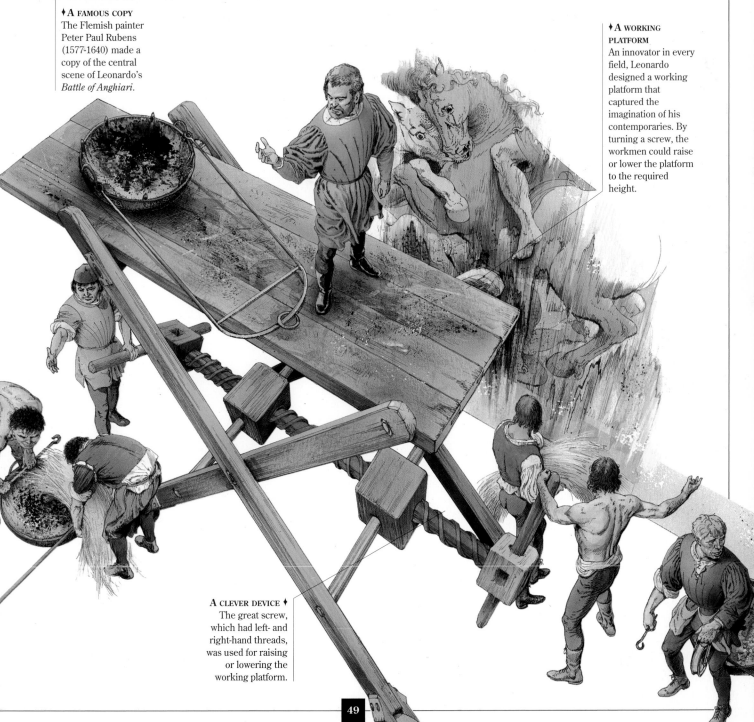

✦ A WORKING PLATFORM
An innovator in every field, Leonardo designed a working platform that captured the imagination of his contemporaries. By turning a screw, the workmen could raise or lower the platform to the required height.

A CLEVER DEVICE ✦
The great screw, which had left- and right-hand threads, was used for raising or lowering the working platform.

THE MONA LISA

The world's most famous painting is shrouded in mystery. But it is of no great importance whether the subject of the portrait is "Monna Lisa", wife of Florentine banker Francesco del Giocondo, or a favorite courtesan of Giuliano de' Medici. The lady with the enigmatic smile and intense gaze is depicted in a loggia (indoors). In the background is a magical, dream-like landscape of rocks and water.

EARLY EXPERIMENTS ✦
In this early drawing of the countryside around his native village of Vinci (see page 7), Leonardo's interest in views from above is already evident.

✦ THE WORK
Oil on wooden panel, 77 x 53 cm (30 x 21 inches). Louvre, Paris. Shortly after his return to Florence in 1503, Leonardo began work on a portrait that was to occupy him, off and on, for the rest of his life. The unfinished painting followed him to Milan, Rome and finally France. Antonio De Beatis mentions seeing it when he visited Leonardo at Cloux in 1517. The painting passed through many hands, until finally Napoleon assigned it to the Louvre in 1805. Stolen in 1911 and brought back to Italy, it was exhibited in Florence, Rome and Milan before its final return to France. So subtle was Leonardo's technique that his brushstrokes are invisible, even when the painting is examined under X-rays. The work must have required infinite patience. The Mona Lisa has always been an object of curiosity. Imaginative artists have portrayed the lady in the most unusual guises. She is shown as nude in one seventeenth-century copy (above) and, in modern times, Salvador Dalí painted her with a moustache.

✦ A STORM
This study of a deluge reveals Leonardo's interest in

atmospheric phenomena, and their effects on the quality of light.

Leonardo used "aerial" perspective in composing the landscape behind the Mona Lisa. That is, the further away things are, the more colors fade and lines become blurred. This gives a sense of depth. The *landscape has a magical atmosphere, with the bridge on the right the only sign of human existence. A different perspective is used for the figure, with her steady gaze and expressive mouth.*

MOUNTAIN RANGES ✦
In this preparatory drawing for the *Virgin and Child with St Anne*, we seem to view these mountain peaks from an airplane - a standpoint favored by Leonardo.

MOUNTAINS ✦
In this Madonna from 1480 - Alte Pinakothek, Munich - the quality of the atmosphere creates the sense of distance between the viewer and the mountains in the background.

✦ WATER
Leonardo was fascinated by the phenomenon of evaporation. In his misty landscapes, water and mountains appear to merge into each other.

✦ PERSPECTIVE
The landscape fades away into the muted blues and greens of the horizon. This effect is a result of the refraction of light in the atmosphere.

✦ AIR IS BLUE
Leonardo maintained that air is blue. The more distant an object, the more air between it and the observer: hence objects in the far distance take on a blue appearance.

LOOKING INTO ✦
THE DISTANCE
In Leonardo's *Bacchus* of 1515 - Louvre, Paris - the outlines of objects in the background soften with distance, until finally they merge into their surroundings.

HYDRAULICS

In Leonardo's day waterways were far more important than they are today. It was quicker and cheaper to transport goods by boat, because of the poor state of the roads and the inefficiency of existing vehicles. Canals were also useful for irrigation, and, where there was a fall in level, water power could be harnessed to drive grinding and fulling mills. Lying inland, Florence would benefit from an effective link with the sea, and for over a century the Florentines had dreamed of building a waterway to the Tyrrhenian Sea. The Arno ran dry in summer, and even in winter navigation was difficult because of the river's winding, irregular course. On his return to Florence, Leonardo studied how to build a navigable canal which would rejoin the Arno near Pisa, an ancient sea-going republic and rival of Florence. In considering this plan, Leonardo could draw on the wealth of experience he had acquired in Milan. There he had carried out many projects to improve Lombardy's canal network.

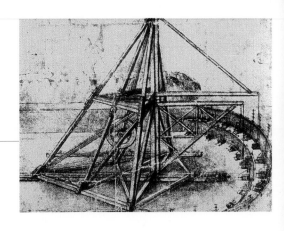

MACHINES, NOT MEN ✦
Realizing that men equipped only with spades and shovels would take years to complete so vast a project as diverting the Arno, Leonardo designed great excavating machines to hasten progress.

MOTIVE POWER ✦
Barges were towed along the canal by men and horses.

FILLING THE LOCK ✦
The sluices are opened, the lock fills with water, and the barge rises to the higher level.

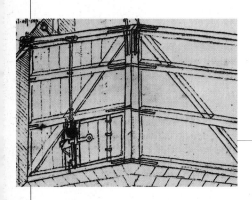

✦ THE INVENTOR
Leonardo is credited with the invention of many hydraulic devices, in particular the lock. Locks make it possible to control the water level in a confined section of canal, and so raise and lower boats from one level to another.

MOORING ✦
The barge is moored with ropes to the side of the lock.

ENTERING A LOCK ✦
The gates are open, and a barge travelling upstream enters the lock.

☞ *In 1503 Florence embarked on a debilitating war against her neighbor, Pisa. Niccolò Machiavelli, Florentine minister of war, had for some time been thinking of diverting the Arno, which runs through both cities, as a way of damaging Pisa's livelihood. Leonardo studied the problem and drew up a well-illustrated report. According to an old tradition, he was actually commissioned to begin the work, but this is improbable: to divert the river would have taken two thousand laborers forty thousand working days. The task was beyond Florence's means, and would have taken years to complete. In fact, the war ended in 1509. Leonardo's notes nevertheless demonstrate his ability in problem-solving.* ☞

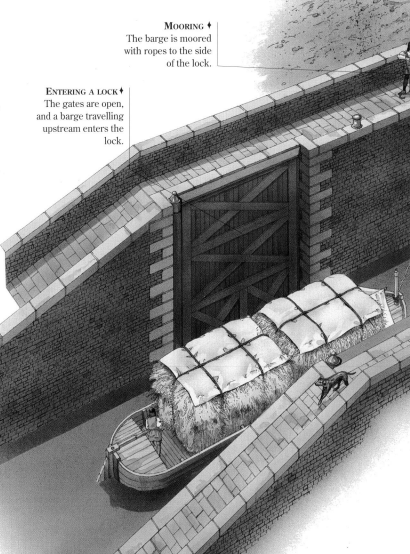

THE CANAL ✦
The Arno, with its seasonal flow, was difficult to navigate. Leonardo planned a canal fed by the streams descending from the Apennines. The canal would have begun in Florence and rejoined the Arno near Pisa.

✦ THE TUNNEL
It would have been necessary to drive a tunnel nearly one mile long under the hill of Serravalle.

HOW A LOCK WORKS ✦
1. The sluices are opened and water fills the lock.
2. The lock is full.
3. The exit gate is opened and the boat continues its journey.

CANAL BRIDGE ✦
Canals often had to cross rivers.

SAINT ANNE

Seated on the knees of Saint Anne, Mary is depicted lifting the baby Jesus, who in turn is attempting to sit astride a struggling lamb. As she watches the child at play, Saint Anne - the mother of Mary - contemplates the miracle of the incarnation. The theme of the three generations was common in northern Europe, and eventually became popular with Italian painters, particularly in Florence.

♦ FORM
The figures merge and it is difficult to say where one begins and another ends: Mary's arm could belong to Saint Anne, their legs are intertwined, and the Child's thigh is continued in the leg of the lamb.

♦ THE WORK
Oil on wooden panel, 168 x 130 cm (5.5. x 4.25 feet). Louvre, Paris. The *Virgin and Child with St Anne* is the final version of a subject on which Leonardo had been working for some time. He had already produced two sketches and, possibly, an earlier painting. Leonardo painted the panel towards the end of his second stay in Milan, between 1510 and 1513. It accompanied him to France, together with the *Mona Lisa* and

St John the Baptist.
He kept the three paintings by him until his death. Francesco Melzi, the pupil who inherited his works, brought the *St Anne* back to Italy, but in 1629 cardinal Richelieu, minister of Louis XIII, purchased it and took it to France as a gift for his sovereign. In 1801 it was added to the Louvre collections.

♦ MOVEMENT
The figures are as if bound up together in a single movement: the Child is trying to grasp the lamb, while Mary restrains him, watched by Saint Anne. The group

tends towards the right-hand side of the picture, where their eyes also seem to converge on a single point. The observer is left with an acute sense of instability.

Leonardo treated the subject in a completely new way: in terms of composition, and of the interpretation he seems to be suggesting. The figures are as if interwoven, forming a compact mass *with the structure of a pyramid. Leonardo had already used this arrangement, but here he gives the group a dynamic sense of movement. Three preparatory drawings are shown on the left.*

COLOR ♦
Warm and cold tones are perfectly balanced, creating a magical equilibrium of predominantly blue and brown tones.

♦ A SYMBOL OF CHRIST'S PASSION

In the religious ceremonies of the Old Testament, an animal offered in sacrifice had to be without spot or blemish. For Christians, the lamb became the symbol of Christ's sacrifice on the cross. By showing the infant Jesus embracing the creature, Leonardo suggests the purpose for which Christ came: innocent as a lamb, he was born to give his life as a sacrifice.

♦ THE VIRGIN

The Virgin Mary leans forward with all the solicitude of a mother wanting to protect her baby. By this simple, gentle gesture, Leonardo represents the instinct of a mother seeking to avert the tragic destiny awaiting her child.

♦ FIRST THOUGHTS

In this 1498 drawing in the National Gallery, London, the allusion is more explicit: Saint Anne points upwards to indicate that this is God's will.

MASOLINO AND ♦ MASACCIO, 1420

In this static, pyramid-shaped arrangement, Saint Anne is depicted as an old woman, solemnly dominating the composition.

♦ SAINT ANNE

Supporting the whole group, the dignified figure of Saint Anne looks on with an expression of sweet resignation. For Leonardo, she represents the Church. The primeval landscape in the background suggests the passage of time: Saint Anne knows that Christ's sacrifice is inevitable, and feels pity for her daughter.

FLIGHT

◆ **THE WING-BEAT OF BIRDS**
Leonardo started by studying the way birds beat their wings.

◆ **HOW BIRDS FLY**
Finding it impossible to design wings light enough to be worked by human muscle power, Leonardo turned his attention to the gliding flight of birds.

Strangely enough, it is Leonardo's most fantastic project - his attempt to create a flying machine - that best demonstrates the way his mind worked. He began by observing birds, studying the anatomy of their wings, and the function and arrangement of their feathers. Watching them in flight, he noted that the wing-beat was different for take-off, forward flight and landing. His first idea was that a man might fly by flapping a large pair of wings, but he soon realized that human muscle power was insufficient. He next considered a mechanical propulsion system worked by a spring, but it was apparent that the spring would unwind too quickly for sustained flight. He therefore returned to his study of birds, observing how large birds of prey are lifted up by air currents. He took into account the importance of atmospheric conditions: wind speed and direction, and meteorological and aerodynamic factors. Finally, he concluded that, in the absence of an engine - not invented until centuries later - the best prospect for human flight lay in fixed-wing gliding. He then designed a machine similar to a modern hang-glider.

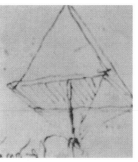

FUTURE INVENTIONS ◆
Leonardo anticipated the helicopter and the parachute.

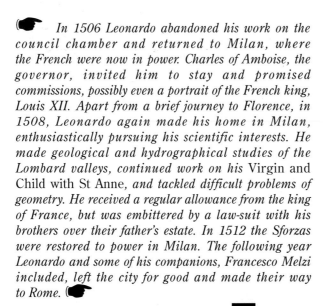

👉 *In 1506 Leonardo abandoned his work on the council chamber and returned to Milan, where the French were now in power. Charles of Amboise, the governor, invited him to stay and promised commissions, possibly even a portrait of the French king, Louis XII. Apart from a brief journey to Florence, in 1508, Leonardo again made his home in Milan, enthusiastically pursuing his scientific interests. He made geological and hydrographical studies of the Lombard valleys, continued work on his* Virgin and Child with St Anne, *and tackled difficult problems of geometry. He received a regular allowance from the king of France, but was embittered by a law-suit with his brothers over their father's estate. In 1512 the Sforzas were restored to power in Milan. The following year Leonardo and some of his companions, Francesco Melzi included, left the city for good and made their way to Rome.* 👉

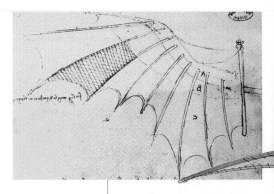

WING WITH FLAPS ◆
Leonardo observed that, when birds come in to land, their feathers are held tightly together. From this he wrongly deduced that birds in normal flight spread their feathers to allow air to pass through. And so he designed a wing with flaps that would open on take-off and close on landing.

A FLYING MACHINE ◆
The wings were worked by the hands and feet of the pilot.

SPRING-DRIVEN ◆
Leonardo designed spring-driven wings which would flap up and down like those of a bird.

FIXED WING ◆
A fixed wing, with appendages to control the machine. Leonardo had adopted the principle of the hang-glider.

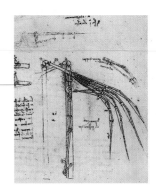

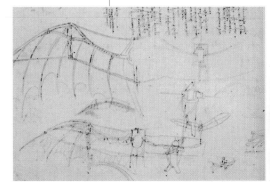

♦ **EXPERIMENTS**
Leonardo's studies
on flight were
accompanied by a
series of experiments
on the use of
artificial wings

IMPROVEMENTS ♦
Leonardo tried out
other materials and
improved the
framework. He was
moving towards the
concept of gliding.

MECHANICS

Leonardo's interest in mechanical engineering is amply proved by the thousands of his drawings that remain. When these were first published, a hundred or so years ago, they created a sensation, and many people saw Leonardo as having anticipated almost all modern inventions, from the helicopter to the bicycle. We are now more aware of his debt to earlier inventors, and to his contemporaries: many of the machines he drew had already been built, or at least existed in the minds of imaginative engineers. Leonardo was original in having understood that the working of any machine, be it a crane or a water-mill, depends on a limited number of mechanisms: springs, connecting rods, cams, gears, and so on. The way to obtain better machines was therefore to study and improve their component parts.

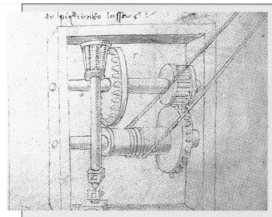

✦ A LIFTING MACHINE
A drawing of a type of winch, by Francesco di Giorgio, architect, engineer and friend of Leonardo. It gives a general idea of the winch and its gearing system. Compared with this, Leonardo's drawings were more detailed and explored how machines worked.

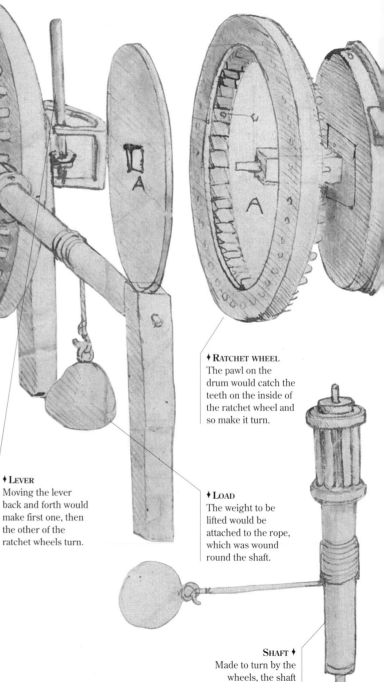

✦ LEONARDO'S DRAWINGS
On page 59 are study drawings by Leonardo of different mechanisms. The drawing on this page is one he made of another kind of winch for lifting things. On the left he shows what the machine looks like. Then, on the right, he gives an exploded version in an attempt to explain how the machine works.

☛ *In 1513 Leonardo arrived in Rome, where he was a guest of the Florentine cardinal Giuliano de' Medici, brother of the new pope Leo X. The greatest artists of the day had gravitated to Rome. Bramante died there in 1514, and Raphael took over the responsibility for building St Peter's. Leonardo was not obliged to paint, but designed the stage sets for some of the lavish Roman entertainments. He continued his scientific studies, particularly mathematics, studying the problem of squaring the circle and beginning a treatise on geometry. In 1514 or 1515 Leo X gave him the task of draining the swampy, unhealthy countryside around Rome - a project to which he devoted two years. Louis XII of France died in 1515 and his successor, Francis I, offered Leonardo hospitality at the French court. After one more year in Rome, in 1517 Leonardo set off for France, where he was to live out the rest of his life.* **☛**

✦ RATCHET WHEEL
The pawl on the drum would catch the teeth on the inside of the ratchet wheel and so make it turn.

✦ LEVER
Moving the lever back and forth would make first one, then the other of the ratchet wheels turn.

✦ LOAD
The weight to be lifted would be attached to the rope, which was wound round the shaft.

SHAFT ✦
Made to turn by the wheels, the shaft would wind in the rope.

◆ DRUM
Each half of the double drum has a pawl, which would engage with the ratchet teeth in one direction only. As each wheel rotated, the dowels would turn the shaft, lifting the load.

CAM ◆
A cam transfers the movement of a rotating shaft to another part of the machine. In some internal combustion engines, cams open and close the valves.

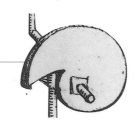

COUPLING ◆
Leonardo designed many kinds of coupling. Their purpose is to connect two mechanical parts.

◆ OPPOSING RATCHET WHEEL
This wheel would rotate in the opposite direction to its partner.

PULLEY ◆
A pulley is a wheel with a rope or belt on its rim. Pulleys can be used for lifting weights and for transmitting power.

CHAIN ◆
Drive chains are used to transmit power from one part of a machine to another. The most obvious example is a bicycle chain.

CLUTCH ◆
A clutch, consisting of two parts which can be connected and disconnected, is used to engage and disengage a mechanism.

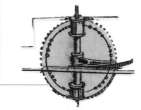

COG-WHEELS ◆
Cogs are vital components. They transmit power from one shaft to another and, depending on their size, increase or decrease the speed of rotation.

BEARINGS ◆
Leonardo designed many kinds of ball and roller bearing, to reduce friction.

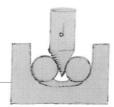

WORM ◆
Leonardo called the worm of a helical gear a "perpetual screw." This type of gear transmits power between shafts at right angles to each other, and permits large reductions in rotational speeds.

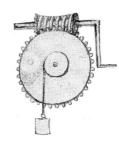

ESCAPEMENT ◆
A device which regulates the motion of rotating mechanisms, used most often in clocks.

TEETH AND DOWELS ◆
A close-up of the teeth and dowels of the ratchet wheel.

SCREW ◆
A screw combining a right-hand and a left-hand thread doubles the speed of a mechanism.

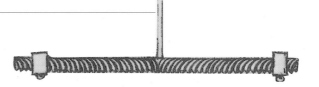

FRANCE

Leonardo's story ends in France, at the court of Francis I, where even in the last months of his life he engaged in one of his favorite activities: designing the sets and machinery for lavish entertainments. When he died at Cloux, not yet seventy years of age, honored by king and courtiers alike, his legacy to posterity was immense. Leonardo was one of the greatest painters of all time, a sculptor, a brilliant engineer, architect, scientist and musician. More than that, his extraordinary gifts, never before combined in a single person, laid the foundation for a new vision of man and his environment. Leonardo was the first "modern human." His questing mind was never satisfied, but sought always to probe further into the unknown, to overcome the restrictions of fixed modes of thought and behavior and extend the frontiers of human knowledge.

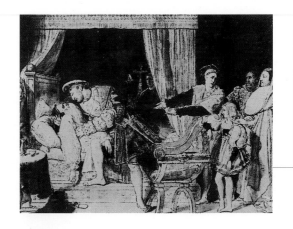

✦ LEONARDO'S DEATH
This famous drawing by the French painter Dominique Ingres (1780-1867) depicts Leonardo's death. Although Francis I is shown at the bedside, the king was not in fact present during his last moments. It is true, however, that he was devoted to Leonardo.

✦ ROBOTS
Leonardo had a passion for automata. To mark a celebration in honor of Francis, he constructed a mechanical lion. At the crucial moment the lion opened to eject its load of white lilies, symbol of the French crown.

AMBOISE ✦
Leonardo spent the last years of his life close to the royal residence of Amboise at Cloux.

REMORANTIN ✦
A plan for the château of Remorantin, which Leonardo undertook for Francis's wife. It was never built.

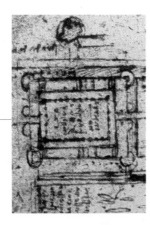

ST JOHN ✦
This *St John the Baptist* - executed after 1510 and now in the Louvre - was Leonardo's last known painting. The artist brought it with him to France, and bequeathed it to his friend and pupil Francesco Melzi.

✦ MELZI
Francesco Melzi, Leonardo's favorite pupil and assistant, watches the reaction to Leonardo's contrivance.

✦ WHAT LEONARDO LOOKED LIKE
Above: the figure of Plato in Raphael's *School of Athens* (Vatican), thought to be a portrait of Leonardo. Left: a supposed self-portrait, drawn by Leonardo in 1512. The artist looks older than his years.

✦ CHAMBORD
The château de Chambord. There is no definite evidence, but Leonardo may have influenced its design.

☞ *Francis I was well aware of Leonardo's genius, and heaped honors upon him. He gave him a princely residence at Cloux, near Amboise; granted him a pension; and bestowed on him the title of first painter, architect and mechanic of the King. Despite losing the use of one arm, Leonardo showed that his appetite for work was undiminished. For a celebration to honor the king, he built a mechanical lion; he helped organize other royal festivities; and he produced studies for irrigation projects in various French cities. In 1519 his health took a turn for the worse. In April he made his will, leaving all his manuscripts to Francesco Melzi. He died on May 2, 1519. Legend has it that Francis I, who admired him greatly and regarded him almost as a father, hurried to his bedside at Amboise to pay his last respects.*

◆ KEY DATES

1452	Leonardo born at Vinci on 15 April, natural child of ser Piero, a notary, and Caterina, a peasant girl in service with the family.
1469	Joins the workshop of Andrea del Verrocchio, in Florence, where he learns the techniques of drawing, painting and sculpture.
1473	Now a member of the painters' guild of St Luke. Executes the first work that can be ascribed to him with certainty: a drawing of the Arno valley.
1478	Paints an altarpiece for the Palazzo della Signoria, Florence. Failure of the Pazzi conspiracy against the Medicis; Lorenzo de' Medici's authority confirmed.
1482	Moves to Milan, where he is commissioned to create a colossal equestrian statue in memory of Francesco Sforza, and employs his talents in many other fields.
1492	Designs costumes for the wedding of Ludovico il Moro and Beatrice d'Este. Death of Lorenzo the Magnificent. Columbus sails to the New World.
1495	Begins painting the *Last Supper* in the refectory of Santa Maria delle Grazie, a monastery in Milan. Decorates parts of the Sforza castle.
1499	Leaves Milan with the mathematician Luca Pacioli. Stays at Vaprio, then Mantua, where he makes two portraits of Isabella d'Este.
1500	In March, returns from Venice to Florence, where he lodges at the Servite convent of the Santissima Annunziata.
1502	Serves Cesare Borgia as architect and engineer during military campaigns in the Romagna region. Studies fortification systems and war machines.
1503	Back in Florence, paints the *Mona Lisa*. The Florentine Republic commissions him to paint the *Battle of Anghiari* in the Palazzo Vecchio.
1504	Works on the *Battle of Anghiari*. Michelangelo completes his *David*. Raphael moves to Florence, and is deeply influenced by Leonardo's work.
1508	Returns to Milan and devotes himself to geology and anatomy. In Rome, Michelangelo is commissioned to paint the Sistine ceiling.
1513	Leaves for Rome, where he spends three years in the service of Pope Leo X. Pursues mathematical and scientific studies.
1514	Draws up plans for draining the Pontine marshes. Death of Bramante; Raphael succeeds him as architect of St Peter's.
1517	Francis I, the new king of France, having reconquered Milan, invites Leonardo to his court. Leonardo takes up residence at Cloux, near Amboise.
1518	Designs the stage sets for the wedding of Lorenzo de' Medici and a niece of the French king. Takes part in celebrations for the Dauphin's baptism.
1519	Charles V elected Holy Roman Emperor. A sick man, Leonardo makes his will on 23 April, naming his painter friend Francesco Melzi as executor. Dies at Cloux on 2 May.

◆ LEONARDO'S NOTEBOOKS

Right up to the end of his life Leonardo continued his scientific studies and made prodigious quantities of notes. Several times he attempted to set them in order, but none of the books he embarked on was ever finished, and his observations remained fragmentary, unconnected and at times contradictory. On Leonardo's death, this priceless collection of writings, many of them illustrated with drawings and sketches, passed to Francesco Melzi, who began to catalogue them. The work was extremely difficult: Leonardo's notes were usually very short, and often intended only for his own use. He sometimes repeated himself in different places, copied extracts from other writers' works and, years later, would fill in empty spaces in earlier manuscripts. His notes were not always dated. Reordering his writings on a chronological basis was clearly very difficult. Melzi nevertheless managed to reorganize at least part of the material in a logical way and, following the master's original intentions, compiled the *Treatise on Painting*, which now constitutes the Vatican Library's CODEX URBINAS. When Melzi died, in 1570, the manuscripts went various ways, and some were lost, dismembered or mutilated. Roughly 3500 pages have survived, mostly written on both sides of the paper and illustrated with drawings. Some are in the form of small note-pads, which Leonardo used for making rapid observations. There are also more substantial exercise books intended for specific studies, but they generally degenerated into collections of miscellaneous notes, and a large number of loose sheets. Most are written in an apparently indecipherable hand, which some of Leonardo's contemporaries took to be a form of secret code. It is in fact mirror writing: the artist wrote from right to left using his left hand.

THE "ATLANTIC" AND WINDSOR CODICES. Some decades after Melzi's death, the Milanese Pompeo Leoni, official sculptor to King Philip II of Spain and art collector, tried to reassemble some of the scattered manuscripts. He catalogued and numbered a good part of Leonardo's writings and a large number of individual sheets, and collected them into two substantial volumes. The first, kept in the library of Windsor Castle, is a compilation of some six hundred drawings, including studies for drapery and for the *Last Supper*. It also contains a plan of the town of Imola – the first such survey carried out on scientific lines – and almost all Leonardo's anatomical studies. The second volume, kept in the Ambrosian Library in Milan and universally known as the "Atlantic" Codex, possibly on account of its size (in Greek mythology, Atlas was the giant who supported the world on his shoulders), contains drawings and writings on scientific subjects. It includes notes on artillery and on offensive and defensive weapons, plans for a self-propelled carriage (still referred to as "Leonardo's automobile") and early drawings for a flying machine. There is also a curious sketch of a bicycle, surprisingly like modern versions, drawn on the reverse of one of Leonardo's sheets by a pupil, who was copying an original by the artist, now lost.

MANUSCRIPTS A-M AND ASHBURNHAM CODEX. In 1635 the Atlantic Codex found its way to the Ambrosian Library in Milan, together with twelve other manuscripts identified by the letters A to M. In 1796 Napoleon decreed that all these volumes be expropriated and sent to the library of the Institut de France in Paris. Only the Atlantic Codex was eventually returned. The oldest of all these compilations is manuscript B, dating from 1488, which contains drawings of war machines, boats, bridges and flying machines. 1490 and 1491 are covered by manuscripts C and A respectively, the latter devoted largely to painting and physics. A part of Manuscript A today forms the separate codex known as Ashburnham, on painting. Manuscripts H and I, which also belong to Leonardo's first Milanese period, are concerned with grammar and lexicology. The others – D, E, F, G, K, L and M – are devoted to scientific topics.

THE TRIVULZIANO CODEX. This is one of the oldest collections of Leonardo's writings, dating from his early years in Milan. Kept in the Castello Sforzesco, it contains notes on grammar and lexicology, and long lists of words, mainly deriving from Latin. Leonardo had not received much formal education, but knowledge of Latin was indispensible for reading most scientific texts. This codex bears witness to his desire to master it.

THE FORSTER MANUSCRIPTS. Three small notebooks, kept at the Victoria and Albert Museum, London. The most important, Forster I, consists of fifteen pages, dating from 1490, sewn into a bigger notebook compiled in 1505. It contains diagrams of hydraulic devices, demonstrating Leonardo's fascination with the world of water. The other two are devoted to Euclidian geometry, which Leonardo learned from his friend Luca Pacioli.

MADRID I AND MADRID II. Not discovered until the 1960s, these two codices, inventory numbers 8937 and 8936, are kept in the National Library, Madrid. The first, begun during Leonardo's early years in Milan, contains illustrations of machinery, particularly for textile manufacture, and mechanical components (screws, chains, cogs, pulleys, fly-wheels, ball bearings, gears, clock parts). The second includes a report on the problems of casting his bronze horse, the project for diverting the waters of the Arno, and plans for the fortification of Piombino.

HAMMER (FORMERLY LEICESTER) CODEX. The writings and many of the drawings in this codex are concerned with a topic of special fascination to Leonardo: water and its dynamics: flow, currents, whirlpools, rapids. There is also material on astronomy and geology, with theories about the structure of the earth and the way its surface changes.

CODEX ON BIRD FLIGHT. Kept in the Biblioteca Reale in Turin, this collection was compiled around 1505 and contains studies and drawings of birds, their anatomy and their mode of flight in different atmospheric conditions. There are also pages devoted to quite different subjects, in particular mechanics, hydraulics and architecture.

ARUNDEL MANUSCRIPT. Kept at the British Museum, this is a compilation of notebooks on various subjects recorded by Leonardo in the final decades of his life. In his treatment of water, he returns to the theme of the Hammer Codex and the drawings of the Deluge owned by Queen Elizabeth II. Leonardo planned to enlarge on this subject in a work entitled *Libro primo delle acque*.

◆ LIST OF WORKS INCLUDED IN THIS BOOK

The works reproduced in this book are listed here, with their date, when known, the museum or gallery where they are nowheld, and page number. The numbers in bold type refer to the Credits on page 64, which give further information about some of the works. Where no gallery is shown, the work is in a private collection. Abbreviations: Atlantic Codex, AC; Arundel Codex, ARC; Windsor Codex, WC; codex on bird flight, BFC; Madrid I, MI; Madrid II, MII; Manuscript B, MB; Manuscript L, ML.

ANONYMOUS
1 *Nude Mona Lisa*, 17th century (Kaupe collection, Pallanza) 50.
ANDRES DEL CASTAGNO (c.1421-1457)
2 *Last Supper*, 1450 (refectory of the convent of Santa Apollonia, Florence) 43.
APOLLONIO DI GIOVANNI (c.1415-1465)
3 *Banquet in a Courtyard*, c.1460 (Biblioteca Riccardiana, Florence) 29.
BELLINI, GIOVANNI (c.1432-1516)
4 *Pietà*, c.1460 (Museo Correr, Venice) 16.
BOTTICELLI, SANDRO (1445-1510)
5 *Adoration of the Magi*, 1480 (Uffizi Gallery, Florence) 27; 6 *Annunciation*, c.1470 (Louis F. Hyde collection, Glen Falls, New York) 18; 7 *Birth of Venus*, 1482 (Uffizi Gallery, Florence) 16; 8 *Head of Angel*, c.1480 (Musée des Beaux-Arts, Rennes) 15.
BRUNELLESCHI, FILIPPO (1377-1446)
9 *Crucifix*, c.1410-15 (Gondi chapel, church of Santa Maria Novella, Florence) 10; 10 *Sacrifice of Isaac*, bronze panel for door of Florence Baptistry, 1401 (Bargello Museum, Florence) 10.
DALI, SALVADOR (1904-1979)
11 *Mona Lisa with Moustache*, 50.
DOMENICO, VENEZIANO (byname of Domenico di Bartolomeo) (early 15th century-1461)
12 *Annunciation*, 1445-48 (Fitzwilliam Museum, Cambridge, England) 19.
DONATELLO (byname of Niccolò di Betto Bardi) (1386-1466)
13 *Crucifix*, c. 1410-15 (church of Santa Croce, Florence) 10; 14 *The Feast of Herod*, 1427 (cathedral baptistry, Siena) 11; 15 *Equestrian statue of Gattamelata*, c. 1446-50 (Piazza del Santo, Padua) 31.
GHIBERTI, BUONACCORSO
16 Drawing of the swivel crane used in building the dome of Florence cathedral (Zibaldone 105 r.) 20.
GHIBERTI, LORENZO (1378-1455)
17 *Sacrifice of Isaac*, bronze panel for door of Florence Baptistry, 1401 (Bargello Museum, Florence) 10.
GHIRLANDAIO (byname of Domenico Bigordi) (1449-1494)
18 *Last Supper*, 1480 (church of Ognissanti, Florence) 43.
GIOTTO (c.1267-1337)
19 *St Francis expelling the devils from Arezzo*, 1297-99 (upper church of St Francis, Assisi) 12.
GOZZOLI, BENOZZO (1420-1497)
20 *One of the Magi, as a youth*, 1459. Detail, with portraits of members of the Medici family (Chapel of the Palazzo Medici-Riccardi, Florence) 28.
INGRES, DOMINIQUE (1780-1867)
21 *Death of Leonardo*, 1818 (Musée du Petit Palais, Paris) 60.
LEONARDO
– Paintings
22 *Adoration of the Magi*, 1481-82 (Uffizi Gallery, Florence) 26-27; 23 *Annunciation*, 1472-75 (Uffizi Gallery, Florence) 18-19; 24 *Annunciation* for Pistoia Cathedral, 1488 (Louvre, Paris) 18; 25 *Bacchus*, 1515 (Louvre, Paris) 51; 26 *La Belle Ferronière*, 1490-95 (Louvre, Paris) 39; 27 *Benois Madonna*, c.1478 (Hermitage Museum, St Petersburg) 38; 28 *Last Supper*, 1495-97 (Santa Maria delle Grazie, Milan) 42-45; 29 *Mona Lisa*, c.1503-1505 (Louvre, Paris) 38, 50-51; 30 *Madonna with the Carnation*, 1480 (Alte Pinakothek, Munich) 51; 31 *The Musician*, c.1490 (Pinacoteca Ambrosiana, Milan) 39; 32 *Portrait of Cecilia Gallerani (Lady with an Ermine)*, 1488 (Czartoryski Museum, Cracow) 39; 33 *Portrait of Ginevra de' Benci*, 1474 (National Gallery of Art, Washington, D.C.) 38; 34 *Portrait of Isabella d'Este*, 1500 (Louvre, Paris) 39; 35 *St John the Baptist*, 1513-16 (Louvre, Paris) 61; 36 *The Virgin and Child with St Anne*, 1510-13 (Louvre, Paris) 54-55; 37 *The Virgin of the Rocks*, 1483-86 (Louvre, Paris) 32-33; 38 *The Virgin of the Rocks*, 1503-06 (National Gallery, London) 32.
– Drawings and studies
39 Cartoon for *The Virgin and Child with St Anne*, 1498 (National Gallery, London) 55; 40 Compositional study for *The Virgin and Child with St Anne* (Accademia Gallery, Venice) 54; 41 *The Deluge*, c.1516 (WC 12380) 50; 42 Drawings of costumes for the "festa del paradiso", 1490 (Royal Library, Windsor) 31; 43 Drawing of hanged man, connected with the execution of Bernardo Baroncelli, c.1479 (Musée Bonnat, Bayonne) 29; 44 Drawing of a plough, Leonardo's personal emblem (Royal Library, Windsor) 6; 45 Drawings of regular bodies for Luca Pacioli's *De divina proportione*, 1496-1503 (ML) 40; 46 Drawing of roof for Milan Cathedral, 1487-88 (AC 310 v-b.) 35; 47 Drawing of the swivel crane used in building the dome of Florence Cathedral (AC 965 r.) 20; 48 *Female head* (Gabinetto dei disegni e delle stampe, Uffizi Gallery, Florence) 18; 49 *The Flood*, c.1516 (WC 12380) 50; 50 *Grotesque portrait*, c.1515 (Christ Church, Oxford, inv. 0033) 42; 51 *La Scapigliata (lady with hair undone)*, 1490 (Pinacoteca Nazionale, Parma) 39; 52 *Landscape of the Arno Valley*, 1473 (Gabinetto dei disegni e delle stampe, Uffizi Gallery, Florence) 7; 53 Map of Pisa and mouth of the Arno, c.1503 (MII 52 v., 543 r.) 53; 54 Perspective study for the *Adoration of the Magi*, c. 1481 (Gabinetto dei disegni e delle stampe, Uffizi Gallery, Florence) 27; 55 Plan for casting the Sforza monument (MI 157 r.) 31; 56 Plan for the Château de Remorantin, 1517-18 (ARC 269 r.) 61; 57 Plans for symmetrically designed churches (MB 17 v.) 35; 58 Preparatory drawing for *Adoration of the Magi*, c.1481 (ARC) 26 a.; 59 Preparatory drawing for *Adoration of the Magi*, c.1481 (Ecole des Beaux-Arts, Paris) 26 c.; 60 Preparatory drawing for the *Adoration of the Magi*, c.1481 (Fitzwilliam Museum, Cambridge, England) 26 b.; 61 Preparatory drawing for the drapery covering the knees of *The Virgin and Child with St Anne* (Royal Library, Windsor) 54; 62 Preparatory drawings for an equestrian monument, 1508-10 (WC 13356) 31; 63 Preparatory drawing with mountain ranges for *The Virgin and Child with St Anne*, 1498 (WC 12410) 50; 64 Preparatory drawing for *Portrait of Isabella d'Este* (Royal Library, Windsor) 38; 65 Preparatory drawing with storm over a valley for *The Virgin and Child with St Anne* (Royal Library, Windsor) 54; 66 Preparatory study for the *Last Supper*, c.1495 (WC 12542 r.) 42; 67 *Self-portrait*, 1512 (Biblioteca Reale, Turin) 61; 68 Study for angel in *The Virgin of the Rocks*, c.1483 (Biblioteca Reale, Turin) 38; 69 Study of angel's head for *The Virgin of the Rocks*, c.1483 (Royal Library, Windsor) 32; 70 Study of the arm, c.1512 (Royal Library, Windsor) 37; 71 Study for armored vehicle (British Museum, London) 47; 72 Study for ball and roller bearings (MI 101 v.) 59; 73 Studies of bird flight (BFC 7 v.; 8 r.) 56; 74 Studies of the cardiac muscle, c.1512 (Royal Library, Windsor) 36; 75 Study for chains (MI 10 r.) 59; 76 Study for cogged wheels (MI 5 r.) 59; 77 Study for coupling (MI 62 r.) 59; 78 Studies of the cranium, c.1512 (Royal Library, Windsor) 37; 79 Study of drapery, c.1478 (Louvre, Paris) 15; 80 Study of escapement (MI 12 r.) 59; 81 Study for excavating machine (AC 1 v.b.) 52; 82 Study for figure of St James in the *Last Supper*, c. 1495 (WC 12552) 42; 83 Study for flying machine (AC 276 r.b.) 56; 84 Experiments for artificial wings (MB 88 v.) 56; 85 Studies of fetuses, c.1512 (Royal Library, Windsor) 37; 86 Study for foundry (WC 12647) 46; 87 Studies for heads for *The Battle of Anghiari*, c.1504 (Szépnuiveszeti Museum, Budapest) 49; 88 Study of horseman with lance, c.1483 (WC 12653) 46; 89 Study of horses and riders for *The Battle of Anghiari*, c. 1504 (Louvre, Paris) 49; 90 Study for lock gate (AC 240 r.c.) 52; 91 Study for machine gun (AC 56 v.) 47; 92 Study of machine for converting alternating to continuous motion (AC 30 v.) 58-59; 93 Study for mortar (AC 9 v. top) 46; 94 Study for parachute (AC 381 v.a.) 56; 95 Study for perspectograph (AC 1 b r.a.) 13; 96 Study of plants for *The Virgin of the Rocks*, c. 1483 (Royal Library, Windsor) 32; 97 Study for propeller (MB 83 v.) 56; 98 Study for pulley (MI 87 r.) 59; 99 Study of rearing horse, c.1490 (WC 123582) 24; 100 Study of rocks and aquatic birds for *The Virgin of the Rocks*, c.1483 (Royal Library, Windsor) 32; 101 Study for screw (MI 58 r.) 59; 102 Study for Serravalle tunnel (MI11 r.) 53; 103 Study of the thorax, c.1512 (Royal Library, Windsor) 37; 104 Study of towers (MII 93 v.) 47; 105 Study for a wing (AC 22 v. b.) 57; 106 Study for articulated wing (AC 308 r.a.) 57; 107 Studies for a wing with apertures (AC 74 r.; 309 v.b.) 56; 108 Study for integrated wing (AC 313 r.a.) 57; 109 Study for worm gear (MI 17 v.) 59; 110 Vitruvian man, c.1492 (Accademia Gallery, Venice) 36.
– Works attributed to Leonardo
111 *Lady with pearls*, now thought to be a work of the Bolognese school (Pinacoteca Ambrosiana, Milan) 39.
LIPPI, FILIPPO (c.1406-1469)
112 *Annunciation*, 1437-40 (church of San Lorenzo, Florence) 19.
LIPPI, FILIPPINO (1457-1537)
113 *Adoration of the Magi*, 1496 (Uffizi Gallery, Florence) 27.
LORENZO DI CREDI (1459-1537)
114 *Portrait of old man* recognized as Perugino, c.1490 (Gabinetto dei disegni e delle stampe, Uffizi Gallery, Florence, inv. 237E) 15.
MARTINI, FRANCESCO DI GIORGIO (1439-1502)
115 Page from *Treatise on military and civil architecture* (Biblioteca Laurenziana, Florence) 30; 116 Page from *Treatise on military and civil architecture* with lifting machine. (Biblioteca Laurenziana, Florence) 58.
MASACCIO (byname of Tommaso di ser Giovanni di Mone Cassai) (1401-1428)
117 *Adoration of the Magi*, 1426 (Staatliche Museen, Berlin) 26; 118 *The Tribute Money*, 1427-28 (Brancacci Chapel, church of Santa Maria del Carmine, Florence) 11; 119 *The Trinity*, 1427 (church of Santa Maria Novella) 12.
MASOLINO DI PANICALE (c.1383-1440) AND MASACCIO
120 *The Virgin and Child with St Anne*, 1420 (Uffizi Gallery, Florence) 55.
NANNI DI BANCO (1380/90-1421)
121 *Four Crowned Saints*, 1412-16 (Orsanmichele, Florence) 10.
PAOLO UCCELLO (byname of Paolo di Dono) (1397-1475)
122 *The Battle of San Romano*, 1456-1460 (Uffizi Gallery, Florence) 10.
PIERO DELLA FRANCESCO (1415/20-1492)
123 *Annunciation* (Galleria Nazionale dell'Umbria, Perugia) 12; 124 *Baptism of Christ*, c.1448-50 (National Gallery, London) 13.
RAPHAEL (Raffaello Sanzio) (1483-1520)
125 *The School of Athens*, c.1508 (Stanza della Segnatura, Vatican) 61; 126 Preparatory drawing for *The Dispute over the Sacrament* with portrait of Bramante, 1509 (Vatican Museum, Rome) 34.
RUBENS, PETER PAUL
127 Copy of the central section of *The Battle of Anghiari* (Louvre, Paris) 49.
UTILI, GIOVANNI BATTISTA (1465/70-1516)
128 *Three Archangels with Tobias*, 1470. Detail showing the construction site of Santa Maria del Fiore (Bartolini and Salimbeni collection, Florence) 21.
VAN DER GOES, HUGO (1435/40-1482)
129 *Adoration of the Shepherds*, 1476-78, detail (Uffizi Gallery, Florence) 11.
VAN EYCK, JAN (c.1390-1441)
130 *Giovanni Arnolfini and his wife*, 1434 (National Gallery, London) 11.
VERROCCHIO (byname of Andrea di Francesco di Cione) (1435-1488)
131 *David*, c.1465 (Bargello Museum, Florence) 22; 132 *Doubting Thomas*, c.1483 (Orsanmichele, Florence) 22; 133 *Equestrian Monument to Bartolomeo Colleoni*, 1497-88 (Campo dei Santi Giovanni e Paolo, Venice) 24, 31; 134 *Winged putto*, 1475-80 (courtyard of Palazzo Vecchio, Florence) 22; 135 *Study of male nude*, c.1470 (Gabinetto dei disegni e delle stampe, Uffizi Gallery, Florence) 14.
VERROCCHIO AND LEONARDO
136 *Baptism of Christ*, 1472-75 (Uffizi Gallery, Florence) 16-17; 137 Study for head of Venus. Sketch for *Venus and Cupid*, c.1475 (Gabinetto dei disegni e delle stampe, Uffizi Gallery, Florence) 15.
VIGONNISE BARB
138 *Portrait of Luca Pacioli* (Capodimonte Museum, Naples) 40.

The original and previously unpublished illustrations in this book may only be reproduced with the prior permission of Donati-Giudici Associati, who hold the copyright.

The illustrations are by: Giovanni Bernardi (pp.8-9), Simone Boni (pp.20-21), L.R. Galante (pp.40-41, 46-47), Roberto Lari (pp.30-31), Andrea Ricciardi (pp.6-7, 28-29, 34-35, 52-53), Sergio (cover, pp.4-5, 12-13, 14-15, 16-17, 22-23, 24-25, 36-37, 44-45, 48-49, 60-61).

All efforts have been made to trace the copyright-holders of the other illustrations in the book. If any omissions have been made, this will be corrected at reprint.

Thanks are due to the following institutions and individuals for their permission to reproduce photographs: Alte Pinakothek, Munich; Biblioteca Reale, Turin; Collezione Bartolini e Salimbeni, Florence; Czartoryski Museum, Cracow; Fitzwilliam Museum, Cambridge, England; Galleria degli Uffizi, Florence; Galleria Nazionale dell'Umbria, Perugia; Hermitage Museum, St Petersburg; Louis F. Hyde Collection, Glen Falls, New York; Musée Bonnat, Bayonne; Musée du Louvre, Paris; Musei Vaticani, Rome; Museo Civico Correr, Venice; Museo di Capodimente, Naples; Museo Nazionale del Bargello, Florence; National Gallery, London; National Gallery of Art, Washington, D.C.; Pinacoteca Ambrosiana, Milan; Pinacoteca Nazionale, Parma; Staatliche Museen, Berlin; A.D.E.: 26d, 31d, 32a-c, 33d, 34c, 35a-b-c, 38e, 39b, 41d-e, 48e, 50e, 51c-h, 52a-b, 53a-b, 54a, 55b, 56e-m; Archivio Giannini: 16b, 18c, 19e, 26a, 27b, 31c, 32b, 35f, 38a-b-c, 39c, 40b-d, 41a, 42d, 44a, 46a-b-c-d, 49a, 50b, 51d, 56a-c-f-g-h-i-n, 57a, 59f, 61a-b;

Photo SCALA/Florence: 2, 4, 5, 7, 9, 15, 17, 18, 20, 22, 23, 26, 27, 28, 29, 30, 31, 32, 34, 35, 36, 67, 112, 113, 119, 120, 121, 122, 123, 125, 129, 131, 135, 136.
Marco Quattrone: 19

Thanks are due to the Istituto di Scienza delle Costruzioni of the Faculty of Architecture, University of Florence, for granting permission to publish the models of Leonardo's machines reproduced on page 20.

2014
Year A–II

THE ALMANAC FOR PASTORAL LITURGY

SOURCEBOOK

FOR SUNDAYS, SEASONS, AND WEEKDAYS

Joseph DeGrocco	Graziano Marcheschi	Jakob K. Rinderknecht
Maureen A. Kelly	Jill Maria Murdy	Denise Simeone
Julie M. Krakora	Michael R. Prendergast	S. Anne Elizabeth Sweet, OCSO
Corinna Laughlin	Robert C. Rabe	

LITURGY
TRAINING
PUBLICATIONS

Nihil Obstat
Very Reverend Daniel A. Smilanic, JCD
Vicar for Canonical Services
Archdiocese of Chicago
February 18, 2013

Imprimatur
Reverend John F. Canary, STL, DMIN
Vicar General
Archdiocese of Chicago
February 18, 2013

The *Nihil Obstat* and *Imprimatur* are declarations that the material is free from doctrinal or moral error, and thus is granted permission to publish in accordance with c. 827. No legal responsibility is assumed by the grant of this permission. No implication is contained herein that those who have granted the *Nihil Obstat* and *Imprimatur* agree with the content, opinions, or statements expressed.

CONTENTS

INTRODUCTION

Overview of *Sourcebook*

SOURCEBOOK *for Sundays, Seasons, and Week-days 2014: The Almanac for Pastoral Liturgy* provides guidance regarding the various liturgical elements (music, environment, prayers, readings, etc.) so that communities can prepare liturgies rooted in the vision of the Second Vatican Council. The practical suggestions are oriented to assist parishes and other communities to celebrate the liturgy in the best possible way—thoughtfully, deliberately, and with confidence and faith in the God who has claimed us in Baptism and who desires us to worship him in spirit and in truth: "God is Spirit, and those who worship him must worship in Spirit and truth" (John 4:24).

Sourcebook is organized to help you follow liturgical time in sequence. It begins with Advent, which is the start of the liturgical year, and it continues with Christmas Time. Next begins Ordinary Time, so-named because the Sundays are designated by their ordinal (counted) numbers.

Sourcebook tags the Sundays in Ordinary Time after Christmas Time and up until Lent as "Ordinary Time (During Winter)." This is not an official description or designation, but merely a chapter heading *Sourcebook* uses to differentiate between the two parts of Ordinary Time.

Next you will find Lent, followed by the Sacred Paschal Triduum, and then Easter Time. After the Solemnity of Pentecost, Ordinary Time resumes. *Sourcebook* refers to this longer stretch as "Ordinary Time (During Summer and Fall)." When Ordinary Time concludes, the next liturgical year begins, so this chapter takes us right up to the end of the liturgical year. A supplemental liturgical music preparation sheet and a check-list for those who serve during the Triduum are available online at www.ltp.org/t-resources.aspx. These sheets may be reproduced and distributed to your ministers for free.

Within each of the chapters of *Sourcebook*, you will find two sections: "The Liturgical Time" and "The Calendar." "The Liturgical Time" was formerly called "The Seasons" and is organized into several parts:

◆ *The Meaning:* the theological meaning and history of liturgical time

◆ *The Saints:* how the living witness of the saints can deepen and enrich liturgical time

◆ *The Liturgical Books:* what the *Lectionary for Mass, The Roman Missal,* and other ritual texts tell us about liturgical time; information particular to the third edition of *The Roman Missal* is under this same category

◆ *The Liturgical Environment:* ideas for the appearance of worship spaces

◆ *The Liturgical Music:* the musical expression of liturgical time and how to enhance it

◆ *Devotions and Sacramentals:* ideas to foster the parish's devotional life while emphasizing the primacy of the liturgy

◆ *Liturgical Ministers:* tips and formational notes for all liturgical ministers

◆ *A Prayer for Meetings during . . . :* Seasonal prayers to use to begin or end meetings; these can be used at liturgical ministry meetings or by worship committees, parish councils, parish staffs, and other parish organizations

◆ *Children's Liturgy of the Word:* how to prepare the Sunday children's Liturgy of the Word

◆ *The Parish and the Home:* how to carry liturgical time from the parish to the domestic Church (at home)

◆ *Mass Texts:* original prayers for the Order of Mass (where options are permitted)

"The Calendar" is a straightforward almanac for each day of the liturgical year. You can look up any day of the year and find basic liturgical information as well as ideas for how to celebrate it. The primary purpose of *Sourcebook,* however, is to help you celebrate Sundays, solemnities, feasts, and all of liturgical time. For this reason, you will find most of the material in "The Calendar" devoted to Sundays, solemnities, and feasts, which include the following three sections:

◆ *Lectionary for Mass:* an explanation of how the Scriptures of the day relate to what is being celebrated

◆ *The Roman Missal:* insights into the prayers and suggestions about options; particular notes are provided for the third edition of the Missal

◆ *Pastoral Reflection:* spiritual reflections about the day, drawing from the Scriptures or the liturgical observance; may be used as homily sparkers, bulletin notes, or to guide discussion at liturgy committee meetings

Other days include additional sections:

◆ *"About this . . .":* what the Church is celebrating on this day and why

◆ *Today's Saint:* Biographies of the saints celebrated on that day

About the Authors

◆ Msgr. Joseph DeGrocco, pastor of Our Lady of Perpetual Help Church, Lindenhurst, NY and former professor of liturgy and director of liturgical formation at the Seminary of the Immaculate Conception in Huntington, NY, holds an MA in theology (liturgical studies) from the University of Notre Dame and a Doctor of Ministry from the Seminary of the Immaculate Conception. He is the author of *A Pastoral Commentary on the General Instruction of the Roman Missal,* the *Dictionary of Liturgical Terms, The Church at Worship: Theology, Spirituality, and Practice of Parish Liturgy,* is a regular contributor to the "Q & A" column in *Pastoral Liturgy* (all from LTP), and is a member of his diocese's Liturgical Commission. He has provided commentaries on *The Roman Missal.*

◆ Maureen A. Kelly has an MA in theology from the University of Louvain in Belgium, and has held parish, diocesan, and national positions in catechesis. She has written articles for catechetical magazines and authored *Call to Celebrate: Eucharist, Reconciliation and Confirmation* (Harcourt Religion Publishers); *Christian Initiation of Children: Hope for the Future* (Paulist Press); *Children's Liturgy of the Word* and the *What's New about the Mass* series of booklets for children, teens, and their teachers (both LTP). Maureen has contributed to the sections on the "Sacraments of Initiation" and "Children's Liturgy of the Word."

◆ Julie M. Krakora received her BA in theology from Marquette University and her MA in pastoral studies from Loyola University in Chicago. She has actively been in ministry for the past 14 years and loves to write anything that will bring people closer in relationship with God. She is the author many LTP pastoral resources. She has provided the "Pastoral Reflections."

◆ Corinna Laughlin is director of liturgy for St. James Cathedral, Seattle. She is a frequent contributor to this *Sourcebook* in addition to co-authoring several volumes in *The Liturgical Ministries Series* from LTP. She holds a doctorate in English from the University of Washington and a BA from Mount Holyoke College. Corinna provided reflections on the 50th anniversary of CSL.

◆ Graziano Marcheschi speaks nationally on liturgy and the arts, Scripture, and lay ministry. He is the executive director of University Ministry at Saint Xavier University, Chicago and formerly served as director of lay ministry formation for the Archdiocese of Chicago. He holds an MA in drama from the University of Minnesota, an MDIV from Loyola University Chicago, and a DMIN from the University of St. Mary of the Lake.

◆ JILL MARIA MURDY provides "The Liturgical Music" sections. She serves as director of music for a Catholic parish. Her background includes monastic liturgy, small rural and very large urban parishes. Murdy holds a BA in music from Dickinson State University, and an MA in Theology from the University of Notre Dame. She is an accomplished speaker and award-winning prolific author. Her website is www.jillmaria.com.

◆ MICHAEL R. PRENDERGAST is a seasoned pastoral musician and liturgist with experience at the parish, cathedral, and diocesan levels. He is a frequent speaker and clinician for conferences, dioceses, and parishes. He has edited and authored numerous books and articles, including *The Liturgical Ministry Series: Guide for Liturgy Committees* (LTP), co-authored with Paul Turner. Michael holds advanced degrees in theological studies and liturgy. Michael is coordinator of liturgy at St. Andrew Church in Portland, Oregon; an instructor in the Lay Ministry Formation program for the Archdiocese of Portland; and an instructor in the theology department at the University of Portland. He is also a team member for the North American Forum on the Catechumenate. Michael is founder and executive director of Sacred Liturgy Ministries, a liturgical consulting firm; find out more at www.sacredliturgyministries.org. Michael has written the sections on the "Rite of Penance," the "Rite of Marriage," the "Order of Christian Funerals," the "Book of Blessings," "Liturgical Ministers," and "Devotions and Sacramentals."

◆ ROBERT C. RABE is a high school theology teacher in Chicago. He serves the Church in a variety of capacities, including retreat facilitation, instructor in diaconal and lay formation programs, and author and editor of theological resources for both adults and youth. Holding an MDIV from Saint John's School of Theology, Robert possesses a solid background in scriptural interpretation. His publications include *Daily Prayer 2007* (LTP), *The Bible: The Living Word of God*, and the *Year of Grace 2012* (LTP), and he is a contributing author to *Sourcebook for Sundays, Seasons, and Weekdays 2011* (LTP). He recently earned an MED in Catholic School Leadership and Supervision. Robert has provided the seasonal overviews of the saints.

◆ JAKOB KARL RINDERKNECHT is a doctoral student in systematic theology at Marquette University. He has been involved with parish liturgical ministry across the country and coordinated liturgical environment for the 2011 Southwest Liturgical Conference. His research interests include sacramental and ecumenical theology and their expression in the life of the local Church. Jakob provided the reflections on the "Liturgical Environment."

◆ DENISE SIMEONE has worked in parish and diocesan work in Albany, New York and Kansas City, Missouri. She is director of Mission and Program Development for the National Catholic Reporter Publishing Company. She writes a monthly column for *Celebration Magazine* on the Sunday psalms and is co-author of LTP's annual *Foundations for Preaching and Teaching*. Denise has provided the "Parish and the Home" sections.

◆ S. ANNE ELIZABETH SWEET, OCSO, PHD, is a Cistercian nun at the monastery of Tautra Mariakloster in Norway, who writes regularly on Scripture and liturgy in both the United States and in Norway, including a weekly blog (reflection) on the Sunday readings at www.klosterliv-monasticlife.org. She has provided the majority of the Scripture commentaries for this year's edition.

50th Anniversary of the *Constitution on the Sacred Liturgy*

WEDNESDAY, DECEMBER 4, 2013 is an important day for all who are involved in preparing for the celebration of the Church's liturgy: it marks the 50th anniversary of the promulgation of the *Sacrosanctum Concilium*, the *Constitution on the Sacred Liturgy of the Second Vatican Council.*

Compared to other Church councils, the output of the Second Vatican Council was vast: 16 documents, touching on virtually every aspect of Church life and governance. The Council Fathers talked about everything from how the Church understands and uses modern communications media to how she understands and uses the

Scriptures. There are documents on relations with non-Catholics and with non-Christians, on the priesthood and the religious life, on bishops and on the laity. The documents of the Council are a treasure trove of wisdom and guidance for the Church as she continues to preach the timeless message of Christ in ever-changing times.

Liturgy was the first topic on the agenda when the Council opened in October 1962, and the first document it produced was *Sacrosanctum Concilium,* promulgated at the conclusion of the second session by Pope Paul VI.

Why start with liturgy? Perhaps because when the Council began, liturgical reform had already been underway for more than 50 years. Dom Prosper Guéranger, who re-established the French Benedictines at Solesmes and helped revive interest in Gregorian chant, was on the vanguard, and the beginning of the 20th century saw the flourishing of liturgical scholarship and an increased emphasis on active participation. The Liturgical Movement received official sanction with Pope Pius XII's encyclical *Mediator Dei* (1947), which paved the way for the Council's reforms.

Liturgy was, therefore, an "easy" topic to begin with, since so much work had already been done to prepare for reform. But there was still considerable debate, especially around the use of Latin, the reform of the Mass and the Breviary (the Liturgy of the Hours), and the giving of Communion under both kinds. In the end, the Council Fathers found common ground: the final text passed overwhelmingly, with 2,147 in favor, and only four opposed.

The Constitution is a general document, laying out core principles for understanding and celebrating the liturgy. While it highlights areas to be addressed in the reforms, it does not get into many specifics about the manner in which the liturgy was to be restored to ancient models and adapted to modern times. That would be the task of the Consilium, a group of bishops aided by experts in a wide variety of fields, from music to Latin to sacred art, who met from 1964 until 1970. Their task was to take the teachings of the Constitution and bring them to life in the reform of the rites. Here are some of the highlights of the Council's teaching:

- The Constitution emphasizes that the liturgy is all about the Paschal Mystery: Christ's Passion, Death, and Resurrection. The Paschal Mystery is at the heart of every liturgy: thus, every liturgy—every Mass, every Baptism, every funeral, Lent as well as Easter—

is about Christ's victory over death. We are sharers in that Mystery by our Baptism and our participation in the Eucharist.

- Christ is present in the liturgy in various ways: in the priest offering the Mass, in the sacraments, in the Word proclaimed, and in the gathered assembly, praying and singing together (CSL, 7). Three of these four "presences" of Christ had been pointed out in Pope Pius XII's *Mediator Dei* (1947) long before the Council. But one of them is new: "He is present in his word." This new awareness of the importance of the Scriptures would have significant ramifications for the liturgical reforms.

- The liturgy is the most important thing we do as the people of God: it is both "the summit toward which the activity of the Church is directed" and "the font from which all her power flows" (CSL, 10). We celebrate the liturgy so that we can be strengthened and empowered to go forth and evangelize the world. We evangelize so that more and more people may come to the table and give worship to God.

- The participation of the people really matters. It is not enough to follow the rubrics, though that is important: "something more is required than the mere observation of the laws governing valid and licit celebration; it is their duty also to ensure that the faithful take part fully aware of what they are doing, actively engaged in the rite, and enriched by its effects" (CSL, 11). The participation of the people becomes the guiding principle for the reforms of the liturgy. "In the restoration and promotion of the sacred liturgy, this full and active participation by all the people is the aim to be considered before all else" (CSL, 14).

Out of these concepts at the core of the Constitution came a great variety of reforms, including the clarification of the Mass and other rites in keeping with the core value of "noble simplicity" (CSL, 34); the development of the Sunday and weekday Lectionaries and the vastly increased use of Scripture in the liturgy; the restoration of the catechumenate and the development of the RCIA; the reform of the liturgical year with the restoration of the original meaning of Lent as a season of preparation for Baptism; the restoration of ancient but largely forgotten parts of the Mass like the Prayer of the Faithful and Communion under both kinds; the reform of the funeral rites to emphasize the participation of the deceased in the Paschal Mystery of Christ; the allowance for variation in national rites, to "respect and foster the genius and talents of the various races and peoples" (CSL 37)—what we have come to know as "inculturation"; and the opening up of our churches and our liturgy to the best in contemporary sacred music, art, and architecture.

In an address to the Council Fathers on November 18, 1965, near the end of the Fourth Session of the Council, Pope Paul VI said, "Discussion is coming to an end, and understanding is beginning. The disturbance wrought by ploughing a field is followed by the well-ordered labors of cultivation. The Church is settling down with the new norms she has received from the Council . . . . This is the period of the true 'aggiornamento' proclaimed by our predecessor of venerable memory, John XXIII" (quoted in Xavier Rynne, *The Fourth Session*, p. 307). Implementation was not always as smooth or "well-ordered" as Pope Paul VI hoped. In some places, overenthusiasm led to anomalies out of keeping with the genuine spirit of the reforms. In other places, stubborn resistance to change kept the reforms from flowering as they should. But over the years, reflection on the *Constitution on the Sacred Liturgy* has led us to a deeper understanding of the liturgy and of the importance of our shared prayer in building up the Body of Christ. Fifty years later, this holy work continues.

Overview of the The Roman Missal

THE Missal is the collection of prayers, chants, and instructions (rubrics) used to celebrate Mass. This includes prayers such as the Sign of the Cross and opening greeting; Collects; Gloria; Creed; Eucharistic Prayers; Holy, Holy, Holy; Memorial Acclamations; and the final blessing. The majority of the prayers we recite or sing at Mass are contained in this book and it is these prayers that are currently being retranslated from the original Latin into English.

In the early Christian Church, many of the Mass prayers were memorized and handed down orally. Scribes eventually collected the prayers and recorded them in *liber sacramentum* (book of sacraments or sacramentaries). Other books were used for the Scripture readings: Lectionaries and a *Book of the Gospels* (Evangeliary) for the Scripture readings, and additional books for the chants and antiphons. Slight changes and additions developed as manuscripts were handed on and hand

scribed. Eventually the chants, Scripture readings, prayer texts, and instructions were compiled into a single volume, the *Missale Plenum* (complete Missal). When Johannes Gutenberg invented the movable printing press in 1470, this allowed the Mass texts to become standardized and published universally. In 1474, the first *Missale Romanum* (Roman Missal) was printed in Latin and the texts contained in this volume evolved over the five ensuing centuries.

Because the amount of Scripture proclaimed at Mass increased following the Second Vatican Council (1962–1965), the *Missale Romanum* (Roman Missal) was divided into two separate books: *The Lectionary for Mass* (four volumes of Sacred Scripture) and *The Sacramentary* (prayers, chants, and instructions [rubrics] for the celebration of the Mass). The new English translation of the *Missale Romanum* changed the name of the book from *The Sacramentary* to *The Roman Missal*.

Overview of the Lectionary for Mass

THE *Lectionary for Mass* is the ordered selection of readings, chosen from both testaments of the Bible, for proclamation in the assembly gathered for worship. Lectionaries have been used for Christian worship since the fourth century. Before the invention of the printing press in the fifteenth century, the selection and order of the readings differed somewhat from church to church, often reflecting the issues that were important to the local communities of the time.

For the four centuries between the Council of Trent (1545–1563) and the Second Vatican Council (1963–1965), the readings in most Catholic churches varied little from year to year and were proclaimed in Latin, a language that many no longer understood. The Second Vatican Council brought dramatic changes. It allowed the language of the people to be used in the liturgy and initiated a revision of the Lectionary. The Bible became far more accessible to Catholics and once again a vibrant source of our faith and tradition.

The new Lectionary that appeared in 1970 introduced a three-year plan that allowed a fuller selection of readings from the Bible. During Year A, the Gospel readings for Ordinary Time are taken from Matthew, for Year B from Mark, and for Year C from Luke.

The Gospel for Year A: Matthew

Matthew, whom Christian Tradition has long associated with the tax-collector of the same name in Matthew 9:9 writes sometime around the year 80 AD. We know that he writes after the Roman destruction of the Temple in Jerusalem (70 AD) and at a time when Jewish Christians were no longer allowed in the synagogue, as he speaks repeatedly of "their" synagogues (for example, see Matthew 10:17). Jewish Christians were faced not only with articulating a new identity for themselves, but also with having to decide what should be asked of Gentile believers.

Matthew's sources include Mark, whose basic structure he follows as well as some sayings of Jesus from a source also known to Luke. Matthew also has some material of his own. The way he uses and adapts his sources gives us an insight into the situation of his community.

Matthew begins his account of the Gospel speaking of Jesus's *genesis* (thus, echoing the Greek name of the first book of the Bible that recounts the beginnings both of creation and of the Jewish people). Note that Matthew traces Jesus's genealogy to Abraham, the father of the chosen people (see Matthew 1:1). He also identifies him as the son of David (see Matthew 1:1), thus, setting the stage for proclaiming him as the Messiah. Of particular note in the genealogy is the mention of five women: Tamar, Rahab, Ruth, Bathsheba (although she is only identified as the "wife of Uriah" [see verse 6]), and Mary the Mother of Jesus.

Note that it is Joseph, the husband of Mary, who is named in the line of descent. Indeed, it is Joseph who is the major focus in the narratives of Jesus's infancy and childhood. Already in the infancy narratives, Matthew begins to demonstrate that Jesus is the fulfillment of the prophecies of old (for example, Isaiah 7:14 in Matthew 1:23). Jesus is Emmanuel, God-with-us, as he will remind the disciples at the end of the Gospel (Matthew 28:20). Similarly, already in the infancy narratives there is hint of the mission to the Gentiles that is so strongly emphasized in the final words of the Gospel (for example, the Magi in 2:1–12, 28:19).

Matthew presents Jesus as the authoritative teacher throughout his public ministry and there are five major discourses of instruction (Matthew, chapters 5–7; 10; 13; 18; 24–25). The first of these,

in chapters 5–7, is the Sermon on the Mount. It is actually a collection of sayings and teachings concerning what those who would inherit the Kingdom of Heaven must be and do.

Chapter 10 focuses on the mission of the disciples. The disciples are first and foremost those who must "learn" from Jesus (as the Greek word implies). Only then are they subsequently sent out as *Apostles* (from the Greek word "to send")—but they remain disciples! Note that the commission given them at the end of the Gospel is first of all to "Go . . . and make disciples of all nations . . ." (Matthew 28:19).

Several parables about the kingdom of heaven are grouped in chapter 13. Even Jesus's use of parables to teach is viewed by Matthew as the fulfillment of Scripture (see Psalm 78:2 in Matthew 13:35), as is the failure of some of the Jews to believe in Jesus (see Isaiah 6:9–10 in Matthew 13:14).

Chapter 18 addresses relationships within the Church—and it is Matthew alone of the evangelists who uses the word *ekkēlsía* with reference to the Christian community (see Matthew 18:17; see also Matthew 16:18). Of particular importance here is the teaching on forgiveness (see Matthew 18:16–18, the "you" is plural; the authority is given to the community).

Chapter 23 is a denunciation of the Jewish leaders for their hypocrisy. Much of this material is unique to Matthew's account of the Gospel. It is here also, that we find Jesus's insistence that his disciples remain disciples (Matthew 23:8). He alone is the authoritative teacher.

The Parousia or end-time is the subject of the parables and teachings in chapters 24–25. Christians are called to vigilance in the face of its unknown time. Other parables and teachings are of course found outside these five major discourses.

Many of Jesus's miracles are grouped together in chapters 8–9, for the most part. These follow upon chapters 5–7 which stress Jesus as the authoritative teacher. Matthew presents Jesus's healing ministry as fulfilling Isaiah's words concerning the Chosen Servant of the Lord: "He took away our infirmities and bore our diseases" (Isaiah 53:4 in Matthew 8:17).

Matthew's Passion narrative begins in chapter 26. Consistent with what we might call an "anti-Jewish" tone in his Gospel, Matthew places the blame for the Death of Jesus on the Jewish people (see Matthew 27:25). Remember, though, Matthew himself was Jewish as were many in his community, though at the time he wrote they had been excluded from the synagogues because of their belief that Jesus was the Messiah. Matthew alone stresses Pilate's innocence (Matthew 27:24). Matthew alone tells of Judas's attempt to right the wrong he had done in betraying Jesus (Matthew 27:3–10).

Most significant among the unique details given by Matthew are the occurrence of an earthquake at both the Death (Matthew 27:51) and the Resurrection of Jesus (Matthew 28:2). At Jesus's Death, the quake split open tombs and the bodies of many of the righteous who had died were raised. After Jesus's Resurrection, these risen righteous ones appeared to many (Matthew 27:52–53). Indeed, a new age had begun in human history.

From the storeroom of Matthew's account of the Gospel (Matthew 13:52), we find both the old and the new, numerous Old Testament quotations which Jesus fulfills as well as new interpretations of the old and indeed, new commands. Nothing of the old is abolished (Matthew 5:17); but what it means to be righteous is brought into sharper focus (Matthew 5:20). In this year of Matthew, may we, contemporary disciples of Jesus, take his teachings to heart. Truly blessed shall we be if we put Jesus's words into practice (Matthew 7:21). The Kingdom of Heaven is ours.

—S. Anne Elizabeth Sweet, ocso

Overview of Children's Liturgy of the Word

CHILDREN's Liturgy of the Word is liturgy. It is ritual! This rite enables children to encounter the Word of God at a cognitive level. What transpires in this ritual should resemble what is going on in the adult assembly. After the Collect, the priest celebrant invites the prayer leader to come forward to receive the children's Lectionary. It is also customary to have the children come forward to hear the words of dismissal (see the optional dismissal prayers in this *Sourcebook*). The prayer leader then takes the Lectionary and processes, with the children following, to the space where the Liturgy of the Word is to be celebrated.

Children's Liturgy of the Word is not a catechetical session. Although the ritual is full of liturgical catechesis, it should not become another religious education class. If you follow the principle that children's Liturgy of the Word should reflect what is going on in the main liturgical assembly, then those who prepare and lead this ritual should strive to be prayer leaders, not catechists.

Children's Liturgy of the Word does not distinguish age groups. It is for children of all ages (pre-school through those who have not yet received first Eucharist) to gather together, with younger children learning from older children.

Craft activities and handouts shouldn't be used at children's Liturgy of the Word. There are some great activity sheets on the market, but consider adding them to the bulletin or distributing them during catechetical sessions or religious education meetings. You might have those who prepare children's Liturgy of the Word write a column for the parish bulletin or post to the parish website. These writers could simply cite the readings that will be used and summarize a few points they will be making in their reflection. Add questions that the family can discuss on their way home from Mass or at mealtime that day or in the coming week. A good resource to help you prepare liturgies with children is *Children's Liturgy of the Word 2013– 2014 A Weekly Resource* (LTP).

—Robert W. Piercy, Jr.

Overview of the Saints

WINDING throughout the liturgical year is the observance of the sanctoral cycle. This is the cycle of solemnities, feasts, and memorials in which we remember and honor God's holy ones— the Blessed Virgin Mary and the saints. These are the Apostles and martyrs, the evangelists, and the Fathers of the Church. They are popes and religious founders, peasants and statesmen. They are men and woman, clerics and married people, the elderly and the young. All of them have lived some aspect of Christ's Paschal Mystery in a unique and powerful way.

These holy men and women, the heroes of our faith upon whose shoulders we stand (the pillars of the Church), are revered and memorialized as members of the "great multitude, which no one could count, from every nation, race, people, and tongue," who stand now before the throne of the Lamb, dressed in white and waving palm branches (Revelation 7:9). In this, they also stand with us each and every time we gather around the banquet table of the Lamb. As we praise and thank God through the complete praise and thanksgiving of Christ in Eucharist, we join the saints in their eternal praise of God through Christ.

through it. In the evening the community again comes together to give God praise for blessings received throughout the day and to ask him for protection through the coming night.

Overview of the Liturgy of the Hours

THE Liturgy of the Hours, the Divine Office, the Breviary are all terms that refer to what the *General Instruction of the Liturgy of the Hours* (GILOH) calls the official, daily prayer of the Church with Christ and to Christ (see GILOH, 2). The Hours are principally a prayer of praise, and secondly of petition. As the prayer of the Church, the Hours are the very prayer of Christ, since Christ's prayer is *always* a prayer of praise to the Father and petition for the salvation of the world. In the praying of the Hours, the Church fulfills her baptismal obligation to do as Christ commanded—to pray. The GILOH notes that in praying the Hours, the baptized members of Christ's Body (the Church), through the Holy Spirit, are united with the perfect prayer of Christ to the Father.

The full celebration of the Liturgy of the Hours covers the passing of the day and includes the Office of Readings, Morning Prayer (Lauds), Daytime Prayer (midmorning, midday, and mid-afternoon), Evening Prayer (Vespers), and Night Prayer (Compline). Over the course of these celebrations, the whole day is sanctified and offered to God in praise and thanksgiving. In this day-to-day prayer all time is made holy.

Although the Liturgy of the Hours is the official daily prayer of the Church, few communities celebrate it as part of the regular liturgical life of the parish. It is thought to be the prayer of the clergy rather than the prayer of everyone. Many, however, do celebrate some portion of the Hours at various liturgical times of the year. During the "high seasons" (for example, Advent/Christmas Time, Lent/Triduum/Easter) many parishes will offer Morning Prayer or Evening Prayer on one day of the week.

Morning and Evening Prayer are the two hours that are the "hinges" upon which the whole liturgy moves through the day. In the morning the community, ideally, gathers to commend the day to God, to ask God to bless it and lead them

Overview of the Sacraments

THE whole liturgical life of the Roman Catholic Church revolves around the celebration of Eucharist and the other sacraments. There are seven sacraments in the Church: Baptism, Confirmation, Eucharist, Reconciliation, Anointing of the Sick, Marriage, and Holy Orders.

The sacraments are communal celebrations of the Church, grace-giving encounters with Christ that articulate what God is doing in our lives now. Sacraments mark the peak moments of our lives. They celebrate the grace of God that calls us to conversion and membership in the Church and gifts us with the Holy Spirit, that offers us reconciliation and healing, that calls some to leadership in the Church community and others to the vocation of Christian Marriage, and invites us into the mystery of Christ's suffering, Death, and Resurrection.

In Christ, God became visible and tangible. In the Church, Christ, and hence God, remains visible and tangible among us. The Church in turn becomes visible and tangible in the seven signs. They are Christ's hands that now touch us and Christ's words that now ring in our ears. Those who prepare sacramental celebrations have the sacred and serious responsibility of doing these well, of familiarizing themselves with the rites and understanding them fully. Read the introductory notes of the ritual text (the *praenotanda*); know the signs and symbols, the rubrics and prayers, and the shape of the ritual well. Invite collaboration, encourage ministries, and allow grace to flow.

Overview of the Order of Christian Funerals

THE Order of Christian Funerals is an event that unfolds over time, in stations. Beginning with the first moment that the family encounters the deceased, all the way to the moment when that person's mortal remains reach their final resting place, the Church honors the one who has died and walks with those who mourn.

Some people prepare their funerals in advance. Parish ministers should be ready to prepare the funeral liturgy efficiently, on short notice, with good collaboration among clergy, musicians, sacristan, funeral director, parish bereavement committee, and members of the family. It is a difficult time for those in mourning to prepare the liturgy, although some families will welcome the chance to be involved in the liturgical preparations. The parish should have a reliable process already in place that conforms to liturgical norms and standards. This is often a powerful moment of evangelization.

In 1997, the National Conference of Catholic Bishops approved an appendix to the *Order of Christian Funerals* in light of pastoral circumstances concerning the cremated remains of a body. The text *Appendix: Cremation with Reflections on the Body, Cremation, and Catholic Funeral Rites by the Committee on the Liturgy* is exceptionally helpful in explaining how the funeral liturgy is celebrated with cremated remains. One liturgical difference, for example, is that no pall is used, since this represents the clothing of the body with the baptismal garment.

Sensitive ministry to the bereaved calls upon the gifts of a variety of people, including clergy, pastoral ministers, musicians, and bereavement counselors. Not all of these ministries are strictly liturgical, but all will ultimately have an impact on liturgy as they shepherd people through this passage in life.

Overview of the Book of Blessings

THE *Book of Blessings* (BB) provides multiple orders of blessing for various needs and occasions. The book for use in the dioceses of the United States of America contains those from the Roman volume (*De Benedictionibus*) as well as blessings proper to the United States of America.

It would be helpful to review the *Book of Blessings* periodically to see how the parish calendar can incorporate blessings during the year.

Blessings are liturgical prayers that flow from the Word of God. In addition to the usual blessings for people, buildings, objects, and special occasions, there are some entries that might surprise you, such as blessings for victims of crime, for sick children, or for those suffering from addiction. People who need such blessings will not usually ask for them; therefore, the parish staff ought to be attentive to these orders of blessings and the needs of the faithful. In the right setting, such prayers can be wonderful. A blessing is an event of worship, and so calls for a variety of ministries. Be attentive to musical selections, scheduling liturgical ministers, and encourage parishioners or a small community to attend.

Overview of the Liturgical Environment

THE liturgical environment must be in balance with the religious and devotional art of a community. The signs, symbols, and elements of the environment must be dignified and beautiful. They need not be expensive, and because of the transitory nature of liturgical time, prudence should be used in expenditures. At the same time, a budget that appreciates the importance of the liturgical environment to the community's prayer is essential. Dignity and beauty is inherent in the natural world: the variety of grasses and herbs; the textures of stone, wood, and glass; the multiplicity of fruits and vegetables; the grandeur of rivers, lakes, and oceans; the majesty of the stars, the moon, and the sun. Care should be taken to use natural materials whenever possible and practical. The climate of your region will produce natural symbols that speak to you. Harvest in your community may mean pumpkins and wheat, or it may mean oranges and grapefruits. Coral and seashells will suggest water in coastal communities, while cattails and native gravel will remind inlanders of rivers and lakes. Using local resources limits the need for artificial symbols, but when these are chosen, care must be taken to assure that beauty is preserved.

During liturgy, symbols take four forms: action, word, images, and music. The postures we assume show our relationship to God and community; the words we pray and music we sing communicate beliefs, emotions, and tone. As ministers of the liturgical environment, you are concerned primarily with images. Attending to the other forms of symbols, and consulting with music ministers in particular, can reinforce the symbols' power. Whatever symbols are selected for the liturgical environment, they must speak for themselves.

Overview of Liturgical Music

WITHIN our day-to-day secular existence, singing is increasingly viewed as something best "left to the professionals." The very act of standing and singing together is counter-cultural. However, our ministerial mission is to help shape the sung prayer of the People of God. Whether we serve in a large parish with thousands of families and multiple choirs or a tiny congregation with only a few cantors; whether our primary instrument of worship is a pipe organ or a rhythm ensemble or a single piano; whether our repertoire is built mostly of hymns and chant or consists primarily of contemporary-styled music, our fundamental purpose and mission remains the same. We are here to enable, empower, and sing with our assemblies, to guide their sung prayer through the peaks, valleys, and level ground of the Year of Grace.

The musical sections of this *Sourcebook* are intended to build upon the liturgical commentary and address some of the concerns, both practical and theoretical, particular to music ministry. Musicians will still want to (and should) examine the sections of *Sourcebook* not specifically addressing the musical issues of shaping sung worship. Remember that part of what we do as music ministers is to shape an aural environment for worship that enhances and harmonizes with the visual and tactile environment already present. The liturgical music sections provide some concrete suggestions for songs, hymns, chants, and/or service music appropriate for particular liturgical times.

Overview of Devotions and Sacramentals

ONE of the paths setting Catholics apart from many other Christians is the principle of sacramentality. Sacramentals are associated with the Church's official rituals. They include public and private devotions, religious signs, symbols, gestures, prayers, rituals, images, music, and natural or synthetic objects. While not always inherently religious (e.g., water, a color, or a posture), they become sacramentals, or sacred, in their religious use. They are not part of the Church's official liturgy of sacraments and prayer, but are used to worship God, honor the saints, or seek divine favor. Sacramentals allow us to touch the invisible mystery of God in a physical way.

The reverent use of sacramentals, such as keeping holy water or blessed palms in the home, can also be devotional. The list could go on. Usually devotions spring up as popular piety and are later sanctioned and regulated by the Church if they are judged to be particularly beneficial and foster a very personal love for the mysteries celebrated in the liturgy. They are to always be viewed in relation to the liturgy. The *Constitution on the Sacred Liturgy* (CSL) highly endorses devotion; however, it notes that they should always "be so fashioned that they harmonize with the liturgical seasons, accord with the sacred liturgy, are in some way derived from it, and lead the people to it, since, in fact, the liturgy, by its very nature far surpasses any of them" (CSL, 13). The Stations of the Cross, for example, allow us to meditate on the Passion of the Lord while walking in a "pilgrim way," and the Rosary reflects on the mysteries of Christ through the experience of Mary. Novenas can strengthen our appreciation for the intercession of the saints, and call us to holiness of life.

ADVENT

The Meaning

THE primary liturgical environment is the natural environment. In the northern hemisphere, Advent falls as daylight is fading away to the shortest days of the year. Our awareness of this is less than it once was because of the prevalence of electric lighting and the 24/7 culture of the Internet, international business, and the news cycle. Of course your parish may be more or less aware of the natural day, depending on where you are located and how parishioners make their living. While in Anchorage, the day shortens to a mere five and half hours, Honolulu still sees ten and a half hours of daylight on December 21. Similarly, people who make their living outdoors and those whose moods are more affected by the absence of daylight will notice these changes more, but Advent is a chance for all Christians to become aware of the growing darkness.

Advent is a season of waiting, of stillness, of reflection, and of expectation. Dwindling daylight sets the stage for these actions and the liturgical year wisely makes use of them. We have just celebrated the Solemnity of Our Lord Jesus Christ, King of the Universe, which brought the annual cycle to its eschatological end. Advent continues the eschatological hope of this solemnity, but awaits the dual coming of Christ: as the infant of Bethlehem and in his promised return. This is why the Lectionary focuses on both John the Baptist's proclamation of Jesus and Jesus's parables of the coming Bridegroom. As we wait in the colder and darker days of the year, we look for the light of the coming Messiah and the fullness of the kingdom of God.

The Lectionary for Mass

ADVENT is about longing and desire . . . not for material gifts—though that may be the reality for many—but longing and desire for the full realization of God's kingdom. Advent looks to the day that is coming (so says the First Reading for the First and Second Sundays). For the prophet Isaiah, it was the day when the rule of the Messiah or Christ, the anointed Davidic heir, would bring a time of peace and well-being to the Israelite people. From the Christian perspective, given the birth of the Messiah, that day is the day of his return in glory, when God's kingdom would be fully realized. Advent is about being ready and watchful for the Lord's coming in glory—as the Gospel for the First Sunday (see Matthew 24:37–44) bids us.

The first Christians longed for that day. Paul expected it within his own lifetime (see Romans 13:11; 1 Corinthians 10:11). The First Letter to the Corinthians ends with the prayer that the Lord will come (see 1 Corinthians 16:22). The Book of Revelation, the last book of the New Testament, ends with the promise of its realization (see Revelation 22:20).

At every Mass, we acclaim in our Eucharistic acclamations: "we proclaim your death . . . until you come again." But is that coming something we ever even think about . . . much less long for? Our Advent liturgies sound a wake-up call if only we would hear. The Lord will come whether we are ready or not.

Perhaps that is why John the Baptist, the main focus of the Gospel for the Second and Third Sundays, is such a helpful Advent figure for us. We need to hear his command "Prepare the way of the Lord" just as did those to whom he first spoke (see Matthew 3:3; 11:10). We need to prepare his way in our hearts, in our families and in our everyday world as well as in the world at large—and that

takes time, action, and commitment. Remember, John asked his listeners for evidence of their readiness and repentance (see Matthew 3:8).

The weekday readings of Advent offer us an interfacing of texts that emphasize the Lord's coming to us and the necessity of our coming to him and being receptive him. This can only happen if we are ready and prepared!

Do we make ready the way of the Lord's coming to us in the Word of Scripture by taking time to read it prayerfully? Do we prepare ourselves for the Lord's coming to us in eucharist—or is it something that has become routine, taken for granted? Do we take time for prayer in our daily lives, thus creating a space and a place where we can meet the Lord and he, us? Do we go out to meet the Lord as he comes to us in those who are poor and needy?

The Gospel for the Fourth Sunday focuses on Joseph as a man whose openness of heart to God and obedience to his Word led him to take Mary as his wife, thus preparing the way for a family and a home in which the Savior could be born and grow and made ready for the mission that would be his. Are our families and homes places where those who bear the name Christian can grow in faith and Christian values?

Mary's openness of heart to God and obedience to his Word is highlighted on the Solemnity of the Immaculate Conception of the Blessed Virgin Mary on December 8. On this day, we remember how God poured out his grace upon Mary from the beginning of her existence so that she might be ready to receive his Word and give flesh to his Son. Her ongoing care for her children in every time and place, but especially for the Mexican and Hispanic peoples, is commemorated on the Feast of Our Lady of Guadalupe on December 12.

The last week of Advent focuses on how God accomplishes his plan of salvation in and through the life not only of Mary but of others as well, people whose hearts are open to God's call and obedient to his Word. They are models for us of how God accomplishes his plan of salvation through people, who in the daily activities of their lives are faithful to God's commands and obedient to his Word. And so may we be as we await the fulfillment of his plan of salvation when he comes again in glory.

May this Advent find us giving a real priority to preparing the way of the Lord first of all in our own hearts, then in the lives of our families and friends. May we allow this Advent to be a time when we come into touch with our deepest longings and desires—those that no material gift can fill, but only God. May this Advent be a time when we give a little more thought to what it means when we say "we proclaim your death . . . until you come again." May this Advent be a time when we commit ourselves to be people faithful to God's commands and obedient to his Word, people through whom the Lord's plan of salvation is accomplished in our world today as we wait and pray, "Come, Lord Jesus."

The Roman Missal

Advent texts in *The Roman Missal* are found as the first segment of the Proper of Time. Every day has its own Mass—a proper Entrance Antiphon, Collect, Prayer over the Offerings, Communion Antiphon, and Prayer after Communion are provided. Formularies begin with the First Sunday of Advent and end with the Morning Mass for December 24. Starting with December 17, date-specific Mass formularies are given, and must be used, for the corresponding day, that is, December 17, December 18, December 19, and so on. Consequently, use of the non-date specific weekdays of Advent (for example, Monday of the First Week of Advent, Wednesday of the Second Week of Advent, etc.) is discontinued and the date-specific Mass formularies are used, except for the Fourth Sunday of Advent, when that Mass replaces whatever date it falls on.

The Collects reflect the overall sense of joyful expectation and this thematic movement from the Second Coming to the Nativity. Images and phrases such as the Christian people having "the resolve to run forth to meet your Christ / with righteous deeds at his coming" (First Sunday of Advent), to the request for their being found to be "worthy of the banquet of eternal life" (Wednesday of the First Week of Advent), and of their hastening, "alert and with lighted lamps, to meet him when he comes" all give expression to the theme of the Second Coming, while, as of the Third Sunday of Advent, the Collects shift to speak of "faithfully await[ing] the feast of the Lord's Nativity" and go on to refer specifically to the Virgin Mary (for example, December 19

and 20) and the Incarnation (for example, Fourth Sunday of Advent, and December 20 and 22).

Communities may wish to consider marking the liturgical time by consistent use of selected texts. For example, if one form of the greeting is usually used, priest celebrants might consider switching to another form during Advent. Although for the Penitential Act, any invocations may be used for the third form (#6 in the Order of Mass), option I as found in the Sample Invocations for the Penitential Act in Appendix VI at the back of the Missal might be most appropriate, as those invocations highlight past, present and future comings of Christ. Option II, using phrases such as "mighty God and Prince of peace," "Son of Mary," and "Word made flesh" might also be a good choice, although this set of invocations might also be better left for Christmas Time.

Many priest celebrants find that Advent is a good time to use Eucharistic Prayer for Reconciliation II on a frequent or regular basis. This is particularly appropriate during the first part of Advent which is focused on the Second Coming of Christ and the definitive establishment of the Kingdom of God. The second Eucharistic Prayer for Reconciliation mentions hatred overcome by love, of revenge giving way to forgiveness, and of discord being changed to mutual respect. It also describes the eschatological gathering, where the Virgin Mary, the Apostles and saints, and people "of every race and tongue / who have died in your friendship" are brought together to share in an unending banquet of unity "in a new heaven and a new earth, where the fullness of your peace will shine forth."

The first or second acclamations for "The Mystery of Faith," insofar as they both refer to Christ's coming again, might be preferable over the third option for this liturgical time.

The Gloria is omitted during Advent, except for the Solemnity of the Immaculate Conception and the Feast of Our Lady of Guadalupe. The Creed, usually omitted on weekdays, is said on the Solemnity of the Immaculate Conception.

There are two seasonal Prefaces, the first two in a series of Prefaces found in the Order of Mass as part of the Eucharistic Prayer. Preface I of Advent, which speaks of the two comings of Christ, is used from the First Sunday of Advent to December 16 and in other Masses during Advent that do not have their own proper Preface, and Preface II of Advent, which describes the expectation of Christ's coming and specifically mentions the Nativity, is used in Masses of Advent from December 17 to December 24. These Prefaces may still be used even if Eucharistic Prayer for Reconciliation II is used.

There is an option to use a Solemn Blessing over the people that is specific to Advent; priest celebrants should give due consideration to using this three-part blessing, at least on Sundays. It can be found in the section "Blessings at the end of Mass and Prayers Over the People" which immediately follows the Order of Mass in the Missal. There is also the possibility of selecting one of the 26 choices for a Prayer over the People.

Children's Liturgy of the Word

IN order to help children carry the deep reverence that they feel for the sacred space of the church into their space for the Liturgy of the Word, careful attention must be given to liturgical environment. The space should be arranged and decorated as a liturgical space, not a classroom or play space.

Try to decorate the space so that it feels continuous with the liturgical environment of the space where the main assembly is worshipping. The prayer table, lectern cloths, and banners should be of colors appropriate to the liturgical time. You may also incorporate symbols to reinforce different liturgical seasons. For example, you may use an Advent wreath during this liturgical time.

If you are using a classroom, rearrange the chairs and move desks out of the way. Remember to consider the space in relation to the movement associated with the celebration so that you and the children can participate in the procession and the proclamation of the Word with ease and grace. Put away any toys or games, and do your best to temporarily remove or cover up any distracting posters or displays. Create a space where the Lectionary, candle, and any other liturgical symbols are prominent and easily seen.

The Saints

THIS time of preparation has us celebrate one solemnity (Immaculate Conception of the Blessed Virgin Mary), one feast (Our Lady of Guadalupe), four obligatory memorials (St. Francis Xavier, St. Ambrose, St. Lucy, and St. John of the Cross), and five optional memorials (St. John of Damascus, St. Nicholas, St. Damasus I, St. Peter Canisius, and St. John of Kanty). Through each of these saints God reveals himself in unique and multifaceted ways. Our celebrations of these saints should emphasize that they are reflections of the glory of God suited to speak to different times and places.

◆ IMMACULATE CONCEPTION: This solemnity is celebrated this year on December 9 and is not a Holyday of Obligation because its usual date (December 8) is the Second Sunday of Advent. On this day, we celebrate the teaching that Mary, even as she was conceived by her mother, was specifically and uniquely prepared and called to be the Mother of God, the instrument of God's self-revelation in Christ Jesus. She is proclaimed as a singular bright spot in the dark night of human sin—a moon reflecting the brilliant sunny light of God. Her light invites us to be reflections of the glory of God, delivering the presence of Christ in our time, and to be bright spots in our world of darkness and confusion. This celebration occurs nine months before the feast of the Nativity of Mary (September 8). The Immaculate Conception is the patronal feastday of the United States of America and the national basilica bears this title. As is recommended for all of Advent, flowers and other physical ornamentation of the church should be restrained so as to continue the theme of Advent and highlight the solemnity of Christmas when it arrives.

◆ OUR LADY OF GUADALUPE: As patroness of the Americas and especially of Mexico, Our Lady of Guadalupe's feast is celebrated on December 12. This feast commemorates the apparitions of the Blessed Virgin Mary, as a dark-skinned American Indian pregnant woman, to St. Juan Diego, also an American Indian, in 1531. This image of the Blessed Virgin has inspired faith and hope for countless indigenous peoples and all peoples of the Americas. Our Lady of Guadalupe has become a symbol that the revelation of Christianity was truly meant for the peoples of the Americas—for all nations—as well as for the Europeans who brought this faith here. Just as the Christian call goes out to all the world, so too should our care and concern envelop all races, rich and poor alike. All communities should take time and effort to reflect on the message of Guadalupe, not just those of Hispanic origin.

◆ OBLIGATORY MEMORIALS: These four saints commemorated this Advent illumine our world even today as they did in their own times. St. Francis Xavier, as one of the original Jesuits and one of the greatest missionaries in the history of the Church, brought the light of Christ to the peoples of India, Japan, and other areas of the East. His life story is full of the various and numerous methods that he used to proclaim the message of revelation. St. Ambrose, who illumined his time as a preacher, writer, and bishop, is recognized now as a Doctor of the Church. His preaching encouraged the young St. Augustine to convert from his former ways and to become a Christian. St. John of the Cross famously wrote about the themes of darkness and light in the spiritual life, while living through the darkness of persecution for his beliefs. St. Lucy, whose very name means light, died as a martyr lighting the way to ultimate faithfulness to the closeness of our God. Each of these heroes of faith encourages us by their life, words, and prayers to attend to the revelation of God and to be heralds of that revelation to all.

◆ OPTIONAL MEMORIALS: While these celebrations are optional, it is always possible to mention these saints in Advent Homilies and/or the Universal Prayer (Prayer of the Faithful) since their messages compliment and support the themes of Advent. St. John Damascene, a Doctor of the Church, taught about the closeness of God in his support of icons—physical representations of Christ and the saints. St. Nicholas, the basis of Santa Claus, is the very image of giving and self-sacrifice. There are many ethnic and cultural traditions surrounding this memorial that could be encouraged in keeping with Advent themes. St. Damasus was instrumental in encouraging St. Jerome to produce a translation of the New Testament into Latin, the language of the less educated, further allowing revelation to spread among the people. St. Peter Canisius, another Doctor of the Church, who was known for his brilliant teaching, produced several catechisms aimed at bringing knowledge of the faith to as many people

as possible. St. John of Kanty, the patron saint of Lithuania, was a university professor who championed the idea approaching disagreements with courtesy and moderation—virtues that are most important in this time of preparation!

The Liturgy of the Hours

ADVENT is the perfect time to introduce the celebration of the Hours to your community's liturgical prayer. Begin simply by scheduling celebration of the Hours on the four Sundays of Advent. When celebrating the Hours, the parish community enters into the rhythm of the liturgical year and experiences more fully the Paschal Mystery.

For those who are just beginning praying the Hours, consider acquiring a copy of *Shorter Christian Prayer*, available from Catholic Book Publishing Company. Oregon Catholic Press (OCP) has recently released a new collection *We Shall Praise Your Name: 25 Theme-Based Biblical Prayers based on the Liturgy of the Hours* by Paule Freeburg, dc and Christopher Walker (illustrated by Jean Germano). This collection is a good resource meant to assist with the introduction of children and adults to the Hours. The images in this book, by Jean Germano, influenced by the twelfth-century St. Albans Psalter, honor the ancient tradition of adorning the prayer books of the Church with illuminated miniatures.

Since Morning and Evening Prayer are the chief hours of the day (the hinge hours) consider adding the basic structure of the Hours (invitation, hymn, psalm, reading, Gospel canticle, intercessions, and blessing) to all activities that occur during the liturgical time, including parish meetings, retreats, or Advent festivals. Find a good musical setting of the Canticle of Zachary (used in Morning Prayer) and the Canticle of Mary (used in Evening Prayer). Use these settings at celebrations of the Eucharist, Hours, other sacramental celebrations as well as during public devotions, such as *Los Posadas*. Consider including a Spanish or bilingual musical setting of the Canticle of Zachary such as "*Cántico de Zacarías*/Canticle of Zechariah" by Suzanne Toolan, RSM, from World Library Publications (www.wlp.jspaluch.com) or the Canticle of Mary "Let It Be Done to Us/ *Tu Voluntad, Señor*" by Bob Hurd or "Luke 1:

Benedictus" by Pedro Rubalcava, both from OCP (www.ocp.org) to the parish repertoire.

Consider using the prescribed hymn *Conditor alme siderum*/"Creator of the Stars at Night" or *Veni Emmanuel*/"O Come, O Come, Emmanuel," which both contain lovely poetry of the season, whenever you gather to celebrate Evening Prayer. For Morning Prayer consider hymns such as "On Jordan's Bank," (WINCHESTER NEW); "Come Thou Long Expected Jesus," (STUTTGART); "The King Shall Come When Morning Dawns," (MORNING SONG); or "The King of Glory," (Traditional Israeli Folk Song).

Consider using the optional responses to the intercessions "Come, Lord, and not delay" (Evening Prayer I on Saturday) or "Come, stay with us, Lord" (Evening Prayer II on Sunday). Perhaps you could consider using one of these texts as a response to the Universal Prayer (Prayer of the Faithful) at Sunday and daily Eucharist as well. The office of readings from December 17–24 and the O Antiphons, that serve to introduce the Canticle of Mary during Evening Prayer, bring a richness to these final days of Advent as we await to usher in the Prince of Peace.

Advent begins with Evening Prayer I on Saturday, November 30, 2013 and ends with mid-afternoon Prayer on December 24, 2013.

The Rite of Christian Initiation of Adults

MOST inquirers come to the process of the Rite of Christian Initiation of Adults with many queries—among them, questions on prayer: How do I pray? When should I pray? Does prayer really work? Does God hear my prayers? Will God answer my prayers? What if I pray and I don't feel anything or hear anything?

Inquirers come with many and diverse experiences of prayer. Some have had no experience whatsoever. Others may be more comfortable with rote prayer or prayers that can be read. Still others who come from the evangelical tradition, for example, might be more comfortable with spontaneous prayer. This is why the initial interview is an opportunity to see what, if any, experience the person has had with prayer. Persons who speak to God throughout the day may not consider their conversation to be prayer, because it isn't formal-

ized or written down. One person going through the process, for example, was asked by the initiation director if prayer was a significant part of his life. "No," was the answer. "Really?" the initiation director said. "You never talk to God." He replied, "Of course, I talk to God. I talk to him when I get up, and I thank him for the beautiful day! I thank him for the precious gift of my wife, who is the greatest treasure in my life. I thank him for changing the light from red to green when I am in a hurry. I thank him throughout the day when I need him and even when I don't. I do not sit down and read anything, but I talk to God all day long." The initial interview will help to point out how prayer has already played a role in the inquirers' lives and what might still be needed to help them feel comfortable, "calling on God in prayer."

—Adapted from an article by Kathy Kuczka © LTP, 2011.

The Sacraments of Initiation

ADVENT is a perfect time for providing opportunities for groups preparing for the Sacraments of Initiation to take a welcome break to enter into prayer. You may wish to provide some reflective short daily prayer meditations on the hopes and anxieties of the Jewish people who waited in faith and hope for the Messiah. Certainly parents presenting children for Baptism, Confirmation, and first Holy Communion will relate to the anxieties of Mary and Joseph who were surrounded by mystery and so many unanswered questions as they awaited the birth of Jesus.

At the same time, John the Baptist challenges his listeners to "prepare the way" (Matthew 3:3) and to change our hearts. Perhaps schedule a prayerful evening of reflection prior to the parish Advent celebration of the Sacrament of Penance and Reconciliation. It would be helpful to include an examination of conscience for those parents and young people preparing to celebrate the Sacraments of Initiation.

Though most preparation sessions are tailored to a specific age group and sacrament, adding a ritual experience for all those involved can be very effective especially during the Advent season. Ritual experiences are always transformative and they provide a dimension to catechesis that is based on personal experience and reflection. Any week of Advent will work, but perhaps earlier in the season when things are calmer might be the most practical and convenient for families.

Since Baptism is the door to life, the first sacrament on which all the others hinge, "breaking open" the rite—its symbols and gestures, Scripture texts, and prayers can be offered as a focus. It will touch the hearts of participants in unexpected ways. Encourage all parishioners to attend. Send special invitations to parents seeking Baptism for their children, candidates for Confirmation, first Holy Communion, and the Catechumens. Prepare the ritual experience in the context of a celebration of the Word of God. Since this occasion is not Mass, you are afforded more flexibility and creativity. The key to holding events like this is careful preparation and the willingness to let the Spirit take control.

Preparing a ritual experience includes several elements: music, proclamation of the Word, symbol, and ritual gestures. Choose a presider from the parish staff or from the parish community who has a gift for good presiding and the ability to prepare a theologically sound reflection. Include the Renewal of Baptismal Promises as the focus of the ritual. Use readings and prayers from the *Rite of Baptism for Children* or the *Rite of Christian Initiation of Adults*. At the conclusion of the ritual distribute reflection questions about the celebration. Provide time for quiet reflection and then ask open-ended questions such as "What did you hear during the celebration?" "What touched you?" "What surfaced for you that perhaps you had never thought about before?" Following a brief sharing among the entire group, catechists and facilitators could then assemble in specific focus areas (RCIA, Baptism preparation, family groups for first Holy Communion). This would afford the opportunity to unpack the experience according to age level and specific sacrament. Enlist the help of the parish liturgy director and music director to prepare the experience. Liturgy is a collaborative effort.

The Rite of Penance

COMMUNAL penance services are popular in Advent. It is common for parishes to celebrate Form II, the Rite for Reconciliation of Several Penitents with Individual Confession

and Absolution. People should be catechized, so when they confess their sins they should do so in a timely manner, since the priest can only offer "suitable counsel" (RPen, 55) which does not mean an extended time for counseling. Few communities have yet to discover the value of celebrating the entire rite which calls for the Proclamation of Praise for God's Mercy, the Concluding Prayer of Thanksgiving, the Concluding Rite, and Blessing. In many places the people simply leave following the individual confession and absolution. We know that sin affects the whole community and we are used to gathering to listen to the proclamation of the Word of God and ponder the words of the Homily where the social dimensions of sin are called to our attention. In addition we have a General Confession of Sins using the *Confiteor*, we sing a litany or an appropriate song, and pray together the Lord's Prayer (see RPen, 54). When we omit the Proclamation of Praise for God's Mercy we fail to recognize the "good works which will proclaim the grace of repentance in the life of the entire community" (RPen, 56). This could be likened to coming to the celebration of the Mass but foregoing the Eucharistic Prayer.

The readings and psalms of Advent are ripe with images of light and darkness and the call to conversion especially in the texts about John the Baptist. The penitential intercessions (see RPen, 204) may be used for the General Confession of Sins. Consider the musical setting, "Lead Us to Act Justly" by Michael R. Prendergast and Joseph B. Sullivan available from Oregon Catholic Press (OCP), which uses the official text from the rite. This collection models what the rite is asking us to do and moves us away from intercessions that begin with the words such as "for the times we failed . . . . " Appendix II, section II from the rite includes a Common Penitential Celebration for Advent. These penitential celebrations have been referred to as non-sacramental celebrations since even if they are led by a priest they do not include individual confession and absolution. These penitential celebrations, which can be led by a lay leader of prayer or a deacon, are meant to gradually lead the community, (especially children) to the celebration the Rite of Reconciliation of Individual Penance, Form I or the Rite for Reconciliation of Several Penitents with Individual Confession and Absolution. The Advent repertoire of hymns, songs, and psalms are rich with images of God's reconciling mercy.

The Pastoral Care of the Sick

THE people of God should know that they can ask for the Sacrament of the Anointing of the Sick and, "as soon as the right time comes, to receive it with full faith and devotion" (PCS, 13). Ritual Masses of Anointing are not permitted on the Sundays of Advent (see PCS, 131–148). Ritual Masses may be celebrated on the weekdays of Advent except for the Immaculate Conception. Anointing outside of Mass may happen at any time (see PCS, 111–114). The Universal Prayer (Prayer of the Faithful) should include a prayer lifting up the sick and suffering of the parish and the world each week. Priests who go to homes, hospitals, or care centers could be accompanied by members of the parish, including pastoral musicians who could lead in the singing of one of the psalms, responses, and litanies from the ritual text. Consider bringing the parish bulletin or an audio recording of one of the Advent liturgies or if appropriate an Advent wreath to be placed in the sick person's room.

The Rite of Marriage

WHEN Marriages are celebrated on one of the Sundays in Advent, the Mass of the day is used along with the nuptial blessing and final blessing (see *Rite of Marriage* [RMar], 11). Weddings may not take place on Immaculate Conception (a Holyday of Obligation [see RMar, 11]). Ritual Masses may be celebrated on the other days of Advent.

Encourage couples to plan their colors and choice of flowers to be synonymous with the Advent liturgical environment. One suggestion would be to ask the couple to add a garland of flowers to the Advent wreath. Music ministers who assist couples with preparing the wedding liturgy might introduce them to the plethora of Advent hymns and carols and encourage their use in the celebration. Remind engaged couples that the celebration of the rite should find a home in the season (see RMar, 11).

The Order of Christian Funerals

THE *Order of Christian Funerals* (OCF) presumes full and fruitful use of *Pastoral Care of the Sick*. The OCF picks up both ritually and contextually where PCS leaves off. The OCF is primarily about the ministry of consolation, offering comfort in time of grief or distress. Christians who minister consolation to the bereaved do so in the context of their own faith. Those who console need to have an understanding of death as embedded in the Paschal Mystery of Christ.

Funeral rites is the term designated to refer to all the liturgical celebrations in the *Order of Christian Funerals*. The OCF is a collection of several rites for Christian burial. *Funeral liturgy* is the term designated to refer to a "funeral Mass" (Eucharist) and "funeral liturgy outside of Mass" without Eucharist.

Funeral Masses may not be celebrated on Immaculate Conception. The color of the vestments used for funerals include white, violet, or black. Psalm 25, one of the seasonal common psalms for Advent, is a good choice for funerals and is one of the appointed psalms from the *Order of Christian Funerals*. Many of the readings in the OCF contain rich images of Advent.

The OCF contains over 40 prayers that may be used as Collects at the funeral liturgy including prayers for those who died after a long illness, a stillborn child, a child who died before Baptism, one who died by suicide, or for the spouse of a non-Christian married to a Catholic, to name a few. Be sure to take advantage of the many options found in the OCF.

The Book of Blessings

THE *Book of Blessings* call for the full, conscious, and active participation of the gathered Church in the celebrations of blessings. It states: "it is ordinarily not permissible to impart the blessing of any article or place merely through a sign of blessing without either the word of God or any sort of prayer being spoken" (BB, 27). The structure of blessings usually takes the following form:

- Introductory Rites: song, Sign of the Cross, and greeting
- Introduction: brief explanation of the blessing and its significance
- Reading of the Word of God: with a Psalm and a brief Homily or reflection
- Intercessions: following the form used in the Liturgy of the Hours or at Mass
- Prayer of Blessing: the conclusion to the Intercessions
- Concluding Rites: blessing of all and a suitable song unless the blessing is celebrated within Mass

Part V of the ritual book includes the Blessings Related to Feasts and Seasons. Blessings for Advent includes the Order for the Blessing of an Advent Wreath (Chapter 47). If the blessing occurs during the celebration of the Mass the blessing follows the Universal Prayer (Prayer of the Faithful). The Blessing of the Advent Wreath is also found in *Catholic Household Blessings & Prayers* in Part III, Days and Seasons.

The Liturgical Environment

Of course, the first thing most of us think about in connection with Advent is the wreath. This devotion is an important part of many families' Advent prayer—gathering around the dinner table to light candles, hearing the Scriptures, and praying. It is also usually a fixture in our churches, announcing the coming Messiah in its growing light. Because the Advent wreath is a devotion, it does not need to be central in the liturgical space, particularly if it will be disruptive to the flow of the liturgy or the movement of ministers and people. Consider where the wreath might be placed where it will be seen throughout Advent—not just during Mass. It is preferable to have one wreath for a parish rather than many. Also consider using sanctuary lamps that can be left burning throughout the season as a quiet witness. Of course, like all items for liturgy or devotion, there is a preference for natural materials in constructing an Advent wreath. Oftentimes, stores that sell Christmas trees will give you the trimmed branches from the bottom of the trees for free. These are usually quite fresh and, when mixed with garland, offer a nice contrast of different kinds of greenery. Other items, such as

pomegranates, apples, lavender, or locally growing berries (cranberries, holly, etc.) can brighten up a wreath. Regularly misting the wreath with a spray bottle of water will help keep it fresh. The wreath is blessed only once.

The liturgical color for Advent is violet, with rose as an option in the third week. Advent violet is ideally a bluish shade, sometimes called royal purple. This differentiates the Advent violet from the redder shades of Lent, which transitions to the scarlet of Holy Week. Advent violet might remind the viewer of the pre-dawn sky, further situating Advent as a period of waiting for the return of the light.

Not all parishes have rose vestments. In this case violet can be used throughout Advent. While the immediate reason for rose (the introit, *Gaudete*) is not used in most parishes, the three-year Lectionary cycle does place readings about joy in the coming Savior in the middle of Advent. The rose in the midst of the darkness also draws from the natural environment; just as rose colors the sky before the sun is seen, this joyful rose is brought into the dark sanctuary before Christmas.

The Liturgical Music

The music in Advent should be subdued. *Sing to the Lord: Music in Divine Worship* (STL) reminds us: "At other times, the liturgical season calls for a certain musical restraint. In Advent, for example, musical instruments should be used with moderation and should not anticipate the full joy of the Nativity of the Lord" (114).

For more contemporary ensembles within, it may be good to think of an "unplugged" mentality, returning to acoustic instruments and hand drums.

The Gloria is not sung during Advent execpt for on Immaculate Conception and Our Lady of Guadalupe.

For a list of Advent music suggestions visit www.LTP.org/resources for a free PDF.

The Liturgical Ministers

PLAN to provide spiritual formation for liturgical ministers during Advent. Consider LTP's *Keeping the Seasons / Celebremos los tiempos litúrgicos*, a multi-use CD-ROM that contains bilingual catechesis, prayer, and spiritual nourishment for Advent and Christmas Time. *Keeping the Seasons / Celebremos los tiempos litúrgicos* includes ready to print Advent greeting cards that you can custom design and send to liturgical ministers and volunteers in the parish thanking them for their dedicated service to the people of God.

Advent is the perfect time to celebrate the Liturgy of the Hours with liturgical ministers and the entire community. Encourage liturgical ministers to use OCP's *Morning and Evening Prayer for the Commute* by Christopher Walker and Paule Freeburg, dc or GIA's *My Morning Prayer* and *My Evening Prayer* with music by various artists. These recordings of Morning and Evening Prayer can help to keep ministers linked to the Church's daily prayer.

Plan now to train new ministers of hospitality for Christmas, so that all who cross the threshold of the church will feel welcomed and embraced with the love of Christ. Include students returning from college or former parishioners home to be with family or friends, to serve as ministers during the Christmas break.

Care for the greens of the Advent wreath to make sure the foliage and branches remain fresh each week. Review orders for Christmas flowers and plants, and make sure ministers of the liturgical environment receive a schedule indicating the times when the church and parish campus will be prepared. Christmas falls on a Wednesday in 2013 (2014 liturgical year) so ministers will have some breathing room to prepare the space. Be attentive to areas of the campus that might be used for overflow seating, parking and traffic flow, fire lanes, and snow removal in the parking lot.

Devotions and Sacramentals

ADVENT is filled with rich devotional and sacramental traditions. The Advent wreath is an important domestic Church custom and a blessing of the Advent wreath is contained in *Catholic Household Blessings & Prayers* and the *Book of Blessings.* The Jesse Tree flows from the story of Jesse in Isaiah 11:1–10 and David in 1 Samuel 16:1–13. Jesse is the father of David, beginning a line of descendants that will lead to Jesus, the Messiah. Ornaments may be placed on the tree that trace the stories of the first covenant that lead to the birth of Jesus. Some of the symbols on the ornaments include the dove, apple, ark, a bag of grain, a ram, and the burning bush, to name a few. Throughout Advent, a different ornament can be added to the tree each day and a then a Scripture reading representing the ornament of the day is read. *Faith Magazine,* a publication of the Catholic Diocese of Erie, Pennsylvania, includes the story of the Jesse tree. You can find a link to download patterns for ornaments by going to www.eriercd.org/jessetree.htm.

December 6 is the optional Memorial of St. Nicholas, Bishop. Many customs and traditions have come from Europe, one of which is placing an orange or tangerine and a candy cane, which is in the shape of a bishops' staff, in the socks and shoes of children the evening before his memorial. As a family, set aside an unused shoe for the remainder of Advent and fill it with your spare change. During Christmas Time, use the money to perform random acts of kindness for the needy.

December 7 is the Memorial of St. Ambrose, Bishop and Doctor of the Church. St. Ambrose was the author of many hymn texts including the rich Advent text "Savior of the Nations Come."

A novena to the Immaculate Conception normally begins on the Feast of St. Andrew on November 30 and ends on December 8. The novena was originated by Pius XI in 1936 as a response to the threat of communism and fascism—in particular, Nazism. On December 8, 2015 the Church will mark the 50th anniversary of the close of the Second Vatican Council. Begin preparing for the ways in which you will mark this anniversary in your parish. Consider setting aside time to revisit the documents of the Council and mine the key teachings found within them. Use this day to reflect on some of the titles of Mary including; Mary New Advent, Mary New Dawn, and Mary, Mother of the Church.

On December 12, we celebrate the Feast of Our Lady of Guadalupe, which begins with the Mass of the Roses where the *Las Mañanitas*, a song of greeting meant to "wake" the Virgin, is sung. The use of roses is in reference to the sign that the Virgin gave to St. Juan Diego (whose memorial is usually observed on December 9, but since December 8 falls on a Sunday in 2013, the Solemnity of the Immaculate Conception is transferred to December 9 because this day is the patronal feastday of the United States) as a proof of the her appearance. *Catholic Household Blessings & Prayers* includes a prayer in honor of Our Lady of Guadalupe.

On December 13, we commemorate the Memorial of St. Lucy, Virgin and Martyr. St. Lucy is associated with festivals of lights. Her memorial points outs the light we hope for in Jesus Christ. Since she is the patron saint of those afflicted by diseases of the eye it would be an appropriate day to celebrate the Sacrament of the Anointing of the Sick with those suffering from any form of ailments of the eye.

Advent is filled with a number of novenas including *Las Posadas* (meaning "lodging") which begins on December 16 at midnight (or earlier in the evening). Each evening of the novena, a young couple dresses as the Virgin Mary and St. Joseph. Singing songs, the community accompanies the couple who are in search of shelter as the birth of Mary's child draws near.

Simbang Gabi is the novena of the Filipino community, which also begins on December 16. The church bells are rung to announce the beginning of the novena. The Mass of the Rooster or *Misa di Gallo* (meaning "night of worship") consists of the celebration of the Eucharist on each of the nine days before the Solemnity of the Nativity of the Lord. The celebration includes paper lanterns (*parol*)—symbols of lights that were carried by the Filipino people in rural parts of their country.

LTP's *Children's Daily Prayer* provides prayers and activities to assist children and families in keeping the days of Advent. LTP's *Keeping the Seasons / Celebremos los tiempos litúrgicos* are reproducible resources for Advent and Christmas Time that will support the devotional and prayer life of the domestic Church.

The Parish and the Home

MANY of us know what it is like to catch a glimpse of the fragileness of life: a serious health diagnosis, an accident or close call, the loss of a job or loved one or a relationship. We know how quickly life can change—really in an instant. In that moment we realize what is important to us or what we have neglected or left incomplete. We understand how precious life is. Perhaps we wish we had stayed more alert, more focused, and more awake to the life right in front of us.

"Therefore, stay awake! For you do not know on which day your Lord will come" (Matthew 24:42). Jesus spokes these words to his disciples. Our parish communities hear them as we begin a new liturgical cycle on the First Sunday of Advent. How do we engage the members of our households, families, classrooms, and communities? How can we help them recognize God's message of Good News so we are ready and attentive to do our part to build the reign of God?

Advent is the time for pausing and taking stock. As we celebrate the beginning of the Church's new year we are aware of the pulls of the secular culture and world around us. Much of that tension is of our own making as we juggle the demands of the holiday season with the message of the coming Emmanuel. Holiday decorations bombard us months in advance; Christmas songs seem to endlessly surround us. Even religious institutions, schools, and churches give mixed messages with early holiday parties and gift-giving. It is difficult to keep the deep reflective timing.

Preparing for Advent, particularly with those parishioners who are newly engaged or married or with households that have recently or will celebrate the birth of a first child, is a graced moment. They often are at a particularly vulnerable time. They have a new appreciation for values, traditions, and family customs. They are asking questions: What is important to us? How should we raise our child? How can we live our faith? What is the purpose of life? They may very well recognize the dangers of the material excess of Christmas Time. They are primed to make changes, create new customs, reflect on rituals, and begin Advent practices.

These parishioners need a community's help: Create a forum for them to talk with others about these ideals. Help them meet other families who have made changes to their celebrations of the Christmas holiday. Sponsor a hands-on workshop where they can create an Advent wreath (before Advent) and demonstrate ways it can build family reflection and prayer. Teach Advent songs and prayers. Send them home with materials and information about the customs of St. Nicholas (December 6) and St. Lucy (December 13) or *Las Posadas* (December 16–24). Present images that deepen the understanding of Mary's Immaculate Conception (December 8) and Our Lady of Guadalupe (December 12). Make it fun. Give them an anchor to grip when the world wants to shove and rush them into the holiday frenzy.

Mass Texts

◆ DISMISSAL TEXT FOR CHILDREN'S LITURGY OF THE WORD

As decorations go up in your homes
    and throughout our neighborhood,
it will be hard for you to keep your eyes on Jesus
and to remember he's the "reason for the season."
But don't let anything fool you,
and don't let anything distract you,
because the reason we put up trees and wreaths
    and manger scenes,
the reason we celebrate with gifts and joyful meals,
is because of a great miracle:
God became like each of us
so that we could become like God.
Go now in peace to hear God's Word.

◆ DISMISSAL TEXT FOR THE CATECHUMENS

You who seek union with Christ's Church
will now go forth to do what this season asks
    of each of us:
wait and rejoice.
As we await the celebration of Christ's birth
    and his coming in glory,
we rejoice with you that he has called you to himself
and chosen our community to nurture you
    in the faith.

As you reflect on today's Word from Scripture,
rejoice that God has chosen to write your name
    within the Book of Life.

◆ SEASONAL TEXTS FOR PRAYER OF THE FAITHFUL

Invitation to Prayer:

We sing "Silent Night" but hurry through busy, noisy days during this holy season. Our God invites us into silence so that we can contemplate his mercy made so visible in his Son, Jesus. Relying on that mercy we now speak our needs in full confidence that God is never deaf to our prayers and never slow to come to our assistance.

Intercessions:

For the needs of Christ's Church and for all who exercise the responsibility of pastoring; that God's people be nourished and the Gospel proclaimed through the worthy service of holy ministers, let us pray to the Lord.

For civic leaders who shoulder the responsibility of maintaining the peace and providing for the common good; that their service be marked by selfless commitment to the good of society, let us pray to the Lord.

For the poor who daily are deprived of basic necessities and who hunger for the justice of which the prophets spoke on God's behalf; that justice might flow like a mighty river ridding us of the greed and corruption that always make the poor their first victims, let us pray to the Lord.

For those who suffer from the effects of physical and mental illness; that the healing hand of Christ might bring them wholeness and peace, let us pray to the Lord.

For our families; that the child of Bethlehem might be enshrined in our homes as the Prince of Peace, let us pray to the Lord.

Response: You who are hope's fulfillment, hear our prayer.

Concluding Prayer:

As Israel waited in hope for the coming
    of her Savior,
we wait in confident hope that all we ask
is already given through the infinite mercy
    of the Father of our Lord, Jesus Christ,
through whom we ask these prayers.

December
Month of the Divine Infancy

 **1** (#1, LM) violet
First Sunday of Advent

The Lectionary for Mass

◆ FIRST READING: "In days to come . . . " (Isaiah 2:15). Advent bids us look to a future time. For the people of Isaiah's time, living in the wake of the destruction of the city of Jerusalem and their beloved Temple, this future time would be a time of restoration—and more. All nations will come to hear the Lord's teaching. The Lord will judge all nations and inaugurate a time of peace. Hear the invitation that is given to us as well: Come . . . listen to the voice of the Lord. Come, walk in his light.

◆ RESPONSORIAL PSALM 122 is fittingly a joyful, pilgrimage hymn to the Temple in Jerusalem. Note the echoes of themes from the First Reading: judgment, peace, and prayer for the well-being of Jerusalem.

◆ SECOND READING: Note the urgency in Paul's words: time is running out! And indeed, the Christians of his day expected the Second Coming of the Lord to be within their lifetime. Paul calls the Romans to a spirit of watchfulness, to be clothed in light rather than darkness, to live as those who bear the name of Jesus and in whom he dwells.

◆ GOSPEL: A similar urgency is heard in today's Gospel, only here, within the context of an unknown time of the coming of the Son of Man (a title used throughout the Gospel accounts with reference to Jesus). Jesus calls his followers to watchfulness and readiness. They must be prepared to welcome the Son of Man.

The Roman Missal

"Grant your faithful, we pray, almighty God, / the resolve to run forth to meet your Christ / with righteous deeds at his coming . . . ." With these words from the Collect, the mood for the new liturgical time is set. There is a great sense of urgency, of expectation, and of longing, because Christ is coming, and we are to meet him with our righteous deeds.

A certain sense of excitement and expectation should be evident in the tone of voice used by the priest in his liturgical greeting and in his words of extemporaneous introduction to the Mass of the day. It is, after all, the beginning of a new liturgical year in the Church, and so there is great anticipation about all that lies ahead in the upcoming Year of Grace. Ample use of Advent hymns at this liturgy and at every liturgy throughout the time will give musical voice to the longing in every worshiper's heart.

The Gloria is omitted, as it is for every Sunday of Advent. The Creed is said or sung.

The Prayer over the Offerings, which will be repeated on the Mondays and Thursdays of Advent up to December 16, acknowledges that the offerings we make at the Eucharist are gathered from among the gifts first given to us by God. This can be taken to mean both the material elements for the bread and wine ("fruit of the earth," "fruit of the vine" and "work of human hands")

and the spiritual offerings of our lives, both of which have their origin in divine bounty. Additionally, the prayer emphasizes the connection between our earthly offering ("what you grant us to celebrate devoutly here below") and our participation in the heavenly liturgy (that said offering may "gain for us the prize of eternal redemption").

Preface I of Advent is the Preface prescribed for today, and aptly so, as it lays out for us the two comings of Christ, namely, his first coming, when he assumed the lowliness of human flesh, and his Second Coming, the day that we watch for as we look forward to inheriting the "great promise" which is the foundation for our hopefulness. Our confidence in the future and our daring to hope are well-founded, for they are grounded in Christ.

The Prayer after Communion, which will be repeated on the same days as the Prayer over the Offerings, reminds us that our participation in the sacred mysteries gives us the proper orientation to the things of this world: we are to remember that they are passing things, and, in recognizing that, we should "love the things of heaven and hold fast to what endures."

Give strong consideration to using the Solemn Blessing for Advent at the end of Mass, option #1 among those blessings; it gives powerful expression to Advent themes.

The Missal itself is silent on the blessing of the Advent wreath; the Advent wreath is a home custom that has made its way into the celebration of the Eucharist over time. If the blessing of the wreath is to take place at Mass, consult the *Book of Blessings* for the proper procedure and texts; it can be found in Part V: "Blessings Related to Feasts and Seasons," Chapter 47, Order for the Blessing of an Advent Wreath (First Sunday of Advent), I, Order of Blessing within Mass. The blessing and lighting of the first candle takes place as the conclusion to the Universal Prayer on this First Sunday. On the other Sundays the appropriate number of candles is lit either before Mass begins or immediately before the Collect, without any additional rites or prayers.

Pastoral Reflection

Fully live the experience that begins upon us this day, which is one of waiting in joyful hope—knowing with absolute certainty that something miraculous is upon us. This week, treat your friends and family with the same joy and warmth you will easily offer on Christmas day. Verbally affirm those around you, for this is the action of Christ within us. Live each minute as if it was your "final" moment with Jesus as our teacher observing you to pass the final of your life!

The Anniversary of CSL

This Wednesday, December 4, will mark the fiftieth anniversary of the promulgation of the *Constitution on the Sacred Liturgy*. How might you celebrate the 50th anniversary of CSL in your parish community?

◆ EXPLORE CSL AND ITS LEGACY. CSL is not easy reading. It has wonderful passages, accessible to all, but it also has juridical sections that may be less useful for parish groups. There are resources out there that will help you to highlight what's most important in CSL.

◆ HOST A LITURGICAL WEEK (OR A LITURGICAL DAY). In the years leading up to the Council, the annual Liturgical Week brought together the leading lights of the Liturgical Movement and thousands of priests, religious, and lay faithful to explore the liturgy together. They participated in the Mass and in other liturgies as well, experiencing the fullness of the Church's prayer. You might begin a Liturgical Day with the Office of Morning Prayer, then have a keynote on CSL or some

other aspect of the liturgy. There could be times for reflection and quiet prayer, tours of the liturgical art of the parish, opportunities to sing or learn about liturgical music, presentations on the history of the liturgy, and a concluding celebration of the Eucharist. What better way to celebrate CSL than to celebrate what it celebrates—liturgy, art, and tradition?

◆ REVIEW YOUR LITURGICAL CELEBRATIONS HONESTLY. Each month during this anniversary year, you might gather key staff and liturgical ministers to look at the liturgy in light of some of the key concepts and teachings of CSL and do a little "examination of conscience." Ask yourselves: How do people participate in the Mass? What is strong? What could be stronger? Refer to CSL, 14. Is the liturgy the source and summit of parish life? Refer to CSL, 10. Does it truly nourish a vibrant life of service in parish and beyond? How are you doing on music? Refer to CSL, 112–121. Do the liturgies in your parish "shine with a noble simplicity?" Refer to CSL, 34. The *Constitution on the Sacred Liturgy* called for honest evaluation of the effectiveness of the liturgy in the Church as a whole. Today, it calls us to do the same.

M
O **2** (#175) violet
N **Advent Weekday**

The Lectionary for Mass

◆ FIRST READING: Isaiah loves images of life—such as the lustrous branch of the Lord mentioned today, and the abundant fruit of the earth—to be given to the survivors of the devastation of Jerusalem. So it will be "on that day" (Isaiah 4:2)—that often repeated phrase throughout Isaiah, pointing to a future day of restoration and fulfillment of all that God had promised. Indeed, it will be a time of a new exodus, a new deliverance, as the imagery of

the cloud by day and the fire at night suggests, when the Lord's glory will shelter and protect all.

◆ RESPONSORIAL PSALM 122 is a pilgrimage psalm, sung as pilgrims made their way to the Temple. Notice the emphasis on praying for peace, particularly apropos for a city that has suffered destruction.

◆ GOSPEL: "Comings" are likewise mentioned throughout today's Gospel. (This is not evident in the English translation, but both Jesus's entry into Capernaum and the centurion's approach to Jesus are forms of the Greek verb meaning "to come.") Jesus the healer offers to come to the centurion's house to heal his servant. Protesting his unworthiness and knowing the authority his own word carries, the centurion asks only for a healing word from Jesus because he believes in its power.

The Roman Missal

All the texts are proper for today. The Collect speaks of being alert as we await the advent of Christ; echoing the scriptural imagery of the bridegroom coming and knocking, we pray that we will be found "watchful in prayer." The Prayer over the Offerings and the Prayer after Communion are the same as used yesterday, the First Sunday of Advent.

T
U **3** (#176) white
E **Memorial of St. Francis Xavier, Priest**

The Lectionary for Mass

◆ FIRST READING: Today's text begins and ends looking to "that day" (Isaiah 11:1) of the Lord when his messianic promise will be realized. Jesse, the father of King David, and his longed-for descendant who would reestablish the nations and restore peace is likewise mentioned in both of these places. The first half of the reading describes the qualities of this anointed one; in particular, his endowment with the Spirit of the Lord and the gifts the Spirit brings. His reign will be marked by harmony among people, within nature, and between humankind and nature. The glory of this messianic era will be recognized not only by Jews, but also by Gentiles.

◆ RESPONSORIAL PSALM 72: The antiphon reiterates the qualities of the messianic king's reign. Indeed, these qualities are characteristics of God: justice, concern for the poor and the afflicted. Note also the reference to the Gentiles. All tribes of the earth shall be blessed, all nations shall praise him.

◆ GOSPEL: Luke portrays Jesus as the Spirit-endowed Messiah spoken of in today's First Reading. Today's text focuses on the depth of the relationship between Father and Son and the communication between them, all of which Jesus shares with those who follow him. Thus, his disciples are truly blessed, for they see and hear the fullness of what the prophets and kings of old longed for.

The Roman Missal

Since today's memorial is obligatory, the orations from *The Roman Missal* are those found in the Proper of Saints, for December 3, and the color worn is white. However, on obligatory memorials, it is permissible to use the Collect of the seasonal weekday as the concluding prayer to the Universal Prayer; this allows the sanctoral celebration to still maintain its context within the liturgical season, and it is strongly recommended that the priest take advantage of this option. Also, since there is no proper Preface assigned for today, Preface of Advent I may be used, and this would be another way of keeping a link with the season, although the Preface of Holy Pastors or Preface I or II of Saints could also be appropriate choices.

All of the orations in some way refer to St. Francis Xavier's missionary work and ask that we too may have the same zeal for souls and bear witness to the Gospel as effectively as did this Jesuit priest.

Today's Saint

St. Francis Xavier (1506–1552), a native Spaniard, was one of the founding members of the Society of Jesus (the Jesuits). Francis Xavier felt called to be a "spiritual soldier" through missionary endeavors to Christianize foreign lands and convert the hearts of unbelievers. One of the many honors Francis received in his life was his appointment by the pope as *apostolic nuncio* (an ambassador of the Church) to the East. He traveled to many places, including India, the Philippines, and Japan. In his travels, Francis tended to the needs of the sick and infirm, revitalized the liturgical and sacramental life of already existing Christian populations, and drew people to faith in Jesus Christ.

WED 4 (#177) violet
Advent Weekday

Optional Memorial of St. John Damascene, Priest and Doctor of the Church / white

The Lectionary for Mass

◆ FIRST READING: God's words, addressed to a people enshrouded in the darkness of sorrow and death, bring a message of hope: the God for whom they wait will come, bringing salvation and providing an abundant feast for his people on his holy mountain. What joy will be theirs!

◆ RESPONSORIAL PSALM 23 is a beautiful song of confidence and trust in the Lord who shepherds us through the valley of darkness and death to an abundant feast. Truly we can know that we will live in the house of the Lord all the days of our life.

◆ GOSPEL: On a mountain in Galilee, Jesus removes the darkness and sorrow of those with physical afflictions and provides a meal for the hungry crowd that has followed him. What joy was theirs as they glorified God for the salvation they experienced in Jesus. Do we allow him to remove the darkness and sorrow that enshroud us and to provide for our needs as well?

The Roman Missal

If the optional memorial is celebrated today, the Collect is proper from the Proper of Saints; the Prayer over the Offerings and Prayer after Communion may be taken from Wednesday of the First Week of Advent, which would be preferable in order to keep the sense of the liturgical time. However, these other two orations may also be taken either from the Common of Pastors: For One Pastor, or from the Common of Doctors of the Church. Either way, since this is an optional memorial, consider using Preface I of Advent to keep the sense of the liturgical time.

Today's Saint

Monk, Doctor of the Church, theologian, scholar, poet, hymnologist, liturgist—these are just a few of the roles St. John (657–749) fulfilled as a faithful son of the Church. Most notably, he is remembered for his avid defense of the use of sacred art in churches, monasteries, and homes. Born only five years after the death of Muhammad, John was thrust into conflict, particularly regarding the heresy iconoclasm. The iconoclastic heresy, which sought to destroy all images of devotion, resulted from the misinterpretation on the part of the emperor and many others that Christians were using sacred art as a means of idol worship. St. John composed three treatises with the goal of lifting up images of Christ, the saints, and Mary as a doorway to the mystery of God's saving work.

Anniversary of *CSL*

Today is the 50th anniversary of CSL, the first monumental document of the Second Vatican Council.

THU 5 (#178) violet
Advent Weekday

The Lectionary for Mass

◆ FIRST READING: "On that day" (Isaiah 26:1)—the phrase is a repeated refrain in our readings this week. On that day the Lord comes with power to save his people and a song will be sung throughout the land. The people of Israel, a just and faithful people, enter the holy city. It is a time of freedom for the oppressed and downtrodden, the destruction of the high and lofty, and the lifting up of the poor and needy.

◆ RESPONSORIAL PSALM 118 is a song of thanksgiving for the merciful deeds of God. The theme of trust (heard two times in the First Reading) pervades the first stanza. The second speaks of opening the gates so God's people can enter. The third focuses on the salvation that accompanies the arrival of the one who comes in the name of the Lord.

◆ GOSPEL: Entering the kingdom is today's focus. The requirements are doing the will of the Father and acting on the words of the Lord that one has heard. Does not building on the rock evoke the firm purpose of the First Reading? What is our house or "where we're at," as the expression goes, built on?

The Roman Missal

A sense of urgency and the need for divine help is conveyed in today's Collect, as we ask God to "stir up" his power. Our sins interfere with our reception of what God wishes to give to us, but those sins are overcome through the mercy of God. The Prayer over the Offerings and Prayer after Communion are the same as those used on Sunday and Monday of this week.

FRI 6 (#179) violet
Advent Weekday

Optional Memorial of St. Nicholas, Bishop / white

The Lectionary for Mass

◆ FIRST READING: "On that day . . . the deaf shall hear . . . the blind shall see . . ." (Isaiah 29:18). Earlier in Isaiah 29:9, (not included in today's reading) the blind are those who have blinded themselves in a metaphorical rather than physical way. That longed-for day of the Lord will be a day of healing and insight, of rejoicing in the Lord, of freedom from oppression. This is the saving work of the Lord in our midst.

◆ RESPONSORIAL PSALM 27: The Lord is light for those unable to see, the salvation of all who are oppressed and afflicted. Psalm 27 speaks of deep confidence in the Lord. Note the three "seeing" words in the last two stanzas. The psalm ends with the very fitting Advent exhortation to "wait for the Lord."

◆ GOSPEL: Today's account of the healing of the blind men is a nice complement to both the First Reading and the Responsorial Psalm. Notice that the blind men "followed" (an image of discipleship) Jesus into the house. By seeking the presence and touch of the Lord they receive sight. This experience of salvation was too much to contain, and they spread this Good News throughout the land.

The Roman Missal

It is likely that the optional Memorial of St. Nicholas will be referenced in some way, since he is such a popular saint in connection with this time of year. If the optional memorial is celebrated, the Collect is proper from the Proper of Saints, but consider taking the Prayer over the Offerings and Prayer after Communion from Friday of the First Week of Advent, in order to keep the a strong Advent connection. However, it is also possible to use the Common of Pastors: for a Bishop for these other two orations. Either way, since this is an optional memorial, consider using Preface I of Advent to keep the sense of the liturgical time.

Today's Saint

Little is known about Nicholas, the "wonderworker," other than the fact that he lived sometime during the fourth century and was bishop of the city of Myra in Asia Minor. There is some evidence that he was imprisoned during the Diocletian persecutions, and later condemned Arianism, a heresy that denied the Son was co-eternal with the Father. Many stories exist about St. Nicholas, but the best known is the one about a poor man who could not feed or clothe his three daughters. Upon hearing of this man's dire situation, St. Nicholas tossed three bags of gold through his window one evening so the man could tend to his daughters' needs. Modern folklore about Santa Claus, Kris Kringle, and Father Christmas are based on the stories of St. Nicholas and his great love for and generosity toward children.

SAT 7 (#180) white
Memorial of St. Ambrose, Bishop and Doctor of the Church

The Lectionary for Mass

◆ FIRST READING: God's words are addressed to a people who experience sorrow and affliction. God promises them that he will hear them when they cry out, will reveal his way and instruct them when they turn to him. "On that day"— the day of salvation . . . is a salvation manifest even in nature. That day of his coming, a day of destruction of evil and of arrogance, will be a day of healing for God's people, healing of the wounds of their chastisement.

◆ RESPONSORIAL PSALM 147 is a hymn of praise. The second and third stanzas in particular echo the themes of healing and deposing the mighty from the First Reading. Note the theme of waiting in the antiphon.

◆ GOSPEL: While we had mention of flocks of animals in today's First Reading, it is the Jewish people themselves who are the sheep in today's Gospel. Jesus saw them as sheep without a shepherd. In today's passage, Jesus's healing work is paramount, and the Apostles are sent and empowered to continue this mission.

The Roman Missal

All of the orations are proper for today, found at December 7, the Memorial of St. Ambrose, in the Proper of Saints section of the Missal. It would be a good idea to use the Collect for Saturday of the First Week of Advent as the conclusion to the Universal Prayer, in order to highlight a connection with liturgical time.

The Collect draws a connection between the reason we venerate St. Ambrose and a constant need in the Church for priestly vocations: after we recognize St. Ambrose as "a teacher of the Catholic faith / and a model of apostolic courage," we then ask God to "raise up in your Church men after your own heart / to govern her with courage and wisdom."

The Prayer over the Offerings asks for the gift of the Holy Spirit, in that through our participation in celebrating these mysteries, we will be filled with the same light of faith that enlightened St. Ambrose. Thus, the transformation that is always part-and-parcel of our participation in offering the Eucharist is implicitly affirmed.

The Prayer after Communion has an Advent ring to it as it asks that our participation in this Eucharist may bring us strength to hasten fearlessly along the paths we are asked to travel so that "we may be prepared for the delights of the eternal banquet."

Today's Saint

St. Ambrose (339–397) was esteemed as a man of ardent faith with a flair for diplomacy. He was unanimously chosen as bishop of Milan at a time when the Church was in upheaval over the Arian controversy. He was an unlikely choice: although a professed Christian, he had not yet been baptized. Throughout his life he boldly rebuked emperors such as Theodosius and Valentinian, warriors like the ruthless Maximus, and unfaithful Christians. He prevented wars and invasions, demanded repentance on the part of sinful leaders, and brought people and nations together when reconciliation seemed impossible. St. Ambrose, a prodigious writer of homiletics, is counted as one of the four original Doctors of the Church, along with St. Augustine, St. Jerome, and St. Gregory.

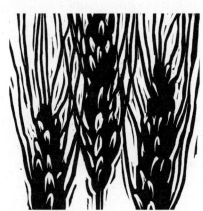

☼ **8** (#4) violet
Second Sunday of Advent

The Lectionary for Mass

◆ FIRST READING: A stump— a seemingly lifeless sign of what once was flourishing. So must Jerusalem and the house of David have seemed to the people of Isaiah's day after the Babylonian conquest. Yet what hope is heard in the prophet's words. The roots are deep and there is life in the stump of Jesse, even though it may not be evident. New life will sprout from it, a Davidic heir, on whom the Spirit of the Lord will rest. His rule will be marked by fidelity and justice for all people. It will be a time of great peace for all of creation. It will be a time of blessing for all people, Gentiles as well as Jews.

◆ RESPONSORIAL PSALM 72: We will hear today's psalm often in Advent, so apropos with its focus on the king and his reign. Note how the stanzas reiterate all the characteristics of the king and his reign described in Isaiah's words.

◆ SECOND READING: What a great advertisement for the Scriptures! All that was previously written— for Paul, this would have been what we know as the Old Testament— was written for our instruction and encouragement in hope and endurance. Most of Paul's words in today's text, however, have to do with welcoming one another . . . especially the Gentiles (or non-Jewish) people who desire to embrace the Christian faith. How are we called to welcome others of different ethnic or religious origins today?

◆ GOSPEL: John the Baptist had a pivotal role in preparing the way for the imminent coming of the Lord. John called those who would hear him to conversion, to "good fruit[s]" (Matthew 3:10) evident in their lives. It was not enough—and indeed a mistake—to be assured of their righteousness just because they were Jews. The one who comes will come as Judge. The one who comes will baptize with the Holy Spirit and with fire—the potential for powerful change and transformation in the lives of all who believe.

The Roman Missal

In the ranking of liturgical days, a Sunday of Advent takes precedence over a solemnity of the Blessed

Virgin Mary, so the Second Sunday of Advent is celebrated today, and the Solemnity of the Immaculate Conception is transferred to tomorrow, December 9.

The Gloria is not sung or said today. The Creed is said or sung today.

A sense of urgency continues to be conveyed in the Collect as we pray that nothing may "hinder those / who set out in haste to meet your Son." However, any progress we make in our Advent journey of running to meet Christ is not due to our own merits, as noted in the Prayer over the Offerings. In fact, since we can do nothing on our own, we recognize our need for rescue through God's mercy. The Prayer after Communion is another prayer that asks that our participation in this Eucharistic offering will help us to be able to distinguish with wisdom the difference between the things of earth and the things of heaven, holding firm to the latter.

Preface I of Advent is the Preface assigned for today and so is the one to be used. Consider using the Solemn Blessing for Advent at the end of Mass.

Pastoral Reflection

What holds you back from being the best version of yourself? What situations, beliefs, and past actions fester the angst that twists at your soul? John the Baptist lived an austere life so as to better experience God. He knew that water cleanses the body and fire would ignite the soul. Take a step inward this week and be mindful of all that needs to be healed from the past and in the present.

(#689)   white

Solemnity of the Immaculate Conception of the Blessed Virgin Mary, Patronal Feastday of the United States of America

MON 9

TRANSFERRED FROM SUNDAY

About this Solemnity

Today we celebrate Mary's Immaculate Conception; that is, her total freedom from original sin from the moment of her conception. This freedom from the sin of Adam and Eve is shown in today's Gospel. In Mary's response to the angel, she shows her willingness to place herself fully in God's hands, even when it promises to be difficult and requires great faith and trust.

Please note that the obligation to attend Mass today has been lifted.

The Lectionary for Mass

◆ FIRST READING: A stark contrast can be drawn between the responses of Adam and Eve to God in today's First Reading and that of Mary in today's Gospel. Adam and Eve had reason to fear God because of their disobedience; Mary, who had found favor with God, had no reason to fear. Adam and Eve's disobedience led to punishment; Mary's receptivity and obedience, to salvation. Adam and Eve's sin resulted in enmity between the woman and the serpent (the evil one); Mary's offspring was to be holy. Eve became the mother of all the living; Mary became the Mother of the Son of God—and of all who would be reborn in him.

◆ RESPONSORIAL PSALM 98 is a hymn of praise to God the King. He has done, and is doing, marvelous deeds. Ever faithful to his covenant of old, he brings salvation not only to Israel but to all nations.

◆ SECOND READING: This is yet another contrast with today's First Reading given Paul's emphasis on the blessings believers have received

---

in Christ. We were chosen (mentioned two times) even before the foundation of the world (and the fall of the first human creatures) to receive God's salvation and to be a people of praise.

◆ GOSPEL: Mary was "full of grace" and "found favor with God" (Luke 1:28) when she received the angel's message that she was to be the Mother of Jesus, the Son of the Most High. Mary was perplexed, "greatly troubled" (Luke 1:29) the text says, at what this means, at how it could be. It can be, and is, through the power of God. In contrast with Adam and Eve, who asserted their own will over and against God, Mary humbly acquiesced in the face of the mystery: I am God's servant.

The Roman Missal

Today both the Gloria and the Creed are sung or said, due to the celebration of the solemnity. The texts for the Mass are found in the Proper of Saints.

That Mary was preserved from the stain of original sin from the moment of her conception is the theme echoed throughout the prayers for the Mass. The Collect refers to Mary as "a worthy dwelling for your Son" because she was preserved "from every stain / by virtue of the Death of your Son;" thus is Mariology situated within Christology. Yet, Mary is always seen within the context of the Church, as the model disciple, and hence the second part of the Collects asks for her intercession that we too "may be cleansed and admitted to your presence."

The Prayer over the Offerings echoes the petition of the Collect as it again asks that through Mary's intercession "we may be delivered from all our faults." Be careful of the phrase "prevenient grace" in this prayer; it can be a bit of a tongue-twister! Priest celebrants will want to practice this prayer carefully.

The Preface is found right there along with the other texts for the day. As is common because it expresses the reasons we are giving thanks to God at this celebration, the Preface is a rich source for the meaning and theology of the solemnity we are celebrating, and it can be a splendid source for homiletic themes. Again recalling that the meaning of the solemnity is found in Mary's being preserved "from all stain of original sin," the Preface also expresses Mary's place in the life of the Church as the disciple placed "above all others / to be for your people an advocate of grace and a model of holiness."

Finally, the Prayer after Communion again asks that just as Mary was preserved from sin, so too might we, now through our participation in the sacrament, be healed of the wounds of sin.

It would be a good idea to use the Solemn Blessing at the end of Mass suggested for today, which is the one titled "The Blessed Virgin Mary," number 15, the first choice under the "For Celebrations of the Saints" section.

Pastoral Reflection

Mary, the chosen one of God—pure, holy, open, and willing—listened to the angels even though she was uncertain. In her absolute surrender to the will of God, she became the prime example for each of us to trust and let go of our path and walk steadily into the arms of God given strength by the Spirit. Her gift is not singular, but one which is already transferred to your heart. What causes you to doubt? Who are the angels who speak to you with words of wisdom, but in fear (or pride) you don't want to listen? What stirs your soul so deeply that you could dance with the angels while gifting this world? The impossible is possible because of God and listening hearts like Mary's. Spend time in precious silence stilling your soul to hear the

words of God. If you can hear the words, respond with Mary, "I am the handmaid of the Lord" (Luke 1:38). If you cannot yet hear a tangible response, work on the practice of stilling your soul as Mary taught.

TUE 10 (#182) violet
Advent Weekday

The Lectionary for Mass

◆ FIRST READING: The word of the Lord is addressed to a devastated Jerusalem, many of whose citizens are in exile. God's word comforts his people. Her time of punishment (the Exile) is ended. A new era is about to begin. God is coming with power. God's people must prepare the way for him. And note, the God who comes with power, comes likewise in tenderness, like a shepherd lovingly caring for his flock and carrying the very young in his arms.

◆ RESPONSORIAL PSALM 96, a joyful hymn of praise, acclaims the glory and power of God the King. All of creation rejoices at his coming.

◆ GOSPEL: The image of shepherd mentioned at the end of today's First Reading is fulfilled in Jesus, the good shepherd. Today's Gospel emphasizes in particular Jesus's seeking out—and finding—the sheep that is lost.

The Roman Missal

We are progressing along in our Advent journey as evidenced by the first specific mention of the Nativity in the Collect; these days can be seen as a kind of movement slowly advancing from the first phase of Advent into the second phase. The Prayer over the Offerings and the Prayer after Communion are the same ones used on this past Sunday.

WED 11 (#183) violet
Advent Weekday

Optional Memorial of St. Damasus I, Pope / white

The Lectionary for Mass

◆ FIRST READING: Israel in exile felt, perhaps, abandoned by God. All of God's promises seemed to be a thing of the past. Today's text emphasizes not only the power of God the Creator, but the tender care he shows to all his creation. This care embraces and strengthens his chosen people—if only they place their hope in him.

◆ RESPONSORIAL PSALM 103 is a song of praise and thanksgiving for all the blessings received from God. Notice the blessings specifically mentioned: forgiveness, healing, and redemption.

◆ GOSPEL: In light of today's First Reading, we could easily hear the word *hope* in place of the "come" of today's Gospel. That is to say, we are invited to come in hope to our God. In him alone we will find true rest from all that burdens us.

The Roman Missal

If you are celebrating the optional memorial, then use the Collect for St. Damasus I from the Proper of Saints. The Prayer over the Offerings and Prayer after Communion, however, may be taken from Wednesday of the Second Week of Advent, and this might be considered the preferable choice for the sake of keeping the sense of the season. If desired, however, these two orations may be taken from the Common of Pastors: For a Pope. Consider using Preface I of Advent in order to situate this memorial within the season.

Today's Saint

St. Damasus I (+ 384): Two significant historical events formed the backdrop of this saint's life: the witness of courageous martyrs during the Diocletian persecutions and the granting of religious freedom to Christians by Emperor Constantine. St. Damasus I reigned as pope for 24 years. He is remembered for revitalizing devotion to the relics of martyrs by adorning catacombs, building churches, making shrines more accessible, and marking the resting places of the martyrs with unique inscriptions and epigrams. He is also remembered for his innate ability to bring about uniformity and peace in an empire recently characterized by persecution and infiltrated with paganism. Among his many other accomplishments, St. Damasus is credited with encouraging St. Jerome to produce a new translation of the Latin Bible, called the Vulgate.

THU 12 (#690A, 707–712) white
Feast of Our Lady of Guadalupe

About this Feast

Behind the miraculous appearance and icon that define Our Lady of Guadalupe, is a story of persistence and courage. When Our Lady appeared to Juan Diego, she sent him to the bishop to request that a church be built. Juan Diego, an indigenous peasant farmer, had no status, power, or influence with which to impress the bishop, yet he followed Our Lady's request. Risking rejection or even ridicule, he returned twice with his amazing story of the vision. With the blooming flowers packed in his tilma (poncho), and the miraculous icon that emerged beneath them, Our Lady helped Juan Diego make his point. The story teaches us trust, and the certainty that when God calls us to proclaim his kingdom, we are surrounded by the grace we need to see our mission through. May we persist in sharing the Good News, even in the face of great challenges.

The Lectionary for Mass

◆ First Reading: Today's reading from Zechariah takes on new meaning in light of today's feast of Our Lady of Guadalupe and her appearance to the humble peasant, Juan Diego. This visitation of God's Mother was an occasion of deep joy, as nations of Hispanic peoples join themselves to the Lord through her, celebrating his presence among them.

◆ Canticle: Today's response is a hymn from the book of Judith, the Jewish woman who saved her people from destruction at the hands of the foreign enemies. Christians see her as prefiguring Mary, the Mother of God, who had a preeminent role in saving humanity from eternal destruction.

◆ Second Reading: We hear of the vision of the Christian prophet John about a woman in the heavens, traditionally interpreted as Mary, the Mother of God. Her child, rescued from the devil's fury, is ruler of the nations and enthroned with God. The woman is led to a place God has prepared for her.

◆ Gospel: Two choices are given, both from Luke 1: the Annunciation to Mary or the visitation of Mary and Elizabeth. Both focus on the marvelous deed of Mary, the Mother of Jesus, in her "yes" to be the Mother of the Lord, thus saving her people from eternal destruction.

The Roman Missal

The orations for this Mass are found in the Proper of Saints. The Collect, Prayer over the Offerings, and Prayer after Communion are all proper for today, so they replace the Advent texts. The Gloria is sung or said today. The Creed is not said.

The Collect reminds us that, insofar as Our Lady appeared to the humble peasant Juan Diego, the celebration of this feast is tied to a lively faith that seeks "the progress of peoples in the ways of justice and peace." Living a life of faith exemplified by those virtues of justice and peace is what lies behind the petition expressed in the Prayer over the Offerings: "grant that this sacrifice / may strengthen us to fulfill your commandments / as true children of the Virgin Mary."

The Preface assigned for today is either Preface I or II of the Blessed Virgin Mary, but perhaps the references to God's extension of his "abundant mercy from age to age" and his looking on "the lowliness of your handmaid" make Preface II a more appropriate choice for today's celebration.

The Prayer after Communion continues the theme of peace mentioned in the Collect and the Prayer over the Offerings, yet it also nicely echoes the place of this Marian feast within Advent time as it mentions the glorious dawning of the day of the Lord: "may we who rejoice in Our Lady of Guadalupe / live united and at peace in this world / until the day of the Lord dawns in glory."

FRI 13 (#185) red
Memorial of St. Lucy, Virgin and Martyr

The Lectionary for Mass

◆ First Reading: Isaiah must have written these words after spending some time on the seashore, where nature spoke to him of Israel's relationship with God. Today's text emphasizes God's role as "Teacher," and the commandments are what is taught. If Israel obeyed, their prosperity would be like a flowing river with its abundant harvest of fish. Israel's descendants would be as numerous as the sands on the seashore (as God had earlier told Abraham in Genesis 22:17); their vindication, like the waves of the sea—at times powerful, at times gentle—rolling over and washing all that they encounter.

◆ RESPONSORIAL PSALM 1: We hear a continuation of the theme of the Lord as teacher, and the happiness and prosperity of those who obey him. Notice that we also have more images from nature: the flourishing tree and the chaff.

◆ GOSPEL: There is a sad irony in today's text. No matter who the messenger or what the message, the generation of Jesus's contemporaries failed to respond. God's wisdom, personified in Jesus, will ultimately be made known.

The Roman Missal

For today's obligatory memorial, the Collect is taken from the Proper of Saints section in the Missal, for December 13, the Memorial of St. Lucy. The Prayer over the Offerings and the Prayer after Communion are taken from either the Common of Martyrs: For a Virgin Martyr or from the Common of Virgins: For One Virgin. It would be a good idea to use the Collect of the seasonal weekday, Friday of the Second Week of Advent, as the concluding prayer to the Universal Prayer to maintain the connection to liturgical time. Also, since there is no proper Preface assigned for today, Preface of Advent I may be used, and this would be another way of keeping a link with the season, although certainly the Preface of Holy Virgins and Religious or one of the Prefaces for Holy Martyrs could also be appropriate choices.

Today's Saint

Even from a young age, St. Lucy (c. + 304) had a burning desire to serve God and an infinite love for the poor. Living in Syracuse, a city in Sicily, she fell prey to the Diocletian persecutions, which eventually resulted in her martyrdom. She resisted a man, believed to be a Roman soldier, who tried to rape her. He, in turn, denounced her as a Christian and had her tortured and killed. Numerous legends revolve around

her death. One well-known legend is that she tore out her eyes to resist her attacker. Her name comes from the Latin, *lux / Lucia*, meaning *light*; therefore, many northern countries honor her at this time of year when darkness is pervasive. Sweden celebrates the virginity and martyrdom of St. Lucy during a festival of light with a sacred procession of young girls clothed in white dresses with red sashes, and crowned with lit candles.

(#186)   white
Memorial of St. John of the Cross, Priest and Doctor of the Church

S A T **14**

The Lectionary for Mass

◆ FIRST READING: The focus in both readings today is Elijah. His brief but powerful prophetic ministry is recounted in 1 Kings 17–19, 21 and 2 Kings 1–2. The Lectionary text omits Sirach's summary of Elijah's miracles in verses 5–7. The focus is not so much on his ministry as on his mysterious translation (being taken up) into heaven via a fiery chariot (Kings 2:11). This gave rise to an expectation that he would return before the coming of the Messiah. Sirach alludes to this expectation in verse 10 of today's reading. The "it is written" can be found in Malachi 3:23–24, the last words of the Old Testament.

◆ RESPONSORIAL PSALM 80: Three images for Israel are found in today's Psalm: the "flock" of the Lord, who is shepherd (see verse 2); the vine (see verse 15, see Isaiah 5:1–7); and the "son of man," referring to Israel as a nation of people. The psalm is a prayer for help and protection. Both the antiphon and the closing stanza speak of Israel's distance from the Lord. The psalmist knows that God's help is needed even to turn back to him.

◆ GOSPEL: Today's text opens on the note of the expectation of Elijah's return before the coming of the Messiah. Jesus proclaims John the Baptist as the Elijah figure who came preaching repentance before his coming, but whose message was not heeded.

The Roman Missal

All three of the orations, the Collect, the Prayer over the Offerings, and the Prayer after Communion, are proper for today and found at December 14 in the Proper of Saints section of the Missal. Consider once again using the Collect of the seasonal weekday as the concluding prayer to the Universal Prayer to continue the sense of Advent time. Preface of Advent I, of Holy Pastors, or one of the two Prefaces of Saints would all be appropriate options to use for the Preface.

All of the orations echo the mystical theology associated with St. John of the Cross. The Collect references his "outstanding dedication to perfect self-denial / and love of the Cross," asking that we might imitate those spiritual virtues. The Prayer over the Offerings requests that "we, who celebrate / the mysteries of the Lord's Passion, / may imitate what we now enact." The Prayer after Communion hails St. John as one through whom God has "wonderfully made known the mystery of the Cross" and prays that we may cling faithfully to Christ as we draw strength from participating in the offering of this Sacrifice.

Today's Saint

St. John of the Cross (1542–1591), a Carmelite priest and Doctor of the Church, is hailed as one of the greatest mystical theologians in Church history. Along with his spiritual friend, St. Teresa of Avila, he set out to reform the Carmelite Order to its original spirit—a life of simplicity centered on interior prayer. St. John was persecuted by his Carmelite brothers, eventually imprisoned because his reforms challenged their comfortable lives of opulence and indulgence. During his imprisonment he composed a beautiful poem, known as *The Dark Night*, which expressed his intense desire for God. St. John composed other well-known mystical texts, including *The Ascent of Mount Carmel* and *The Living Flame of Love*. SS. John and Teresa founded a new branch of the Carmelites, known as the Discalced (meaning "without shoes") Carmelites.

☀ 15 (#7) violet/rose
Third Sunday of Advent

The Lectionary for Mass

◆ FIRST READING: "Here is your God, / he comes with vindication . . . / he comes to save you" (Isaiah 35:4). The coming of the Lord will be a time of full blossoming of the earth, total healing of human infirmities, and restoration of all that had been lost. What hope these words gave to Israel in exile. This frightened, wounded people will return to their homeland, their beloved Zion (Jerusalem), with great joy and song.

◆ RESPONSORIAL PSALM 146: The antiphon is adapted from the First Reading (see Isaiah 35:4). Psalm 146 is a hymn of praise. Note the marvelous deeds for which the Lord is praised in each of the three stanzas.

The promises heard in today's First Reading are experienced as fulfilled. The Lord is king in Zion.

◆ SECOND READING: Patience is mentioned four times in today's reading. For those to whom James writes, there seemed an endless delay as they awaited expectantly the coming of the Lord. Can we identify with this attitude? Or is it something foreign to us? Are we expectantly awaiting the Lord's coming? James also insists that the members of his community be patient with one another. Should they need models of patience, let them look to the prophets. Some of them had to wait a long time for the fulfillment of God's promises!

◆ GOSPEL: Jesus's answer to the question of John's disciples echoes the words of the prophet Isaiah. In fact, Jesus's words and deeds bear witness to their fulfillment. Jesus also gives testimony to John the Baptist's important role in the history of salvation. His presence and ministry is the fulfillment of the prophecy of Malachi: the Lord's messenger will prepare his way—and so John has done.

The Roman Missal

It is the Entrance Antiphon for this Mass that gives it its name of *Gaudete Sunday*: "Rejoice in the Lord always; again I say, rejoice. / Indeed, the Lord is near." The theme of rejoicing is picked up again in the Collect, as we pray that as we are faithfully awaiting the Solemnity of the Nativity of the Lord, we may be enabled "to attain the joys of so great a salvation / and to celebrate them always / with solemn worship and glad rejoicing." Thus, does the shift into the second phase of Advent make a marked progression with the Collect's specific mention of awaiting the Nativity.

The Gloria is once again omitted. The Creed is said or sung.

The Prayer over the Offerings, although assigned for several days throughout Advent, has possibly not been heard much due to its being replaced by sanctoral texts. It is a beautiful prayer that acknowledges that our "sacrifice of worship"—which should be offered not only at liturgy, but "unceasingly," for example, in the sacrifice of the living of our lives—was begun in sacred mystery and asks that such sacrifice should serve in accomplishing God's saving work.

Even though the rubrics indicate that the priest celebrant has a choice between Prefaces I and II of Advent, only Preface I can be used today. Preface II is not used until December 17. If the Third Sunday of Advent falls on December 17 or after, Preface II can be used.

The Prayer after Communion asks that the sustenance found in the Eucharist may both "cleanse us of our faults and prepare us for the coming feasts," thus acknowledging the movement we have made during Advent in approaching the coming feast of the Lord's Nativity as mentioned in the Collect.

The Advent Solemn Blessing at the end of Mass is a good choice for today.

Pastoral Reflection

Jesus boldly left behind concrete pieces of evidence of the absolute reality of who he was and is—the Messiah, God among us. What evidence could friends and family use to testify of your steadfast commitment to following Jesus? Each day this week, be conscious to leave proof behind of your desire to emulate Jesus. Your proof may not be as miraculous as curing the blind, yet maybe you can help others see God more clearly this week through your actions, to hear more fully the love of Christ through your words. In loving humbleness, the actions you offer will bring Jesus truly alive.

MON 16 (#187) violet
Advent Weekday

The Lectionary for Mass

◆ First Reading: The last line of today's reading is now doubt the reason for the text's inclusion in the Lectionary text. The star advancing from Jacob and the staff rising from Israel point to the Messiah. Balaam was a prophet summoned by the king of Moab to curse Israel because he feared their military prowess. However, when God's spirit came upon him, Balaam could not curse, but only bless Israel and speak of a king yet to come. Christians see this text fulfilled in the birth of Jesus, a descendant of Jacob and the Messianic king long awaited.

◆ Responsorial Psalm 25: If we read the story of Balaam from the beginning of Numbers 22, we see that Balaam is a man who exemplifies the prayer of Psalm 25. Having learned the Lord's will concerning Israel, Balaam could not speak a word against them. They were a people on whom God's kindness and compassion rested from of old.

◆ Gospel: Jesus, like Balaam, speaks with the authority of God—so too, did John the Baptist. The hypocrisy and deceit of the Jewish religious authorities who question Jesus is obvious and they do not want to be caught in their own ruse. Have we taken the authority of John and of Jesus to heart?

The Roman Missal

There is still one more day before the specific formularies for late Advent weekdays begin, so today's texts are taken from Monday of the Third Week of Advent, and Preface I of Advent is assigned for today.

The Collect is a plea that the darkness of our hearts may be enlightened by being visited with the grace of the Son, thus giving voice to a typical Advent motif of light and darkness. The Prayer over the Offerings and the Prayer after Communion have been heard before in Advent, on Monday and Thursday of the first week.

TUE 17 (#193) violet
Advent Weekday

The Lectionary for Mass

◆ First Reading: The setting of today's reading is Jacob's deathbed testament to his twelve sons. Jacob, whose name was changed to Israel, is the grandson of Abraham and Sarah. The descendants of his twelve sons comprise the twelve tribes of Israel. Here, the tribe of Judah is given priority. The references to the scepter and to the reception of the homage of the peoples (nations) have led to a royal or messianic interpretation of the text.

◆ Responsorial Psalm 72 is a royal psalm, a prayer for the king, for justice and peace, in and through his reign. How fully this is realized in the reign of God inaugurated by Jesus!

◆ Gospel: Today's Gospel is Matthew's account of the genealogy of Jesus. Note Judah's name, fourth in the list, after Abraham, Isaac, and Jacob. Note also that the first verse mentions David, to whom the promise of an everlasting throne was first made. The genealogy we hear today was of utmost importance for the Jewish Christians, and served as evidence of Jesus's messianic identity. Note also the names of the five women: Tamar; Rahab; the wife of Uriah, whose name was Bathsheba; Ruth; and Mary. Their stories all have some element of the exceptional about them.

The Roman Missal

Now we begin the special Mass formularies for the last days of Advent, leading to the celebration of the Nativity of the Lord. Skip the remainder of the Missal pages for the Third Week of Advent and go to the section titled, "The Weekdays of Advent," using today the formularies for December 17.

The Collect gives expression to the wondrous "interchange" that has taken place in the mystery of the Incarnation: since the Son has "taken to himself our humanity," may he "be pleased to grant us a share in his divinity." Thus, the implications of what we are preparing to celebrate at the Nativity begin to unfold: Christ came and died and rose for us that we might become like him, indeed, so that we might become divine.

The Prayer over the Offerings highlights that partaking in the Eucharistic meal, "these venerable mysteries," is being nourished with the bread of heaven.

Preface II of Advent is the Preface to be used today, and for the remainder of Advent.

The Prayer after Communion asks that the Eucharistic banquet we have just shared in may have a real effect in our life, namely, that "aflame with your Spirit, / we may shine like bright torches / before your Christ when he comes." That's a good spiritual intention for the last days of Advent, that the holiness of our life may shine brightly as a welcome for Christ.

WED 18 (#194) violet
Advent Weekday

The Lectionary for Mass

◆ First Reading: Jeremiah's words would have deeply touched the hearts of his exiled people, for he speaks of a coming day of salvation when the Exile would be over and the people would return to their land. It would be nothing less than deliverance from slavery, as was the Exodus from Egypt earlier in their history. And how do his words touch our hearts? What exile do we experience? For Israel of old, a future Davidic king would bring deliverance, and his reign would be characterized by wisdom, righteousness, fidelity to the Lord, security, and salvation. How do we, today, experience the reality of that kingdom? How do we still await it?

◆ RESPONSORIAL PSALM 72: Characteristics of this hoped-for king are further elaborated in today's Responsorial Psalm, a royal prayer for the king. The antiphon celebrates the justice and peace that all will experience during his reign.

◆ GOSPEL: See page 26, Fourth Sunday of Advent.

The Roman Missal

The orations used are those specifically assigned for December 18.

Notice how the Collect for today uses the motif of old and new: although we "are weighed down from of old by slavery beneath the yoke of sin," we pray that we "may be set free by the newness / of the long-awaited Nativity / of your Only Begotten Son." Humanity is made new in Christ, not just once in history, but even today—especially in the celebration of the liturgy, "making the work of our redemption a present actuality" (*CSL*, 2; quoting Hebrews 13:14).

The sense of being made new is echoed in the Prayer over the Offerings, which references the healing we received by the Death of Christ. The Prayer after Communion draws our attention "to the coming solemnities of our redemption." Preface II of Advent is used again.

T H U 19 (#195) violet
Advent Weekday

The Lectionary for Mass

◆ FIRST READING: The reading recounts the appearance of an angel of the Lord to the barren wife of Manoah, promising the birth of a son. She is given special instructions regarding her pregnancy and the upbringing of her son. These instructions are in fact taken from Numbers 6:2–8, pertaining to the *Nazirite* (meaning "sacred" or "vowed") consecration to the Lord. When he grew up, Samson had a significant role to play in the deliverance of Israel from the power of its Philistine enemies.

◆ RESPONSORIAL PSALM 71 is both a prayer of confidence and a prayer for deliverance, prayed by one who is elderly. These themes are heard in the first two stanzas of the psalm. Both the antiphon and the third stanza proclaim God's praise for his wondrous deeds.

◆ GOSPEL: Juxtaposed with the announcement of Samson's birth is that of John the Baptist. Elizabeth, like the wife of Manoah, was unable to conceive. Like Samson's parents, Zechariah and Elizabeth were righteous. Note how the description of John's future mission and behavior evoke the Nazirite prescription heard in today's First Reading. John, filled with the Spirit, will go before the Lord, preparing "a people fit" (Luke 1:17) for him through their repentance. Note also that both Zechariah and Elizabeth are advanced in years, a nice link to today's psalm. Zechariah's angelic messenger even gives a sign that his words are true: Zechariah will be made mute, unable to speak, until the silence is broken by the birth of his child.

The Roman Missal

The use of the special formularies for late Advent weekdays continues, as the prayers are taken from those assigned specifically for December 19. The impending celebration of the Nativity is noted in the Entrance Antiphon, as "He who is to come will come and will not delay."

The Collect specifically references the mystery of the Incarnation, noting that the radiance of divine glory was revealed to the world "through the child-bearing of the holy Virgin." The Prayer over the Offerings acknowledges that the offerings we bring (and we can infer both material and spiritual offerings are meant) are small, but nonetheless made holy by God's power. The Prayer after Communion asks that the effects of our sharing in the Eucharistic banquet be evident in the purity of our minds.

Preface II of Advent is used once again.

F R I 20 (#196) violet
Advent Weekday

The Lectionary for Mass

◆ FIRST READING: See page 25, Fourth Sunday of Advent.

◆ RESPONSORIAL PSALM 24: See page 25, Fourth Sunday of Advent.

◆ GOSPEL: Mary is the one who preeminently allowed the Lord to enter into the whole human race by her "yes" to God's call. Of her, Jesus, the Son of the Most High and the Savior of all people, would be born through the power of God's Holy Spirit.

The Roman Missal

The orations used are the specific formularies for December 20, continuing the use of the special texts for the late Advent weekdays.

The Virgin Mary is referenced in the Collect, as the prayer recognizes her example in saying "yes" to becoming the "dwelling-place of divinity." The prayer asks that we may hold fast to God's will in the same way she did.

The Prayer over the Offerings asks that our participation in this mystery (for example, this celebration) may allow us to possess the gifts we have been awaiting in faith.

The Prayer after Communion speaks of the fruits of the heavenly gift of the Eucharist, namely, renewal and the "joy of true peace."

Preface II of Advent is assigned for today.

SAT 21 (#197) violet
Advent Weekday

Optional Memorial of St. Peter Canisius, Priest and Doctor of the Church / violet

The Lectionary for Mass

◆ FIRST READING (OPTION 1): Christian tradition, beginning with Origen of Alexandria in the third century, has loved to interpret the Song of Songs, a biblical love song, as pertaining to Christ (the lover) and the Church (the beloved). How fitting, then, to have this text about the "coming" of the Lover on this twenty-first day of December. Notice that the Lover invites the Beloved to come and meet him.

◆ FIRST READING (OPTION 2): In Zephaniah, joy resounds. The Lord, the King of Israel, the Savior, is in your midst (mentioned two times). Note that Israel experiences joy at this presence, and the Lord rejoices in his people.

◆ RESPONSORIAL PSALM 33: The theme of joy continues in this song of praise. The themes of waiting for the Lord's coming and the joy of those who are the Lord's own are voiced in the third stanza.

◆ GOSPEL: The theme of joy resounds. Even the child in Elizabeth's womb leaps for joy at the presence of the Lord in Mary's womb. We must be a people of faith, believing that the Lord's promise will be fulfilled.

The Roman Missal

The Mass formularies are taken from those specific to December 21. If, however, the Memorial of St. Peter Canisius is to be observed, then the Collect may be taken from the Proper of Saints for December 21, St. Peter Canisius, replacing the Advent Collect. The other prayers, however, must come from the Proper of Time. Advent Preface II must be used. The Collect of the saint acknowledges his defense of the Catholic faith and praises his strength "in virtue and in learning."

The Advent Collect makes reference to the two comings of Christ: it acknowledges our rejoicing "at the coming of your Only Begotten Son in our flesh" and it asks that "when at last he comes in glory," we may "gain the reward of eternal life." The Prayer over the Offerings speaks of the transformation of the offerings that is to occur; as they are transformed "into the mystery of our salvation," the implication is that we who receive those gifts will also be transformed, for example, saved. The Prayer after Communion prays that our "participation in this divine mystery" will result in protection and abundant health in mind and body.

Today's Saint

St. Peter (1521–1597), born in Holland and educated in Louvain, firmly believed in responding to the Protestant reformers in a non-threatening, compassionate manner. Pope Leo XIII called St. Peter "the second apostle to Germany after Boniface" because of his ability to foster dialogue between opposing sides during the Reformation and enliven faith in the hearts of distressed Catholics. He published his *Catechism* in 1551, which is a series of three scholarly works that convey the tenets of the Catholic faith without ever referencing his opponents. As an avid believer in the power of the written word, St. Peter wrote extensively and encouraged others to defend the truth with pen and paper as well.

22 (#10) violet
Fourth Sunday of Advent

The Lectionary for Mass

◆ FIRST READING: God's presence with his people is nowhere more evident than in the promised child who will bear the name Emmanuel: God-with-us. God's promised sign comes in a time of great affliction when the kingdom of Judah feared destruction at the hands of her enemies. The child is a sign that Jerusalem would be spared and her enemies destroyed.

◆ RESPONSORIAL PSALM 24: Today's Psalm juxtaposes the power and might of the Creator with God's nearness to his people: "Let the Lord enter; he is the king of glory" (antiphon; Psalm 24:7c, 10b). As we draw nearer to the Solemnity of the Nativity of the Lord (Christmas) we rejoice in the marvelous way that the Lord has entered into our human history by becoming one of us. The second stanza sets forth what is required of the one who would enter into his presence—and here we should think not only of his presence here and now, but also in the age to come. May we always be among those who seek the face of the Lord our Savior. May we always live as those who can stand in his holy place.

◆ SECOND READING: We hear the beginning of Paul's letter to the Romans. Paul stresses his call to be an Apostle of Jesus, who is the fulfillment of all that was prophesied in the Scriptures (Old Testament). His reference to Jesus as descended from David is particularly important, as this points to Jesus as the promised Davidic Messiah or Anointed One. As the prophets of old foretold, salvation is offered not only to the Jews, but also to the Gentiles.

◆ GOSPEL: Matthew's account of the events preceding Jesus's birth focus on the angelic appearances to Joseph of the house of David, assuring him that Mary's child was conceived through the Holy Spirit. The child, whose birth is the fulfillment of the prophecy of Isaiah regarding the soon-to-be-born Davidic heir of today's First Reading, is Jesus the Savior, "Emmanuel . . . 'God is with us'" (Matthew 1:23).

The Roman Missal

Today the Mass texts are taken from the Fourth Sunday of Advent, found just after Friday of the Third Week of Advent; do not use the texts for December 22. The Gloria is not said today, omitted for the last time in this liturgical time, as it will return with the celebration of the Nativity. The Creed is said or sung.

The Collect is, of course, the familiar prayer that concludes the Angelus. The prayer reveals a sophisticated and complete Christology in that it connects the Incarnation with the Paschal Mystery: we are led from the Annunciation, through the Incarnation to a sharing in the Passion and Resurrection. It's a stark reminder to us that although at different times throughout the liturgical year we highlight or emphasize particular aspects of the mystery of Christ's life, at its core liturgy is always about the Paschal Mystery, and it is this mystery that is celebrated at every liturgy, regardless of the season or occasion.

The Prayer over the Offerings invokes the action of the Holy Spirit, asking that just as the Spirit filled "with his power the womb of the Blessed Virgin Mary," so too may he sanctify (for example, with his transformational power) the gifts we have placed upon the altar. The Spirit at work in the Annunciation is the same Spirit at work in our liturgy today.

Preface II of Advent is the required Preface.

In the Prayer after Communion, we acknowledge the nearness of the celebration of the Nativity, praying that as that feast day draws near, "we may press forward all the more eagerly / to the worthy celebration of the mystery."

Strong consideration should be given to using the Advent Solemn Blessing at the end of Mass.

Pastoral Reflection

The simplicity of the Gospel still relates to those who are betrothed to objects (cell phones, laptops, iPods) or spend too much time at work, exercising, or socializing without upholding one's soulful needs to spend time with God. This week, be conscious of how you spend your time, and how the Holy Spirit lives within you. Like Joseph, awaken your spirit to heed the commands given, be it in Scriptures that you read daily this week or through the evidence God leaves to guide your life.

MON 23 (#199) violet
Advent Weekday

Optional Memorial of St. John of Kanty, Priest

The Lectionary for Mass

◆ FIRST READING: Today's reading is actually the closing words of the Old Testament. It ends with the promise of a messenger from the Lord who is sent to prepare the way of the Lord. He is likened to Elijah, who centuries earlier had preached a message of repentance. Elijah's mysterious translation into heaven via the fiery chariot gave rise to the tradition that he would return to earth before the coming of the Messiah.

◆ RESPONSORIAL PSALM 25: Two days before Christmas, our antiphon, from Luke, reminds us that the day of our redemption, the coming of the Lord Jesus, is near. The prayer voiced in the stanzas of the psalm ask for the Lord's instruction and guidance in knowing the way to meet him.

◆ GOSPEL: Throughout the Gospel accounts, John the Baptist is associated in one way or another with the prophet Elijah. Today's Gospel recounts his birth. and the mysterious signs accompanying his birth.

The Roman Missal

Today we return to the specific Mass formularies for late Advent weekdays, and so the texts used are those specific to December 23. If, however, the Memorial of St. John of Kanty is to be observed, then the Collect may be taken from the Proper of Saints for December 23. The Prayer over the Offerings and the Prayer after Communion must, however, must come from the Proper of Time Advent Weekday December 23, and Advent Preface II must be used.

The Collect acknowledges both the nearness of the celebration of the Nativity and the continued closeness of Christ who came in the flesh, asking that we may receive mercy "from your Word, / who chose to become flesh of the Virgin Mary / and establish among us his dwelling." In another acknowledgment of the closeness of the Nativity, the Prayer over the Offerings asks that the oblation offered bring about our reconciliation with God so that "we may celebrate with minds made pure / the Nativity of our Redeemer."

Eschatology is emphasized and images from the parables of Jesus are used in the Prayer after Communion, as petition is made that "those you have nourished with these heavenly gifts" may be ready, "with lighted lamps, / to meet your dearly beloved Son at his coming."

Today's Saint

St. John eloquently empowered people to bridge the ponderings of the mind with the feelings of the heart. In terms of his own spiritual journey, he followed the simple, austere practices of the desert fathers—never clinging to material goods, fasting whenever possible, and living in contemplative awareness. Because St. John was deeply respected by colleagues and students, many years after his death his academic gown was used at the investiture of each new doctor of the university.

T U E **24** (#200)   violet
Advent Weekday (Morning Mass)

The Lectionary for Mass

◆ FIRST READING: Israel's King David is at the height of his reign in today's reading—his kingdom at peace and prosperous. Reflecting on the splendor of his own palace, the realization dawns: the Ark of the Covenant, that sign of God's presence with his people, is housed in a tent . . . . David proposes to build a fitting house, a temple for the Lord. But God has other plans. The verses chosen for today's reading shift the focus from a house (Temple) for God to God's promise of an everlasting house (dynasty) for David.

◆ RESPONSORIAL PSALM 89 is a hymn of praise and thanksgiving for the covenant God has made with David. The second and third stanzas speak directly of this.

◆ GOSPEL: Today's Gospel is Zechariah's hymn of praise at the birth of John the Baptist. Note the reference to the Davidic covenant and the recounting of God's promises to Israel. The child's mission is to prepare the way for him who is "dawn from on high" and mighty Savior.

The Roman Missal

The texts for this Mass are taken from the assigned prayers for December 24, with Preface II of Advent being used again for the last time this year.

CHRISTMAS TIME

The Liturgical Time

The Calendar
December 24 (evening), 2013 to January 12, 2014

The Meaning / The Lectionary for Mass

RECENTLY a young mother wrote to me, "This is the first year that Susie is in the 'know' about Santa Claus. Maybe she'll be able to focus more on Jesus this Christmas, but for children, Santa is a hard act to top." I was deeply touched by her words: first by her own sense of what Christmas is really all about, and secondly, by her desire that her young daughter share this same awareness. I wondered if there aren't many more children—and adults as well—who share Susie's difficulty.

Why is this so? As I pondered the question, it occurred to me that the reality of the Incarnation, God becoming one of us, is of such magnitude that we cannot begin to comprehend it. It is way over our heads, so to speak.

On the other hand, the tiny, helpless baby who is God-with-us . . . a baby is so common, so ordinary, that despite the initial "ooohs" and "aaahs," apart from the parents, isn't it easy for the rest of us just to take it all for granted?

The twelfth-century Cistercian, Abbot Guerric of Igny, sums up the dilemma well: "Do you wish to see God emptied of himself? See him lying in the manger. 'Behold our God,' says Isaiah . . . (25:9). 'Where?' I ask. 'In that manger,' he says. It is an infant I find there. Do you mean to say that this is he who declares 'I fill heaven and earth' (Jeremiah 23:24), for whose majesty the whole breadth of heaven is narrow? I see a child wrapped in swaddling clothes. Do you mean to say this is he who is clad in the glory and beauty of unapproachable light, clothed with unbounded light as with a garment (Psalm 103:1ff)? I hear him crying. Is this he who thunders in the heavens, at the sound of whose thunder the angelic powers lower their wings (Ezekiel 1:25)? . . . So indeed it is. This is our God; but he has been emptied out in order to fill you, and he has willed to fall short of himself, as it were, in order to restore you" (*Guerric of Igny: The Liturgical Seromons* Book 1, Cisctercian Publications, 1970. Published by the Liturgical Press: Collegeville, MN).

Yes, it is something so extraordinary, we can hardly comprehend it. Yet it appears so ordinary that it is easy to overlook it. The Scriptures of Christmas Time invite us to sharpen our focus, to see with the eyes of our heart, who this child really is and what he means for our lives.

The readings for the Vigil of the Solemnity of the Nativity of the Lord stress the "newness" of what God is doing in entering into a relationship so intimate with his people that it is described in terms of the love of a bridegroom for his bride (see Isaiah 62:1–5). Extraordinarily new, yes—in a way far exceeding anything we could imagine . . . but at the same time, the fulfillment of God's promises of old (see Acts of the Apostles 13:23 and Matthew's genealogy in chapter one).

The readings for the Mass during the Night proclaim that in the birth of the child prophesized by Isaiah, the burdens of darkness and gloom that enshroud humanity are pierced by light (see Isaiah 9:1–6). Similarly, the light of glory fills the night sky at the birth of Jesus the Savior (see Luke 2:1–14). Do we see this light in our hearts?

Both the First and the Second Readings for the Mass at Dawn speak of God our Savior—and the Second Reading ascribes the title to Jesus as well. Do we recognize our own need for a Savior? Luke's account tells us that when the shepherds heard the news of the angels' revelation they went in haste to find the Child. Do we go in haste to his Word? To prayer? To worship him at the Eucharistic assembly?

What a *Word* God has spoken to us in Jesus (see John's Prologue, the Gospel for the Mass during Day)! Do we see the Word God speaks as glad tidings (see the First Reading for the Mass during the Day, Isaiah 52:7–10), as far exceeding

any Words God spoke in the past (see Hebrews 1:1–6, the Second Reading)? His Word, his coming, brings joy not only to human hearts—but to all the earth as well (see the Responsorial Psalms).

On the Feast of St. Stephen, we celebrate the feast of one who not only received the Word, the gift of Jesus, but who gave his own life for the sake of Jesus's name in return (see Acts of the Apostles 7:59). In our own day as well there are Christians who experience the reality described in the Gospel of the day (see Matthew 10:17–22), facing suffering and persecution and even death because of the name of Jesus.

The Feast of St. John, Apostle and Evangelist, sets before us the gift of a deeply personal experience, indeed, a relationship, with the Lord Jesus. Christian tradition identifies John with the beloved disciple of the Gospel (see John 13:23; 20:4.8) and the three letters of the New Testament, which bear his name.

The tragedy of the death of the Holy Innocents, cut off from life at such a young age, must not obscure the reality of the fullness of life that would be theirs since they died in Jesus's name (see Matthew 2:13–18). Accordingly, the Church celebrates them as martyrs. As the Responsorial Psalm attests, the snare was broken and they were freed (see Psalm 124:7).

The readings for the Feast of the Holy Family invite us to reflect on the quality of relationships within our own families (see Sirach 3:2–6, 12–14; Psalm 128; Colossians 3:15–21). The Gospel for this year (Matthew 2:13–15, 19–23) portrays the Holy Family as among those who are forced to flee their homeland and seek refuge in another land. What anguish and fear must have seized them—not only when they fled to Egypt, but even on their return when it was still unsafe for them to settle in Judea.

The Solemnity of Mary, the Holy Mother of God, can likewise be thought of as a "family" feast, focusing as it does on Mary's motherhood. Mary held all of the words and events concerning her Son in her heart, pondering their meaning, that she might see and understand. Her "mothering" of Jesus included forming him to be a person of prayer open to the call of God. Isn't that what all parents are called to do for their children?

The Solemnity of the Epiphany of the Lord immediately brings to mind the journey and the gifts of the Magi, guided by a star whose meaning they readily knew (see Matthew 2:1–12). Matthew's account of this event makes clear that God's salvation is for Gentiles as well as Jews, as the Second Reading from Ephesians likewise emphasizes.

This year we have a full week between the Solemnity of the Epiphany of the Lord and the Feast of the Baptism of the Lord. The "Epiphany theme" is heard throughout the week in the repetition of Responsorial Psalm 72. The First Readings are a continuation of the First Letter of John begun during the Octave of the Nativity of the Lord. It is a beautiful letter to read at this time, stemming as it does from the witness and conviction of one who knew the Lord when he walked on the earth, who heard his teaching and witnessed his marvelous deeds. All is handed on to new generations of believers that they—that we—might see more clearly what the coming of Jesus and the salvation he accomplished means for human life and history. The letter likewise deals with the internal challenges and external threats facing the community. The Gospel for these days tell of events of the first days of Jesus's public ministry. The glory, the light, becomes visible. The promises of the prophets are fulfilled.

Christmas Time ends with the Feast of the Baptism of the Lord, the event that the Gospel accounts portray as initiating Jesus's public ministry. In a sense, the feast recapitulates the readings we've heard throughout the season: Jesus is the beloved Son of God on whom God's Spirit rests. He is the fulfillment of God's promises of old: the revelation of God's power and glory, the Savior in our midst, bringing comfort and care, healing, wholeness, and peace to God's people. He became what we are in order that we might become what he is, beloved sons and daughters of God, his chosen servants, filled with his Spirit that we might carry on the mission that he has begun.

The Roman Missal

THE texts for the days of Christmas Time are located in two different places in the Missal. A segment for Christmas Time follows the Advent segment in the Proper of Time section at the front of the Missal. Here can be found Mass formularies for the four Masses for the Nativity—the Vigil Mass, the Mass during the Night, the Mass at Dawn, and the Mass during the Day; for the Sunday within the Octave of the Nativity, which is the Feast of the Holy Family of Jesus, Mary, and Joseph; for the Sixth and Seventh Days within the Octave; the Solemnity of Mary, the Holy Mother of God; for two Masses for the Epiphany of the Lord—a Vigil Mass and a Mass during the Day; and for the weekdays of Christmas Time. Finally, Mass formularies are also given for the Sunday after the Epiphany, which is the Feast of the Baptism of the Lord.

Other texts for Christmas Time are found in the Proper of Saints. In that section can be found the obligatory feasts of St. Stephen, St. John the Apostle and Evangelist, and The Holy Innocents. Other texts found in this section are those for the obligatory Memorials of SS. Basil the Great and Gregory Nazianzen and Elizabeth Ann Seton, and optional memorials for St. Thomas Becket, and St. Sylvester, and the Most Holy Name of Jesus, St. André Bessette and St. Raymond of Penyafort.

If a particular form of the greeting was used all during Advent, priest celebrants might consider switching to another form during Christmas Time and using that one consistently. For the Penitential Act, although any invocations may be used for the third form (#6 in the Order of Mass), Option II in the section of sample invocations for the Penitential Act found in Appendix VI of the Missal, with phrases such as "mighty God and Prince of peace," "Son of Mary," and "Word made flesh," would seem to be a very appropriate choice, as they echo Christmas themes. Option I might be considered another appropriate choice insofar as those invocations highlight past, present, and future comings of Christ: "you came to gather the nations into the peace of God's kingdom; you come in word and sacrament to strengthen us in holiness; you will come again in glory with salvation for your people."

Eucharistic Prayer I, the Roman Canon, has proper inserts that should be used when this prayer is prayed at Masses on the Nativity of the Lord and throughout its Octave, and on the Epiphany of the Lord. The first or second acclamations for "The Mystery of Faith," insofar as they both refer to Christ's coming again, might be preferable over the third option, although that option does use the word "Savior," which would echo the notion of the Savior who is born for us.

The Gloria returns at the celebration of the Nativity and is sung or said every day throughout the Octave.

There are three Prefaces for the Nativity of the Lord, any of which might be equally appropriate on the solemnity itself, during its Octave, and on the other weekdays of Christmas Time, even if that day might otherwise have its own proper Preface (unless, according to the rubrics, in "Masses that have a proper Preface concerning the divine mysteries or divine Persons"). Preface I of the Nativity of the Lord focuses on Christ as the Light of the World and as the visible image of the invisible God. Preface II highlights the mystery of the Incarnation; while this Preface also speaks about the invisible divinity being made visible in Christ, it goes on to focus on the "awe-filled mystery" of the One who was "begotten before all ages." In that mystery of the Incarnation, all that was cast down is raised up, all unity is restored to creation and humanity is called back to the heavenly kingdom. Preface III highlights the "holy exchange that restores our life" as human nature is assumed by the Word. Additionally, there is a Preface of the Epiphany of the Lord that is used in the Masses of the Solemnity of the Epiphany and may also be used in Masses after the Epiphany up to the Saturday preceding the Feast of the Baptism of the Lord. The Preface for the Baptism of the Lord is found in the Proper of Time section with the other formularies for that Mass.

Several special three-part Solemn Blessings specific to this liturgical season are given in the section for "Blessings at the End of Mass and Prayers over the People." There is one for the Nativity of the Lord (#2), one for the beginning of the year (#3), and one for the Epiphany of the Lord. As always, one of the choices of the Prayers over the People may also be used.

Children's Liturgy of the Word

THE celebration of the Liturgy of the Word with children begins with the dismissal of children from the main assembly. The children should first gather with the main assembly to celebrate the Introductory Rites. Between the conclusion of the Collect and the beginning of the First Reading, the priest celebrant should formally send the children to their separate space. Seasonal examples of dismissal text are provided in this *Sourcebook* at the end of each seasonal overview under "Mass Texts."

You will need to establish procedures for a quick and quiet procession from the church

to where you celebrate the Liturgy of the Word with children. Confer with the music director regarding an acclamation for the assembly to sing during this time. Pay attention to the procession from the main assembly into your space, helping the children to see it as a sacred, ritual act that seamlessly transitions them from one part of the Mass to another. You will want to keep an eye on how things are progressing in the main assembly. Assign an assistant to coordinate the timing of the Liturgy of the Word with children with that of the main assembly. By the time the main assembly is reciting the Creed, the children should be reciting the Creed, too. The children should return to sit with their families after the Liturgy of the Word is finished, but before the Liturgy of the Eucharist begins. When you return the children to the main assembly, be sure to watch for those who are having trouble finding their families.

The Saints

A child is born for us, and a son is given to us; his scepter of power rests upon his shoulder, and his name will be called Messenger of great counsel.

—Entrance Antiphon
Solemnity of the Nativity of the Lord,
At the Mass during the Day

WHAT an image of dichotomies—a child, a baby carrying a heavy scepter of power! Christmas is full of dichotomies, full of surprises, and rich in messages of great counsel. Our Savior has come. What a wondrous time! The Savior of all arrives as a helpless child and that speechless infant is the "Messenger of great counsel." Our God announces the message of love in countless and imaginative ways. The saints of this season are some of the ways that God continues to send this message. Besides the great Solemnity of the Nativity of the Lord, there are two others (Mary, the Holy Mother of God, and Epiphany of the Lord), five feasts (St. Stephen; St. John; The Holy Innocents; Holy Family of Jesus, Mary, and Joseph; Baptism of the Lord), two obligatory memorials (SS. Basil the Great and Gregory Nazianzen, St. Elizabeth Ann Seton), and four optional memorials (St. Sylvester I, Most Holy Name of Jesus, St. André Bessette, and St. Raymond of Penyafort).

On January 1, we celebrate the Solemnity of Mary, the Holy Mother of God. As strange as it seems that a crying babe has come to rescue us, stranger still is it that a peasant girl should be the God-Bearer, the Theotokos. This day also is the last of the Octave Days of Christmas. Only Christmas and Easter are celebrated with octaves, eight days highlighting the centrality of these celebrations to our faith. Liturgies on these days should strive to embody the specialness of the season and the message it represents. St. John, the Evangelist, (December 27) by tradition the youngest of the Apostles, through his writings became a messenger of the Good News. Legend says that he survived a poisoning attempt after he blessed the cup of poisoned wine. That has given rise to the tradition of blessing and sharing wine on his feast day. St. Elizabeth Ann Seton was a messenger of the Good News by establishing Catholic schools in the United States. And in the spirit of Christmas dichotomies, St. André Bessette, a religious brother who spent most of his life at menial labor, became a great healer and was instrumental in building the great Oratory of St. Joseph in Canada. All celebrations of the Christmas saints should highlight the wonders that God works in the midst of human frailty and simple lives. The message is the same, but the messengers are very different. Perhaps that is God's way of speaking to each of us in our own need—giving to each of us the child with power to carry the scepter of God's infinite love.

The Liturgy of the Hours

THE most common practice for celebrating the Liturgy of the Hours in parish communities in our time seems to be during the major seasons. Many communities gather for the celebration of Sunday Evening Prayer during the Advent and Christmas Time or during Lent/ Sacred Paschal Triduum/Easter Time. In addition, many communities, especially those without resident priests, gather to celebrate Morning or Evening Prayer, with or without the reception of Holy Communion.

Christmas Time runs from Evening Prayer I for the Nativity of the Lord through Evening Prayer II of the Feast of the Baptism of the Lord. The celebration of the birth of Jesus, the mani-

festation to the astrologers from the east, and the inauguration of Jesus's mission as he comes out of the Jordan River are inseparable parts of the great mystery of the Incarnation.

Consider using the prescribed hymns, chants, and carols when celebrating the Hours during Christmas Time including "A Child is Born in Bethlehem," "*Puer natus* in Bethlehem" (Plainchant, Mode I); "Go Tell it on the Mountain" (Traditional Spiritual); "O Come, All Ye Faithful" (Adeste Fideles); or "What Child Is This" (Greensleeves). The *Hymnal for the Hours,* published by GIA Publications, is an invaluable source for both psalm tones, propers, and hymnody for celebrating the Hours.

The prayers of Christmas Time remind us that Christ is not a helpless infant, but rather a mediator and Messiah born for the salvation of all peoples. In the latter part of Christmas Time we hear new and significant titles for Christ such as "New Adam" and "Sun of Justice." The antiphons for Morning Prayer and Evening Prayer for Epiphany of the Lord are especially rich in their imagery. For example, the antiphon for Morning Prayer reads: "Today the Bridegroom claims his bride, the Church, since Christ has washed her sins away in Jordan's waters; the Magi hasten with their gifts to the royal wedding; and the wedding guests rejoice, for Christ has changed water into wine, alleluia."

The Rite of Christian Initiation of Adults

THE precatechumenate is a time of evangelization and "initial conversion that cause a person to feel called away from sin and drawn into the mystery of God's love" (RCIA, 37). Because prayer is an instrument of conversion, it is essential to help inquirers begin not only to learn about prayer, but to experience prayer. Our faith tradition is filled with a variety of expressions of prayer: private, devotional, Scripture-based, rote, spontaneous, communal, liturgical, silent, contemplative, etc. A prayer-enriched precatechumenate will expose the inquirers to these various styles of praying. Since there is no definite time for the precatechumenate, there is sufficient time to engage the inquirers with alternative modes of prayer.

The rite's only guideline concerning prayer in the period of evangelization and precatechumentate comes from RCIA, 40: "During the precatechumenate period, parish priests (pastors), should help those taking part in it with prayers suited to them, for example."

Focus on softening the environment with candles, fabric, flowers, or plants. Inquirers may not yet feel comfortable praying in a group. An environment that lives up to the hospitality called for in this period will go a long way toward inviting people to pray.

Music is one of the Church's primary ways of praying. Think about opening or closing a session with a song or a refrain from a song. Even if you don't have a strong song leader on the team, there are plenty of CDs and MP3 downloads available to help facilitate group singing. Especially pray the psalms, which are the Church's ancient hymnal.

Use the various colors and symbols (big and bold) that flow from the liturgical year. Pray the Collect from the Mass to help set the "seasonal" tone and to remind inquirers what liturgical time the Church is celebrating. Check the liturgical calendar to see which saint the Church is celebrating either on the date or during the week the precatechumenate gathers. For example, if you gather on December 6, the optional Memorial of St. Nicholas, you might incorporate a single prayer or ritual action that reflects the life of this saint.

—Adapted from an article
by Kathy Kuczka © LTP, 2011.

The Sacraments of Initiation

THE Advent liturgies provide a perfect opportunity for sacramental catechesis. The stories of a baby in a manger, angels singing, Magi bearing gifts, and a guiding star capture our hearts and imaginations. Find times to gather around the crèche, even informally, with parents preparing for the Baptism of their child and also those preparing children and young people for the other Sacraments of Initiation. Meeting around the crèche provides a good springboard for sharing reflections, thoughts, and feelings about Christian parenting. Children and young people are drawn to the crèche. Spend a catechetical session gathered with them around the crèche and have them reflect

and share their thoughts about the Christmas liturgies, and home traditions.

Any of the solemnities of Christmas Time are appropriate for the celebration of the Baptism of children, especially Epiphany and Baptism of the Lord, which focus on our status as God's beloved and adopted children.

By signing us with the gift of the Spirit, Confirmation makes us more completely the image of the Lord and fills us with the Holy Spirit, so that we may bear witness to him before all the world and work to bring the Body of Christ to its fullness as soon as possible.

Very often these candidates are required to complete a certain number of community service hours as part of their overall preparation. This time when school is out presents a wealth of opportunities for such service that can lead to "hands on" catechesis and more involvement in the community.

Involve Confirmation candidates in the transition of the church from Advent to Christmas. Engaging these candidates in some of the behind the scenes preparations such as working with art and environment, hospitality, even sacristy preparations, will communicate their place and importance in the community. As they are "doing" they are also learning the meaning behind why we do what we do. Being present and visible also will allow the larger community to get to know them and what their gifts are, leading to relationships that are supportive and affirming.

The word *Bethlehem* literally translates from the Hebrew as "House of Flesh" or "House of Bread." A manger is an eating place for farm animals. What great images for children preparing for First Eucharist! First Holy Communions are often scheduled during Easter Time, however Christmas Time is a perfect time for children to understand that there are poor among us—bread broken to heal a broken world.

The Rite of Penance

AT Christmas Time some who have been estranged from the Church find a way back home to the Eucharistic table. Communities should be attentive to the language used in the bulletin, through public announcements, and above all the Homily so that people of "every race and tongue" will feel welcomed and accepted at the "Sacrifice of perfect reconciliation" (Eucharistic Prayer II for Reconciliation). It would be helpful to schedule the celebration of the Rite of Penance in the last days of Advent leading up to the Solemnity of the Nativity of the Lord so people will have an opportunity to confess their sins and receive absolution. The parish website should list the times the sacrament is celebrated and the number to call to schedule a time to celebrate the sacrament with a priest.

The Pastoral Care of the Sick

THE Church should take time to be personally present to the sick and suffering in the community, especially those in hospitals and care centers and the homebound. Share Christmas festivities with these folks, bring them the parish bulletin, a poinsettia, an audio tape of one of the Christmas liturgies, or a CD of Christmas carols. Some parishes bring knitted or crocheted shawls, blankets, hats, or slippers to the sick and homebound during Christmas Time.

Ritual Masses are not permitted on the solemnities during Christmas Time. Make sure the parish has trained and properly appointed lay ecclesial ministers who can bring Holy Communion and Viaticum to the sick and the dying. Catechize people so that they know to ask for the Sacrament of Anointing of the Sick at the beginning of a serious illness and Viaticum when death is close.

The Rite of Marriage

THE Rite of Marriage may not be celebrated on the Solemnities of the Nativity of the Lord; Solemnity Mary, the Holy Mother of God; or Epiphany of the Lord. If the rite is celebrated on other Sundays or solemnities within Christmas Time, the Mass of the day is used along with the nuptial blessing and final blessing from the rite (see RMar, 11/use the texts from the third edition of the Missal). When the rite is celebrated on a Sunday or solemnity only one reading from the *Rite of Marriage* may be used. In addition to the celebra-

tion of the rite during Mass, Form II, the Rite for Celebrating Marriage Outside of Mass and Form III, the Rite for Celebrating Marriage Between a Catholic and an Unbaptized Person, may be used when an appropriate pastoral need arises.

Remind the couples about the Christmas Time environment and encourage them to prepare their colors and flowers to accent the seasonal setting. As part of Marriage preparation consider sharing photos of the church decorated for Christmas from past years with the couple. Marriages celebrated in Christmas Time should look and sound like Christmas. Especially at Christmas Time, but in every season, encourage the couple to make a gift for the poor. A suggested donation between $250.00 and $500.00 should not be unrealistic considering the amount of money that is usually spent on clothing, jewelry, catering, and receptions. Of course, treat every situation pastorally and sensitively.

The Order of Christian Funerals

CHRISTMAS Time is an especially difficult time to experience death. Death can change the meaning of Christmas forever for mourners. Funerals may not be celebrated on the Solemnities of the Nativity of the Lord or Mary, the Holy Mother of God. If the parish office is closed between the Nativity of the Lord and New Year's Day make sure a member of the parish is available to minister to families, as soon as possible after the time of the death of a loved one. Make sure that someone responds to voice mail or e-mail messages in a timely manner. Providing a phone number in the case of emergency in the parish bulletin and on the parish website is most helpful.

The Book of Blessings

THE Order for the Blessing of a Christmas Manger or Nativity Scene (BB, chapter 48) and the Order for the Blessing of a Christmas Tree (BB, chapter 49) may be used in Christmas Time. A blessing of a manger or Nativity scene and the blessing of a Christmas tree is also found in *Catholic Household Blessings & Prayers* in Part

III, Days and Seasons. Other appropriate blessings during Christmas Time might include the Order for the Blessing of Homes during the Christmas Season (BB, chapter 50); the Order for the Blessing of a Family (BB, chapter 1) which would be especially appropriate for the Feast of the Holy Family; the Order for the Blessing of Travelers (BB, chapter 9); the Order for the Blessing of Religious Articles (BB, chapter 44); and the Order for the Blessing of Rosaries (BB, chapter 45).

The Liturgical Environment

As you prepare for Christmas, many of the choices have likely already been made in past years, but you may consider if there are areas in which there might be improvements to be made. Such changes should usually be made slowly, which may require planning to implement them over several years' time.

The crèche should be set up in a location where it is not impeding the movement of the assembly or the liturgical ministers and where it does not distract from the central liturgical actions. Depending on your space, an appropriate location may be in the back of the church or in a side chapel, or even in the narthex. The space directly in front of the altar is best avoided. Wherever it is, the crèche should be carefully set up so that it is an attractive and welcoming invitation to reflect on the season. Placing some of the plants for the liturgical space as part of the crèche can help make this happen.

The poinsettia with its red and green foliage has come to be a cultural marker of Christmas Time, and there is nothing wrong with this. However, you might consider also using plants that make use of the liturgical colors of white and gold. There should always be a preference for real, living plants in the church, just as in all other liturgical times. While many parishes have opted for artificial trees and garlands because of considerations of cost, mess, and even the local fire code, consider what real plants can be used in the liturgical space given your budget, the amount of care you will be able to provide, and the light available.

Light is an often underused aspect of liturgical preparation, and Christmas is the perfect time to make good use of it. Christmas should be a bright light shining in the darkness of mid-winter. The white and gold liturgical colors work well with this emphasis without requiring any special equipment. Extra candles may be placed throughout the church, although be careful where they are placed, particularly with the other additions to the space. The seven-day candles that are made for sanctuary lamps are generally safe, and may be used along with other candles or votive lights. Placing any of these within white or gold chimneys makes them not only safer, but highlights the liturgical colors of the liturgical time.

While some modifications need to be made for the various feast days that fall within the liturgical time, there should be a noticeable continuity throughout Christmas Time. The density of feasts and solemnities means that the space must be somewhat flexible in its set-up. In preparing the environment, planning ahead and leaving space for these changes to the environment can allow these feasts to be celebrated beautifully, but without too much difficulty.

The Liturgical Music

"Joy to the World" the season has come! After the Advent restraint, now is the time to go large and lovely with Christmas Time. Bring out the brass, strings, timpani, and other instruments as you are able to create rich and beautiful celebrations.

Be hospitable. Do you need to create a more complete worship aid that includes hymns and Mass settings rather than a listing of page numbers? Overflow crowds may mean that many will not have access to hymnals, and there will surely be some who are not familiar with the Mass settings of your parish. Traditional carols are a very important part of the season as well. Give the congregation things they can sing "by heart" and save a few special pieces for the prelude or somewhere else. For a list of Christmas Time music suggestions please visit www.LTP.org/resources for a free PDF.

Liturgical Ministers

SINCE many ministers may be away at Christmas, don't overextend other ministers. Be sure to schedule ministers as family units and invite students returning from college to serve as well. Inquire with various groups in the parish to see if they are willing to help with ministry of hospitality. Various parish ministers, especially musicians, sacristans, priests, and deacons are often present for two or more liturgies on Christmas Eve or Christmas Day. Consider preparing a place where these ministers can have some down time and provide simple food and beverages for these co-workers in the vineyard.

Devotions and Sacramentals

MANY ethic traditions abound in Christmas Time including adding candles on the table (from Slavic countries), paper lanterns (South America), placement of holly on the table (Ireland), the sharing of the Oplatky (a piece of bread that looks like a large host of sacred images—a Polish and Slavic tradition). In the section on Christmas Time in *Catholic Household Blessings & Prayers* we find the blessing for the following: the Christmas Tree and the blessing of the Christmas manger or Nativity scene.

It is customary on Epiphany to mark the doors of the home following in the steps of the Magi—whose names according to legend are Caspar, Melchior, and Balthazar. While singing the carol "We Three Kings" form a holy procession with the family walking from room to room and inscribe over each door the numbers of the new year with the initials of the Magi: 20+C+M+B+14. The letters form an acronym for *Christus mansionem benedicat*, "May Christ bless this house." Children will be enthralled watching their parents etch letters and numbers over their doors with chalk. Consider concluding your time of prayer by singing the *Te Deum*, the text of the beloved hymn, "Holy God We Praise Thy Name."

The Parish and the Home

THIS is the season to invite our families to celebrate the Christmas mystery. If we have remained fixed during our earlier December weeks on the reflective rituals of Advent we are ready to celebrate through the feasts of the Holy Family of Jesus, Mary, and Joseph and the Solemnity of the Epiphany of the Lord. Now is the time for a parish Christmas party, be it a potluck meal or a share-your-holiday-leftovers dinner.

St. Matthew gives us a unique picture of the journey of Joseph to protect his family and bring them to safety. This can be a time for families to tell the stories of their own relatives or ancestors who may have come to this country in search of a better place for themselves and their families. They often wished simply to protect themselves and their families as they sought a healthy and secure place to raise their children. The topic of immigration can be a volatile one in many places but we are given no better example than in the story of Joseph trying to find a safe haven in a foreign land for his family protected from the threat and danger of Herod. Through Matthew's account heard on the Feast of the Holy Family we can help our parish family see their role in protecting all families regardless of the country of their birth.

The story of Herod is a springboard to invite people to collect items for newborn babies born in poverty or waiting for adoption or for the mothers to be who may find it difficult to carry a pregnancy to fruition without the help of a community. Many Catholic Charities and other Catholic or community social service agencies sponsor drives for baby diapers, supplies, clothing, and baby equipment.

At this time many people realize the need to do more. Parishes can help their communities by continually offering opportunities to serve. Displaying places to volunteer with pictures, easy access to information, and people in the community to talk with or volunteer alongside make it easier for people to connect their desire with action. Some parishes invite their members to consider a pledge of service as a part of their stewardship appeal. We set a great example as a community for the many young people who routinely are asked to do service hours through school and Confirmation programs.

Mass Texts

◆ **Dismissal Text for Children's Liturgy of the Word**

The glow of Christmas still fills our homes
and we continue to celebrate the great truth that
    God came to live among us.
But to live with us, Jesus must find a home
and the only home he wants is right here within
    our hearts.
Let's pray that the Scriptures you will now hear
will help open your hearts so wide
that Jesus will be able to enter and there make his
    home with you.

◆ **Dismissal Text for the Catechumens**

Our celebration of Jesus's birth in the manger
    at Bethlehem
reminds us he must be born as well within
    our hearts.
You have committed to allowing your heart
    to become a manger
in which Christ can rest and be a part
    of your daily life.
May your reflection on his Word enable you
    to keep room for Christ within your heart
so he may more and more become the heart
    of your world.

◆ **Seasonal Texts for the Prayer of the Faithful**

Invitation to Prayer:

The angels sang his praise when he was born
and now they sing forever before his throne
    of glory.

Yet though he reigns in the heavenly court,
he is not too far to see our every need
or too distant to hear our every plea.
Let us offer our prayers to him whom saints and
    angels worship.

Intercessions:

That the Church Christ established on the foundation of the Apostles and with the blood of martyrs and all her leaders throughout the world might serve God's people faithfully, we pray:

That the leaders of nations and governments might humbly recognize that their governance is an expression of God's ultimate rule over all the earth, we pray:

That those in need of material sustenance, spiritual consolation, or of emotional comfort might find it through the generous hearts and open hands of God's holy people, we pray:

That those who have died will know the peace and joy of standing before the brilliance of God within the glory of his kingdom, we pray:

That our parish will never fail to recognize the Christ who walks among us even in the guise of the stranger and the outcast, we pray:

Response: O come, let us adore him.

Concluding Prayer:

Merciful Jesus, by taking on human flesh
and living humbly within the family at Nazareth
you affirmed the goodness of human life.
In this joyful season, free us from all that would
    rob us of joy
and hinder us from singing your praises
together with the saints and angels of heaven
where you live and reign for ever and ever.
Amen.

December
Month of the Divine Infancy

T U E
24
(#13)   white
Vigil of the Solemnity of the Nativity of the Lord

About this Solemnity

The events surrounding Jesus's birth are found only in Matthew's and Luke's accounts. In John's account, which was written later than the others, there is a totally different presentation of Jesus coming into the world, as "the Word became flesh" (John 1:14). The other Gospel accounts stress the humanity of Jesus, while John's prologue stresses the divinity. The essence of the prologue that is important to proclaim is that God took on human flesh. God became incarnate in Jesus.

The Vigil Mass

The Lectionary for Mass

◆ FIRST READING: Jerusalem, the city once desolate and forsaken, will shine with the glorious light of the Lord—and all nations see it. Joy abounds as God renews his covenant of love with Jerusalem, his bride.

◆ RESPONSORIAL PSALM 89 is a song of praise, acclaiming the deeds of the Lord, celebrating God's covenant with David and the promise that his throne will last forever.

◆ SECOND READING: Our Second Reading consists of excerpts from Paul's proclamation of the Gospel to the Jews in Antioch. We hear the high points of Israel's history: the Exodus from Egypt, the anointing of David as king, the covenant made with him, and finally, the presentation of Jesus as this promised descendant whose coming was heralded by John the Baptist.

◆ GOSPEL: Matthew's genealogy of Jesus traces his ancestry back not only to King David, but to Abraham, the father of the Jewish people. The second part of the Gospel (and the shorter option) consists of Matthew's account of the events preceding Jesus's birth, focusing on the angelic appearances to Joseph, assuring him that the child was conceived through the Holy Spirit. The child, whose birth is the fulfillment of the prophecy of Isaiah, is Jesus the Savior, God with us.

The Roman Missal

The Gloria is sung or said; given the festivity of the occasion, the musical setting used should be a magnificent one indeed, as the text echoes the words of the heavenly host praising God's glory.

The prayers for the Vigil Mass very much maintain the sense of vigiling as they speak of waiting and looking forward. The Collect mentions that we are gladdened "year by year / as wait in hope for our redemption" and asks that we may "merit to face him confidently / when he comes again as our Judge."

During the recitation or singing of the Creed, all are to kneel at the words "and by the Holy Spirit was incarnate," up to and including the words "and became man." Don't let the assembly be caught by surprise by this such that very few kneel or such that it winds up being awkward and haphazard. After leaving a silent pause after the Homily, the priest may offer a spontaneous introduction to the Creed that explains how and when the kneeling is to take place, so that all might properly participate in this gesture that highlights the Incarnation.

The Prayer over the Offerings continues to "look forward . . . / to the coming festivities," asking that our response to "the beginnings of our redemption" that are made manifest in them may be to serve God "all the more eagerly."

There is a choice from among three for the Preface at this Vigil Mass—Preface I, II, or III of the Nativity of the Lord. These can be found immediately following the two Advent Prefaces. Preface I uses the motif of Christ as Light, describing how "in the mystery of the Word made flesh / a new light of your glory has shone upon the eyes of our mind." In this light, "we recognize in him God made visible" and are "caught up through him in love of things invisible." Considering that the Vigil Mass will in many places take place in darkness, this might be an especially appropriate choice for those communities, although the theological motif of Christ as Light is certainly universally applicable. Preface II highlights how all things have been restored through the Incarnation: Christ, appearing visibly and in time has raised up all that was cast down, restoring "unity to all creation" and calling "straying humanity back to the heavenly Kingdom." Preface III uses the beautiful phrase of the "holy exchange," describing how "when our frailty is assumed by your Word / not only does human mortality receive unending honor / but by this wondrous union we, too, are made eternal."

Note that if Eucharistic Prayer I, the Roman Canon, is used, there is a proper form of the *Communicantes* that is used—it is the first insert, with the heading "On the Nativity of the Lord and throughout the Octave." The text, "In communion with those whose memory we venerate, / especially the glorious ever-Virgin Mary, / Mother of our God and Lord, Jesus Christ" is replaced by the insert beginning, "Celebrating the most sacred night (day) / on which blessed Mary . . . ." Then, upon completion of the insert text, the prayer resumes with the line, "and blessed Joseph, her Spouse . . . " as indicated by the marking.

The Prayer after Communion asks "that we may draw new vigor / from celebrating the Nativity of your Only Begotten Son" as it acknowledges that it is through the Paschal Mystery of that Son that "we receive both food and drink."

Given the festivity of this liturgy, it would be fitting to use the formula of Solemn Blessing at the end of Mass, using form #2, "The Nativity of the Lord."

25

(#14, #15, #16)   white

Solemnity of the Nativity of the Lord

The Lectionary for Mass

Mass during the Night

◆ First Reading: Isaiah describes the life situation of an oppressed people in time of war. In the midst of darkness, a shining light is seen, a light that brings joy. The light is associated with the birth of a child, an heir to the Davidic throne. Notice the names given to him—they point to the mission he is to accomplish and the role he will have on behalf of the people. All is the work of God. Christian tradition sees this fulfilled in Jesus of Nazareth, whose birth we celebrate today. In the midst of our winter darkness, we celebrate Jesus, the Light of the World.

◆ Responsorial Psalm 96: The antiphon is taken from Luke's account of the birth of Jesus and is the angel's proclamation to the shepherds: "Today is born our Savior . . . ." The psalm acclaims God's kingship over all creation and all nations. Notice how all creation joins in this hymn of praise.

◆ Second Reading: Two comings of the Lord are juxtaposed in this reading. The first coming of Jesus is mentioned in the first line ("the grace of God has appeared," Titus 2:11). Note also the reference to Jesus's work of redemption at the end of the reading. The focus of the

reading, however, is on Jesus's Second Coming at the end of time, with particular reference to how believers are to live in anticipation of that coming.

◆ Gospel: Luke stresses, first of all, Joseph's Davidic ancestry, thus the journey to Bethlehem. Luke also portrays Mary and Joseph as travelers lacking a room of their own, forced to take shelter in a stable where animals live. (Might we think of them as homeless? As street people?) Some simple shepherds living in a nearby field first receive news of his birth from the proclamation of the angels. The scene is far from comfortable and luxurious. The infant Jesus has a manger for a crib—how symbolic—for he will come to be recognized in the breaking of the bread, in the food given in memory of him.

The Roman Missal

Although for many communities this Mass will be "Midnight Mass," it is interesting that the Latin name for this Mass translates to simply "Mass during the Night." Certainly the tradition of Mass at Midnight holds a special place in the hearts of many Catholics.

As with all Masses for this solemnity, the Gloria is sung or said.

The Collect makes reference to "this most sacred night" being made "radiant with the splendor of the true light." The motif of darkness and light is further employed as the prayer goes on to petition "that we, who have known the mysteries of his light on earth, / may also delight in his gladness in heaven."

During the recitation or singing of the Creed, all are to kneel at the words "and by the Holy Spirit was incarnate," up to and including the words "and became man."

The Prayer over the Offerings makes reference to the "holy exchange" in terms of the request that through that exchange, "we may be

found in the likeness of Christ, / in whom our nature is united to you."

See the notes under the Vigil Mass for a discussion about the three options for the Preface. Again, while any of the three Prefaces are appropriate, one might consider the first, focused on "Christ the Light," as having a particular pertinence to this celebration, especially in view of the Collect. Also, Preface III could be a good choice; its mention of "the holy exchange" would echo the Prayer over the Offerings as explained above.

Note that if Eucharistic Prayer I, the Roman Canon, is used, there is a proper form of the *Communicantes* that is used.

The Prayer after Communion gives voice to our joy at participating in the Nativity and asks that we "through an honorable way of life [may] become worthy of union with him."

Use the Solemn Blessing at the end of Mass, form #2, "The Nativity of the Lord."

The Nativity of our Lord Jesus Christ from the *Roman Martyrology*

The text for this proclamation can be found as the last item in Appendix I of the Missal (immediately before the Rite for the Blessing and Sprinkling of Water in Appendix II). The proclamation, coming from the *Roman Martyrology*, declares in a formal way the birth of Christ, using references from Sacred Scripture. Beginning with Creation, it correlates the birth of the Lord to major events in both sacred and secular history, giving believers a context for salvation history. The text is either sung (preferably) or recited. The Missal specifies that at Mass it is to be done before the beginning of Christmas Mass during the Night, although it may also be done on December 24 during the celebration of the Liturgy of the Hours. A key point is that when done at the

Mass during the Night (which for many parishes would be Midnight Mass) it may not replace any part of the Mass. Thus, the proclamation is done before Mass begins and the Introductory Rites (indeed, the rest of the Mass) occurs as usual. Since the rubrics do not specify any particular minister to proclaim the announcement, it may be done, depending on circumstances, by a deacon, cantor, reader, or, if necessary, even the priest himself. It is arguable whether or not the ambo is an appropriate place from which to sing or recite the proclamation, although it would appear to be allowable to do so based on the precedent that, according to the rubrics, *The Announcement of Easter and the Moveable Feasts* announced on the Epiphany of the Lord is to be done from the ambo.

Mass at Dawn

The Lectionary for Mass

◆ FIRST READING: Isaiah's words are first spoken to an exiled people, soon to return to their homeland as a result of the Lord's salvific work among them. Once considered by themselves—and others—as people whom the Lord had forsaken, they are given a new identity as those holy and redeemed. Today, we celebrate the coming of Jesus as Savior and the new identity we receive through participation in his life.

◆ RESPONSORIAL PSALM 97: The antiphon's mention of light evokes the second stanza of the psalm as well as the image of the glory of the Lord shining around the shepherds in the field. To this light, the angelic proclamation "the Lord is born for us" is joined. The psalm is one that celebrates the kingship of the Lord over all creation—how appropriate in light of the birth of the newborn king of the Jews.

◆ SECOND READING: The appearance in the first line refers to the birth of Jesus. Paul emphasizes that God's salvific act on our behalf stems from his mercy, not our merit. Closely connected with the birth of Jesus is the theme of our rebirth in Baptism and our renewal through the gift of God's Spirit—the means through which we receive the gift that is offered.

◆ GOSPEL: We see the shepherds receiving and acting upon the message of the angel. They are, perhaps, the first to seek Jesus in Luke's account. Finding him, they become bearers of the Good News to others—these early shepherd witnesses to Jesus. The shepherds praise and glorify God. Mary ponders the meaning of it all in her heart, something she will do repeatedly in Luke's account of Jesus's childhood.

The Roman Missal

The Gloria is sung or said; given the festivity of the occasion, the musical setting used should be a magnificent one indeed, as the text echoes the words of the heavenly host praising God's glory.

The Collect for the Mass at Dawn is replete with the imagery of light: it references our being "bathed in the new radiance of your incarnate Word"; it mentions "the light of faith, which illumines our minds"; it asks that that same light of faith "shine through in our deeds."

During the recitation or singing of the Creed, all are to kneel at the words "and by the Holy Spirit was incarnate," up to and including the words "and became man."

The Prayer over the Offerings prays for the gift of transformation, as it petitions that our offerings be worthy so that "just as Christ was born a man and also shone forth as God, / so these earthly gifts may confer on us what is divine." The notion of sacramentality that is communicated in this prayer—the

idea of earthly realities manifesting divine realities—is striking.

In view of that, perhaps Preface I of the Nativity, with its emphasis on light, shining glory, and the divine being made visible, is the most appropriate choice among the three possible Prefaces, although, with reference to the discussion above under the Vigil Mass section concerning the three options for the Preface, it could be argued that any one is as appropriate as any other.

Note that if Eucharistic Prayer I, the Roman Canon, is used, there is a proper form of the *Communicantes* that is used.

The Prayer after Communion asks that our celebration of the Nativity may deepen our faith so that we may love "the hidden depths of this mystery" more and more.

Use the Solemn Blessing at the end of Mass, form #2, "The Nativity of the Lord."

Mass during the Day

The Lectionary for Mass

◆ FIRST READING: The reading begins and ends on the note of salvation—that which is accomplished by the Lord—not just for Jerusalem, but for all nations. First, we have the announcement of salvation and the proclamation of the Lord's kingship. Then, there is the eye-witness of what God is doing and the jubilant response of praise.

◆ RESPONSORIAL PSALM 98: Our antiphon acclaims the salvation of our God, now seen by all nations. These themes are further elaborated in the stanzas of the psalm. Note also the reference to God's covenant fidelity in accomplishing salvation and the joyful, musical response of praise.

◆ SECOND READING: This beginning of the letter to the Hebrews takes us full circle: from God's promises to the prophets of old, through its fulfilment in the coming of Jesus his Son into the world, to the heavenly exaltation of Jesus when he had accomplished his mission on earth. Note also the affirmations about the Son: his active part in creation and in sustaining the world; the glory he shares with the Father.

◆ GOSPEL: We hear the beginning of John's account. Note the presence of themes we just heard in Hebrews: the son's pre-existence, his active part in creation, the glory he shares with God. References to the ministry of John the Baptist are interspersed in today's text, as is the theme of the light and enlightenment that Jesus brings. The reading ends on the note of the grace and glory we have received from him and our call to become more and more his children through the gift of his grace

The Roman Missal

The Gloria is sung or said; given the festivity of the occasion, the musical setting used should be a magnificent one indeed, as the text echoes the words of the heavenly host praising God's glory.

The Collect speaks of the "holy exchange" between divinity and humanity, even though it does not use those exact words. Using the same words of the prayer when the priest or deacon mixes a little water into the wine, the prayer, after acknowledging how God both created and restored the dignity of human nature, petitions "that we may share in the divinity of Christ, who humbled himself to share in our humanity."

During the recitation or singing of the Creed, all are to kneel at the words "and by the Holy Spirit was incarnate," up to and including the words "and became man."

The Prayer over the Offerings notes that we make our oblation on this solemn day that manifests "the reconciliation / that makes us wholly pleasing in your sight," thus

alluding to the restoration and healing that comes to us through Christ.

See the notes under the Vigil Mass for a discussion about the three options for the Preface. While any one is as appropriate as any other, there may be a particular fittingness to using Preface III of the Nativity, insofar as it echoes the Collect with its mention of "the holy exchange."

Note that if Eucharistic Prayer I, the Roman Canon, is used, there is a proper form of the *Communicantes* that is used.

The Prayer after Communion asks that the Savior born this day, who is "the author of divine generation for us" may also be "the giver even of immortality."

Use the Solemn Blessing at the end of Mass, form #2, "The Nativity of the Lord."

Pastoral Reflection

Luke 2:15–20 (reading for the Mass at Dawn) is about a birth and a promise, made known to the people. Jesus was found by the shepherds, heralded by the angels, protected lovingly by his parents. First, find and purposefully name the gifts (glorious light) in the person you might struggle with this week. In the parties and unwrapping of gifts, make yourself known to God. Present the inner core of your heart, something that cannot be wrapped but can be given or promised (spending five extra minutes in conversation with God, sitting quietly and offering your prayers for another, sacrificing something to help another.) Then, like Mary, you can reflect on the love God has poured into your life and all others and be amazed by your life.

26 (#696) red
Feast of St. Stephen, the First Martyr

The Lectionary for Mass/ Today's Saint

◆ FIRST READING: Today's reading is excerpted from the two chapters of the Acts of the Apostles where we meet Stephen, the first person named among those chosen to assist the Apostles with the daily distribution to those in need. He is described as a man filled with faith and the Holy Spirit (see Acts of the Apostles 6:5). Today's reading jumps from Acts of the Apostles 6:10, which notes the wisdom with which Stephen spoke, to 7:54–59, which describes his martyrdom. Omitted are the accusations of blasphemy made by his opponents (named at the beginning of the reading) and his consequent trial before the Sanhedrin (Jewish council). The immediate reference to the "this" that so infuriated the Sanhedrin (verse 54) is his charge against the Jewish leaders for their obstinacy in refusing to believe in Jesus and putting him to death. Stephen is sustained by his vision of the glorified and exalted Christ at the right hand of God. This was blasphemy to the Jewish leaders and deserved punishment by death. Stephen's prayer as he dies is that of Jesus: into your hands, I "commend my spirit" (Luke 23:46).

◆ RESPONSORIAL PSALM 31: The antiphon is the prayer of Stephen (and Jesus) as they die. Psalm 31 is a song of confidence and a prayer for deliverance from enemies.

◆ GOSPEL: Stephen was among the first to experience severe opposition from his own people. Believers thus share in the suffering of Christ. The verb "hand over" is the same verb used in the Passion narratives. Jesus gives assurance of the Spirit's presence in such times and the promise of salvation to those who endure.

The Roman Missal

The texts for this Mass are found in the Proper of Saints section of the Missal, at December 26; all the orations are proper to the day.

Since today is a day within the Octave of Christmas, the Gloria is sung or said at this Mass.

The Collect acknowledges St. Stephen as a man who prayed for his persecutors (which of course he did in imitation of Christ) and petitions God that we may learn to love our enemies as a consequence of our worship.

One of the three Prefaces of the Nativity is used today. Since we are within the Octave of the Nativity, be sure to use the proper form of the *Communicantes*, if Eucharistic Prayer I, the Roman Canon, is used.

The Prayer after Communion is a prayer of thanksgiving to God as it makes explicit reference to the Nativity, noting that we are saved through that mystery, and as it goes on to express our joy at the "celebration of the blessed Martyr Stephen."

F R I **27** (#697) white
Feast of St. John, Apostle and Evangelist

The Lectionary for Mass

◆ FIRST READING: "We have heard . . . we have seen . . . and touched with our hands . . . " (1 John 1:1). John's proclamation of Jesus is rooted in the reality of a personal experience of the Lord. He has found life—eternal life—in fellowship with Jesus. His desire and hope is that others will receive the Word and have life. In this is his joy.

◆ RESPONSORIAL PSALM 97: The antiphon echoes the theme of joy (note also the references to "glad" in the last two stanzas). The psalm celebrates the kingship of the Lord. All of creation joins in praise.

◆ GOSPEL: The text takes us to the end of Jesus's life, to the tomb, in fact. Tradition holds that John is the "other disciple" (John 20:2) and the one with whom Jesus had a special bond. It is he, the beloved disciple, who sees and believes.

The Roman Missal

The texts for this Mass are found in the Proper of Saints section of the Missal, at December 27, and all the orations are proper to the day.

Since today is a day within the Octave of Christmas, the Gloria is sung or said at this Mass.

All of the orations echo Johannine themes: the Collect mentions grasping with proper understanding what has been brought to our ears; the Prayer over the Offerings uses imagery such as "banquet," "supper," and "the hidden wisdom of the eternal Word"; and the Prayer after Communion references the Word made flesh, asking that that same Word, "through this mystery which we have celebrated, / ever dwell among us."

One of the three Prefaces of the Nativity is used today. Since we are within the Octave of the Nativity, be sure to use the proper form of the *Communicantes* ("On the Nativity of the Lord and throughout the Octave") if Eucharistic Prayer I, the Roman Canon, is used.

Today's Saint

St. John (first century), Apostle and fourth Evangelist, is called the "beloved disciple" because of his close relationship with Jesus. Throughout his account of the Gospel, St. John, named as the son of Zebedee and brother of St. James the Greater, makes an appearance at significant moments in Jesus's life; specifically, at the Last Supper, the Garden of Gethsemane, the foot of the Cross, and the upper room. These appearances point to the intimate relationship he had with our Lord. His account of the Gospel is quite different from the synoptic accounts (Matthew, Mark, and Luke) due to his high Christology

(divine emphasis), which is proclaimed through symbolic language and poetic form. The eagle is the chosen symbol for John's account, ultimately representing the depth and height to which the human spirit must soar in order to grasp the meaning of John's text. Among his many important contributions to the Church, other scriptural writings are attributed to his name, including three epistles and the Book of Revelation.

S A T **28** (#698) red
Feast of the Holy Innocents, Martyrs

The Lectionary for Mass

◆ FIRST READING: Having fellowship with the Lord means that his light and life are evident in our behavior. Only in this is there true fellowship with him. John calls all believers to honest self-appraisal and recognition of their sinfulness, and correspondingly, to appeal for forgiveness to Jesus, our Advocate with the heavenly Father. He lived, and died, that we might have the light of eternal life.

◆ RESPONSORIAL PSALM 124: Today's psalm is one of thanksgiving for deliverance from the enemy. We can think of it as applying not only to our own deliverance, accomplished by Jesus, from the snares of the devil, but also to the deliverance of the Holy Innocents through death to life everlasting. In all ways and at all times, our help is in the Lord.

◆ GOSPEL: While there is no mention of the event described in today's Gospel in historical sources, such an action is entirely in keeping with the character of Herod the Great as it is described elsewhere. Herod is enraged at the possibility that his throne will be usurped and seeks immediately to wipe out any perceived opposition. Note how Matthew describes the events as fulfilling the Scriptures, an important point for his Jewish Christian community. Note, too, how the history of the Jewish people is relived in Jesus: he is taken down to Egypt, that his life might be spared (as were the sons of Jacob), and is later called "out of Egypt" (Matthew 2:15).

The Roman Missal

The Mass formularies for today are found in the Proper of Saints section of the Missal, at December 28; all the orations are proper to the day.

Since today is a day within the Octave of Christmas, the Gloria is sung or said at this Mass.

The Collect relates how the Holy Innocents proclaimed not by speaking, but by dying, and it goes on to ask that we may live our faith not only through confession on our lips, but also through our manner of life. The Prayer over the Offerings reminds us that the salvation offered through the saving mysteries brings justification "even to those who lack understanding," a reference to the Holy Innocents. The Prayer after Communion echoes the Collect in acknowledging that the Holy Innocents "were crowned with heavenly grace" even though they were "unable to profess your Son in speech." The prayer asks that we may be recipients of that same salvation as we have received the "holy gifts" of the Eucharist.

One of the three Prefaces of the Nativity is used today. Since we are within the Octave of the Nativity, be sure to use the proper form of the Communicantes ("On the Nativity of the Lord and throughout the Octave") if Eucharistic Prayer I, the Roman Canon, is used.

Today's Saints

Herod the Great, fearing for his throne after the Magi told him about the birth of Jesus, ordered the execution of all male children in Bethlehem, hoping that Jesus would be among those killed (see Matthew 2:16–18). According to

Matthew, this fulfilled the prophecy of Jeremiah (31:15): "In Ramah is heard the sound of sobbing, bitter weeping! Rachel mourns for her children." The haunting "Coventry Carol" refers to this episode as it asks, "O sisters too, how may we do, / For to preserve this day / This poor youngling for whom we sing / By, by, lully, lullay."

(#17)   white

29 Feast of the Holy Family of Jesus, Mary, and Joseph

About this Feast

This liturgical feast has been on the Church calendar about a hundred years, often on different dates. It is a "devotional" or "idea" feast that was inaugurated by Holy Family associations. Everything we know about the Holy Family, which is not much, comes from the Gospel accounts read over the three years. It celebrates the unity and love so evident in the family of Joseph, Mary, and Jesus.

The Lectionary for Mass

◆ FIRST READING: We may think of today's reading as an elaboration of what it means to honor one's father and mother as commanded by God to Moses (see Exodus 20:12). In addition, we hear the blessings that will come to the one who faithfully observes this command of the Lord.

◆ RESPONSORIAL PSALM 128: In the mentality of the Old Testament, to fear the Lord was to reverence the Lord and be obedient to his commandments. As in the First Reading, we hear the blessings that will come upon the one who is obedient to the Lord.

◆ SECOND READING: If only each of us could take these exhortations on the manner of living a Christian life to heart. What a difference it would make in our relationships with one another! Love, reverence, respect, forgiveness, and peace—all are hallmarks of the Christian family. Verses 18–21 (the end of the longer form of the reading) are technically called a "household code"— reflecting the cultural values and the tradition of a time and place when wives were submissive to their husbands. The next verse (verse 22, not included in today's reading) addresses the relationship between slaves and their masters.

◆ GOSPEL: Like his people before him during the time of Joseph the Patriarch (see Genesis 45–46), the child Jesus was taken down to Egypt that his life might be spared. Like his people before him, Jesus, too, was led out of Egypt. In order to protect him from any danger or threat to his life, Joseph took Jesus and his Mother to settle in Nazareth in Galilee, the northern region of Israel. Thus, the adult Jesus was known as *"the Nazorean"* (Matthew 2:23).

The Roman Missal

The texts for this feast are located in the Proper of Time section of the Missal, immediately after the Christmas Mass during the Day.

The Gloria is sung or said at this Mass on the Sunday within the Octave of the Nativity of the Lord.

The Collect praises the Holy Family as a shining example and asks that "we may imitate them / in practicing the virtues of family life and in the bonds of charity." The Prayer over the Offerings makes another petition for our families as it asks that, "through the intercession of the Virgin Mother of God and Saint Joseph, / you may establish our families firmly in your grace and your peace." Imitation of the Holy Family is invoked a third time, in the Prayer after Communion, and that prayer also requests that "after the trials of this world, / we may share their company for ever."

Because this feast occurs on a Sunday this year, the Creed is said.

One of the three Prefaces of the Nativity is used today. Given that all the orations ask that our families may be changed to imitate the virtues of the Holy Family, perhaps an argument could be made that Preface II of the Nativity, with its mention of Christ restoring unity to all creation and calling humanity back after it has strayed, is an appropriate choice over the other two.

Since we are still within the Octave of the Nativity there is a proper form of the *Communicantes* if Eucharistic Prayer I, the Roman Canon, is used. As on Christmas, it is the first insert, with the heading "On the Nativity of the Lord and throughout the Octave."

Some parishes have the custom of using the Prayer of Blessing from the Order for the Blessing of a Family in the *Book of Blessings* as a Prayer over the People at the end of Mass (see *Book of Blessings*, 65–67). However, there may be pastoral advantage to keeping the context of this Feast being a Christmas celebration, and to therefore using the Solemn Blessing for the Nativity of the Lord (#2 in the "Blessings at the End of Mass and Prayers over the People" section of the Missal). Perhaps if it is desirable to highlight the blessing of families, materials could be distributed or printed in the parish bulletin for a home rite of blessing among the family members at home, along the lines of what

is found in *Catholic Household Blessings & Prayers* (published by the United States Conference of Catholic Bishops).

Pastoral Reflection

It is a tall order to believe that our subconscious, our dreams, has anything to do with our daily life. Psychologists, and God, too, would disagree! God finds uncanny ways to speak to us. While the essence of the Gospel today is allowing the father (Joseph) to protect his family, it is also about trusting wholeheartedly in God, no matter what. When you go to sleep tonight, place your deepest needs into God's hands. Ask for an answer. Wait to receive a response. It may not come in the expected manner, but God's loving heart always responds. As the Divine Parent of all in heaven, God protects. Allow God to do this loving job for your life. For this to happen, you have to offer, trust, and then believe.

(#203) white

MON 30 Sixth Day within the Octave of the Nativity of the Lord

The Lectionary for Mass

◆ FIRST READING: There is a beautiful inclusiveness in John's words, embracing—and addressing—people of all ages in the community. And surely there is an inherent call for each group addressed: to know the Father—and to "know" here is not just intellectual, but an experiential knowledge, a being-in-relationship with the other; to know him who is from the beginning, a reference to the Word as well as to the Father—echoing John's account of the Gospel (John 1); to be strong and victorious when encountering the Evil One. Believers are called to discern between what is from the Father and what is of the world.

◆ RESPONSORIAL PSALM 96: We might think of today's psalm as describing what should be the response of those who know the Father: praise and adoration before the Lord, the King, the Creator, and Judge.

◆ GOSPEL: The call to live faithfully is a lifelong call. In today's First Reading, children, youth, and parents are named. In today's Gospel, it is the elderly, specifically an 84-year-old woman. Anna faithfully lived what perhaps came as a later call (in her widowhood?) to ceaseless prayer and adoration in the Temple. Most importantly for Luke's readers and for us, she was a prophet who recognized and proclaimed the child Jesus as the one who would redeem Israel.

The Roman Missal

Today's Mass formularies are found in the Proper of Time section of the Missal, at December 30; all the orations are proper to the day.

Since today is a day within the Octave of Christmas, the Gloria is sung or said at this Mass.

The Collect reiterates the theme of newness that has been expressed before as it asks that the Nativity may set us free from the "ancient servitude" which "holds us bound / beneath the yoke of sin." The Prayer over the Offerings implores that what we profess with devotion and faith may come to reality through the mysteries we celebrate. The Prayer after Communion speaks to the transformative action of the Eucharist, asking that through our partaking in the sacrament, "we may be made fit to receive your gift / through this very gift itself."

One of the three Prefaces of the Nativity is used today. Since we are within the Octave of the Nativity, be sure to use the proper form of the *Communicantes* ("On the Nativity of the Lord and throughout the Octave") if Eucharistic Prayer I, the Roman Canon, is used.

T U E 31 (#204) white
Seventh Day within the Octave of the Nativity of the Lord

Optional Memorial of St. Sylvester, Pope

The Lectionary for Mass

◆ FIRST READING: John and his community thought that they were living in the end time. We may well be without realizing it. People of Jewish and early Christian tradition believed that the end times would be characterized by the presence of false teachers. John's community has experienced this, and his words today are reassuring: you do have knowledge, knowledge of the truth, and you have the anointing of the Spirit. Do not waver in the face of those who would oppose you.

◆ RESPONSORIAL PSALM 96 recounts the joyful response of all creation to the Lord's coming. We think not only of his first coming, but also his last.

◆ GOSPEL: Today's reading is the same as for the Mass of Christmas Day. In light of today's First Reading, note the mention of opposition to the Word and the contrast between those who believe and those who do not. Truth comes through Jesus. Believers have received from his fullness. Because he became one of us, we receive his grace to become as he is, a child of God.

The Roman Missal

The texts for December 31 can be found in the Proper of Time. Since today is a day within the Octave of Christmas, the Gloria is sung or said at this Mass.

The Nativity of the Son of God is acknowledged as "the beginning and fulfillment of all religion" in the Collect, and the prayer then goes on to ask that "we may be numbered / among those who belong to him." The Prayer over the Offerings petitions God that our participation in this offering may lead us to give "fitting homage to your divine majesty" and unite us in mind and heart. The Prayer after Communion uses the motif of the difference between things that pass away and things that are eternal, asking that we strive to trust more deeply in the eternal. Notice too how the prayer has a link to the end of the calendar year, as it speaks of experiencing the remedies God provides "both now and in the future."

One of the three Prefaces of the Nativity is used today. Since we are within the Octave of the Nativity, be sure to use the proper form of the *Communicantes* ("On the Nativity of the Lord and throughout the Octave") if Eucharistic Prayer I, the Roman Canon, is used.

It is also possible to celebrate the optional Memorial of St. Sylvester. In this case, the Collect is proper to the memorial and can be found in the Proper of Saints, at December 31. The remaining orations may come either from the Mass for December 31 or from the Common of Pastors: For a Pope. In any event, one of the Nativity Prefaces should still be used.

Today's Saint

Very little is known about St. Sylvester I. He was pope from 314 to 335 during the era of Constantine, when the Church was able to come out of hiding after years of persecution. During his pontificate some of the great churches in Rome were built, such as the Lateran Basilica and the original St. Peter's Basilica on the Vatican Hill (the present St. Peter's Basilica was constructed between 1506 and 1626). The First Council of Nicaea in 325, at which the Nicene Creed was adopted, occurred during his papacy. Sylvester did not attend, but he sent two legates.

January
Month of the Holy Name

W E D 1 (#18) white
The Octave Day of the Nativity of the Lord Solemnity of Mary, the Holy Mother of God
HOLYDAY OF OBLIGATION

About this Solemnity

We are still in the midst of Christmas Time, and today the Church celebrates the solemnity of Mary, the Holy Mother of God. One of the most outstanding characteristics of Mary is her willingness to know and do God's will. While we would like to follow her example, we wonder how she was so sure of it. Today's Gospel gives a clue. She reflected on events that happened and were happening. She meditated. In our busy lives today, we often overlook meditation as a prayer. Many grow up not knowing how to meditate, which is regrettable. Today the children will get a taste of one way to participate in meditation.

Lectionary for Mass

◆ FIRST READING: We hear the words the Lord gave to Aaron, his priest, to use in blessing the Israelites. How truly these words are fulfilled in the Christ event, as the face of the Lord shines upon us in and through Jesus. In his humanity, he possesses the fullness of the divine radiance. Peace—the Hebrew *shalom*—connotes the fullness of well-being, God's preeminent gift in Christ. All who follow Christ now bear his name.

◆ RESPONSORIAL PSALM 67 is a prayer for God's blessing. Note the echoes of the First Reading in the first line. This joyful hymn of praise acclaims God's salvation for all the nations.

◆ SECOND READING: Jesus's birth happened at the fullness of time, ordained by God for the revelation of his salvation. The text emphasizes Jesus's humanity and his Jewish identity as well as his divine sonship. What is more, it proclaims our adoption as children of God through him. Jesus's Spirit dwells in our hearts, crying out Abba—the Aramaic word for "Daddy"—to the Father.

◆ GOSPEL: The visit of the shepherds to the manger is center stage in today's Gospel. These people, so receptive to the Good News they received from the angels, in turn become bearers of the Good News themselves. What is significant on this solemnity is the Gospel's comment about how Mary reflected in her heart on all that was said. She is truly one who "listens" to God in all of life.

The Roman Missal

The texts for this Mass are found in the Proper of Time section (the beginning of the Missal). The Gloria is sung or said, since it is the Octave of the Nativity. The Creed is said or sung.

The Collect recognizes the Blessed Virgin Mary as the one "through whom we were found worthy / to receive the author of life" and asks for her intercession. The Prayer over the Offerings notes that just as we find joy in this solemnity, so too may we rejoice in eternal life. The Prayer after Communion prays that the heavenly sacrament we have received with joy may lead to eternal life.

The Preface assigned for today is Preface I of the Blessed Virgin Mary. The first paragraph of that Preface contains a choice that must be made among various phrases, according to the particular celebration; in this case, the phrase "on the Solemnity of the Motherhood" is the one to be used. For the last time this year, the proper form of the

Communicantes for the Nativity of the Lord and its Octave is to be used if Eucharistic Prayer I, the Roman Canon, is chosen.

The Prayer after Communion refers to Mary as the "Mother of your Son" and "Mother of the Church" as it asks that we may be led to eternal life through our sharing in the Sacrament.

Interestingly, the formula of Solemn Blessing that is suggested at the end of Mass is the one for "The Beginning of the Year." Certainly the fact that this Mass is celebrated on New Year's Day (or New Year's Eve) makes this an appropriate choice, as the beginning of the new calendar year is an event that should be recognized, and one might argue it is therefore the preferred choice. Other possible Solemn Blessings, however, could be the one for "The Nativity of the Lord" (since it is the Octave of Christmas), "The Blessed Virgin Mary" (since it is a Marian feast), and even "Ordinary Time I" (since it is the blessing of Aaron and connects with the First Reading).

Pastoral Reflection

Mary is the epitome of a woman who gave her life entirely to God, listened to God's voice and never doubted. Because of this, she knew her Son long before he was even born. Through the courage and witness of his Mother, Jesus, the name above all names, entered the world—our world. If you are able to have a conversation with your mother, ask her how she felt when you were born. Listen once again to the reason you were given your name. Or, look up your name to discover the meaning for yourself. If you have children of your own, share why they were named as they are. Names create strong identities. How does your name define your path in life?

Memorial of SS. Basil the Great and Gregory of Nazianzen, Bishops and Doctors of the Church

T H U 2

The Lectionary for Mass

◆ FIRST READING: False teachers who would deceive believers and lead them away from the truth of Jesus are a major concern. Repeatedly we hear the word "remain" (mentioned six times), which can also be translated as "live," "dwell," or "continue." Remain true to Christ's teaching so as to live or dwell in him and the Father. Keep his word so that the Father and the Son are at home in you. Remain in the anointing of his Spirit.

◆ RESPONSORIAL PSALM 98: Our abiding with the Father and the Son is the result of the saving power of God at work in our lives. This Christmas Time we celebrate not only his coming to the earth, but his presence in our lives. All creation, all Israel, all the nations, and we ourselves, have seen the saving power of God. We sing his praise.

◆ GOSPEL: Today's Gospel sounds like Advent, with the centrality of John the Baptist. True teachers point to Christ, his coming, his presence, his teaching, and not to themselves.

The Roman Missal

The prayers for this Mass, all proper for the day, are found in the Proper of Saints section of the Missal, at January 2. Since we are now outside the Octave, the Gloria is no longer sung or said on weekdays. The Collect asks that we may follow the example and teaching of Bishops SS. Basil and Gregory, putting it into practice in charity; the Prayer after Communion echoes that, asking that through our partaking of the Eucharist, "we may preserve in integrity the gift of faith / and walk in the path of salvation you trace for us."

The Preface chosen could certainly be one of the three Prefaces of the Nativity, highlighting that we are still in Christmas Time.

Today's Saints

SS. Basil and Gregory became close friends as students in Athens. Together they fought against the Arian heresy, which denied the full divinity of Christ. Their writings also aided the Church's understanding of the Holy Spirit and the Trinity. With Basil's brothers, Gregory of Nyssa and Peter of Sebaste, they are among the Capadocian Fathers. Gregory is known as "the Theologian" by the Eastern Churches. Basil is known as the father of Eastern monasticism and had a great influence on the development of liturgy, East and West.

F R I **3** (#206) white
Christmas Weekday

Optional Memorial of the Most Holy Name of Jesus / white

Today's Optional Memorial

The name of Jesus is important. It means "God saves." His family does not choose the name of Jesus; rather, God gives it to him before his birth: "You are to name him Jesus," the angel tells Joseph in a dream, "because he will save his people from their sins" (Matthew 1:21). Jesus's name is both his identity and his mission. Jesus's name is powerful: "Whatever you ask in my name, I will do," he tells his disciples (John 14:13). In the letter to the Philippians, St. Paul sings a hymn to the power of Jesus's name: "God greatly exalted him and bestowed on him the name that is above every name, / that at the name of Jesus every knee should bend, of those in heaven and on earth and under the earth, / and every tongue confess that Jesus Christ is Lord, to the glory of God the Father" (Philippians 2:9–11).

The Lectionary for Mass

◆ First Reading: The central section of today's text pertains to the great love God has bestowed upon us in making us his children (for example, sharing something of his very own life with us). What is more, his will is that his children become as he is. Framing this central section is instruction on how to live and become like him: by being righteous (in right relationship with God) and keeping ourselves pure (unblemished by sin).

◆ Responsorial Psalm 98, a joyful hymn of praise, is used often in Christmas Time as a Responsorial Psalm. Not only have the Jews seen the fulfillment of God's promises, but all nations have seen his glory.

◆ Gospel: John the Baptist introduces Jesus as the Lamb of God. The attribution will be important in John's account where Jesus is crucified at the hour that the Passover lambs are sacrificed for the annual celebration of Israel's redemption from slavery. John further testifies that Jesus is endowed with the Holy Spirit and will baptize those who come to him with this same Holy Spirit. Notice also the reference in the second line of the Gospel to Jesus's preexistence, which was already mentioned in the Prologue of this Gospel account. Finally, in the last line, there is yet another title, another confession of faith: Jesus is the Son of God.

The Roman Missal

If the Christmas Time weekday is celebrated, the texts are found in the Proper of Time at the beginning of the Missal, for Tuesday during the Weekdays of Christmas Time. Be sure you use the proper Collect—two options are given. The one for "Before the Solemnity of the Epiphany" is the one to use. Two options are also given for the choice of the Preface; one of the Prefaces of the Nativity is the correct choice

to make, since that is the choice that is to be made this year as today falls before the Solemnity of the Epiphany.

The orations for the optional memorial are found in the Proper of Saints section, at January 3. All three of the prayers make explicit reference to the name of Jesus. One of the Nativity Prefaces should still be used.

S A T **4** (#207) white
Memorial of St. Elizabeth Ann Seton, Religious (U.S.A.)

The Lectionary for Mass

◆ First Reading: Do we act in righteousness; that is, do our actions and decisions put us in a right relationship with God as the Law and the Gospel teach us? The one who lives in God commits no sin since God's life within that person becomes more fully alive. Note the specific behavior that is mentioned: love for the brother or sister.

◆ Responsorial Psalm 98: Today's verses call upon seas, rivers, and mountains to join the hymn of praise. Note the emphasis on God's righteous judgment.

◆ Gospel: In the first line we hear again, "Behold, the Lamb of God" (John 1:36) as John the Baptist shows his disciples the way to Jesus. They, in turn, become disciples of Jesus. How beautiful are these words: "Come, and you will see" where I live and stay with me (John 1:39). Like John the Baptist, Andrew shows his brother Simon the way to the Messiah, Jesus then gives Simon a new name.

The Roman Missal

All of the prayers are proper for today and are found in the Proper of Saints section at January 4. Although one of the two Prefaces of the Saints could be used, the preferred choice would be to stick with one of the Nativity Prefaces, in order to maintain the sense of Christmas Time.

The prayers for the Mass echo the attributes of St. Elizabeth Ann Seton, as the Collect references the saint's "burning zeal" and asks that we may find God "in daily service with sincere faith." and as the Prayer after Communion asks that "we may be inflamed with a burning desire for the heavenly table, / and by its power consecrate our life faithfully to you."

Today's Saint

Even though Mother Seton was raised in a faithful Episcopalian family, she felt drawn to the Catholic faith. Upon her conversion, which happened after the death of her husband, she wanted to give her life more fully to God and the education of the poor. She was a woman of many firsts: she is the foundress of the first group of women religious in the United States of America (Sisters of Charity); she started the first Catholic school, ultimately laying the foundation for the American parochial system; and she was the first American-born person to be canonized a saint.

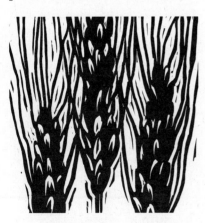

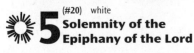
(#20)   white
5 Solemnity of the Epiphany of the Lord

About this Solemnity

The solemnity of the Epiphany of the Lord has several themes. First, we have the wise men being guided through darkness by the light of the star. Second, we have the star as a sign that leads the wise men to Jesus. Third, we have the manifestation of God to Gentiles, not just Jews pointing to the reality that Jesus came for all people. Fourth, we have the mystery that God does reveal his very self in human flesh. Young children relate better to the themes of signs and being a sign of Jesus to others. It is important to keep repeating those themes throughout the year.

The Lectionary for Mass

◆ FIRST READING: It was the shining star that led the three Magi from the east to Jerusalem, thus fulfilling the words of the prophet Isaiah heard in today's First Reading. In Isaiah's day, the shining light signified the dawn of a new period in the nation's history after the exile, a time of rebuilding and resettling the land. Joy abounds—so much that the human heart cannot contain it and the face glows. Jerusalem's glory is visible not only to herself, but to all the nations.

◆ RESPONSORIAL PSALM 72 is a prayer for the king, most fitting on this day when we celebrate the manifestation of the newborn king to those from far off lands who come bearing gifts (see the third stanza). Indeed, they represent the "every nation," the Gentile nations of today's antiphon. Note how the first, second, and fourth stanzas are apt descriptions of Jesus's future ministry.

◆ SECOND READING: Paul has been entrusted with God's grace. He has been given stewardship of this grace as he proclaims the Gospel in the world of his day. The fullness of his message is that Gentiles as well as Jews are offered salvation, coheirs and members of the same family of God.

◆ GOSPEL: It was commonplace in antiquity that a new star signalled the birth of a new ruler. It is this shining light that led the Magi (astrologers or wise men; no mention of them being kings) to seek the newborn king. King Herod, an easily threatened and insecure person, was far from overjoyed at the news and deceitfully tries to ascertain the child's whereabouts, so that he might be killed—as Herod typically did with any would-be contenders to his throne. We meet the theme of joy again when the overjoyed Magi find the child—the same expansive joy as we heard in Isaiah. As was the case with Joseph, a dream instructs the Magi, and the child's life is spared. Note also Matthew's inclusion of a citation from the Old Testament, thus demonstrating the fulfilment of the Scriptures that the child was to be born in Bethlehem.

The Roman Missal

There are two different Masses for this solemnity, one for the Vigil on the day before the solemnity, and one for the Mass during the Day; be sure to use the correct formularies.

At the Vigil Mass

The Entrance Antiphon for the Vigil Mass, coming from Baruch 5:5, not only sets the tone for this celebration, but also uses the words that are the basis for a line in Eucharistic Prayer III: "Arise, Jerusalem and look to the East / and see your children gathered from the rising to the setting of the sun."

The Gloria is sung or said today. The Creed is said or sung.

Light, splendor, brightness, shining, appearance: these are the themes that are conveyed in the three orations for this Mass. The Preface used is the Preface of the Epiphany of the Lord, which is found after the third Preface of the Nativity. There is no mention that the proper form of the *Communicantes* for the Epiphany of the Lord is to be used if Eucharistic Prayer I, the Roman Canon, is prayed. This is because the Vigil Mass is a distinct Mass with its own set of texts and, as it were, its own focus. The proper form of the *Communicantes* for the Epiphany of the Lord only refers to "the most sacred day" whereas the form for the Nativity of the Lord, for example, has the option of using either "night" or "day." Thus, the insert should not be used at the Vigil Mass. Aside from that, there is a certain validity to using Eucharistic Prayer III at this Mass, with echo of Baruch in the line "from the rising of the sun to its setting."

The same principle would apply for *The Announcement of Easter and the Moveable Feasts* (the "Epiphany Proclamation"—see below, At the Mass during the Day). Since no mention is made of it here but it is mentioned at the Mass during the Day, it is something that is envisioned to be done only on the day itself, not at the Vigil.

Be sure to use the Solemn Blessing at the end of Mass, the one for The Epiphany of the Lord (#4).

At the Mass during the Day

The Gloria is sung or said today. The Creed is said or sung.

The famed star of Scripture and of song is mentioned in the Collect, as the prayer asks that just as the star was the guide for the revelation of God's only begotten Son to the nations, so may we too "be brought to behold the beauty of your sublime glory."

A rubric for the Mass during the Day suggests announcing the moveable feasts of the upcoming year. This proclamation can be found as the next-to-last item in Appendix I of the Missal, just before the Nativity Proclamation. It is sung or said from the ambo by a deacon or a cantor immediately after the Gospel. Although optional, this is a wonderful practice to include as

it brings to the forefront the importance that the rhythm of liturgical time should hold in every Catholic's life; it can serve as a springboard for a catechesis on the liturgical year. As the Epiphany is all about the manifestation of the coming of God in the flesh, so too do we acknowledge how the Paschal Mystery is manifested in the various feasts and times throughout our year.

The Prayer over the Offerings makes a beautiful connection between the gifts of gold, frankincense, and myrrh once offered by the Magi and the gifts we offer today at this sacrifice, namely, the gift of "he who by them is proclaimed, / sacrificed and received, Jesus Christ."

The Preface assigned for today is the Preface of the Epiphany of the Lord, which can be found after the Preface III of the Nativity of the Lord.

The Prayer after Communion uses the motif of light to ask that we might better understand and dwell in "the mystery in which you have willed us to participate."

For the Final Blessing, be sure to use the Solemn Blessing for the Epiphany of the Lord (#4).

Pastoral Reflection

Today's Gospel uses the word homage many times and yet it is not a word or concept we use very often in current time. What does "to pay homage" mean to you? To whom would you pay homage and how would you choose to do this? In our lives we each have a guiding light (person, concept, idea, goal) that helps us move forward. Be conscious of what star you have chosen to follow and if it is not worthy of being paid homage to, search diligently for a more affirming star. Another word, "prostrated" is used even less often and is rich in meaning. The wise ones prostrated themselves before Jesus and his parents. Their journey satisfied, they laid

their lives before the Holy One. Kneeling is but one prayer posture to submit ourselves humbly to God.

MON 6 (#212) white
Christmas Weekday

Optional Memorial of St. André Bessette, Religious / white

The Lectionary for Mass

◆ FIRST READING: In this season of celebrating the Lord's coming to earth, John's words to the Christian community echo Jesus's words to his disciples the night before he died, assuring them of his presence with them even after his return to his heavenly Father. Like ourselves, John's community lived in this post-resurrection time. The first part of today's reading, verses 22–24, focuses on: prayer in Jesus's name (v. 22; John 14:13; 16:23); the command to love one another (v. 23, John 13:34; 15:12–17); the importance of remaining in Jesus (v. 24, John 15:4–10); and the gift of the Spirit to believers (v. 24; John 16:13–15). The second part of the reading deals with the necessity of discernment in recognizing whether or not a spirit (or a teacher) is of God. John sets forth specific criteria for discernment. The community would seem to be threatened by the danger of these false teachers. John's words are reassuring, reminding them that they have received the Spirit of truth and they belong to God

◆ RESPONSORIAL PSALM: In its original context, Psalm 2 was about the Davidic king. At this time, it can readily be applied to Jesus, the Messiah. Juxtaposed with today's First Reading, it can be applied to all who believe in the name of Jesus, who have received his Spirit, and belong to God. We are in the world, but we belong to God and must live accordingly.

◆ GOSPEL: At the beginning of his public ministry, Jesus enters fully into the "world," all the while belonging to God and proclaiming the Good News of the kingdom of God. As he will do throughout his Gospel, Matthew cites texts from the Old Testament to demonstrate to his Jewish Christian community that Jesus is the fulfillment of all that was promised of old. Jesus's healing ministry goes hand in hand with his preaching. His light overcomes the darkness enshrouding both body and soul.

The Roman Missal

If the Christmas Time weekday is celebrated, the texts are found in the Proper of Time at the beginning of the Missal, after the Epiphany Mass during the Day, for Monday during the Weekdays of Christmas Time. Be sure you use the proper Collect—the correct one to use is the second one, for "After the Solemnity of the Epiphany." For the Preface, you may use either the Preface of the Epiphany or one of the Prefaces of the Nativity. It might be advantageous to use the Preface of the Epiphany, in order to highlight these last days of Christmas Time. This option will be the same for each Christmas weekday between now and Saturday.

If the optional memorial is celebrated, the proper Collect is to be used, as found in the Proper of Saints, at January 6. The other prayers may be taken from the Common of Holy Men and Women: For Religious, or from the Christmas Time weekday.

Today's Saint

St. André Bessette (1845–1937) modeled his life on that of St. Joseph, to whom he had a great devotion. As a brother of the Congregation of the Holy Cross in Montreal, he was given the post of doorkeeper at Notre Dame College, a post he kept for 40 years. A simple, holy man, André had a special gift of praying over the sick. His prayers were answered, sometimes in miraculous ways, and people began to come to him in large numbers. He gave all the credit to St. Joseph, and he dreamed of a shrine to St. Joseph on Mount Royal. He lived to see the building of the magnificent Oratory of St. Joseph begun. By the time of his death he was receiving some eighty thousand letters per year from people begging for his prayers. When he died, a million people filed in procession past his coffin. Today, the Oratory of St. Joseph at Mount Royal receives two million pilgrims each year. André Bessette was beatified by Pope John Paul II in 1982 and canonized by Pope Benedict XVI on October 17, 2010.

TUE 7 (#213) white
Christmas Weekday

Optional Memorial of St. Raymond Penyafort, Priest

The Lectionary for Mass

◆ FIRST READING: Notice how many times the word "love" occurs in the space of these four verses. God is love; God's love initiated and accomplished the plan of our salvation; God's love lives on in our love for one another.

◆ RESPONSORIAL PSALM 72 is a prayer for the Davidic king, that his reign will be marked by God's justice and peace. It is most appropriate for this liturgical time when we celebrate the birth of the Messiah and his manifestation as the Savior of all people. God's concern for the poor and afflicted is mentioned twice in the verses chosen for today. That concern was given flesh in Jesus, who came and lived among us, giving himself as an offering for sin, that we might live fully in God's love and life. Now it is up to us to live in such a way that his kingdom can be realized among us.

◆ GOSPEL: Today's Gospel recounts one incident when Jesus showed a special concern for those who were "needy" not only physically but in mind and soul, "like sheep without a shepherd." He feeds their hungry minds with his teaching and feeds their bodies with the meager provisions at hand to provide abundantly. Note the Eucharistic overtones in Jesus's blessing, breaking, and distributing the bread.

The Roman Missal

If the optional memorial is celebrated, the Collect is taken from the Memorial of St. Raymond, as found in the Proper of Saints at January 7. The other orations may be taken from the Common of Pastors: For One Pastor, or from the Christmas Time weekday.

Today's Saint

As a Dominican priest and scholar, St. Raymond traveled far and wide to convert non-believers, change the hearts of heretics, and infuse the great universities of Europe with solid theological instruction, resulting in a presence of the Dominicans at the universities of Oxford and Cambridge. Recognized as a visionary leader, St. Raymond was elected third master general of the Dominican order, following in the footsteps of Blessed Jordan of Saxony. His spiritual aptitude and theological literacy reached beyond the walls of the Dominicans to other areas: He served as spiritual director to the pope, Archbishop of Tarragona, and compiler and reviser of Church laws (canon law).

WED 8 (#214) white
Christmas Weekday

The Lectionary for Mass

◆ FIRST READING: The theme of "remaining" in Jesus and in God is prominent in the Johannine literature (see, for example, John 15), and the word "remain" occurs four times in today's text. "Remaining" in Jesus and in God is the mark of discipleship. Today's reading elaborates on what this means. God is love, so if we wish to remain in God, we must remain in love—in God's love for us, in total love for God and faith in Jesus, and in love for one another. We must strive for this love to be brought to perfection, that is, to maturity, in us.

◆ RESPONSORIAL PSALM: Once again we hear echoes of the Epiphany in today's Responsorial psalm (second stanza), which was also the Psalm for that feast. Notice the reference to the rescue of the poor who cry out (third stanza). This is what the disciples do in today's Gospel—they cried out and Jesus rescued them.

◆ GOSPEL: After feeding the multitude, Jesus withdrew into solitude on the mountain for prayer. After praying, he went down to the shore and saw the distress of his disciples who were out on the lake in the midst of the storm. Walking on the sea, he came to their aid. The ability to walk on the sea is an attribute of God in Job 9:8. Jesus's words "It is I" (ego eimi) echoes the divine self-revelation to Moses in Exodus 3:14. Mark is depicting Jesus manifesting his glory for those who have the ability to see and understand.

The Roman Missal

The prayers for today are found in the Proper of Time.

THU 9 (#215) white
Christmas Weekday

The Lectionary for Mass

◆ FIRST READING: John's words are strong. If anyone says he loves God but hates his brother or sister, he is a liar (and that hate can be expressed in actions as well as in words). Simply put, the measure of our love for God is our love for one another. Loving one another is not an option, it is a commandment from God. We are not left to our own abilities in doing this: we have been begotten by God and his grace operates within us. We need only believe.

◆ RESPONSORIAL PSALM 72: Note the reference to fraud and violence in the second stanza. Is this not the hate that Jesus has overcome and that we are to overcome through our love for one another? In mutual love, there is true blessing.

◆ GOSPEL: Jesus returned to Galilee where he had grown up and lived as an adult. Note the reference to his empowerment by the Spirit. Today we see him attending a synagogue service in Nazareth where he reads from the prophet Isaiah. The text is programmatic of what his whole mission would be. Indeed, Isaiah's prophecy was fulfilled in Jesus.

The Roman Missal

Again the prayers are found in the Proper of Time.

FRI 10 (#216) white
Christmas Weekday

The Lectionary for Mass

◆ FIRST READING: Throughout the Johannine writings, there is an inherent tension between the world, or the flesh (understood as anything opposed to Christ and the Spirit), and the way of truth and life inaugurated by Jesus. Thus, we find the word "victor" in the first line of the reading. The thrust of the reading, however, validates Jesus as truly the Christ, the one sent and attested to by God, who gives eternal life to all who believe. Perhaps we are hearing words intended to reassure believers who feel threatened by false teachers, who were a problem in the Johannine community. John's whole purpose in writing was to remind them that those who believe in Jesus have eternal life—now.

◆ RESPONSORIAL PSALM 147: The reference to God's Word in the second and third stanzas echoes the theme of the "testimony of God" (1 John 5:9) heard in the First Reading. How privileged are God's people for the revelation they have received.

◆ GOSPEL: Lepers were outcasts in society, as they still are in many places in our world today. Jesus healing brought about not only a physical cure, but a restoration to human community. Note the reference to the man falling "prostrate" before Jesus in adoration and supplication.

The Roman Missal

The location of the texts for this Mass, the correct Collect to use, and the suggested Preface to choose all follow what is described in the previous two days.

SAT 11 (#217) white
Christmas Weekday

The Lectionary for Mass

◆ FIRST READING: Today's text reiterates the themes of belonging to God, prayer, discernment, and truth. Note also today the mention of prayer for a brother or sister whom we see sinning. The reading ends with a warning about idols. Asking ourselves if we have any idols is always worthwhile. What do we worship, or idolize in our thoughts and actions, with our time, money, and energy?

◆ RESPONSORIAL PSALM 149: Today's psalm is hymn of praise sung by the children of Jerusalem (Zion), the children of God. God delights in them! It's as if God says to each one of us: "You are mine. I take delight in you."

◆ GOSPEL: Today's Gospel contains the only reference to Jesus baptizing, a claim later refuted in John 4:2. It is a non-issue for John the Baptist. He gladly defers to the presence and the ministry of the Christ whose way he prepared. In Christ's presence, John's joy has been made complete.

The Roman Missal

The prayers for this Mass are in the Proper of Time. The Preface of the Epiphany would still be a preferred choice.

(#21)   white

12 Feast of the Baptism of the Lord

About this Feast

The Feast of the Baptism of the Lord proclaims a theophany, a revelation or manifestation of the divine Sonship of Jesus by his anointing and appointing to his messianic office. It is the feast that proclaims the Baptism that elevates believers to the status of sons and daughters of God.

The Lectionary for Mass

◆ FIRST READING: Today's reading from Isaiah focuses on the Lord's chosen servant, endowed with his Spirit that he might accomplish his prophetic mission through word and deed. Note the mildness of the Servant's manner: he is gentle healer and proclaimer of God's salvation. His presence is awaited by all the peoples of the earth.

◆ RESPONSORIAL PSALM 29: In its origins, this psalm was a Canaanite hymn to Baal the storm god (notice the reference to thunder in the third stanza). It was adapted by the Israelites to acclaim God's power over all creation—in particular the waters that come down from heaven and cover the earth.

◆ SECOND READING: We hear Peter's speech in the house of the Gentile Cornelius. The story in its entirety in Acts of the Apostles 10 merits reading. Peter's words are a summary of the Gospel account of the words and deeds of Jesus. Note also how the description of Jesus's ministry echoes Isaiah's description of God's servant.

◆ GOSPEL: Jesus comes to the one who prepared his way, seeking to receive his baptism, a sign not of sinfulness but of righteousness, his right relationship with God and total commitment to his kingdom. Here at the beginning of his ministry, we see God's Spirit descending upon him and hear the voice of the Father affirming his beloved, with whom he is pleased.

The Roman Missal

Consider the Rite for the Blessing and Sprinkling of Water. Sing or say the Gloria and the Creed.

There are two options for the Collect. The first prayer asks that we, as children by adoption, may always be "well pleasing" to God.

The second prayer asks that just as Christ is recognized outwardly like us, so too may we be inwardly transformed to be like him. The Prayer over the Offerings also speaks of transformation, asking that "the oblation of your faithful / may be transformed into the sacrifice of him" who willed "to wash away the sins of the world" (an illusion to blood/water imagery).

The Preface is given right there along with the other Mass formularies for the day as it recapitulates not only scriptural references to the baptism of the Lord, but also the meaning of that baptism in understanding who Christ is as the Servant who "has been anointed with the oil of gladness / and sent to bring the good news to the poor."

The Prayer after Communion reminds us that, having been nourished with the sacred gifts, we must be God's children "in name and in truth" by "faithfully listening to your Only Begotten Son."

Pastoral Reflection

The human psyche is similar for all people, even if we don't want to believe in our shared reality. We all desire approval and need love from our parent(s). Today's Gospel speaks of the most beautiful relationship that is desired in our hearts. If you are a parent, be this same kind of bold, embracing, and affirming parent to your child. Purposely seek out opportunities (or times) to tell your child that you are well pleased with them. If you never received this kind of attention from your parent(s), living or deceased, name all the gifts and traits they gave to you to be this blessed creation of God's. You are loved deeply and God is well pleased. Are you well pleased with yourself? Focus on the innate gifts you have been given as a chosen child of God.

ORDINARY TIME (DURING WINTER)

The Meaning / The Lectionary for Mass

On Christmas, we celebrated the dawning of the Light to those who dwelt in darkness. The light of a star guided the Magi to Bethlehem to see the newborn king—the first time that the light of Christ was revealed to the Gentiles. And right in the middle of this period of Ordinary Time this year, on the fourth Sunday, we celebrate the Feast of the Presentation of the Lord. Forty days after his birth, the child Jesus was brought to the Temple in Jerusalem in accord with the law of Moses. It was here that Simeon, a just and righteous man inspired by God's Holy Spirit, recognizes him as the Anointed of the Lord, a light of revelation to the Gentiles, and the glory of Israel.

Christmas Time ends with the Feast of the Baptism of the Lord, a feast that also marks the beginning of the "ordinary" days of Jesus's ministry—extraordinary as they were, marked by his powerful words and deeds. Fittingly, both John the Baptist and Jesus share the focus of the Gospel for the Second Sunday in Ordinary Time.

John's mission of preparing the way for Jesus continued after the baptism, gradually fading away to give way to the one who was the true Light of the World (see John 1:7–9). On the third Sunday, we hear from the beginning of Matthew's account of Jesus's public ministry. Note how Matthew sees the presence and ministry of Jesus to be the great light spoken of by the prophet Isaiah. On the fifth Sunday, Jesus teaches his disciples of every time and place that we are now the light of the world, burning with his light, of course. On the sixth and seventh Sundays, we hear something of what we must be and do in order to burn with that light.

What a difference it makes in our lives, when we experience the light that is of Christ and it begins to burn within us. Nowhere is this more evident than in the life of St. Paul, whose "conversion" we celebrate on January 25. "Conversion," yes—but not from "non-religious" to "religious;" rather, his was a conversion from a zealous Jew who did not believe that Jesus was the Messiah to a man who would stop at nothing in proclaiming that Jesus was not only Messiah, but Lord and God whose light transforms us (see 2 Corinthians 3:18).

Our daily readings from Mark's account of the Gospel take us from the beginning of Jesus's public ministry to the middle of his journey to Jerusalem before his Death—a fitting place to stop as we begin our Lenten journey. In these first ten chapters we see the almost magnetic attraction Jesus has for the people. He is literally swarmed by crowds that desire to listen to his word, to touch and be touched by his healing power. We also witness Jesus in major—and victorious—confrontation with the powers of evil.

But life is far from easy for him. The people of his hometown cannot accept him as a prophet. After all, they know his family. They watched him grow up and learn his father's carpenter trade. Some of his relatives, observing his growing popularity and his tirelessness in teaching and healing, think that he is out of his mind. There is constant controversy and criticism from the religious leaders of his people. His disciples, whom we no doubt look on as privileged people, struggle to know exactly who Jesus is and what all that he does really means. Jesus even calls them faithless and takes them to task for it. They are also keenly interested in what they will get in return for following him (see the Gospel for the Tuesday before Ash Wednesday).

Jesus encountered many difficulties in ordinary life and how much we can identify with him in these. There is much to learn as well from the way Jesus handled these hard times.

On the weekdays of the first five weeks, our First Readings tell the story of the establishment of the monarchy in Israel, beginning with the birth of Samuel, the prophet who was instrumental in its beginning and who anointed both Saul and David as king. We hear of God's promise of an everlasting dynasty to David and of the succession of his son Solomon who built the Temple in Jerusalem. Throughout all these events, there are the everyday human struggles; there are words and deeds that are good and virtuous, as well as choices that are sinful. There are calls to conversion and numerous manifestations of the fidelity and mercy of God. These stories, these personalities have much to reveal about our own lives.

In the sixth and seventh weeks, we read from the letter of James, whose words likewise focus on behaviors and choices in our everyday lives. On Monday and Tuesday of the eighth week, we read from the beginning of the first letter of Peter. All of these texts serve as a perfect lead-in to the conversion to which we are called in Lent: a more committed following of Christ's teaching and imitation of his life, as we not only shine more brightly as the light of the world, but are more and more aflame with the unfading glory of the inheritance that will one day be ours (see the first reading from 1 Peter for Monday of the eighth week).

The Roman Missal

THIS first segment of Ordinary Time begins on Monday, January 13, with the First Week in Ordinary Time and continues until Tuesday, March 4, inclusive; Ash Wednesday is March 5. One Ordinary Time Sunday is replaced by the Feast of the Presentation of the Lord. As a Feast of the Lord, this day has a higher rank than a Sunday in Ordinary Time, and therefore is celebrated on Sunday, February 2 in place of the Sunday.

The Mass formularies for this segment of Ordinary Time are found in the "Ordinary Time" section that follows the "Easter Time" section in the Missal. Each Sunday has its own proper Collect, Prayer over the Offerings, and Prayer after Communion, as well as Entrance and Communion Antiphons. There are no formularies for ferial weekdays. Customarily, priests will repeat the

prayers from the previous Sunday, although there is no hard-and-fast rule about this; in fact, orations from any Sunday in Ordinary Time may be used on any ferial weekday (see *The General Instruction of the Roman Missal* [GIRM], 363). Note that there are no formularies for the "First Sunday in Ordinary Time," since the Sunday that begins the First Week in Ordinary Time is always either the Feast of the Baptism of the Lord or the Solemnity of the Epiphany of the Lord (in some years, Feast of the Baptism of the Lord is celebrated on the Monday after Epiphany); thus, orations used for weekday Masses during the First Week in Ordinary Time should come from the page titled accordingly.

In addition, Masses for Various Needs and Occasions and Votive Masses may also be chosen, although these should be used in moderation (see GIRM, 369). Unless expressly indicated to the contrary, the weekday readings and the chants between them may continue to be used with Masses for Various Needs and Occasions and Votive Masses, thus allowing the continuous flow of the Lectionary selections to be observed. Of course, use of the orations for Masses for Various Needs and Occasions provides an excellent opportunity to use one of the four forms of the Eucharistic Prayer for Various Needs; the Missal provides guidelines to match one of the four forms of the Eucharistic Prayer with a corresponding Mass formulary. Also, don't forget the traditional Saturday commemoration of the Blessed Virgin Mary may be observed during Ordinary Time.

If particular texts were used for Advent and Christmas Time, it would be a good idea for communities to use other options. For example, it might be good to use the simpler greeting of "The Lord be with you," especially on weekdays. Also, Ordinary Time might be a good opportunity to use a wider selection of invocations for the Penitential Act. Appendix VI gives a variety of sample invocations, and originally-composed ones might also be used. Perhaps the Confiteor ("I confess to almighty God . . . ") might consistently be used, although this might also be better left for Sundays in Lent given its explicit references to admission of sin. Additionally, perhaps the less-widely-known, "Have mercy on us, O Lord. / For we have sinned against you. / Show us, O Lord, your mercy. / And grant us your salvation," might be used, with advanced notice given to the assembly so everyone can be prepared. If this form is used, remember that the *Kyrie, eleison* (Lord, have mercy) still needs to be said after it since those particular invocations were not used.

For Sundays, there are eight Prefaces to choose from, and they begin after Preface II of the Ascension of the Lord. Any Preface may be used on any Sunday, so the priest should select a Preface based on how well its theme connects with or otherwise echoes the readings and his Homily. Preface I focuses on the Paschal Mystery and the People of God, as it describes how, having been freed "from the yoke of sin and death," we have been summoned "to the glory of now being called / a chosen race, a royal priesthood, / a holy nation" and a people whose purpose is "to proclaim everywhere your mighty works." Preface II deals, in a general way, with the mystery of salvation as it recounts the Incarnation, Passion, and Resurrection. Preface III, subtitled "The salvation of man by a man," speaks of how, in becoming human, the "cause of our downfall" became "the means of our salvation." Preface IV rehearses the history of salvation by calling to mind Christ's birth, suffering, Resurrection, and Ascension, and how each of those mysteries brings salvation to us. Preface V takes a wider focus as it deals with creation itself, recalling God's creation of the world, his arranging of times and season, and of his forming man in his own image to rule over creation, and to praise him. Preface VI, "The pledge of the eternal Passover," explicitly mentions the Paschal Mystery and our share in it, as eternal life is pledged to us even now, through our having received the firstfruits of the Spirit. Preface VII highlights the obedience of Christ that restored those gifts that had been lost through humanity's sinful disobedience. Preface VIII of Sundays has an ecclesiological theme as it emphasizes the people gathered together "through the Blood of your Son and the power of the Spirit" to be made into "the body of Christ and the temple of the Holy Spirit."

Although the orations from the previous Sunday may be used during the week in Ordinary Time, the Sunday Prefaces are not; on Ordinary Time weekdays, one of six Common Prefaces is to be used. These Prefaces do not immediately follow the Sunday ones; instead, they are found a little further on in the Missal, following those for the Most Holy Eucharist and for the various categories of saints. As with the Sunday Prefaces, the Common Prefaces may also be selected by theme, as they connect with the readings of the day and with the Homily. Common Preface I speaks of the renewal of all things in Christ achieved through his self-emptying. Common Preface II tells of how humankind has been created through the goodness of God and redeemed through the mercy of God. The creation of the human race is mentioned again in Common Preface III, but this time in connection with the human race being created anew and, because of that, the rightness of serving God. Common Preface IV relates how our praise of God is itself a gift from him, and how our thanksgiving to God aids us in salvation. Common Preface V proclaims the mystery of Christ in terms of his Death, Resurrection, his coming again in glory. Common Preface VI is actually the proper Preface for Eucharistic Prayer II, and it too proclaims the mystery of Christ, this time by recounting how Christ is the "Word through whom you made all things," the one who, incarnate by the Holy Spirit and born of the Virgin, was sent as Savior and Redeemer, and who, when he "stretched out his hands as he endured the Passion," not only broke the bonds of death and manifested the Resurrection, but also won a holy people.

If the priest wishes to use a Solemn Blessing at the end of Mass, there are six options provided, and any one may be chosen at his discretion. It might be preferable use a Solemn Blessing only on Sundays, so as to draw a distinction between weekdays and Sundays, allowing the weekdays to be simpler than Sundays.

In addition to the aforementioned Feast of the Presentation of the Lord on February 2, the only other days to take particular note of outside of the usual memorials are the Day of Prayer for the Legal Protection of Unborn Children on Wednesday, January 22, the Feast of the Conversion of St. Paul the Apostle on Saturday, January 25, and the Feast of the Chair of St. Peter the Apostle on February 22. More specific information about each of those days can be found in the "Calendar" section a little later in this book.

Children's Liturgy of the Word

LIVE music led by trained music ministers is ideal. Although it is not always possible to have a parish musician or song leader available for the celebration of the Liturgy of the Word with children, it is worthwhile to consult your parish liturgy or music director about this option. He or she might be able to suggest someone who would be willing to be the music minister. If there is no option for live accompaniment or a trained cantor to lead your group, do your best to facilitate an atmosphere of joyful song on your own. You might bring in musical instruments such as chimes or bells that the children can use as you sing. If the children are too young to learn entire songs, you might sing with them by using a "call and response" method, singing one line to them and then inviting them to sing it back to you. Or, if no one is available you can use a recording as accompaniment.

The Saints

THIS season does not highlight a particular aspect of salvation history or event in the life of Christ, rather we celebrate the universal call to holiness and our vocation to offer thanksgiving and praise to God for all the myriad ways that God gathers us and saves us. This can be particularly seen in the three feasts of this season.

First, in celebration of the Conversion of St. Paul, the Apostle (January 25), we remember the ministry of the father of missionaries, St. Paul of Tarsus, Apostle of the Gentiles. St. Paul was truly instrumental in gathering thousands "from the nations" into the community of believers. His writings continue today to gather billions into the flock of Christ. On this day, it would be quite appropriate to highlight how Christianity has spread throughout the world and point out the incredibly international character of the Church.

The second feast, the Presentation of the Lord (February 2), commemorates the act by which the Blessed Virgin Mary and St. Joseph fulfilled the law by bringing the child Jesus to the Temple. It was there that Simeon and Anna both testified that this child was the Messiah, the Light of the Nations. A time-honored way to celebrate this day is with the blessing of candles for use throughout the year in church and at home and a procession with candles. The blessed candles should remind us that we too are meant to be lights for our world and the procession speaks to our call to carry our light beyond the everyday boundaries of our lives—to push and stretch ourselves beyond the comfortable.

The third feast is the Chair of St. Peter the Apostle (February 22). Here we celebrate the leadership role of St. Peter. The chair is a symbol of leadership, teaching authority, and service of a bishop. Considered the first bishop of Rome, St. Peter exemplifies for us the servant leadership we as Christians are called to exercise in our ministry of the baptized. We must lead others by example to give thanks and praise to God by our service to others. Today would be a great day to bring schoolchildren to the local cathedral and point out the *cathedra*, or "chair" symbolizing the bishop's leadership role in the diocese.

This year, Ordinary Time (during Winter) includes nine obligatory memorials and eleven optional memorials. Each of these holy people took responsibility for announcing the whole message of the Gospel and living out the message of salvation. Several of these heroes of the faith are remembered as martyrs, those who gave up life rather than deny their beliefs and live inauthentic lives. Those who gave God glory by giving up their lives are St. Agnes, St. Agatha, St. Paul Miki and Companions, St. Fabian, St. Sebastian, St. Vincent, and St. Blaise. While numerous legends abound concerning the earliest martyrs, these are fine opportunities to explain the notion of patron saints, to teach the concept of the intercession of the saints, and to promote healthy appreciation of devotions and customs that are associated with various cultures and ethnicities (for example, the French honor St. Vincent as the patron of vintners perhaps because his name contains the French word for *wine*—"vin," and he is celebrated on the traditional day for the beginning of planting grape vines). A popular devotion that crosses cultural divides is the blessing of throats on the optional Memorial of St. Blaise derived from the legend that this holy bishop saved a boy from choking on a fish bone. These devotions are part of our Catholic heritage and should be nurtured, explained, and developed within the context of the Gospel message and Tradition of our faith.

There are four Doctors of the Church (those saints given the title by the pope because of their holiness, the orthodoxy of their thought, and the usefulness of their writings to the faithful) whom we commemorate during this liturgical time: St. Hilary, who defended the early Church against false teachings; St. Francis de Sales, whose writings explained how the spiritual life was accessible to all the faithful; St. Thomas Aquinas, whose teachings helped explain many doctrines of the Church;

and St. Peter Damian, who worked tirelessly to reform the clergy and monasteries. These holy men and women, along with founders of religious congregations, teachers, priests, and missionaries, all led lives aimed at living out the Christian vocation to offer thanksgiving and praise to God in all the actions and words of their lives. This, too, is our call. Our God has gathered from among the nations many models and companions along the way in the saints celebrated during this liturgical time.

The Liturgy of the Hours

MUSICAL resources abound for implementing the celebration of the Hours. Consider any of these resources, which together offer a plethora of diverse musical settings of psalms, hymns, canticles, antiphons, and other texts of the Hours. These include: "Praise God in Song" (various), "Light and Peace" (Haas), and "Holden Evening Prayer" (Haugen) from GIA publications. "Lord, Open My Lips" (Consiglio) and "O Joyful Light" (Joncas), are from Oregon Catholic Press, Portland Oregon (ocp.org). "God of Light be Praised" (various) and "Jesus When the Sun Goes Down" (Janco) from World Library Publications. "Pray Without Ceasing" (Various) from Liturgical Press and the "Mundelein Psalter," from Liturgy Training Publications. These resources are invaluable when introducing the Hours with full musical options.

These weeks of Ordinary Time are found in Volume III of the *Liturgy of the Hours*. If you are just beginning to celebrate the Hours, read the *General Instruction of the Liturgy of the Hours* found in the beginning of Volume I, the Advent and Christmas Season (it is also found in *The Liturgy Documents, Volume II: Essential Documents for Parish Sacramental Rites and Other Liturgies* [LTP]). Secondly, look at the "Ordinary," which begins on page 649 in Volume II: Ordinary Time, Weeks 1–17. Here you will find the basic outline for the Hours. Each part of a typical celebration of the Hours contains an invitatory, hymnody, psalmody, readings, responsories, Gospel canticles, intercessions, Lord's Prayer, and dismissal. The book will guide you through the structure and provides the *rubrics* (the Latin word for "red") and the text of the celebration. Once you are familiar with this basic structure you can set the ribbons in the book as you move through the four-week cycle of psalmody and the texts for the days' celebration. The other ribbons can be set to the texts for the day or the liturgical time.

A relatively new observance in the liturgical calendar is the day set aside as the Day of Prayer for the Legal Protection of Unborn Children (January 22). This would be a most appropriate day to celebrate Evening Prayer in the community. Consider inviting other parishes from your deanery or vicariate as well as other Christian ecclesial communities to gather with you to pray for the dignity of each human person. Encourage parishioners to bring diapers, formula, clothes, blankets, bottles, baby food, and cereal and donate them to a shelter for battered and abused women and children.

The Feast of the Presentation of the Lord falls on a Sunday in 2014. Again, here is an opportunity to celebrate Evening Prayer in the parish. Consider adding an extended *Lucernarium* (Service of Light) to the celebration and bless the candles to be used in the parish for the next year as well as candles to be used in the domestic Church.

The Rite of Christian Initiation of Adults

PASTORAL musicians are charged to discover ritual music that can be sung robustly by the gathered faith community, so both they and those coming for the Easter sacraments know that the community is standing together with them in their journey. Primary to the celebrations of the Sacraments of Initiation are sung acclamations and psalmody. Acclamations have been described as shouts of joy arising from the midst of the assembly or "assents to God's word and action" (STL, 115a). The psalms foster "meditation on the word of God," (GIRM, 61), and aid the Church in entering into the signs and actions of the rites. When the assembly robustly sings the acclamations and psalms during the ritual, we are not only responding to God's Word, but we are affirming the ritual action that has just taken place. This affirmation is our assent to the active transforming work of the Holy Spirit in our lives and in the lives of those who are seeking the Easter sacraments.

It is hoped that both catechumens and members of the elect are dismissed from the Sunday Eucharist each week. Of all the acclamations, psalms, litanies, and songs used for the RCIA, the dismissal acclamation/song is one of the most important pieces to sing. Since ritual music invites the community to encounter the ritual action, find one acclamation to use at the dismissal year after year. This should be done especially when the dismissals are from various liturgies in a parish from week to week. Even when the musical leadership of multiple Masses in the parish is done in various styles (contemporary, traditional, bilingual), and by different pastoral musicians, find one acclamation that will work for all Masses and stick to it. A few pastoral musicians will find this to be a challenge, but remember, musicians are present to help facilitate the prayer of the gathered Church. This gathered Church includes both catechumens and elect, and if they hear a different acclamation from week to week, the dismissal may seem disjointed and unfamiliar. Both the assembly and those journeying toward the Easter sacraments need to be able to identify with a common acclamation for this ritual moment.

The RCIA employs a great deal of conversation, and the pastoral musicians of the community are called to enter into this conversation, with candidates, the elect, and members of the RCIA team and catechists for the rites to be celebrated fully and robustly as we stand together in Christ.

The following three resources are a must for pastoral musicians and RCIA teams: "Chosen in Christ Elegídos en Crísto: Music for Christian Initiation/Música para la Iniciación Cristiana," edited by Jerry Galipeau, WLP; "Christ We Proclaim: A Music and Liturgy Resource for the Rites of Christian Initiation," edited by Christopher Walker, OCP; and "Who Calls You By Name: Music for Christian Initiation, Volumes I and II," composed by David Haas, GIA.

—Adapted from an article
by Michael R. Prendergast © LTP, 2009.

The Sacraments of Initiation

IN northern climates, this point in the year can be cold, dark, and pretty bleak. Candles or a blazing fire provide a glow that warms the heart and spirit. In the Rite of Baptism, a candle is lit from the Paschal candle. The liturgical symbol is light. This symbol is brought to life through the ritual gesture of passing that light from one to another. This is used in the Rite of Baptism; following the blessing of the fire at the Easter Vigil; and on the feast of the Presentation of the Lord (sometimes referred to as Candlemas Day) as we process with lighted candles recognizing Christ present in our midst. In Baptism the light of faith is passed from the godparents to the newly baptized while the priest celebrant prays:

> You have been enlightened by Christ.
> Walk always as children of the light
> and keep the flame of faith alive in your hearts.
> When the Lord comes, may you go out to meet him
> with all the saints in the heavenly kingdom.

Breaking open this symbol and gesture with those preparing for Baptism, Confirmation, and first Holy Communion can be a powerful and meaningful experience.

For the celebration of the Presentation of the Lord, (February 2) invite the candidates to brainstorm the kinds of light (both positive and negative) we experience daily such as: sunlight, electric lights, headlights on a vehicle, reflectors on a bike, fire, candles on a birthday cake, and so on. Have fun with this and elicit creative responses.

Have participants name any references to light they can think of from the Scriptures. (It is a good idea for the facilitator to have several prepared ahead of time to help get the conversation started.) Summarize with a discussion focusing on their responses. Use the following questions as conversation starters: Why is light so important in our lives? When can light be destructive? How do we waste light? When does light bring us joy? Light is a symbol for faith—what does light say about faith? Why is faith so important in our lives? When can our faith be destructive? How is faith joyful? Point out that we never know the impact our words and actions may have on another. This is what it means to "pass the light" of God's love to others.

Another special day to consider during this time is the optional Memorial of St. Blaise (February 3). On this memorial, two unlit candles are used to bless throats, seeking immunity or healing for all diseases of the throat. This ritual also provides a wonderful springboard for reflection and discussion on how we use our voices. We can choose to be loud, soft, harsh, loving, or gentle. We raise our voices to speak out against injustice, as well as in joyful praise.

Take time to show them the candles to be used in the blessing of throats. All of us remember what it is like to have a cold, sore throat, or cough and that even though medicine helps to make us better, we can ask God to make us better as well. This may also be a time to celebrate a ritual of anointing within a celebration of the Word. Prepare ahead, so a priest or deacon will be available to do the anointing. Use one of the minor Rites of Anointing from the RCIA.

The Rite of Penance

PERHAPS to honor the Week of Prayer for Christian Unity, the parish could schedule one of the non-sacramental penitential celebrations (Appendix II, section III) where the naming of the sins against the unity of Christians could be voiced and the celebration could include prayers for a greater understanding between Christians, Jew, Muslims, and other people of good will. Consider including reading sections from the Second Vatican Council's "Decree on Ecumenism" (*Unitatis Redintegratio*) and the "Declaration on the Relation of the Church to Non-Christian Religions" (*Nostra Aetate*). Take your lead from Pope John Paul II, who on behalf of the Church, asked forgiveness for sins committed against Jews, heretics, women, Gypsies, and native peoples on March 12, 2000.

On January 23 the Church sets aside a day observing a time of Prayer for the Legal Protection of Unborn Children in the United States. Consider celebrating one of the non-sacramental penitential celebrations found in Appendix II, section III of the *Rite of Penance*. Invite people to bring diapers, formula, clothes, blankets, bottles, baby food and cereal to be shared with women who may be considering terminating their pregnancy.

The Pastoral Care of the Sick

ILLNESS in winter can make it difficult for the sick and elderly to get to Mass so keep in touch with those who may be absent from the Sunday assembly. When Ritual Masses for the Anointing of the Sick are held, consider the need for adequate transportation including transport of people in wheelchairs. Arrange for the people to sit in every other pew or row of chairs and leave enough room around those in wheelchairs so that the priest(s) can move freely throughout the assembly. Encourage the priest(s) to be generous with the oil; then have a number of other ministers follow each priest, inviting them to continue massaging the oil into the persons head and hands. Invite those from your community who work in health care and the healing arts to assist in this role.

The optional Memorial of St. Blaise is a fitting day to celebrate the Anointing of the Sick. Likewise, February 11, the optional Memorial of Our Lady of Lourdes, would be another appropriate day to celebrate the sacrament. Be sure to include the singing of the beloved LOURDES HYMN "Immaculate Mary" in the day's celebration and locate a hymnal that contains all seven verses.

The Rite of Marriage

THE Rite of Marriage may be celebrated at the Vigil Mass of Sunday. This is becoming very popular in many places. We find several reasons to support this phenomena: a) sacraments are celebrations of the whole community therefore celebrating the rite in the context of the wider community supports this teaching of the Church; b) in communities where several Marriages occur in a given year and where both priests and deacons may already have a very full Mass schedule for a given weekend, they may be restricted from adding additional Masses to the weekend calendar; and finally c) in locales where a priest serves several faith communities and must often travel great distances, the Rite of Marriage is often celebrated at the Vigil Mass of Sunday or even on a Sunday since the priest may have to move on in a timely manner to serve the next community entrusted to his pastoral care. Yes, the celebration of Marriage at the Vigil Mass of Sunday fulfills the obligation to participate in the Mass. Consider the announcement of banns in the parish bulletin and website and encourage the whole parish to pray for those couples preparing to celebrate the sacrament.

Consider using the blessing for engaged couples from the *Book of Blessings* (Chapter VI) several times throughout the year. Alert couples that you are doing this and encourage their attendance and participation at the Sunday celebration of the

Eucharist. Include the names of those preparing to celebrate the sacrament in the Universal Prayer (Prayer of the Faithful). The Rite of Marriage may be celebrated on the Feasts of the Baptism of the Lord (January 12, 2014) and the Presentation of the Lord, (February 2, 2014).

Consider preparing wedding guidelines that are pastorally sensitive, thorough, and welcoming. Share these guidelines with the couple early in the process so they have a clear understanding of both the expectations of the universal Church, the local Church (the archdiocese), and the parish. A parish wedding coordinator or a wedding team should work with couples. Consider training sponsor couples to journey with those preparing to celebrate the sacrament. Music ministers and those who assist the couple with preparing the wedding liturgy should meet with the couple as early in the process as possible. Prepare a set of FAQs that can be given to the couple early on. One of the first questions couples ask is "how much does it cost to get married in this church?" Consider providing the couple with one suggested fee allowing for one check to be given to the church. This can alleviate issues that sometime arise over stipends, gifts, or donations. With one check, written to the parish, it can later be divided up to cover the expenses of the use of the parish facility, a stipend for the priest or deacon, the wedding coordinator, and the musicians.

The Order of Christian Funerals

THE Vigil (see OCF, 54–81) is the time when the community keeps watch with the family in prayer. This is the first major ritual moment in the funeral process. The Vigil is the moment when the assembly offers its first formal act of consolation to the bereaved by focusing the story of the deceased, in a faith dimension, and by joining that story with the story of the Church.

Vigils can be celebrated in the home, the funeral home, or the church. The church is the preferred setting for the Vigil. The time of the Vigil is rather flexible; however, it must be celebrated at a time not attached to the time of the funeral liturgy. The choice of the presiding minister is not limited to an ordained minister so a priest, deacon, or lay leader of prayer can lead the Vigil for the deceased. There are two major parts to the Vigil: 1) the Liturgy of the Word which includes First Reading, Responsorial Psalm, Gospel, Homily, and/or reflection and sharing; and 2) the prayers of intercession, which include the litany, Lord's Prayer, and concluding prayer followed by reflection and sharing. The minor parts are the Introductory Rite, which include the greeting, song, invitation to prayer, Collect; and the Concluding Rite, which include a blessing and an optional closing song. Consider extending the Vigil in private for several hours—perhaps to midnight—or even through the night. This practice is gaining popularity in many places.

The Vigil may also be celebrated within the context of the Office of the Dead, Morning, or Evening Prayer (see OCF, 348–395). These official liturgical prayers may be celebrated in the presence of the body in the church, the home, or the funeral home.

Families will need assistance in preparing the liturgies and choosing appropriate Scripture and music selections, and help with preparing the Universal Prayer (see OCF, 401). The Funeral Mass may be celebrated in the evening; this can be seen as a pastorally sensitive accommodation so that more family and friends of the deceased may participate, especially those in situations where bereavement leave is not provided by an employer. If the body is housed in the church overnight, security and insurance should be put into place.

In places where the ground is still frozen, the Rite of Committal may need to be delayed until after the ground is thawed.

The Book of Blessings

THE blessings found in part VI, Blessings for Various Needs and Occasions, are intended for those who carry out a particular ministry in the parish: those who exercise pastoral service, lectors and readers, altar servers, sacristans, musicians, ushers, extraordinary ministers of Holy Communion, parish pastoral council members, officers of parish societies, new and departing parishioners, those receiving ecclesiastical honors, and those being inaugurated as public officials. These blessings serve to recognize the importance of liturgical and pastoral service to the parish and

to parish organizations. These blessings are appropriate to use at any time of the year. The Order for the Blessing of Students and Teachers (Chapter 5) would be appropriate for use during Catholic Schools Week, January 26–February 1, 2014. The Order for the Blessing of Articles for Liturgical Use (Chapter 39) could be used to bless candles on the Feast of the Presentation. The Order for the Blessing of Throats on the Feast of St. Blaise on February 3 is found in Chapter 51 (an optional memorial in the dioceses of the United States).

The Liturgical Environment

THOSE who work in the Church often need a quick chance during this time to catch a breath from the stresses of Christmas Time and to relax before the busy days of Lent. There is something right about this, and there is no need that the environment become a source of stress. It might be wise to cut back on many things, including plants in the sanctuary. Use potted plants that you already have. The natural environment is also catching its breath at this point of the year, patiently waiting for the beginnings of spring; for now, things are resting.

Of course, even providing a quiet liturgical environment requires some forethought and work. When Christmas Time ends with the Feast of the Baptism of the Lord, it should end in the space also. The distinctive plants and environment of Christmas Time should not be left in the space for Ordinary Time. The crèche needs to be removed, poinsettias should be adopted out to good homes, and the Christmas greenery should be removed. If you used real trees and garland and your local fire ordinances will allow it, you can celebrate the end of the Christmas Time in a very traditional way by hosting a bonfire. Such fires were annual occurrences around Epiphany in many European communities, and further play up the light imagery of the season. This can also be a fitting way to encourage the celebration of the entire Christmas season. If you do something like this, proper preparation in clearing space and having a plan to control and extinguish the fire is an absolute necessity.

As the liturgical space is changed back from white to green, the color used might reflect the darker greens of the evergreens that are the only natural color in much of the northern hemisphere at this time of year. Attending to the Lectionary and to the proper prayers may suggest particular aspects of the environment that can be highlighted in the worship space, although such changes should not detract from the central place of the Word and the Eucharist.

Particular observances that take place within Ordinary Time (during Winter), such as the Feast of the Presentation of the Lord (February 2), and St. Blaise (February 3), should receive some special additions to the space, appropriate to their solemnity. The Feast of the Presentation is historically celebrated with the blessing of candles to be used in the coming year. Different kinds of candles can make a beautiful addition to the liturgical environment. If the blessing of throats is to be celebrated, candles will need to be prepared for this rite as well, and they can be included in the candles prepared for blessing the day before.

The Liturgical Music

AFTER all the excitement of Christmas, you may welcome simplifying the liturgies a little bit. In the Church, this concept is known as progressive solemnity. *Sing to the Lord* 110-112 states, "Progressive solemnity means that 'between the solemn, fuller form of liturgical celebration, in which everything that demands singing is in fact sung, and the simplest form, in which singing is not used, there can be various degrees according to the greater or lesser place allotted to singing.'"

Continue to sing the Gloria. One might consider using a different Mass setting for the season, of course that may depend on how you are rebuilding your Mass repertoire since the changes in *The Roman Missal*. Those are pastoral decisions you'll need to make depending on where your community is.

Music suggestions for Ordinary Time are provided on www.LTP.org/resources. Visit this site for your free PDF.

Liturgical Ministers

THIS is a good time of year to provide training for liturgical ministers and to tighten up liturgies before Lent. In 2014 you will find eight Sundays in Ordinary Time (during Winter). Invite the homilists and preachers in your community to reflect on the texts of the liturgy, the various parts of the Mass, and how the different liturgical ministries support the full, conscious, and active participation of the gathered Church.

On the Second Sunday in Ordinary Time (January 19, 2014), reflect on the baptismal call to ministry and the presence of Christ in the gathered Church; on the Third Sunday in Ordinary Time (January 26, 2014), reflect on the ministry of the bishop, priest, and deacons and the presence of Christ in the priest celebrant; on the Fifth Sunday in Ordinary Time (February 9, 2014), reflect on the presence of Christ in the proclamation of the Word; on the Sixth Sunday in Ordinary Time (February 16, 2014), reflect on the presence of Christ "par-excellence" in the bread and wine, totally transformed into his Sacred Body and Blood; on the Seventh Sunday in Ordinary Time (February 23, 2014), reflect on the baptismal call to ministry and service and hold a ministry fair in the parish following each weekend liturgy so you can sign up new members for various liturgical, catechetical, and social ministries in the parish.

On the Saturday before the Eighth Sunday in Ordinary Time (March 2), gather all parish ministers together for a ministry seminar. Include new and seasoned ministers in the training sessions. Consider beginning the day with registration and a continental breakfast followed by Morning Prayer at 9:00 AM; at 9:30 AM invite an inspirational speaker to reflect on baptismal ministry and include about fifteen minutes for small group discussion and then report back to the large group at 10:45. At 11:00, have a short break and then gather the various ministers, so folks can hone their skills, deepen their sense of Eucharist, and prepare themselves to climb the holy mountain of Easter. At 12:30, gather everyone together for a concluding prayer, blessing, and a hymn or song that will send people out into mission, such as "Lord You Give the Great Commission" (ABBOT'S LEIGH) or "The Summons" (KELVINGROVE). On the Eight Sunday in Ordinary Time, include a blessing for all who exercise pastoral service in the parish (see Part VI of the *Book of Blessings*).

The Feast of the Presentation of the Lord (February 2) falls on a Sunday this year. Invite people to bring candles from home to be blessed. Encourage families to light a candle at the dinner table during the evening meal.

Make sure all is prepared for the great ninety days of Lent, Triduum, and Easter. Create a checklist that would include such things as: who orders palms and have they considered providing eco-friendly palms; who burns last year's palms and prepares ashes; who distributes ashes to the sick and homebound; will prayer cards be used and distributed; will the church provide devotional materials such as books to celebrate the Way of the Cross; will LTP's *Keeping the Seasons* be used; will the church host a parish mission; will Morning or Evening Prayer be celebrated in the parish; will people shadow the parish liturgist and sacristans to learn about the work of those who prepare the liturgy; who will review the schedule for Lent, Triduum, and Easter Time and prepare printed cards with the liturgical, devotional, and other celebrations or events held during the ninety days; will Operation Rice Bowl be given out to support the work of Catholic Relief Services; what resources will be provided to the community to assist them in observing prayer, fasting, and almsgiving in the domestic Church and in the workplace; who will provide ongoing liturgical catechesis through the parish bulletin and website; how will parish staff alert the community to pray for and gather for the various rites with inquirers, catechumens, candidates, elect, and neophytes during these ninety days; who will work to provide continuing catechesis about the distinction between catechumens and candidates; have the Paschal candle, candles for the elect, and the assembly been ordered; is the paschal candle large enough to "evoke the truth that Christ is the light of the world" (*Paschale Solemnitatis* [PS], 82); if an order of service will be used for any of the liturgies of the ninety days, have the proper copyright permissions been secured?

Devotions and Sacramentals

JANUARY is the month set aside by the United Nations for poverty awareness. The United States Conference of Catholic Bishops contains resources at the following link http://old.usccb.org/cchd/povertyusa/povamer.shtml. The Week of Prayer for Christian Unity is held between January 18–25. For over one hundred years the Franciscan Friars of the Atonement have been providing resources for this week of prayer (www.atonementfriars.org/index.html). Also, see the section on prayer for Christian Unity in *Catholic Household Blessings & Prayers*. November 21, 2014 will commemorate the 50th anniversary the Second Vatican Council's ecumenical document, *Unitatis Redintegratio*. Given this upcoming anniversary, it would be an excellent occasion for spending the next eleven months studying this document and along the way find opportunities to draw together with other Christians for prayer, joining together in acts of justice and peace, and gather for camaraderie and solidarity. Catholic Schools week is January 26–February 1, 2014 and resources can be found at http://www.ncea.org.

February is Black History Month. Consider studying the lives of several African saints and blesseds including St. Augustine of Hippo (August 28); St. Benedict the Black (April 4); SS. Perpetua and Felicity (July 10); and St. Josephine Bakhita (February 8), to name a few. February 2 is the Feast of the Presentation of the Lord, the date for candles to be blessed for use in the Church and home. You will find a domestic Church ritual for receiving the blessed candles in the home in *Catholic Household Blessings & Prayers*. It is also an appropriate day to bless mothers and those who are pregnant (see DPPL, 121) and to honor those who have consecrated their lives to the Church (see DPPL, 122). February 3, the optional Memorial of St. Blaise, bishop and martyr, is the day when the Church blesses throats (see BB, chapter 51).

The Church has a venerable tradition of devotion to the Blessed Sacrament including: perpetual adoration, exposition of the Blessed Sacrament, and Benediction.

Celebrate *Mardi Gras,* which literally means "Fat Tuesday," in French. The name comes from the tradition of slaughtering and feasting upon a fattened calf on the last day of Carnival. The day is also known as *Shrove* Tuesday (from "to shrive," or hear confessions), Pancake Tuesday, and *Fetter Dienstag*. The custom of making pancakes comes from the need to use up fat, eggs, and dairy before the fasting and abstinence of Lent begins.

The Parish and the Home

"**B**EHOLD, the Lamb of God" (John 1:29). In a way, we are given our marching orders for the Second Sunday in Ordinary Time. John the Baptist gives his witness about Jesus for all to hear and believe. Everything he does points to Jesus as the one who was to come in fulfillment of God's promise of salvation. In our parish households and communities we too can examine how our lives point faithfully to Jesus; how they give witness to our fidelity to God's call.

In the following Sunday Gospel we hear Jesus pick up the Baptist's message proclaiming: "Repent, for the kingdom of heaven is at hand" (Matthew 4:17). Jesus goes on to call his first disciples who became a part of his mission announcing the Good News and curing people of every disease and illness. Pretty tall orders but we can begin in our neighborhoods and towns to bring the Good News. How do we do that? The messages we hear this wintertime before Lent are strong: Blessed are the peacemakers, the persecuted, and the merciful. You are salt. You are light. Go be reconciled with your brother or sister or neighbor before you come to the altar. Love your enemies. Pray for your persecutors. Seek first God's reign and the way of holiness.

What if we were to invite parishioners to examine their call to discipleship? When did they first hear God's call? If they could name the mission of their household what might it say? We could hang these "mission statements" in the parish hall, gathering space, or classrooms or feature them in the bulletin or on the website. The passage from Joshua 24:15 comes to mind: "As for me and my household, we will serve the Lord." This is a good season to examine our mission as disciples, even perhaps as a parish. How do we deepen the sense of mission and commitment to bringing about God's reign before we come to our Lenten time of examining our lives?

A parish could rekindle the opportunities for service at these times, making new opportunities available to parishioners. Many people come away from the holiday season knowing they are blessed and grateful for what they have. They may feel more compelled to share out of that sense of blessing and may even have more time to devote to an ongoing project after Christmas. Perhaps we have whet their appetites and given them a taste of the many needs right in our own backyards. Show examples of places they can serve as families, as groups of young people, as retirees. Use pictures, social media, and personal invitations. Ask people to tell their stories of how serving and giving to others has touched or even changed their lives.

Offer a few opportunities to watch a movie in the parish. It is much easier today to stream movies through a computer and projector making it a more realistic screening experience. There are many good movies that will not be viewed by people in a theater but have value for discipleship. Diocesan offices and websites often have a list. This would be an easy undertaking for a small task force of parishioners and is a time-limited project for those who cannot serve on a long-term parish committee. *Romero, Rise and Dream, Secret Lives: Hidden Children, Remember the Titans* are just a sampling of the many titles available.

Mass Texts

◆ CHILDREN'S LITURGY OF THE WORD

Every kind of growth takes effort: we grow physically be eating well and exercising; we grow intellectually by studying and listening; and if our spirits are to grow, we have to open our ears and open our hearts so we can hear and learn what God wants to teach us. The Word of God is food for our spirits that helps our spirits grow in grace and wisdom, as Jesus did when he was a child. Go now to hear God's Word and to be nourished by its message.

◆ DISMISSAL TEXT FOR RCIA

Without growth there is no life. And in the spiritual life we either move forward or we lose ground. Through your journey on the path of inquiry, catechumenate, and election, you have committed yourselves to steady growth in knowledge and practice of the faith. We rejoice with you in your commitment and pray with you for an abundant outpouring of God's grace upon your effort. May your time of breaking open the holy Word of God we've just proclaimed strengthen you and deepen your appreciation of God's mercy in calling you to himself.

◆ Seasonal Texts for Prayer of the Faithful

Invitation to Prayer:

No season is without growth for even in the frozen ground the silent seed is waiting and the love of God shines down to ready the soil for spring's awakening. Let us pray for the constant growth that signals a vibrant life within the Church and in our world.

For the leaders of the Church, that they constantly strive to better know the Lord that they might better serve him and all his holy people, we pray: We count on you, O Lord, to shine your grace upon us.

For our civic leaders, both local and national, that the Spirit purify their motives and guide their decisions as they work for the good of all, we pray: We count on you, O Lord, to shine your grace upon us.

For families where young lives begin to grow and for the parents divinely charged with their care, may the example of the Holy Family teach us to establish

homes where love dwells amidst harmony and joy, we pray: We count on you, O Lord, to shine your grace upon us.

For the forgotten and the lonely, especially those suffering from physical or mental illness, that mercy become incarnate through our compassion action, we pray: We count on you, O Lord, to shine your grace upon us.

For those who call this parish home, that they will find here a shelter in time of need, an oasis in time of drought, and a place where our love of God is constantly nurtured, we pray: We count on you, O Lord, to shine your grace upon us.

Concluding Prayer:

In confidence we come to you, O Lord,
for you are the source of all that nurtures and
    sustains us.
Nourish us at your table
that we might become the nourishment we receive.
We ask this in Christ our Lord.
Amen.

January
Month of the Holy Name

Except for the days of the First and Thirty-fourth Weeks in Ordinary Time, The Roman Missal does not provide prayer texts for the weekdays in Ordinary Time. Instead, priest celebrants and those who prepare the liturgy may select from among the prayers provided for the Sundays in Ordinary Time. Your diocesan Ordo will provide suggestions. On days celebrated as optional memorials, prayers may be from the Sundays of Ordinary Time, the Proper of Saints, or the Commons. On all Saturdays during Ordinary Time that do not have an obligatory memorial, a memorial to the Blessed Virgin Mary may be celebrated. The prayers may be selected from the Common of the Blessed Virgin Mary. Commentary below is only provided for Sundays, solemnities, feasts, and obligatory memorials.

M O N 13 (#305) green
Weekday (First Week in Ordinary Time)

Optional Memorial of St. Hilary, Bishop and Doctor of the Church / white

The Lectionary for Mass

◆ FIRST READING: We begin a series of readings from the books of Samuel. Today, we meet Elkanah, the father of Samuel, and Hannah and Peninnah, Elkanah's two wives. Hannah, especially loved by Elkanah, was barren, a disgrace for an Israelite woman since children were seen as a blessing from the Lord. Peninnah had borne many children and so taunted Hannah for her barrenness. Hannah experienced deep anguish and grief, not only because of her barrenness, but because of Peninnah's reproaches.

◆ RESPONSORIAL PSALM 116 is a prayer that accompanied a sacrifice in the Temple. In today's First Reading, Elkanah and his wives go to the Temple of the Lord in Shiloh precisely in order to worship the Lord and offer sacrifice—as was their yearly custom. The psalmist, aware of all that God has done for him, publicly proclaims God's praise.

◆ GOSPEL: We hear Mark's account of the beginning of Jesus's public ministry. John the Baptist, having been arrested, is no longer on the scene. Jesus's ministry begins in Galilee, the northernmost part of the country. Throughout Mark, Jesus will gradually make his way to Jerusalem where his Passion, Death, and Resurrection will take place. Here at the beginning of his ministry, Jesus announces the proximity of God's kingdom and asks for repentance and faith. He calls his first disciples to assist in his ministry.

The Roman Missal

If the optional memorial is not being celebrated, the orations are taken from the page titled "First Week in Ordinary Time," located in the "Ordinary Time" section of the Proper of Time (there is no page for Sunday of the First Week in Ordinary Time).

Today's Saint

St. Hilary was the Bishop of Poitiers, France, during the era of the Arian heresy, and he fought for the correct understanding and expression of the divinity of Christ. He was known as the "hammer against Arianism" and the "Athanasius of the West," after the Bishop of Alexandria who fought the heresy in the East. The Christian world was so divided by Arianism that Hilary was exiled twice. His great contribution was the successful expression in Latin of the theology about Christ, or Christology, that had been developed in Greek.

T U E 14 (#306) green
Weekday

The Lectionary for Mass

◆ FIRST READING: Entering the Temple at Shiloh, Hannah turns to the Lord in her grief and sorrow. She begs for a son and promises to dedicate him to the Lord if her prayer is granted. Eli the priest, looking on, at first misjudges her, thinking that she was drunk. Learning of her sorrow and misery, Eli blesses her. Note that Hannah's prayer and Eli's word of blessing moved her beyond her downcast state and the withdrawal and isolation described in yesterday's reading. Her trust was rewarded and she conceived a son.

◆ CANTICLE: Today's response is Hannah's prayer of thanksgiving when she offers her weaned son to the Lord in fulfillment of her vow (verse 11 of today's reading). Hear her prayer of thanksgiving within the context of her previous barrenness and rivalry with Peninnah.

◆ GOSPEL: The "followers" in the first line of today's Gospel are Simon and Andrew, James and John, whose response to Jesus's call was described in yesterday's reading. Jesus goes first to the synagogue, that gathering place for prayer and study of the Scriptures. Note how Mark contrasts Jesus's teaching ability with that of the scribes. Jesus has an authority that they lack. The Lectionary translation omits the word *immediately* found in the Greek text of verses 21 and 23. Right at the beginning, the opposition of the realm of evil to Jesus is evident. The evil spirits know who Jesus is and rightly fear that he has come to destroy them. Nothing more is said of the man who was healed. The focus is on Jesus and his power over evil—something that led those who saw and heard him to ponder who he was.

The Roman Missal

Because *The Roman Missal* does not include prayer texts for the week-days of Ordinary Time, there will be no Missal commentary for ferrial weekdays. Instead, please refer to your local *Ordo* for suggestions.

W E D 15 (#307) green
Weekday

The Lectionary for Mass

◆ FIRST READING: We hear the call of Samuel, the young son of Hannah, as he served in the Temple under the guidance of Eli the prophet. Note the comment of how in those days revelations of the Lord were uncommon, and also of how Samuel did not yet know the Lord. The verb know here connotes personal experience or relationship. Samuel was one quick to respond and be open to the instructions of his mentor. What a beautiful model Eli is for all the elderly in their relationships with children as one who teaches them to know the Lord.

Because of Eli, Samuel is introduced to the Lord and learns to ask the Lord to speak to him.

◆ RESPONSORIAL PSALM: Samuel's response to the call he heard was, "Here I am." It is likewise the prayer of the psalmist: "Here I am, I come to do your will." The Lord speaks to the one who waits with openness. Obedience is more pleasing to the Lord than ritual offerings with no personal involvement. Like Samuel (last line), the psalmist speaks the Lord's word.

◆ GOSPEL: Today's text recounts several events in one of the early days of Jesus's ministry. What warmth is conveyed in the picture of Jesus in the home of his disciple-friends, Simon and Andrew. What tenderness and compassion Jesus showed by healing the mother of Simon's wife, and also to all who gathered at the door—finding in him the way to healing and wholeness. (Notice

that Jesus's power over demons and evil spirits is mentioned three times.) We glimpse the source of Jesus's healing power and teaching authority in his time alone in prayer. Note that he rises early and seeks solitude so as to have this time, which was so very important for what he was sent to do.

T H U 16 (#308) green
Weekday

The Lectionary for Mass

◆ FIRST READING: The reading recounts the events of two battles in a Philistine attack on Israel, whose defeat is interpreted as God's punishment for sins. The last line of the reading speaks of the death of the two sons of Eli, Hophni, and Phinehas. In 1 Samuel 2:12–36 (not included in the Lectionary) there is an important piece for understanding this story. Here we hear of Hophni and Phinehas's wickedness in taking for themselves some of the meat offered for sacrifice in a manner not in accord with tradition. In effect, they took the best for themselves first. Eli was aware of this but did nothing. The revelation given to the young Samuel (see 1 Samuel 3:11–18, also excluded from the Lectionary) predicts the punishment and Hophni and Eli's deaths. The Ark of the Covenant, a chest containing the tablets of the law of Moses, was Israel's most sacred possession. It represented God's presence among them. Its loss was unbelievable tragedy.

◆ RESPONSORIAL PSALM 40 is a communal lament, prayed by Israel in the wake of defeat in battle (first stanza). The last stanza voices Israel's fervent prayer as they lie prostrate before the Lord.

◆ GOSPEL: We witness a similar gesture of prayer in the leper who kneels before Jesus, begging for deliverance from his affliction. What

the Scriptures call leprosy is much broader than what we now know as Hanson's disease. It included any number of skin afflictions. Fear of contagion was paramount and lepers were isolated. (Notice that Jesus's compassion for the man leads him to touch him.) The instruction to go to the priest accords with Leviticus 13–14, for the priest's declaration was necessary for the healed leper to be readmitted to the community. At the end of today's text we hear Jesus's command of silence to the leper. The nature of Jesus's Messiahship would only be gradually revealed and understood.

F R I 17 (#309) white
**Memorial of
St. Anthony, Abbot**

◆ FIRST READING: The young servant of the Lord, Samuel, grew up to become a judge in Israel. In terms of biblical history, the judges were men and women who both arbitrated disputes and served as military leaders (see the Book of Judges for their stories). In his old age, Samuel appointed his two sons as judges, but they were not just judges. As a result, the people rejected them and asked Samuel to appoint a new leader. They did not want another judge, but a king, so that they could be like all the other nations. Samuel was distressed by their request, and in today's reading we hear the results of God and Samuel's discussion of the matter. God acquiesces even though he was not pleased with the request. The people, in fact, were replacing his sovereignty with those of a mere mortal.

◆ RESPONSORIAL PSALM 89 acclaims the everlasting covenant God made with David. David was Israel's second king and perhaps its greatest. In today's First Reading we hear of the very beginnings of the monarchy.

◆ GOSPEL: Jesus's acclaim grows. As we heard yesterday, it was impossible for him to enter a town without drawing a crowd, and today that crowd is at the door of his home. The thatched grass roof of his house provided an alternative route for the paralyzed man and his friends who could not get as close as they wished. Today's text portrays Jesus not only as teacher of the Word, but as healer, as one who forgives sins and as one who knows the thoughts of the human heart. How charismatic he must have been; what power and authority was manifest in his words and deeds. The people had never seen anything like it.

The Roman Missal

The Mass texts are proper for today and can be found in the Proper of Saints at January 17. The orations all echo the virtues of St. Anthony's life: his "wondrous way of life in the desert" and the need for self-denial in order to love God above all things (Collect); being free from "earthly attachments" so that "we may have our riches in you alone" (Prayer over the Offerings); and the saint's "glorious victories / over the powers of darkness" (Prayer after Communion). Although no particular Preface is indicated in the rubrics for today, certainly one should be chosen from among the two Prefaces of Saints or the Preface of Holy Virgins and Religious.

Today's Saint

Early in his life, St. Anthony of Egypt (251–356) discovered the importance of solitude in knowing oneself in relationship to God. Solitude provides the vehicle through which one battles demons and removes worldly distractions that distance the heart from the will of God. St. Anthony journeyed in the desert for nearly thirty years where he lived a life of solitary prayer and self-discipline—a life of utter dependence on God. After his time in

the desert, he emerged as a man of balance, ready to share all he learned regarding the human thirst for God. Realizing that the spiritual life takes root within a community of believers, he founded a group of monks. While serving as abbot, a spiritual father, to the monks, St. Anthony mentored them in the ways of contemplative prayer and helped them overcome illusory thinking. His dynamic personality continued to attract individuals. As a result, he counseled a steady stream of pilgrims and laid the foundation for many monasteries.

S A T **18** (#310) green
Weekday

Optional Memorial of the Blessed Virgin Mary / white

The Lectionary for Mass

◆ FIRST READING: We meet Saul who would become Israel's first king. In verses not included in today's reading, we hear of how Saul, failing to find the lost animals, sought out Samuel, a reputed prophet of the Lord, for help. Today's reading picks up in verse 17, with the Lord confirming his choice of Saul as the one to be anointed with oil and so designated as ruler of the people. Saul is also charged with delivering God's people from their enemies.

◆ RESPONSORIAL PSALM 21 is a prayer for Israel's king. It is the Lord's strength, not his own, that gladdens the heart of the king. The king, by virtue of his selection by the Lord and the anointing that signifies it, stands in special relationship with the Lord. The king is to be a blessing for all God's people.

◆ GOSPEL: Again we have a large crowd gathering around Jesus, and again, he teaches them. We hear also of the call of Levi (Matthew). Tax

collectors were a despised lot, for they were agents of the Roman government and also used their position to supplement their own income. This unlikely—and to some, unrighteous—man was called by Jesus. The official religious leaders strongly object to Jesus's table fellowship with Levi and his friends, since sharing a meal with someone was a sign of acceptance and relationship. In the minds of the Pharisees and scribes, those who are righteous separated themselves from sinners. Yet, Jesus welcomed sinners and entered into their company. At the end of today's text, he tells why.

19 (#64) green
Second Sunday in Ordinary Time

The Lectionary for Mass

◆ FIRST READING: We hear the reflections, the awareness, the understanding of the call and mission of one specially chosen by God, even before his birth, to be the Lord's servant. His mission was not only on behalf of Israel, his own people, entrusted as he was to bring them back to the Lord, but for all the nations. God's servant would be their light, revealing the ways of God's salvation.

◆ RESPONSORIAL PSALM 40: Our antiphon is the beautiful response of one who has heard and accepted God's call. The verses of Psalm 40 chosen for today touch on the theme of waiting to hear God's answer to the prayer of one's heart, of waiting to hear what one should say or do. The psalmist is totally open and disposed to the Lord's will. It is his joy and delight.

◆ SECOND READING: Notice how often the word "call" occurs in today's Second Reading: Paul's "call" to be an Apostle; the community's "call" to be holy. All believers are "called" to "call" on the name of the Lord. In him, we find grace and peace.

◆ GOSPEL: The "call" or "vocation" of Jesus and John the Baptist are juxtaposed today—calls that are integrally related. Note how John the Baptist recognized his call to be the forerunner of Jesus, God's Chosen One. How important it was for John, how important it is for us, to recognize and proclaim the presence of Jesus among us. Jesus's call, his mission, is to be the Lamb of God, the one who would take away the sin of the world. In John's account of the Gospel, Jesus accomplishes this through his Death on the cross, at the hour when the Passover lambs were sacrificed. Endowed with God's Holy Spirit, Jesus, the Son of God, baptizes us into the life that is his own. In this, we are chosen, we are called to be his servants.

The Roman Missal

The Mass texts for today are found in the "Ordinary Time" section of the Proper of Time. The Gloria is sung or said today. The Creed is said or sung.

The Collect acknowledges God as the one who governs "all things," and so asks him to "bestow [his] peace on our times." The Prayer over the Offerings reiterates how "whenever the memorial of this sacrifice is celebrated / the work of our redemption is accomplished." The Prayer after Communion highlights the unity of the faithful that is

a constitutive element in the meaning of the Eucharist as it asks God to pour the Spirit of love on us so that those who have been nourished by the "one heavenly Bread" may become "one in mind and heart."

Any one of the eight Prefaces of the Sundays in Ordinary Time may be selected for today. In light of the First Reading and the Gospel, Preface I, "The Paschal Mystery and the People of God," might be a good choice. Another good choice might be to use Eucharistic Prayer IV; the opportunities to use this prayer are limited, since the use of its proper Preface is required and therefore use of this prayer is precluded when another Preface is assigned. The sweeping review of salvation history and references to Jesus's mission in this Preface would make this an appropriate choice for this Sunday.

Pastoral Reflection

To be humble and wise like John the Baptist is a gift we each need to acquire. John had popularity and a large following, but he knew the kingdom to come was not about him. He was but a messenger baptizing simply, while a strong force was yet to come. In this new civic calendar year, be conscious of your choices and need for accomplishment in this world. Bless yourself with holy water each day this week with a prayer asking that you, too, can willingly submit to the baptism of fire that Jesus provides and follow eagerly in the footsteps of his teachings.

M O N | 20 | (#311) green **Weekday**

Optional Memorials of St. Fabian, Pope and Martyr / red; St. Sebastian, Martyr / red

The Lectionary for Mass

◆ FIRST READING: It was difficult for Saul to be totally submissive to the Lord and obedient to his word, especially when he thought his idea

was a good (or better) one. God had commanded total extermination of Israel's enemies, along with all of their possessions. Saul was victorious in battle, but failed in obedience. To God, obedience is better than sacrifice. Obedience is the offering of self that the Lord seeks.

◆ RESPONSORIAL PSALM 50: The upright and the obedient see the saving power of God. From the perspective of the Biblical author, Saul was neither. The stanzas of today's psalm echo Samuel's words to Saul in today's First Reading and reiterate the importance of obedience.

◆ GOSPEL: On the heels of the account of a meal shared with sinners, Mark sets the issue of fasting—or more particularly, the observation that Jesus's disciples do not. Fasting is a religious practice that signifies both repentance and self-denial, and receptivity for the coming of God. As noted earlier, marriage was a Biblical symbol of the covenant God had made with Israel. Wedding celebrations are neither the time nor the place for fasting. So it was for Jesus's disciples: the Bridegroom was in their midst. The "new" thing God was doing in Jesus called for a new way of looking at the old traditional practices.

Today's Saints

The Church celebrates the lives of two holy men today, SS. Fabian (+250) and Sebastian (+288), both of whom were martyred for their faith. Very little is known about each of these martyrs, yet they continue to capture the hearts of Catholic Christians everywhere. St. Fabian was elected pope in 236, even though he was not a priest. During his pontificate, Emperor Decius came into power and began persecuting Christians who would not return to pagan worship. St. Fabian was the first among many killed under this emperor's violent reign. While serving as a soldier,

St. Sebastian was persecuted at the hands of Diocletian. According to legend, he was pierced with arrows so that he would die a slow and painful death, but this attempt on his life was unsuccessful due to his athletic stamina. He eventually became well enough to confront the emperor regarding the way Christians were being treated. This led to his execution.

TUE 21 (#312) red
Memorial of St. Agnes, Virgin and Martyr / red

The Lectionary for Mass

◆ FIRST READING: With Saul rejected as ruler of Israel, a new king is needed. Today's reading recounts God's instruction to Samuel. The new chosen one is from the sons of Jesse in Bethlehem. Note that the Lord's selection is not who Samuel—or we—might think it would be, for the Lord looks not at appearances but at the heart. David is singled out and anointed as king. From that day on, he is filled with the Spirit of the Lord.

◆ RESPONSORIAL PSALM 89 recounts the story of God's covenant with David. Today we hear of his selection as king when but a youth, his anointing, and his special relationship with God as Father in which he stands because of his kingship.

◆ GOSPEL: Controversy with the Pharisees, those strict interpreters of the law, continues. At issue are laws pertaining to the Sabbath and Jesus's disciples presumed violation of them. Jesus shrewdly points out biblical precedent for exceptions to the law. The Sabbath was made for the sake of humankind. Jesus, Son of Man, has authority over it.

The Roman Missal

The Collect is the only oration proper for today, and it is found at January 21 under the Proper of Saints. The prayer has Pauline echoes in its assertion that God chooses "what is weak in the world to confound the strong." The other orations are taken either from the Common of Martyrs: for a Virgin Martyr or from the Common of Virgins: For One Virgin. Although no particular Preface is indicated in the rubrics for today, certainly one of the two Prefaces of Holy Martyrs should be considered as likely choices, although the Preface of Holy Virgins and Religious could be another candidate.

Today's Saint

St. Agnes (291–304) lived a very short life, but each and every moment was filled with inestimable worth. She felt called to consecrate her virginity to Christ in a culture that lived according to the flesh rather than the spirit. When St. Agnes refused numerous marriage proposals because of her espousal to Christ, she was tried and beheaded. Two words embody the whole of her life: faithfulness and purity. No human being or earthly promise could shatter St. Agnes's commitment to her beloved God, nor could any hatred or vengeance taint her virginal heart. Devotion to St. Agnes gained popularity in the Middle Ages, along with other virginal saints like Ursula, Dorothy, and Barbara. In religious art, she is often depicted with a lamb, symbolizing the spotless (pure) sacrifice she made for the Lord.

WED 22 (#313) green
Weekday

Day of Prayer for the Legal Protection of Unborn Children (U.S.A.) / white or violet

About this Day of Prayer

On this day, the Church gives us prayers rooted in hope as the United States mourns the loss of millions of lives by abortion. In the Mass for Peace and Justice, we pray that all governments, especially our own, seek a truly just society, one in which the common good of all people, including the most vulnerable, is sought. In a very real way, we pray for the end of this genocide, the victims of which we remember with our violet vestments and mournful hymns. Why, then, did the 2011 Missal introduce this new option of praying instead with joyful white vestments, in thanksgiving for human life? Does this not cheapen their needless death? On the contrary: It celebrates their brief lives, reminding us also of the beauty and sacredness of the lives around us, who have not yet been lost. We remember, we intercede, we hope—and the Church leads us in all three (written by Claire M. Gilligan).

On this sensitive day, we should remember that there may be members of our parish who are still in the process of reconciling with God and the Church because they have had an abortion. If able, provide counselors to support those who have participated in an abortion. Using this day to condemn rather than to show mercy can cause pain. We are called to show compassion and God's mercy as we restore all and renew all in Christ's love and life. You might also host a Rosary for life.

The Lectionary for Mass

◆ FIRST READING: The context of today's reading is young David's visit to his three older brothers who are serving in Saul's army and encamped for battle opposite the Philistines. Saul is disheartened by the taunting challenge of Goliath, the Philistine warrior. David, never having been in the army, wants to respond to the challenge. His credentials? He has killed the lion and the bear who would take one of his flocks. Trusting in the power of the Lord, and not in sword or armor, David kills Goliath with slingshot and stone. It is the Lord who has fought on Israel's behalf.

◆ RESPONSORIAL PSALM 144: This psalm of thanksgiving echoes the theme of the Lord as warrior, as fighting on Israel's—and David's—behalf. The last stanza is particularly appropriate for David the harpist (see 1 Samuel 16:16–18).

◆ GOSPEL: Today's Gospel follows immediately after yesterday's text. Again, there is controversy with the Pharisees over observance of the Sabbath. We can only surmise how the man's physical disability impacted his everyday life. As Mark tells the story, one almost gets the sense of Jesus and the Pharisees aligned in battle opposite one another. Notice that Jesus is angry. He realizes they were watching him, wanting to accuse him. Indeed, as the last line indicates, they sought to put him to death. Like their ancestors, the Pharisees were hardened of heart. They could not receive the salvation Jesus came to bring.

The Roman Missal

The prayers for this Mass are taken from the Masses and Prayers for Various Needs and Occasions, from one of two formularies: either the Mass "For Giving Thanks to God for the Gift of Human Life" (#48/1), in which case white vestments are worn, or the Mass "For the Preservation of Peace and Justice" (#30), in which case violet vestments are worn.

The Mass "For Giving Thanks to God for the Gift of Human Life" has two different sets of orations from which to choose. All the prayers, though, express the Church's concern for the dignity of life and the need to both reverence and give witness to that dignity. The Mass "For the Preservation of Peace and Justice," while having only one Prayer over the Offerings and Prayer after Communion, has four different Collects from which to choose.

Consider using the infrequently-heard Eucharistic Prayer for Use in Masses for Various Needs; the fourth form, "Jesus, Who Went About Doing Good," would seem to be a good choice: the Preface speaks of how Jesus always showed compassion for children and for the poor, and how he became a neighbor to the oppressed; in the petitions, the prayer asks God to "Open our eyes / to the needs of our brothers and sisters" and to make the "Church stand as a living witness / to truth and freedom, / to peace and justice." These are all themes that are applicable to this day.

THU 23 (#314) green Weekday

Optional Memorial of St. Vincent, Deacon and Martyr / red; Optional Memorial of St. Marianne Cope, Virgin / white

The Lectionary for Mass

◆ FIRST READING: David proved to be a most successful warrior—and initially, Saul was most pleased. Today we hear of Saul's anger and resentment toward David. Saul was jealous because David was receiving more acclaim for his deeds in battle than Saul was. This drove Saul to murderous intentions. Jonathan, Saul's son, loved David very much and warned David of his father's evil intent. Jonathan successfully intervened with his father on David's behalf. Saul agreed that he would not kill David.

◆ RESPONSORIAL PSALM 56 is a song of confidence in battle. The last two stanzas are most apropos for David when Saul agrees to spare his life.

◆ GOSPEL: Great crowds continue to gather around Jesus—so many, that in today's Gospel Jesus asks that a boat be readied for him. There, at least, he would have some space from the crowd. Today's Gospel is a bit of a summary statement of Jesus's healing ministry and of his power over evil spirits who know his true identity. The command to secrecy (last line) indicates that it is not yet time for Jesus's true identity to be revealed.

Today's Saint

St. Vincent was from Saragossa in third-century Spain. He is also known as Vincent the deacon and served under St. Valerius, bishop of Saragossa. He was martyred in 304 during the persecution by the emperor Diocletian. Just before he was killed on a gridiron or grill, he was offered his freedom if he would throw a copy of the Scriptures on the fire that was prepared for him, but he refused. After witnessing Vincent's faith and heroism, his executioner converted to Christianity.

St. Marianne Cope (1838–1918) was born in West Germany, but a year after her birth the Cope family emigrated to the United States of America to seek work and educational opportunities. From a young age, she felt the call to enter religious life, which led to her decision to enter the Sisters of St. Francis in Syracuse, New York. She had a deep affection for the suffering and sick. Marianne was instrumental in the establishment of two of the first hospitals in the central New

York area—hospitals that were open to all people regardless of ethnicity, religion, or race. While serving as superior general of her religious community, she accepted an invitation to care for the sick, especially those afflicted with leprosy, in Hawaii. Marianne joined the mission to Hawaii where she helped establish homes for leprosy patients and cared for St. Damien De Veuster of Moloka'i who contracted leprosy because of his ministry to the sick. Following the death of St. Damien, Marianne continued his compassionate ministry of care for leprosy patients. Marianne lived the Franciscan call to serve the "crucified," the most vulnerable, in society. The inclusion of her "feast day" as an optional memorial for the dioceses of the United States was approved by the Vatican in early 2013.

(#315)   white
FRI 24 Memorial of St. Francis de Sales, Bishop and Doctor of the Church

The Lectionary for Mass

◆ FIRST READING: Saul, jealous and hateful of David, seeks to kill him. Today's reading gives us a glimpse of David's character that is almost unbelievable. With the man who seeks to take his life within easy reach, David refuses to harm him. His enemy, the king, is God's anointed. Saul is a bit overwhelmed by David's goodness, as he should be. At the end of today's reading, the man who sought to kill prays a blessing instead in the face of the kindness shown to him.

◆ RESPONSORIAL PSALM 57: The first line of today's psalm in the Hebrew text actually attributes it to David when he sought refuge from Saul in the cave. The prayer is one of confidence, with firm trust in God's deliverance.

◆ GOSPEL: Today's Gospel event takes place on a mountain; that favored place for prayer and the encounter with God in biblical tradition. Jesus summons his disciples and designates twelve of them for a special ministry. Note what they are chosen for: 1) to be with Jesus, that is, to learn from him; 2) to proclaim the Good News of the Kingdom of God; and 3) to have authority over the realm of evil— an important aspect of Jesus's own ministry in the Gospel according to Mark.

The Roman Missal

The orations are proper for today and are to be found in the Proper of Saints at January 24. The prayers include mention of St. Francis de Sales by way of his gentleness, his meekness, his charity, and his being inflamed with the Holy Spirit. Although no particular Preface is indicated in the rubrics for today, the Preface of Holy Pastors would make sense, since St. Francis was a bishop.

Today's Saint

St. Francis de Sales (1567–1622), bishop of Geneva, contributed immensely to the development of spirituality through the publication of his book, *An Introduction to the Devout Life.* Living at a time when manuals on spirituality were written primarily for clerics and members of religious orders, St. Francis's book provided a practical path to holiness for people from all states of life. He challenged the prevailing belief that only a select few could obtain sanctity. Along with his accomplishments in the area of an everyday, or lay, spirituality, he cofounded with St. Jane Frances de Chantal the Order of the Visitation of Holy Mary, a religious community of nuns that would move beyond traditional enclosure to a healthy blend of prayer and service to the poor. Together, SS. Francis and

Jane, with their close friends SS. Vincent de Paul and Louise de Marillac, transformed the face of the Church in France. St. Francis has been named a Doctor of the Church.

(#519)   white
SAT 25 Feast of the Conversion of St. Paul the Apostle

About this Feast/Saint

Today's feast celebrates God's triumph, even in the most unlikely circumstances. Before St. Paul meets the Risen Lord on the Road to Damascus, he is Saul, dedicated to viciously persecuting the followers of Jesus Christ. Imagine yourself among those early Christians, and hearing that Saul, one of the most feared enemies of your community, has encountered the Lord and changed his life entirely to serve him from then on. Although certainly astonishing, the conversion of St. Paul is also deeply inspiring, for it tells us that God does not hold our mistakes against us, but rather calls us to turn our minds and hearts to follow his Son instead. The conversion of St. Paul is proof that no one is too far beyond the call of the Lord to follow, and that in Christ, change for the better is always possible.

The Lectionary for Mass

◆ FIRST READING: Two options are given for the First Reading. Both are Paul's account (as reported by Luke) of his experience of the Risen Christ on the road to Damascus and the important identification of Jesus with believers. In the first option, we hear of Paul's Jewish heritage and membership in the Pharisaic sect. The second option focuses on Ananias's understandable fear and hesitance about going to Saul. Nonetheless, he is obedient.

Both readings speak of Paul's experience of the bright light (identified with the Lord) and his hearing the Lord's voice (note the discrepancy, though; in Acts 9 Paul's companions hear the voice as well). Both readings contrast Paul, the zealous and aggressive defender of Judaism with the blinded man who needed to be led by the hand. Paul's blindness is the result of his experience of the Risen Christ manifest in light—so bright that, literally, Paul was unable to see. Paul is led by the hand literally by his companions and figuratively by Ananias, whose word "led" Saul to Baptism and an understanding of his call and mission from Jesus.

◆ RESPONSORIAL PSALM 117: The antiphon is from Mark's account of the Gospel, the Risen Christ's commission of his disciples. Psalm 117 is a psalm of praise, calling upon all peoples, Gentiles as well as Jews, to sing God's praise.

◆ GOSPEL: Jesus sends the Twelve to the whole world (Gentiles as well as Jews) to proclaim his Good News and to baptize those who believe. Their divine commission will be confirmed by signs, and they will continue Jesus's work of healing and exorcism.

The Roman Missal

All the Mass texts for this feast are proper and are located in the Proper of Saints at January 25.

The Gloria is sung or said today. The Creed is not said.

As might be expected, all the prayers make reference to St. Paul's conversion, preaching, and faith in one way or another; the Prayer after Communion specifically asks that the sacrament we have received "stir up in us that fire of charity / with which the blessed Apostle Paul burned ardently / as he bore his concern for all the Churches." Our participation in the Eucharist should transform us to have that same "fire of charity" for all our brothers and sisters in the Body of Christ, and for all Churches.

The Preface that is assigned for today is that of Preface I of the Apostles. A Solemn Blessing is suggested at the end of Mass, the one titled "The Apostles" (#17). Strong consideration should be given to using it.

☀ **26** (#67)   green
**Third Sunday
in Ordinary Time**

The Lectionary for Mass

◆ FIRST READING: Isaiah's words were first spoken in the wake of the Assyrian conquest of northern Israel (see verse 23). The darkness of the conquest, its destruction and distress, is now replaced by glory and light as a result of the Lord's marvelous deeds on Israel's behalf. Subsequent verses 5–6, not included in today's reading, associate this with the birth of a child, heir to the Davidic throne.

◆ RESPONSORIAL PSALM 27: Fittingly, today's Responsorial Psalm acclaims the Lord as light and salvation. His protection and help casts out fear in times of distress. The prayer of the second stanza, expressing such longing to see the Lord, is fulfilled whenever we turn to Jesus.

◆ SECOND READING: The divisions in the Corinthian community based, it seems, on rivalries stemming from self-designated status, literally tear the community apart. Paul begs that the divisions cease and that the unity befitting the Lord's community be realized. They must take the Lord, who emptied himself and died the meanest of deaths, as the wisdom of their lives.

◆ GOSPEL: Isaiah's words (First Reading) are cited by Matthew in today's Gospel. Their juxtaposition with the beginning of Jesus's ministry casts Jesus as this Light. We hear Jesus calling his first disciples who immediately respond to him. Jesus's ministry of teaching and healing brought enlightenment and smashed the yokes that burdened the people.

The Roman Missal

The Mass texts for this Sunday are found in the "Ordinary Time" section of the Proper of Time. The Gloria is sung or said today. The Creed is said or sung.

The Collect asks that God may direct our actions so that "in the name of your beloved Son / we may abound in good works." In the Prayer over the Offerings we are asking God to accept our offerings so that, in sanctifying them, "they may profit us for salvation." The Prayer after Communion asks that, as a result of receiving the grace of being brought to new life (for example, in the Eucharist), "we may always glory in your gift."

Any one of the eight Prefaces of the Sundays in Ordinary Time may be selected for today. Preface I, "The Paschal Mystery and the People of God," with its references to being summoned and called out of darkness, might be a connection with the Gospel.

The deacon's or priest's use of the third option for the dismissal formula, "Go in peace, glorifying the Lord by your life," would make a nice connection with the Prayer after Communion.

Pastoral Reflection

Peter and Andrew immediately dropped their nets, their livelihood, to follow the renegade Jesus and two more brothers then followed. If Jesus were to walk through your town today, what would you have to immediately drop to spread a great message? There are many lights (people) who chase our darkness away. Disciples are meant to be this light at all times. Understanding the need for companionship, Jesus's first disciples were pairs—brothers. Who is your spiritual "pair" that you might want to come with you to feel more secure in walking a new path? If this person does not know how important they are to how you want to follow Christ Jesus, take time to affirm their discipleship and how it helps you be a better follow of Jesus.

MON 27 (#317) green Weekday

Optional Memorial of St. Angela Merici, Virgin / white

The Lectionary for Mass

◆ FIRST READING: David is acclaimed king by all the tribes of Israel and anointed as king by their elders. Note the two images used in the description of David's kingly role: shepherd, very pastoral; and commander, pointing to military strength. Verse 5, the last line of the first part of the reading, can be confusing. In chapter 2 of 2 Samuel we are told of David's acclamation as king by the tribe of Judah. In chapter 5, all the tribes of Israel acclaim him as king. David has united all of Israel and captured Jerusalem (Zion, city of David).

◆ RESPONSORIAL PSALM 89, a lengthy psalm, focuses on God's covenant with David. Today's chosen verses speak in particular of God's choice of David and the promises made to him.

◆ GOSPEL: Jesus manifests power over demons and provokes controversy and confusion over his identity. The scribes accuse Jesus of being possessed and of being a tool of Satan. Jesus responds with a parable that invites them to recognize the illogic of their reasoning and subtly warns them against not recognizing the power of the Holy Spirit.

Today's Saint

Several miraculous occurrences, including restoration of sight and visions, surrounded the life of St. Angela Merici (1474–1540), a native of Desenzano in northern Italy. She was profoundly impacted by one vision in which she saw a great company of virgins and saints singing and playing instruments while descending from a staircase in the heavens. Based upon this vision, St. Angela founded a group of consecrated women known as the Ursulines, dedicated to the education of young women, especially the poor. They were named after the fourth-century martyr and protector of women, St. Ursula, to whom St. Angela had a special devotion from an early age. Unlike the traditional customs practiced by those in religious orders, the members of this community did not wear habits, take vows, or live behind an enclosure. The women often resided with their own families, but met for instruction. St. Angela was gravely concerned that customary practices or rules not hinder the women from freely serving those in need.

TUE 28 (#318) white Memorial of St. Thomas Aquinas, Priest and Doctor of the Church

The Lectionary for Mass

◆ FIRST READING: One of King David's first acts in Jerusalem was to bring the Ark of the Covenant from the house of Obededom, where it had been staying since the Philistines had sent it away from their midst (see 1 Samuel 6), into Jerusalem. The Ark is brought up in procession amid much celebration, with sacrifice, with song and dance. All the people participate in the sacrifice not only through their presence, but by sharing in the food that David gave them.

◆ RESPONSORIAL PSALM 24 was no doubt used to accompany a procession with the Ark of the Covenant in the Temple. Note the repetition of "King of Glory." The Israelites believed that God was invisibly present in the Ark of the Covenant.

◆ GOSPEL: Discipleship (listening to the words of Jesus and doing them) puts one in a relationship with Jesus that is stronger than the ties of natural family.

The Roman Missal

The Collect is proper for today and is to be found in the Proper of Saints at January 28. The first part of the oration recognizes St. Thomas Aquinas's zeal for holiness and study of sacred doctrine; the second part asks God to grant "that we may understand what he taught / and imitate what he accomplished." The other prayers are taken either from the Common of Doctors of the Church or from the Common of Pastors: For One Pastor. The Preface to use is either the Preface of Holy Pastors or one of the two Prefaces of Saints.

Today's Saint

St. Thomas Aquinas (1225–1274), a Doctor of the Church, felt drawn to the charism of the Dominicans, even though his parents wanted him to become a Benedictine monk. As a young Dominican, his reserved demeanor led his classmates to believe he was unintelligent; therefore, they called him the "dumb ox." Little did they know St. Thomas was a brilliant man who would write the *Summa Theologica*—a theological masterpiece that explicates the truths of the Catholic faith by demonstrating the intimate relationship between reason and revelation. His intellectual genius and method of theological inquiry was greatly influenced by his mentor and teacher St. Albert the Great. The person once thought to be "dumb ox" became known as the "angelic doctor" due to his profound impact on theological thought, as far reaching as the Second Vatican Council and contemporary theologians like Karl Rahner.

W E D 29 (#319) green Weekday

The Lectionary for Mass

◆ FIRST READING: Today's reading is the Lord's response to King David's desire to build a house (Temple) for God (see 2 Samuel 7:1–3, verses omitted in today's reading), spoken through Nathan the prophet. It is not the Lord's will that David build the Temple, but rather that his son do this. The Lord reaffirms his choice of David as king and his fidelity to him and promises to build an everlasting house (dynasty) for him (2 Samuel 7:12–14).

◆ RESPONSORIAL PSALM 89 acclaims the covenant God made with David, in particular his promise of an everlasting dynasty for David.

◆ GOSPEL: The parable of the sower and the seed is a familiar one. As Jesus teaches the crowd, he himself is the sower of the seed of the Word, as are all who proclaim the Gospel after him. The parable's interpretation invites us to examine our own receptivity to the Word of God. What type of ground is our heart? Sandwiched between the parable and its interpretation is Jesus's private teaching to his disciples. Note their privileged, or rather, blessed status, as recipients of God's revelation. The text from Isaiah serves to explain why so many did not hear and take the Word to heart.

T H U 30 (#320) green Weekday

The Lectionary for Mass

◆ FIRST READING: Today's reading follows upon yesterday's text and is David's prayerful response to God's Word spoken through Nathan. David is overwhelmed by God's goodness and fidelity to him and comes before him to give thanks and seek God's continued blessing for himself and for his people.

◆ RESPONSORIAL PSALM 132 is a prayer for King David, recalling his fidelity and his desire to build a dwelling place (Temple) for God. The covenant God established with David is likewise recalled. Zion (Jerusalem) is God's special dwelling place, the site of his Temple.

◆ GOSPEL: Two short parables and an enigmatic saying invite the listener to further reflection. Note the emphasis on hearing. Both images, the lamp and the measure, are familiar items from everyday life. What do we take in? What do we "put out" for others?

F R I 31 (#321) white Weekday Optional Memorial of St. John Bosco, Priest

The Lectionary for Mass

◆ FIRST READING: We have heard of several instances of David's integrity, even to the point of sparing the king who sought to take his life. In today's text, David's weakness comes to the fore. He gives in to his lustful desire, then seeks to cover up his wrong, even to the point of staging the death of Uriah, Bathsheba's husband. (Note, in contrast, Uriah's integrity in refusing to make an exception for himself and spend the night with his wife while his soldiers are encamped at the gates of the city.)

◆ RESPONSORIAL PSALM 51: The first two lines of the psalm in the Hebrew text (not part of today's response) attribute this psalm to David in the context of his sin with Bathsheba. It is a heart-felt prayer of repentance and petition for forgiveness.

◆ GOSPEL: Jesus appeals to his listeners' experience of nature to teach them the mystery of the growth of the Kingdom of God. Signs of the growth of a seed are visible, and while scientists today may be able to explain the process of growth, the force underlying it remains mysterious. Jesus's parables teach people with images and invite them to ponder their meaning. Can we hear with these same ears today?

Today's Saint

God gifted St. John Bosco (1815–1888) with the ability to read and interpret the signs of the times. Living during rapid industrialization and growing anti-clericalism, he became very concerned about the emotional and spiritual livelihood of people, especially the plight of the young. St. John worked to provide positive and affirming environments, including orphanages and oratories, where the young could learn and recognize their infinite potential. In the spirit of his favorite hero, St. Francis de Sales, he founded the Salesians, a religious congregation devoted to works of charity, with an emphasis on empowering young people to become strong pillars of faith in a culture of instability. His work among young men living in the slums proved to be a worthy endeavor. Whether he was presiding at Mass or playing games with children or carrying the sick to hospitals, it was obvious he lived until his "last breath . . . day and night, morning and evening" for the neglected and abandoned (as quoted in *Butler's Lives of the Saints: January, New Full Edition*, p. 229).

February
Month of the Passion of Our Lord

S A T **1** (#322) green
Weekday

Optional Memorial of the Blessed Virgin Mary / white

The Lectionary for Mass

◆ FIRST READING: Today's reading follows immediately upon the text we heard yesterday. The Lord sends the prophet Nathan to David. By means of a parable about the ewe, Nathan has David judge his own deed. Faced with his guilt, David acknowledges his sin. The sickness and death of the child conceived through his illicit union is understood to be a punishment for his sin.

◆ RESPONSORIAL Psalm: As we did yesterday, today we hear penitential Psalm 51. In our response, we pray with David for a clean heart. Our repentance, our steadfastness, our praise—these are not what we do of ourselves, but God's grace accomplishes them within us.

◆ GOSPEL: We see a very tired Jesus in today's Gospel—so tired that he sleeps peacefully through a raging storm at sea, whose waves were drenching the inside of the boat. The professional fishermen, for whom storms at sea must not have been unknown, are terrified. It is they who turn to Jesus for help now. They expected him to do something but are overwhelmed by his power over the natural elements. Who is Jesus, they wonder?

(#524)   white
2 **Feast of the Presentation of the Lord**

About this Feast

The Feast of the Presentation of the Lord is rooted in everyday life. In faithful observance of the law of Moses, Mary and Joseph present Jesus in the Temple to consecrate him to the Lord. There they met the righteous Simeon and the prophet Anna, for whom Temple worship was part of everyday life. God rewarded their fidelity by allowing them to see the one who was Savior and to hold him in their arms. When the ceremony of presentation was completed, Mary and Joseph and Jesus returned to their hometown. There, they created a home and a family life. There, Jesus grew up, becoming strong and wise, and the grace of God was upon him.

The Feast of the Presentation of the Lord, on February 2, is also called Candlemas Day. According

to Luke's account of the Gospel, Simeon recognized Jesus as the Messiah in the Temple and declared him "a light for revelation to the Gentiles, and glory for your people Israel" (Luke 2:32). This sparked the tradition of blessing enough candles to last an entire year. This led to candle processions in churches and in the streets, which became known as "Candlemas."

The Lectionary for Mass

◆ FIRST READING: *Malachi* is not so much a proper name but rather a Hebrew word that means "my messenger." This very short prophetic book (three chapters) targets the Temple priests in particular for their lack of fidelity to the Lord and their "unfit" sacrificial offerings. The messenger who will "come" to God's Temple will be like fire (light) refining and purifying Israel so that they may offer worthy sacrifice to God. Today's feast celebrates Jesus as that messenger.

◆ RESPONSORIAL PSALM 24: Today's psalm in its origins most probably was a hymn used when the Ark of the Covenant—signifying God's presence with his people—was carried in procession in the Temple.

◆ SECOND READING: Jesus is portrayed as the "merciful and faithful high priest" (Hebrews 2:17) who offers fitting sacrifice to God. The reading stresses his oneness with his brothers and sisters when he embraced human life and death. Like his brothers and sisters, he knows temptation and as a result is sure help for us in our own.

◆ GOSPEL: Echoes of today's other two readings are heard in the Gospel: purification, sacrifice, the Lord coming to the Temple—light. Simeon, echoing themes first voiced in the Old Testament, proclaims Jesus as a light for the Gentiles and glory (another image of light) for

Israel. There is also the note of purification and refining with reference to the child's destiny: "for the fall and rise of Israel" (Luke 2:34) and the revelation of the thoughts of human hearts.

The Roman Missal

Everything is proper to today's feast, so all texts and rubrics are found at February 2 in the Proper of Saints.

The Blessing of Candles and the Procession

The Missal calls for this Mass to begin with the blessing of candles and a procession, in one form or another. Two possibilities are given in the Missal: "The Procession" and "The Solemn Entrance." With this feast occurring on a Sunday this year, there is no real reason for the more elaborate form, "The Procession," to not take place at at least one Mass.

First Form: The Procession

All should gather in a place apart from the worship space where the procession will go to—for example, a smaller church, or perhaps a space in the parish hall, or perhaps even the gathering space of the church. The gathered faithful are to be already holding candles, so either the people bring candles with them or candles are handed to them as they gather. The priest, wearing white Mass vestments (although he may wear a cope at this point instead of a chasuble), and the ministers enter. There is no mention of a procession or of any singing, so the priest and the ministers just informally take their places. First, light everyone's candles and while this is done the antiphon suggested in the Missal (*Ecce Dominus noster*—"Behold, our Lord will come with power, to enlighten the eyes of his servants, alleluia"), or some other appropriate song, is sung. If another song or chant is used, the words should speak of the imagery of light.

After the candles are lit and the singing is concluded, the priest begins with the Sign of the Cross and one of the usual forms of the Greeting for Mass. Then he gives an introductory address; he may use the exact words as provided in the Missal at #4 for the Feast of the Presentation of the Lord, or he may use similar words. The address as given in the Missal notes the passing of forty days since the celebration of the Nativity and recalls how "Today is the blessed day / when Jesus was presented in the Temple by Mary and Joseph." It goes on to speak of the meaning of this feast as Jesus "coming to meet his believing people" and how Simeon and Anna, enlightened by the Holy Spirit, recognized him. It ends with the exhortation that we should "proceed to the house of God to encounter Christ," particularly as we shall recognize him in the breaking of bread until he comes again. Whether the priest uses the exact words in the Missal or similar words, the point of the address is to encourage the faithful "to celebrate the rite of this feast day actively and consciously."

After the address, the priest extends his hands and blesses the candles using the exact words of one of the two prayers of blessing given at #5 in the Missal (Feast of the Presentation of the Lord). In the first prayer, which specifically recalls Simeon and which refers to "the Light for revelation to the Gentiles," the priest makes the gesture of blessing with the Sign of the Cross where indicated; there is no such gesture in the second prayer, which speaks more generally about light and God's glory.

Next, the priest sprinkles the candles with holy water without saying anything. Then he puts incense into the thurible for the procession, receives his lighted candle from the deacon or another minister, and the procession begins with the words of invitation from the Missal, given by

the deacon, or, if there is no deacon, by the priest himself.

With everyone carrying lighted candles, the procession, in the usual order (that is, thurifer, crossbearer, candlebearers, and so on), moves into the worship space while an appropriate antiphon or song is sung. This Missal offers two suggestions for antiphons: "A light for revelation to the Gentiles and the glory of your people Israel" or "For my eyes have seen your salvation, which you have prepared in the sign of all the peoples." Latin text for the first option is provided in the Missal.

When the priest arrives at the altar in the church, he venerates it and incenses it, if incense is being used. He then goes to the chair where he changes from the cope into the chasuble, if he wore a cope for the procession. The Gloria is then sung, after which the priest prays the Collect, and Mass continues as usual.

Second Form: The Solemn Entrance

When the procession as described above is not going to take place, then the assembly gathers in the church as they usually do, holding candles. The priest, along with the ministers and a representative group of the faithful, goes to a place in the church that is visible to the rest of the assembly. They can be at the doors of the church or even somewhere inside the church itself. Notice that it is presumed that more than just the priest and ministers will gather and move in procession; a certain number of the faithful are expected to participate in this. The priest wears white Mass vestments; no mention is made of using a cope in this form of the entrance.

The priest and the others arrive at the place for the blessing of candles, without any music or formal procession. Once they are in place, everyone's candles are lit, with an antiphon or song being sung, as described above (this may take a little bit of thinking-through ahead of time, so that it is not done haphazardly; ushers can be of assistance here). Once everyone's candles are lit, the priest begins in the same way as in the first form above, with the Sign of the Cross, Greeting, introductory address, and blessing of candles and sprinkling, followed by the procession, accompanied by singing; he uses the same texts as designated for the first form of procession. As in the first form, the priest incenses the altar when arriving there, if incense is being used, and then he goes to the chair, at which point the Gloria is sung and Mass continues in the usual manner.

At the Mass

The Collect makes a connection between Christ's being presented "on this day in the Temple / in the substance of our flesh" and the request that, by God's grace, "we may be presented to you with minds made pure."

Since this feast falls on a Sunday this year, the Creed is to be said.

The Prayer over the Offerings draws a parallel between the offering of the Son, offered as the Lamb without blemish for the life of the world, and the offering we make now with exultation, asking that our offering here and now be pleasing to God, as was the offering of the Son.

The Preface, found right along with the other texts for this Mass in the Proper of Saints, is a brief one, succinctly stating that the "co-eternal Son was presented on this day in the Temple / and revealed by the Spirit / as the glory of Israel and the Light of the nations." Because of this, "we, too, go forth, rejoicing to encounter your Salvation." This going forth to encounter salvation occurs on many levels: certainly in the journey of our life, but also as we continue forth with the offering

of this sacrifice, where we will encounter Christ in the salvific power of the Paschal Mystery made present in the Church's anamnesis of the Eucharistic Prayer and in Christ's Real Presence in the Eucharist. This would be a good occasion to chant the introductory dialogue and Preface, in order to highlight the festivity of this liturgy.

Simeon is mentioned again, this time in the Prayer after Communion, as we pray that just as his expectation was fulfilled "that he would not see death / until he had been privileged to welcome the Christ," so too may we meet the Lord in the gift of eternal life.

Pastoral Reflection

Rituals are momentous reminders of the transformations completed and paths still to come. In today's Gospel, the ritual of presentation, in which Jesus is fully given his name, happens and his identity is fully recognized by the wise prophet, Simeon and prophetess, Anna. Both had waited their whole lives to have God's promises fulfilled. They seemed to hold a sacred space and gave due blessing in the ritual of presenting Jesus to his Jewish faith. Who knows your identity so fully that they present your life and richness back to you; or remind you of your true self when you have forgotten? Gift each of them with some form of thanks this week. Similarly, which young child in your life can you choose to unceasingly pray for to grow into their identity in God? Start a quiet journey with/for them. Finally, Anna fasted day and night and gave constant glory to God while she awaited the birth of Jesus. What depth can you lay claim to that keeps you rooted in your knowledge of God?

Optional Memorials of St. Blaise, Bishop and Martyr / red; St. Ansgar, Bishop / white

The Lectionary for Mass

◆ FIRST READING: Absalom, son of David, was a power-hungry man who successfully managed to win the people's loyalty away from King David. Eventually, Absalom conspired to become king in David's place. When he heard about this, David fled for his life, weeping and mourning over his son's treacherous act. As he fled, a man came out cursing and stoning David. His soldiers wanted to retaliate and kill him, but David would not let them. Perhaps this man was sent from the Lord. In any event, David chose to leave judgment in the Lord's hands and prayed for deliverance from his affliction.

◆ RESPONSORIAL PSALM 3: The biblical editor of the Psalter attributes this psalm to David as he fled from Absalom in the incident described in the First Reading. David put his trust solely in the Lord, and in the very act of trusting, he found strength and confidence (third stanza).

◆ GOSPEL: Once again, Jesus demonstrates his power over the world of the demonic and restores to health a man described as wild, unrestrainable, and self-destructive. Note the change in the possessed man's demeanor and behavior as a result of his healing encounter with Jesus. Subsequently, the healed man went and proclaimed all that Jesus had done for him.

Blessing of Throats

The optional Memorial of St. Blaise is the traditional day for the blessing of throats. Although the Missal is silent on it, the *Book of Blessings* states that throats may be blessed at Mass, following the Homily and the Universal Prayer. For pastoral reasons, it may take the place of the final blessing of the Mass. The formula of blessing is: "Through the intercession of St. Blaise, bishop and martyr, may God deliver you from every disease of the throat and from every other illness: In the name of the Father, and of the Son, and of the Holy Spirit. Amen."

Today's Saints

Although St. Blaise (+316) and St. Ansgar (801–865) were separated by time, they both wanted to care for souls. While serving as Bishop of Sebastea, in Armenia, St. Blaise was a visible witness of the Gospel, which eventually led to his martyrdom during the persecutions of Diocletian. His feast day is commemorated with a blessing of throats because legend says that he cured a young boy choking on a fish bone. St. Ansgar, born in France, was a monk with a missionary spirit. He longed to travel to distant lands to draw more and more souls to the saving message of Christ. His missionary endeavors were directed toward Scandinavian territory, thus earning him the title Patron of Denmark. He is credited with organizing missions to Denmark, Sweden, and Norway, and building the first Christian church in Sweden. Due to his excellent leadership and preaching skills, St. Ansgar was appointed Archbishop of Hamburg.

TUE 4 (#324) green
Weekday

The Lectionary for Mass

◆ FIRST READING: David's magnanimity is once again evident in his grief over the death of his son Absalom, despite his intent to seize his kingship. David's way of thinking and acting was certainly a far cry from what his men expected. His example calls us to examine our own attitudes toward the misfortunes of those who try to harm us.

◆ RESPONSORIAL PSALM 86: This psalm is a prayer for God's help and comfort in a time of sorrow and affliction. Note the request for a "glad heart" in the second stanza. Perhaps we can also hear the reference to God's forgiveness (third stanza) in terms of those who delighted in Absalom's death.

◆ GOSPEL: There are two miracle accounts in today's Gospel, one "framed" by the other. Both are powerful stories of faith and trust in the power of Jesus (despite the lack of faith shown by some at Jairus's house). Jesus's touch—and touching him—brings healing and life. How might we experience this touch in our day?

WED 5 (#325) red
Memorial of St. Agatha, Virgin and Martyr

The Lectionary for Mass

◆ FIRST READING: It is difficult to see what is wrong with David's action in taking a census. Is this not good military leadership? However, verses not included in today's lesson indicate that the census is not God's will. David was told this but persisted nonetheless with his own plan. Accordingly, he was punished by the Lord. The biblical author interpreted the plague at harvest time as the divine punishment. David repents of his sin and asks that the punishment due to him not be inflicted on the people.

◆ RESPONSORIAL PSALM 32 is a song of repentance attributed to David. Acknowledging his guilt, David trusts in the mercy of the Lord.

◆ GOSPEL: Jesus is at home in Nazareth, and his fellow citizens think that they know all there is to know about who this man is. Their assumptions and presumptions become a stumbling block to faith in Jesus and to the reception of his healing works. It is faith that elicits the divine power that is at work in Jesus.

The Roman Missal

The Mass text that is proper for today is the Collect, and it can be found in the Proper of Saints at February 5. The prayer highlights St. Agatha's courage in martyrdom and her chastity. The Prayer over the Offerings and the Prayer after Communion will come either from the Common of Martyrs: For a Virgin Martyr or from the Common of Virgins: For One Virgin. For the Preface, one of the two Prefaces of Holy Martyrs would be a good choice.

Today's Saint

Agatha was born in Sicily, probably around the year 231, and is one of the women mentioned by name in Eucharistic Prayer I. According to legend, she was the daughter of a prominent family and was very beautiful. The Roman senator Quintianus wished to marry her, but when Agatha spurned him, he had her put in a brothel. In spite of this, Agatha held to her Christian faith. Quintianus then had her tortured by having her breasts cut off. She eventually died in prison in 253. St. Agatha is the patron of the city of her martyrdom, Catania, and is invoked against the fire, earthquakes, and eruptions of Mount Etna. In recent years, because her breasts were cut off as part of her torture, she is considered the patron saint of breast cancer patients.

THU 6 (#326) red
Memorial of St. Paul Miki and Companions, Martyrs

The Lectionary for Mass

◆ FIRST READING: Knowing that his death was close at hand, King David gives his farewell words to Solomon, his son, urging him to be faithful to God's covenant laws. If he does so, he will be blessed. If Solomon's descendants are likewise faithful, there will always be a Davidic descendant on the throne in Jerusalem, for so God has promised in his covenant with David. At David's death, Solomon became king of Israel.

◆ CANTICLE: Today's response comes not from the Book of Psalms, but from a hymn in 1 Chronicles 29. It is David's prayer of praise to God after he and all the people freely offered their gold, silver, and jewels to God to be used in the construction of the Temple in Jerusalem. Note the designation of Solomon as king in 1 Chronicles 29 and also the Chronicler's account of David's death.

◆ GOSPEL: Jesus commissions the Twelve who are sent out two by two. Mark emphasizes that Jesus has given them power to cast out demons (unclean spirits), that is to say, Jesus gives them a share in his own authority and power. And as we hear at the end of the reading, they exercise this power. They also preach repentance, as does Jesus. Note the mention of anointing the sick with oil for healing—evoking our own sacrament of the sick.

The Roman Missal

The Collect, which is proper for today, is found in the Proper of Saints at February 6. The prayer refers to God as "the strength of all the Saints," and asks that through the intercession of St. Paul Miki and companions, "we may hold with courage even until death / to the faith that we profess," just as they did. The Prayer over the Offerings and the Prayer after Communion are taken from the Common of Martyrs: For Several Martyrs. For the Preface, use one of the two Prefaces of Holy Martyrs.

Today's Saints

St. Paul Miki (+1597), a Jesuit priest, was one of the twenty-six martyrs of Japan. Feeling threatened by the growing influence of the Jesuits, the local governor had members of the Christian community arrested and thrown in jail. They were forced to walk six hundred miles from Kyoto to Nagasaki as a deterrent to other Christians, but they sang the *Te Deum* as they went. At Nagasaki they were crucified. When Christian missionaries returned to Japan in the nineteenth century, they found that a secret Christian community had survived by transmitting their beliefs and prayers from generation to generation.

FRI 7 (#327) green
Weekday

The Lectionary for Mass

◆ FIRST READING: We hear Sirach's praise of King David. In effect, the reading is a summary of those deeds recounted in the Books of Samuel. What a beautiful tribute to him are the words "with his whole being he loved his Maker / and daily had his praises sung." David's contribution to Israel's worship is also acclaimed. Indeed, many of the psalms are attributed to David.

◆ RESPONSORIAL PSALM 18 is attributed to David, prayed after his escape from his enemies. David trusted in the Lord as his refuge and was blessed abundantly.

◆ GOSPEL: Mark's account of Herod's musings on Jesus's identity provides an occasion for telling of the death of John the Baptist. Today's text offers an interesting character study of Herod, son of Herod the Great. He is said to have "feared" John, recognizing his righteousness and holiness. Herod's weakness was his determination to uphold his own image before his guests—even at the cost of John's death—rather

than act in accord with the truth he knew in his own heart.

SAT 8 (#328) green
Weekday

Optional Memorials of St. Jerome Emiliani / white; St. Josephine Bakhita, Virgin / white; Blessed Virgin Mary / white

The Lectionary for Mass

◆ FIRST READING: While in the Temple, Solomon heard the Lord speaking to him in a dream, promising to give him whatever he desired. Solomon's greatness is evident in his response. He asks not for riches, but for an understanding heart (literally, a "listening" heart) that he might judge and govern God's people rightly. God answered his prayer, and indeed Solomon was renowned for his wisdom (see 1 Kings 3:16–28; see also the Books of Proverbs and Wisdom, which are attributed to Solomon).

◆ RESPONSORIAL PSALM 119 acclaims the wisdom of God's law; almost every verse of this longest psalm in Scripture extols some aspect of the Torah (law and teaching) of God. Our antiphon beautifully reflects Solomon's prayer.

◆ GOSPEL: Jesus's disciples had been hard at work faithfully carrying out the mission with which they had been entrusted: preaching, repentance, expelling demons, healing the sick (see Mark 6:7–13). No doubt, they were physically and mentally tired. How welcome Jesus's invitation to go apart by themselves with him for some rest must have been. The urgency heard so often in Mark's account of the Gospel is evident in the description of the people as "hasten[ing]" ahead of Jesus and his disciples to this deserted place. Instead of showing frustration or even annoyance on seeing them there, Jesus shows compassion. Sensing their hunger for his word, he began to teach them.

Today's Saints

While being held as a political prisoner, St. Jerome Emiliani (1481–1537) had a conversion experience in which he repented for his past sinful ways and devoted his life to Mary. After a miraculous escape he developed a special love for the unfortunates of society, concentrating on the needs of orphans and prostitutes. He founded a religious community, Clerks Regular of Somasca, with the intent of providing food, clothing, housing, and catechesis for the needy. St. Jerome is credited with developing the question-and-answer format for teaching catechism.

St. Josephine Bakhita (1869–1947), born in the Sudan, was enslaved at the age of ten and eventually sold to an Italian consul. Later in life she felt drawn to the Catholic faith through interaction with the Canossian Sisters. Following her conversion, she joined the sisters to live a life fully devoted to Jesus Christ and works of charity. She gained increasing popularity due to her exceptional spiritual practices, which led to her canonization.

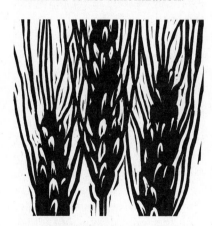

(#73)   green
9 Fifth Sunday in Ordinary Time

The Lectionary for Mass

◆ FIRST READING: Isaiah's words call God's people to action! And in Jesus's teaching in Matthew 25 on the end time, these commands become the criteria of judgment. Through faithfully observing them, the light that comes from God shines forth, and it is the motif of light that figures prominently in the today's Responsorial Psalm and Gospel as well. Note that the observance of God's law becomes not only a source of light—and enlightenment—for the faithful, but of healing and vindication as well.

◆ RESPONSORIAL PSALM 112: Our antiphon beautifully expresses how we need the light of goodness from one another. As in today's First Reading, righteousness or being in right relationship with God is established through the faithful observance of God's commands, particularly those pertaining to the poor and needy. Through this fidelity, the just person can stand confidently before the Lord and know deep peace.

◆ SECOND READING: In today's continuation of readings from the First Letter to the Corinthians, Paul reflects on his own call and mission. His personal enlightenment, we might say, is Jesus, the crucified one, in whom the glorious power of God was made manifest in Risen life. We can truly say that it is Jesus, who is the Light of Paul's life and he is totally committed to letting that light shine forth through his own weakness.

◆ GOSPEL: Jesus compares the presence and ministry of his disciples to salt, which enhances the taste of food, and to light, which is a necessity if we are to see our way in the darkness. If salt or light lose their effectiveness, they are worthless. So, too, with the disciples—and we are among them. Note that in the context of Matthew's account, today's passage comes after the Beatitudes (Matthew 5:1–12) and before Jesus's teaching about the true fulfillment of the law (Matthew 5:17–48). It is only through fidelity to his teaching that we can truly be the salt of the earth and the light of the world.

The Roman Missal

The Mass texts for today are found in the "Ordinary Time" section of the Proper of Time. The Gloria is sung or said today. The Creed is said or sung.

The Collect asks that the Lord will keep us safe as we rely "solely on the help of heavenly grace." The Prayer over the Offerings prays for the transformation of the created realities we offer, that is, bread and wine, so that just as they are material sustenance for us, so too may they become "the Sacrament of eternal life." The Prayer after Communion highlights the unity of the faithful that is to be the result of their participation in the Eucharist. Being united in the one Body of Christ through "the one Bread and the one Chalice" (a presumption that the chalice is offered to the assembly at all Masses?) is the way that we "joyfully bear fruit / for the salvation of the world."

Any one of the eight Prefaces of the Sundays in Ordinary Time may be selected for today. In keeping with the themes presented in the Gospel, however, Preface I, "The Paschal Mystery and the People of God," with its mention of the people called out of darkness to proclaim God's mighty works, or Preface V, with its reference to humanity's charge to "for ever praise you in your mighty works," are two choices that would work well.

Pastoral Reflection

Comparing all ordinary moments in life, when are you the happiest? How do you feel at this moment in time? What allows you to be this free and joyful? Similarly, what makes this feeling of joy fade? This innate joy is the light, the salt, and the gift you give the world. We are only truly happy and shine brightly when we are living full as God wants us to live, given our unique gifts in this life. When we are not living in our giftedness, our light fades and our lives lose their personality. Be comfortable sharing the light you are. Allow the flavor of your life to remain rich. This week use your life uniquely to glorify God at all times.

MON 10 (#329) white
Memorial of St. Scholastica, Virgin

The Lectionary for Mass

◆ FIRST READING: Today's reading tells of the dedication of the Temple, which Solomon built in Jerusalem. The Ark of the Covenant was enthroned in the innermost part of the Temple called the Holy of Holies. Although the Lectionary doesn't include details about the building process or a description of its interior, a perusal of these in 1 Kings 6–7 gives us a sense of the Temple's grandeur. Innumerable sacrificial offerings were made on this great day of dedication. After the enthronement of the Ark, a dark cloud filled the Temple—a sign for Solomon and all the people that God dwelt there.

◆ RESPONSORIAL PSALM 132 was sung by pilgrims making their way to the Temple. The "it" of the first line of the first stanza is the Ark of the Covenant. Perhaps this psalm accompanied a procession with the Ark of the Covenant, which was enthroned in the Holy of Holies.

◆ GOSPEL: Once again, we sense the urgency in Mark's account. People "immediately" recognize Jesus and "scurry" to bring their sick to him. Jesus's reputation as healer has spread. Particularly interesting is the reference to the fact that people only had to touch the tassel of his cloak to be healed. This mention of touch is reminiscent of the woman with the hemorrhage in an earlier chapter who was healed when she touched Jesus.

The Roman Missal

The Mass text that is proper for today is the Collect, found in the Proper of Saints at February 10. The Prayer over the Offerings and the Prayer after Communion are taken either from the Common of Virgins: For One Virgin, or from the Common of Holy Men and Women: For a Nun. For the Preface, choose either the Preface of Holy Virgins and Religious or one of the Prefaces of Saints.

Today's Saint

Information regarding the life of St. Scholastica is rather meager, but her legacy continues to live on. She was the twin sister of St. Benedict, the father of Western Monasticism. From a young age (480–547 AD) she expressed a deep desire to dedicate her life to God through the monastic vows: obedience, conversion of life (poverty and chastity), and stability. She founded and supervised a monastery of nuns near her brother's monastery at Monte Casino. Once a year St. Scholastica and St. Benedict would meet somewhere between their two monasteries to pray and discuss spiritual matters. Just prior to her death she met with her brother one more time. As the time came for him to leave, she prayed that somehow his visit would be extended. All of a sudden, a violent thunderstorm broke forth from the heavens, preventing St. Benedict from departing. Her prayers were answered—they spent the entire night pondering the deeper mysteries of life.

TUE 11 (#330) green
Weekday

Optional Memorial of Our Lady of Lourdes / white

Today's Optional Memorial

Today we commemorate the Virgin Mary's appearances in 1858 to Bernadette Soubirous, a 14-year-old peasant girl. This created an uproar in the small town, and Bernadette was repeatedly questioned and pressured by the local officials to recant her story. The parish priest told her to ask the lady's name. Bernadette returned and said, "I am the Immaculate Conception," a title for Mary, of which Bernadette would have known nothing. One of the lady's requests was that a chapel be built on the site of her appearance. Eventually a large church was built there (Lourdes, France), which is now a popular pilgrimage site (visit their website: http://fr.lourdes-france.org).

The Lectionary for Mass

◆ FIRST READING: Our readings continue from 1 Kings 8. Today we hear Solomon's prayer on the day of the dedication of the Temple. Solomon appeals to the mercy of the God of the covenant that the Temple may have his protection and blessing and that he hear the prayers of the people who worship there.

◆ RESPONSORIAL PSALM 83 extols the beauty of the Temple and expresses a pilgrim's longing to be and dwell there, singing the praises of the Lord.

◆ GOSPEL: The heart of today's Gospel is to be found in Jesus's citation of the words of the prophet Isaiah: "they honor me with their lips"—and we might add, "and their practices"—"but their hearts are far from me" (Isaiah 29:13). It is so easy to rationalize, to justify oneself. But God looks not at the appearances of external rituals in which the Pharisees, who set themselves apart, took such great delight, but at their hearts.

WED 12 (331) green
Weekday

The Lectionary for Mass

◆ FIRST READING: Solomon's wisdom is acclaimed in today's reading, which recounts the visit of the Queen of Sheba. In effect, she had to come and see for herself if all that she had heard about Solomon was true. Note that the word wisdom occurs four times in addition to the attestation that there was nothing the queen could ask that Solomon couldn't answer. Note also the references to the prosperity of Solomon. This is the fulfillment of what God had promised when Solomon prayed for wisdom. At the end of her visit, the queen praises Solomon's God and attests to the blessings of those who are privileged to hear Solomon's wisdom.

◆ RESPONSORIAL PSALM 37: Today's psalm is one that tells of the blessings bestowed on the just and wise person. The psalm speaks of both the way in which we can become just and wise, and the blessings of the Lord upon such a person.

◆ GOSPEL: Ritual cleanness and the necessary purifications—something of immense importance to the Pharisees—was the subject of yesterday's Gospel controversy. Today, we hear a teaching from Jesus that follows upon this, first to the crowds, then to his disciples. What really makes a person unclean in the eyes of God is not contact with external objects, but rather, what is within the heart. Thirteen different matters of the heart involving thoughts, attitudes, words, and actions are named as things that render us impure or defiled before God. All of God's people are called to purity of heart.

THU 13 (#332) green
Weekday

The Lectionary for Mass

◆ FIRST READING: In an earlier reading, we heard the beautiful tribute to Solomon that his heart was with the Lord. In today's text, we see that his single-hearted focus has become divided. As a result of the influence of his foreign wives, Solomon had turned to idolatrous worship of other gods. Solomon will be punished by the Lord. At his death, the kingdom will be divided. However, in fidelity to his covenant with David, the Lord promises that one tribe will endure.

◆ RESPONSORIAL PSALM 106 is another song of instruction, which basically tells the story of Israel's fidelity and infidelities. The first stanza of today's response is both an exhortation to righteousness and a prayer for God's help. The second and third stanzas describe the very kinds of things that went on at Solomon's idolatrous shrines.

◆ GOSPEL: The first line of today's Gospel gives us a glimpse of something we see often in Mark's account—Jesus's attempts to be alone and unrecognized. Clearly his ministry of preaching, exorcism, and healing was draining. Yet, we never see him turn anyone away. We see, too, how Jesus's understanding of his mission is continually refined by his experiences and encounters with people. The woman he meets in today's Gospel is a Gentile. Like so many others, after having heard about Jesus, she comes to him seeking healing for her daughter. She is not to be put off because she is Gentile. This time it is she who tells a parable, which leads Jesus to respond to her needs.

FRI 14 (#333) white
Memorial of SS. Cyril, Monk, and Methodius, Bishop

The Lectionary for Mass

◆ FIRST READING: The prophet Ahijah, tearing his new cloak into twelve pieces, confirms the Lord's judgment against Solomon with a prophetic action. The twelve pieces symbolize, of course, the twelve tribes of Israel. At Solomon's death, the kingdom would be divided and Jeroboam would become king of the northern kingdom.

◆ RESPONSORIAL PSALM 81: Both today's responsorial antiphon and the first stanza of the psalm echo the first commandment of the Mosaic covenant—which Israel did not keep. Because of the infidelity of their idolatry, Israel was handed over into the hands of their enemies.

◆ GOSPEL: Jesus's ministry among the Gentiles continues. Today, a deaf and mute man is brought to Jesus to be healed. It is interesting that Jesus took the man away by himself to heal him. The healed man must have told the story far and wide. Mark wrote his account in Greek some thirty-five to forty years after the Resurrection, but included in today's account is the Aramaic word *Ephphatha*—a word in Jesus's native tongue.

The Roman Missal

All the texts for this Mass text are proper for this day, and they are found in the Proper of Saints at February 14.

The Collect makes explicit reference to SS. Cyril's and Methodius's mission to the Slavic peoples. The Prayer over the Offerings speaks of the transformation that we pray will occur as a result of entering into the Sacrifice: "grant that these gifts may become the sign of a new humanity, / reconciled to you in loving charity." It's a reminder that at the heart of all Christian missionary work is the belief that the sharing in the life of Christ makes all things new, and that one of the fruits of living in Christ's love is reconciliation. The Prayer after Communion refers the universality of the Eucharist: God is the "Father of all nations," the one who makes us "sharers in the one Bread and the one Spirit." As a result of our one sharing in the Eucharist, we pray that "the multitude of your children, / persevering in the same faith, / may be united in building up the Kingdom of justice and peace."

No rubric assigns a particular Preface for this Mass; since the two saints are honored together and one is a monk while the other one is a bishop, one of the two general Prefaces of Saints would probably be the best choice.

Today's Saints

SS. Cyril (827–869) and Methodius (815–884) were brothers bound not only by biology, but by their longing to evangelize the unenlightened heart. Their missionary zeal led them to Slavic territories where the seeds of Western Christendom had yet to be planted. At the time, the Western Church only recognized the Hebrew, Greek, and Latin languages; therefore, they were charged with the task of translating the Bible and liturgical texts into Slavonic. Because Slavonic did not have a written language, the brothers had to develop a script, which later became known as the Cyrillic alphabet, named after St. Cyril. Shortly after his brother died, St. Methodius was consecrated a bishop. Because SS. Cyril and Methodius are venerated in both the East and West, they are considered the patrons of ecumenism.

S A T 15 (#334) green
Weekday

Optional Memorial of the Blessed Virgin Mary / white

The Lectionary for Mass

◆ FIRST READING: A person hungry for power will do anything to get it and anything to keep it, as is evident in today's First Reading. Fear that the peoples' pilgrimages to God's Temple in Jerusalem would sway their loyalty to King Rehoboam there, Jeroboam constructed two idolatrous shrines in the north where the people could worship. Jeroboam's infidelities included the consecration of priests who were not Levites—also in violation of God's law. Accordingly, Jeroboam and his house would be punished.

◆ RESPONSORIAL PSALM 106 is a historical psalm that recounts Israel's infidelities. Jeroboam's sin in making golden calves evokes the sin of his ancestors long before in the Sinai desert. We are called to look at our own infidelities, our own golden calves. In the words of our antiphon, let us cry out for God's mercy.

◆ GOSPEL: We see Jesus's great sensitivity to the needs of others evidenced in today's Gospel. He is not just an indifferent observer; his heart, his inner being, is moved by their plight. Mark's way of telling the story of the feeding of the multitude (giving thanks, breaking the loaves and distributing them) clearly evokes the Eucharist and calls us to reflect on it as food for our own journeys. There is also a lesson to be learned from the way Jesus takes what is at hand, however meager it is, and with prayer, finds in it what is needed.

☀ 16 (#76) green
Sixth Sunday in Ordinary Time

The Lectionary for Mass

◆ FIRST READING: There are two foci in today's reading from Sirach. The first is the fundamental choice that every human being has in life: to choose life or to choose death. The second is on the wisdom of the God who sees, knows, and understands all.

Keeping God's commandments leads to life; disobeying them ends in death. Our fundamental orientation of life is confirmed through numerous choices—some big, some small—made each and every day of our lives. It is something worth pondering. And, as today's reading concludes—God leaves us totally free.

◆ RESPONSORIAL PSALM 119 acclaims the wisdom of God's law. Our antiphon (see verse 3) attests to the blessedness and happiness of those who choose to follow it. The last two stanzas given for today (verses 17–18, 33–34) are basically a prayer for the gift of wisdom from God.

◆ SECOND READING: Today's Second Reading also treats of God's wisdom, contrasting it with the transitory wisdom of this age. Drawing on words from Isaiah 64:3–4 and inspired by God's Spirit, Paul speaks of the extraordinarily unimaginable future God has prepared for those who love him.

◆ GOSPEL: The Pharisees prided themselves on their observance of the law—with literal precision. They deemed themselves as "righteous" (see Matthew 5:19) because of it. Jesus asks for more than obedience to the mere letter of the law. That "something more" leads us into the deeper meaning, the true spirit of the law, and into true righteousness. Note the pattern of Jesus's speech: "You have heard . . . but I say to you . . . " (Matthew 5:21, 22). This is the way to the Kingdom of Heaven.

The Roman Missal

The Mass texts for today are found in the "Ordinary Time" section of the Proper of Time. The Gloria is sung or said today.

The Collect asks that our lives "may be so fashioned by your grace / as to become a dwelling pleasing to you." The prayer can serve as a reminder of the connection between liturgy and life—the point of participating in worship is not to engage in ritual actions for their own sake, but rather so that our participation in ritual worship will change us to live life as God asks us to live it, so that he will truly "abide / in hearts that are just and true." The Prayer over the Offerings reiterates that such transformation should be the heart of the oblation we make; as we make our offering in union at Mass with Christ's, "may it become for those who do your will / the source of eternal reward." The prayer reminds us, however, that nothing is automatic; transformation can only occur when we are open to doing God's will. In the Prayer after Communion we pray that, "having fed upon these heavenly delights" of the Eucharist, "we may always / long for that food by which we truly live."

Any one of the eight Prefaces of the Sundays in Ordinary Time may be selected for today. Perhaps Preface VII would be a good choice in view of the Gospel reading's emphasis on correct behavior and living a moral life.

Pastoral Reflection

There is nothing simple about the Ten Commandments and yet in everyday simple actions, without full consciousness, we may each break one. Jesus's words today are strong. He came to teach a new way of living, to not just know the law, but to fully live the law as it was meant to be lived. We are to be examples for others to uphold the law, thus making it easier for our neighbors to comply. Yet, when we fall, we must be aware of that nature and quickly and consciously do something about our misgivings. At Mass every Sunday, we offer a sign of peace. If the person you need to forgive is not present, call that person to mind so that your heart will soften and you will be able to forgive. Consciously cleanse your body of all things that pull you from God. Be purposeful in your words, thoughts, actions, and reactions. For all you say and do is meant to be guided by the Spirit dwelling in you. In this way, you can allow your "yes" to mean yes and your "no" to mean no, because God makes the choice with you, not against you.

M O N 17 (#335) green Weekday

Optional Memorial of the Seven Holy Founders of the Servite Order / white

The Lectionary for Mass

◆ FIRST READING: During the next two weeks, we hear from the letter of James. Today's text touches upon several themes: the need for perseverance in trials, the need for the wisdom that comes from God, the need for persistent prayer in faith. James warns people against being of two minds, that is, divided in their commitment to the Lord. James's words about the transitory nature of life and riches are good preparation for our Lenten journey.

◆ RESPONSORIAL PSALM 119: True life is found in the Lord, the source of all life. True life is accessible for all in the Word of the Lord. Today's psalm acclaims the wisdom and benefits of God's law.

◆ GOSPEL: Today we see Jesus undergoing a sort of trial with the Pharisees who are arguing with him. They are clearly a people of closed minds, not at all open to the wisdom of God as manifest in the teaching and actions of Jesus.

Today's Saints

The Founders of the Order of Servites were seven young men with one vision—to "be of one mind and one heart" (*Rule of St. Augustine;* the adopted Rule of the Servites, available from www.domcentral.org/trad/rule. htm), through common prayer, works of charity, and a special devotion to Mary, the Mother of God. Living in thirteenth-century Florence, the Founders of the Order of Servites (Friar Servants of Mary) were inspired to abandon their homes and businesses to seek a life of prayerful seclusion, eventually establishing themselves on Monte Scenario, called the "sounding mountain." These Friar Servants of Mary paid homage to Mary by living a humble and simple life. Their lifestyle drew young men from all over, which ultimately led to their establishment as a religious order. In the eighteenth century, a holy woman by the name of St. Juliana Falconieri was attracted to the lives of the seven holy founders and decided to consecrate her life to God, laying the foundation for the Servite Sisters.

T U E **18** (#336)   green
Weekday

The Lectionary for Mass

◆ FIRST READING: James calls us to look at the desires within us that lead us into sin and encourages us to persevere in times of temptation. God wills us to bring us to new and eternal life through the Word of truth of the Gospel. Let us be open to these words and take them to heart as we prepare for our Lenten journey.

◆ RESPONSORIAL PSALM 94: It is indeed a blessing to be instructed by the Lord, and the law of God and the Gospel of Jesus are preeminent means of instruction. Today's psalm calls us to strive for uprightness of heart and assures us of God's mercy in those times when we feel that we are slipping.

◆ GOSPEL: How frustrated Jesus was with his disciples for their lack of understanding of his words and deeds. He goes so far as to accuse them of having hardened hearts—just like their ancestors in their desert wanderings after the Exodus. Jesus warns them against the leaven of the Pharisees and of Herod. What "leaven" must we be on guard against? What signs have we failed to see? What words have we failed to hear?

W E D **19** (#337)   green
Weekday

The Lectionary for Mass

◆ FIRST READING: James knows only too well the dangers that so easily accompany speech. Accordingly, he exhorts his listeners to be slow; literally, to delay speaking and to "bridle [their] tongue[s]." So much damage is done to human relationships by impetuous and thoughtless speech, not to mention the hurtful words that are too often deliberately spoken. On the other hand, believers should be quick to listen and to welcome the Word of God with its power to save. But listening to the Word is not enough; one must act on it.

◆ RESPONSORIAL PSALM 15 is a wisdom psalm, instructing those who pray it on what must be done if we would live on God's holy mountain. Notice the references to speech in the stanzas of the psalm as well as to righteousness and care for the poor and afflicted, also of concern in today's First Reading.

◆ GOSPEL: Again we see Jesus taking the afflicted person off by himself in order to heal him. Emphasis is given to the power of Jesus's touch—and indeed, notice how many times hands are mentioned in today's reading. As was the case in one of last week's Gospel accounts, spittle is used as a healing ointment, consistent with the belief in Jesus's day of its healing properties.

T H U **20** (#338)   green
Weekday

The Lectionary for Mass

◆ FIRST READING: James's concern with what believers "do" continues. Today, the issue is how the rich and poor are treated in their assemblies. James has a clear picture of what is going on and he does not approve. His instruction is firm: "show no partiality" to the rich. The command to love our neighbors includes the poor as well as the rich. The poor are to be honored as much as the rich for it is the poor who are rich in faith and love of God.

◆ RESPONSORIAL PSALM 112 acclaims the blessedness and blessings of the one who fears or reverences the Lord and keeps his commands through good works.

◆ GOSPEL: As he makes his way to yet another city, Jesus asks his disciples who the people that have been coming to him in such numbers think he is. Some think he is John the Baptist returned from the realm of death, others Elijah, whose coming before the Messiah was expected by the Jews (see Malachi 3:23–24). Peter acknowledges that he is the Christ or Messiah—which, of course, Jesus is. Immediately, however, Jesus begins to teach his disciples what his Messiahship would mean—definitely not what Peter had in mind. Jesus's rebuke of Peter is strong and his command is clear. Peter must "get behind" Jesus; Peter must follow Jesus's way to Jerusalem.

F R I **21** (#339)   green
Weekday

Optional Memorial of St. Peter Damian, Bishop and Doctor of the Church

The Lectionary for Mass

◆ FIRST READING: James's emphasis on action continues, and once again the litmus test is treatment of the poor. Believers must translate their faith into action through their works. Indeed, this is what Abraham the father of believers did when he was willing to sacrifice his son Isaac (see Genesis 22) in obedience to God's command.

◆ RESPONSORIAL PSALM 34: Throughout the Scriptures, God has special care and concern for the poor. Psalm 34, in particular, acclaims this and gives thanks and praise for the salvation and deliverance received.

◆ GOSPEL: Jesus continues his teaching on what it means to follow him: nothing less than denying oneself, taking up one's own cross, and entering into the mystery of Death and Resurrection. In this—and only this—will we find salvation. In doing this, we will be lovingly welcomed by Jesus when he comes in glory. Mark and the believers of his day believed that this coming would be within their lifetimes.

Today's Saint

St. Peter Damian (1007–1072), born to a large Italian family, entered a Camaldolese Benedictine monastery comprising hermit monks who followed an austere life of fasting and prayer. Dedicating himself to the study of Scripture and the Fathers of the Church, he gained a reputation among the hermits as being both a gifted scholar and spiritual guru. Although he lived in a monastery, removed from the world, St. Peter was a powerful voice of reform in the Church. He spoke out against clerical abuses, challenged bishops to recommit themselves to their vocation, and announced the need for a reformed papacy. Recognized for his ability to lead, he was made Abbot of his monastery and later installed as Bishop of Ostia. As bishop, he never lost sight of his calling to be a monk. He was so influential in the Church that Pope Leo XII declared him a Doctor of the Church.

S A T 22 (#535) white Feast of the Chair of St. Peter the Apostle

About this Feast

The chair of a bishop, called the *cathedra*, is the symbol of his foundational ministry to be a teacher of faith to his church community. What then can we learn from Peter, the rock of our Church? His extraordinary confession of faith in this passage teaches us courage to confess truth, even if it may sound far-fetched by everyday standards. Peter listened to the Spirit of God in his heart and proclaimed Jesus as Christ, Son of the Living God. When Jesus asks "Who do you say that I am?," each of us is presented with the same question. What is the Spirit of God prompting us to proclaim?

Today's feast, attested to as early as the mid-fourth century, has its roots in the *Parentalia*, or commemoration of dead relatives and friends

celebrated between February 13 and 22. At this commemoration, a chair, or cathedra, was left empty for particular deceased persons. Since the actual date of Peter's death was unknown, it came to be remembered on February 22, eventually becoming a celebration of his taking over the pastoral responsibility of the Church of Rome.

The Lectionary for Mass

◆ First Reading: Peter exhorts his fellow presbyters (those in leadership) to willingly and eagerly shepherd the believers who are entrusted to them. Presbyters are to be examples of service, not domination. Note that although they hold leadership roles, they are nevertheless subordinate to Christ, the "chief Shepherd" (1 Peter 5:4), to whom they are accountable and who will give them their reward, a share in his glory, when he is revealed at the end of time. Note the twofold mention of this revelation. The early Christians lived in ardent hope and expectation of it.

◆ Responsorial Psalm 23: Today's psalm focuses on the Lord as Shepherd, a fitting response to the first reading with its reference to Christ the "chief Shepherd" (see 1 Peter 5:4). Have you ever noticed how much of a servant or minister the shepherd of Psalm 23 is? Everything that he does is for the care and well-being of the sheep. Pray this psalm, imagining yourself as the sheep who receives such loving care.

◆ Gospel: In today's Gospel, Peter confesses Jesus as the Christ or Messiah, the long-awaited son of David—and the Son of the living God. Jesus attributes this profound confession of faith to a gift of grace, a revelation from the Father. Peter was known as Simon when first called by Jesus, and that name occurs in today's text as well. His new name, "Peter," is no doubt derived

from the Greek word for "rock"—thus the word play in verses 17–18.

Peter is given a foundational role in the establishment of the "Church" (and here is the first time the word is used in the Gospel according to Matthew), or the assembly of those who are called, as the Greek word implies. Also implied is a relationship between the Church and the "Kingdom of heaven" (Matthew's phrase for the Kingdom of God; see verse 19). The words "bound" and "loose" (verse 19) pertain to the exercise of authority (but see Matthew 18:18, which gives this role to the community). Today, however, Peter's authoritative leadership role is the focus of our feast.

The Roman Missal

Everything is proper to today's feast—all texts are found at February 22 in the Proper of Saints.

The Gloria is sung or said today.

All of the orations include mention of St. Peter, as might be expected, focusing on his teaching and on our need to hold fast with integrity to the faith that has been both confessed and taught by Peter. In fact, this idea of the Church's faith being built upon the faith of Peter is expressed in the liturgy even before the orations: in the Entrance Antiphon, taken from Luke's account of the Gospel, we hear, "The Lord says to Simon Peter: / I have prayed for you that your faith may not fail, / and, once you have turned back, strengthen your brothers."

The Collect presents an image of the surety and strong foundation that we can have when we rely on the faith confessed by Peter, as particularly evidenced by the role that Jesus gave to Peter after the Apostle's confession of faith in the Lord: we ask that "no tempests may disturb us" because we have been set "fast / on the rock of the Apostle Peter's confession of faith." Again acknowledging that it is only through Peter's teaching that the Church can hold the faith in all its integrity, the Prayer over the Offerings also recognizes St. Peter as the shepherd of the Church.

The Prayer after Communion speaks of the Eucharistic celebration as "this redeeming exchange," asking that our nourishment "by communion in the Body and Blood of Christ . . . may be for us a Sacrament of unity and peace." Thus does the prayer bring to the fore the importance of unity that is at the heart of both the Petrine ministry, even down to our day in the role of the pope, and the celebration of the Eucharist.

The Preface assigned for today is Preface I of the Apostles, which expresses how through the blessed Apostles God continues to watch over the Church to protect his flock always.

It is suggested in the Missal to use a Solemn Blessing at the end of Mass, the formula of blessing titled "The Apostles." It would be a good idea to use this today.

Pastoral Reflection

Today we celebrate a promise that Christ has given to us—the promise that we may put our trust and faith in the teaching authority of Peter and his successors. Peter is the rock and foundation upon which God has built his "house." What confidence our Lord has in Peter! If the Son of God is willing to place his confidence in poor, weak, Peter, should we be any less willing to trust in the promise of Christ?

23 (#79) green
Seventh Sunday in Ordinary Time

The Lectionary for Mass

◆ First Reading: Our reading opens with the command to "be holy" (Leviticus 19:1) because the Lord our God is holy. It continues with the practical spelling out of how we are or become holy as we cooperate with God's grace in heeding his commands. The commands set forth in today's reading have to do with the way we speak and act toward others. The commands are simple: We are to love our neighbor.

◆ Responsorial Psalm 103: The verses chosen for today's response tell us what God is like in his dealings with his human creatures. They spell out for us just how we should be toward others if we are to be holy as the Lord our God is holy, and perfect as our heavenly Father is perfect (today's Gospel).

◆ Second Reading: Paul's words likewise treat of our holiness—only in this case, our holiness is based on the fact that God dwells in us. Thus, Paul says, we are God's temple. It is reality that we should keep in mind in our relationships with one another, lest we, through irreverence, meanness, dishonesty, or whatever, "destroy" the temple of God that they are.

◆ Gospel: Like deserves like, deemed the law in terms of retaliation for evil, but Jesus radically overturns this: do not give like for like, rather absorb the evil and respond in love. Give more than what is asked of you. This is the radical law of love in the Kingdom of God.

It is easy to love those who love us, to show kindness to those who are kind to us. But the Gospel demands more of us: We are to love our enemies and do good to those who persecute us—whatever shape that may take in our daily lives. It is only in so doing that we are truly Jesus's disciples, and that we become like our heavenly Father who shows unconditional benevolence toward all. The Greek word *perfection* in the last line of today's text, means not so much "flawlessness" as "maturity" and "wholeness."

The Roman Missal

The Mass texts for today are found in the "Ordinary Time" section of the Proper of Time. The Gloria is sung or said today.

In the Collect we pray that as we ponder spiritual things, such spiritual thoughts will not remain merely in the mind, but rather, that they will be put into concrete practice, so that "we may carry out in both word and deed / that which is pleasing to you." In the Prayer over the Offerings, we both acknowledge that celebrating these mysteries is "the observance that is your due" and, at the same time, ask that the celebration "may profit us for salvation." We must always remember that our worship adds nothing to God's greatness, and God in no way needs or is dependent on us, and we are the ones who gain when we have our lives ordered correctly and make the proper place for worship and offering sacrifice to God. The Prayer after Communion prays that the mystery we have just celebrated will truly be experienced in our lives—presumably, one can reason, in the concrete practice of our virtues, as was expressed in the Collect.

In keeping with today's Gospel proclamation to love our enemies and pray for those who persecute us, using Eucharistic Prayer for Reconciliation II could be a good possibility. If Eucharistic Prayers I, II, or III are going to be used, then Preface II of the Sundays in Ordinary Time, with its reference to God's "compassion for the waywardness that is ours" might be a good choice.

Pastoral Reflection

Have you ever heard today's Scripture quoted when you experience something unjust? The outer layer of words, "turn the other cheek" (see Matthew 5:39: "When someone strikes you on (your) right cheek, turn the other one to him as well"), seems to say that we shouldn't fight back and allow the person hurting us to have easy access to be wounded again. Yet, Jesus is not saying we should allow someone to walk all over us. He is saying that we need to be conscious of what is worthy of our efforts and time and to be the same person in all situations. Who gets underneath your skin? How can you turn your cheek and do the opposite of their actions *to* them, being kind when they are cruel? Is it possible to be the hospitable person at all times, to everyone you meet? Consistency matters and allows your light to remain bright.

M O N 24 (#341) green Weekday

The Lectionary for Mass

◆ FIRST READING: James's exhortation to wisdom is reminiscent of the wisdom writings in the Old Testament such as Proverbs, Sirach, and the Book of Wisdom. True wisdom is that which "comes from above" and is rooted in God's law. James is quite clear on what this wisdom is like—and what it is not like. By its fruit you shall know it. Are we among those who have the wisdom from above?

◆ RESPONSORIAL PSALM 19: The second half of Psalm 19, from which the stanzas of today's response are taken, acclaim the law of the Lord and lists its numerable attributes. Note the references to wisdom, purity, and truth in the stanzas of today's response—all echoing today's First Reading.

◆ GOSPEL: What a contrast between the disciples' lack of faith and the faith of the father of the possessed boy! Jesus teaches his disciples—and us—that there is a close relationship between faith and prayer. Don't miss Mark's somewhat passing comment about the crowd's amazement on seeing Jesus as he came down the mountain after the transfiguration experience. Was Jesus still radiant after his time of intense prayer?

T U E 25 (#342) green Weekday

The Lectionary for Mass

◆ FIRST READING: James hits us straight on with the realities of the wars and conflicts that exist between people, as well as nations and even within the individual person. The result is sin.

James exhorts those who hear his word in every age to draw near to God, to cleanse their hands of sin, to purify their hearts and no longer be of two minds. It is time for conversion, for single-hearted focus on the Lord and undivided commitment to his way.

◆ RESPONSORIAL PSALM 49: Today's psalm instructs us to rely on the Lord, rather than on our own devices in dealing with the anxieties, the uncertainties, and even the violence that beset us. The one who strives to live justly can be assured of the Lord's support.

◆ GOSPEL: Both today's First Reading and Gospel share a common theme—the necessity of humbling

oneself before the Lord and before one another. What a clashing juxtaposition there is between Jesus's teaching on his imminent Death and Resurrection—the result of being handed over by one of his own—and the disciples arguing about who among them is the greatest. We must become servants; we must receive those who are small and powerless. In them, we receive and welcome the Lord.

W E D 26 (#343) green Weekday

The Lectionary for Mass

◆ FIRST READING: James's words pose some very good questions for our own self-examination. Do we think and plan like the Christians he addresses—as if we ourselves have mastery and control of our days and our lives? Where does the Lord fit into it all? It is well to take James's advice to heart: "if the Lord wills it . . ." (James 4:15)—and only then are we able to accomplish any of our plans.

◆ RESPONSORIAL PSALM: Our antiphon is from Matthew's Sermon on the Mount (Matthew 5:3). We are truly poor in spirit if we know our dependence on God, such as James exhorts Christians in today's First Reading. As Psalm 49 wisely points out (first stanza of today's response), all people are dependent on God, without exception, without class distinction. All will die. All will come before God in judgment.

◆ GOSPEL: Today's text offers us another insight into the very human character of the disciples (remember how Jesus called them faithless in Monday's text?). Today, they see themselves as a rather elitist group. No, Jesus tells them—if someone has performed an act of power in Jesus's name, that person is one with and for Jesus.

THU **27** (#344) green
Weekday

The Lectionary for Mass

◆ FIRST READING: Most people who hear James's words today may not consider themselves wealthy—at least in comparison with those our society deems so. Yet, in comparison with the majority of the people in the world today, we are indeed rich. Hear James's words about wealth in this light. What do we use or wear that was manufactured by workers, perhaps in other countries, who are exploited by big and wealthy corporations? What do we eat that was harvested by workers who have been exploited? To do so is to be an accomplice in the crime. God hears the cries of the poor.

◆ RESPONSORIAL PSALM 49: Our antiphon is the same as yesterday's, and our psalm, a continuation of Psalm 49. More words of woe for the rich who live mindlessly of the poor, who live off the poor. Their judgment is at hand.

◆ GOSPEL: Commitment to conversion and integrity is likewise the subject of today's Gospel. Nothing at all is worth the cost of losing everlasting life! (Gehenna, or hell, is its opposite.) Jesus is not suggesting self-mutilation, but he is clearly putting things in vivid perspective! The final line of today's Gospel is likewise a vivid image: live so as to be a "good" seasoning, a "good" preservative for peace in your dealings with one another.

FRI **28** (#345) green
Weekday

The Lectionary for Mass

◆ FIRST READING: James's words sound a new note, not about wealth, but about our relationships with one another, and in particular, about behaviors that are destructive of those relationships. On these we will be judged. James calls believers to tolerance, as difficult as it may be at times, and to perseverance in being and doing good. We are not to swear, but rather to speak truthfully and in integrity.

◆ RESPONSORIAL PSALM 103: Today's psalm of praise acclaims the mercy and compassion of God, qualities that we are to show in our relationships with one another. Note how today's verses describe God's dealings with us. This is how we are to be with one another.

◆ GOSPEL: Jesus asks more of his disciples than did the law of Moses. The case in point in today's Gospel is divorce. According to the law of Moses, this is permissible on certain grounds. According to Jesus, who came to fulfill the law, it is not.

March
Month of St. Joseph

SAT **1** (#346) green
Weekday

Optional Memorial of the Blessed Virgin Mary / white

The Lectionary for Mass

◆ FIRST READING: These concluding words of James's letter offer practical advice about prayer in several circumstances of life. James's point is clear: prayer is most efficacious. Note the reference to the anointing of the sick, a practice likewise attested in Mark 6:13. How do we implement his advice in the final words of today's reading? How can we bring back one another to the truth when we have strayed from it? Do you have the courage to speak, to act?

◆ RESPONSORIAL PSALM 141: Today's psalm is a prayer for the evening sacrifice, a fitting response to James's exhortation on prayer. Imagine your prayer as the smoke of incense, gently wafting its way heavenward. Perhaps the guard of the mouth for which the psalmist prays is warning against any words spoken that are not akin to prayer, to praise, to upbuilding one another. Our eyes should be turned to God, for God's eyes are upon us.

◆ GOSPEL: If only we knew the reasons why the disciples objected to people bringing children to Jesus! Whatever the reason, Jesus did not approve of their so doing. Jesus wanted people to bring children to him. More important than knowing why the disciples objected is knowing why a child is the model of acceptance of the kingdom for disciples of all ages. What do you think?

☀ **2** (#82) green
Eighth Sunday in Ordinary Time

The Lectionary for Mass

◆ FIRST READING: The prophet's words are addressed to Israel in exile, to a people who have experienced the loss of homes, Temple, and land. No wonder it seemed that God had forsaken his people. Far from it. God's loving care for Israel can be compared to—and even surpasses—that of a mother for her infant. It is almost unthinkable that a mother could forsake her helpless infant, though sadly this can happen. Never will God forsake his people.

◆ RESPONSORIAL PSALM 62: Today's antiphon is virtually a command: "Rest in God alone. . . . " Good words to speak, to command our souls. God will never forsake us or let us down. God is the only one about whom we can say this with assurance. Note how many times the word "only" is used. Note the images used to describe this security.

◆ SECOND READING: The Corinthian community was torn by division and factions that often centered on loyalties or dislike of various teachers. To be sure, Paul lacked the eloquence of some of his co-workers in Corinth (see for example, 1 Corinthians 3:3–5). It is in this context that today's reading should be seen. Paul asserts his trustworthiness as servant and steward of the mysteries of God in his proclamation of the Gospel.

◆ GOSPEL: Like the prophet Isaiah, Jesus calls his disciples to confident trust in the providential and loving care of God—here twice named their heavenly Father. Such an attitude stands in stark contrast with putting all one's efforts and energies in mammon (the opening words of the Gospel)—or worrying as if everything depended on ourselves. I wonder how the disciples felt when Jesus called them people "of little faith" (and trust). Would he say the same of us?

The Roman Missal

The Mass texts for today are found in the "Ordinary Time" section of the Proper of Time. The Gloria is sung or said today.

The Collect asks that God's peaceful rule may direct the course of our world, and that under such protection the Church "may rejoice, / untroubled in her devotion." The Prayer over the Offerings recognizes that the outward gifts we offer (bread and wine) are meant to

be signs of the inward, spiritual sacrifice we bring to the Sacrifice of the Mass, which, if course, must be the sacrifice of "our desire to serve you with devotion." The prayer then goes on to ask that what is granted to us in the offering "as the source of merit / may also help us to attain merit's reward"—in other words, we pray that our participation in the offering will itself be the source of our transformation. The Prayer after Communion connects the nourishment we have received through the Sacrament here and now with the heavenly liturgy, asking that having been fed now "in the present age, / you may make us partakers of life eternal."

Preface VI of the Sundays in Ordinary Time, "The pledge of the eternal Passover," might be a good choice today insofar as it speaks of our closeness to God—"in you we live and move and have our being"— and of our experiencing God's care as a daily effect; this could connect with the Gospel theme of not being anxious, and trusting in God's care for us.

Pastoral Reflection

In our time and age, with the economy causing much worry and forcing even simple choices like not making an extra trip with gas prices being too high, how do we follow the words of Jesus today? Whom do you serve—the demands of common culture or the consideration of Christ? Culture all too easily causes stress. God promotes peace. What can you choose to give to God this week? Look at your lifestyle and your everyday choices. Critique why you do what you do and whom it serves, culture or Christ. God desires serene souls and joyful spirits. With God all things are possible. How do you lose control of your life so God can gain control?

M O N **3** (#347) green

Weekday

Optional Memorial of St. Katharine Drexel, Virgin / white

The Lectionary for Mass

◆ FIRST READING: The first letter of Peter opens with a prayer of praise for the new birth and promised inheritance that Christians have received through the Resurrection of Jesus. This reality brings a joy much deeper than the trials and sufferings that are bound to be a part of a life lived in the footsteps of the one who suffered, died, and rose from the dead.

◆ RESPONSORIAL PSALM 111: God has indeed remembered his covenant forever. In Jesus, the promises of old are fulfilled in a way beyond all human imagining. Thanksgiving (stanza one) can be our only response. In Jesus, God has delivered his people (stanza 3) from the power of death and brought them into the fullness of life.

◆ GOSPEL: Eternal life is the desire of this would-be disciple of Jesus, a man faithful to fulfill the law and commandments, but whose heart is deeply attached to all that he owns—so much so that he is unable to follow Jesus.

Today's Saint

St. Katharine Drexel (1858–1955), a wealthy and worldly heiress from Philadelphia, did not spend her fortune on houses or jewelry, but on the establishment of institutions and missions dedicated to the marginalized. Due to her financial means, she had the privilege of traveling to various parts of the country in which she became keenly aware of the oppression of Native Americans and African Americans. She dedicated her entire life, including the founding of a religious community known as the Sisters of the Blessed Sacrament, to the empowerment of these people through education (i.e., launching the first Catholic college for African Americans, and starting one hundred forty-five Catholic missions and twelve schools for Native Americans). Regarding the purpose of the Sisters of the Blessed Sacrament, St. Katherine said, "Ours is the spirit of Eucharist— the total gift of self" (as quoted on the website of the Archdiocese of Philadelphia, www.archdiocesephl .org/rigali/cardhom/drexel04. htm).

TUE 4 (#348) green
Weekday

Optional Memorial of St. Casimir / white

The Lectionary for Mass

◆ First Reading: Jesus the Messiah and Lord has come! He whom the prophets awaited and proclaimed has come into our midst. He has brought eternal life to all who would believe. Do we recognize what is ours? Do we live accordingly? Do we live in joyful and confident expectation of Jesus's Second Coming at the end of time when the fullness of our life with him will be realized?

◆ Responsorial Psalm 98: The psalmist breaks forth in a joyful hymn of praise in the realization of God's salvation. Is our response to what Jesus has done for us one of joy and praise?

◆ Gospel: There is something so human and real about Peter. He tells Jesus that he's given up everything to follow him—unlike the man who couldn't part from his possessions. He asks him, "What are we going to get in return?" And the Lord says, "All that you have given up will return to you in abundance and you will have eternal life. There is also something else: Persecutions. You will suffer because you follow me" (author's paraphrasing). The members of Mark's community knew the reality of persecution because of their faith in Jesus. In the early Church, this faith could cost you your life. But the return will be abundant: eternal life.

Today's Saint

St. Casimir was a prince of Poland and of the Grand Duchy of Lithuania. Born in the royal palace in Kraków, he was heir apparent to the throne. When the king went to Lithuania, Casimir was left in charge of Poland from 1481 to 1483, and it is said that he ruled with great justice and prudence. Casimir was known for his piety and devotion. Weakened by fasting, he developed a lung disease that was probably tuberculosis, and died. St. Casimir is buried in the cathedral of Vilnius, in Lithuania.

LENT AND HOLY WEEK

The Liturgical Time

The Calendar
March 5, 2014–April 17, 2014

The Meaning/The Lectionary for Mass

LENT calls us to repent of all that obscures God's life within us and to believe in the Good News of the Gospel: the Good News of the forgiveness that is offered, the Good News of God's love that is greater than anything we have done or failed to do, the Good News of the eternal life that has already begun for us through the Death and Resurrection of Jesus and in which we share through Baptism. Lent calls us to life: to become more and more in touch with the reality of God's life within us, to awaken to the glorious destiny that is ours and to hasten toward it. This is the pre-eminent theme we hear in the Sunday Lectionary for Year A.

The Gospel reading for the First Sunday of Lent is always the account of Jesus's temptation in the desert. Matthew's account offers us some details of the nature of the temptations as the tempter tries to get Jesus to misuse or show off his power and to worship someone, something other than God. Are these not our temptations, too? Matthew's account likewise shows us how Jesus remained faithful to God. Note how his knowledge of the Scriptures helped him in this regard.

On the Second Sunday of Lent, we glimpse Jesus's glory on the mountain of transfiguration.

We glimpse the glory that is our destiny in him as well (see 2 Corinthians 3:18). We hear the voice of the Father: "This is my beloved Son with whom I am well pleased. Listen to him." Jesus shows us the way to be pleasing to the Father as his beloved sons and daughters. We need only heed his words.

The beautiful story of Jesus's encounter with the Samaritan woman at Jacob's well is the Gospel reading for the Third Sunday of Lent. If we but knew the gift of God. If we but recognized the water that is offered us, "welling up to eternal life" within us. Would we not hasten and drink abundantly?

Jesus's gift of sight to the man born blind, the Gospel for the Fourth Sunday of Lent, calls us to examine the ways in which we are blind. Do we really want to see? How deep is our faith in Jesus? Come to him and receive the gift of sight he so longs to give.

The powerful account of the raising of Lazarus is the Gospel for the Fifth Sunday of Lent. Yes, Jesus's power extends even to the realm of the dead and he can and does bring life out of death. What might this mean in our own lives right now?

We witness Jesus's own entrance into the realm of the dead with the reading of the Passion narrative on Palm Sunday. With the crowds that welcomed him into Jerusalem, we acclaim our king as he comes into the city where his passage through death into life will be accomplished.

The First Readings on the Sundays of Lent trace the story of God's plan of salvation for humankind: their creation and fall; the formation of a Chosen People beginning with the call of Abraham; Israel's desert journeys after the Exodus (how quickly God's people—ourselves among them—forget the marvels done on their behalf); the anointing of David as king during Israel's monarchical period; and the promise of re-creation during the lifeless days of exile. Note how the Second Reading on Sundays both echoes what was heard in the First Reading and gives hints of themes that will be treated more at length in the Gospel!

On weekdays, we will notice that the First Reading—always from the Old Testament during Lent—and the Gospel are closely connected. So, too, is the Responsorial Psalm, an often neglected part of the Liturgy of the Word. See yourself as the one called to conversion and repentance—you are. See your family, your parish community, as the people called to conversion and repentance—you

are. See yourself as the one in need of healing—you are. See yourself as the one who receives Jesus's healing touch—you can. See yourself as the one whom Jesus forgives—you are. See yourself as the one called to forgive—you are.

Beginning with the fourth week, the Gospel accounts are from John, whose emphasis is very different from that found in Matthew, Mark, and Luke. We hear clearly how Jesus was sent from heaven to do the works of the Father; and of how the Father was at work in him. We hear of the healings Jesus performed; these are signs that manifest his glory and reveal his divinity. We hear of the growing controversy between Jesus and the Jewish religious leaders, reaching a high point during Holy Week.

On Palm Sunday, we hear the account of Jesus's entry into Jerusalem from the Gospel according to Matthew. Note the continuation of Matthew's emphasis on how Jesus is the fulfillment of all that was prophesied in the Old Testament. The people jubilantly proclaim Jesus's Kingship. His entrance into the city had a powerful effect on all who dwelt there, prompting them to ask his identity. Note the crowds' response: "This is Jesus the prophet, from Nazareth in Galilee."

The First Reading focuses on the Suffering Servant "who did not turn back" but remained faithful (whether referring to the prophet Isaiah himself or to Israel as a nation). It points to Jesus, the Suffering Servant of God (see Isaiah 50:4–7). There are four such texts in Isaiah, and in the course of the week, we will hear the other three (see Isaiah 42:1–7; 49:1–6, 52:13–53:12).

The liturgy of the last week of Lent calls us to welcome Jesus as the prophet who speaks and lives the message of our salvation. It invites us to walk and pray with him into the mystery of death and eternal life. Yes, we are dust and unto dust we shall return . . . but not forever. Jesus "gave up" his life spirit to God (see Matthew 27:50) that he might breathe it, transformed in the glory of God, upon us.

Know that Lent is not so much about what we do for God . . . as it is about what God wishes to do for us: re-creating us in his love and life. Our sacrifices, our Lenten practices are important, yes, for they help us to focus on God; our acts of self-denial create an opening for God's creative work in us. It is this new life—our life recreated in and by the Risen Christ—that we will celebrate at Easter. Enter, then, into these forty days with joy.

The Roman Missal

THE texts for Lent in *The Roman Missal* are found immediately following the Mass for the Sunday after the Epiphany of the Lord, the Feast of the Baptism of the Lord. Like Advent and Christmas Time, every day for Lent and Holy Week has its own Mass. Each day has a proper Entrance Antiphon, Collect, Prayer over the Offerings, Communion Antiphon, and Prayer after Communion. Formularies begin with Ash Wednesday and continue up to and including the texts for the Chrism Mass on Thursday of Holy Week (Holy Thursday), after which the section for the Sacred Paschal Triduum begins.

This year, two solemnities replace the Lenten days: St. Joseph, Spouse of the Blessed Virgin Mary, on Wednesday, March 19, and the Annunciation of the Lord, on Tuesday, March 25.

The *Universal Norms on the Liturgical Year and the General Roman Calendar* (UNLY) explains that "Lent is ordered to preparing for the celebration of Easter, since the Lenten liturgy prepares for celebration of the Paschal Mystery both catechumens, by the various stages of Christian Initiation, and the faithful, who recall their own Baptism and do penance" (27). Thus, it is not surprising to find both penance and initiation as themes that emerge in the Missal texts throughout the time of Lent.

Careful selection of texts by parish liturgy committees can greatly enhance a community's entrance into the proper Lenten spirituality. Given the penitential nature of Lent, it would make sense to highlight the Penitential Act. You might consider using the Confiteor more frequently, or perhaps even exclusively, if your community uses it rarely at other times of the year. Lent would also be a good time for singing the Penitential Act as a way of highlighting it. Musical notation is provided in the Missal for singing all three components, that is, the priest's introduction, the invocations by the priest, deacon, or another minister, and the priest's conclusion (the absolution). Notice how a minister other than the priest or deacon may announce the invocations before the assembly's response of "Lord, have mercy" or "Christ have mercy;" taking advantage of this option could greatly enhance the singing if a cantor, for example, were more musically adept than the priest or deacon. Of the sample invocations given in

Appendix VI, Forms III, IV and perhaps V seem to especially correspond to the Lenten themes. Additionally, using the Greek *Kyrie, eleison* and *Christe, eleison* rather than the English words could be another way to highlight the Penitential Act during this liturgical time.

Of course, the Alleluia is omitted at every occasion, including solemnities and feasts, throughout the entirety of Lent. The Gloria is also omitted, although it is used on the Solemnities of St. Joseph and the Annunciation, and at the Chrism Mass.

Priest celebrants, liturgists, and preparers need to know their way around *The Roman Missal* during Lent in order to take full advantage of different options and to be sure they are using the correct texts. There are four Prefaces of Lent, designated I–IV. Prefaces I and II can be used on weekdays (except for Ash Wednesday) and should be used on Sundays that do not have their own Preface prescribed. Prefaces III and IV are used on the weekdays of Lent, including Ash Wednesday. Specific Prefaces are prescribed for the First and Second Sundays of Lent, placed with the orations (not with the Prefaces), as well as for the Third, Fourth, and Fifth Sundays of Lent (also located right there with the orations) when the Year A readings are used (that is for the scrutinies). When the Year A readings are not used, Prefaces I or II of Lent are used on those three Sundays, not the Preface that is given immediately following the Prayer over the Offerings (read the rubrics carefully). Also, there are two Prefaces of the Passion of the Lord: the first is used during the Fifth Week of Lent, and the second is used on Monday, Tuesday, and Wednesday of Holy Week.

It must also be noted that when the scrutinies are celebrated, proper texts (including Collect, Prayer over the Offerings, and Prayer after Communion) for the First, Second, and Third Scrutiny respectively are to be used; these can be found in the section Ritual Masses: I. For the Conferral of the Sacraments of Christian Initiation, 2. For the Celebration of the Scrutinies.

Given the importance of this liturgical time, Lent might be a good time to regularly chant the introductory dialogue and Preface to the Eucharistic Prayer, if this is not already being done. Also, Lent is a good time to use one of the Eucharistic Prayers for Reconciliation, especially the first one, with its explicit references to God's constant offer of pardon to sinners, to the present time being a time of grace and reconciliation to turn back to the Lord, and to Jesus's willingness "to be nailed for our sake to the wood of the Cross" as he out-stretched his arms on the Cross "to become the lasting sign of your covenant." Even though those prayers have their own Prefaces, it is permissible to use the Preface of Lent that might be prescribed for that day and yet still use the remainder of one of the Eucharistic Prayers for Reconciliation. Consider using Eucharistic Prayer for Reconciliation I more frequently.

Any of the three acclamations for "The Mystery of Faith" are fitting for Lent: the first and third call specific attention to the Paschal Mystery as they mention the Lord's Death and Resurrection, while the second connects participation in the Eucharistic Banquet with the proclamation of the Lord's Death. One might argue that the third option, with its particular mention of the Cross, has a certain obvious link to the season and might be especially or perhaps even exclusively used throughout all of Lent and, perhaps even throughout all of Easter Time, to connect the forty days of Lent with the fifty days of Easter Time. Whichever acclamation is chosen, communities should consider using a different one than is used at other times, or at least changing the musical setting.

Finally, every day of Lent has a proper Prayer over the People. The custom of a daily prayer over the people in Lent seems to have originated in the *Gelasian Sacramentary* of the seventh century and, after not being included in the Missal of Paul VI, has reappeared with the third edition of *The Roman Missal*. A rubric indicates that the prayer is optional on weekdays; the prayer is required on Sundays, however, including Palm Sunday of the Passion of the Lord. Note the proper structure when a Prayer over the People or a Solemn Blessing is used at the end of Mass: after the priest says, "The Lord be with you," and the people respond, "And with your spirit," the deacon, or, in his absence, the priest himself, says the invitation, "Bow down for the blessing." Then the priest outstretches his hand over the people and says the prayer, with all responding "Amen."

Children's Liturgy of the Word

MANY adults find it challenging to lead a prayerful experience with children. Some may bore or confuse the children with abstract concepts or too much talking. Others might become overwhelmed by the children's energy and will allow the Liturgy of the Word to devolve into playtime. Maintaining a prayerful, liturgical environment while holding the children's attention can be a difficult skill to master.

Try to refer to the children by name, and tell them what they may call you. As you get to know them, try to remember to recognize the big things in their lives, such as birthdays, the deaths of relatives, or the births of new siblings. You might choose to recognize these milestones in the Prayer of the Faithful.

Communicating with confidence and good body language can help you to immediately capture and hold the children's attention. Stand erect and use expansive hand and arm gestures. Be aware of your facial expressions. Avoid any feelings of self-consciousness as you sing or pray with the children. The children will sense your discomfort and will respond accordingly. Instead, project yourself confidently and joyfully and the children will follow suit.

During the Homily or reflection, you can interact with children by asking them questions. It is best to avoid questions that can be answered with a simple yes or no in favor of more evocative questions. Listen to the children's responses with the goal of affirming and celebrating their experience of God in their lives, rather than worrying about correct answers. You might occasionally need to clarify a child's response, but you should avoid correcting or negating them.

If you ask a question or invite the children to bring forth prayers and are met with silence, welcome and respect it. It is not necessary to fill all of the time with talking or singing. Silence is prayer. You might pause after the Scripture readings or allow silent time during the Homily or reflection when the children do not immediately respond to a question. It is okay for them to think or just to be with the questions and listen to the Holy Spirit working within them.

The Saints

THE saints of this season trusted in the Lord and many were well acquainted with affliction. SS. Perpetua and Felicity (March 7), a North African noblewoman and her servant, suffered persecution and martyrdom shortly after both had given birth. St. John of God (March 8) was abandoned as a child and later suffered from mental instability, but through his trust in God he accomplished many acts of charity for the sick and founded a religious order. St. Patrick (March 17) was kidnapped and sold into slavery before he became the Apostle of Ireland. St. Cyril of Jerusalem (March 18) was both exiled for many years and was bitterly attacked because of his teachings. He is now considered a Doctor of the Church because of his brilliant catechesis despite his harsh treatment by his contemporaries. Each of these saints points out that often the very circumstances of life can be a type of penance. However, that penance only reaches its potential in a person's life—becomes salvific—when that person trusts in the mercy of God to deliver them from affliction.

Some saints show their gladness and rejoice in the Lord through their preaching, teaching, and writing. St. Francis of Paola (April 2), a Franciscan, spent much of his life as hermit but later was sent by the pope to accomplish peace between warring nations. St. Isidore of Seville (April 4), the last of the Fathers of the Church, was a proponent of education, especially among the clergy, and was a prolific writer whose work was influential throughout much of the Middle Ages and beyond. St. Vincent Ferrer (April 5), a Dominican friar, was a renowned preacher and devoted himself to preaching the need for penance. He was also instrumental in promoting Church unity during a time of great discord. St. John Baptist de la Salle (April 7) left a life a luxury to commit himself to educating the poor along with his followers in his newly founded religious congregation of the Brothers of the Christian Schools. Finally, St. Stanislaus (April 11) was a bishop who was martyred for speaking out against a king's ill treatment of his subjects. Even though these commemorations are treated as optional memorials during Lent, all of these heroes of the faith are excellent guides for our Lenten journey. Whether we need to see the potential and hope for God's mercy in the afflictions of our lives or whether we need to be encouraged to sing out our gladness and rejoicing in mercies already received, the saints supply us with endless grace-filled witness and assistance on our pilgrimage of faith.

The Liturgy of the Hours

DURING Lent the Church is called to embrace a spirit of repentance and *metanoia* ("a change of heart") or conversion. Consider offering celebrations of Morning or Evening Prayer at convenient times when members of the parish can gather for communal prayer. If you do not have a Sunday Evening Eucharist in your community, gather people together for the celebration of Evening Prayer as a fitting conclusion to the Lord's Day. Invite other parishes in your vicariate or deanery or other Christian Churches in your area to join you for these Celebrations. Consider inviting religious leaders or those with a certain theological expertise to preach at these celebrations.

Since Wednesdays and Fridays are traditional days of fasting in the Church and many parishes hold gatherings on Wednesdays and Fridays of Lent, consider including celebrations of the Hours. Encourage people to bring nonperishable food or toiletries to be given to the local St. Vincent de Paul society. The usual pattern in many parishes is to celebrate the Way of the Cross on the Fridays of Lent. Pope Paul VI, in his apostolic exhortation, *Marialis cultus* (MC), noted, "exercises of piety should be harmonized with the liturgy, not merged into it" (MC, 31). There are times when communities try to attach the Way of the Cross to a liturgy such as adoration and Benediction of the Blessed Sacrament or the Liturgy of the Hours. This should be discouraged.

On Ash Wednesday, the psalms of Wednesday of week 4 are specified for use in praying the Hours. There is an exception at Morning Prayer, where one finds the option of psalms, canticle, and antiphons for Friday of Week III. Since the readings are recurring for the first four weeks of Lent consider using shorter passages of the readings, for example, from the Book of Exodus as found in the Office of Readings. The ritual text divides the season into two parts; before Holy Week and Holy Week.

Continue to provide catechesis on the Hours for the entire community. When focusing on the intercessions, for example, instruct the people that the intercessions at Morning Prayer serve to dedicate the day to the Lord while the intercessions at Evening Prayer function in the same way as those at the celebration of the Eucharist. Consider a sung response to the intercessions using one of the many options for Lent such as "Lord, have mercy on your people" and since the Lord's Prayer flows from the intercessions consider chanting the Lord's Prayer if your community hasn't already been doing this.

Any hymns that speak of the forty days of Lent are especially appropriate for the weeks of Lent. Passiontide hymns are fitting for Fridays of Lent and toward the end of the season following the Fifth Sunday of Lent through Holy Week. Look for texts that proclaim the entire Paschal Mystery. The hymns found in the book of the Hours for Lent include, "Lord, Who Throughout These Forty Days" (ST FLAVIN); "When I Survey the Wondrous Cross" (ROCKINGHAM); " Keep in Mind" (LUCIEN DEISS); "Let All Mortal Flesh Keep Silence" (PICARDY); "The Glory of These Forty Days" (ERHALT' UNS, HERR); and "Take Up Your Cross" (WINCHESTER NEW). When Holy Week begins additional hymns are recommended including: "Were You There" (WERE YOU THERE); "O Sacred Head, Surrounded" (PASSION CHORALE); "I Shall Praise the Savior's Glory" or "Pange, Lingua, Gloriosi" (PANGE, LINGUA Mode III); "Crown Him With Many Crowns" (DIADEMATA); and "All Glory Praise and Honor" (ST. THEODULPH).

The Rite of Christian Initiation of Adults

THE scrutinies provide instruction on the mystery of sin, aiding the elect in growing in awareness and acknowledgment of sin and developing a sense of repentance. That instruction is followed by "bringing out" and strengthening of what is good. As the elect go through the three scrutinies, they should grow in their understanding of sin. RCIA, 143 states: "From the first to the final scrutiny the elect should progress in their perception of sin and their desire for salvation." They learn to seek Christ's presence. Their spirit is filled with Christ as "the living water," as "the light of the world," and as "new life." In the final part of the scrutiny, through the rites of exorcism (or healing), the elect are freed from the effects of sin and the obstacles to Christ and are thereby drawn to what is good and Christ-like.

With this preparation, the elect are ready to move on to the rites of initiation. After initiation the newly baptized continue their faith journey and spiritual development; and in doing so, they may celebrate the Sacrament of Reconciliation when the Spirit moves them.

RCIA, 459–472, sets out a penitential rite for candidates as an optional rite to help candidates make their preparation for the Rite of Reception. This penitential rite, can "serve to mark the Lenten purification of baptized but previously uncatechised adults who are preparing to receive the Sacraments of Confirmation and Eucharist or to be received into the full communion of the Catholic Church." This penitential rite, which may be celebrated on the Second Sunday of Lent or a weekday of Lent is to be kept separate and distinct from the scrutinies of the elect. In preparing for the penitential service consideration should be given to the nature of the liturgical service. Possibly, the parish may decide to celebrate the rite before a parish communal penance service.

—Adapted from an article by Ross Privitelli © LTP, 2012.

The Sacraments of Initiation

WE can take our cues from the *Rite of Christian Initiation of Adults* and adapt some of the rites pertinent to this period of enlightenment for the elect, to candidates preparing for the next stage in their own initiation. The parish liturgist will be a big help in assisting those responsible for catechizing these young people to tailor some of the rituals for them according to understanding and appropriateness. These adapted rituals could be set in the context of a retreat and/or celebration of the Word. These rites might be an enrollment of names during a school Mass; a preparation for the celebration of Penance modeled after a scrutiny preparation; catechesis and ritual presentation of the Creed and/or Lord's Prayer. Some of these might also be done within the context of an all-school Mass, or simply within a Liturgy of the

Word. Work with the candidates in preparation, using the prayers from the RCIA as a springboard for their own reflection.

Lent is also a good time to help children get into the habit of doing some journaling. Pose a question or two, for example from the Rite of Election:

◆ Have you found strength in God's grace? When?

◆ Have you found support in our community's prayers and example? How?

◆ Do you wish to enter more fully into the life of the Church through the Sacrament of _____? Why?

Doing this with one or more of the rites will help these candidates and their parents to appreciate the seriousness of the initiation sacraments, and to ponder a little more deeply the mystery they are entering more fully into.

During Lent, the Coss stands front and center, casting its shadow on all of us. The ritual gesture for the symbol of the Cross is signing. In Baptism we are signed with the Cross and claimed by Christ as his own. On Ash Wednesday we are signed with ashes, acknowledging that we have tarnished our baptismal promises and once again make the conscious effort to "turn away from sin." We make the Sign of the Cross at the beginning and end of every Mass. Every time we are signed with the Cross, we are signed in God's name.

Use the ritual of Signing of the Cross often during Lent. Have children sign themselves and each other.

Place a clear glass bowl of holy water in your meeting space and each time you meet during Lent do a ritual where each person comes to the water in a prayerful way and makes the Sign of the Cross.

One or two times during Lent sign each participant in your group on the forehead with the Sign of the Cross.

On Good Friday, many communities use a large wooden cross for adoration. Consider placing a cross or crucifix on the prayer table where young people can see it. Explain the importance of the cross as a sacramental.

At the beginning of Lent explain the significance of almsgiving both inside and outside the parish community. Help young people understand that they too have a responsibility to tithe to their parish community. Help them choose an activity they can do as a group that would be appropriate to their age and would be a help to persons in need.

The Rite of Penance

WHEN scheduling Lenten Penance services, collaborate with neighboring parishes and institutions so that celebrations are held on varied days and during a range of weeks within Lent. Prepare early to make sure enough confessors are available to celebrate the sacrament in each community. Consider celebrating the sacrament during a daylight hour for those who may not be able to come out of their homes in the evening. Provide transportation for parishioners who may not otherwise have a way to get to the church and be prepared to celebrate the sacrament with people who have special needs. Consider the Lenten environment and place a candle with a piece of seasonal fabric on a small table or stand at the station of each confessor. In Appendix II, section II from the *Rite of Penance* you will find a Common Penitential Celebration for Lent that could be celebrated with children of various ages especially those who are preparing to receive the sacrament for the first time as well as those who are preparing for the Easter sacraments.

The Pastoral Care of the Sick

ON Ash Wednesday ashes may be brought to the sick and homebound and when a priest makes a pastoral visit on this day it may also be an appropriate day for anointing. Consider bringing along a copy of *"What Am I Doing for Lent this Year?"* (LTP) and a devotional resource for praying the Way of the Cross. Chapter 52 from the *Book of Blessings* contains the order of prayer for a layperson to use while bringing ashes to the homebound.

Lent is a most appropriate liturgical time to celebrate the Anointing of the Sick because it clearly shows the Paschal dimension of Christian suffering. The Lenten readings, especially the Gospel account of the man born blind, rain down images of God's healing embrace. Those who wish to celebrate the Sacrament of Penance should have the opportunity to do so before being anointed (see PCS, 133). The litany (see PCS, 138) and the prayer over the oil (140) can be chanted with the people taking up their responses, which will bring a greater solemnity to the celebration. Seven prayers following the anointing respond to a variety of pastoral settings (see PCS, 125, A–F).

The elect and candidates preparing for the Easter sacraments may be anointed if they are experiencing a serious illness. The people of God should be instructed that any baptized person can be anointed and "those preparing for serious surgery, the elderly whose infirmity declines further, and seriously ill children should ask for sacramental anointing" (PCS, 138). During the celebration of daily Mass in the parish is a most appropriate time to celebrate the sacrament. The section on Christ the physician in the *Catechism of the Catholic Church* (see CCC, 1503–1505) contains an especially rich spirituality of healing and suffering through God visiting his people (see also Luke 7:16; cf. Matthew 4:24).

The Rite of Marriage

MARRIAGES may not be celebrated on Ash Wednesday, the Sundays of Lent, and Palm Sunday of the Passion of the Lord. On March 19, the Solemnity of St. Joseph, Spouse of the Blessed Virgin Mary and March 25, the Annunciation of the Lord, the Mass of the Day is used, with one reading from the *Rite of Marriage* (see RMar, 67–105).

In Lent there are no Alleluias, no flowers, no pulling out all the organ stops. However, while white vestments may be used at the wedding liturgy, the mantra for celebrating weddings in Lent must be *restraint*. In the celebration of the Rite of Marriage we can find many connections and references to the primary themes of Lent. Some of these would include the giving of alms as an act of love, the role of the covenant in salvation history, and the covenant between husband and wife. In addition in the nuptial blessing we find themes of covenant, establishment of married life, "the one blessing that was not forfeited by original sin or washed away in the flood" (RMar, 33) and in the universal prayer a concern for the "afflicted and the needy" and the joy of "generous friends" (RMar, 125).

The Order of Christian Funerals

THE Church has a long-standing prohibition of eulogies at funerals: "A brief homily based on the readings should always be given at the funeral liturgy, but never any kind of eulogy" (OCF, 141). The homilist is to keep in mind with delicate sensitivity not only the identity of the deceased and the circumstances of the death, but also the grief of the bereaved, the focus of the Christian funeral rite is the saving mystery of Jesus's Death and Resurrection. Attentive to the grief of those present, the Homilist should dwell on God's compassionate love and on the Paschal Mystery of the Lord, as proclaimed in the Scripture readings (see OCF, 27).

If the Church limits the length and number of eulogies at funerals, why is it that this practice continues to be a problem in many parishes? Although what sometimes happens is not what the Church envisions, the justification comes in a statement made in the OCF: "a member or a friend speak in remembrance of the deceased before the final commendation begins" (OCF, 170).The words are to be brief, highlighting an aspect of the deceased's life of faith. If there is a desire for a more lengthy eulogy or sharing of memories, then this should take place at the Vigil or the funeral reception. Priests should read ahead of time for the text or outline of any proposed eulogy and make changes in length or content, if necessary.

A Funeral Mass may be celebrated on Ash Wednesday but not on the Sundays of Lent. The singing of Alleluias is prohibited in Lent so the review of texts from hymns and songs that may contain this word is advised. Many of the funeral Gospel texts are drawn from Passion narratives of John and would be especially appropriate choices for Lent. The Lenten environment is simple and flowers are not allowed in the church except for the Solemnities of St. Joseph and the Annunciation.

The Book of Blessings

THE Order for the Blessing and Distribution of Ashes—Ash Wednesday—is found in chapter 53. The Order for the Blessing of the St. Joseph's Table (March 19) is found in chapter 54. The Order for the Blessing of Pilgrims (chapter 8); the Order for the Blessing of Children not yet Baptized (chapter 1, 4); and the Order for the Blessing of Catechumens (chapter 4, 3) are also appropriate for use during Lent. *Catholic Household Blessings & Prayers* also includes various blessings and prayers for use during Lent.

The Liturgical Environment

THE color of Lent is violet. A redder violet than that of Advent may be used. This changes to rose for the Fourth Sunday of Lent, called *Laetare Sunday,* which can be seen as a kind of transition. Historically, statues and crucifixes in the liturgical space were veiled from the Fifth Sunday of Lent on, and this is still an option in the dioceses of the United States. If you do decide to use veils in your church, consider carefully how to do this. Particularly in more ornate spaces, it is simply impossible to veil everything, and the practice can lead to a haphazard look unless you are very intentional about how it is done. Veiling is not required by the rubrics and should not be done until the Fifth Sunday in any case.

Several common practices regarding the environment in Lent require discussion. First, some parishes have made a habit of emptying the font and the holy water stoups for the duration of Lent, or even replacing the water with sand. The practice was the subject of a dubium to the Congregation for Divine Worship and the Discipline of the Sacraments in 2000. The congregation responded that the practice is to be discontinued. They do note that the font may be emptied after the Evening Mass of the Lord's Supper, as a preparation for the blessing of new baptismal water, which takes place at the Vigil, but this practice is not to be extended to the entire season of Lent. Emptying the font and any stoups actively detracts from the baptismal character of Lent. Our Lenten fasting ought not include a fast from the sacraments or the sacramentals of our liturgical life, but a return to them.

Another area in which we might want to reconsider our Lenten practice is the potential overuse of desert imagery in our liturgical environment. The Lenten season does begin with the reading of Jesus's temptation in the desert, but this temptation did not take place in the American Southwest and the readings of the rest of the season do not remain in the desert. We might reconsider if sand and cacti are the best environment to help the assembly enter into Lent, particularly in areas of the country where these are not the local environment. What aspects of "spring waiting" and "new growth" are present in the environment in which your church is located? Consider making use of those. If Lent is an annual invitation for Christians to return to and be strengthened in their Baptismal vocation, how might that be highlighted?

Preparation for Holy Week and the Sacred Triduum requires early preparation. Palms for the Palm Sunday procession, for example, need to be ordered early if you are using them. While we are used to the long thin fronds, the rubrics ask simply for branches. A parish might consider if there is need for them to import palm fronds from abroad, instead considering the use of local branches in the procession, if this is feasible in your location. Parishes who do desire to use palms might consider seeking out sustainable (eco-)palms, which can be ordered through a variety of sources online with sufficient preparation.

The Palm Sunday procession begins in a location other than the sanctuary, and this location requires attention as well. Because the beginning of the procession includes a reading from the Gospel, considering how well people will be able to hear it is important and amplification may be necessary, particularly outdoors. If your parish has a secondary enclosed location where people can gather to begin the service before processing to the church, this might be considered.

The Liturgical Music

AS a penitential season, Lent should be the most subdued time of year. Keep the music simple, and avoid any excess instrumentation. The Gloria is not said or sung (except on the Solemnity of St. Joseph). We fast from the Alleluia and use alternative refrains. The playing of the organ and other musical instruments is allowed only to support the singing. Do not be afraid to integrate more silence into your Lenten liturgies. Aside from the obvious parts of the liturgy, you might consider omitting the closing song during Lent.

Music suggestions are available as a free PDF on www.LTP.org/resources.

Liturgical Ministers

IN addition to the members of the assembly make sure all the liturgical ministers in the parish are knowledgeable of the initiation rites and model robust responses when the various rites of the catechumenal process are celebrated during this season of purification and enlightenment. Make sure rehearsals have been scheduled for all initiation rituals including scrutinies, anointings, and celebrations of the Word of God so that all ministers and sponsors are well prepared and those involved clearly understand their role. Mull over the possibility of sending one or two lectors from the parish out with the elect to break open the Word following the dismissal. This will accomplish at least three things: give the regular RCIA catechists or team members a break, allow the elect to experience the breaking open of the Word with another disciple of Christ, and potentially expand the pool of RCIA team members in your parish. Make sure schedules for liturgical ministers are given well in advance of the season.

Consider gathering with the parish lectors to break open the readings of the season and ask different readers to proclaim some of the texts for Lent while giving each other feedback. Use a responses such as: *I really like how you _____, I appreciate your understanding of the prophets words that helped to evoke _____ or, you may want to consider _____ when proclaiming this text in the future.* Make sure feedback is given in a nonjudgmental or non-threatening manner.

Have processional routes been mapped out for the various Lenten liturgies? Identify who will help facilitate the church on the move. Who will prepare the Triduum schedule for the website and what will the parish do to encourage greater participation in the liturgies of the Three Days? What time will the Easter Vigil be scheduled for? Remember the *Universal Norms on the Liturgical Year and the General Roman Calendar* tells us that the Vigil "should begin after nightfall" (UNLY, 21). Visit this link http://aa.usno.navy.mil/data/docs/RS_OneYear.php, from the United States Naval Observatory, to see what time the sun will set in your region on April 19, 2014.

Encourage each minister in the parish to invite a Catholic who no longer attends Mass to join them on the First Sunday of Lent. Welcome these brothers and sisters (without making them feel guilty for being away), host a coffee klatch following each Mass and have people voice the reason why they have been away. Be prepared to hear peoples' needs and meet them where they are at. Consider implementing a program such as Catholics Come Home (www.catholicscomehome.org) or check out the tips found at this link from the USCCB: usccbmedia.blogspot.com/2012/04/tips-for-welcoming-returning-catholics.html.

Devotions and Sacramentals

ON the traditional days of fasting (Wednesday and Friday) the *Directory of Popular Piety and the Liturgy* (DPPL, 130) upholds the venerable practice of reading from holy Scripture especially the accounts of the Lord's Passion. *Paschale solemnitatis* (PS) reminds us that "devotional exercises which harmonize with the Lenten season are to be encouraged . . . they should foster the liturgical spirit which the faithful can prepare themselves for celebration of Christ's paschal mystery" (PS, 20).

The practice of fasting and abstinence in the United States is that every person 14 years of age or older must abstain from meat (and items made with meat) on Ash Wednesday, Good Friday, and the Fridays of Lent; every person between the age of 18 and 60 must fast on Ash Wednesday and Good Friday (see the *Catechism of the Catholic Church* [CCC], 1250–1252).

The Stations of the Cross or the Way of the Cross, the *Via Crucis,* is a popular devotion to accompany the final events in the life of Jesus (see DDPL, 134–145). Consider *The Way of the Cross* (LTP) that contains the traditional Jerusalem stations, the scriptural stations used in Rome, and the stations with the women of the Gospel. Why three settings of the Way of the Cross? DPPL,

134 envisions adaptation of the stations to reflect on certain aspect of Christ's Passion. *Catholic Household Blessings & Prayers* contains both the traditional and biblical Way of the Cross.

The *Via Matris*, which reflects the seven sorrows of the Blessed Virgin Mary, is an exercise on the seven "stations" or moments when Our Lady journeyed in her faith and expressed the agony of her life (see DPPL, 136–137). Be sure to include the singing of the *Stabat Mater* when praying the *Via Crucis* or the *Via Matris*.

Consider additional gatherings in the parish during Lent including a simple soup lunch or supper followed by a time of prayer and reflection on Catholic social teaching or the practice of *Lectio Divina* focusing on the Gospel accounts of the season on the Passion of Christ. Prayer around the cross following the pattern of the monks at Taizé has become a venerable tradition in many communities. The use of iconography or other Christian art can be used to aid in contemplation and reflection on the sacred texts.

Many communities have a St. Patrick's Day (March 17) parade followed by a traditional Irish dinner of corned beef and cabbage. As a sign of your Lenten concern for the poor, consider serving a meal at a homeless shelter or bringing a hot meal to a person living on the street. You will find the rich prayer of St. Patrick's Breastplate in *Catholic Household Blessings & Prayers*.

The Solemnity of St. Joseph Spouse of the Blessed Virgin Mary (March 19) is a traditional day in Italian parishes to bless breads, pastries, and other foods for the poor. This devotion is based on Italian women praying to St. Joseph while waiting for their husbands' safe return from sea or war. The women refrained from eating meat until their husband's return. The *Book of Blessings* includes a blessing for breads, pastries, and other foods as does *Catholic Household Blessings & Prayers*.

On the Solemnity of the Annunciation of the Lord it is fitting to pray for religious communities under Mary's patronage.

Catholic Household Blessings & Prayers includes a prayer for the domestic Church for the placing of the blessed palm branches in the home. The chapter also contains the four Songs of the Suffering Servant from the Book of Isaiah, which are particularly suited for reflection during this most Holy Week.

The Parish and the Home

FIND a way to visibly mark Lent as a parish community and various households. Perhaps it is to fill the church or school hallways with signs that can be duplicated in homes and workplaces. One nonverbal way might invite parishioners to hang pieces of violet paper marked with crosses even made with ashes (similar to the mark on our foreheads on Ash Wednesday) in the places at home we might notice them: bathroom mirror, kitchen table, car dashboard, over our bed, school locker, office, desk, or anywhere that we might be reminded that this season calls us to daily reflection of how we are living our lives. A computer or phone application (app) could even be designed for parishioners who are away at college or the military. Ask your teenagers to design or find it; they would be excited to be asked. When parishioners gather for liturgy or meetings and see the same signs in the parish facility it resonates that the domestic Church is a part of the larger Church community.

There are many websites that offer a daily spiritual reflection with words, photographs, or images. Offer a listing on the parish website or send an e-mail link. Invite your teens to create a list for the parish. Encourage their creativity and focus in the areas in which they are already involved. Young people wish to be of service, and this taps a natural ordinary activity for them.

Lent coming during late spring this year offers the opportunity to use the symbol of growth from seeds, bulbs, or plants. We have forty days of Lent. Watching the growth that happens to plant life over forty days reminds us that though it might seem insignificant at one glance growth does happen to a growing seed over time. So it is with us— it reminds us of the power of daily work, daily habits, and taking one step at a time.

Lent invites us to focus on prayer and reflection, fasting, and almsgiving. We can offer people a list of forty steps, forty things to do in these areas: ways to enhance prayer and reflective life; ways to fast from the things that harm our spirit and inner life; and ways to give alms, or time, or share our gifts. Concrete ideas help people focus on the importance of making a change that offers renewal and new life. But often we are uncertain where to start.

A list can even be turned into cards that can be pulled from a basket each day for reflection. We don't have the same focal point as the Advent season offers with the wreath, but we can give people a symbol of remembrance such as basket of rocks, cross, seed, nails, crown of thorns. One parish even gave their parishioners a walking stick to invite them to walk alongside Jesus during Lent.

Often families make lighter meals during Lent such as a weekly soup supper or meatless meal. This could be a good opportunity for a household to cook extra for a weekly meal and share it with others such as a homebound parishioner, soup kitchen, or shelter or perhaps to volunteer during this season to serve meals. The sharing of meals, not only with disciples, but also with those who were at the very edges of society was a central part of Jesus's interaction with people. Whether they are the homeless, the poor, those in migrant camps, or wherever we are aware there is need—that is where Jesus calls us to go. Our work during Lent will give us the inspiration and commitment to continue our journey with Jesus for these forty days.

Mass Texts

◆ Children's Liturgy of the Word:

During the weeks of Lent, God reminds us nothing
    is more important in our lives than he is.
Many things try to get our attention—television,
    games, friends, toys—
But none is more important than the one who
    made us
and who loves us, even more than our own parents
    can love us.
In Lent we remember what it means to be children
    of God.
Go now and listen to God's Word
that speaks to each one of us about the goodness
    of God.

◆ Dismissal Text for RCIA

Lent is a desert of time rather than place.
The grains of sand moving through an hourglass
remind us each moment of life is precious and
    irretrievable.

We rejoice that you have chosen to use your time
to grow in your knowledge and love of the Lord.
Go forth in confidence that the we who
    remain behind
rejoice that soon you will be washed in the blood
    of the Lamb.
One day, may we stand together on the shores
    of the kingdom,
ready to meet the Lord who made us all and called
    us in his love.

◆ Seasonal Texts for Prayer of the Faithful

Invitation to Prayer:

Because God's love for us is unbounded
and far greater than the love of a mother
    for her child,
we dare approach the throne of mercy
and make our needs known to our
    compassionate Father.

For the Church who is your Bride, that she may worthily proclaim your Gospel through the acts of generous love of your ministers and of all your holy people, we pray: Lord of mercy, hear our prayer.

For political leaders who are entrusted with the care and prosperity of the peoples of the earth, that they might serve generously, motivated not by partisan interests or selfish pursuits, but by the common good, we pray: Lord of mercy, hear our prayer.

For the poor of this world, that lives will be bettered by our generous sharing from our bounty and even from our need, we pray: Lord of mercy, hear our prayer.

For the sick, that through prayer and compassionate care they may be restored to physical and mental well-being, we pray: Lord of mercy, hear our prayer.

For those who have died, especially those who have died without the comfort of loved ones at their side that they may enter the fullness of the kingdom and rejoice forever in the company of the angels and saints, we pray: Lord of mercy, hear our prayer.

Concluding Prayer:

In all things you call us to put our trust in you,
    O God.
Hear us as we humbly entreat your mercy,
you who know us by name and love us beyond
    our imagining.
Through Christ our Lord.
Amen.

March
Month of St. Joseph

WED 5 (#219) violet
Ash Wednesday

About Ash Wednesday

In the early Church, when Lent was a time for the reconciliation of public penitents, the penitents would come to the church at the beginning of Lent; that is, on Ash Wednesday. They would wear a penitential garment, suggesting sackcloth, and be sprinkled with ashes. Then they would be ritually expelled from the assembly to do their penance for forty days, returning to the church on Holy Thursday, when they would be readmitted to the sacraments.

With time, the expulsion of penitents disappeared, but the ashes remained and became a call to penance of all the faithful. In the Scriptures, sackcloth and ashes are the signs of penance.

The practice of using ashes from the palms of the previous year's Palm Sunday is a relatively new element of the liturgy, first appearing in the twelfth century. It adds another layer of meaning to this rich rite, reminding us of where we are headed—to the glory of Easter.

The Lectionary for Mass

◆ First Reading: It is not enough to perform external rituals of repentance unless the heart is pierced by sorrow. All of Israel, even its youngest members, are called to seek mercy from the Lord.

◆ Responsorial Psalm 51: Fully aware of sinfulness, the psalmist prays for God's help and for the clean heart, which alone can see God.

◆ Second Reading: The Word of God calls out: Be reconciled to God. Now is the favorable time, the right time! Do not fail to receive God's grace. Today is the day of salvation.

◆ Gospel: Prayer, fasting, and works of mercy are the traditional acts of Lenten repentance. They are not to be performed for the acclaim of others but rather done in secret, that the heavenly Father may reward us.

The Roman Missal

All the prayers and texts are proper for the day and can be found at Ash Wednesday in the Lent section of the Proper of Time toward the beginning of the Missal.

The Entrance Antiphon sets the theme and tone for the entire Lenten journey, which begins today: the focus is on God's mercy, as he calls us to repentance and looks with love on the creatures he has created; such is the very nature of God.

There is no Penitential Act today, since it is replaced by the distribution of ashes.

The Collect speaks of the "campaign of Christian service" that is begun today—a campaign that is begun with fasting. The proper focus of Lent is laid out for us: it is a time to "take up battle against spiritual evils" so that "we may be armed with weapons of self-restraint." Over and over again throughout the entirety of Lent the Mass prayers will remind us that the journey of Lent is more than just "giving something up," and it is more than just simply doing outward acts of penance; rather, the prayers call us to a true metanoia, a change of life with practical consequences for the way we live.

The rite for the blessing and distribution of ashes takes place after the Homily. The priest celebrant, with any necessary ministers (for example, the bookbearer, and someone to hold the vessel with water, if needed), goes to the place where the vessel(s) with ashes is (are). Hands remain joined for the introduction (the rubric for which does *not* indicate "these or similar words"), and then he leaves a brief period for silent prayer. Then, with hands extended, he prays one of the two prayers of blessing. While both prayers contain the gesture of making the Sign of the Cross over the ashes, the gesture has a somewhat different focus in each of the two prayers: in the first, the priest is asking the grace of God's blessing on those "who are marked with these ashes," and in the second, the blessing is invoked more specifically on the ashes themselves. Consequently, the gesture should match the action according to the words of the prayer.

The prayers very clearly speak of the journey of conversion. The first prayer, during which the people are blessed, highlights the Lenten observances of acts of humility and works of penance that the faithful will undertake; and it asks for God's blessing that those who undertake these practices "may be worthy to come with minds made pure / to celebrate the Paschal Mystery of your Son." The second prayer focuses more on the ashes and their purpose and meaning: receiving the ashes on our heads is an acknowledgement that "we are but ashes / and shall return to dust." Therefore, we ask, that as a result of our observance of Lent, our gain may be twofold—not only pardon for sins, but also "newness of life / after the likeness of your Risen Son."

After the prayer, the priest sprinkles the ashes with water, but this is done in silence, without his saying anything.

Either one of two formulae is used to impose ashes: "Repent, and believe in the Gospel" or "Remember that you are dust, and to dust you shall return." Although there is no stated rule about it, there might be a certain logic in using the first formula if the first prayer of blessing is used, and the second formula if the second prayer is used, since in some way the themes of the prayers and the formulae of imposition seem to correspond to each other. Say the words of imposition exactly as they are given; don't alter them or try to "personalize" the phrase; it is the Church who calls each of her members to repentance, not you personally. The rubric states simply that ashes are placed on the head of all those present who come up, as the formula is said. Customarily, this is done by the priest (or deacon or minister) dipping his (or her) thumb in the ashes, and then tracing the ashes on the person's forehead in the Sign of the Cross, although technically, there is nothing that requires this. (Interestingly, we know, for example, that historically ashes have also been sprinkled on the top of peoples' heads.)

Singing is to take place during the imposition of ashes, and several possibilities are spelled out in the Missal. There are three suggested antiphons that can be used in connection with the verses of Psalm 51; a responsory is also suggested, or, another appropriate song may be sung.

Be sure to provide the means for priests and other ministers to wash their hands after the distribution of ashes. Pre-moistened towelettes sometimes work better than plain water, although water and towels should also be available.

After the imposition of ashes (and the ministers washing their hands), the Universal Prayer takes place; the Creed is not said. After the Universal Prayer, Mass continues as usual.

If the blessing and distribution of ashes takes place outside Mass, then all proceeds as described above, including all the readings and their chants as at Mass, but then, after the Universal Prayer, the priest simply blesses and dismisses the faithful, using the Prayer over the People

given at the end of the Mass formularies. Interestingly, there is no specific mention in the rubrics that the Our Father is prayed when the blessing and distribution of ashes occurs outside Mass; they simply direct that the rite is concluded with the Universal Prayer, the Blessing, and the Dismissal of the faithful.

The Prayer over the Offerings highlights the journey of conversion we are undertaking at the beginning of Lent and are marking by the offering of this sacrifice, a journey that will come to its completion in the days of the Sacred Paschal Triduum; we ask that "we may turn away from harmful pleasure / and, cleansed from our sins, may become worthy / to celebrate devoutly the Passion of your Son."

The Preface to be used today is either Preface III or Preface IV of Lent. Preface III speaks of the fruits of self-denial: pride that is humbled and works of kindness, specifically in feeding the poor; Preface IV speaks of how bodily fasting serves to "restrain our faults, / raise up our minds, / and bestow both virtue and its rewards." Both Prefaces are short and to the point, in keeping with the starkness of this day's liturgy. Also, today might be a good day to use the Eucharistic Prayer for Reconciliation I, with or without its proper Preface, to highlight the tone of the liturgical time, and to provide a stark contrast with Ordinary Time if this prayer has been used rarely, if at all, recently.

For the dismissal, the priest is to use the Prayer over the People. There is no indication that this dismissal text is optional. The prayer is prayed with the priest's hands extended over the people. The prayer asks that God will pour out on us "a spirit of compunction" as a result of our doing penance, again pointing to the inward, spiritual conversion that should take place as a result of the outward actions.

The actual blessing and dismissal take place as usual.

A visit can be scheduled to all the sick and homebound on Ash Wednesday to share already-blessed ashes. There is a simple order in the *Book of Blessings,* chapter 52. A priest, deacon, or lay minister may distribute ashes, but the lay minister excludes the prayer of blessing. The lay minister should bring already-blessed ashes.

Pastoral Reflection

While made in the image and likeness of God, we are not God and thus have lives in need of cleansing. Today begins the preparation to go deep within, care more for others, and create a clean space for God to reside. All you do is meant to have your life be more in synch with Christ's path, not for the praise of the world. The less fortunate are always among us to teach us to return to God, listen to their needs. Choose a cause this Lent. Create a date with God each day and spend time in true conversation (prayer). Clear your body of toxins and excess food so that you "live simply so others can simply live." Study the lives of the saints this Lent. Their lives are great models of all we are called to be this day.

THU 6 (#220) violet
Thursday after Ash Wednesday

The Lectionary for Mass

◆ FIRST READING: Like Israel of old, we have a choice: life or death, blessing or curse. Are we willing to take God's Word to heart and live accordingly?

◆ RESPONSORIAL PSALM 1: Fidelity to God's law is the source of true happiness and flourishing life. The one who is faithful thrives, like a beautiful tree with deep roots and leafy branches in abundance.

◆ GOSPEL: Jesus sets the paradox before us: true life comes only through death. It was the way for him, so must it be for us.

The Roman Missal

All the texts are proper for today. The Collect asks for God's help and inspiration so that what we do (especially during the time of Lent) may always begin in God and be brought to completion by him. The Prayer over the Offerings asks for pardon such that, having received that pardon, the "offerings we set upon this sacred altar" may truly be oblations that give honor to God. Use one of the four Prefaces of Lent. While any one of the four is appropriate, since today's account of the Gospel speaks explicitly of denying oneself, perhaps Preface III, with its explicit mention of self-denial, would be a good choice. The Prayer after Communion acknowledges the blessings we have received from God while beseeching from him "pardon" and "salvation."

There is a Prayer over the People provided every day during Lent for the end of Mass. While the prayer is optional on weekdays, it is a good practice to use these special prayers to highlight the liturgical time. The prayer acknowledges that God has "made known to your people the ways of eternal life;" within the context of Lent, we can think of those ways of eternal life being the ways of penance (prayer, fasting, and almsgiving). The prayer goes on to ask that that same path to eternal life may lead to God who is "the unfading light."

FRI 7 (#221) violet
Friday after Ash Wednesday

Optional Memorial of SS. Perpetua and Felicity, Martyrs / violet

The Lectionary for Mass

First Reading: God calls the people to account for their meaningless rituals of fasting and acts of penance.

Though performing the externals, they have failed to obey God's commandments. Fidelity to the law's demands for justice is the sign of true repentance.

◆ RESPONSORIAL PSALM 51: The repentance God desires is conversion of the heart.

◆ GOSPEL: Both the prophet Isaiah and the Book of Revelation describe God's covenant with Israel in terms of a bridegroom and bride. A question about fasting leads to Jesus's self-revelation: He is the Bridegroom, the fulfillment of God's covenant promises.

The Roman Missal

The Collect of the Lenten weekday acknowledges that we have begun works of penance; this is in keeping with the nature of these weekdays before the First Sunday of Lent acting as a kind of introduction to the liturgical time. The prayer asks for perseverance, "that we may have strength to accomplish with sincerity / the bodily observances we undertake." The Prayer over the Offerings for the day prays for interior conversion to occur as a result of the sacrifice we offer this day: "that it may make our intentions acceptable to you / and add to our powers of self-restraint." The Lenten Prayer after Communion petitions for healing and forgiveness, in that it asks that as a result of our partaking in the Eucharist, "we may be cleansed of all our misdeeds, / and so be suited for the remedies of your compassion."

One of the four Prefaces of Lent is used today. While any one of the four is appropriate, you might consider using Preface IV, since it specifically mentions fasting, and would therefore echo the Gospel.

Even though the Prayer over the People is optional on weekdays, it would be good to use it, to highlight the liturgical time.

If the optional Memorial of SS. Perpetua and Felicity is to be observed today, then the proper Collect is used, as found at March 7 in the Proper of Saints; the other orations and the Preface are taken from the weekday of Lent (see GIRM, 355a). In this case, then, the Collect of the Lenten weekday can be used as the conclusion to the Universal Prayer.

Today's Saints

In the year 203, SS. Perpetua and Felicity were martyred in the amphitheater at Carthage. Their crime was professing faith in Jesus Christ. Perpetua was a wealthy noblewoman, the mother of a young son; Felicity was a humble slave girl, who gave birth to a daughter just a few days before she died. These women, so different in their circumstances, were united in their death. The names of these heroic women are included in Eucharistic Prayer I, alongside the names of Apostles and martyrs. They lived today's account of the Gospel, praying for their persecutors.

SAT 8 (#222) violet
Saturday after Ash Wednesday

Optional Memorial of St. John of God, Religious / violet

The Lectionary for Mass

◆ FIRST READING: God calls Israel to fast from evil deeds, especially those that violate the well-being of others. Israel must be a people who are faithful to God if they are to flourish and find life and rest, if they are to be restored and rebuild what has been destroyed.

◆ RESPONSORIAL PSALM 86: Of ourselves, we are poor and helpless. We need God, his help and his deliverance. We need to learn God's wisdom.

◆ GOSPEL: No one is rejected by Jesus, not even the scorned tax collector, hated because of his allegiance to the Romans and his self-serving practices. It is not because he is virtuous that he—and we—are called, but because Jesus knows our need. May we be open to the healing he offers us.

The Roman Missal

The Lenten Collect entreats God for protection, asking him to "look with compassion on our weakness." The Prayer over the Offerings asks for inner purification through the sacrifice "of conciliation and praise," which will be offered. The Prayer after Communion prays that the nourishment we receive in the Eucharist "may be for us a help to reach eternity."

One of the four Prefaces of Lent is used today, and any one of the four is appropriate. Preface II of Lent might be especially considered for use, since its references to the renewing and purifying of hearts and to being "freed from disordered affections" would go well with the Gospel story of the call and conversion of Levi.

Even though the Prayer over the People is optional on weekdays, it would be good to use it, to highlight the liturgical time.

If you will be observing the optional Memorial of St. John of God today, then use the proper Collect found at March 8 in the Proper of Saints; the other orations and the Preface are taken from the weekday of Lent, however. Consider using the Collect of the Lenten weekday as the conclusion to the Universal Prayer.

Today's Saint

St. John of God was a Portuguese friar who became a leading religious figure. After a period in the army in Spain, he began to distribute religious books, using the new Gutenberg printing press. At one point, John had an intense religious experience that resulted in temporary insanity. He was thrown into a mental institution, and while there, he realized how badly the sick and the poor were treated. Once he recovered, he spent the rest of his life caring for them. In Granada he gathered a circle of disciples around him who felt the same call and founded what is now known as the Brothers Hospitallers of St. John of God.

(#22)   violet
9 First Sunday of Lent

The Lectionary for Mass

◆ FIRST READING: The "patching" of verses from Genesis 2–3 invites us to focus on several realities about human existence. First, humanity is formed from the clay of the earth ("dust [we] are . . .") and enlivened by the very breath of God (2:7). Secondly, God created a place of beauty and delight—again from the clay of the earth—where humanity would live. Thirdly, very early on in their existence, human creatures listened to a voice other than God's. It was a choice that changed their life with drastic consequences that would have been forever—had God not sent Jesus.

◆ RESPONSORIAL PSALM: We acknowledge our sinfulness, our failures to listen to God's voice, and pray for the gifts of a clean heart and a steadfast spirit. Gifts—because only with God's grace will we possess these. In light of the Genesis account of the human creature being enlivened by God's spirit or breath, note the reference to "your holy spirit" in the last line of the third stanza.

◆ SECOND READING: Paul's words spell out the consequences of Adam's sin—and the ramifications of the gift of Jesus's life and obedience even to the point of death. As a result of Adam's sin, all die. As a result of Jesus's obedience, all are brought to justification and to life.

◆ GOSPEL: Like all humanity, Jesus was tempted to listen to a voice other than that of his heavenly Father. The Gospel identifies the tempter as the devil or Satan, that fallen angel now leader of the powers of evil (see Revelation 12). Note carefully the nature of the temptations. The devil is almost taunting Jesus to misuse or abuse his power, to "show off," to exalt himself. Note how the Scriptures are a tool that Jesus uses in resisting temptation (yet note that the devil can quote Scripture too!). Matthew's account of the temptations is framed by references to God's power at work in Jesus's life as he is led by the Holy Spirit into the desert—and no doubt that same Spirit remained with him during his temptations—and ministered to by God's angels after he had endured and triumphed over his temptations.

The Roman Missal

The Gloria is omitted today. The Creed is said.

The Collect on this First Sunday of Lent sets the program, as it were, for the liturgical time that lies ahead and has the character of a prayer that is inaugurating something to be undertaken. We pray that "through the yearly observances of holy Lent," our understanding of "the riches hidden in Christ" may grow, and that our conduct may reflect those riches of living life in Christ. The Prayer over the Offerings also has the characteristic of launching the sacred time of Lent as it acknowledges that the offerings we make this day "celebrate the beginning / of this venerable and sacred time." Consequently, the prayer asks that we be given the right dispositions to make the offering properly. The Prayer after Communion speaks of the nourishment that comes to us in the Eucharist in terms of the three traditional virtues of faith, hope, and charity, noting the good effect that is had on each; it then, in a clear allusion to today's account of the Gospel, goes on to ask "that we may learn to hunger for Christ, / the true and living Bread, / and strive to live by every word / which proceeds from your mouth."

The Preface to be used for this Mass is given on the pages right there along with the other texts for the Mass. The reason this Preface, "The Temptation of the Lord," is used today is obvious, since the Gospel reading for the First Sunday of Lent is always the account of the temptation of Jesus from one of the Gospel accounts. Consider chanting the Introductory Dialogue and the Preface today; if this is not the regular practice of your community, this can be a way of powerfully drawing attention to the solemnity of Lenten time (but be sure to prepare and rehearse your assembly as needed, if your people are not familiar with the responses!).

The Prayer over the People is required, not optional, on the Sundays of Lent, and the text is given right after the Prayer after Communion.

Sending of the Catechumens for Election

The Rite of Christian Initiation of Adults includes an optional Rite of Sending of the Catechumens for Election. If your diocese celebrates the Rite of Election on the First Sunday of Lent, as suggested by the RCIA, then consider celebrating this Rite of Sending in your parish.

Celebrating the rite is yet another way to catechize the entire parish about the meaning of RCIA and the journey the catechumens (soon-to-be elect) undertake. Also, the rite provides yet another opportunity for the catechumens to be supported in prayer by, and to receive the good wishes of, those who will soon be their brothers and sisters in Baptism. The rite takes place after the Homily at Mass and is described in numbers 106–117 in the RCIA.

Pastoral Reflection

Temptations. The devil. Angels. These are words and concepts that come with unique conversation depending on who you are. Jesus was tempted today by the devil (a real being) and, after defeating the evil one, was ministered to by the angels (another true reality.) What temptations in your life need to be reduced to dust? The devil can take on many forms. Are you aware of how evil can enter your life and appear good? Walking in the light of God, fed only by God's Word and commands, we will not fall prey and can rely upon the support of those walking with us. There are "earthly angels" in the guise of friends to keep us walking straight and God's angels among us to guide our steps. In these forty days of Lent, open your eyes to all that is influencing you to be anything other than the perfect child of God that you are called to be.

MON 10 (#224) violet
Lenten Weekday

The Lectionary for Mass

◆ FIRST READING: Our reading opens with the command to "be holy" (Leviticus 19:2) and continues with the practical spelling out of how to do this as we cooperate with God's grace in heeding his commands. The command is simple: we are to love our neighbor.

◆ RESPONSORIAL PSALM 19: Today's antiphon comes from the Gospel according to John. Jesus's words are indeed Spirit and life! The last stanza of today's psalm can be seen in connection with the practical commands set forth in today's First Reading regarding our behavior toward others.

◆ GOSPEL: How we treat others in their needs and suffering is the criterion for our judgment at the end of time. Are we among the righteous or the unrighteous, according to Jesus's principles of judgment? His message is simple. What we do—or don't do—for other people in their need is what we do—or don't do—for the Lord. Eternal life or eternal punishment is at stake.

The Roman Missal

Today's Collect acknowledges the conversion and instruction that we need if we are going to benefit from our Lenten penances; the prayer thus reminds us that any growth in the spiritual life we make during Lent is not the result of our own efforts, but are the result of God's action in us. The Prayer over the Offerings prays that "this devout oblation be acceptable to you, O Lord," so that our "manner of life" may be sanctified. As is common for the Prayer over the Offerings, we are reminded that the worship we offer at Mass should not stay within the confines of the liturgical action, but must have an effect in our everyday life, changing our everyday actions to be more loving and Christ-like. The Prayer after Communion speaks of the healing that comes through our reception of the sacrament, a healing that keeps us safe in both mind and body.

The Preface to use is one of the four Prefaces of Lent. While any one of the four is appropriate, Preface I, with its mention of "works of charity" would work well today in tandem with the Gospel reading.

Even though the Prayer over the People is optional on weekdays, it would be good to use it, to highlight the liturgical time.

TUE 11 (#225) violet
Lenten Weekday

The Lectionary for Mass

◆ FIRST READING: The image of rain and snow watering the earth and bringing forth fruit, thus accomplishing the purpose for which they were sent by the Lord, is an apt illustration of the fruitful effect God intends his Word to have in the minds and hearts of those who hear it.

◆ RESPONSORIAL PSALM 34 is a prayer of thanksgiving and praise for God's deliverance. In light of today's First Reading, it is interesting to note the words in the stanzas of the psalm. There is the Word-in-action of God's deliverance in the first stanza. There are the words of the poor, the just, and the afflicted that are not without fruitful effect when addressed to the Lord.

◆ GOSPEL: One does not need many words for prayer—only confidence and trust. Today Jesus teaches us how to pray. This prayer (Our Father) also requires words-in-action expressed in forgiveness. In fact, our willingness to forgive is the "condition" of God's forgiveness of us—at least in the last line of today's account of the Gospel.

The Roman Missal

The Collect calls our attention to "the chastening effects of bodily discipline," specifically, the way such discipline brings clarity to our minds (which can be made "radiant" as a result) and strengthens our yearning for God. This prayer is yet another reminder of the inward transformation that is the goal of our outward Lenten practices. The Prayer over the Offerings acknowledges that the gifts we bring are from God's bountiful goodness; it then asks that the offerings of bread and wine, "temporal sustenance," be transformed to give us eternal life. The sacramental principle is being referred to here, as the prayer prays that tangible signs be transformed to convey spiritual realities of grace. The Prayer after Communion prays that today's celebration of the mysteries may help us to keep the proper perspective in life: namely, that "by moderating earthly desires / we may learn to love the things of heaven."

Any one of the four Prefaces of Lent can be used today.

Even though the Prayer over the People is optional on weekdays, it would be good to use it, to highlight the liturgical time.

WED 12 (#226) violet
Lenten Weekday

The Lectionary for Mass

◆ FIRST READING: The story of Nineveh's immediate faith-filled and penitential response to Jonah's call to conversion is most impressive. And Jonah was only one day into his journey! How quickly Jonah's word had spread. How willingly the Ninevites responded—from the king on down. How quick, how complete is our response to the call of repentance?

◆ RESPONSORIAL PSALM 51 is one of the penitential psalms, focusing as it does on the humble sinner's prayer not only for forgiveness, but also for a renewed and purified heart.

◆ GOSPEL: The people of Jesus's generation could hardly be likened to the Ninevites when it came to responding to God's call. With hearts and minds closed to Jesus's words, they face a judgment of condemnation. The queen of Sheba traveled a great distance to hear the wisdom of Solomon (1 Kings 10). Jesus—greater than Solomon—was in their midst, yet they failed to recognize the wisdom of his teaching.

The Roman Missal

The Collect for today asks that the good works of our bodily self-denial may bear fruit by our being "renewed in mind"—again emphasizing the need for the outward behavior to have an effect on our interior disposition, our spiritual life. The Prayer over the Offerings asks that just as God makes the gifts offered become the sacrament, so too may he "let them become for us an eternal remedy." The prayer can remind us that regardless of the objective truth of the offerings of bread and wine becoming the Body and Blood of Christ, nothing automatic happens to us as a result of the transformation of those elements; instead, they will only be the "eternal remedy" they are supposed to be in our lives if we are open to them and cooperate with God's grace—and that only happens with the proper interior conversion and disposition. The Prayer after Communion prays that the nourishment of the sacrament may "bring us unending life."

Any one of the four Prefaces of Lent can be used today. While any one is appropriate, the First Reading and the Gospel, with their emphasis on responding to the call to conversion, might make Preface II of Lent, with its focus on Lent as "a sacred time / for the renewing and purifying of their hearts," or Eucharistic Prayer for Reconciliation I with its proper Preface (". . . you constantly offer pardon / and call on sinners / to trust in your forgiveness alone . . . / Even now you set before your people / a time of grace and reconciliation . . ."), good choices for today.

Even though the Prayer over the People is optional on weekdays, it would be good to use it, to highlight the liturgical time.

THU 13 (#227) violet
Lenten Weekday

The Lectionary for Mass

◆ FIRST READING: Esther was a Jewish woman who became the wife of the Persian king Ahasuerus. As queen, she was in an exceptional position to save her people from the threat of extinction at the hands of Haman, an official in the Persian court. The prayer we hear today was uttered by Esther prior to her audience with the king to intercede on behalf of her people. Note how what Esther learned as a child concerning the saving acts of God in human history gave her strength and courage in her present undertaking.

◆ RESPONSORIAL PSALM 138 is a prayer of thanksgiving for the Lord's favorable answer to a cry for help. The thankful awareness of God's saving deeds in the life of the one who prays is echoed in each stanza. How can we make the awareness, the thanksgiving of this prayer, our own?

◆ GOSPEL: A word of assurance from the Lord: "ask" and you will receive. The heavenly Father wishes only good things for his children. Do we confidently look for the good in whatever the circumstances of our lives?

The Roman Missal

The Collect acknowledges our complete and utter dependence on God and asks that he may bestow on us "a spirit of always pondering what is right and of hastening to carry it out." More than just good intentions is needed during Lent; we must be sure to follow through with concrete actions so that, as the prayer goes on to ask, we may "be enabled to live according to your will." The Prayer over the Offerings expresses the proper stance of humility we should bear when offering the Sacrifice, as it entreats God for mercy for those "who approach you in supplication" and that he might "turn the hearts of us all towards you." The Prayer after Communion prays that the sacred mysteries we have been given in the Eucharist may be "a healing remedy for us, / both now and in time to come."

Any one of the four Prefaces of Lent can be used today.

Even though the Prayer over the People is optional on weekdays, it would be good to use it, to highlight the liturgical time.

FRI 14 (#228) violet
Lenten Weekday

The Lectionary for Mass

◆ FIRST READING: Ezekiel's words give great hope to sinners who turn from their wickedness to a life of righteousness. God will "forget" the sins of their past. There is warning in today's text for those who are righteous if they turn from a virtuous life to one of wickedness: God will forget their good deeds. Dare we accuse God as unfair? Do not overlook the immense importance of the present moment.

◆ RESPONSORIAL PSALM 130: Echoing a theme from the First Reading, today's psalm asks: if the Lord remembers sin, who can live? Psalm 130 is a psalm of repentance and confident trust in the Lord's mercy.

◆ GOSPEL: Virtuous (righteous) living is likewise a major concern in today's account of the Gospel. Jesus clearly spells out what he means by righteousness, at least regarding the questions of anger toward another, and forgiveness. Reconciliation with another has priority—even over sacrifice.

The Roman Missal

In today's Collect, we ask that we may be "so conformed to the paschal observances" that the penance ("bodily discipline") we have begun may be fruit "in the souls of all." The use of the word "paschal" in this third edition of *The Roman Missal* highlights for us the Lent and Easter connection and reminds us that we do penance during Lent not for its own sake, but for the sake of sharing more deeply in new life with, through, and in Christ who is risen. In asking God to accept our sacrificial offerings, the Prayer over the Offerings reminds us that it is God's will that we are reconciled to him, and our salvation is restored, through the offering of the Eucharistic Sacrifice. The Prayer after Communion uses the captivating phrase "holy refreshment of your Sacrament" in asking that the Eucharist cleanse us of old ways and "take us up into the mystery of salvation."

Any one of the four Prefaces of Lent can be used today. Consideration might also be given, in light of the Gospel's call for us to be reconciled with one another (especially before bringing our gifts to the altar), to using Eucharistic Prayer for Reconciliation II, as it describes in its Preface how it is through the power of the Spirit "that enemies may speak to each other again, / adversaries join hands, / and peoples seek to meet together" and how the Spirit "takes away everything that estranges us from one another."

Even though the Prayer over the People is optional on weekdays, it would be good to use it, to highlight the liturgical time.

SAT 15 (#229) violet
Lenten Weekday

Lectionary for Mass

◆ FIRST READING: The salvation of the present moment, the now, today, is central in our First Reading. We agree to live wholeheartedly as God's people, faithful to the demands of his covenant. God promises us glory and praise if we live as a faithful people, sacred to the Lord.

◆ RESPONSORIAL PSALM 119: The stipulations of the covenant agreement are spelled out in the law. Psalm 119 acclaims the wisdom of God's law and the blessedness of those who faithfully observe it.

◆ GOSPEL: The command to hate our enemies is not expressed, at least not in these words, in the Old Testament. Neighbors were members of one's own people. Enemies were those who injured, harmed, or threatened in some way. Certainly we find hatred of the wicked expressed in the Old Testament, but Jesus asks more than did the law of Moses. One's enemies are to be loved. The heavenly Father loves both the just and the unjust. Jesus's disciples must be as "perfect" (mature) as their heavenly Father.

The Roman Missal

Today's Collect prays for the turning of our hearts toward the eternal Father so that "we may be dedicated to your worship." That dedication, however, includes "carrying out works of charity," thus pointing to an understanding of worship that goes beyond liturgy to include the "liturgy of one's life," for example, living a life of love, which is the sacrifice pleasing to God. The Prayer over the Offerings, in acknowledging that we are restored by "these blessed mysteries," also asks that they "make us worthy of the gift they bestow." Thus, we are reminded that our participation in offering the sacrifice is not through our own merit, but because we have been made worthy of that participation only as a gift from God in the first place. The Prayer after Communion prays for "unceasing favor" and "salutary consolations" for those who have shared in the "divine mystery" of this celebration of the Eucharist.

Any one of the four Prefaces of Lent can be used today. While any one is appropriate, one could find in either Preface I or Preface III echoes

of today's account of the Gospel's challenge to be perfect as our heavenly Father is perfect.

Even though the Prayer over the People is optional on weekdays, it would be good to use it, to highlight the liturgical time.

☀ **16** (#25) violet
Second Sunday of Lent

The Lectionary for Mass

◆ FIRST READING: God begins to form a people for himself, beginning with the call of Abraham. (Notice that the second part of verse 4, omitted by the Lectionary, tells us that Abraham was 75 years old—however that was reckoned—when he received this call!) What is most significant is Abraham's prompt obedience in the face of the call—and the promise—of the Lord. All the communities of the earth did indeed find blessing in him—and in his descendant, Jesus (see Matthew 1:1).

◆ RESPONSORIAL PSALM 33: How fitting is today's response, given the unhesitating trust that Abraham placed in God's Word. The Hebrew word translated as *mercy* is "hesed" or "covenant love." The verses of Psalm 33 chosen as today's response extol the trustworthiness of the Lord's Word, and his protection and deliverance of those who reverence him—all of which were fulfilled in Abraham's life.

◆ SECOND READING: Hardships are part and parcel of life. Hardships are especially a part of trying to live a life in accord with Gospel values and teaching. Endure these, carry these—ultimately they have no power over us. Life and immortality is ours through Jesus, our Savior.

◆ GOSPEL: Mountains are privileged places of encounter with God. So it was for Moses, for Elijah, and for Jesus. So it was also for Jesus's companions when they glimpsed the divine glory that was his as well as the presence of Moses and Elijah. How important it was that Israel listen to the words God gave to Moses. How important that Jesus's disciples listen to the words of God that he speaks. According to the prophet Malachi, Elijah would come preaching a message of repentance before the coming of the day of the Lord. In the verses immediately after the Transfiguration, Jesus tells his disciples that Elijah had already come in the person of John the Baptist (Matthew 17:12–13). Yes, the day of judgment, the day of salvation, is imminent in the person of Jesus. How important it is that we listen to the words of the one who is not only judge but the beloved Son who is pleasing to the Lord. How important it is that we take his words to heart.

The Roman Missal

The Gloria is omitted today.

The Collect for the Second Sunday of Lent clearly connects with the Gospel reading of the Transfiguration. The prayer's opening address to God refers to him as the one who has "commanded us / to listen to your beloved Son." It goes on to ask that we might be nourished "inwardly by your word," gain "spiritual sight made pure" and therefore "rejoice to behold your glory." The imagery in the prayer all but puts us in the Transfiguration scene. The Prayer over the Offerings makes a strong connection between Lent and Easter as it looks forward to "the celebration of the Paschal festivities;" we ask that we may be prepared for those festivities by being cleansed of our faults and sanctified in body and mind through the offering of this Sacrifice. The Prayer after Communion is a prayer of gratitude, expressing thanksgiving that "As we receive these glorious mysteries," we are allowed "while still on earth / to be partakers even now of the things of heaven." The prayer reminds us that the Church's celebration of the Eucharist is also a participation in the heavenly, eschatological banquet.

The Preface to be used for this Mass is given on the pages right there along with the other texts for this Mass. Titled "The Transfiguration of the Lord," the Preface clearly recalls and gives the meaning of the Transfiguration: "to show, even by the testimony of the law and the prophets, / that the Passion leads to the glory of the Resurrection." Thus is the centrality of the Paschal Mystery reaffirmed. Consider chanting the introductory dialogue and the Preface today; if this is not the regular practice of your community, this can be a way of powerfully drawing attention to the solemnity of Lenten time (but be sure to prepare and rehearse your assembly as needed, if your people are not familiar with the responses!).

The Prayer over the People is required, not optional, on the Sundays of Lent, and the text is given right after the Prayer after Communion.

Pastoral Reflection

While today's marvelous experience is all about Jesus's identity, how can it relate to your life? Jesus's face shone like the sun. When do you allow God's presence to glow fully with you so that you glow in Christ? The disciples were in awe and a cloud cast a shadow upon them. When have you experienced God's love and were so dumbfounded that you

couldn't fully receive the gift and the intensity of the light was then reduced? God speaks to all and speaks easily with Jesus. A conversation necessitates that one party speaks and another party listens. Do you allow time to listen to God? For in the listening you will then be like the disciples, receiving the power of God, and will fall prostrate to worship. Glow with God this week. Listen to God in prayer. Even if you cannot hear what you want, create a personal form of praise to God—through writing, song, nature, or acknowledging God working through another person.

◆ St. Patrick's Day: Parades, corned beef and cabbage, and service projects usually mark this special day of our favorite Irish saint. This year, St. Patrick's Day falls on a Monday. Remember to celebrate this saint and to think of the outreach associated with him. Consider serving at a local food pantry as part of your Lenten concern for the poor.

MON 17 (#230) violet
Lenten Weekday

Optional Memorial of St. Patrick, Bishop / violet

The Lectionary for Mass

◆ First Reading: Today's First Reading is, in effect, a confession of sin, an acknowledgment that God's people have broken the covenant through their disobedience. They have heeded neither the law nor the prophets. The "scattering" (exile) of God's people (outside the land of Israel) is considered punishment for sin. There is mention of God's mercy, compassion, and forgiveness—but the emphasis in today's text is clearly on the people's guilt.

◆ Responsorial Psalm 79: Fittingly, our antiphon pleads that the Lord will not deal with his people as they deserve. The context of the

psalm is the aftermath of the destruction of Jerusalem and the Temple—viewed as punishment for sin by biblical authors, as is the subsequent exile. The first two stanzas ask for God's forgiveness.

◆ Gospel: The Gospel according to Luke stresses the mercy and compassion of God. This is the emphasis in Jesus's teaching in today's text with the command that his followers incorporate this same mercy and compassion in their dealings with one another. The last line of the Gospel is a strong call to self-examination.

The Roman Missal

The Collect of the Lenten Weekday acknowledges that the reason we "chasten our bodies" is for the sake of "the healing of our souls," again reminding us that the outward practices of Lent must penetrate into our inner life. The prayer goes on to ask that we will be enabled to abstain from all sins and have our hearts strengthened so we can "carry out your loving commands." The Prayer over the Offerings, in asking God to accept our prayers, also asks that we might be "set free from worldly attractions." The Prayer after Communion asks that this sharing in Communion may both "cleanse us of wrongdoing / and make us heirs to the joys of heaven."

One of the four Prefaces of Lent is used today. While any one of the four is appropriate, Preface I might be a good one to pick up on the themes of the First Reading and the Gospel today.

Even though the Prayer over the People is optional on weekdays, it would be good to use it, to highlight the liturgical time.

If the optional Memorial of St. Patrick is observed today, then the proper Collect is used, as found at March 17 in the Proper of Saints; the other orations and the Preface are taken from the weekday of Lent (see GIRM, 355a). In this case, then, the Collect of the Lenten weekday can be used as the conclusion to the Universal Prayer.

Today's Saint

Many legends have developed around St. Patrick (390–460), from driving snakes out of Ireland, to using the shamrock to explain the Trinity; however, his popularity stems beyond these stories, to his missionary zeal and astonishing ability to inspire faith. He was sold into slavery at a young age and eventually freed, and so he wanted people enslaved by doubt and skepticism to know the liberation found in Jesus Christ. Although he had little education, he was appointed Bishop of Ireland. His many accomplishments include the conversion of Ireland, ordination of clergy, consecration of virgins, and organization of missions to evangelize Europe. St. Patrick's life has a universal appeal; therefore, his feast day is celebrated by the Roman Catholic Church, the Church of England, the Episcopal Church in America, and the Evangelical Lutheran Church in America. He also makes an appearance on the Russian Orthodox calendar. Today is a solemnity and holyday of obligation in Ireland.

T U E **18** (#231)   violet
Lenten Weekday

Optional Memorial of St. Cyril of Jerusalem, Bishop and Doctor of the Church / violet

The Lectionary for Mass

◆ FIRST READING: The cities of Sodom and Gomorrah were notorious for their wickedness, as were the people of Isaiah's day. The first part of today's reading consists of eight commands. In fulfilling these, true righteousness and purity is to be found in God's eyes. In the second part of the reading, God, as it were, invites us to sit down and talk things over. God tells us what can

"come" to us ("become," mentioned two times) if we listen to him. The possibility is held out to us; the choice is ours.

◆ RESPONSORIAL PSALM 50: Like the First Reading, the Psalm is concerned with true righteousness. The ritual offerings are in place but the dispositions of heart (the true sacrifice of praise) are not. It is this that God desires. See all of the third part of Psalm 50 for the details of what is required.

◆ GOSPEL: How hard it is to obey those whose example is not consistent with their teaching, yet that is what Jesus says his hearers must do. The Pharisees are faulted for their hypocrisy, for calling attention to themselves and expecting preferential treatment. This is not to be the way of Jesus's followers who are called to humble service.

The Roman Missal

The Collect brings to the fore our utter and complete dependence on God as it reminds us that without God "moral humanity is sure to fall." Consequently, the prayer goes on to ask that God's constant help might keep us from all harm and be brought to salvation. The Prayer over the Offerings acknowledges that these mysteries that we celebrate are the means by which God works his sanctification within us; therefore, we ask that we may "be cleansed of earthly faults / and led to the gifts of heaven." The Prayer after Communion for the Lenten Weekday asks that "the refreshment of this sacred table" may bring both "an increase in devoutness of life" and "the constant help of your work of conciliation."

One of the four Prefaces of Lent is used today. While any one of the four is appropriate, perhaps either Preface II, with its references to having our hearts purified and our

being "freed from disordered affections," or Preface III, with its reference to humbling "our sinful pride," would work well today.

Even though the Prayer over the People is optional on weekdays, it would be good to use it, to highlight the liturgical time.

If you wish to observe the optional Memorial of St. Cyril of Jerusalem, then use the proper Collect found at March 18 in the Proper of Saints but take the other orations and the Preface from the weekday of Lent (see GIRM, 355a). The Collect of the Lenten weekday can be used as the conclusion to the Universal Prayer.

Even though the Prayer over the People is optional on weekdays, it would be good to use it, to highlight the liturgical time.

W E D **19** (#543)   white
Solemnity of St. Joseph, Spouse of the Blessed Virgin Mary

About this Solemnity/Saint

St. Joseph (first century) was an honorable and just man who took the Blessed Virgin Mary, the Mother of Jesus, as his wife. While engaged to Mary, Joseph found out that she was pregnant, but he knew he was not the father. After an angel appeared to him in a dream, in which he was told that the child was from the Holy Spirit, he courageously moved forward, and still planned to marry his beloved Mary and protect the soon-to-be Messiah. St. Joseph, a carpenter by trade, appears at various points in the four Gospel accounts, including Luke's genealogy (see Luke 3:23), the infancy narratives (see Matthew 1—2; Luke 1—2), and the flight into Egypt (see Matthew 2:13–15). Although he disappears from the Gospel after Jesus's early years, he continues to be a source of inspiration and veneration for many.

The Lectionary for Mass

◆ FIRST READING: David wants to build a "house" or temple for God. Nathan the prophet, instructed by God, tells David that his son will do this. God promises instead to build a house or a dynasty for David. From his line shall come the Messiah, whose kingdom will endure forever.

◆ RESPONSORIAL PSALM 89: The psalmist sings of God's love and fidelity, which is shown in his promise to David of an everlasting covenant and an everlasting kingship.

◆ SECOND READING: Abraham, father of the chosen people, is justified, that is, put in the right relationship with God, not because of his works but because of his faith. Abraham had faith even when—especially when—asked to believe in what seemed impossible.

◆ GOSPEL: Great faith was required of Joseph in the face of the incomprehensible events concerning his espoused wife, and in subsequent years, the actions of her Son. Though not understanding, Joseph humbly and patiently complied with what God asked. In this he is model for us all.

The Roman Missal

All the Mass texts for this solemnity, which are proper for the day, are found in the Proper of Saints at March 19. The somberness of Lent is put aside today, and the Gloria is sung or said.

That God chose St. Joseph to watch over the Holy Family and care for Jesus is echoed in the Collect, as that prayer reminds us that the beginnings of human salvation were entrusted to the "faithful care" of St. Joseph. However, the prayer asks that just as the beginnings of salvation were entrusted to the care of St. Joseph, so may the Church "constantly watch over" the continued unfolding of those mysteries. The Church, as the guardian

and caretaker of the mysteries of salvation, is herself entrusted to the guardianship and care of St. Joseph, as Patron of the Universal Church.

The Creed is said or sung today in observance of the solemnity.

The Prayer over the Offerings focuses on the theme of offering worthy service. The parallel is drawn in petitioning God that "just as Saint Joseph served with loving care / your Only Begotten Son, born of the Virgin Mary, / so we may be worthy to minister / with a pure heart at your altar." The "we" in the prayer refers to all who offer the sacrifice, not just the ordained or other liturgical ministers; rather, all who bring the offering of their sacrifice to be joined with Christ's sacrifice are the ones who minister at the altar and therefore must beg for a pure heart, so that a worthy sacrifice may be offered.

The Preface assigned for today is given right there along with the other Mass texts for the Solemnity of St. Joseph in the Proper of Saints. Its title is "The mission of St. Joseph" and it speaks of the saint as a "just man" and a "wise and faithful servant." Although we often recognize and preach about Mary's *fiat*, let's not forget that in his own way Joseph too had to make a fiat that required openness, trust, and abandonment to the will of God, and so he is rightly called "just" and a "wise and faithful servant."

The Prayer after Communion continues the theme of protection associated with St. Joseph as it asks God that "the family you have nourished / with food from this altar" may be defended "with unfailing protection" and that the gifts we have been given from God may be kept safe.

Today might be a day to use Eucharistic Prayer I, the Roman Canon, since Joseph's name is mentioned in the prayer.

Pastoral Reflection

Surely Joseph was surprised at his role in the plan of salvation. Are we, too, surprised at our role? Do we try to respectfully decline? Does God offer us uncomfortably bold opportunities to serve? Joseph can be our model and inspiration at accepting our responsibilities in the plan of salvation. We can enter situations fraught with danger and turmoil confident that Jesus's earthly father has walked before us.

Honoring St. Joseph

We remember the foster father of Jesus, or, as his title has been reflective of in recent calendars, the spouse of Mary, on March 19 each year. On this solemnity, it is the custom to bless bread, pastries, and other foods to be given to the poor (see BB, 1679). Some Italian parishes have the custom of having meatless dishes to share during a potluck. This comes from the time when the Italian women prayed to St. Joseph for their husbands' safe return while at sea or at war. The women would refrain from eating meat until their husbands returned. While there are many traditions and customs, see the *Book of Blessings*, 1691, for the Litany of St. Joseph that may be said during this break from the Lenten fast. Ask schoolchildren and religious education students this day to attend Mass or participate in a St. Joseph's Table celebration to remind us of the importance of this holy and righteous man. If St. Joseph is the patron of the parish, a low-key celebration of coffee, juice, and pastries might be appropriate. If the parish has an image of St. Joseph, place flowers and candles around it. If the parish is not doing a traditional St. Joseph's Table, the assembly could be encouraged to bring food for the poor to Mass. Before the final blessing, people can be invited to bring their offerings forward and place them in baskets. The Litany of St. Joseph could be sung at this time. Then the blessing prayer is said over the baskets and the final blessing and dismissal is given.

THU 20 (#233) violet
Lenten Weekday

Lectionary for Mass

◆ FIRST READING: By their fruits you shall know them. Today's First Reading from Jeremiah contrasts the dryness and barrenness of the one rooted in the transitory and mortal with the fruitfulness and stability of the one rooted in the Lord. The word translated as "tortuous" literally means "deceitful" or "fraudulent." The Lord searches out the human mind and heart. In Lent, especially, so must we search our minds and hearts.

◆ RESPONSORIAL PSALM 1: Our antiphon echoes the true blessedness and happiness of the one firmly rooted in the Lord. The stanzas continue this theme and point to God's law as the ground in which we must remain firmly planted.

◆ GOSPEL: In today's parable, the theme we have already heard continues, as Abraham points to the law and prophets as sure guides to everlasting blessedness. The rich man is faulted not because he is rich, but because he looked away from the needy man who was daily at his door. In this, he failed to show the concern for the poor that the law and the prophets command. The poor man, totally ignored in his earthly life, was comforted in the bosom of Abraham.

The Roman Missal

Today's Collect brings to mind how the purification we undergo during Lent can restore us to innocence, as it asks that being caught up in the fire of the Holy Spirit, "we may be found steadfast in faith and effective in works." The Prayer over the Offerings again highlights the necessary connection between our exterior behaviors of Lenten disciplines and our interior dispositions and conversion: those disciplines are supposed to both be a sign of and bring about the inward, spiritual realities. The Prayer after Communion prays that the sacrifice we have just celebrated may truly be active and strong within us.

Any one of the four Prefaces of Lent assigned for the day could be used equally appropriately. Even though the Prayer over the People is optional on weekdays it would be good to use it today to highlight the liturgical time.

FRI 21 (#234) violet
Lenten Weekday

The Lectionary for Mass

◆ FIRST READING: The jealousy, coldness, and attempt to do away with the one who triggers these emotions is, sadly, perhaps all too common an experience, especially within families. We also hear echoed, or rather, prefigured, what will happen to Jesus, the beloved Son, centuries later, even to being stripped of his garment. The reference to Joseph as a dreamer pertains to verses 5–11, which are not included in today's reading.

◆ RESPONSORIAL PSALM 105: Today's psalm tells a bit more of Joseph's story: how the "evil" inflicted upon him by his brothers worked unto good in the hands of God. It was truly a "marvel done by the Lord," as the antiphon says. Joseph's ability to interpret dreams won his release from his Egyptian prison and led to a position in Pharaoh's royal court.

◆ GOSPEL: Today's text is another example of the destructive power of uncontrolled passions and emotions. By killing the son, the tenants could acquire the vineyard for themselves. Like Joseph's brothers and the chief priests and Pharisees, the tenants plotted the destruction of another for their own gain. Jesus is the Son sent by the Father to obtain the fruit of the work of the tenants. The citation of Psalm 118:22–23 points to Jesus as the rejected stone who became the cornerstone (foundation stone) of God's new people.

The Roman Missal

The Collect notes the purifying effect that the practice of penance has, and so goes on to ask that being purified, we may be led "in sincerity of heart / to attain the holy things to come." The Prayer over the Offerings again connects the offering of our worship at the sacrifice of the Mass with the way we live our everyday lives in a reciprocal relationship: it asks that God's grace may both prepare us "for the worthy celebration of these mysteries," and that we may be led to the celebration "by a devout way of life." The Prayer after Communion expresses how the Eucharist is a foretaste of the fullness of the kingdom yet to come as it asks that "Having received this pledge of eternal salvation," we may "attain the redemption you promise."

Any one of the four Prefaces of Lent would be equally appropriate today. Even though the Prayer over the People is optional on weekdays it would be good to use it today to highlight the liturgical time.

SAT 22 (#235) violet
Lenten Weekday

The Lectionary for Mass

◆ FIRST READING: The reading is a prayer: God is the shepherd, and the people who desire to be led and cared for by him are his flock. What was of old, the marvels of the Exodus, is recalled. The prophet prays to see such wonderful signs again. The prayer arises from a situation of distress and affliction. The second part of the reading/prayer acclaims God as one who forgives and delights in so doing. God will cast the sins of those who repent into the depths of the sea, remembering them no more.

◆ Responsorial Psalm 103 praises God's benefits: forgiveness, healing, and deliverance from that which threatens to destroy. From the depths of the sea to the heights above the earth, as far as east is from west—it is the image of a cross, his unbounded love, his immeasurable forgiveness.

◆ Gospel: The well-known parable of the prodigal son is, perhaps, better named the parable of the lavish and loving father. Once we realize how we have wasted our inheritance, let us make our way to his waiting embrace.

The Roman Missal

The Collect for today twice uses a this life/next life to come contrast; first, it acknowledges that in being granted "glorious healing remedies while still on earth" we are already "partakers of the things of heaven;" second, it asks that we might be guided through this present life to be brought "to that light in which you dwell." The Prayer over the Offerings points to the fruits that can be gained from our participation in this sacrifice, namely, being restrained from "unruly desires" and being led "onward to the gifts of salvation." The Prayer after Communion directs our attention to the inner workings of the sacrament, specifically our request that it "fill the inner depths of our heart" and "make us partakers of its grace."

Prefaces I–IV are the choices once again today. While any one is appropriate, perhaps Eucharistic Prayer for Reconciliation I, with its own Preface, would be a good choice for today, insofar as that Preface tells how God is rich in mercy, offer-

ing constant pardon, how he never turned away despite how humanity broke the covenant again and again, and how now is a time for turning back. These themes would complement the parable of the lost son in today's account of the Gospel.

☀ 23 (#28) violet Third Sunday of Lent

The Lectionary for Mass

◆ First Reading: Today's reading is set in the context of Israel's desert wanderings before they arrive at Mt. Sinai. God's marvelous care for them as evidenced in their exodus from slavery in Egypt seems to have been forgotten. In fact, the people are dissatisfied and resentful. Ever faithful to his people, God, who shortly before enabled them to pass through the waters of the Red Sea out of slavery into freedom, now gives them water from the rock to sustain their lives.

◆ Responsorial Psalm: Our antiphon highlights the theme of *today* as the day to hear God's voice in obedience and trust. Today is the day of salvation. Note the reference to Massah and Meribah (from today's First Reading) in the last stanzas of the psalm.

◆ Second Reading: We are placed in right relationship with God through God's initiative and grace. Faith is the way of our access to God and gives rise to hope for the glory of God for which we are destined.

All is God's initiative and love, in Jesus who gave his life for us.

◆ Gospel: If only we knew the gift of God, and who is saying to us "give me a drink. . . ." John's account of Jesus's encounter with the Samaritan woman would have us reflect on the reality of our own baptismal life. Do we really know the gift we have been given? Do we know, are we in personal relationship with Jesus who is the giver of life? Today's account of the Gospel calls not only the catechumens who are preparing for Baptism, but all of us who will renew our baptismal vows at the Easter Vigil, to drink freely from the water that Jesus gives. It is the fountain of eternal life (see John 7:37).

The Roman Missal

The Gloria is omitted today. There are two sets of Mass formularies that might be used today: one is the Mass for the Third Sunday of Lent; the other is "For the First Scrutiny."

The Collect for this Sunday mentions the three traditional Lenten practices of prayer, fasting, and almsgiving and identifies them as a remedy for sin. After doing so, the prayer asks that God, looking "graciously on this confession of our lowliness," may lift us up by his mercy, despite the fact that we are "bowed down by our conscience." The Prayer over the Offerings reminds us that if we are going to "beseech pardon for our own sins," then we must be willing to forgive our neighbor; the two are connected.

There is a Preface that is given on the pages right there along with the other texts for this Mass— "The Samaritan Woman." It is to be used when the Gospel story of the Samaritan woman is read. Referring explicitly to the Samaritan woman, this Preface speaks of the thirst for faith, and of how faith is in the first place a gift given by God. Consider chanting the introductory dialogue and the Preface today; if this is not the regular practice of your community, this can be a way of powerfully drawing attention to the solemnity of Lenten time (but be sure to prepare and rehearse your assembly as needed, if your people are not familiar with the responses!).

The Prayer after Communion relates how the Eucharist we receive here and now on earth is a foretaste and sign of the heavenly reality that it sacramentalizes. The prayer uses an interesting appellation for the sacrament: "the pledge / of things yet hidden in heaven." We ask that our participation in the Paschal Mystery celebrated in the Mass comes to "true completion."

The Prayer over the People is required, not optional, on the Sundays of Lent, and the text is given right after the Prayer after Communion.

First Scrutiny

If your parish is celebrating the First Scrutiny with the elect, then, according to a rubric in the Missal, the proper prayers should be used; these Mass formularies are found in the "Ritual Masses" section of the Missal, under segment I—For the Conferral of the Sacraments of Initiation, #2—For the Celebration of the Scrutinies, A—For the First Scrutiny. Here is provided a Collect, a Prayer over the Offerings and a Prayer after Communion, in addition to Entrance and Communion Antiphons. The Preface assigned is the Preface of the Third Sunday of Lent, the same Preface found at that Mass as described above. There are also special inserts to be used in the Eucharistic Prayers, particular ones for Eucharistic Prayers I, II, and III (since those insert texts are given separately from the Eucharistic Prayer itself, some preparation will have to be done to avoid an awkward delay caused by the flipping of pages back and forth; the insert text can be copied onto a card and affixed or

attached in some way to its proper place in the Eucharistic Prayer being used). There is no Prayer over the People given for the Mass for the First Scrutiny; however, this does not mean one cannot be used. Presumably, the priest would have a choice from either the Prayer over the People for the Third Sunday of Lent or even Solemn Blessing #5, "The Passion of the Lord."

The Mass orations for the First Scrutiny are beautiful prayers that focus intently on the elect's approaching initiation. The prayers refer to the elect directly, in the Collect as "these chosen ones," in the Prayer over the Offerings as "your servants" and in the Prayer after Communion as "those you are to initiate through the Sacraments of eternal life." The Collect describes how they will be "fashioned anew through your glory" as the dignity that was lost by original sin will be restored when they "come worthily and wisely to the confession of your praise." The Prayer over the Offerings is the same prayer that was used on Friday of the Second Week of Lent, but it takes on a whole new layer of meaning used in this occasion as it includes those who are preparing for the sacraments. The Prayer after Communion asks the Lord to give help and protection to those whom he is preparing to initiate.

For the actual ritual of the scrutiny itself, consult RCIA, 150–156. The scrutiny takes place after the Homily.

Pastoral Reflection

The richness of today's account of the Gospel truly takes volumes to unpack in imagery and intention. Place yourself in the shoes of the woman, for we each have a past we want to hide and yet God knows everything about us. The world shuns the sinful, and yet the least among us are the ones who fully "get God's mercy" usually quicker than the

"profoundly religious." Reach outside of your circle of influence this week and have a conversation or meal with someone you might usually overlook. Be conscious of how you are seen by others, how God sees you, and how you see yourself. If you were to look into the water of the well, would your image be refreshing to others? Ask God for the "water" you need to be fully you; and once you are refreshed in God's nourishment, be this person of vibrant grace at all times.

M O N 24 (#237) violet
Lenten Weekday

The Lectionary for Mass

Please note that the optional readings for the Third Week of Lent may be used on any day this week (#236).

◆ FIRST READING: The Gentile Namaan is healed of his leprosy by the prophet Elisha. But before he can be healed, he must set aside his own ideas and, listening to the word of the prophet, obey.

◆ RESPONSORIAL PSALM 42: Like the deer that yearns for life-giving streams, the psalmist thirsts for God and prays for enlightenment on the way to God's dwelling place.

◆ GOSPEL: People everywhere have difficulty accepting the word of the prophet, especially when he or she is someone they know. The people of Jesus's hometown are so enraged by his words that they seek to kill him.

The Roman Missal

The Collect for today notes how the Church needs God's compassionate cleansing and protection, because without it, the Church cannot stand secure; the prayer reminds us that unlike any human society or association, the existence of the Church is rooted in God, and without that divine union, she does not exist.

The Prayer over the Offerings refers implicitly to the holy exchange that takes place in the Liturgy of the Eucharist: we offer our gifts of bread and wine as tokens of our service, indeed, of our very selves, and we pray that they will be transformed into the "sacrament of salvation." The Prayer after Communion prays that our sharing in the sacrament will result in purification and unity.

Any one of the four Prefaces of Lent can be used today. While any one is appropriate, you might also consider using Eucharistic Prayer for Reconciliation II with its own Preface. The themes of universality and of salvation being extended to those thought to be outsiders as presented in the readings would be continued in phrases such as the Church's being "an instrument of your peace among all people" and bringing together "those of every race and tongue" to "the unending banquet of unity" that are found in the second part of the Prayer.

Even though the Prayer over the People is optional on weekdays, it would be good to use it, to highlight the liturgical time.

(#545) white

T U E 25 Solemnity of the Annunciation of the Lord

About this Solemnity

It is Luke who tells of the angelic annunciation to Mary of Jesus's birth (1:26–38). Through the angel Gabriel, the Spirit of God comes to Mary in the most unfeasible way, asking the impossible. As a young woman engaged to be married, being found pregnant would have meant her death in the culture of the time. She risks hurting Joseph, bringing shame on their families, and setting herself up for execution, because she is sure of one thing: God calls her to be Mother to the Son of God. Mary is special because her faith is stronger than her fear. She does

not see the road ahead but knows that God wills for her to journey it nonetheless. Trusting in God above all, she consents her will, becoming the first and most important vessel of bringing Christ's presence into the world.

The Lectionary for Mass

◆ FIRST READING: Christian tradition has long seen this text of the prophet Isaiah fulfilled in Mary of Nazareth. In his account of the Gospel, Matthew says so explicitly (1:22–23). In its original context, the child to be born was the son of Ahaz the king and would be heir to the Davidic throne at a time when the kingdom of Judah feared total annihilation. It was a sign of assurance that God's promises would be fulfilled. God was indeed still with his people and acting on their behalf.

◆ RESPONSORIAL PSALM 40: Today's antiphon is particularly appropriate given Mary's acceptance of the angel's word. God desires a listening heart, an obedient heart above all.

◆ SECOND READING: Our responsorial Psalm 40 is cited in today's Second Reading from Hebrews. Jesus's obedient response, "Behold, I come to do your will," echoes that of his Mother. How much her faith and devotion to God must have been a living example for her Son as she taught him by word and deed from the earliest days of his life to be an obedient servant of the Lord. His obedience to his heavenly Father, even to the point of giving his own life as a sacrifice, inaugurated a new covenant with our God.

◆ GOSPEL: The Word of the Lord is sent to yet another woman betrothed to one of David's descendants. God has not forgotten his promise of an everlasting throne of David. The humble virgin of Nazareth has found favor with God. She shall conceive by the power of the Holy Spirit and bear a Son. He will

rule over God's people. His kingdom shall be everlasting. Truly, as no other Davidic king before him, he is indeed the Son of God in a most unique way.

The Roman Missal

All the Mass texts for this solemnity are proper for the day and can be found in the Proper of Saints at March 25. As with the Solemnity of St. Joseph last week, the somberness of Lent is again put aside. The Gloria is sung or said.

The theology underlying the words of the Collect reflects the understanding that as a result of the Incarnation, humanity is given a share in divinity. Not unlike the prayer the priest prays at the mixing of a little water into the wine, ("By the mystery of this water and wine / may we come to share in the divinity of Christ / who humbled himself to share in our humanity"), this Collect asks, insofar as God willed that his Word should take on human flesh, that we "may merit to become partakers even in his divine nature."

The Creed is said today in observance of the solemnity. Today is one of two times (the other being at the Masses on the Nativity) when all genuflect, instead of bow, at the words "and by the Holy Spirit was incarnate of the Virgin Mary and became man." Be sure your assembly is prepared for this; the priest can give a brief explanation of this in his introduction to the Creed.

The Prayer over the Offerings highlights that it is the Church that is making this offering (notice what this means in terms of liturgical theology—the entire assembly makes the offering, not just the priest), and, in so doing, she (the Church) is recognizing that her life began with the Incarnation of the Son. In God's acceptance of this offering, we pray that the Church "may rejoice to celebrate his mysteries on this Solemnity."

The Preface assigned for today is given right there along with the other Mass texts for the Solemnity of the Annunciation of the Lord in the Proper of Saints. Titled "The Mystery of the Incarnation," it relates Mary's hearing "with faith" about the Christ who was to be born "by the overshadowing power of the Holy Spirit." The text goes on to relate how, by bearing the child in her "immaculate womb" the promises made to the children of Israel were fulfilled and the hope of the world was realized.

The Prayer after Communion expresses our confession in Jesus as "true God and true man" as among the "mysteries of the true faith," and asks that we may attain eternal joy "through the saving power of his Resurrection."

No Solemn Blessing or Prayer over the People is designated for the end of Mass, but if you desired to use one, certainly Solemn Blessing #15, "The Blessed Virgin Mary," would be appropriate for today.

Pastoral Reflection

This sign of hope and God's love interrupts our liturgical time of repentance with the promise of redemption. When we despair that there is no way we can reverse our sinful ways, God reminds us of his loving plan. A Savior, who will sacrifice his life for our selfish choices, gives us the chance of eternal life with God. The miracle of the Annunciation draws us forward toward the miracle of the Resurrection.

WED 26 (#239) violet
Lenten Weekday

The Lectionary for Mass

◆ FIRST READING: Fidelity to the covenant, expressed in obedience to God's commands, is the way to wisdom, to life, and to the realization of all that God has promised. God is especially near to the people he has made his own.

◆ RESPONSORIAL PSALM 147: The heart of the close relationship God has established with Israel is the word, the law, he has spoken to them.

◆ GOSPEL: Jesus came not to abolish the law of old, but to fulfill it. In fact, later in this chapter in Matthew's account, he teaches the people that fulfilling the law means doing more than the letter of the law requires.

The Roman Missal

Today's Collect reminds us that we can look on our Lenten observance as a school of prayer, and it also speaks of our being nourished by God's Word. Thus, the prayer goes on to ask that in that schooling and nourishment we may be totally devoted to God, and united with him (and with one another) in prayer. The Prayer over the Offerings entreats God to accept the prayers of his people along with the sacrificial offerings they make, and it asks God to defend those who celebrate those mysteries "from every kind of danger." The Prayer after Communion requests that as a result of our being fed at the heavenly banquet of the Eucharist, we may be cleansed and made worthy to receive God's promises.

Any one of the four Prefaces of Lent designated for today could be used to equal benefit.

Although the Prayer over the People is optional on weekdays, it would be good to use it, to highlight the liturgical time.

THU 27 (#240) violet
Lenten Weekday

The Lectionary for Mass

◆ FIRST READING: "Listen . . . pay heed . . ." (Jeremiah 7:23–24) so God commanded his people. Yet from the beginning of their existence as a people of God at the time of the Exodus, up to and including Jeremiah's day, they have failed to do so. Can the same be said of us?

◆ RESPONSORIAL PSALM 95: The theme of listening is echoed in today's text, particularly in the antiphon and the last stanza of the psalm. Only through true obedience to God's Word can we offer a fitting sacrifice of praise; only then, do we truly let ourselves be guided by the Lord our shepherd.

◆ GOSPEL: The controversy surrounding Jesus centers on the source of his power. There are those who would say that he is in league with Satan. But why would Satan weaken his own hold on people? How could others among the Jews have power to cast out demons if it were not for God working through them? The last line of today's text calls us to particular self-examination. Are we with Jesus or against him? How do our everyday lives answer that question?

The Roman Missal

There is somewhat of a sense of urgency in today's Collect, which takes note of the journey we are on toward the celebration of Easter. Referring to that upcoming feast as "the worthy celebration of the Paschal Mystery," the prayer asks that as that feast draws closer, "we may press forward all the more eagerly" toward it. Thus, we are again reminded of the ultimate purpose of our Lenten journey, which is to share in the risen life of Christ celebrated at Easter. The Prayer over the Offerings asks that we be cleansed "from every taint of wickedness" in

---

order that the gifts we offer will be pleasing to God. The Prayer after Communion points out that those who receive the sacrament are raised up; the prayer then goes on to ask that, so raised, "we may come to possess your salvation" both in what we celebrate and in the way we live life as disciples.

Any one of the four Prefaces of Lent would be equally appropriate today.

Continue to use the Prayer over the People given for the day at the end of Mass, to highlight the liturgical time.

FRI 28 (#241) violet
Lenten Weekday

The Lectionary for Mass

◆ FIRST READING: It is interesting to observe how often the prophet Hosea uses the words heal and return in close proximity. It is only in returning to the Lord that true healing, in every sense of the word, is to be found. The truly wise one knows this and walks in the paths of the Lord.

◆ RESPONSORIAL PSALM 81: Returning to the Lord means listening and obeying his Word. We hear the Lord reminding Israel of what he has done for them in the stanzas of today's psalm and calling them to hear and obey. Then they will find life and blessing. What foreign gods do we worship? What are we called to hear and obey?

◆ GOSPEL: Omitted from the Lectionary reading is the beginning of verse 28 with its interesting observation:

the scribe is drawn to Jesus by the way he so skillfully refuted the Sadducees over the question of resurrection (see Mark 12:18–27). Note also that this same scribe affirms the correctness of Jesus's understanding of the most important commandments of the law. The scribe, in turn, receives Jesus's affirmation: you are close to the kingdom of God.

The Roman Missal

The Collect for today specifies what we want God's grace to do for us: we ask that "we may be constantly drawn away from unruly desires" and more closely obey the "heavenly teaching," which has been given to us as a gift. In the Prayer over the Offerings we ask that the offerings will be pleasing to God and beneficial for us. In the Prayer after Communion we pray that as a result of sharing in the sacrament, God's strength will be at work in us completely, "pervading our minds and bodies" and bringing us "the fullness of redemption."

Any one of the four Prefaces of Lent can be used today. While any one is appropriate, perhaps Preface II has a certain resonance with the Gospel, with phrases in the Preface such as the renewing and purifying of our hearts, and our being freed from disordered affections.

Continue using the Prayer over the People given for the day as a way of underscoring Lenten time.

SAT 29 (#242) violet
Lenten Weekday

The Lectionary for Mass

◆ FIRST READING: The first part of today's reading sounds like true words of repentance, even if the motive does seem a bit self-centered. Perhaps that is why the Lord compares Israel's piety to the morning dew that quickly passes away.

◆ RESPONSORIAL PSALM 51: Our antiphon is the last line of the reading, only here "love" (Hosea 6:6; literally "covenant love") is rendered as "mercy" (antiphon). Again, there is the reminder: sacrifice apart from a contrite heart means nothing.

◆ GOSPEL: Who is righteous (in right relationship) with God? It is God who decides, not us. The Pharisee, even if his assertions were true, looked—and prayed—to himself and not to God. He looked down on others. The tax collector lowered his eyes before God, acknowledged his sinfulness, and asked mercy. In humbling himself, he was exalted by God.

The Roman Missal

The Collect connects our observance of Lent with what they are oriented toward, namely, celebrating with joy the Paschal Mystery at Easter; that is the focus our hearts should be set on. The Prayer over the Offerings prays simply that it is by God's grace that we can approach the celebration of the mysteries, and so we ask that our minds may be made pure. The prayer includes an interesting phrase about the mysteries, as it asks that we may offer God "fitting homage in reverently handing them on." The phrase can remind us of how our celebrations of the Eucharist are not isolated actions, but instead should be seen as actualizations that perpetuate the one offering made by Christ, that offering made present in our space and time through the Spirit. The Prayer after Communion asks for heavenly assistance so that we might seek God with all our hearts and be granted what we request. Perhaps too we can hear the phrases "minds made pure" and "fitting homage" in light of the virtue of humility that is emphasized in the Gospel.

While any one of the four Prefaces of Lent can be used today, perhaps Preface III with its reference to God's will that we "humble our sinful pride" would echo the Gospel reading.

Even though the Prayer over the People is optional on weekdays, it would again be good to use it.

☀ **30** (#31) violet or rose
Fourth Sunday of Lent

The Lectionary for Mass

◆ FIRST READING: In this story of the anointing of David as king of Israel, we hear an important message—God looks not at appearances, but at the human heart. The least likely candidate for king in human eyes is precisely the one God has chosen.

◆ RESPONSORIAL PSALM 23 is a much loved and comforting psalm. In the context of today's liturgy, it points to the shepherd David's call to shepherd (rule) God's flock, Israel.

◆ SECOND READING: Once you—we—were darkness, but now, because of our Baptism, we are light. Paul calls us to live as what we are and tells us how. Is the darkness overshadowing us? "Wake up!" he commands.

◆ GOSPEL: John 9 opens with a premise that was a widely held view in Jesus's day—affliction is punishment for sin. It is a view that Jesus corrects: no, through this affliction, through the healing that he will bring about, the work of God will be seen. Note the cost of faith in Jesus: expulsion from the synagogue. This was the case in the evangelist's day, the lot of many Jews who had come to believe in Jesus. Sadly, our faith in Jesus can at times cost us as well.

The Roman Missal

Traditionally, this Fourth Sunday of Lent marks a joyful relief amidst the seriousness and somberness of the many weeks of preparation for Easter. Hence, today is called *Laetare Sunday*, a name that comes from the Entrance Antiphon for this Mass, from Isaiah 66: "Rejoice, Jerusalem, and all who love her. / Be joyful, all who were in mourning; / exult and be satisfied at her consoling breast." The Missal tells us that to mark *Laetare Sunday*, rose-colored vestments may be worn, and the altar may be decorated with flowers. However, the Gloria is still omitted today.

Also, as with the previous Sunday, there are two sets of Mass formularies that might be used today: one is the Mass for the Fourth Sunday of Lent; the other is "For the Second Scrutiny."

The Collect for this Sunday recalls how God has reconciled the human race to himself through his Word; salvation was accomplished through the Paschal Mystery of the Word-made-flesh, Jesus. It is because of God reconciling us to himself (something we could not have accomplished) that we can make the petition the second part of the Collect offers: that "the Christian people may hasten / toward the solemn celebrations to come." Thus, does the prayer orient us toward Easter.

The Prayer over the Offerings mentions the joy that characterizes today as it notes that we place our offerings before God "with joy." We are also reminded of the inherently missionary nature of the Eucharist—how it is not something just for ourselves, but rather how it impels us to look outward to serve the world—as the prayer goes on to note that we present these offerings "for the salvation of all the world."

The Preface that is given on the pages right there along with the other texts for this Mass, "The Man Born Blind," is to be used today.

Do not use Preface I or II of Lent; that is meant for other years when that Gospel is not read. Using the motif of humanity's being led out of darkness into "the radiance of the faith," the Preface relates how being "born in slavery to ancient sin" (that is, original sin) is to be in darkness, and how we are led out of that darkness "through the waters of regeneration." The theme of the Sacrament of Baptism as enlightenment could not be clearer here, a reference so appropriate as the Church approaches the Easter Vigil when the elect will be baptized and the faithful will renew their baptismal promises. Consider chanting the introductory dialogue and the Preface today; if this is not the regular practice of your community, this can be a way of powerfully drawing attention to the solemnity of Lenten time. Be sure to prepare and rehearse your assembly as needed, if your people are not familiar with the responses!

The Prayer after Communion continues the focus on light as it acknowledges how God enlightens everyone who comes into the world, and it asks that he will illumine our hearts so "that we may always ponder what is worthy and pleasing to your majesty and love you in all sincerity."

The Prayer over the People is required, not optional, on the Sundays of Lent, and the text is given right after the Prayer after Communion.

Second Scrutiny

If your parish is celebrating the Second Scrutiny with the elect, then, according to a rubric in the Missal, the proper prayers should be used; these Mass formularies are found in the "Ritual Masses" section of the Missal, under segment I—"For the Conferral of the Sacraments of Initiation, #2"—"For the Celebration of the Scrutinies, B"—For the Second Scrutiny. Here is provided a Collect, a Prayer over the Offerings, and a Prayer after Communion, in addition to Entrance and Communion Antiphons. The Preface assigned is still the Preface of the Fourth Sunday of Lent, the same Preface found at the Mass described above. A rubric notes that there are also special inserts to be used in the Eucharistic Prayers, particular ones for Eucharistic Prayers I, II, and III, and the texts for those may be found at the texts for the First Scrutiny. Since those insert texts are given separately from the Eucharistic Prayer itself, some preparation will have to be done to avoid an awkward delay caused by the flipping of pages back and forth. The insert text can be copied onto a card and affixed or attached in some way to its proper place in the Eucharistic Prayer being used.

There is no Prayer over the People given for the Mass for the Second Scrutiny; however, this does not mean one cannot be used. Presumably, the priest would have a choice from either the Prayer over the People for the Fourth Sunday of Lent or even Solemn Blessing #5, "The Passion of the Lord."

In the Collect for the Second Scrutiny, we ask God to give the Church "an increase in spiritual joy" (echoing the joyfulness of Laetare Sunday); it also makes reference to the elect, asking "that those once born of earth may be reborn as citizens of heaven." The Prayer over the Offerings continues the tone of the Sunday as it notes how we place the offerings, "which bring eternal remedy," with joy before the Lord and, in so doing, we pray that we may fittingly present them "for those who seek salvation." Thus, the elect preparing for initiation are at the heart of the Church's prayer at the offering of the Sacrifice this Sunday. The Prayer after Communion petitions the Lord to sustain, correct, protect, and direct us.

For the actual ritual of the scrutiny itself, consult RCIA, 164–170. The scrutiny takes place after the Homily.

Pastoral Reflection

What is your greatest sense: sight, hearing, taste, smell, or touch? Can you imagine going at least a day without the ability to utilize what is innately you? Even if it is just for one activity in your day, see if you can accomplish something that relies on each one of those senses without utilizing it. How do you smell roses, if you cannot smell? Or see your loved one if you do not have eyesight? Simple moments are priceless, yet the man in today's account of the Gospel was branded sinful because he could not see, shunned by his parents for speaking the truth of healing, and also saved by a faith he was not taught, but claimed. Speak the truth when it is not easy to do so. Stand for a cause even without support. In doing so, you live today's account of the Gospel, trusting what cannot be seen, but is made known.

MON 31 (#244) violet
Lenten Weekday

The Lectionary for Mass

Please note that the optional readings for the Fourth Week of Lent may be used on any of the remaining days of this week (#243).

◆ FIRST READING: The prophet's words stem from the period of exile in Babylon and proclaim a message of hope. God is "about" (Isaiah 65:17; an important adverb of time!) to create something new and what joy it brings—both for the people and for God. Note how many times words related to "joy" occur. The past is forgotten as God brings about a new creation.

◆ RESPONSORIAL PSALM 30: Fittingly, today's response is a song of thanksgiving for the experience of deliverance from death (first stanza) and sorrow (second and third stanzas). God has answered the psalmist's prayer.

◆ GOSPEL: Today's text tells of the second sign or miracle Jesus performed in the Gospel according to John (there are a total of seven recorded). Galilee was a region inhabited by many non-Jewish (Gentile) people. The royal official, unlike many of Jesus's own people, believed in his healing power and sought deliverance for his son who was near death (note the link with today's Responsorial Psalm). Unlike many of the Jews we meet in John's account, this official believed in the word that Jesus spoke and his son was healed. What power in Jesus's Word! What powerful things can happen as a result of faith in Jesus!

The Roman Missal

The Collect speaks of the renewal of the world that takes place through the sacred mysteries and, acknowledging God's eternal design, asks that he will give his help to us now. Thus, does the prayer convey a confidence in the future that God provides for us, a future that is beyond our reckoning since the mysteries through which God renews the world are "beyond all telling." We may read into this text a Christian optimism that has its foundation in the Resurrection of Christ. The Prayer over the Offerings continues this sense of optimism in the future and new life because of God's saving activity as it asks that as a result of the offering, "we may be cleansed from old earthly ways / and be renewed by growth in heavenly life." The Prayer after Communion asks for renewal and perseverance as the Eucharist renews us "within and without."

Any one of the four Prefaces of Lent is equally appropriate today.

Although the Prayer over the People continues to be optional on weekdays, its consistent use would mark the daily liturgies of Lent in a significant way.

April
Month of the Holy Eucharist

T
U
E **1** (#245) violet
Lenten Weekday

The Lectionary for Mass

◆ FIRST READING: Exiled in Babylon, Ezekiel is led, in a vision, to the Temple in Jerusalem. Accompanied by his heavenly guide, he sees a stream of life-giving water flowing from the Temple where God dwells—a stream so abundant that it becomes a mighty river. On its banks are trees laden with fruit and leaves that bring healing.

◆ RESPONSORIAL PSALM 46 acclaims Jerusalem, the city where God dwells, the city whose strength is the Lord. It is a city watered by life-giving streams. Such was the vision of both Ezekiel in today's First Reading and John in the Book of Revelation (see 22:1–2).

◆ GOSPEL: What a remarkable thing Jesus has done in today's account of the Gospel. With a word, he healed the man who waited helplessly to be immersed in the healing waters of Bethesda, thus doing the work of the Father. We see in the story the belief that disease was punishment for sin as well as the growing antagonism between the Jews and Jesus because of his healing work on the day of the Lord.

The Roman Missal

In another reminder of how the journey of Lent leads to the celebration of new life through Christ at Easter, today's Collect speaks of being prepared "to welcome worthily the Paschal Mystery" as a result of having our hearts shaped during this liturgical time by "the

venerable exercises of holy devotion." The Prayer over the Offerings acknowledges that the gifts we offer at the Eucharist are gifts that the Lord himself has first bestowed on us; thus, the prayer notes how those offerings serve to "attest to your care as Creator," and we ask that they "effect in us the healing / that brings us immortality." The Prayer after Communion points to the purification and renewal of our minds and help for our bodies, "now and likewise in times to come," that comes to us through "this heavenly Sacrament" of the Eucharist.

Any one of the four Prefaces of Lent is equally appropriate today. In light of the First Reading, Preface I would be a most appropriate choice. The First Reading reflects on the use of water as a symbol reminding us of the healing and new life that comes to us through Baptism and the Gospel account's emphasis on Jesus who brings healing and restoration, and as a reminder of the Sacraments of Initiation celebrated at the Easter Vigil. Preface I of Lent refers to awaiting "the sacred paschal feasts," and our participation in the mysteries by which we have been reborn, and being led "to the fullness of grace / that you bestow on your sons and daughters."

Although the Prayer over the People continues to be optional on weekdays, its consistent use would mark the daily liturgies of Lent in a significant way.

W
E
D **2** (#246) violet
Lenten Weekday

Optional Memorial of St. Francis of Paola, Hermit / violet

The Lectionary for Mass

◆ FIRST READING: The Lord delivers his people from all their afflictions through the life and work of his chosen servant. This is the focus of the first two verses of the reading. Then, we hear what that

deliverance and comfort will look like as the people are lovingly shepherded by their God who has not forgotten them, and never will.

◆ RESPONSORIAL PSALM 145: Fittingly, this song of praise highlights the mercy God shows toward his people. The first line of the first stanza, in fact, is the very way God describes himself to Moses on Mount Sinai. The last line of the last stanza, with its theme of calling on the Lord, is a nice connection with the first line of the First Reading.

◆ GOSPEL: Each stanza of today's Responsorial Psalm makes mention of God's work. Today's account of the Gospel, a continuation from yesterday, shares this focus with its emphasis on Jesus doing the work of his Father, in particular, the work of healing and giving life. Do not miss the point: the one who believes in Jesus has eternal life now, the passage from death to life has been accomplished. We wait, of course, for its full realization in the resurrection of life, which is to come after our physical deaths.

The Roman Missal

The Collect focuses on our need to admit our guilt and seek pardon for our sins; we can do so with confidence, however, for the prayer rightly names God as the one who "reward[s] the merits of the just / and offer[s] pardon to sinners." At this point in Lent, if we have grown weary of the need to do penance, this prayer can refresh and renew the theme of repentance. The Prayer over the Offerings uses motifs contrasting the old and the new, asking that "the power of this sacrifice" will "mercifully wipe away what is old in us, / and increase in us grace of salvation and newness of life." The prayer can remind us that each and every celebration of the Eucharist, insofar as it is our participation in the Death and Resurrection of Christ, is an opportunity to receive new life from God in being raised up with Christ through the offering of the sacrifice. The Prayer after Communion for the Lenten Weekday identifies the Eucharist as a heavenly gift that bestows "a heavenly remedy on your people," asking that it not bring judgment on those who receive that gift; thus, we are reminded of the need to receive the Eucharist worthily, not presumptuously.

One of the four Prefaces of Lent is used today. While any one of the four is appropriate, perhaps, in light of the Collect's focus on repentance, either Preface III, with its direct reference to self-denial and humbling our sinful pride, or Preface IV, with its mention of how bodily fasting restrains our faults, would be good options.

Even though the Prayer over the People is optional on weekdays, it would be good to use it, to highlight the liturgical time.

If you wish to observe the optional memorial of St. Francis of Paola, then use the proper Collect found at April 2 in the Proper of Saints, but take the other orations and the Preface from the Lenten Weekday (see GIRM, 355a). The Collect of the Lenten Weekday can be used as the conclusion to the Universal Prayer.

Today's Saint

From a young age St. Francis of Paola (1416–1507) longed for a solitary life marked by complete and utter dependence upon God. While living as a hermit he adopted an austere life, focusing on two spiritual disciplines: fasting and prayer. Underlying his spirituality was the belief that one must empty oneself, as Jesus did upon the Cross (kenosis/self-emptying), in order to fully understand his or her dire need for God. Fasting (one of the three disciplines of Lent) serves as a reminder that nothing can fill the hungering

of the soul except the healing love of the Lord.

Although St. Francis of Paola was attracted to the Franciscan friars, he longed for a more contemplative life grounded in solitude and asceticism. Building upon the Franciscan tradition, he founded the hermits of Brother Francis of Assisi, which eventually became known as the Minim Friars, meaning "the least" of all God's servants. The community had a strong devotion to the five wounds of Christ and the Virgin Mary.

Due to his reputation for holiness and the miraculous, King Louis XI of France requested St. Francis's spiritual guidance as he was preparing for death. St. Francis spent the last 25 years of his life advising kings and restoring peace between France and its neighboring countries. Many miracles connected to the sea have been attributed to his name; therefore, he is the patron of navigators and naval officers.

THU 3 (#247) violet
Lenten Weekday

The Lectionary for Mass

◆ FIRST READING: The people of Israel forsake God and make an idol in his place with their own hands while Moses is on Mount Sinai. Angered, God is determined to destroy them. Moses pleads on behalf of the people, asking God to remember the covenant he made with their fathers, Abraham, Isaac, and Jacob. God hears and relents.

◆ RESPONSORIAL PSALM 106: This same incident is recounted in today's Responsorial Psalm. Like Israel of old, we have forsaken God and worshipped idols of our own making. We, too, plead for his mercy.

◆ GOSPEL: Continuing the text of John 5, we hear Jesus confront the Jews on their refusal to believe in him, the one sent by the Father, who comes in the name of the Father and with the voice of the Father, the one who gives life. Jesus is the one to whom the whole law of Moses points and in whom it is fulfilled. If only they—and we—could hear.

The Roman Missal

The Collect for today sets a tone of humility and it reminds us of the purpose of our Lenten penance: it should correct us and school us in doing good works. The prayer also asks for perseverance so that we might "come safely to the paschal festivities." Again there is the undertone in this prayer of calling upon the Lord for help as we continue through the long haul of Lent. The Prayer over the Offerings asks for cleansing and protection through the offering we make in sacrifice. The Prayer after Communion again points to the purification that comes to us through the sacrament, as it asks that we be granted "freedom from all blame." The sense of how participation in the Eucharist brings new life and heals us from our burdens is highlighted as the prayer asks "that those bound by a guilty conscience / may glory in the fullness of heavenly remedy."

Although any one of the four Prefaces of Lent is equally appropriate today, perhaps Preface I of Lent would work particularly well to echo the orations, with that Preface's mention of "minds made pure," being reborn, and being led to "the fullness of grace."

Although the Prayer over the People continues to be optional on weekdays, its consistent use would mark the daily liturgies of Lent in a significant way.

FRI 4 (#248) violet
Lenten Weekday

Optional Memorial of St. Isidore, Bishop and Doctor of the Church / violet

The Lectionary for Mass

◆ FIRST READING: The wicked cannot tolerate the just. Their witness condemns them. Accordingly, the wicked seek to destroy the just one to see if God will indeed take care of him.

◆ RESPONSORIAL PSALM 34: The Lord does not abandon the just into the hands of their foes, but delivers them.

◆ GOSPEL: Mistakenly, the Jews think they know Jesus's identity. They fail to realize that he has not come on his own but is sent by the Father.

The Roman Missal

The Collect for the Lenten Weekday reminds us that the penances we undertake during Lent are gifts that have been given to us from God as "helps for us in our weakness." As a result, those helps have healing effects on us, effects that we should receive with joy and reflect in the way we live daily "a holy way of life." The Prayer over the Offerings asks for cleansing so that we might approach the source of this sacrifice with purity; thus, does the prayer remind us that our worship can never be mere outward ritual, but must always draw us more deeply into the mystery being celebrated. The Prayer after Communion for the weekday uses the contrast between old and new to ask that we leave former ways behind and "be renewed in holiness of mind." The prayer reminds us that reception of the sacrament is never a passive reception but must represent the offering of self and openness to transformation of a life that is continually being renewed in Christ.

Any one of the four Lenten Prefaces that are designated as options for today would be as good a choice as another.

Even though the Prayer over the People is optional on weekdays, it would be good to use it, to highlight the liturgical time.

If you wish to observe the optional Memorial of St. Isidore, then use the proper Collect found at April 4 in the Proper of Saints but take the other orations and the Preface from the weekday of Lent (see GIRM, 355a). The Collect of the Lenten Weekday can be used as the conclusion to the Universal Prayer.

Today's Saint

St. Isidore of Seville (560–636 is credited with organizing the Church of Spain through various councils and synods. His theology of the Trinity and Incarnation were the basis for a Creed that was approved at the Fourth Council of Toledo (633 AD). Along with these two noteworthy accomplishments, he also revised the Mozarabic Rite—the accepted liturgy of Spain—and opened cathedral schools for the training of priests. St. Isidore was named a Doctor of the Church due to his extensive writing, including doctrinal summaries, etymological studies, and rules for religious communities.

SAT 5 (#249) violet
Lenten Weekday

Optional Memorial of St. Vincent Ferrer, Priest / violet

The Lectionary for Mass

◆ FIRST READING: The prophet is taken by surprise when he realizes the opposition against him. His enemies seek to take his life. Jeremiah can only entrust himself to the Lord.

◆ RESPONSORIAL PSALM 7: The psalmist, too, knows the rage of his foes and cries out for God's help and protection. God is a sure refuge.

◆ GOSPEL: Those who hear Jesus are perplexed. Could Jesus be the long-awaited one, the Messiah? But they didn't expect a prophet, a Messiah, from Galilee. What are they to make of the authority with which he speaks? Who is Jesus for us?

The Roman Missal

The Lenten Collect once again reminds us that without God we can do nothing: "without your grace / we cannot find favor in your sight." The Prayer over the Offerings points out that even in bringing our oblations we are not yet perfected, and we may in some way be defiant of God's will; nonetheless, in our offering to God, we pray that he will assist us in conforming our will to his own. This prayer, then, reminds us of the willingness to have our will transformed. This must be an inherent part of participating in the offering of the sacrifice. The Prayer after Communion for the Lenten Weekday again asks for purification so that we may be pleasing to God.

One of the four Prefaces of Lent is used today. While any one of the four is appropriate, perhaps Preface II, with its references to having our hearts purified and our being "freed from disordered affections," would be a good choice for today.

Even though the Prayer over the People is optional on weekdays, it would be good to use it, to highlight the liturgical time.

If you wish to observe the optional Memorial of St. Vincent Ferrer, then the proper Collect for this memorial is taken from April 5 in the Proper of Saints. The other Mass prayers are taken from the Lenten Weekday (see GIRM, 355a). The Collect of the Lenten Weekday can be used as the conclusion to the Universal Prayer.

Today's Saint

St. Vincent Ferrer (1350–1419), a native of Valencia and a Dominican friar, lived during the Great Western

Schism in which there were several claims to the papacy. Noted for his eloquent preaching, he worked tirelessly to bring unity in the midst of the papal controversy. At first he did not attain success in settling the conflict, but his political savvy eventually aided in the restoration of papal unity and peace. He embarked on missionary journeys through Spain, France, and Italy, preaching a message of repentance and the fear of hell.

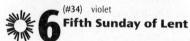

6 (#34) violet
Fifth Sunday of Lent

The Lectionary for Mass

◆ FIRST READING: The words of the prophet Ezekiel address an Israel in Exile. The "death" of their exiled status will end when the Lord raises them up and restores them to their homeland. They will live because God will put his Spirit in them. It is an image of re-creation.

◆ RESPONSORIAL PSALM 129: It is because of the Lord's mercy that we have received the fullness of redemption. Psalm 129 originates during the time of the Babylonian Exile. The psalmist describes his affliction and expresses his trust in the Lord's deliverance.

◆ SECOND READING: The motif of being enlivened by God's Spirit is likewise heard in today's Second Reading. "Flesh" is used here with reference to anything opposed to God. In Baptism, we have received the Spirit of God, which gives us life, eternal life. In the age to come, this same Spirit who raised Jesus from the dead will raise our mortal bodies also.

◆ GOSPEL: John goes to great lengths to let us know that Lazarus, the beloved friend of Jesus, was really dead, all the more to heighten the extraordinary power of God at work in Jesus—power even over the realm of death. So would God's glory be manifest. Jesus is "the resurrection and the life" even in this age. Today's account of the Gospel account bids us to look at what is dead within us, perhaps even with a stench! We hear today Jesus's command: Come forth from the tomb. Let yourself be untied so that you can go free.

The Roman Missal

The Fifth Sunday of Lent can be seen as a turning point in the Lenten journey as we enter the final days of the liturgical time, with less than two weeks left before we begin the Sacred Paschal Triduum. The Missal contains a rubric pointing to a practice that can serve as a visual reminder to the assembly that we have reached this point in Lent: the practice of covering crosses and images in the church may be observed beginning with this Sunday. Images and statues are covered until the beginning of the Easter Vigil; crosses, however, are uncovered sooner, remaining covered only until the end of the Celebration of the Lord's Passion on Good Friday. Consider doing this in your church so that the faithful continue to be engaged in the somberness and tone of Lent through the visible environment of the worship space.

Also, as with the previous two Sundays, there are two sets of Mass formularies from which to choose today: use either the Mass for the Fifth Sunday of Lent if you are not celebrating the Third Scrutiny, or the Mass for the Third Scrutiny if you are celebrating that ritual.

The Gloria continues to be omitted today.

With the celebration of the Lord's Passion approaching, the Collect for today specifically mentions how "your Son handed himself over to death." Recalling that act of love, the prayer asks that we may "walk eagerly in that same charity." The events of the Paschal Mystery are to be for all Christians, not just some remote example lived by Jesus, but rather the actual pattern of living that is grafted onto our lives, a pattern that we imitate daily.

The Prayer over the Offerings prays that because God has "instilled in your servants / the teachings of the Christian faith," we may be purified "by the working of this sacrifice." We can glean from this prayer several different levels of meaning. The phrase "teachings of the Christian faith" can certainly call to mind for us those who are being formed in the faith as they prepare for the Sacraments of Initiation; it can also remind us of our own formation and education in Christianity, a gift that has been instilled in us by the Lord himself, through the Holy Spirit, through those who formed and educated us. We can also remember that "the teachings of the Christian faith" are more than just doctrinal principles, but rather include a whole way of living life and looking at the world. The purification we ask for should involve the transformation to embrace Christian living in all its aspects.

The Preface that is given on the pages right there along with the other texts for this Mass, titled simply "Lazarus," is the Preface that is to be used today, since it is Year A, and the Gospel account of Jesus raising Lazarus is the text assigned for the day. Do not use Preface I or II of Lent; those options are meant for other years when the Lazarus reading is not used. The

Preface makes reference to the new life, which Christ gives us through the sacred mysteries, as he takes pity on us just as he wept for his friend Lazarus. Consider chanting the introductory dialogue and the Preface today; if this is not the regular practice of your community, this can be a way of powerfully drawing attention to the solemnity of Lent (but be sure to prepare and rehearse your assembly as needed, if your people are not familiar with the responses!).

The Prayer after Communion is ecclesial in its focus, as it prays that through the sacrament "we may always be counted among the members of Christ, / in whose Body and Blood we have communion." The prayer is a reminder to us of a proper Eucharistic theology that understands Communion not only as union with Christ, but also as union with his Body, the Church; the liturgical act of receiving Holy Communion, although intensely personal, is never private—it is always a corporate action of the Body.

The Prayer over the People is required, not optional, on the Sundays of Lent, and the text is given right after the Prayer after Communion.

Third Scrutiny

If your parish is celebrating the Third Scrutiny with the elect, then, according to a rubric in the Missal, the proper prayers should be used; these Mass formularies are found in the section "Ritual Masses," under segment I—For the Conferral of the Sacraments of Initiation, #2—For the Celebration of the Scrutinies, C—For the Third Scrutiny. Here we find a Collect, a Prayer over the Offerings, and a Prayer after Communion, in addition to Entrance and Communion Antiphons. The Preface assigned is still the Preface of the Fifth Sunday of Lent, the same Preface described above. A rubric notes that there are also special inserts to be used in the Eucharistic

Prayers, particular ones for Eucharistic Prayers I, II, and III, and the texts for those may be found at the texts for the First Scrutiny. Since those insert texts are given separately from the Eucharistic Prayer itself, some preparation will have to be done to avoid an awkward delay caused by the flipping of pages back and forth. The insert text can be copied onto a card and affixed or attached in some way to its proper place in the Eucharistic Prayer being used. There is no Prayer over the People given for the Mass for the Third Scrutiny; however, this does not mean one cannot be used. Presumably, the priest would have a choice from either the Prayer over the People for the Fifth Sunday of Lent or even Solemn Blessing #5, "The Passion of the Lord."

The elect are specifically mentioned in all three of the orations for this Mass for the final Scrutiny. The Collect makes explicit reference to their initiation as it prays that "these chosen ones" who have been "instructed in the holy mysteries" may "receive new life at the font of Baptism / and be numbered among the members of your Church." Of course, as we pray for those preparing for initiation, we cannot help but call to mind our own initiation and so be renewed in our own commitment to the faith. The Prayer over the Offerings acknowledges the faith that is already at work in the elect, noting that God has instilled in them as his servants "the first fruits of Christian faith." The Prayer after Communion prays for unity among all God's people, asking that as they submit themselves to God, they may obtain the grace of living out their joy at being saved and "remember in loving prayer those to be reborn." It is the role of all the faithful to pray for those preparing for the sacraments; the work of supporting those coming to the faith is work that belongs to every member of the Church.

For the actual ritual of the Scrutiny itself, consult RCIA, 171–177. The Scrutiny takes place after the Homily.

Pastoral Reflection

Jesus was human; a man with depth of emotions ranging from love to sadness, patience to anger. If our God could be honest about his emotions, develop friendships that stirred his heart, and could deal with disciples who just "couldn't get it," how much more are we called to do the same? Our human nature, while sinful, is full of great life and light if we walk in and with the Light of Jesus Christ. Who are your best friends for whom you would do anything? How can you be both aware of the depth and breadth of your emotions, yet conscious of controlling them if and when necessary? Today Jesus wept in love and was perturbed with impatience. Be conscious of all that is within you this week and how each moment brings you closer to the living God.

MON 7 (#251) violet
Lenten Weekday

Optional Memorial of St. John Baptist de la Salle, Priest / violet

The Lectionary for Mass

Please note that the optional readings for the Fifth Week of Lent may be used on any of the remaining days of this week (#250).

◆ First Reading: Two options are given for today's First Reading about the unjust accusation against the God-fearing (righteous) woman, Susannah, made by two wicked elders of Israel who lusted after her. In the longer form, we hear of their plot to have her as their own and her cry for help. The shorter form begins at this point with her prayer that God will reveal the truth and her life will be spared. The hero of the story is the young Daniel. Endowed by God with wisdom, he objects to the false trial and arranges instead a trial of the two wicked elders, who condemn themselves with their own words. Susannah's life is spared, and the wicked elders receive the punishment they intended to inflict on her.

◆ RESPONSORIAL PSALM 23: How fitting is today's antiphon, for Susannah did indeed walk through a dark valley of unjust accusation, which nearly led to her death. Psalm 23 is a song of confidence acclaiming the Lord as Shepherd. He was indeed at her side, hearing her cry for help and rescuing her from death.

◆ GOSPEL: Today's account of the Gospel presents Jesus as the Light of the World, the light that overcomes all darkness, the light of life. The mention of testimony and judgment echoes themes in today's First Reading. Jesus, too, knew false accusation. His testimony to the truth was not accepted. In this instance (today's account of the Gospel), his life is spared for his "hour" had not yet come.

The Roman Missal

As we begin the last days of Lent, the Collect for the Lenten Weekday invites us to more and more deeply focus on entering into the Paschal Mystery and to dying and rising with Christ, particularly as that mystery will be celebrated during the Sacred Paschal Triduum, which is rapidly approaching. Thus, the prayer asks that Christ's passage will be ours: "grant us so to pass from former ways to newness of life, / that we may be made ready for the glory of the heavenly Kingdom."

The Prayer over the Offerings reminds us that the fruit of bodily penance must be "a joyful purity of heart." We might ask ourselves, after all these days of Lent so far, whether such joyful purity of heart has truly increased in us as a result of our Lenten practices. It is that same joyful purity of heart that is

supposed to be the acceptable offering brought to the sacrifice. The Prayer after Communion for the Lenten Weekday asks God that we may be cleansed of our faults through the sacraments, and, in an image of being raised up with Christ, requests that we may "hasten our steps upward toward you."

In keeping with the shift to the period of late Lenten time, starting today there is no longer a choice among Prefaces; rather, Preface I of the Passion of the Lord is the Preface assigned for today. It speaks explicitly of the Passion of Christ and of the "wondrous power of the Cross" that reveals both God's judgment on the world and the "authority of Christ crucified." Consider using this Preface even if you are using one of the Eucharistic Prayers for Reconciliation (you are not required to use the Preface that goes with the Eucharistic Prayer for Reconciliation).

Continue to use the suggested Prayer over the People at the end of Mass, even though it is optional, especially in these final days of Lent.

If you wish to observe the optional Memorial of St. John Baptist de la Salle, then use the proper Collect found at April 7 in the Proper of Saints, but still take the other orations and the Preface from the weekday of Lent (see GIRM, 355a). The Collect of the Lenten Weekday can be used as the conclusion to the Universal Prayer.

Today's Saint

Most people have never heard of St. John Baptist de la Salle (1651–1719), and yet have been profoundly shaped by his educational methodology. He established standard educational practices that we take for granted; that is, teaching to a group of individuals simultaneously, instruction in the vernacular, and giving reports regarding student progress. Moved by pity for

poor children in France, St. John resigned his office and gave away his wealth to establish a religious institute called the Institute of the Brothers of the Christian Schools. The purpose of the institute was to teach the poor so they could realize their innate dignity as children of God and rise above their impoverished circumstances. Today, St. John Baptist de la Salle's brothers serve in all parts of the world as teachers, social workers, counselors, and retreat facilitators.

TUE 8 (#252) violet
Lenten Weekday

The Lectionary for Mass

◆ FIRST READING: Wandering in the desert, the people of Israel lose heart (and patience) and complain against God and Moses. As punishment, God sends poisonous serpents, which bite the people. Many die from the serpents' bites. Recognizing their sin, the people plead that God relent. The people are healed by gazing on the mounted serpent as instructed by God.

◆ RESPONSORIAL PSALM 102: In the midst of their distress, perhaps after their exile in Babylon as the second stanza of the psalm suggests, Israel cries out for God's help.

◆ GOSPEL: Who is this man, Jesus? His hearers do not understand. Today Jesus tells us much about himself: he is from above, not of this world; he is sent by the Father who is always with him. What is more, Jesus is the great "I AM," the name God revealed to Moses in the burning bush. The "lifting up" of the Son of Man (on the Cross) parallels the lifting up of the serpent. Both were a source of healing and life.

The Roman Missal

The Collect today contains an important petition, namely, that we may persevere in obeying God's will. Again, the prayer seems to recognize our need for encouragement and strength to maintain the long discipline of Lent. There is an interesting result of that perseverance that is mentioned: so that "the people dedicated to your service / may grow in both merit and number." Perhaps this phrase could remind us of the importance of giving good example to those preparing for initiation; our witness as we persevere through Lent can have a direct effect on their coming into the faith.

The Prayer over the Offerings recognizes the reconciliation that is brought about between God and humanity as a result of our participation in the sacrifice; through it, we can ask God, who is full of compassion, to pardon our offenses. The Prayer after Communion notes how a constitutive dimension of being human is to seek what is divine.

The Preface assigned for today is Preface I of the Passion of the Lord, as it will be every day this week. Use this Preface even if you are using one of the two Eucharistic Prayers for Reconciliation (you are not required to use the Preface that goes with the Eucharistic Prayers for Reconciliation).

Although the Prayer over the People continues to be optional on weekdays, its continued use would mark this late Lenten Weekday in a significant way.

W E D 9 (#253) violet
Lenten Weekday

The Lectionary for Mass

◆ FIRST READING: Daniel's three companions are condemned to death by being thrown into a fiery furnace for their refusal to worship the idol set up by the Babylonian king Nebuchadnezzar. They were willing to sacrifice their bodies rather than disobey God's law. God sent his angel to be with them and kept them safe in the midst of the fire.

Seeing this, Nebuchadnezzar acknowledged the power of their God.

◆ CANTICLE: Today's text is actually from the Book of Daniel, the hymn sung by the three men in the furnace, when they realized that the flames were not harming them.

◆ GOSPEL: Today's account opens with a beautiful definition of discipleship: remaining in Jesus's word. The rest of today's text focuses on the Jews' misunderstanding of Jesus's teaching. They still cannot recognize that he is from God, the fulfillment of God's promises all the way back to Abraham.

The Roman Missal

Today's Collect first speaks of the interior transformation that should be taking place in us as a result of our Lenten penance, namely, that our hearts should be enlightened, and then goes on to ask that God will hear us when we cry out to him.

The Prayer over the Offerings gives voice to the holy exchange that is inherent in the Eucharist: it asks God to receive back the sacrificial offerings he first gave to us, and, in so doing, to make them "remedies for our healing." Picking up on the Prayer over the Offerings' reference to the offerings as a remedy, the Prayer after Communion asks that the mysteries we have received may "bring us heavenly medicine," purging all evil from our hearts. We can call to mind that the early church often referred to the Eucharist as the "medicine of immortality" (see, for example, chapter 20 of Ignatius of Antioch's Letter to the Ephesians).

The Preface assigned for today is once again Preface I of the Passion of the Lord. Remember to use this Preface even if you are using one of the Eucharistic Prayers for Reconciliation (you are not required to use the Preface that goes with the Eucharistic Prayer for Reconciliation). Also continue to use the Prayer over the People for the day.

T H U 10 (#254) violet
Lenten Weekday

The Lectionary for Mass

◆ FIRST READING: God renews his covenant relationship with Abraham. A covenant is a type of agreement in which two parties pledge themselves to one another and which entails responsibilities on the part of both. God pledges loyalty to Abraham and promises his descendants land. Note the name change, signifying Abraham's special role.

◆ RESPONSORIAL PSALM 105: The psalmist calls the descendants of Abraham to remember their covenant responsibilities and reminds them of all God has done for them.

◆ GOSPEL: The controversy over Jesus's identity continues in today's reading, with the Jews identified as descendants of Abraham. Jesus refers to himself as "I AM," the name by which God revealed himself to Moses. This is who Jesus is, he who is from the beginning.

The Roman Missal

The Collect places before us in a powerful way our need for God: it states that we plead before him and we place our hope in his mercy. It also asks for perseverance in "holy living," reminding us again that the sacrifice we celebrate at the Eucharist must be put into the concrete practice of love and self-giving in our daily lives. Only then can we rightly ask, as we do in this prayer, to "be made full heirs of your promise." The Prayer over the Offerings reminds us of the missionary nature of the Eucharist, calling us beyond just our own needs, as it asks that the sacrificial offerings may both "profit our conversion / and the salvation of the world." That the offering of the Eucharist is the Church's work for the salvation of the whole world must never be forgotten. The Prayer after Communion expresses both the earthly and the heavenly effects of the Eucharist, as it is the sacrament by which we are fed "in the present age" and through which we hope to be made "partakers of life eternal."

As with the other days this week, the Preface assigned for today is Preface I of the Passion of the Lord, and it should be used even if you are using one of the Eucharistic Prayers for Reconciliation (you are not required to use the Preface that goes with the Eucharistic Prayer for Reconciliation).

Also as with the other days of Lent, continue to use the Prayer over the People.

FRI 11 (#255) violet
Lenten Weekday

Optional Memorial of St. Stanislaus, Bishop and Martyr / violet

The Lectionary for Mass

◆ FIRST READING: In this text, one of the "confessions" of Jeremiah, the prophet acknowledges the threats of his foes who seek his downfall. He likewise acknowledges his deep trust in the Lord. In the last verse, we hear his acclamation of praise for God's deliverance.

◆ RESPONSORIAL PSALM 18 echoes the prayer of Jeremiah: in the midst of overwhelming distress, trust in God and the experience of his deliverance.

◆ GOSPEL: In today's account of the Gospel, part of a controversy that actually begins in verse 22, the Jews are in a dilemma over Jesus's identity. They do not understand his claims to be one with the Father, to be the Son of God, to be sent by the Father, even though his works bear witness to this. While some Jews think that he is blaspheming, others believe.

The Roman Missal

There are two options for the Collect today. The first prayer is a prayer for pardon, asking that we will be set free from "the bonds of the sins / we have committed in our weakness." The second option notes how in this liturgical time the Church imitates the Blessed Virgin Mary "in contemplating the Passion of Christ," and therefore the prayer goes on to ask that through her intercession "we may cling more firmly each day / to your Only Begotten Son and come at last to the fullness of his grace." Thus, in a certain sense, this second prayer puts us at the foot of the Cross along with Mary, clinging to Jesus even throughout his Passion and Death, and prepares us well to enter into the celebration of Holy Week. The Prayer over the Offerings highlights the place of worship at the center of Christian life, as it asks "that we may be worthy / to serve ever fittingly at your altars, / and there to be saved by constant participation." "Constant participation" can remind us that life itself is to be liturgical, as the offering of our life as a sacrifice to God is to occur not only at the ritual celebration, but as a way of life every day. The Prayer after Communion asks that we might have the "unfailing protection" the sacrifice brings to us so that it will "always drive far from us / all that would do us harm."

The Preface assigned for today is Preface I of the Passion of the Lord; remember to use it even if you are using one of the Eucharistic Prayers for Reconciliation (you are not required to use the Preface that goes with the Eucharistic Prayer for Reconciliation). Continue to use the Prayer over the People as well.

If you wish to observe the optional Memorial of St. Stanislaus, then use the proper Collect found at April 11 in the Proper of Saints, but take the other orations and the Preface from the weekday of Lent

(see GIRM, 355a). The Collect of the Lenten Weekday can be used as the conclusion to the Universal Prayer.

Today's Saint

Noted for his compassionate concern for the poor and for his wise counsel, St. Stanislaus (1030–1079) was appointed Bishop of Krakow. His consecration as bishop was met with great joy on the part of the people. While serving as bishop he spoke out against King Boleslaus, an unjust and cruel man who incited fear in the people of Poland. St. Stanislaus, outraged by the oppressive behavior of the monarch, declared that an unjust king has no place in the Church. In response, the king defamed his reputation, eventually ordering guards to kill him, but they refused. The king took matters into his own hands by stabbing him with a sword. St. Stanislaus, the martyr, is the patron saint of Poland and the city of Krakow.

SAT 12 (#256) violet
Lenten Weekday

The Lectionary for Mass

◆ FIRST READING: God's Word is addressed to the Jewish nation in exile. The prophets saw the exile as punishment for sin (see verse 23). God promises a return to the land, the unification of all the tribes, the restoration of the Davidic line, and an everlasting covenant.

◆ CANTICLE: Today's response is a canticle taken from the prophet Jeremiah, that was spoken during the time of the Babylonian exile, and reiterates the promise of restoration and return.

◆ GOSPEL: Controversy over Jesus heightens after the raising of Lazarus. The Jewish leaders fear the demise of Israel at the hands of the Romans. Ironically, the Death of

Jesus results not in demise or destruction but in the "gathering" (a motif in each of today's Scriptures) of the scattered people.

The Roman Missal

Today's Collect begins with a clear reference to Baptism, as it states that God has made "all those reborn in Christ / a chosen race and a royal priesthood." It then goes on to ask that we will be given "the grace to will and to do what you command." The Prayer over the Offerings notes that the gifts we offer come from our fasting; here we can be especially reminded that since the acceptable sacrifice to God is a humble and contrite heart, our fasting and other Lenten penances should have that precise effect, producing hearts (and lives) that can be a gift offered to God. The Prayer after Communion prays that the nourishment we have received in the Body and Blood of Christ "may make us sharers of his divine nature." It thus highlights the transformative aspect of Eucharistic Communion, namely, that we become what we receive. The divine life given to us in our Baptism (referred to in the Collect) is nurtured and strengthened in the Eucharist.

Preface I of the Passion of the Lord is assigned for the last time today, and it should be the Preface used even with one of the Eucharistic Prayers for Reconciliation (you are not required to use the Preface that goes with the Eucharistic Prayer for Reconciliation).

Use the Prayer over the People, even though it is optional, to reinforce the themes of the liturgical time.

(#37, Gospel; #38)   red

13 Palm Sunday of the Passion of the Lord

About Palm Sunday

Branches of palm, olive, or sometimes even budding willow, are ancient symbols of victory and hope, as well as of new life. The procession celebrating Jesus's entry into Jerusalem overflowed with praise and excitement, as onlookers waved these triumphant branches and proclaimed their blessings. Yet, in a few days, they will cry "Crucify him!" The crowd's change of heart illustrates the problem of holding God to our expectations. The crowd expected a liberating leader, the Messiah, to free them from Roman oppression. Jesus instead takes up his Cross and invites us to do the same. Through his Death and Resurrection he is indeed a liberator, but from Death and sin, not from Rome. But unable to see past their need, the crowd's disappointment turns into anger and a death order. As we enter Holy Week, Palm Sunday teaches us to let God be God, and to trust in God's wisdom not only to meet but shatter and exceed our expectations.

The Lectionary for Mass

◆ GOSPEL AT THE PROCESSION WITH PALMS: Matthew is ever ready to demonstrate that Jesus fulfills all the prophecies of the Old Testament, in this case, Zechariah 9:9. The prophet's words acclaim the coming of Zion's (Jerusalem's) king, the Davidic king. In the opening words of his account of the Gospel, Matthew emphasizes Jesus's descent from David (see Matthew 1:1)—and in today's text, the crowd cries out "Hosanna to the Son of David . . . Jesus the prophet, from Nazareth. . . ." The acclamations here are joyous, in praise of the one whose words and deeds were so powerful, whose coming had so long been awaited.

◆ FIRST READING: One of the four so-called "suffering Servant Songs" of Isaiah (we will have the others in the course of the week) depicting a prophet who willingly submits to shame and disgrace in carrying out his ministry with God's help. In the context of today's liturgy, Isaiah's words point to Jesus, the suffering prophet from Galilee. Throughout his ministry, Jesus's words were meant to rouse and give hope to a weary people. Faithfully, he listened to the Father in prayer. Faithfully he carried out his mission. Hear how Isaiah's words about the prophet's sufferings are echoed in Matthew's account of Jesus's Passion.

◆ RESPONSORIAL PSALM 22: The words of today's antiphon are placed on the lips of the crucified Jesus in Matthew's account of the Passion. Did Jesus feel abandoned by God? The psalm is a prayer of lament uttered in the depths of great distress. Note how the psalmist's descriptions of his suffering are echoed in the Gospel account of Jesus's Passion and Death. Note the confident change of tone in the last stanza of the psalm. The psalmist had moved—or been carried—through his suffering into a new stance in life. So, too, was Jesus. So, too, can we be.

◆ SECOND READING: Today's text is an early Christian hymn that concisely summarizes the Christian mystery: though divine, Jesus willingly embraced human likeness and was obedient to God, even unto a shameful Death. "Because of this" he was exalted by God. And as a result, all creation reverently acknowledges him as Lord.

◆ GOSPEL: This year on Palm Sunday we hear Matthew's account of Jesus's suffering and Death. Matthew follows Mark's account closely while at the same time incorporating information from his own sources, such as Judas's remorse and suicide (see Matthew 27:3–10), the dream of Pilate's wife about Jesus (27:19), Pilate's assertion of his own innocence with regard to Jesus's Death (see Matthew 27:24–26), and the placement of a guard of soldiers at Jesus's tomb in order to prevent his body from being stolen and his Resurrection asserted (see Matthew 27: 52–66).

As in Mark, all takes place at Passover, the annual commemoration of the deliverance of the Israelites from slavery in Egypt. As Jesus celebrates this feast with his disciples, he will undergo his own Passover from Death to Life. He will be "handed over" (note how often the verb occurs) by one from his own circle of disciples as well as by the religious leaders of his people. And in a very real sense, he likewise hands himself over to the Father: ". . . your will be done" (Matthew 26:42).

The sufferings of his Passion are not only physical. In addition to the betrayal just mentioned, "all" of his disciples abandon him and flee at the moment of his arrest. He is denied by Peter, the very one whom he had earlier made the head of his Church, the community of his followers. How would Jesus have felt in the experience of betrayal and abandonment by his closest friends at this time?

On the other hand, in contrast to Jesus's male disciples who betrayed, denied, and abandoned him, there are the "many" (the use of the word

here is unique to Matthew) women disciples who had "followed" Jesus from Galilee, including Mary Magdalene, Mary the mother of James and Joseph, and the unnamed mother of the sons of Zebedee (Matthew 27:56; see 20:20–28). They are present at Jesus's burial and Mary Magdalene and "the other Mary" remained there, sitting facing the tomb. It is these two who come to the tomb on the morning of the day after the Sabbath (Matthew 28:1). Their actions have much to say about discipleship and the fidelity and fears of disciples—of those who were contemporaries of Jesus as well as ourselves today.

Matthew depicts Jesus's Death (and Resurrection) as "earthshaking" events (Matthew 27:51–54; 28:2). The earthquake signaled the inauguration of the end time (see Matthew 24:7; Revelation 16:18) as does the Resurrection of the dead (Matthew 27:51–53; see also Daniel 12:1–4). The earthquake was also associated with manifestations of the presence of God in the Old Testament (see, for example, Judges 5:4, Psalm 77:19) and it is this that prompts the centurion and his companions to acclaim: "Truly, this was the Son of God" (Matthew 27:54).

The Roman Missal

A careful reading of the Missal by all those involved in the preparation of today's liturgy will help ensure a smooth flow to the ritual. All the texts are found in the "Holy Week" section of the Missal that follows Saturday of the Fifth Week of Lent in the Proper of Time.

All Masses today take place with the Commemoration of the Lord's Entrance into Jerusalem, "to accomplish his Paschal Mystery," in the words of the Missal; that Commemoration takes place using one of three forms: The Procession, The Solemn Entrance, or The Simple Entrance. The Missal indicates that the Procession (the first form) or

the Solemn Entrance (the second form) takes place before the principal Mass, and that the Solemn Entrance, but not the Procession, may be repeated before other Masses that are usually celebrated with a large gathering of people (note, therefore, that the Missal envisions the first form, the Procession, taking place only once, whereas the Solemn Entrance may be used at as many Masses as is deemed pastorally advantageous in light of the gathering of the people).

First Form: The Procession

This form of the commemoration takes place with all gathering at a place other than inside the church to which the procession will go—either a smaller church, or perhaps a parish center room, or perhaps even outside. The faithful already hold palm branches.

The priest and the deacon wear red vestments; the priest may wear a chasuble, or he may wear a cope and then change into a chasuble when the procession is over. At the appointed time, the priest, deacon, and other ministers go to the place where everyone is gathered. The Missal does not indicate that this is any kind of a formal procession *per se*, so it can be an informal gathering of the clergy and ministers as they arrive at the place of beginning. The Missal does state, however, that "meanwhile" (while the ministers are assembling, or perhaps even while all are gathering, not just the ministers, to create a prayerful environment as all arrive) an antiphon or an appropriate song is sung; the antiphon suggested is from chapter 21 of Matthew's account of the Gospel: "Hosanna to the Son of David; blessed is he who comes in the name of the Lord, the King of Israel. Hosanna in the highest."

After this singing and when all have arrived, the priest begins with the Sign of the Cross and the usual liturgical greeting for Mass, followed by an introductory address. For this introduction, he may use the words given in the Missal (#5, at Palm Sunday of the Passion of the Lord); if he uses his own words, it is important that he convey the invitation for the faithful to participate actively and consciously in the celebration this day.

After the address, the priest says one of the two prayers of blessing. Only the first option includes the gesture of making the Sign of the Cross by the priest; the second one does not. The first prayer specifically asks God to bless the branches, and then goes on to ask that we "who follow Christ the King in exultation, may reach the eternal Jerusalem through him." The second option focuses more on the people "who today hold high these branches to hail Christ in his triumph," asking for their faith to be increased and their prayers to be held, so that they "may bear fruit for you by good works accomplished in him." Whichever prayer is used, however, the branches are next sprinkled after the prayer, in silence.

Then the deacon, or the priest if there is no deacon, proclaims the Gospel account of the Lord's entrance according to the proper cycle of Lectionary readings in the liturgical year; the Missal states this is done "in the usual way," meaning that there should be the greeting "The Lord be with you" and the announcement "A reading from the holy Gospel according to . . ." as is always done. Incense may also be used here. The third edition of *The Roman Missal* has the texts for this first Gospel reading right there in the Missal, which makes things much easier.

The Missal notes that after the Gospel, a brief Homily may be given. The key word concerning this Homily would seem to be "brief," if one were to be given at all—it's optional. Then an invitation is given by either a priest, deacon, or lay minister, using the words in the Missal or similar ones, to invite the people to begin the procession.

The procession is led by the thurifer, if incense is used, followed by a crossbearer. The Missal specifically points out that the cross that is carried should be "decorated with palm branches according to local custom." The cross is carried between two ministers with lighted candles. Behind this follow the deacon with the *Book of the Gospels*, the priest, the ministers, and then the faithful (note that the priest celebrant is not at the end of the procession, but rather walks before the people). Singing takes place during this procession, with various options suggested in the Missal; other appropriate songs may of course be chosen.

Keep in mind in your preparations that it will be important to choose music that will be able to be sung easily by the choir and the people as they move along in procession. Think through the route that will be used and how the movement will affect peoples' ability to sing. Think of ways to maintain the singing. *Sing to the Lord: Music in Divine Worship* (STL, 93–94) points out that while recorded music should not normally be used in liturgy, the use of recorded music to accompany communal singing during a procession outside is an exception. Therefore, if necessary, look into resources for having pre-recorded music broadcast. For example, your choir could record the singing ahead of time, and then that recording could be broadcast outside via a bell-tower or some other external speaker system, and that music would support and enhance the assembly's singing while they are processing to the church.

The Missal notes that a second song or a responsory is sung as the procession enters the church; thus, the music should change.

Then, as the procession enters the church, the priest goes to the altar, venerates it, and, if appropriate, incenses it. The people, meanwhile, continue to process into the church. He then goes to his chair, changes from cope to chasuble if necessary, and, when all are in the church, the singing ends. The priest goes right into the Collect of the Mass, and then Mass continues in the usual way; the other Introductory Rites are omitted.

The Second Form: The Solemn Entrance

This form of the entrance is used at Mass when the first form, the procession, is taking place or has taken place at another Mass, or when a procession outside the church cannot otherwise take place for some reason.

In this case, the priest, ministers and, if possible, a small group of the faithful gather somewhere other than the sanctuary, but preferably at a place where the people can see the rite. All are already holding branches in their hands.

An antiphon or another song is sung while the priest approaches the place where the rite is to begin, and then the Sign of the Cross, liturgical greeting, introduction, blessing and sprinkling, and proclamation of the Gospel all occur as described above. After the Gospel, the priest, ministers, and small group of the faithful process solemnly through the church to the sanctuary while an appropriate song is sung. Then, arriving at the altar, the priest venerates it and then goes to the chair, where, omitting the Introductory Rites, he says the Collect of the Mass after the singing ends. Mass then continues in the usual way. The Missal makes no provision for the priest to wear a cope in this form of entrance; he wears the chasuble.

Third Form: The Simple Entrance

Essentially, this form of entrance is the same as any other Sunday: the priest proceeds to the altar while the Entrance Antiphon with its psalm or some other suitable song is sung; he arrives at the altar, venerates it, and then goes to his chair; and then he begins Mass with the Sign of the Cross, greets the people as usual, and Mass continues. In this form, the usual Introductory Rites would occur.

At the Mass

The Collect highlights the theme of humility, as exemplified both in Christ's taking flesh and in his submission to the Cross. It asks that "we may heed his lesson of patient suffering" in order to "merit a share in his Resurrection." This is the mystery we enter into this day and this week, culminating in the Sacred Paschal Triduum. Through the celebration of the liturgy, we seek to participate in the mystery of his dying and rising; through that participation, we seek to be transformed so that our lives may more closely be a reflection of his way of humility.

There are special instructions for the proclamation of the Lord's Passion: it is to be read without candles and without incense, and there is to be no greeting before the proclamation and no signing of the book. It is customary in many places to have several people participate in the reading of the Passion, not just the priest and deacon. However, the part of Christ should, if possible, be read by the priest. Only a deacon asks for the blessing of the priest before reading the Passion, as he does before reading the Gospel. Your community may wish to consider chanting the Gospel; this is a wonderful way of highlighting the solemnity of the day.

The Missal goes on to note that there should be a Homily after the narrative of the Passion, but interestingly the adjective "brief" is used again.

The Creed and the Universal Prayer take place as usual.

The Prayer over the Offerings underlines how our celebration of the liturgy is a participation in the once-and-for-all sacrifice of Christ, which is made present in our time and space, and it asks that through the Passion of Christ, we may have reconciliation with God and feel the effects of God's mercy, even though "we do not merit it by our own deeds."

The Preface assigned for today, "The Passion of the Lord," is given right there in the Missal along with the other texts for this Mass. The Preface is a very succinct proclamation of how Christ, though innocent, "suffered willingly for sinners" in order to save the guilty.

The Prayer after Communion prays that having been nourished with the sacred gift of the Eucharist, we may be led to the fullness of life through Christ's Resurrection. The Prayer over the People, required for today, sets the perfect tone for Holy Week and the Sacred Paschal Triduum as it asks God to look on us as the family "for whom our Lord Jesus Christ did not hesitate to be delivered into the hands of the wicked and submit to the agony of the Cross."

Pastoral Reflection

The essence of everything we are and believe in is shared at length today. A feast has to first be seen in its entirety, with the awestruck sense of all it holds seen in the heart, before the small bites can be taken, tasted, and understood. The bite-size pieces of sustenance come as we will live the Last Supper, walk the Stations on Good Friday, and watch Jesus crucified. Until those known moments, listen deeply to

where you need to "sit" in the story; open your eyes to how you need to grow and which character you might be, and wait in trust that all can be given to God and made new.

MON 14 (#257) violet
Monday of Holy Week

The Lectionary for Mass

◆ FIRST READING: We see the gentleness of the servant in dealing with those to whom he is sent. His mission is to bring enlightenment and liberation not only to Israel, but to all the nations. The servant has been chosen by God and endowed with his Spirit.

◆ RESPONSORIAL PSALM 27: With the Lord as light and salvation, the psalmist confidently and courageously faces his adversaries. There is no cause for fear.

◆ GOSPEL: With lavish extravagance, Mary, the sister of Lazarus, washes Jesus's feet and anoints them with costly oil. Jesus interprets her gesture prophetically, associating it with the day of his burial. Judas, Jesus's betrayer, with self-serving concerns, objects to what she has done, but Jesus sets the matter straight.

The Roman Missal

The Collect today asks that we be "revived" through the Passion of Christ: the prayer acknowledges that weakness and our failure, but also implicitly recognizes that every time we celebrate the Paschal Mystery in liturgy, we share in the new life that is brought to us through the Lord's Passion, Death, and Resurrection. The Prayer over the Offerings reminds us that the mysteries we celebrate here "cancel the judgment we incurred." We can recall that it is through the liturgy that the work of our redemption is accomplished, and therefore we can petition that these same mysteries may "bear for us fruit in eternal life." The Prayer after Communion notes how these sacred mysteries are a remedy to bring us eternal salvation.

The fact that we are now in Holy Week is marked by the assignment of a new Preface—Preface II of the Passion of the Lord is assigned for today. The Preface makes specific mention that "the days of his saving Passion and glorious Resurrection are approaching." In view of this, it might be better to use this Preface and not replace it with the proper Preface if one of the Eucharistic Prayers for Reconciliation is used (you are not required to use the Preface that goes with the Eucharistic Prayers for Reconciliation). In fact, it might be advantageous to highlight a certain starkness of these days of Holy Week through using an economy of words; along those lines, perhaps Eucharistic Prayer II would be a good choice for these last three days before the Sacred Paschal Triduum. Its direct statement of "At the time he was betrayed and entered willingly into his Passion" makes it perhaps especially appropriate for these three days.

T U E 15 (#258) violet
Tuesday of Holy Week

The Lectionary for Mass

◆ FIRST READING: The Lord's servant addresses both Israel and the nations. Even before he was born he was chosen not only to restore the conquered and exiled Israel, but to enlighten the nations with God's Good News of salvation. Though he was disheartened about his ministry, the words of the Lord have given him new courage and vision.

◆ RESPONSORIAL PSALM 71: The psalmist in distress cries out for God's deliverance. God is—and has been even before the psalmist's birth—rock, refuge, stronghold,

and teacher. The experience of salvation leads to grateful proclamation of the Lord's deliverance.

◆ GOSPEL: Jesus is troubled and distressed, knowing that one of his disciples will betray him and a second will deny him. At the same time, he recognizes that his Death will also be his exaltation, his return to the Father, and his glorification. One day, our death will be our return to the Father as well.

The Roman Missal

Today's Collect prays that we may receive pardon through our celebration of "they mysteries of the Lord's Passion." Certainly the prayer reminds us of the forgiveness that comes to us through the Paschal Mystery. However, it uses an interesting phrase: the prayer says, "grant us so to celebrate the mysteries of the Lord's Passion." We can be reminded that nothing automatic happens through the offering of the Eucharist, but rather that the fruitfulness of our participation in the mystery is connected to our openness and offering in making ourselves one with the sacrifice being offered; we must be both properly disposed and properly focused and attentive in order to truly share in the grace of the sacrament. The Prayer over the Offerings asks that we may be given a share in the fullness of the sacred gifts in which we have been made partakers. The Prayer after Communion makes a connection between the earthly liturgy and the heavenly liturgy as it asks that having been nourished by the saving gifts in this present age, we may be made "partakers of life eternal."

Preface II of the Passion of the Lord, first used yesterday, is again assigned for today. A connection can be made throughout these last three days of Lent by using the same Eucharistic Prayer II, appropriate for its simplicity in these days of Holy Week.

W E D 16 (#259) violet
Wednesday of Holy Week

The Lectionary for Mass

◆ FIRST READING: The word the prophet speaks is the word he heard from the Lord—not his own word. The prophet willingly endures the opposition and suffering he experiences in carrying out his mission—knowing that God is his helper.

◆ RESPONSORIAL PSALM 69 is a psalm of lament, vividly describing the sufferings endured by one of the chosen people—all for the sake of God. The last stanza attests the psalmist's confidence that God will deliver him.

◆ GOSPEL: One of Jesus's own will betray him. Jesus is fully aware of this, yet he does not shun his betrayer, but shares the Passover meal with him.

The Roman Missal

The Collect for this Mass continues to powerfully highlight for us the mood of Holy Week and the central mystery we are celebrating during the Sacred Paschal Triduum. First, the prayer expresses how Christ submitted "to the yoke of the Cross." Implicit in this statement is the Lord's free acceptance of Death, a Passion he entered into willingly (as echoed in Eucharistic Prayer II). Second, the prayer takes note of the effects of Christ's sacrifice and our participation in the salvation it won: it asks that the power of the enemy be driven away, and that we might "attain the grace of the resurrection." The Prayer over the Offerings simply entreats that the offerings be received and that we experience the grace of the effects of Jesus's Passion, which is what we celebrate in mystery. The Prayer after Communion is a prayer that asks God to "endow us . . . with the firm conviction" that "we may be assured of perpetual life" through Jesus's Death.

Preface II of the Passion of the Lord, used on the previous two days, is once more assigned for today, and the connection throughout these last three days of Lent can be maintained if, having used Eucharistic Prayer II on Monday and Tuesday, it is used again today.

THU 17 — violet — Thursday of Holy Week (Holy Thursday)

Chrism Mass (#260) white

About the Chrism Mass

Traditionally, the Chrism Mass is celebrated on the morning of Holy Thursday. The priests of the diocese and representatives of each parish gather with the bishop in the cathedral church. During the Mass, the bishop blesses the oil of the catechumens and the oil of the sick, and consecrates the sacred chrism. In many places, celebrating the Chrism Mass on the morning of Holy Thursday can present undue difficulties, and so, especially in dioceses that are far-flung geographically, it is celebrated earlier in Holy Week. (Even if the Chrism Mass does not take place on Holy Thursday, the optional Rite of Reception of the Holy Oils at the Evening Mass of the Lord's Supper is a good way to maintain the strong link between the Chrism Mass and the Paschal Triduum.)

The Lectionary for Mass

◆ First Reading: These words from the prophet Isaiah are addressed to a post-exilic Israel and speak of the inauguration of a new era of freedom, of healing and wholeness, of joy and restoration. The reading is excerpted, so it would be well to read the passage as a whole. It is no doubt the references to "anointing" and "oil" that prompt the selection of this text for the Chrism Mass. Anointing signified the selection of an individual for a particular role or mission within the community. Aaron was anointed as priest (Leviticus 8:12); David was anointed as king (1 Samuel 16:12–13). The anointing of which the prophet speaks in today's text is more figurative, but it does signify his designation and mission. Oil had many uses in daily life and the association of joy with it points to prosperity and blessings (verse 3; see also Psalm 23:5; 104:15). In this new era, God will make a lasting covenant with his people—unlike the covenant they broke in infidelity. All nations will acknowledge the people of Zion (Jerusalem), formerly conquered and exiled, as specially blessed by the Lord.

◆ Responsorial Psalm 89: This short text focuses on David's anointing as king. The second line associates the imparting of God's strength with this sacred anointing. As a result of his anointing, David stands in a unique relationship with his God (second stanza). As a result of our anointing with the holy oils, so too do we.

◆ Second Reading: In this text from the beginning of the Book of Revelation, John, the Christian prophet, speaks of Jesus as the one who has made all believers "priests for his God and Father"— all believers—not just a particular group or tribe as in the Old Testament. A similar assertion is made by Peter in his first letter (see 2:9). All Christians are anointed as priests, prophets, and kings through the Sacraments of Initiation.

◆ Gospel: Luke depicts Jesus reading the words of Isaiah in our first reading today during a synagogue service in his hometown of Nazareth. He presents himself as the one who fulfills Isaiah's prophecy. He is anointed with the Spirit of God, as is made clear at his baptism (see Matthew 3:16; Mark 1:10; Luke 3:22; John 1:32–33). He is designated as the one who is to bring Good News to the poor, freedom to captives and the oppressed, sight to the blind, a time of blessings. So too are we, through the Spirit we have received in the Sacraments of Initiation into the Church.

The Roman Missal

The unique feature of the Chrism Mass is, of course, the blessing of the Oil of the Sick and of the Oil of Catechumens, and the consecration of the chrism, rites which are carried out by the bishop. The rubric in the Missal notes how the Chrism Mass is usually celebrated during the morning of Thursday of Holy Week, although, should it prove too difficult for the clergy and people to gather on this day, the Mass may be celebrated on another day near to Easter. Dioceses covering a large geographic area, for example, might have to contend with the question of the feasibility of extensive traveling of clergy and faithful in light of the liturgy that must also be celebrated that evening.

One of the important aspects of the Chrism Mass is the way it manifests the priests' communion with their bishop, and therefore the Missal takes special note of the high desirability that all priests participate in the Mass as far as is possible, and that minimally priests from various sections of the diocese be present. As *The Roman Pontifical* explains, "The Chrism Mass is one of the principal expressions of the fullness of the Bishop's Priesthood and signifies the close unity of the Priests with him." ("The Rite for the Blessing of Oils and the Consecration of Chrism," 1). For many dioceses the Chrism Mass is one of the highlights of the year as it manifests the true nature of the Church as the liturgical assembly, priests, deacons, and faithful, gathered around the bishop.

The Missal notes that according to traditional practice, the Blessing of the Oil of the Sick takes place before the end of the Eucharistic

Prayer, but the Blessing of the Oil of Catechumens and the Consecration of the Chrism takes place after Holy Communion. There is also the option, "for pastoral reasons," of moving this entire rite so that it takes place immediately after the Liturgy of the Word, for example, at the end of the Renewal of Priestly Promises. The actual rite for the blessing and consecration of the oils is not found in the Missal; instead, the texts are found in *The Roman Pontifical*.

The Entrance Antiphon for the Mass, taken from Revelation 1:6, notes how Christ "has made us into a kingdom, priests for his God and Father." Thus is highlighted the theme of the priestly nature of the Church, as the members of the Church are the ones who are given a share in the priesthood of Christ the High Priest through the sacraments in which the holy oils are used; it is the people who, belonging to Christ, will be blessed and anointed with the holy oils. The Collect affirms this theme of every baptized person's sharing in the priesthood of Christ as it states, "O God, who anointed your Only Begotten Son with the Holy Spirit and made him Christ and Lord, graciously grant that, being made sharers in his consecration, we may bear witness to your Redemption in the world."

The Gloria is sung or said.

There is a rubric in the Missal that specifies what the Homily preached by the bishop should focus on: starting from the readings proclaimed in the Liturgy of the Word, the bishop is to speak about priestly anointing, urging the priests to be faithful to their office. Thus, the Homily, while obviously addressed to the entire assembly, is to be an exhortation on the meaning of the ordained ministerial priesthood in its

service to the people of God. Inasmuch as the Homily leads into the Renewal of Priestly Promises, the bishop may wish to include in his preaching an explicit invitation for the priests to do this.

The form for the Renewal of Priestly Promises is given in the Missal as the bishop addresses three questions to the priests and they respond "I am." The promises are clearly renewals of the promises made at the ordination of priests ("the promises you once made"). Thus, after affirming their desire to renew their promises, the priests promise to "be more united with the Lord Jesus and more closely conformed to him" through the sacred duties they perform, duties "towards Christ's Church which, prompted by love of him" they "willingly and joyfully pledged" on the day of their Ordination. Their recommitment to these sacred duties is further spelled out in the next question, which asks about the priests' resolve "to be faithful stewards of the mysteries of God in the Holy Eucharist and the other liturgical rites" as, "following Christ the Head and Shepherd, not seeking any gain, but moved only by zeal for souls," they "discharge faithfully the sacred office of teaching." After those questions, the bishop asks the people to pray both for their priests and for him in his apostolic office; each request for prayer is acknowledged by the people with their response of, "Christ, hear us. Christ, graciously hear us." This renewal is always a very moving moment for the entire assembly and it crystallizes a focus for the Chrism Mass, giving the morning Mass a unique identity apart from the Mass of the Lord's Supper in the evening.

The Creed is not said or sung.

The Prayer over the Offerings asks that the power of this sacrifice recreate us, specifically by petitioning that it "mercifully wipe away what is old in us and increase in us grace of salvation and newness of life." In some ways, this might be seen as a summary of the sacramental life that is celebrated using the holy oils and hence the goal of ministry exercised by ordained priests: in all the sacraments, insofar as they make real and effective the saving power of the Paschal Mystery, Christians die and rise with Christ, dying to what is old and sinful and rising with him to share in his newness of life.

The Preface assigned for the Chrism Mass is titled "The Priesthood of Christ and the Ministry of Priests," and therefore it recapitulates first how Christ was anointed High Priest by the Holy Spirit, and then, in turn, since the Father decreed "that his one Priesthood should continue in the Church," not only are all Christ's people made sharers in a royal priesthood, but how "with a brother's kindness he also chooses men to become sharers in his sacred ministry through the laying on of hands." Thus, is Holy Thursday reaffirmed as the traditional day on which Christ instituted the priesthood. The responsibilities of sharing in the sacred ministry are again elucidated in terms of the functions and qualities of the priest: he is called to renew in Christ's name "the sacrifice of human redemption," to set before God's children the paschal banquet, to lead them in charity and to nourish and strengthen them with the Word and the sacraments. In so doing, priests give up their lives for God and for the salvation of their brothers and sisters and so strive to be conformed to the image of Christ himself.

SACRED PASCHAL TRIDUUM

The Meaning / The Lectionary for Mass

THE three days of the Paschal Triduum are really one celebration, focusing on three aspects of one and the same mystery: Christ's passage through Death into eternal life. This is the mystery in which we share through our Baptism. This is the mystery into which we are called not only at the moment of our physical deaths but throughout our lives: allowing ourselves to be handed over by the events and circumstances of life that seem so nonsensical and even unjust; being willing to pass through the darkness of the uncertainties and the unknowns; being raised in the midst of it all into a new life by the power of God at work in us.

The Triduum begins with the evening Mass of the Lord's Supper on Holy Thursday. The Entrance Antiphon of the Mass calls our attention to what it is all about: the cross of Christ, our salvation, our freedom, our life (see Galatians 6:14). According to the Synoptic Gospel accounts (Matthew, Mark, Luke), Jesus's last supper was a Passover meal commemorating Israel's deliverance from slavery in Egypt (see Exodus 12–15). The Gospel according to John offers a different chronology. The last days of Jesus's life are during Passover time, but the last supper is not a Passover meal. Rather, Jesus dies at the hour the Passover lambs are sacrificed (thus, his title: the Lamb of God).

Accordingly, we hear the account of the first Passover in our First Reading for Holy Thursday. The Passover and subsequent Exodus from Egypt was Israel's first experience of God as Savior and deliverer. Both the antiphon for the Responsorial Psalm and the Second Reading are from 1 Corinthians, the earliest New Testament account of the community's celebration of the Eucharist. (Paul's letters actually predate the Gospel accounts.)

The psalm focuses on a cup of salvation offered as part of a thanksgiving sacrifice in the Temple. Drinking cups of wine also came to be part of the Jewish Passover meal ritual. If Jesus's last supper was a Passover meal, Paul's reference to the cup could refer to this. Note also the reference to "remembrance," evoking the memorial of the Passover meal. Only now, the remembrance is of Jesus's Passover from death to life—a Passover that makes the way for our own passage from death to life.

The Gospel according to John does not contain an institution account, *per se*, but rather offers an extensive discourse on Jesus as the Bread of Life in chapter 6. Rather, at his last meal with his disciples before his Death, Jesus washes their feet, the job of a humble servant. This is the Gospel account for Holy Thursday. Jesus's message is loud and clear: this is what they—and we—must do for one another. This service is symbolized in the ritual washing of feet after the Homily. In our service of one another we give our lives on behalf of one another—in memory of Jesus.

In sharing the bread of his life that is broken for us, in drinking of the cup of his blood that is poured out, we are nourished in eternal life; we are united to him and to one another; we commit ourselves to live in a manner that re-members his presence among us. In so doing, we proclaim his Death—and his life of self-giving—until he comes in glory.

The Good Friday celebration is not a Mass but rather a three-part service consisting of the Liturgy of the Word, the Adoration of the Cross, and Holy Communion. The readings point to the self-sacrifice of Jesus as the Suffering Servant described by Isaiah. Note how the details of the servant's appearance point to Jesus at the time of his suffering and Death. Jesus was literally "pierced" by the nails and the soldier's sword on the cross. "By his stripes we were healed." Jesus is the true Lamb of God (see John 1:29) "led to the slaughter." He is the innocent one (see John 19:38), "cut off from the land of the living and smitten for the sin of his people," who gave "his life as an offering for sin." Isaiah's words are pre-eminently fulfilled in Jesus, the prophet from Nazareth.

The antiphon for the Responsorial Psalm is from Luke's account of the Passion, where Jesus is depicted praying these words based on Psalm 31:6 as he dies on the Cross. Psalm 31 is a prayer of confidence and trust in God, prayed by one who is in great distress, one who is in "the clutches of . . . enemies and . . . persecutors." Was this not the experience of Jesus? Note how the words of the second stanza echo the details of the events of Jesus's arrest, trial, suffering, and Death.

The Second Reading from Hebrews presents Jesus as the heavenly high priest who is able to sympathize with us in our struggles because of what he himself experienced. Therefore we can confidently implore him for help in the trials that we undergo. Hebrews' words about Jesus's loud cries and tears call to mind his agony in the garden, as well as his cries from the Cross (see, for example, Mark 15:34). As we hear Hebrews' words, we may ask ourselves: was Jesus saved from Death? True, he died—but he was raised to life again. He was delivered from the power of death—and so are we, because of his Resurrection.

John's account of the Passion is always read on Good Friday. The Crucifixion is Jesus's "hour"— that time to which the whole Gospel is oriented. His lifting up on the Cross is his lifting up in glory (see John 3:14; 8:28; 12:32.34). His ministry, his work on earth is accomplished (see John 19:30). His Mother and the beloved disciple stand at the foot of his Cross, as we do today. We are saved from death and born into eternal life through the blood and water that flow from Jesus's pierced side.

The Easter Vigil is perhaps the high point of the celebration of the Triduum. It is the night of the Passover of the Lord, his passage from the darkness of death into the radiant glory of eternal life. In the readings of the Liturgy of the Word, we hear the story of salvation from the beginning of time. All seven readings are integral in the telling of the story and each has its own Responsorial Psalm (or Canticle) and prayer. The psalm is an integral part of the Word of God we hear tonight: these words that God gives to us are the very words we use in our prayer and praise. The First

Reading is the creation account from Genesis 1–2. We respond with a hymn praising our God for the manifold works of creation. The Second Reading is the heart-rending story of Abraham's willingness to sacrifice his only son to the Lord. Abraham's love of God and obedience to what he asked were so deep that he withheld nothing. And God prevented Abraham from harming his son, thus delivering him from death. Our response, Psalm 16, speaks of the deep peace that comes from trust in the Lord and his guidance. The Third Reading recounts the Exodus from Egypt, a follow-up we might say, to the First Reading from Holy Thursday. The response is the hymn sung by Moses and all the Israelites (including his sister Miriam and all the women who receive special mention in Exodus 15:20–21). The prophet Isaiah describes the covenant relationship between God and Israel as a marriage relationship in the Fourth Reading. What intimate love is conveyed! The text comes from the time of the Babylonian Exile and promises deliverance and restoration to the people. Fittingly, the Responsorial Psalm 30 praises God for the deliverance accomplished for his people. The Fifth Reading is also from the prophet Isaiah and is likewise set in the time of the Exile. Israel is invited to return to the Lord in repentance and to drink abundantly of his wisdom and teaching for in it, they—and we—find life. The response is a hymn from Isaiah extolling God our Savior and the water of salvation he provides. On this night above all nights, we draw it with joy. The Sixth Reading is from the prophet Baruch. We are still in the context of the exile, viewed as punishment for Israel's infidelity. Baruch calls the people to learn the ways and the wisdom of God and to walk in them. These have been made known in the law, Israel's special possession. Our response is Psalm 19, a hymn of praise extolling the law as a priceless treasure. The antiphon is from John's account of the Gospel, and acclaims the words of the Lord as words of everlasting life.

In the Seventh Reading, the words of the prophet Ezekiel promise an end to the exile. God will gather Israel from all the lands into which they were scattered as a result of their infidelities. Note that the restoration is not something Israel deserved, but rather, that God will enact for the sake of his holy name. He will purify his people and give them a new heart and a new spirit.

Three options are given for the response. The first, Psalm 42, is used when Baptisms are celebrated. It focuses on the pilgrim's longing to enter into God's dwelling place (Temple). The antiphon compares this longing to that of a deer for running water, an image that clearly evokes Baptism.

The second option, from Isaiah 12, is also the response to the Fifth Reading. Again, the antiphon's mention of water points to Baptism. The third option, Psalm 51, is a penitential psalm. The antiphon's plea for a clean heart echoes the words of Ezekiel in the Seventh Reading.

The epistle from the letter to the Romans speaks of our own participation (immersion) in Christ's Death and Resurrection through Baptism. In our responsorial antiphon we hear once again the joyful Alleluia, which has been silenced for all of Lent. Psalm 118 is a hymn of praise and thanksgiving for God's victory and deliverance. Verse 22 (the third stanza) is quoted several times in the New Testament with reference to Jesus's Resurrection.

Finally, we hear the Gospel proclamation of that first Easter morning as recounted by Matthew. Jesus's Resurrection, like his Death, was an earth-shaking event. Such signs, associated with the end time in contemporary Jewish literature, signaled the inauguration of a new era in human history. The faithful women disciples who come to the tomb on the morning after the Sabbath encounter the angel of the Lord who announces to them his Resurrection. They are commissioned to tell their brothers and while on their way to do so, encounter Jesus. He, too, sends them to his brothers with word that they will see him again. Is this not what we are all sent to do?

The Triduum concludes with the celebration of Evening Prayer on Sunday. It was the evening of that first day of the week when Jesus appeared to the disciples (see Luke 24:13ff; John 20:19ff). Experiencing him alive, their hearts were filled with joy. It was the evening of that day when Jesus ascended to his heavenly Father (see Luke 24:50–51).

May our participation in this Paschal Triduum strengthen us for all the dyings—and risings—that will be part of our lives in the coming year. In the face of the darkness, the unknown, and the inexplicable, may we know the power of God at work in and through our weakness, bringing us through it to new and transformed life in the victory that he has won.

The Roman Missal

WHEN it comes to preparing for these days, nothing can take the place of carefully reading the prayers and rubrics in the Missal, and this should be the starting point for all those who prepare and minister at these liturgies. Although at first they may seem complicated because the liturgies contain components we only do once a year, there is really nothing that should scare us or that we need overly complicate. A thorough reading of the rubrics, rich discussion and detailed preparation about enacting the choreography in your particular worship space, and competently-run rehearsals for all those involved (including actually walking through the movements, so that a kind of "muscle memory" is facilitated, rather than just simply verbally explaining what will happen) will help ensure that when the time for celebration comes, everyone will be free enough from worry and distraction so that all may prayerfully enter into the ritual. Such preparation reveals how there really is an inner beauty and logic to the liturgies in and of themselves that allow us to encounter the mystery we are celebrating when we allow ourselves to be swept along by the ritual flow. Such careful preparation and rehearsal helps to prevent confusion that creates a kind of "theatrical performance" atmosphere that hinders not only the ministers, but the entire liturgical assembly, from becoming engulfed in the mysteries being celebrated. Be sure to include those who are in charge of the Rite of Christian Initiation of Adults in discussions, so that everyone involved can work together harmoniously from the very beginning of the process.

Those who prepare the liturgies for the Sacred Triduum should consider ahead of time the question of what book will be used at the actual celebration. Certainly, one could make a case for using the Missal book itself, since this is what it is for—it is appropriately noble and dignified, and it is therefore worthy of use; it bears the weight of mystery. However, it is also true that at times the book can be confusing to use, what with its page turns and the listing of various options; this can be especially true when it comes to initiation at the Easter Vigil. Sometimes it becomes necessary to annotate the Missal with post-it notes or other markings, but then doing so begins to detract from the dignity of the book, thus lessening its desirability

as an appropriate tool. Thus, it is not uncommon for parishes to make their own ritual books for the priest celebrant, with the texts the priest will need in order and laid out using only the options selected. Such a book has the advantage of being able to include specific rubrics and choreography as needed for a particular worship space. If such a book is used, however, be sure that it too is one that is noble, dignified, and capable of bearing the weight of mystery. Binders appropriate for this are provided by liturgical supply companies. Here's a hint if you use such binders: use plastic sheet protectors for the pages. Such protectors provide for easy grasping and page-turning since they are thicker than just sheets of paper; be sure to use non-glare ones, to keep it easy for the priest to see the pages.

The rubrics given right at the beginning of the section on the Sacred Paschal Triduum in the Missal are important, as they highlight the centrality of these liturgies. These celebrations are referred to as "the greatest mysteries of our redemption" as they keep the memorial of the Lord "crucified, buried, and risen" (Triduum rubric, 1). Special mention is given to the Paschal fast, which is to be "celebrated everywhere on the Friday of the Lord's Passion and, where appropriate, prolonged also through Holy Saturday as a way of coming, with spirit uplifted, to the joys of the Lord's Resurrection" (ibid.). Parishes would do well to catechize parishioners on the meaning of the Paschal fast, which is different from the Lenten fast. During Lent, we fast as a way of doing penance and of trying to cooperate with the grace of conversion; during the Triduum, we fast as a way of preparing for the great mysteries that are about to be celebrated. The fast during the Triduum is not one of penitence, but one of joy, of, in a sense, almost being too excited to eat, because our focus is totally captivated by the mysteries of redemption being made present to us in our midst. The emptiness of the stomach thus becomes a sign of our openness to die and rise with the Lord in these most holy of days.

The rubrics themselves point to the need for a sufficient number of lay ministers and the need for careful instruction in what is to be done; nothing is to be left to haphazardness. Singing is also given prominence: "The singing of the people, the ministers, and the Priest Celebrant has a special importance in the celebrations of these days, for when texts are sung, they have their proper impact" (Triduum rubric, 2) All, then, should set aside the proper time required to rehearse the singing of texts, including taking the time to prepare the assembly for their sung responses if this is something they are not already familiar with. In fact, the rubric goes on to highlight how the faithful should be given proper catechesis on the rites of the Triduum so that they can truly participate as actively and fruitfully as is intended by the Church. In addition to articles in their bulletin, many parishes hold special workshops or mini-courses on the Triduum for their parishioners, to give them a basic understanding of the liturgies of these days. Such gatherings would be wonderful opportunities to do a *lectio divina* of the Missal prayers with the people, so that they come to their liturgies with their ears, minds, and hearts prepared to receive the proclaimed texts.

Finally, the introductory rubrics end with a challenge to smaller communities. These days are so important that attention is to be given to gathering the faithful in as large an assembly as possible, where the resources for ministers and singing are plentiful. Thus, even though a community may gather regularly for Eucharist, the members of smaller communities must do an honest self-appraisal and ask if they have the necessary resources, specifically in terms of numbers of ministers and musical ability, to carry out the rites with the appropriate festivity and dignity. The Missal gives a certain emphasis to such communities joining with larger ones for these most sacred celebrations: "Consequently, it is desirable that small communities, associations, and special groups of various kinds join together in these churches to carry out the sacred celebrations in a more noble manner" (Triduum rubric, 3).

There are detailed rubrics for each day of the Sacred Triduum.

Children's Liturgy of the Word

MOST parishes do not celebrate Liturgy of the Word with children during the Triduum. Families should be encouraged to bring children to the liturgies of the Triduum if the times are appropriate and they are able to attend to what is happening. Ordinarily these celebrations are the most sensate and the music, rituals, and symbols will engage children.

The Saints

DURING these three days, we celebrate all saints and no saints. The liturgies of the Triduum take precedence over all saints' days, no matter how significant. And yet, during the Paschal Triduum, we are constantly aware of the great company of witnesses who have gone before us, who have witnessed to the mystery of Christ's Passion, Death, and Resurrection by the holiness of their lives.

The Liturgy of the Hours

As we enter into the shortest but most important season of the liturgical year, these days will be enriched in communities that gather to celebrate the Hours along with the one liturgy that unfolds over three days. Even though the days of the Paschal Triduum are some of the most hectic moments in the life of pastoral ministers, setting aside opportunities for celebrations of the Hours can become a prayerful bridge for entering into the celebration of the Three Days.

The Triduum runs from Evening Prayer of Holy Thursday April 17, 2014 through Evening Prayer II of Easter Sunday April 20, 2014. The Easter Vigil takes the place of the Office of Readings. The hymns from the Hours include: "When I Survey the Wondrous Cross" (ROCKINGHAM); "I Shall Praise the Savior's Glory" or "Pange, Lingua, Gloriosi" (PANGE, LINGUA Mode III); "The Word of God Proceeding Forth" (ROCKINGHAM); "O Sacred Head, Surrounded" (PASSION CHORALE); "Alleluia! Sing to Jesus!" (HYFERDOL); "Hail Thee, Festival Day!" (SALVE FESTA DIES); and "The Strife Is O'er" (VICTORY).

The Easter Homily by Melito of Sardis from the Office of Readings on Holy Thursday is a fitting meditation that links the texts of Holy Week to those of the Paschal Triduum. This rich text joins together themes of Incarnation and redemption and celebrates the new Lamb of God who brings together both the old and the new covenants.

On Holy Thursday, Evening Prayer is celebrated only by those who will not participate in the Evening Mass of the Lord's Supper. For those who live in a community without a resident priest, and who would find it too burdensome to travel to the celebration of the Paschal Triduum, people are encouraged to gather and celebrate together certain aspects of the "Three Days." The introduction to the ritual text *Sunday Celebrations in the Absence of A Priest* (SCAP) suggests that those who cannot gather with a mother church in their area "gather as family, that is the domestic Church, or in small faith communities and unite themselves in prayer to the universal church" (SCAP, 95).

During the time following the Evening Mass of the Lord's Supper the tradition of reciting or singing Psalm 22 at different intervals during the celebration of Adoration of the Blessed Sacrament at the altar of repose would be appropriate. If you chant this psalm throughout the night find a good musical setting that weds text and tune and clearly captures the spirit of lament. A fitting conclusion to this period of time is the celebration of Compline or Night Prayer. The ritual book suggests Night Prayer for Sundays after Evening Prayer II, and provides in place of the responsorial the following text: "for our sake Christ was obedient, accepting even death."

The celebration of Morning Prayer on Good Friday and Holy Saturday is highly recommended by the *Ceremonial of Bishops* (296); the *General Instruction of the Liturgy of the Hours* (210); and *Paschale Solemnitatis* (40, 62). Evening Prayer on Good Friday and Holy Saturday is only celebrated by those who do not participate in the liturgies of the Three Days.

When we examine the history of the Liturgy of the Hours, we see a rich and very complicated development, as well as a variety of styles and traditions. Daily monastic prayer with its recitation of the psalms in course, cathedral celebrations, with a more stable and repetitive psalmody as well as heightened ritual, and prayer in the domestic Church with its smaller and less formal communities, have all contributed to the richness of this prayer as it continues to grow in usage and popularity.

The Patristic texts offer wonderful insights into the meaning of the Christian life. St. John Chrysostom's catechesis from the Office of Readings on Good Friday refers to the Sacraments of Initiation and the ancient Homily on Holy Saturday reflects on the account of humanity's fall in Adam, a symbol of darkness, but notes that Christ shatters the darkness when he comes as Light of the World.

Holy Saturday is set aside in many communities as a retreat day for the elect, catechumens,

and candidates. Be sure to include these folks in the celebration of Morning Prayer. Likewise, any members of the parish who will be preparing the Easter environment, musicians meeting for final rehearsals and liturgical ministers who will gather for a walk-through of the great Easter Vigil should be encouraged to gather for Morning Prayer before proceeding to these final tasks before tonight's celebration.

The celebration of Evening Prayer on Easter Sunday evening is strongly endorsed. In some places this celebration has been called Baptismal or Paschal Vespers since it is a fitting opportunity to gather with the neophytes of the community. The liturgical books and their commentaries (*Paschale Solemnitatis*, 98; the *Ceremonial of Bishops*, 371; and the *General Instruction of the Liturgy of the Hours*, 231) all recommend the restoration of this celebration as a completion to the Triduum. A baptismal remembrance is an appropriate adaption to Evening Prayer on this night. The antiphons for the psalms at Evening Payer reflect the synoptic accounts of the Resurrection: Mary Magdalene and the other Mary, "come and see the place where the Lord was buried" and "do not be afraid." To add to the solemnity of the feast consider having a priest or deacon, vested in alb, stole, and cope lead the celebration. Likewise the use of incense, along with festive settings of Easter hymns, psalms and canticles with double or triple Alleluias would be most appropriate.

The Rite of Christian Initiation of Adults

THOSE involved with the implementation of the Rite of Christian Initiation of Adults lament the fact that neither the newly retranslated *General Instruction of the Roman Missal* nor the third edition of *The Roman Missal* mention the dismissal of catechumens at all. It has been a challenge for us to convince our pastors and parishioners of the value of the dismissal of catechumens that is mandated by the Rite of Christian Initiation of Adults. Consistency throughout the Church's official liturgical books would have been of great assistance as we continue to work toward the full implementation of the rite. At present, the only official guidance we have with this issue is found in RCIA, 75.3: ". . . at Mass they [catechumens] may also take part with the faithful in the liturgy of the word, thus better preparing themselves for their eventual participation in the liturgy of the eucharist. Ordinarily, however, when they are present in the assembly of the faithful they should be kindly dismissed before the liturgy of the eucharist begins (unless their dismissal would present practical or pastoral problems). For they must await their Baptism, which will join them to God's priestly people and empower them to participate in Christ's new worship." Catechumens are dismissed because they cannot yet "lift up their hearts" to pray the Eucharistic Prayer. They are not yet a part of the Body of Christ. They have not yet been baptized into the priestly office of Christ and therefore cannot join their voices with the baptized, who unite their hearts in prayer with the celebrant, who voices this priestly prayer to the Father.

Mass is obviously celebrated at Holy Thursday's Evening Mass of the Lord's Supper and at the Easter Vigil. Mass is not celebrated on Good Friday. Holy Communion is distributed, but there is no Mass, no Eucharistic prayer, no Liturgy of the Eucharist. One can draw the conclusion that the dismissal of the elect and catechumens takes place before the Liturgy of the Eucharist on both Holy Thursday and at the Easter Vigil. On Holy Thursday, the dismissal could take place following the washing of the feet and before the General Intercessions (Prayers of the Faithful). At the Easter Vigil, the dismissal could take place following the celebration of Confirmation. (Obviously, the catechumens being dismissed at the Vigil are those who are not being baptized that night but are awaiting Baptism at the celebration of the Vigil during the following year[s] when they are deemed ready.) It makes little sense to have the catechumens present for the renewal of baptismal promises, which follows Confirmation, since they are not yet baptized. This follows the same principle employed at the Service of Light at the Vigil. It is not appropriate that catechumens hold lighted candles because they have not yet been entrusted with the Paschal light in Baptism. Some dioceses mandate that the catechumens be dismissed before the Solemn Intercessions at Good Friday's Celebration of the Lord's Passion. One assumes that the reason for this is that the diocesan leaders feel that the catechumens, not yet the faithful, should not take part in these prayers of the faithful.

—Adapted from an article by Jerry Galipeau © LTP, 2010.

The Sacraments of Initiation

BE sure those who prepare the liturgy and musicians are aware that young people who are preparing for sacraments are being encouraged to attend the celebrations. Encourage families and young people to attend the liturgies of the Triduum. Send home schedules ahead of time and provide childcare for very young children.

Prior to the Triduum inquire whether it would be possible for older children to sit in on a choir rehearsal or a liturgy preparation session for one of the celebrations. Ask the music director to have a cantor come to a session and familiarize children with some of the music that will be used in the Triduum.

Find out if some of the young people can help in the preparations for the Triduum. The preparation and legwork that goes into making it all happen is extensive. There is much to be coordinated and many details need attention. Older candidates for Confirmation as well as high school youth and college students, who might be home on break, could be very helpful. Distribute a simple reflection sheet on the Triduum at the last catechetical session before its celebration. Ask young people to note any of their observations about the Triduum and bring their responses back for the next session. Use them for discussion and as conversation starters.

The Rite of Penance

WHILE many communities do not celebrate the Sacrament of Penance on Good Friday, both Penance and Anointing of the Sick are allowed on this day. Since many people are concerned about their Easter duty, consider scheduling a period of time for the Sacrament of Penance. Take your lead from Pope John Paul II who was pastorally sensitive to people's needs and made a regular practice of celebrating the sacrament on Good Friday. The Sacrament of Penance and the Anointing of the Sick may be celebrated on Holy Saturday (see PS, 75).

The Pastoral Care of the Sick

IT is a venerable tradition to bring Holy Communion to the sick and homebound from the Holy Thursday Table (see PS, 53). Consider placing photos of the sick and homebound in the chapel of repose and encourage those gathered to pray for these members of the community so "they may be more closely united to the celebrating Church" (PS, 53). As part of the environment include a plant such as an African violet or spring flowers such as daffodils or tulips near each photo and then plan to take these flowers to the sick and homebound when Holy Communion is brought to them on Easter Sunday. Holy Communion may be brought to the sick and homebound on Good Friday at any time (see PS, 59). On Holy Saturday, a sick person may be anointed but Communion may only be given as Viaticum (see PS, 75). Provide resources, such as *What Am I Doing for Triduum This Year?* (LTP) when making pastoral visits. The holy oils may be presented as part of the Holy Thursday liturgy. This ritual is not found in the third edition of *The Roman Missal*; however, the text is included in this book on page 151.

The Rite of Marriage

THE Rite of Marriage may not take place during the Paschal Triduum. Make sure this fact is communicated to those who oversee the parish calendar so that no wedding is scheduled for Good Friday or Holy Saturday (see *Paschale Solemnitatis*, 61 and 75). In extreme situations, convalidation of a Marriage is allowed. Occasionally pastoral situations arise, usually having to do with the elect or candidates preparing for the Easter sacraments, but these should be addressed long before the time of the Triduum. On Holy Thursday, a wedding outside of Mass is allowed but good pastoral practice would advise against this except in the case of an urgent pastoral need.

The Order of Christian Funerals

THE Rosary is a common form of the vigil service in many parishes and yet it is not mentioned in the OCF. Perhaps because the Rosary is seen as private devotion rather than as a part of the Church's official liturgy. In areas where the tradition is long established, it might seem most appropriate for the practice to continue. However, in these cases it would be better to incorporate the Rosary or parts of it into the Church's newly prescribed pattern of prayer. There is also the matter of being sensitive to non-Catholics who are gathered to grieve, and whose primary experience of prayer is to gather and reflect on the proclamation of God's Word. Funerals may not be celebrated during the Paschal Triduum (see OCF, 178 and PS, 61). Sensitivity to families is required when communicating this information. Assure the family that the parish will pray for the deceased during Triduum.

The Book of Blessings

THE Order of Blessing of Easter Foods (chapter 54) may be used before or after the Easter Vigil or on Easter morning.

The Liturgical Environment

THE liturgical color for the Evening Mass of the Lord's Supper is white. If the parish has different sets of vestments, this would be a time to bring out the better set, which might also be used for the Easter Vigil and on Easter Sunday. The mood of the celebration is joyous, although it does begin the transition into the Good Friday with the silencing of the bells and instruments after the Gloria. The environment should further this sensibility, but not be too complex, particularly as it will be removed after the liturgy

The manner of the washing of feet should receive careful consideration. It should be set up in such a way as to be central to the assembly's attention and be beautiful, if simple. Vessels for water should also be designed for the practical use to which they will be put. For example, if they are too shallow, it will be difficult not to spill. Towels and chairs will also be necessary. If the church has a wood or stone floor, a carpet brought in for this rite would add both beauty and comfort for those with bare feet, without being too cumbersome. The offering on Holy Thursday is traditionally appointed to be distributed to the poor. If non-monetary gifts are offered, this will require consideration as to how they are to be received.

Enough hosts should be consecrated to allow for the Communion of the faithful on Good Friday.

The altar of repose for the Blessed Sacrament should be carefully constructed, but need not be overly ornate. One church in Minnesota, which has a striking secondary location to use, needs only to add a simple wooden tabernacle and a well-chosen orchid to define a beautiful space. Simplicity can be striking! Because these environments are usually constructed in spaces that were not intended to be used as liturgical space, defining the space is often important. Simple but elegant room dividers or tapestries can provide a background to set the space off well. Good use can be made of the greenery from Palm Sunday, should it still be in good condition, along with some of the plants that have been procured for Easter Sunday and some of the greenery you customarily have in the sanctuary. Along with some candles, these things can form a beautiful, reasonably simple setting for the reposition. It should be in a place distinct from the main liturgical space.

The rubrics call for the altar to be stripped and the removal or veiling of crosses after the liturgy in preparation for Good Friday. Veils should be violet in color. If the font is to be emptied; this may happen at this time also. While the church need not be emptied of furniture and art, generally, simplicity should be the norm for Good Friday. Because people remain to pray before the Blessed Sacrament, any work on the environment should be done in silence, particularly if the place of repose is within earshot.

It is best if the preparations are done after Mass on Holy Thursday, so there should be relatively little to do on this day. The color of the day is red, although the only place this appears is in the vesture of the ministers as the altar is to be bare. Candles should be extinguished and, if possible, removed. A significant cross (only one cross should be used) should be prepared for the procession. It must be light enough that it can be carried. It may be veiled in violet or uncovered. Some parishes hold the cross for adoration while others place a stand at the place of adoration. It may be honored with candles and incense if this is desired. The cross should be left in place throughout the day for peoples' private prayer.

The Blessed Sacrament is brought into the sanctuary for Holy Communion along with a fair linen, corporal, and candles. These are returned to the altar of repose and the sacristy, respectively, after Communion.

The Easter Vigil environment should facilitate the four distinct aspects of the vigil: the Lucernarium, the Liturgy of the Word, the Liturgy of Baptism, and the Liturgy of the Eucharist. The color of the liturgy is white or gold. Whatever is done for environment should highlight, not impede the celebration of the liturgy and draw attention to the principle actions.

One of the most important aspects of environment for the Vigil is light. The Vigil should be celebrated after complete darkness has fallen, and must be completed before dawn. Complete darkness is called "astronomical twilight," and its time at your location can be found on a variety of sites online. Your diocesan Office of Liturgy should also offer guidance on when the Vigil should start. Communities wait for full darkness to put on their expensive fireworks shows because this is the setting they are designed for. The opening rites of the Easter Vigil require no less.

Choose a site for the fire that has sufficient room for the parish to gather and that does not provide unnecessary obstacles to those with difficulty walking. Check the area ahead of time for tripping hazards, removing them as possible or appointing someone to help people requiring assistance. Also consider how people will be able to hear the priest celebrant outside. A sound system is quite possibly necessary.

The fire should be of significant size. This is one of the central symbols of the rite. Consider how to light the Paschal candle from the fire. A taper like those used by altar servers in lighting the candles is useful in this regard. Particularly in dryer locations, be aware of possible fire danger. Someone should be standing by with materials for handling a potential mishap.

The Paschal candle should also be of size proportionate to your space. A church with a soaring roof and cavernous space needs a candle that will not be lost in the space. Place a stand for the candle near the ambo for the incensation of the candle and the *Exsultet*. If you have a second stand, it can be placed by the font. The candle will burn at Mass throughout Easter Time; this is another reason to provide a candle of some size, so that there is more than a stump left at Pentecost for use at Baptisms and funerals throughout the year.

Congregational candles will need to be procured in advance for all the baptized. Smaller candles are less likely to drip, and are favored by some parishes, while others provide larger candles and encourage the faithful to take them home for use during Easter Time.

The primary symbols for the Liturgy of the Word are the ambo, Lectionary, *Book of the Gospels,* and Paschal candle (which takes its proper place by the ambo throughout Easter Time). Consider using light to highlight the ambo during this time. The sound and lights need to be checked ahead of time with both those in charge of them and those who will be reading to prevent mishaps.

Ideally, Baptism of adults should be by immersion, if circumstances allow. It may be possible to build a temporary font that will remain in place for the entirety of Easter Time. Warming the water in the font for Baptism is strongly encouraged.

Those to be baptized may be clothed in a robe, usually of a darker color that will not become transparent when wet. After they are baptized, they may be presented with an alb and taken to a suitable location to change during the congregation's renewal of baptismal promises.

If the baptizing minister is also entering into the font, a dry alb will also be necessary for him to change into. As most churches have floors that become slippery when wet, placing a towel or mat on the floor at the exit of the font is prudent.

Large towels will be necessary, particularly when immersion is practiced. Baptismal candles should also be prepared for each catechumen, along with the chrism in a suitable vessel, and basin and towel for the priest celebrant to wash his hands afterward. The tools for sprinkling the congregation with water should also be prepared. Several small fir branches wired together do a better job of sprinkling water than do the metal aspergilla commercially available, and suggest the life that the water brings.

The Liturgy of the Eucharist is not different from a usual Sunday, although if a congregation has a special set of vessels, this, along with Holy Thursday, would be an appropriate time to use them.

The Liturgical Music

THIS is the highest point of the liturgical year, and it is an incredible endurance marathon for everyone involved with liturgy, but especially for the pastoral musician and church choir. Physical and mental exhaustion can wreak havoc on the voice. Be sure to stress physical care and wellbeing to all your musicians, and heed your own advice.

This is the season that calls for all the musicians in the faith community to come together to form one large choir. The liturgies of the three days are not assigned to different groups. It is one liturgy that unfolds over three days, so all parish musicians should be encouraged to be present. The music used during the Triduum should come back year after year, and the repertoire should be incorporated into the many observances throughout the liturgical year. Pastoral musicians and other liturgical ministers must step up to the plate and show forth the "Church" by celebrating the Triduum as a united community. This may take a few years to accomplish, but this is a once-a-year opportunity to celebrate the Paschal Mystery as "one" community. Over time, it will help musicians from different choirs to build more sincere conversations with one another, not just the perfunctory "hello" on the way in or out of Mass. When the parish musicians embrace this model, they will not only be concerned about the quality of the music, but the quality of relationships with each other and the entire faith community's experience of the heart of our faith, the Paschal Mystery.

Visit www.LTP.org/resources for a free PDF including a list of music for this sacred season.

Devotions and Sacramentals

CONSIDER placing photos of the sick and homebound in the chapel of repose and encourage those gathered to pray for these members of the community so "they may be more closely united to the celebrating Church" (PS, 53). As part of the environment include a plant such as an African violet or spring flowers like daffodils or tulips near each photo and bring these to the sick and homebound on Easter Sunday. During a prolonged

Eucharistic adoration it is appropriate to read "some part of the Gospel of St. John" (Chapters 13–17), (PS, 56). The place for the chapel of repose is not to resemble a tomb, therefore the term sepulcher should be avoided and the Eucharist is not to be placed in a monstrance (see DPPL, 141). Consider placing a bowl, pitcher, and towels in the chapel, concluding the evening with Night Prayer. An Agape meal is more appropriate on this day rather than the Seder supper since Catholics are not Jewish. A venerable tradition in the Church is the visiting of seven churches on Holy Thursday, a reflection of the ancient pilgrimage practice of visiting seven Roman basilicas to obtain a plenary indulgence; often the Rosary is prayed as people move from one church to another.

On Good Friday, Passion plays are popular in several communities. In Spain and Portugal it is a custom to process with the dead Christ through the streets. DPPL cautions against creating hybrid liturgies (see 142 and 143). In some communities images of the Sorrowful Mother such as the Pieta are also carried in procession. DPPL continues by saying "in relation to sacred 'representations' it is important to instruct the faithful on the difference between a 'representation' which is commemorative, and the 'liturgical actions' which are anamnesis, or mysterious presence of the redemptive event of the Passion" (144).

It is customary in some communities to gather with Christians from other ecclesial communions and process through the streets with a large cross. The people stop at various churches or at soup kitchens, homeless shelters, or other institutions that may benefit from a time of prayer. The Good Friday *Tre Ore* (Three Hours) also referred to as the Seven Last Words are popular in some places. St. James Cathedral in Seattle, Washington (http://stjames-cathedral.org) celebrates the *Tre Ore* every Good Friday which includes a reflection on the last seven words of Christ by a theologian of note. People respond in prayer in song and musical selections from the repertoire of the masters written for Holy Week are performed. The Divine Mercy Novena begins on Good Friday.

On Holy Saturday many communities gather for Morning Prayer, which may include some of the minor Rites of the RCIA being celebrated such as the *Ephphetha* prayer (from the Greek meaning "be opened"). In some communities Easter eggs are prepared and butter is carved in the form of a lamb to be used for the Easter feast. For those who cannot participate in the Vigil in the Holy Night of Easter, spend time reflecting on some of the text from this liturgy found in *Catholic Household Blessings & Prayers*.

The Parish and the Home

FAMILIES might consider making a tangible sign of the season such as homemade bread or hot cross buns (decorated with an icing cross). Sharing some of these with neighbors, a homebound parishioner, or residents of a shelter is a good way to connect us with the sharing of a final meal as Jesus did with disciples. This sharing might also help us understand the love Jesus demonstrated for his disciples when he washed their feet and his invitation for them to do the same. While we don't wash dusty feet in the same way that walking travelers once did, we can find ways and do our part to follow the way of Jesus by showing love in our own homes and neighborhoods.

The antiphon for the Responsorial Psalm on Good Friday presents us with Jesus's obedient witness to the Father in the face of suffering and death. Not wavering from his mission to bring about the reign of God, Jesus approached Jerusalem, Gethsemane, and Golgotha with fidelity to do whatever was necessary to demonstrate how much God loved human beings. The cross is a sign of this sacrifice and visibly showing that symbol at home during Lent or Holy Week (perhaps on the dinner table) connects us to the Adoration of the Cross that we do together on Good Friday. An experience of the Stations of the Cross during the week is another way to connect our families with our commitment to walk alongside Jesus as faithful followers.

On Palm Sunday of the Passion of the Lord, we heard the story we celebrate in liturgy during the coming days of Triduum. We heard Matthew's account of Jesus's Passion, Death, and burial beginning with Jesus's approach to Jerusalem and the adulation and cheers of the crowd. Matthew's account of the Gospel for that Sunday ends with the burial of Jesus's body by Joseph of Arimathea. The Gospel account is a good story for personal reflection and prayer throughout the week followed by the remembrance and celebration of the events throughout the liturgies of Triduum.

The Easter Vigil experience, while potentially too long for young children, tells the story of our salvation through, song, reading, and ritual. The Responsorial Psalms serve to deepen our remembrance and our response. The symbols of light in darkness and the markings of the Paschal candle are something that parish households could replicate at home. By drawing on or marking a white pillar candle with signs of their own journey and commitment to follow, a family brings the message of Christ home into their own domestic Church. Lighting it during meals throughout Easter Time demonstrates our willingness to be a light in the world. We remember our own baptismal promises to forsake the darkness of sin and bring the light of Christ into the world as we light our candles.

Mass Texts

Triduum

◆ Dismissal Text for RCIA

The Holy Triduum is a single extended feast that incorporates us into the events of Christ's Death and Resurrection. The mystery of salvation becomes less mysterious when we live it by entering the tomb of the font and then rising to put on the garment of new life in Christ. Your lives manifest this mysterious reality to our community. With gratitude for your fidelity to Christ's call and for the power of your witness we pray that you will fully embrace your new identity in Christ and live it faithfully till the end of your days.

◆ Seasonal Texts for Prayer of the Faithful

Please note the texts below should not be used on Good Friday. Please refer to The Roman Missal *for the Solemn Intercessions on this day.*

During these Three Days, God's love is powerfully manifest to us at the table of the Last Supper, on the hill of Calvary, and in the tomb. Let us turn to the Lord who has provided for our nourishment through Word and sacrament and confidently ask for his mercy:

Response: From our depths, O Lord, we cry to you.

That all leaders in the Church, especially the Holy Father and all bishops throughout the world, will follow the example of Christ, the Suffering Servant, who gave his life for the good of all, let us call out to the Lord:

That the leaders of nations, states, and cities will subordinate their ambition and self-interest in favor of sustained peace, justice, and the dignity of all, let us call out to the Lord:

That families might know the healing and hope that only Christ can offer ensuring that family is always a place where young lives are nourished and protected, where broken relationships are restored, and where love is always at home, let us call out to the Lord:

That all who suffer in body, mind, or spirit might find comfort and healing and become sources of hope and healing for others, let us call out to the Lord:

That those who have died from war, senseless violence, accidents, disease, and old age might reach the banks of the river that flows by the throne of God to receive eternal love and to pray for our salvation, let us call out to the Lord:

◆ Concluding Prayer

Inspired by the rich history of our salvation and buoyed by the stories of our faith that tell of your unfailing love, we present these needs to you, O God, in full confidence that your love will never fail us, for we pray in Jesus's name who lives in glory with you and the Holy Spirit, for ever and ever.

The Reception of the Holy Oils
Blessed at the Chrism Mass

Introduction

1. It is appropriate that the oil of the sick, the oil of catechumens, and the holy chrism, which are blessed by the bishop during the Chrism Mass, be presented to and received by the local parish community.

2. The reception of the holy oils may take place at the Mass of the Lord's Supper on Holy Thursday or on another suitable day after the celebration of the Chrism Mass.

3. The oils should be reserved in a suitable repository in the sanctuary or near the baptismal font.

4. The oils, in suitable vessels, are carried in the procession of the gifts, before the bread and wine, by members of the assembly.

5. The oils are received by the priest and are then placed on a suitably prepared table in the sanctuary or in the repository where they will be reserved.

6. As each of the oils is presented, the following or other words may be used to explain the significance of the particular oil.

7. The people's response may be sung.

Presenter of the Oil of the Sick:

The oil of the sick.

Priest:

May the sick who are anointed with this oil experience the compassion of Christ and his saving love, in body, mind, and soul.

The people may respond:

Blessed be God for ever.

Presenter of the Oil of Catechumens:

The oil of catechumens.

Priest:

Through anointing with this oil may our catechumens who are preparing to receive the saving waters of baptism be strengthened by Christ to resist the power of Satan and reject evil in all its forms.

The people may respond:

Blessed be God for ever.

Presenter of the Holy Chrism:

The holy Chrism.

Priest:

Through anointing with this perfumed Chrism may children and adults, who are baptized and confirmed, and presbyters, who are ordained, experience the gracious gift of the Holy Spirit.

The people may respond:

Blessed be God for ever.

The bread and wine for the eucharist are then received and the Mass continues in the usual way.

April
Month of the Holy Eucharist

THU 17

Thursday of Holy Week (Holy Thursday) Evening Mass of the Lord's Supper

About the Triduum/Evening Mass of the Lord's Supper

This evening Lent ends and the Church enters the Sacred Paschal Triduum, gathering to pray, building toward the prolonged vigiling of Saturday night. This evening's celebration, the Mass of the Lord's Supper, is the threshold liturgy of the Triduum. It commemorates the institution of Eucharist and the priesthood, as well as Jesus's command of love and service. It should be the only parish Mass today, even if varied language groups make up the parish community. Another Mass is celebrated only with permission of the bishop, and it should not dissuade people from attending the principal Mass.

Preparing this liturgy and the others of the Triduum can be enormously stressful if not reviewed well in advance. Avoid scheduling rehearsals during Holy Week; conduct them instead during the last few weeks of Lent. While there should be one overall coordinator for the Triduum liturgies, it helps greatly to have people responsible for each ministry and willing to rehearse each group. Rehearsals calm anxiety and ministers will be able to identify the processional routes, the stations for the washing of the feet, musical cues for movement, the location of readings and petitions, as well as the placement of needed liturgical items.

It is interesting to note that the Missal gives a series of instructions for the whole Sacred Paschal Triduum; these are listed before the rubrics for Thursday of the Lord's Supper. Liturgy committees would do well to take note of these important instructions and reflect on how they can best be implemented in their parish celebrations.

First, the centrality of these days as the preeminent days for celebrating the Paschal Mystery is noted, since on these three days the Church solemnly celebrates "the greatest mysteries of our redemption, keeping by means of special celebrations the memorial of her Lord, crucified, buried, and risen" (rubric for Triduum, 1).

The Paschal fast is also mentioned. The fast is to be kept everywhere on the Friday of the Lord's Passion, but the Missal goes on to recommend that it be prolonged through Holy Saturday. Catechesis about this Paschal fast might be useful for parishioners, because its meaning differs from that of the Lenten fast. While the Lenten fast is centered on penance, conversion, and renewal, the Paschal fast is more focused on preparation and anticipation (in a sense, almost being too excited to eat!); it is a way of preparing to come, "with spirit uplifted, to the joys of the Lord's Resurrection" (rubric for Triduum, 1). The Paschal fast helps us to enter into *kairos*, the "time outside of time" that characterizes the continual anamnesis of the Three Days, which, in some sense, are actually one.

A second rubric cautions that a sufficient number of lay ministers is required in order to fittingly celebrate the Sacred Pashcal Triduum. Thus, what is true all year long must be especially in evidence during the Church's most sacred days, namely, that liturgical celebrations are diversified actions celebrated by the entire Body, and that a variety of ministers is needed, in proper number, so that the fullness of the Church's liturgical ministries may be in evidence. While "good enough is never good enough" is a maxim that should always apply to the Church's liturgical celebrations, the necessity of allowing the rites to be celebrated in all their fullness, which includes an adequate number of lay ministers, is heightened during these days.

In actuality, the point about lay ministers simply underscores the importance of the full, conscious, and active participation of the faithful during the celebrations, and this is the point that is highlighted next. The Missal points out that the "singing of the people, the ministers, and the Priest Celebrant has a special importance in the celebrations of these days, for when texts are sung, they have their proper impact" (rubric for Triduum, 2). Thus, the Missal is calling on communities to sing the rites during these days, and indeed these are the days to sing as many of the texts as possible—maybe even all of them! Furthermore, the full participation of the faithful is so important that the Missal makes a special reminder to pastors to catechize their people about the meaning and order of the celebrations. If we take this seriously, then we understand that catechesis about the Sacred Paschal Triduum through bulletin articles, preaching, workshop sessions, and adult education courses is as important a part of liturgical preparation as are the flow charts, gathering of props and sprucing up of the environment and the vestments.

A third notation specifies that the liturgies of the Sacred Paschal Triduum "are to be carried out in cathedral and parochial churches and only in those chose churches in which they can be performed with dignity, that is, with a good attendance of the faithful, an appropriate number of ministers, and the means to sing at least some of the parts" (rubric for Triduum, 3). For some, this might be a challenge to a radically new understanding of the rites. The liturgies of these days are not formalities or simple prayer experiences that can be performed perfunctorily just for the sake of giving people a nice experience; they are liturgies that are supposed to be powerful expressions of the very heart of what we believe and who we are. Thus, it is essential that these liturgies be celebrated with the dignity and fullness of expression that their nature demands. Small communities and other groupings of the faithful—small communities of religious, nursing homes or other institutions, schools, and even mission parishes may need to ask some very difficult questions about their ability to celebrate these liturgies properly, and perhaps consider joining with larger communities.

The Lectionary for Mass

◆ FIRST READING: Enslaved in Egypt, the Israelites receive instructions from the Lord for the first Passover, an event that was to be perpetually remembered in Israel's history. On this night, the Lord passed over the dwellings of the Israelites marked by the blood of the Lamb, thus sparing their lives. The firstborn of the Egyptians, both human and animal, perished. It is this event that finally changed Pharoah's mind and heart. He not only permitted the Israelites to leave, he sent them on their way (see Exodus 12:31–33). Their deliverance from slavery, their freedom, had begun.

◆ RESPONSORIAL PSALM 116 is a hymn that accompanied a thanksgiving sacrifice. The antiphon reminds us that our Eucharist is also a thanksgiving sacrifice and a sharing in what is offered in communion with the Lord.

◆ SECOND READING: This text is the earliest account of the institution of the Eucharist. Paul hands on the tradition that he has first received from the Church, the Body of Christ, concerning the meal Jesus shared with his disciples the night

he was handed over. This handing over was both his betrayal by Judas and the Jewish leaders having him tried by Pilate. These were but the means of his being handed over into the hands of his heavenly Father. Our Eucharist is a proclamation of his death, because through our participation in it, his mystery becomes our own. So must we do—and live—in his memory, until he comes.

◆ GOSPEL: John's account of the meal the night before Jesus died does not contain an Institution narrative (an account of Jesus's words over the bread and wine). Jesus's Eucharistic teaching is found in the Bread of Life discourse in chapter 6. Rather, John recounts Jesus washing the feet of his disciples—the job of a servant. We are commanded to do the same.

The Roman Missal

Before the Mass texts are given, the Missal lists special instructions that pertain to the celebration of the Evening Mass of the Lord's Supper, some of which are worth highlighting here. First to be noted is that the Mass is celebrated in the evening, "with the full participation of the whole local community and with all the Priests and ministers exercising their office" (Thursday of the Lord's Supper, rubric 1). Thus once again the importance of the community gathering as the one body with a variety of roles and ministries in evidence is affirmed; in fact, it is ancient tradition that all Masses without the participation of the people are forbidden on this day (see PS, 47). Another rubric mentions that flowers are permitted as decorations, but there should be moderation; we are not yet at Easter. This moderation applies to the place where the Blessed Sacrament will be reserved after Mass; *Paschale solemnitatis* specifies that that space must be conducive to prayer and meditation, and therefore demands sobriety, and abuses are to be suppressed

(see PS, 49). Nor is the place of reservation to be made to resemble a tomb, because the chapel of repose is not representing the Lord's burial; rather, it is for the custody of the Eucharistic bread that will be distributed in Communion on the next day (see PS, 55).

The Entrance Antiphon, taken from chapter 6, verse 14 of Paul's letter to the Galatians, sums up the mystery we are celebrating throughout the days of the Sacred Paschal Triduum. It's a mystery that can only be understood by living in its truth: "We should glory in the Cross of our Lord Jesus Christ." How is it possible to find glory in the midst of suffering and death? It's possible because through Christ's suffering and Death "we are saved and delivered." That's the mystery that is the heart of the Christian faith, the mystery that is celebrated in every liturgy, and the mystery that is the *raison d'être* of the Christian life—it is the Paschal Mystery that through Christ, with him, and in him, death becomes life and self-emptying leads to fullness.

The Gloria returns this evening, and it should be sung with joy and fullness; the Missal mentions that bells are rung. Outdoor bells should be rung in the carillon; bells inside the church may be rung by choir members, or altar servers and other ministers, perhaps even by members of the assembly. After this joyous ringing out of the glory of God, the bells are to remain silent until the Gloria of the Easter Vigil. To further highlight the seriousness and uniqueness of the days of the Triduum, a rubric notes that "during this same period [between the Gloria of the evening Mass on Holy Thursday and the Gloria at the Easter Vigil], the organ and other musical instruments may be used only so as to support the singing."

The Collect for this Mass draws our attention to this night's Eucharist being linked to the Last Supper, which is referred to in the Second Reading, with the meaning of the supper being clear: it is the meal Jesus "entrusted to the Church" as "the banquet of his love," "a sacrifice new for all eternity." The effects of participating in that sacrificial banquet are also made clear: we are to draw "from so great a mystery the fullness of charity and of life."

This evening is one of the rare occasions when the Missal specifies for the homilist the themes he is to touch on. The priest's Homily is to shed light on "the principal mysteries that are commemorated in this Mass, namely, the institution of the Holy Eucharist and of the priestly Order, and the commandment of the Lord concerning charity." As will be noted several times below, the connection between participation in the Eucharist and living a life of love cannot be overlooked, and that connection should be at the core of the meaning of this Mass. The institution of the ministerial priesthood is commemorated because of the close connection between priesthood and the Eucharist; it is the priest who acts in the person of Christ the Head (*in persona Christi capitis*) within the liturgical assembly and without whom the Eucharist cannot be celebrated. Notice, however, that there is nothing in the ritual for this evening about priests renewing their promises; the place for that is at the Chrism Mass and it has no place in this liturgy. It is something that is meant to be led by the bishop; there are no texts for it at the evening Mass, and it should not be added.

Sacrificial charity and sacrificial living are ritualized in the Washing of Feet, which, as the Missal notes, follows the Homily. Although technically optional, the ritual has such power that one might rightly question why a community would not celebrate it. The unique power of this startling gesture should be allowed to stand on its own and

should not be obscured by gimmicks or adaptations. Yes, it is uncomfortable, especially (and ironically) not for the one doing the footwashing, but for the one having his or her feet washed (it's not unusual for people to be shy and reticent about doing this); yes, it is countercultural; yes, it can be awkward. However, all three can also be said about Christian humility and sacrificial love. Resist the temptation to weaken the gesture by changing it to a washing of hands. Nor is there any foundation in the Missal for anyone other than the priest celebrant to wash feet; he functions as the sacramental image of Christ the Head at all other parts of the Eucharist, so why should there be the need to mute this representation during this rite, which is part of the Eucharist? True, all are called to wash one another's feet, that is, serve one another, but the same call to service (and unity) is true of every Eucharist, and the priest exercising his liturgical function alone at other times does not negate or lessen the assembly's participation in the mystery; the same is true here. Therefore, also to be avoided is diminishing the power of the gesture by having others, whether they be clergy or laity, join the priest celebrant in washing feet.

The rite is simple and straightforward. The Missal tells us: "The men who have been chosen are led by the ministers to seats prepared in a suitable place. Then the priest (removing his chasuble if necessary) goes to each one, and, with the help of the ministers, pours water over each one's feet and then dries them." Some comments are in order.

Although the Missal uses the word "men" for those who are chosen to have their feet washed, in fact in many United States parishes, women as well as men have their feet washed. The United States Conference of Catholic Bishops has a statement

about the meaning of the Washing of Feet, which would, at least as of this writing, still allow for the practice of including women (see http://www.usccb.org/prayer-and-worship/liturgical-resources/triduum/holy-thursday-mandatum.cfm). Also, no specific number is mentioned, and therefore it need not be limited to twelve. While twelve is a customary number, any number can be used, and the people chosen should adequately reflect the make-up of the community. People of all ages, including young children, may be asked to have their feet washed; people of different races and language groups may be included; at least one of the elect, preparing for initiation at this year's Easter Vigil, may be included.

Next, the only location mentioned is "a suitable place." Therefore, there is no need for this rite to take place exclusively in the sanctuary; in fact, there are several reasons that would argue against that practice. Certainly, the visibility of the rite would be an important factor. Having multiple stations throughout the church would allow for a maximum number of people to be up close to the action as it is taking place. (This is also one way of reinforcing what is true for all liturgy—that the liturgical action takes place in the entire worship space, not just in the sanctuary.) Additionally, there can be something very touching—part of the meaning of humble service—to have the priest celebrant move throughout the assembly, going to those before whom he will kneel, rather than having them come to him. However, the suitability of various locations must be carefully considered: how will chairs be placed and then removed in such a way that this action does not draw undue attention to itself? Will the priest be able to kneel easily enough, and will the necessary ministers have access to assist him? What about numbers of pitchers, basins, and towels—how will they be made available, taken away, and who will see to this? None of these details are insurmountable; they need only be thought through in advance so that specific needs can be prepared for and the action can be carried out smoothly, with a minimum of distraction.

Also of interest is the statement that the priest removes his chasuble if necessary; given the action to be performed, one would think it is necessary, for ease of movement. However, there is no mention of the priest tying a towel around his waist, which is nonetheless a custom that many priest celebrants do; the Gospel for the Mass mentions that Jesus did so before he washed the disciples' feet. The rubric goes on to mention that the priest goes to each person and, assisted by ministers, pours water over each one's feet and then dries them. The plural "feet" is used, which would seem to indicate that both feet of each person are to be washed, not just one. (Many priest celebrants have the custom of kissing the feet of the people as well, after washing them.)

While the rite should not be unduly prolonged, neither should it be hurried; the fact that several examples of antiphons are given in the Missal indicate this. The meaning of the rite is revealed in the antiphons: it is all about Jesus's example of love, humble service, and sharing in Jesus's life by following him.

After the washing of feet, the priest washes and dries his hands, puts the chasuble back on, and the Mass continues with the Universal Prayer as usual. The Creed is not said. After the Universal Prayer, Mass continues with the preparation of the altar and the presentation of the gifts.

Rarely does one find in the Missal a specific rubric about the procession with the gifts, but there is one given here: it is mentioned that gifts for the poor may be presented along with the bread and wine, with those gifts being carried in procession by the faithful. This harkens back to the ancient practice of the Church, where everyone brought something for the offering, and some of the offerings would be set aside for the poor. Such a procession would be a stark reminder of the practical charity that must be a consequence of our participation in the Eucharist—we cannot truly share bread at the Eucharistic table unless we are also sharing bread with the hungry outside the Eucharist. Perhaps these offerings on Holy Thursday can be an impetus for catechizing the faithful at other times about the offering of self that is the heart of our participation in the Eucharistic sacrifice. Certainly the sight of everyone processing forward to bring their gifts to the altar, with the gifts of bread and wine that will be transformed through the power of the Spirit being carried last, would be a powerful sign of the participation of all the faithful. The Missal's suggestion of the antiphon to be chanted, *Ubi caritas*, "Where true charity is dwelling, God is present there" highlights the unity of meaning between the footwashing, which was just completed, and the bringing forward of the offerings for the celebration of the Eucharist.

The Prayer over the Offerings offers a succinct summary of the very essence of liturgical theology: "whenever the memorial of this sacrifice is celebrated / the work of our redemption is accomplished" (one suspects that the homilist could well include this theme in his preaching). To the degree that we are aware of and appreciate what is taking place in our midst here and now (the work of our redemption), that is the degree to which we can be said to be participating worthily in the mysteries.

The Preface assigned for this Mass is Preface I of the Most Holy Eucharist, and the text, with musical notation, is given along with the other texts for this Mass; one could argue that this is revealing the Church's preference for the priest celebrant to chant the Preface (see comments above about singing during the Triduum). The text itself zeroes in on the core of Eucharistic theology. As it recalls Christ offering himself "as the saving Victim," it also notes how the Eucharist was instituted as the pattern of his sacrifice, and therefore the offering of the Eucharist is the memorial of his offering and sacrifice. Participation in the Eucharist means to join one's own offering with the self-offering of Christ that is made present through anamnesis. This is further emphasized as the Preface goes on to note, "As we eat his flesh that was sacrificed for us, we are made strong, and, as we drink his Blood that was poured out for us, we are washed clean."

The complete text for Eucharistic Prayer I, the Roman Canon, is given along with the other texts for this Mass. This allows for an easy use of the special inserts for the *Communicantes* ("In communion with those"), the *Hanc igitur* ("therefore, Lord, we pray"), and the *Qui pridie* ("On the day before he was to suffer"), which are used at this Mass. However, while it might be argued that, given these special inserts, there is a certain preference for using the Roman Canon, it is not required (as indicated by the rubric at number 17, "When the Roman Canon is used . . . "), and so Eucharistic Prayer III could also be used. (Prayer II because of its brevity would not be appropriate, and Eucharistic Prayer IV is disqualified because of its proper Preface.)

There is a special rubric concerning Holy Communion: after distribution, a ciborium with hosts for Communion tomorrow is left on the altar. The Prayer after Communion makes an eschatological reference as it asks that "just as we are renewed by the Supper of your Son in this present age, so we may enjoy his banquet for all eternity." This is the last prayer that will be proclaimed at this liturgy; the transfer of the Blessed Sacrament follows immediately.

The transfer of the Blessed Sacrament is rather simple and direct. After the Prayer after Communion, the Priest, after putting incense in the thurible, goes to the Blessed Sarament and incenses it three times. He puts on a white humeral veil, rises, takes the ciborium, and uses the ends of the humeral veil to cover it.

A procession is then formed, led by a minister with a cross, flanked by ministers with lighted candles; although the people are not mentioned, if the place of repose is in another location, the assembly will join the procession, following these ministers. Other ministers with lighted candles may follow the assembly, preceding the minister carrying the smoking thurible, who is directly in front of the priest carrying the Blessed Sacrament. During the procession, a suitable Eucharistic chant is sung; the Missal suggests *Pange, lingua*, excluding the last two verses (the *Tantum ergo*), and it might be argued there is a certain fondness for using this chant.

Upon reaching the place of repose, the priest places the ciborium in the tabernacle, but leaves the door open. Placing incense in the thurible, he incenses the Blessed Sacrament while kneeling and while the *Tantum ergo* or another Eucharistic chant is sung. After this, the tabernacle door is closed.

Next comes a period of adoration in silence (note that the door is to be closed before the period of adoration). After a period of silence,

the priest and ministers rise, genuflect, and then depart, but with no formal procession—this is simply a functional leaving of the ministers, not a ritual departure. Adoration by the faithful before the Blessed Sacrament continues, but the Missal notes that midnight is a demarcation point for adoration: "after midnight the adoration should take place without solemnity" (rubric 43). However, there is no requirement to continue adoration past midnight, but only "for a suitable length of time during the night." Thus, there is nothing to prevent a parish closing the period of adoration at midnight.

Notice that there is no formal or specific dismissal to this liturgy; thus, emphasizing that the liturgies of the Sacred Paschal Triduum are, in some sense, one continuous liturgy. After the liturgy, at an appropriate time, the altar is stripped and crosses are removed from the church, if they can be; if not, they should be veiled (number 57 of *Paschale solemnitatis* notes that the veil should be red or purple, unless they have already been veiled on the Saturday before the Fifth Sunday of Lent). This stripping is done without any ritual or solemnity.

The Missal makes a final note that if for some reason the Passion of the Lord is not celebrated in the same church on the next day, then Mass ends in the usual way, and the Blessed Sacrament is reserved in the tabernacle as usual, without any procession or adoration.

Pastoral Reflection

The act of washing another's feet does not make practical sense as it did in Jesus's time, but the symbolic act is extremely meaningful. Find a way to truly wash another's feet. If you can make this a physical action of asking to wash and then anoint, do so. If you need to make this spiritual, be present as a servant in total love to another for whom

you usually would not. A true calling of today's Gospel is for our lives to be nourished by the Body and Blood so we can *be* this to others in our words, deeds, and entire lives. Distractions take us away from the prayer we are called to be. Sit in silent prayer. Partake in Adoration this night. Bring a stranger with you and create a bond to call them your friend.

(#40)   red

F R I 18 Friday of the Passion of the Lord (Good Friday)

About Good Friday

On this day, the parish community gathers to prayerfully recall the Death of Jesus "in the hope of their resurrection" (Prayer over the People, Good Friday). Because his Resurrection is inseparable from his Death, the Lord's Passion is truly celebrated. We remember last night's words from St. Paul, "We should glory in the Cross of our Lord Jesus Christ, / in whom is our salvation, life and resurrection, / through whom we are saved and delivered."

A rubric in the Missal describes how the environment in the church expresses the somber mood of the day: the altar should be completely bare, without cross, candles, or cloths. The liturgy is to begin at 3:00 PM or later; a time before 3:00 PM is not envisioned. It is a liturgy consisting of three parts: the Liturgy of the Word; the Adoration of the Cross; and Holy Communion.

The liturgy may be repeated later with the permission of the diocesan bishop, and this is important. For people who work and/or who would otherwise be unable to attend the afternoon liturgy but who are looking to attend a service to mark the day, it would be preferable for them to be able to experience the liturgy of the Church. Certainly devotional celebrations such as Stations of the Cross can be scheduled on this day, but as much as possible we should be encouraging people to pray the official liturgies of the Church. Finally, there is a specific rubric mentioning that this liturgy "by its very nature" may not be celebrated in the absence of a priest; therefore, a deacon may not preside.

The Lectionary for Mass

◆ FIRST READING: The fourth suffering servant song is the picture of one spurned and rejected by others, accounted as nothing, reckoned as a criminal; one who is subjected to harsh treatment, even death. The realization of the true meaning of his life and ministry comes only gradually. Through the Servant's suffering, healing, wholeness, and forgiveness becomes a reality for all. In Jesus, all that is said of Isaiah's servant is brought to new levels of meaning.

◆ RESPONSORIAL PSALM 31: The antiphon is from Luke, the words Jesus utters as he dies. The Psalm tells of the great suffering of the psalmist and expresses great confidence. He entrusts his life to the Lord.

◆ SECOND READING: Jesus struggled, was tempted, suffered, and cried out in anguish to God just as we do. Paradoxically, the God who was able to save him from death did so—not by preventing his Crucifixion, but through it and after it, raising him up in glory to become the source of eternal salvation.

◆ GOSPEL: Jesus has full knowledge of who he is, where he is from, and how he will return there. With a play on words in the Greek, the evangelist portrays Jesus lifted up on the Cross as the moment of his exaltation and glory. In death, Jesus finishes the work he was given by the Father and breathes out his Spirit. The Church is born through the blood and water that poured forth from his side.

The Roman Missal

Just as last night's liturgy had no formal ending, so today's has no formal beginning—one liturgy flows into the next in the unity of these days. Wearing red Mass vestments, the priest and deacon simply go to the altar in silence and, after reverencing it, prostrate themselves; all others in the assembly kneel. Then, after a period of silence, the priest rises and goes to the chair. He should take care to make sure that the period of silence is noticeable. It has been said that true silence begins only when the shuffling, rustling, and other noises end, and so the priest should allow for a prolonged period of true silence on this particular day.

At the chair, the priest prays the prayer. This prayer is not a Collect, and the invitation "Let us pray" is omitted, further showing both the stark nature of this liturgy and the way this liturgy flows from the previous one. The priest has a choice from among two prayers. The first option asks God to remember his mercies and to protect his servants, because they are the ones for whom Christ shed his blood and established the Paschal Mystery. The overt use of the phrase "Paschal Mystery" is striking, and it reminds us of the total mystery we are celebrating through the Sacred Paschal Triduum. The second option asks that just as we have borne "the image of the man of earth" that is, Adam, so too, "by the sanctification of grace," may we "bear the image of the Man of heaven." Bearing the image of Christ is possible because by his Passion he "abolished the death inherited from ancient sin."

The Liturgy of the Word takes place, with the Lord's Passion read in the same way as it was read on Palm Sunday of the Lord's Passion. After the reading of the Passion, a brief Homily is preached; the rubric goes on to mention that at the end of the Homily "the faithful may be invited to spend a short time in prayer" (rubric 10). Certainly this day above all others calls for noticeable periods of silence.

The Solemn Intercessions follow. A deacon or lay minister sings or says the invitation while standing at the ambo. Then all pray in silence for a while, followed by the priest saying or singing the prayer with his hands extended. A rubric mentions that it is traditional for all to kneel for silent prayer after each invitation to prayer, as the deacon may add, "Let us kneel" and "Let us stand." While technically optional, one could argue a certain preference for following this tradition on this day: it highlights the solemnity of the intercessions, and the unusual gesture serves to further mark off the rites of the Sacred Paschal Triduum as rites that occur only once a year to mark our central and holiest days. A key element, however, would be to make sure the people are left to kneel silently for a long enough period of time, lest the kneeling and standing become simply a distracting (and perhaps unintentionally comical) series of down-and-up, down-and-up movements.

There are ten intercessions provided by the Missal: for the Holy Church; for the pope; for all orders and degrees of the faithful; for catechumens; for the unity of Christians; for the Jewish people; for those who do not believe in Christ; for those who do not believe in God; for those in public office; and for those in tribulation. The titles reveal the universality of these prayers as the Church expresses her concern and intercedes for the whole world. It is significant that on one of her most solemn days, the Church spends so much time pleading for the well-being of the entire world.

Following the Solemn Intercessions, which conclude the Liturgy of the Word, comes the second part of the liturgy, the Adoration of the

Holy Cross. The Holy Cross is first shown, and then it is adored; there are two forms for the showing, and there are two ways that the adoration may take place.

In the first form of the showing, the deacon, accompanied by one or more ministers, goes to the sacristy and then returns in procession, accompanied by two ministers carrying lighted candles, carrying the Cross, which is covered with a violet veil, through the church to the middle of the sanctuary. There the priest receives the cross and, after uncovering a little of its upper part, elevates it while singing the "Behold the wood of the Cross . . . ." After responding, "Come, let us adore," the people kneel and adore the cross in silence for a brief period while the priest stands and holds the cross up. Then the priest uncovers the right arm of the cross, again raising it, and then singing "Behold the wood of the Cross . . . " and the rest taking place as the first time. Lastly, he uncovers the cross completely and the same sequence of events occurs. In the second form of showing, the priest or the deacon, accompanied by one or more ministers, goes to the door of the church and takes up the unveiled cross as the ministers take up lighted candles. Then, in procession, they move through the church to the sanctuary, stopping in three locations—just inside the entrance to the church, in the middle of the church, and in front of the entrance to the sanctuary— at which times the priest or deacon elevates the cross, sings "Behold the wood of the Cross" with all responding "Come, let us adore." A rubric states that also in this second form the people are to kneel and adore the cross in silence for a brief moment, as in the first form.

For the Adoration of the Cross, one option is to have the priest or deacon, after carrying in the cross, hand over the cross to ministers to hold at the entrance to the sanctuary, or at some other suitable place, with candles placed to the right and left of the cross. At that location, the priest celebrant, possibly with chasuble and shoes removed, approaches the cross, followed by the clergy, lay ministers, and the faithful, all coming in procession. The sign of reverence to the cross can be varied: a simple genuflection, a kiss, or some other meaningful gesture. Consider inviting everyone to remove their shoes before approaching the cross; there is nothing that forbids this, and the strangeness of this gesture not only reinforces the uniqueness of the days of the Triduum, but also makes a statement about the holiness of the ground we walk in adoring the instrument of our salvation.

It is clearly stated that only one cross should be used for adoration, so parishes should avoid using multiple crosses. When the assembly is so large that approaching individually is not feasible, a second option is given for the adoration. (It should be noted, however, that several people can approach the cross and venerate it at the same time, to accommodate a larger number of participants. There is no need to rush this part of the liturgy, and the music that is suggested [see below] would seem to indicate that more than just a brief time should be accorded to the adoration.) In this second option, the priest, "after some of the clergy and faithful have adored" (the Missal does not specify who these "some" are) takes the cross and invites the people in a few words (of his own choosing—no text is given) to adore the Holy Cross, after which he holds the cross high for a brief time while the faithful adore it in silence. The Missal suggests and gives the texts for an antiphon, the Reproaches, and/or the hymn *Crux fidelis* to be sung during the adoration; other suitable songs may be used as well, and a rubric mentions the *Stabat Mater* as another possibility, in addition to some other "suitable chant in memory of the compassion of the Blessed Virgin Mary."

When the adoration is finished, the cross is carried to its place at the altar, where it stands with lighted candles, which are placed either around the altar, on it, or near the cross. The third part of the liturgy, Holy Communion, now begins with the altar being prepared with a cloth, a corporal, and the Missal being placed on it. While this is being done, the deacon, or, in his absence, the priest, wearing a humeral veil, brings the Blessed Sacrament from the place of repose to the altar while the assembly stands in silence. The Missal specifically notes that the deacon or priest uses "a shorter route," indicating that this is not in any way to be an elaborate procession; it is simply more of a functional bringing the Blessed Sacrament to the altar for Holy Communion, although appropriate marks of honor for the Real Presence are nonetheless used—the humeral veil, and two ministers with lighted candles accompanying the Blessed Sacrament. As the Blessed Sacrament is placed on the altar, candlesticks are placed on or around the altar.

If the deacon brought the Blessed Sacrament to the altar, the priest goes to the altar once the ciborium is uncovered, and he genuflects upon arriving there. He then introduces the Lord's Prayer, which is prayed with its embolism and doxology, followed by a private prayer of the priest, his genuflection, and then the "Behold the Lamb of God . . . " with the response, "Lord, I am not worthy . . . ." Communion is then distributed, during which Psalm 22 or another appropriate song may be sung.

When the distribution of Holy Communion is completed, the Blessed Sacrament is taken by the deacon or another minister to a place prepared outside the church. Of note here is that there seems to be a preference for the priest not to do this; if a deacon is not present, then perhaps another minister would be a more appropriate choice. No mention is made of candles accompanying the Blessed Sacrament, so this too is a simple action of returning the sacrament to its place of repose, and is in no way a procession or movement with a great deal of solemnity; this is in keeping with the tone of the day. If required, the Blessed Sacrament may be placed in the tabernacle, although it would appear the preference is to use a place outside the church.

The liturgy ends as starkly as it began. After the Blessed Sacrament has been removed, the priest prays the Prayer after Communion. Then follows a simple dismissal: the deacon or priest invites the people to bow down for the blessing, the priest extends his hands over the people and prays the prayer; and then they simply depart after genuflecting to the cross. There is no procession by the ministers or the faithful; it is a simple dispersing.

After the liturgy, the altar is stripped, but the cross remains with two or four candlesticks; people should be encouraged to pray before the cross.

Pastoral Reflection

Jesus said: "shall I not drink the cup that the Father gave me?" (John 18:11). Aware of all to come, he did not waiver. Our lives are messy and strength is needed to claim our identity, be strong in it, and walk with God. In the days to come, seek Eucharist under both forms whenever possible. It is the cup of salvation, the Blood poured out, the life sustenance in each of us, which allows us to fully live. In everything you do, don't take the simple for granted—for all is a gift from our hearing to the family members gifted to us.

violet

S·A·T 19 Holy Saturday Morning and Afternoon

About Holy Saturday

Christ was in the tomb; he lay in darkness in the womb of the whole world. Holy Saturday commemorates that day and has a character all its own. It is a quiet day of meditation, reflection, and anticipation, especially for the elect preparing for Baptism. Although there is much to do, don't let it just be a day for decorating the church. During the day, invite people to pray Morning Prayer and vigil in front of the crucifix in the barren church.

There is no Mass during the day, and Holy Communion may be given before the Vigil only as *Viaticum*. Reconciliation and Anointing of the Sick may be celebrated today. Ministers to the sick should make every effort to visit the sick during Good Friday and Holy Saturday, sharing with them some of the readings and bringing the prayers of the community. During the day today we continue the Paschal fast. The elect should be fasting in preparation for their Baptism, and the faithful may join them in solidarity of spirit. This recommendation dates back to about the year 100, where it appeared in *The Didache*. Linked to the past, we continue this discipline in a prayerful spirit. The climax of the Sacred Pashcal Triduum, the Easter Vigil, begins after darkness has fallen, officially forty-five minutes after dark. You can find the exact time for the setting of the sun in your area by consulting http://aa.usno.navy.mil/data/docs /RS_OneYear.php. The Easter Vigil launches us into Easter Time, and it should not be confused with Holy Saturday itself.

The RCIA

The community may gather for Morning Prayer with the elect as they begin their Preparation Rites

(see RCIA, 185–205). A combined Office of Readings and Morning Prayer may take place as it did on Good Friday. If the group is small, gather around the crucifix to pray with a few lit candles. Nothing else is needed. Although the community may gather for prayer at midday or evening, many will use this time to make preparations for the Easter Vigil. The combined Office of Readings and Morning Prayer will give those who gather the opportunity to hear the remarkable Patristic Homily assigned for today, whose author is unknown. "Something strange is happening—there is a great silence on earth today, a great silence and stillness. The whole earth keeps silence because the King is asleep." It depicts Christ's triumphant descent into Sheol (or hell), his meeting with our first parents, and the beginning of the great victory procession by which the souls of the just are liberated by the conquering savior, King Jesus. One imagines, as many icons have depicted, Jesus pulling Adam and Abraham and many others by the hand, leading them out to the consternation of the disbelieving devils. This is what we profess in the Apostles' Creed when we say, "He descended to the dead." In place of the Responsory, the Triduum antiphon from Philippians, "Christ became obedient," is chanted in its fullness. Evening Prayer may be celebrated by the community, on its own, or in conjunction with the Preparation Rites (see below). This is the only Saturday of the liturgical year with its own Evening Prayer. Because the Vigil is to take place at night, some communities may actually start it in the early hours of Sunday morning. This is completely permissible, as long as the liturgy ends before dawn. Especially in those cases, a Saturday Evening Prayer will be welcome.

RCIA, 185 notes that this is a day of prayer, fasting, and reflection for the elect to be initiated at tonight's Vigil. It is preferable that there be no rehearsals for the rites today. Godparents and others should have attended a rehearsal prior to the Triduum so that they can be of assistance to the elect at the evening liturgy. Be sure to conduct the Preparation Rites early in the day. They form an important prelude to Baptism and date back to the early days of the Church. During Lent, the elect received the Creed, *traditio*, from the community of faith and, having meditated on it, commit it to memory. Today they recite the Creed, *reditio*, returning it back to the faithful, demonstrating their readiness for the questions they will hear tonight: "Do you renounce?" "Do you believe?" If you have not yet presented the Lord's Prayer to the elect, you may do so during the Preparation Rites. Augustine testified to this practice at the turn of the fifth century. In the normal course of events, the Presentation of the Lord's Prayer takes place during the Fifth Week of Lent. But if you have too many Lenten evenings committed, moving this presentation to this morning's liturgy is a good option.

If you exercise the option to present the Lord's Prayer today as part of the Preparation Rites, the Gospel for that rite is probably the best one to use. The *Ephphetha* (signing of the senses) and the return of the Creed each recommend Gospel texts also, but hearing three Gospel stories in the same ceremony this morning would be too much. The Presentation of the Lord's Prayer happens in the actual proclamation of the Gospel, so that text should probably take precedence over the others. If infants will be baptized at the Vigil, the *Rite of Baptism for Children* (see RBC, 28) calls for Preparation Rites for them as well. This should involve receiving them at the door, exorcism, and anointing.

The Roman Missal says that adults are anointed with the oil of catechumens during the Vigil if they were not anointed earlier in the day at the Preparation Rites. The *editio typica* (Latin text) of the *Rite of Christian Initiation of Adults* includes this anointing during the Preparation Rites of Holy Saturday, but permits Conferences of Bishops to choose other times for it. The United States edition of the RCIA does not include the anointing during the Preparation Rites at all, but places it during the earlier period of the catechumenate (see RCIA, 98–103). Furthermore, the *National Statutes for the Catechumenate for the United States of America* says, "The rite of anointing with the oil of catechumens is to be omitted in the baptism of adults at the Easter Vigil" (NSC, 16). The best solution would be to ensure that the catechumens are anointed at least once sometime during the period of the catechumenate. That way they need not be anointed with the oil of catechumens on Holy Saturday.

A service combining the reception of infants with preparation of the elect is possible, uniting in one assembly the prayers and expectations of the elect, the parents, the godparents, and the catechists. The format could go as follows, with possible rites listed in RCIA, 185.2, and readings at RCIA, 179–180, 194, 198:

- Gathering hymn, with entire assembly at the entrance
- Reception of infants (*Rite of Baptism for Children* [RBC, 35–41]), the naming and signing of the child
- Procession of all to seating near ambo; refrain or hymn sung by all
- Readings related to Preparation Rites. If you are presenting the Lord's Prayer, choose the texts at RCIA, 179–180. If not, choose a Gospel reading from RCIA, 194 or 198. The Lectionary does not include the selection of readings for the Preparation Rites. You may use its index to find the readings elsewhere in the four-volume set.

- Homily
- Preparation Rites for infants: exorcism (RBC, 49), anointing with oil of catechumens (RBC, 50). If for some reason the adults have not yet been anointed, this would be a good time to do it.
- One or more of the Preparation Rites for adults and children of catechetical age: The *Ephphetha* (RCIA, 199) would come first, then the recitation of the Creed (RCIA, 195).
- Choosing a baptismal name is not celebrated in the United States of America. However, there may be an explanation of the given name of each of the elect. Sometimes, this makes an interesting exercise at this point. Why do the elect have the names they have? You might ask each of them to tell the gathered assembly the story of how their parents chose their name. The priest celebrant might help them reconnect with the values and hopes parents expressed at the time of their birth.
- Prayers of blessing (RCIA, 204)
- Dismissal (RCIA, 205): Note that in the *Rite of Christian Initiation of Adults* the *Ephphetha* appears after the recitation of the Creed, but if both are included in the Preparation Rites, the *Ephphetha* comes first. Some communities invite children today to color eggs, hear and dramatize the Scriptures from the Vigil, and to assist in preparing the worship space. Their participation in the Preparation Rites will be important, especially if there are children of catechetical age in this year's group.

(#41) white

Holy Saturday
Easter Sunday of the Resurrection of the Lord: The Easter Vigil in the Holy Night

S A T **19**

About the Easter Vigil

Shattering the darkness, the great Paschal candle is lit with the Easter fire, five wax nails of incense are imbedded, and it becomes the symbol of the crucified Christ. The Paschal Mystery, already celebrated in various ways since the Evening Mass of the Lord's Supper, is clearly and joyfully announced from the very beginning of the Vigil liturgy. It is in the light of the Paschal candle that the liturgy continues to unfold. The Easter Vigil is the most beautiful of all liturgies. Ranking highest among the celebrations of the liturgical year, it should rank highest in the spiritual life of the parish community, not a small task in places where Christmas is considered the high point. Encourage all parishioners to take part by offering good, solid catechesis and invitations in advance. If the community has been involved in the journey of the catechumens, they will want to be present and surround them for this celebration.

The four parts of the Easter Vigil move us through a gradual unfolding of the Paschal Mystery of Christ. The great fire immediately dispels the gathering gloom. The Liturgy of the Word reveals the path of God's plan throughout salvation history. The Liturgy of Baptism draws the elect through the baptismal waters into the promise of eternal life and renews the baptismal belief of the faithful. The Liturgy of the Eucharist brings the celebration to the climax of the banquet of the Lamb, as we experience the presence of the Risen Christ in our midst.

The Lectionary for Mass

◆ First Reading: The story of our salvation begins at the beginning of time, when God created the beautiful world in which we live, a world filled with life and light. Humankind, created in God's own image and likeness, is the summit of creation.

◆ Responsorial Psalm: There are two options for the Responsorial Psalm. Psalm 104 echoes the creative activity of God heard in the First Reading. In our antiphon, we pray for renewal in God's spirit. Psalm 33 proclaims the earth full of the goodness of the Lord, who

looked on all that he had made and found it good.

◆ Second Reading: Abraham was called by God to be the father of his chosen people. The fulfilment of God's promises rested on Abraham's son Isaac. God's request in today's reading is unexpected and makes no sense: he asks Abraham to sacrifice his beloved and only son. Who cannot but be astounded by Abraham's obedience and total trust in the Lord? It was rewarded not only by the preservation of Isaac's life but by the promised blessing of countless descendants.

◆ Responsorial Psalm 16: Abraham reckoned God as his total inheritance. Note the themes of trust, of deliverance from death, and of life in the stanzas of the psalm.

◆ Third Reading: The Exodus was the event that formed Israel as a nation and prepared Israel to enter into covenant relationship with God. Having been passed over by the angel of death, they now pass through the waters of the sea into freedom. The Egyptians, however, are destroyed in these same waters.

◆ Canticle: Our response is the hymn sung by Moses, Miriam, and all the people in joyful praise of the God who saved them.

◆ Fourth Reading: Throughout Scripture, the covenant relationship between God and Israel is imaged as a marriage relationship. This text from Isaiah is a case in point. Stemming from the time of the Babylonian Exile, a period in history understood as punishment for Israel's infidelities, the Lord reaffirms his love for Israel and his fidelity to the covenant. There is promise of reestablishment.

◆ Responsorial Psalm 30 celebrates God's deliverance of his people. The return from exile was seen by the prophets as a second exodus.

Note the themes of deliverance, new life, and joy.

◆ Fifth Reading: This text is likewise set in the time of the exile, inviting Israel to return to the Lord and to drink abundantly of his wisdom and teaching, for in it we find life.

◆ Canticle: Isaiah joyfully extolls God our Savior and the water of salvation he provides.

◆ Sixth Reading: Still we are in the context of the exile, again viewed as punishment for infidelity. Baruch calls Israel to learn the ways and wisdom of God, as manifest in the Law.

◆ Responsorial Psalm 19 extols the law of the Lord, a priceless treasure. Our antiphon acclaims the words of the Lord as words of everlasting life.

◆ Seventh Reading: The words of the prophet promise an end to the exile. God will gather Israel from all the lands into which they were scattered as a result of their infidelities. Note that the restoration is not something Israel deserved, but rather God will act for the sake of his holy name. He will purify his people and give them a new heart and a new spirit.

◆ Responsorial Psalm 42 (option 1): Three options are given for the psalm. The first, used when Baptisms are celebrated, focuses on the pilgrim's longing to enter into God's dwelling place (the temple). The antiphon compares this longing to that of a deer for running water, an image that clearly evokes Baptism.

◆ Canticle (option 2): The second option, from Isaiah 12, is also the response to the Fifth Reading. Again, the antiphon's mention of water points to Baptism.

◆ Responsorial Psalm (option 3): The third option, Psalm 51, is a penitential Psalm. The antiphon's plea for a clean heart echoes the words of Ezekiel in the Seventh Reading.

◆ Epistle: In this beautiful passage, Paul speaks of our Baptism as an immersion into the waters of Christ's death that we might be raised up into a new life. The tomb has become the womb of eternal life. The challenge for us is to live for God now in the life that is ours in Christ.

◆ Responsorial Psalm/Gospel Acclamation: After withholding Alleluias for forty days, we joyfully sing once again "Alleluia, alleluia, alleluia." We give thanks to God for the marvellous act of raising Christ from the dead and exalting him in glory. Though he is rejected by those who handed him over to death, he is now the foundation stone of our faith. The verses are from Psalm 118.

◆ Gospel: The Resurrection of Jesus, like his death, was an "earth-shaking" event for Matthew the evangelist (see 28:2; 27:51, 54). In Jewish literature of the time, an earthquake signalled the inauguration of the end time. Matthew associates the earthquake with the angel from heaven who opens the tomb when Mary Magdalene and her companion Mary arrive there in the morning after the Sabbath. (Notice that the guards at the tomb see the angel as well as the women but with quite different reactions!) The women are commissioned by the heavenly visitor to announce the Resurrection of Jesus to his disciples. Their obedient response is immediate—and it is while they are in the process of carrying it out that the Risen Jesus himself meets them and commissions them further. May we be as they this Easter morning, met by the Risen Jesus, commissioned with a word for our brothers and sisters, and obediently carrying it out.

The Roman Missal

The Missal gives several introductory and explanatory rubrics for the celebration of the Easter Vigil. Some comments about them are noted here.

This night's Vigil is explicitly described as "the greatest and most noble of all solemnities." The importance and grandeur of this evening celebration cannot be emphasized too strongly, and parishes must resist any temptation to abbreviate the rites or to enact them in a perfunctory way. Feeble excuses such as "it's too long for the people" are in fact insulting to the people of God—their spiritual wherewithal when the rites are done in all their fullness is quite hearty; let's not shortchange the people of God on "this most sacred night."

It is to take place "during the night, so that it begins after nightfall and ends before daybreak on the Sunday. This is an absolutely crucial and non-negotiable point, as strongly stated by PS, 78: "This rule is to be taken according to its strictest sense. Reprehensible are those abuses and practices that have crept into many places in violation of this ruling whereby the Easter Vigil is celebrated at the time of day that it is customary to celebrate anticipated Sunday Masses." The starting time, then, is to be after nightfall: thus, depending on the date of Easter and in what part of the country you live, the time will vary.

The Easter Vigil is made up of four parts: the Solemn Beginning of the Vigil or Lucernarium; the Liturgy of the Word; the Baptismal Liturgy; and the Liturgy of the Eucharist.

First Part: The Solemn Beginning of the Vigil or Lucernarium

The Vigil begins with the church in darkness. The Missal states that "a blazing fire is prepared in a suitable place outside the church," and that the people gather around the fire.

The intent is clear that this is to be a bonfire, more than just a few small flames flickering from a table-top hibachi. As a later rubric describes, the blessing of fire may be adapted if difficulties arise constructing a bonfire. In such cases, the people may gather in the church as usual and at the door of the church the rites of blessing the fire and preparing the candle take place.

The liturgy begins with the Sign of the Cross and the priest offering a greeting to the people "in the usual way"—presumably, using one of the liturgical greetings for Mass; unlike the Good Friday liturgy, the Easter Vigil is a Mass. The priest then instructs the people about the meaning of this night, "in which our Lord Jesus Christ / passed over from death to life," and that we keep this memorial in "the sure hope / of sharing his triumph over death / and living with him in God." The instruction may be given using the exact words in the Missal or similar words of the priest's own choosing.

The priest then blesses the fire, after which the candle is prepared. The rubric simply states that one of the ministers brings the Paschal candle to the priest; while therefore any minister may do this, perhaps it is fitting, if a deacon is carrying the candle into the church, for him to be the one to do this, in a sense taking custody of the candle. The lines of the cross, the alpha and omega, and the numerals of the current year are cut into the candle; this preparation of the candle is not optional. Thus the rite presumes that a real candle that is actually prepared in this way is used; *Paschale solemnitatis* clearly states that it "must be made of wax, never be artificial, be renewed each year, be only one in number, and be of sufficiently large size so that it may evoke the truth that Christ is the light of the world" (PS, 82). Plastic tubes that hold oil canisters and have permanent symbols, where only the last numeral changes from year to year, should be avoided at all costs!

After the cutting of the cross and other signs have been made on the candle, five grains of incense may be inserted in the form of a cross, with the accompanying words. This part is optional.

Next the priest lights the Paschal candle from the new fire with the accompanying words sung or said. A little careful preparation and rehearsal will ensure that all goes smoothly at the beginning of the Vigil; it can become rather awkward managing the various items needed and matching the gestures to the words, and making sure all the necessary things are handy, so think this through ahead of time.

Once the candle has been lit, the procession forms. Ministers take burning coals from the fire and place them in the thurible, and the priest puts incense into the thurible in the usual way. A deacon, if present (otherwise, any other suitable minister), carries the candle. The order of procession is: thurifer with the smoking thurible; then the deacon or other minister with the candle; then the priest with other ministers, and then the people, all carrying unlit candles. Note that the priest precedes the people, and that candles are not yet lit.

The same three stations as used for carrying in the cross on Good Friday are used again: the door of the church, the middle of the church, and in front of the altar. At each station the candle is lifted high and "The Light of Christ" is sung, with the peoples' response. Only the priest's candle is lit after the first "Light of Christ" and its response; then, after the second, the people's candles are lit; after the third, the Paschal candle is placed in its stand that is located next to the ambo or in the middle of the sanctuary.

The Missal is clear that it is at this time that the lights go on in the church, although the altar can-

dles are not yet lit. Although there has arisen the custom of not turning the church lights on until later, usually during the Gloria, it is clear that the rubrics do not call for this. The powerful symbol of the light of the Paschal candle is being emphasized in that once it is brought into church, its brightness completely illumines everything.

With the Paschal candle in its stand, the priest goes to his chair, and after handing his candle to a minister so his hands are free, he puts incense in the thurible and blesses the incense as at Mass. The deacon asks for and receives the blessing from the priest in preparation for singing the Easter Proclamation (*Exsultet*). The blessing is the same one given before the Gospel at Mass, except that the words "paschal praise" are used instead of the word "Gospel." After receiving the blessing, the deacon incenses the book and the candle, and then proclaims the Easter Proclamation at the ambo or at some other lectern; the assembly remains standing and holds lighted candles. The choice as to whether to use the ambo or some other lectern can be made based on the arrangement of your church; presumably, if the ambo were some significant distance from the Paschal candle, it might be advantageous to use a lectern that is right next to the candle.

It is possible for someone other than the deacon to sing the *Exsultet*, with the Missal specifically mentioning the priest celebrant or a concelebrating priest, although a lay cantor is another possibility. One presumes the decision will be made according to which person will be able to proclaim such an important piece best. Note the omission of certain lines in the case of a layperson singing the Proclamation. Immediately after the Proclamation, all extinguish their candles.

Second Part: The Liturgy of the Word

This Vigil is referred to as "the mother of all Vigils," and so nine readings are provided, seven from the Old Testament and two from the New, an Epistle, and a Gospel reading. Considering the importance of this liturgy, all nine readings should be considered, "so that the character of the Vigil, which demands an extended period of time, may be preserved." Liturgy committees and preparers, and indeed all parishioners, should understand that the Solemn Easter Vigil is not just another Mass, nor is it even just "a long Mass;" it is a Vigil, and a Vigil takes time. It is part of the experience of "time outside of time," the sacred time of the Triduum that was begun on Holy Thursday night and is reaching its climax this night. Any attempts to truncate or abbreviate the experience should be avoided. The Missal is clear that using all nine readings is the norm and is preferred. Nonetheless, the Missal does admit of the possibility of reducing the number of readings "where more serious pastoral circumstances demand it." One might take special note of the deliberate use of the word "serious," which is weightier than just preference, impatience or, as noted above, a misguided sense that the people cannot handle it. In the case of a shortened Liturgy of the Word, at least three readings should be read from the Old Testament, both from the Law and the Prophets, and the accompanying Responsorial Psalms should be used; additionally, the reading of chapter 14 of Exodus and its canticle is always to be used—it cannot be omitted.

The priest gives an instruction, using the words of the Missal or his own words, to invite the people to listen to the Word of God "with quiet hearts" and reminding them to meditate on how God has saved his people throughout history and especially by sending his Son as Redeemer.

The Missal gives prayers to follow each of the Scripture readings; in some cases, the priest has a choice between two prayers.

After the last Old Testament reading followed by its Responsorial Psalm and prayer, the altar candles are lit and the priest intones the Gloria. Since the Missal gives the notation for the priest to sing, there would seem to be indicated a preference that the priest do this. After he intones the Gloria, the assembly then takes up the hymn. Bells are rung during the hymn, but no further specification of this given; it simply says "according to local custom," so this can be left open to the creativity of the parish—perhaps the choir rings bells, or servers, or even members of the assembly who have brought their own, or any combination or all of these! When the Gloria is concluded, the priest prays the Collect.

After the Collect, the Epistle is proclaimed. After the Epistle, all rise and the priest solemnly intones the triple Alleluia, with the Missal specifically noting that he raises the tone by a step each time, and all repeat after him. However, if the priest is not capable of singing this properly, it is possible for a cantor to do so. Incense is placed in the thurible as usual, and the deacon receives the blessing as usual. Only incense is carried in procession with the *Book of Gospels*; the Missal explicitly states that candles are not used. Finally, there is a rubric stating that the Homily is not to be omitted. The importance of preaching on this holiest of nights is underscored by this rubric.

Third Part: Baptismal Liturgy

The Baptismal Liturgy begins after the Homily. The rites take place at the baptismal font, so the priest goes there with the ministers, unless there is to be a procession to the font (see below). If, however, the font is in a location where it cannot be easily seen by the faithful, then a vessel with water is placed in the sanctuary. Notice the importance given to the participation of the entire assembly—it is crucial that they be able to see what is going on. This is in keeping with the main thrust of the renewal of the liturgy.

Next, the elect are called forward and presented by their godparents or, in the case of small children, are carried by their parents and godparents. It is admittedly odd that the Missal refers to them as catechumens when, in fact, the terminology used in the *Rite of Christian Initiation of Adults* refers to them as the elect. The Missal does not give any specific texts for this calling forward and presentation.

If there is to be a procession to the baptistery or to the font, it begins now, and the order of procession is clearly noted: a minister with the Paschal candle leads the procession, followed by those to be baptized and their godparents, then other ministers, the deacon, and lastly the priest. (Thus, if there is to be a procession to the font, the priest and the ministers do not immediately go there.) The Litany of the Saints, given in the Missal, is sung during the procession. Names of some saints may be added, especially the saint for whom the parish is named, and other patron saints, for example, of those to be baptized. Also, if there are candidates to be baptized, the priest adds a prayer at the end of the litany.

If there is no procession to the font, the priest addresses the assembly using the words given in the Missal, or words similar to them. The Missal provides a text not only for the case when Baptisms are to take place, but also for the case if no one is to be baptized, yet the font is still to be blessed.

There is a third possibility: that no one is to be baptized, and that no font is to be blessed. In that instance, there is no Litany of the Saints, and the Blessing of Water takes place at once (see below).

After all have arrived at the font and the Litany ends, the priest blesses the baptismal water, with has hands extended during the prayer. The Missal gives the text of the prayer first with musical notation and then without, indicating a certain preference for singing the prayer. The prayer includes the gesture of lowering the Paschal candle into the water either once or three times and then holding the candle in the water for the remainder of the prayer, with an acclamation sung (or said) by the assembly as the candle is lifted out of the water. If no one is to be baptized and if the font is not to be blessed, there is a completely different introduction and blessing prayer for the priest to use.

When Baptisms are to take place, they take place immediately after the blessing of the baptismal water and the acclamation of the people. The Missal first directs the priest to the appropriate ritual (that is, either the *Rite of Christian Initiation of Adults* or *Rite of Baptism for Children*), for the prescribed questions and answers concerning the renunciation of sin. There is also a mention that if the anointing of adults with the oil of catechumens has not already taken place at some point before this (that is, as part of any earlier preparatory rites), then it is to occur now. This, however, conflicts with the *Rite of Christian Initiation of Adults*, 33.7, which states that in the United States, "the anointing with the oil of catechumens is reserved for use in the period of the catechumenate and in the period of purification and enlightenment and is not to be included in the preparation rites on Holy

Saturday or in the celebration of initiation at the Easter Vigil or at another time." As of this writing, this point would seem to be in need of clarification.

Next the priest questions the adults, and the parents, and godparents of children about the faith, again as indicated in the respective rites. Interestingly, the Missal admits of an option that, should the number of those to be baptized be very large, the priest may, immediately after the response of those to be baptized and the parents and godparents of children, also ask for and receive the renewal of baptismal promises of the entire assembly. Presumably, this option is offered as a way of not unduly prolonging the ritual when the numbers are large.

After the professions of faith, the priest baptizes the elect and the children (here the Missal does refer to the adults as the elect!). While no mention is made of the manner of Baptism, it would be good to reflect on what the *Rite of Christian Initiation of Adults* and *Rite of Baptism for Children* ritual books say about the suitability of and preference for immersion.

After the Baptisms, the infants (children under the age of discretion) are anointed with chrism (this is the anointing on the crown of the head, as described in the *Rite of Baptism for Children*). Next, white garments are given to all the newly baptized, adults and children, followed by the lighting of the baptismal candles from the Paschal candle. The Missal states that the Rite of Ephpheta is omitted for the infants.

The explanatory rites completed, there is a procession back to the sanctuary (unless, of course, these rites have occurred in the sanctuary), in the same order as before, and with the newly baptized carrying their lighted candles. The Missal suggests singing the baptismal canticle *Vidi aquam* during this procession, or some other appropriate song.

Finally, the Missal notes that once the procession has returned to the sanctuary, the adults are to immediately receive the Sacrament of Confirmation according to the proper ritual book. (Priests who baptize an adult or a child over the age of discretion have by law the faculty to confirm, and should do so.)

After the Rites of Baptism and of Confirmation are complete, or after the blessing of water if there have been no Baptisms, the renewal of baptismal promises for the assembly takes place (unless this has already been done when those to be baptized did so, as mentioned above). All in the assembly hold lighted candles (although it does not make sense for the newly baptized to participate in this, since they have just done so; it can be powerful for them to watch the "veteran" Catholics renew what they themselves just did for the first time). The introduction to the questions, which may be said by the priest using the exact words in the Missal or other similar words, makes reference both to the Paschal Mystery (the very meaning of what we are doing) and the fact that this celebration comes as the fruition of the Lenten observance; the reference to Lent serves to reinforce a sense of the "Ninety Days," so to speak, of Lent-Easter. Two forms of questions for the renunciation of sin are given, and then there are the traditional questions for the profession of faith, followed by a conclusion by the priest. The priest then sprinkles the assembly with the blessed water while an appropriate baptismal song is sung, perhaps the *Vidi aquam*.

A rubric indicates that during the sprinkling the newly baptized are led to their place among the faithful. In practice, the adults may need some time to put themselves together, especially if Baptism was done by immersion. Drying off, changing clothes, and getting ready to rejoin

the assembly can take place in another location while the assembly renews their baptismal promises and are sprinkled, with the neophytes rejoining the assembly during or immediately after.

After the sprinkling, the priest returns to the chair and the Universal Prayer is prayed in the usual way; the Creed is omitted. The Missal makes specific mention that the newly baptized participate in the Universal Prayer for the first time; it's a significant moment for them as they exercise this important function of the priestly people of God— that of interceding for the needs of others and of the whole world—and its importance should not be lost on them or on the entire assembly.

Fourth Part: The Liturgy of the Eucharist

After the Universal Prayer, the Mass continues as usual with the beginning of the Liturgy of the Eucharist. The Missal makes specific mention of the desirability of having the bread and wine brought forward by the newly-baptized adults and/or by the parents or godparents of newly-baptized children. Thus, is their participation in the offering of the sacrifice for the very first time duly highlighted. Needless to say, high priority should also be given to bringing forward and consecrating all the bread that will be needed for Holy Communion; it is fitting, given the newness of life that is central to this celebration, that any consecrated bread remaining from Good Friday has perhaps been consumed, or at least, is not used for this Paschal celebration.

The Prayer over the Offerings makes yet another explicit reference to the "paschal mysteries," asking that the Lord accept our prayers along with these sacrificial offerings, so that we might be brought "to the healing of eternity" through those mysteries.

Preface I of Easter is the Preface prescribed for this Mass, and the phrase "on this night" is used. The Preface succinctly announces the Paschal Mystery: "by dying he has destroyed our death, and by rising, restored our life."

There are special inserts that are to be used in the Eucharistic Prayer; be careful, as these can be tricky because the inserts are found in the Ritual Masses section toward the back of the Missal, under "I. For the Conferral of the Sacraments of Initiation; 3. For the Conferral of Baptism." Eucharistic Prayer IV would be excluded from use this night, because of its proper Preface, but Prayers I or III would be good choices (II would perhaps not be appropriate to the solemnity of the occasion, due to its brevity, although there is nothing to absolutely forbid it). Eucharistic Prayer I, the Roman Canon, has these three special inserts and proper forms: at the *Mememto Domine* ("Remember, Lord, your servants"), found in the Ritual Masses section; a proper form of the *Communicantes*, used from the Mass of the Easter Vigil until the Second Sunday of Easter, and found right within the text of the Prayer; and a proper form of the *Hanc Igitur* ("Therefore, Lord, we pray") with two variations: one variation is found right within the text of the prayer itself, used from the Mass of the Easter Vigil until the Second Sunday of Easter, and a second variation is found in the Ritual Masses section, with this second variation perhaps being a better choice for use this night if Baptisms have occurred. The inserts for Eucharistic Prayers II and III are found in the Ritual Masses section and are inserted in the places as indicated in the rubrics (there is only one insert for each prayer).

The Missal reminds the priest that before the "Behold the Lamb of God . . . " he may briefly address the newly baptized "about receiving their first Communion and about the excellence of this great mystery, which is the climax of initiation and the center of the whole Christian life." Those words in and of themselves can be the basis for the priest's remarks, and one would think it most beneficial to take advantage of this opportunity to offer extemporaneous remarks to highlight this important moment in the lives of the newly initiated and of the entire community.

The appropriateness of the newly baptized along with their godparents, their Catholic parents, spouses, and the catechists, indeed, the entire assembly, all receiving Communion under both kinds is highlighted, and it is hoped that this is a common practice of the parish.

The Communion Antiphon, taken from chapter 5 of 1 Corinthians, refers to Christ as "our Passover" and enjoins us, since he has been sacrificed, to "keep the feast with the unleavened bread of purity and truth." The Prayer after Communion asks God to pour out on us "the Spirit of your love" so that the nourishment of the Eucharist might make us "one in mind and heart." Once again, unity is emphasized as the goal receiving Holy Communion.

The text for a Solemn Blessing is given and should be used. A rubric indicates that this Solemn Blessing may be replaced by the final blessing formula from the *Rite of Baptism of Adults or of Children*; interestingly, while such a formula is given in the rite for children, there is no such formula in the rite for adults. Use of the formula from the rite for children would make sense if only children were baptized this night; otherwise, stick with the text given in the Missal. Lastly, the dismissal is chanted, by the deacon or by the priest, with the double Alleluia. This solemn dismissal is used throughout the Octave of Easter—that is, also on Easter Sunday, on the weekdays of Easter Week (within the Octave of Easter), and on the Second Sunday of Easter.

It is not used, however, on the other weekdays or Sundays of Easter Time, being used again only at Pentecost.

Pastoral Reflection

With the surprising doubt and deep love of Mary Magdalene, uncover the awesome passion of seeing the Risen Christ in your life tonight. Play the *Hallelujah Chorus* and allow each Hallelujah to infuse you with the joy of our Savior, risen and alive. In your eyes smile with delight and then find a stranger to inspire boldly without saying a word. Live the Resurrection in each moment that you make.

(#42, or Gospel #41, or at an afternoon or evening Mass, Gospel #46)   white

20 Easter Sunday of the Resurrection of the Lord
SOLEMNITY

About Easter Sunday

The celebration of the Resurrection of Jesus Christ continues into Easter Sunday morning. Easter Sunday marks the end of the Triduum and is the first day of the Easter Octave. The celebration of the Triduum concludes after Vespers and the great fifty Days begin. Forty days of fast yield to fifty days of feast. On Easter Sunday, many of those who were present the night before return, especially the neophytes. In addition, there may be many people attending who have not been to church in a while. Have plenty of hospitality ministers to greet and seat them. Have enough seats and enough worship aids so all can participate. Insert words of welcome and a description of the parish into the worship aid or bulletin. Perhaps you will make them feel so welcome that they will return to church because of you.

It is not surprising that in many parishes some of those baptized at the Easter Vigil, those still "wet behind the ears," wake up on Easter Sunday morning and go to Mass. Their excitement cannot be contained. If this is the case, invite the neophytes to wear the white garment donned at the Easter Vigil to Easter Sunday Mass. Some parishes celebrate the receptions into full communion and/or the completion of sacramental initiation at a Mass or Masses on Easter Sunday morning. Others schedule these events on Sundays during Easter Time. This laudable practice helps distinguish the baptized from the unbaptized at the Easter Vigil. Without the additional ceremonies, the Vigil is celebrated much more smoothly, and Easter Time, the great fifty Days, then takes on the characteristic of being an extended time of initiation. Be sure to include the names of the neophytes in the Universal Prayer (Prayer of the Faithful) at the Sunday Masses on Easter Sunday and throughout Easter Time. If the parish celebrates Easter Evening Prayer, consider inviting the neophytes to that celebration.

The Lectionary for Mass

The following commentary was written by Paul Turner © 2013, LTP.

◆ FIRST READING: Beginning this Sunday, and throughout Easter Time, we will read from the Acts of the Apostles, the second of Luke's two-volume work about Jesus and the early Christian community. Our First Reading picks up in the middle of Peter's preaching to his first Gentile converts. In this selection, Peter succinctly summarizes the Gospel from the time of John the Baptist to the disciples' commission to preach the Good News. In reality, Peter's masterful summary here is not limited to his own experience. He reaches back into his tradition, using the prophets' testimony to show that Jesus was the long-awaited Savior and he projects the importance of this event to the end of time in saying that Jesus will be the judge of the living and the dead.

◆ RESPONSORIAL PSALM 118: This is the last of five consecutive Hallel or Alleluia Psalms that were used at special feasts, and most especially at Passover. The verses we pray this Sunday are particularly suited for Easter as they proclaim God's triumph experienced in the lifetime of the believer. As we celebrate the promise that we shall not die, but live, the psalm also reminds us of our responsibility to proclaim the works of the Lord.

◆ SECOND READING, OPTION 1: We can summarize this reading from Paul's letter to the Colossians with the single phrase: "Christ your life" (Colossians 3:4). Paul, like he does in many other places, is reminding the community that their identification with Christ is the absolute center of their lives. They have died to everything else and have been raised in Christ. If that is so, then their gaze should be focused on higher things. In 3:15, Paul explains that they will accomplish that if they allow the peace of Christ to control their hearts.

◆ SECOND READING, OPTION 2: This short citation from 1 Corinthians is taken out of its original context, in which Paul chastised the Corinthians for tolerating immoral behavior in the community. As an Easter reading, it recalls the Passover celebration of salvation. Like fresh dough, the Corinthians are called to be single-minded, focused only on their new life in Christ.

◆ SEQUENCE: This Sunday, the Church sings a sequence—an ancient, poetic song that precedes the singing of the Gospel Acclamation. The Easter Sequence, *Victimae paschali laudes*, is a song of praise to the Paschal Victim that also reflects the Gospel account of Mary's encounter with the Risen Lord. The sequence may be sung each day of the Octave of Easter.

◆ GOSPEL: The Resurrection narratives are foundational to our faith. Like other Gospel episodes, we often imagine them as a unity, filling in details that are missing and passing over details that might be in conflict with one another. Nevertheless, careful attention to details will help us grasp each evangelist's unique message. The Resurrection account in John begins with Mary Magdalene arriving alone at the tomb. Although John tells us nothing about why she went, he does say when: it was dark. Upon seeing the stone removed, she fled to Peter and the other disciple whom Jesus loved, the key disciples in the Gospel according to John. They ran, looked inside the tomb, and realized from the careful placement of the cloths that there had been no robbery. Coming out of the darkness of confusion, they began to believe. But, John tells us, they had not yet understood the meaning of the Scriptures, so they returned home. In the post-Resurrection narrative that follows, which we do not hear in the Sunday Lectionary, the Risen Lord appears to Mary, calls her by name, and tells her to return to the disciples, this time declaring the message of the Resurrection. As Jesus's disciples grasped that message, they realized what God had done for Jesus, for them, and for the whole world.

The Roman Missal

There is a choice from among two of the Entrance Antiphons for today. The first uses the very stark first person: "I have risen, and I am with you still;" the second boldly proclaims that the Lord is truly risen. The frequent use of "alleluia" in each underscores for us the joy and triumph we are celebrating at Easter, an Alleluia joy and festivity that will continue throughout the entire season.

The Gloria is used today, and of course, today is a day for great flourish and solemnity in the selection of musical settings.

The Collect uses the important phrase "on this day." Our participation in the liturgy on this day is our participation in the salvation won for us and made present for us; therefore, it is on this day that God, through his only begotten Son, has "conquered death / and unlocked for us the path to eternity." Therefore, we pray that "we who

keep the solemnity of the Lord's Resurrection" may rise to new life through the renewal brought by the Holy Spirit.

The Creed is said today, although it may be replaced by the rite of the renewal of baptismal promises. Given the close connection between the meaning of Easter and the meaning of Baptism, it would seem there is great pastoral advantage to using this option. The text for it is not given again at the Mass during the Day; the priest will need to refer to the text used at the Easter Vigil.

In the Prayer over the Offerings, we express that we are offering the sacrifice by which the Church "is wondrously reborn and nourished" filled with "paschal gladness."

Preface I of Easter is again, as at the Vigil, the Preface assigned for today. Because of this, use of Eucharistic Prayer IV is again precluded, and perhaps Prayers I or III would be better choices than Prayer II, given the festivity of the day. The only inserts or special forms to worry about are the "In communion with those" and the "Therefore, Lord, we pray" as indicated within the text of Eucharistic Prayer I; there are no other special inserts.

The Communion Antiphon for this Mass is the same one as for the Vigil. The Prayer after Communion asks that, having been renewed by these Paschal Mysteries (linking the Paschal Mystery with the celebration of the Eucharist), the Church "may come to the glory of the resurrection." Thus is an eschatological focus emphasized, as well as the communal nature of participating in the mysteries.

The three-part Solemn Blessing from the Easter Vigil may be used again at this Mass, and the dismissal with the double Alleluia is used, preferably sung.

Pastoral Reflection

It's hard when we have incredible news and no one believes. What would excite those around you about God's love or how can you be an instrument to simply bring a huge smile to someone's face? Bringing their favorite treat, doing something simple but unexpected, treating a stranger. Be creative in sharing great news each day this week. And, while we each may want to be in the spotlight and know we are loved, be conscious to be humble and allow another to shine (like Simon Peter) even if they always seem to be in the light.

EASTER TIME

The Liturgical Time

The Calendar
April 21, 2014–June 8, 2014

The Meaning / The Lectionary for Mass

THE early Church had it right. Fifty days of Easter . . . fifty days of intensely entering more deeply into the mysteries just celebrated . . . fifty days of pondering their reality. For the newly baptized, this was the period of mystagogy, literally, "to move or go through the mystery," that which has been revealed to us through the Death and Resurrection of Christ. It was a time to "go through" that which is made possible and real in our own lives through the Sacraments of Initiation, not only in an intellectual sense as something we should know and understand, but deep within our minds and hearts as something we must live. Could we "cradle" or "veteran" Catholics not benefit as well by such an experience of these fifty days? The readings for this season will offer us many helps in entering more deeply into the mystery that we are called to live as we make our way through Easter's fifty days.

During the Octave, the eight days after Easter, our Gospel accounts tell of the appearances of the Risen Lord. Repeatedly, we hear of the simultaneous fear, struggle to believe, and overwhelming joy the Apostles and disciples experienced. They, too, had to enter into the mystery. The Gloria is sung at every Mass. *Victimae paschali laudes* or the Easter sequence may also be sung or recited on each day of the Octave. This centuries-old hymn is a song of praise to the victorious Lamb of God, the Risen Christ. The Alleluia verse before the Gospel is the same as for Easter Day: "This is the day the Lord has made!" The solemn Easter Alleluias are joined to the closing verses of the liturgy. How can we not put our all into the celebration of Christ's victory over death—a victory in which we have already begun to share?

The First Readings during the Octave are from the Acts of the Apostles as they are throughout Easter Time. We begin with the Apostles preaching on the day of Pentecost after they have received the Holy Spirit. The Church, the community of those who believed that the Risen Christ was Lord and Messiah, had its beginning at this time. Throughout Easter Time, the readings from Acts tell of the Church's expanded growth and those individuals who were instrumental in the spreading of the faith: Peter, James, John, Philip, Paul, Barnabas, Prisca, and Aquila—to name but a few. The Responsorial Psalms are all psalms of victory and deliverance. Pray them from the perspective of the victory and deliverance being your own in the Risen Christ.

Beginning in the Second Week of Easter, the Gospel accounts are from John. It is interesting to hear them in light of the Resurrection. From John 3: God so loved the world that he sent Jesus—not to condemn, but to give life to all who would receive it by being born of water and the Spirit. He is the true and everlasting light that penetrates the darkness of sin and death. He has given us the gift of that light in our Baptism.

Jesus is the Bread of Life, heavenly food for our earthly journey, the food of eternal life, so proclaims John 6 in the third week of Easter. In the fourth week, we see him as our Risen Shepherd who goes before us, offering us life in all its fullness (John 10), as the Paschal Light of the World who overcame the darkness (John 12), as the one who prepares a heavenly place for us and who will come back to take us with him (John 14), as the one who instructs his followers to continue his work, empowered by his presence and his Spirit (John 14). In the fifth, sixth, and seventh weeks we hear from Jesus's Last Discourse in John's account of the Gospel (chapters 15–17). Note the references to the presence and work of the Holy Spirit as we draw closer to Pentecost.

On the Sundays of Easter we hear first from John's account of Jesus's Easter evening appearance to the fearful disciples gathered in the locked room. He wishes them his peace and bestows his Spirit upon them. Thomas was absent, so the Gospel for the Second Sunday continues with another appearance a week later. Believing that the crucified one really lives, having passed through death to the glory of new and eternal life, is at the heart of our faith journey.

On the Third Sunday, we hear Luke's account of Jesus's appearance to the discouraged disciples on the road to Emmaus. So discouraged were they that they had left Jerusalem—and discipleship. Jesus revealed himself to them by explaining the Scriptures and breaking bread with them. Is this not the heart of our own Eucharistic celebrations?

The Fourth Sunday of Easter is Good Shepherd Sunday (John 10). Jesus identifies himself as both the Good Shepherd who not only lays down his life for the sheep but as the "sheepgate" through which they (and we) go in and out, finding security and nourishment.

The theme of Jesus as the Way continues on the Fifth Sunday with our Gospel from John 14. Jesus shows us "the way" to the Father (verse 6). He—all that he lived and taught—is "the Way."

Our reading of John 14 continues on the Sixth Sunday. Jesus speaks of his imminent departure but assures the disciples—and us among them—that he does not leave them orphans, without the support, the protection, the guidance of a loving parent. He will gift them—and us—with the Spirit of Truth.

On the Solemnity of the Ascension of the Lord, we hear the Risen Christ's commission of his disciples before he returns to the Father. Matthew, unlike Luke, does not recount his return or Ascension, but rather emphasizes Jesus's continuous presence with us until the end of the age (Matthew 28:20). These are Matthew's "last words" in his account of the Gospel.

The Gospel for the Seventh Sunday of Easter is from Jesus's prayer for his disciples who will remain in the world after his departure. We hear these words spoken in the context of his last meal with them from the perspective of their fulfillment in his Resurrection.

Easter Time closes with the Solemnity of Pentecost. The First Reading, of course, is Acts' account of the Pentecost after Jesus's Death when the promised Holy Spirit was poured out on the Apostles, Mary the Mother of Jesus, the women who had journeyed with Jesus to Jerusalem (see Luke 8:1–3; 23:49), and members of his family (see Acts of the Apostles 1:11–14). The Gospel is the same as for the Second Sunday of Easter! John has a different chronology than Luke as Jesus gifts his Holy Spirit to the disciples on Easter evening. The Second Reading, from 1 Corinthians, reminds us that the Holy Spirit is a continual gift to believers in every age. The presence and power of the Spirit works within believers in various ways, bringing forth various gifts, all necessary for the functioning of the Church, the Body of Christ. Do we know what our gifts are? Do we use them in service, for the common "benefit"?

Such is the mystery of Easter . . . the marvelous working of God's Spirit, raising Jesus from the dead and working within us with this same power (Ephesians 1:18–20). This Easter, enter more deeply into the mystery. Live it . . . not just for fifty days . . . but every day of your life.

The Roman Missal

U NIVERSAL *Norms on the Liturgical Year and the General Roman Calendar* (UNLY) points out that the fifty days of Easter Time "from the Sunday of the Resurrection to Pentecost Sunday are celebrated in joy and exultation as one feast day, indeed as one 'great Sunday'" (UNLY, 22). The first eight days, the Octave of Easter, are all celebrated as Solemnities of the Lord. As with Advent, Christmas Time, and Lent, every day for Easter Time has its own Mass, so for each day a proper Entrance Antiphon, Collect, Prayer over the Offerings, Communion Antiphon, and Prayer after Communion are given.

The Easter Time section in the Missal begins following the page for Holy Saturday, thus, beginning with Easter Sunday of the Resurrection of the Lord—first, the Easter Vigil in the Holy Night, followed by the Mass during the Day, and then each day of Easter Time starting with the days within the Octave of Easter. Some rubrics are mentioned that are applicable for the entire season. One of these concerns the use of the solemn dismissal with "Alleluia, Alleluia": it is used at the Vigil, at the Mass during the Day, and at Masses throughout the Octave of Easter (see *The Roman Missal*, Sunday of the Resurrection, 69 and 78); it is not, however, to be used at every Mass throughout Easter Time, which is a common mistake made by priests and deacons. After the Second Sunday of Easter, use of the solemn "Alleluia, Alleluia"

dismissal ceases, and it is not used again until Pentecost (both the Vigil and the Mass during the Day). A second rubric to be noted concerns the Paschal candle: "The paschal candle is lit in all the more solemn liturgical celebrations of this period." Given its prominence during Easter Time and its centrality as a symbol of the Resurrection, a legitimate argument could be made that the Paschal candle should be lit at all liturgical celebrations during Easter Time.

Once again, careful selection of texts by parish preparation committees can greatly enhance a community's celebration of the entire fifty days of Easter Time, providing continuity even toward the end of the season when a sort of fatigue about its being "one great Sunday" begins to set in. In the later weeks of Easter Time it is especially important to maintain the particular aspects of the liturgical season that have been used throughout. One of the most obvious examples of this is the Rite for the Blessing and Sprinkling of Water, in place of the Penitential Act, which can be found in Appendix II of the Missal. Although the rite has been moved to an Appendix, it is no less a viable option than it was in the former Sacramentary, where it was placed as an option along with the Penitential Act. It is meant to be used on Sundays, especially in Easter Time, and so it would not be used on weekdays.

The rite begins with the introduction and one of three options for blessing water; during Easter Time, the third option should be used. Where it is the custom to mix salt in the water, the salt is first blessed using the prayer provided in the Missal, and then the salt is poured into the water without any words. Next the priest sprinkles himself, the ministers and the people while an appropriate chant (or song) is sung. After the sprinkling, the singing ends as the priest returns to his chair. It is important for the priest not to forget the concluding prayer that is to be said ("May almighty God cleanse us of our sins, / and through the celebration of this Eucharist / make us worthy to share at the table of his Kingdom"), after which the Gloria is sung (when it is prescribed—which, of course, it is, on Sundays during Easter Time).

If the Rite for the Blessing and Sprinkling of Water is not used, then the Penitential Act occurs as normal. It would be good to highlight a distinction in this Penitential Act between Lent and Easter Time; perhaps, for example, if the Confiteor was emphasized during Lent, then perhaps option III with three invocations could be given prominence, or perhaps used exclusively for this season. Singing the Penitential Act would be a good way to highlight Easter Time, and then returning to reciting it could mark the return to Ordinary Time after Pentecost. Of the sample invocations given in Appendix VI, forms IV, V and VI seem to especially correspond to Easter themes.

The use of "Alleluia" as the Gospel Acclamation resumes, and the Gloria is used as it is prescribed.

There are five Prefaces designated for Easter Time, and these follow Preface II of the Passion of the Lord. Preface I is the Preface assigned to the Easter Vigil, to the Mass on Easter Sunday, and to each of the Masses during the Octave; the priest is to use the proper phrase from among the choices of "on this night" (at the Vigil) "on this day" (on Sunday and during the Octave), and "in this time" (throughout the remainder of Easter Time). Highlighting the Paschal Mystery in a very simple and direct way, this Preface announces that "by dying he has destroyed our death, / and by rising, restored our life." Preface II speaks of aspects of our new life in Christ, in that "the halls of the heavenly Kingdom / are thrown open to the faithful" because of Christ's dying and rising. Preface III speaks of Christ as our eternal intercessor, using Paschal imagery such as "the sacrificial Victim who dies no more" and "the Lamb, once slain, who lives for ever." The fourth Preface uses the motif of restoration as it announces that "the old order [is] destroyed, / a universe cast down is renewed, / and integrity of life is restored to us in Christ." Lastly, Preface V is similar to III in that it highlights Christ as Priest and Victim, describing how he shows himself to be "the Priest, the Altar, and the Lamb of sacrifice" for our salvation.

Easter Time might be a good time to regularly chant the introductory dialogue and Preface to the Eucharistic Prayer. If this was done throughout Lent, it becomes a good opportunity to link the two seasons, highlighting the "ninety days." If it was not done during Lent, then this would be a good time to institute the practice as a way of highlighting the festivity of the season. A community might consider continuing to use the same option as was used during Lent for the acclamation of "The Mystery of Faith," again as a way of emphasizing the theological unity of the Paschal Mystery as it is manifested in liturgical time. Whichever wording for the acclamation is chosen, however, it might be a good idea to change the musical setting to a more festive one.

Various Solemn Blessings appropriate for Easter Time are given in the Missal. There is one proper to the Easter Vigil, given with the texts for that celebration, which can be used again at Masses during the day on Sunday. At all other Masses, the Solemn Blessing for Easter Time, #6 of the Solemn Blessings in the section "Blessings at the End of Mass and Prayers over the People" is used, along with the blessing for "The Ascension of the Lord" (#7) for the Ascension, and for "The Holy Spirit" (#8) for Pentecost.

Children's Liturgy of the Word

You will want to have a number of assistants appropriate to the number of children participating in the Liturgy of the Word in order to help you maintain a prayerful atmosphere. Assistants can help you to process with the children to and from the main assembly and can watch out for any children who are acting out or having trouble sitting still in order to quietly help them. You will want to assign an assistant or two to care for any children who need to use the rest room or who do not want to remain apart from their families and need to return to the main assembly before the end of the Liturgy of the Word. You will also want to assign an assistant to watch the progress of the Liturgy of the Word in the main assembly to be sure that you return at the appropriate time.

Those who participate in the Liturgy of the Word with children need to have some basic training in an awareness of their liturgical roles. The same care should be given to their preparation as is given to those who serve as liturgical ministers in the celebration of the Word to be aware of and comfortable with the fact that they are involved in a full liturgical experience, and not a catechetical session, a time for play, or a child care experience.

When recruiting assistants, music ministers, or any other adults to participate in any aspect of the Liturgy of the Word for children, be sure to check with your parish or diocese to find out about the conditions under which they may work with children. It may be necessary for them to undergo training or background screening. As an adult who has been given the tremendous honor of caring for the spiritual development of children, it is your responsibility to ensure that they can develop their relationship with God in a safe and nurturing environment.

The Saints

"CHRIST is Risen! Truly He is Risen!" The traditional Easter greeting resounds through the ages to our current fifty-day celebration of Christ's Resurrection and our Salvation.

The first recipients of the Holy Spirit and the first heralds of the Resurrection were the Virgin Mary and the Apostles and so it is fitting that the three feasts of this season celebrate the Apostles, SS. Philip and James (May 3), and St. Matthias (May 14), and the Virgin Mary's Feast of the Visitation (May 31). The Church's 1969 revision of the calendar puts the Feast of the Visitation between the celebrations of the Annunciation and the Nativity of St. John the Baptist, highlighting the Virgin Mary's great act of familial charity in visiting her expectant cousin, Elizabeth, even while the Virgin Mary was with child herself. This feast could be an opportunity to remind us all to be more attentive to our extended families, especially those in need. Offerings of charitable support for organizations assisting unwed mothers would be particularly appropriate ways to honor the memory of the Virgin Mary's charity.

The great witness of those who have willingly given up their lives in the service of the faith is exceptionally poignant during this joyful season of remembrance of the triumph of life over death. In all ages and places there have been remarkable individuals who intensely believed that the cross of Christ was a throne of glory and the empty tomb a proclamation of the eternal reign of Christ over life. This year the obligatory memorials of martyrs are for St. Charles Lwanga and Companions (June 3), martyrs from the African nation of Uganda in the late 1800s, and St. Boniface (June 5), "Apostle of Germany" who was martyred in 754. Separated by time and geography, but united in faith and fortitude, the remaining martyrs' commemorations are optional memorials: St. Peter Chanel (April 28), Protomartyr of the South Pacific; SS. Nereus and Achilleus and St. Pancras (May 12), all early willing victims of Roman persecution; St. Christopher Magallanes and Companions (May 21), priests and lay martyrs of Mexico's anti-Catholic campaign of the early 1900s; and SS. Marcellinus and Peter

(June 2), early victims of Rome whose memory is preserved in Eucharistic Prayer I.

The willing offering of one's life is not the only way to proclaim the Easter message. From simple farmers like St. Isidore (May 15) to bishops and popes such as St. Athanasius (May 2), Bishop and Doctor of the Church; St. Augustine of Canterbury (May 27) "Apostle of the English;" and St. Pius V (April 30), the pope who implemented the decrees of the Council of Trent, people of every walk of life have lived in Easter joy proclaiming Jesus Christ risen from the dead. Their example and prayers are joined by the great "Alleluia" sung by vowed religious men and women of every age: St. Damien de Veuster (May 10), missionary to lepers; St. Bernardine of Siena (May 20), Franciscan who cultivated the devotion to the Holy Name of Jesus; St. Rita of Cascia (May 22), an Augustinian nun who previously endured such an unhappy marriage that she is the patron of desperate cases; and St. Norbert (June 6), founder of an order of priests and Church reformer. During this most joyous season there are also opportunities to show further devotion to the Holy Family. St. Joseph, under the title of "The Worker," is celebrated on May 1 when many cultures remember the common worker. The celebration of the Virgin Mary's apparition as Our Lady of Fatima (May 13) highlights devotions to the Rosary and the Immaculate Heart of Mary. Each of these individual commemorations adds to the symphony of praise to God for the freedom given to humanity by Christ's triumph over sin and death. Every Easter Time liturgy adds to the witness of praise and glory given by the saints in heaven and on earth. No matter the particular customs or devotions associated with any saint, all celebrations during this season must proclaim the great Alleluia that Christ is risen! Christ is truly risen!

The Liturgy of the Hours

SEVERAL traditional Easter Hymns are found in the Hours including "The Strife Is O'er," (VICTORY); "At the Lamb's High Feast We Sing," (SALZBURG); "Christ the Lord Is Risen Today," (VICTIMAE PASCHALI); "I Am the Bread of Life," (Suzanne Toolan, RSM); and "Ye Sons and Daughters," (O FILII ET FILAE). A lesser-known hymn found in the Hours is "We Who Once Were Dead" with a poetry that confronts death, gives witness to the Resurrection, and provides rich images of the Lord as our Eucharistic bread.

The Office of Readings, within the Octave of Easter, includes expanded texts of Psalm 19, 66, 104, 118, 119, 136, and 145. The Patristic texts, especially the Easter Homily of Melito of Sardis, offer rich images of lamb, sheep, Passover, king, light, and Word; providing the Church with a lingering taste of the Easter mysteries. The use of the continuous reading from 1 Peter gives witness that parts of this letter were used as an ancient homily to the newly baptized.

Notice how often in the texts during the Octave, one finds the comparison of the old Adam and the New Adam and the linkage of antiphons for the Gospel canticles to the texts of the Gospels used at Eucharist this week. The trilogy of readings from the "Jerusalem Catechesis" roots us in a solid theology of Eucharist, which we fervently celebrate in Easter Time. As we conclude the Octave (the eighth day) on the Second Sunday of Easter we pray the same antiphons, psalms, and canticles from those on Easter Sunday, and 1 Peter 2:9–10 is introduced here and used for the next seven weeks.

As we move through the weeks of Easter we find references to the Gospel, used at the Eucharist, now part of the antiphons for the canticles and a plethora of images that continue to open up the baptismal themes of Easter Time. The exhortations in the patristic readings also lead us to a deeper understanding and appreciation for the intrinsic relationship of the celebration of the Eucharist and love among the members of the Church. St. Justin's description of the Eucharist, from his *First Apology*, offers the beautiful insight that the celebration of the Eucharist makes the Church.

The Rite of Christian Initiation of Adults

Now is the time for mystagogy. Consider the following in your parish when implementing mystagogy.

After initiation, gather the neophytes together in the church to reflect on their experience. Light the Paschal candle again and ask what it was like for the newly initiated to sit in the darkness and then watch the darkness be conquered by the ever-growing light. Light incense for general atmosphere. Open the Lectionary and ask the neophytes which of the readings spoke to them most pointedly.

Invite the neophytes to come to the water of the font and bless themselves before asking what they experienced before getting *into* the water, then being *in* it, and then getting *out* of it. Then bring them to the sanctuary and ask: What was it like processing up the aisle, clothed in white, instead of being dismissed down the aisle? What was it like to stare into the candle flame as you were marked with the chrism and sealed in the Spirit?

With the neophytes standing around the altar, ask: What was it like to bring up the gifts and help set the table for the Eucharistic banquet? And to join in the Eucharistic Prayer? And to come up again to eat and drink for the first time with the community?

These questions make for a full evening of stories and joy, of laughter and tears. It honors the immediacy of the event and begins the mystagogical process of integrating the experience into the neophytes' new life in the Church.

—Adapted from an article by Michael H. Marchal © LTP, 2011.

The Sacraments of Initiation

Easter is the time for initiation: the Baptism of infants, celebrations of Professions of Faith that bring those already baptized in another Christian tradition into full communion, and celebrations of first Holy Communion and Confirmation. If possible, it is ideal to celebrate each of these sacraments with the Sunday assembly. Easter Sunday is a perfect day for celebrating infant Baptism, and full communion for those adults and children who were previously baptized.

If the parish has coffee after Masses have candidates and their families volunteer to serve or be greeters at these gatherings.

If you are preparing first Communion and it is being held at one or more of the Sunday liturgies, be sure to work with the liturgy and music directors ahead of time, as preparations for Easter are well underway by the time Lent starts.

Some communities celebrate first Communion outside the Sunday Mass. When this is the case, work with the liturgy and music directors to plan for the occasion. When attending a parish liturgy for the first time, it might be a good idea for them to wear their distinctive attire to that Mass so the community can also celebrate with them.

However your parish chooses to celebrate the Sacraments of Initiation, children with special needs are often included. Catechists and liturgists need to work with the parents, teachers, and caregivers of these children to be sure they are involved and very much part of the event.

The celebration of Confirmation very much depends on the bishop's schedule and availability. Because Confirmation is the sealing of Baptism, strengthening us to bear witness to the Paschal Mystery, Easter Time, with its baptismal character, is most appropriate for its celebration.

You will also need to look at space in the church. Where will the candidates and their sponsors be seated? Appropriate space will be needed for the bishop to sit as well as priests and deacons who will be participants in the liturgy.

Sacramental symbols should be lavish and placed or highlighted so they are visible. Prepare candidates ahead of time so they are familiar with the flow of the ritual and their responses. Involve candidates as liturgical ministers in this Eucharist as readers, music ministers, and gift bearers.

The Rite of Penance

Since the neophytes are experiencing the fruits of Holy Communion there is no need to rush them into celebrating the Sacrament of Penance (see Catechism of the Catholic Church [CCC], 1391, 1394). Children of various ages especially those who are preparing to receive the Sacraments of Penance and Eucharist for the first time as well as those youth and adults who are preparing to receive the Sacrament of Confirmation would benefit from a Common Penitential Celebration as found in Appendix II, section II from the *Rite of Penance*. In addition, schedule a communal celebration of the sacrament for children based on Form II of the rite. Consult and review the principals found in the *Directory for Masses with Children* (DMC), article 3 and decide what elements should be retained, shortened, or omitted from the rite. Tailor the Examination of Conscience to the children's awareness and make a "better selection of texts" (DMC, 3). Be sure

to provide preparation material for both parents and children who are making themselves ready to celebrate the sacrament.

Consider having a novena between the Solemnities of the Ascension of the Lord and Pentecost and pray for reconciliation and forgiveness in families, neighborhoods, cities, states, nations as well as in the Church. Consider using the text of the Pentecost sequence, *Veni, Sancte Spiritus*: "Heal our wounds . . . wash the stains of guilt away . . . bend the stubborn . . . guide the steps . . ." (*Lectionary for Mass*, 63A). The song "By the Waking of our Hearts" by Paulist Fr. Ricky Manalo with the text "By the waking of our hearts, by the stirring of our souls, may the Spirit of God abide and bring us together in love" (available from Oregon Catholic Press) would be a fitting refrain to sing during the novena.

The Pastoral Care of the Sick

Consider celebrating the sacrament on one of the Sundays of Easter Time during Evening Prayer. Invite those preparing to receive the Sacrament of Confirmation to serve as ministers of hospitality and hosts and following the liturgy provide a festive meal for the sick and their family members. Provide the names of the young people (in large print) on a card for the sick and homebound to take home so that they can pray for these young people preparing to receive the Sacrament of Confirmation. When visiting the sick and homebound during Easter Time, joyfully share the festivity of the season. Upon arrival, greet the person with the singing of the *Easter Alleluia*, bring Easter lilies, newly blessed holy water, a recording of the Easter Masses, a large print issue of *At Home with the Word 2014*, photos of the church decorated for Easter, and cards for the sick and homebound created by children preparing for first Holy Communion.

The Rite of Marriage

THE Rite of Marriage may not be celebrated on Easter Sunday. One may look to the New Testament reading from Easter Time (Acts of the Apostles, the Epistles, and the Book of Revelation) as options to the suggested readings from the Old Testament found in the *Rite of Marriage*. The Paschal candle has pride of place near the ambo during Easter Time. Consider including the candle in the entrance procession. The use of a unity candle is best left for the rehearsal dinner or wedding reception. Encourage couples to choose their colors to be in harmony with the Easter environment and invite them to consider the continued use of various lilies (including calla, oriental, tiger, or peace) as well other spring flowers such as daffodils and tulips or branches from flowering trees. And, considering the church will be decorated in full Easter glory, this can potentially save the couple money for their wedding environment!

The Order of Christian Funerals

THE *Order of Christian Funerals* includes prayers for when the body is transferred to the church or the place of committal (see OCF, 119–127). For example, these prayers can be used to accompany the body to the church for the vigil with the funeral elsewhere, the body to the church for early visitation by the family or friends, or the body to the cemetery from the funeral home. These times of prayer are short and are marked by deep scriptural faith and confidence in God. They can be accompanied by simple gestures, such as the joining of hands at the Lord's Prayer (a gesture that can break the loneliness and isolation of the moment), the touching of the body by the bereaved as a way of leave-taking or saying good-bye, the signing of the body with the Sign of the Cross on the forehead, or the blessing of the body with holy water. These times of prayer could be extended to include a relaxed time for prayer, storytelling, weeping, laughing, Scripture sharing, and so on.

Consider Lectionary readings from Easter Time—they are rich with images of death and new life, and will be helpful with preparing the funeral

liturgy. Consider including the Paschal candle in the entrance procession. The Funeral Mass may not be celebrated on Easter Sunday and the Sundays of Easter including the Ascension of the Lord (if it falls on Sunday) and Pentecost.

The Book of Blessings

BLESSINGS are not about us or our activities, buildings, and/or objects. "Blessings therefore refer first and foremost to God, whose majesty and goodness they extol and, since they indicate the communication of God's favor, they also involve human beings, whom he governs and his providence protects" (BB, 7). This should foster within us a new way of realizing all of creation as a gift and direct us to "profess that as we make use of what God has created, we wish to find him and to love and serve him with all fidelity" (BB, 12).

In Easter Time, these blessings are appropriate to do: Order for the Blessing of Food for the First Meal of Easter (chapter 54); the Order for the Blessing of Homes during the Easter Season (chapter 50); the Order for the Blessing of Mothers on Mother's Day (insert chapter number at P1s); the Order for the Blessing of an Image of the Blessed Virgin Mary (chapter 36, II); Order for the Blessing of Rosaries (chapter 45). Other blessings during Easter Time might include fields and flocks (chapter 26); seeds and plants (chapter 27); travelers (chapter 9); and boats and fishing gear (chapter 22). *Catholic Household Blessings & Prayers* includes blessings and prayers for Easter Time as well.

The Liturgical Environment

THE liturgical color for all of Easter Time is white or gold, with red making a comeback for the Solemnity of Pentecost. This does not mean that the sanctuary need be swathed in white and gold fabric for Easter. Often, such decorations can distract from the liturgical actions, and they often appear to have been thrown together rather than carefully arranged. The Easter environment does not need to be elaborate to evoke the joy of the liturgical time. Indeed, anything that calls attention away from the liturgy itself is to be avoided, while anything that helps draw the eye to the action of the liturgy itself is to be suggested. The use of plants to call attention to the primary liturgical *foci* (altar, ambo, font, Paschal candle) is certainly appropriate.

Another often overlooked aspect of the space is the liturgical assembly itself, which gathers to hear the Word, celebrate the sacraments, and be formed ever more into the Body of Christ. Consideration of how the assembly participates in the liturgical action, and is formed by the liturgical space is worth some consideration in this season of the Resurrection.

Easter Time lasts for fifty days, and as such it is the longest of the seasons other than Ordinary Time. It can be difficult to maintain the festivity throughout the entirety of the season. The liturgical environment can and should assist in maintaining this solemnity. In order to do this, it will be necessary to prepare, setting aside some of the Easter budget for maintaining plants and flowers. If well cared for, many potted plants will last throughout the season, although flowering plants, like lilies, may lose their blooms before Pentecost. If lilies are used, removing the anther from the flowers (the fuzzy yellow parts at the end of the stamen inside the flower), will both help the flowers last longer and make the plants less likely to incite the allergies of parishioners. The addition of some plants throughout the season can help keep the environment looking fresh and inviting. As the Pentecost feast approaches, you might consider adding some more, especially blooming plants in red that will add to the festivity of the day.

The Paschal candle, as has already been mentioned, burns at Mass throughout Easter Time. It may require attention, particularly if there are drafts in your space. Occasionally checking that the follower is fitted properly and that the candle is burning evenly will help it to burn longer.

There are many added liturgies in most parishes during this time: first Holy Communions and Confirmations, weddings, and others. These may bring new elements into the sanctuary, but should not detract from the centrality of the ritual *loci,* nor eclipse Easter Time. As Easter is central to every action of the Church, these liturgies are appropriate during this time, but Easter remains the chief celebration.

The Liturgical Music

DURING these days we have such rich fodder for choosing music based upon the powerful readings, and all the beloved Easter hymns. These days may be filled with Baptisms and first Holy Communions, but keep the musical focus on the Scriptures of the liturgies.

One element that is especially powerful throughout the season is the rite of sprinkling. The blessing of the water may be sung. The song accompanying the sprinkling with blessed water should have an explicitly baptismal character.

It is important to note that the sprinkling rite is its *own* rite. It replaces the Penitential Act and should not be combined with the Gloria.

A list of suggested music for Easter Time is available as a free PDF at www.LTP.org/resources.

Liturgical Ministers

CONSIDER hosting a "liturgy day" at your parish on one of the Saturdays during Easter Time. Collaborate with neighboring parishes in your deanery or vicariate or with the diocesan Office of Divine Worship and join forces to co-sponsor this event. Bring in a guest speaker to address any number of topics related to the Mass and sacraments. Include Morning Prayer, breakouts for individual ministries, and a blessing for ministers (see *Book of Blessings,* chapters 61–63) as part of the day-long program. Be sure to include neophytes in the day's experience and set aside a time for mystagogical reflection throughout the day allowing time for small-group discussion and faith sharing.

Be sure to review the May calendar, since it is often one of the busiest months of the year in people's lives, especially with the celebrations of *Cinco de Mayo,* end of the school year, graduations, Memorial Day, and Mothers' Day. Don't let devotions or the many events in the secular calendar overshadow the fifty days of Easter that are to be celebrated as one great feast (see UNLY, 22). Provide opportunities for the blessing of Easter foods (see *Book of Blessings,* chapter 54) and the blessing of homes (see *Book of Blessings,* chapter 11).

Include college students returning home for summer to participate in the various liturgical ministries in the parish. Provide the link for

Masstimes.org on the parish website and in the bulletin to help parishioners find a nearby church to celebrate Mass if they are vacationing in another part of the country or anywhere else in the world.

Soon after the Lent-Triduum-Easter celebrations have ended, bring together the parish liturgical commission along with parish musicians, priest celebrants, and members of the liturgical environment team to evaluate the seasons—what worked and what didn't work? Invite members of the assembly to participate as well. First, come together in small groups. Ask questions such as: what allowed you to go deeper into the Paschal Mystery? What symbols or rituals spoke to you or stirred up your faith and why? What did you hear or feel as you heard the texts of the Missal or Lectionary proclaimed? Are there any words you or your children are not understanding? Consider writing thank you notes to the various ministers in the parish. Celebrate with simple food and beverages and give thanks for the good work you do on behalf of the holy people of God.

Devotions and Sacramentals

A devotional custom from the Philippines is the "pious exercise of the meeting of the Risen Christ with His Mother: on Easter morning two processions, one bearing the image of Our Lady of Dolours, the other that of the Risen Christ, meet each other so as to show that Our Lady was the first, and full participant in the mystery of the Lord's resurrection" (DPPL, 149). Make sure the parish brings the Eucharist to the sick and homebound on this day. Greet the sick person with the singing of the Easter Alleluia and bring them the plant from the Holy Thursday Altar of Repose or an Easter lily along with recently blessed holy water, a recording of the Easter Mass, photos of the church, and a large print copy of *At Home with the Word*. Consider celebrating Evening Prayer or baptismal vespers on Easter Sunday. If this is not celebrated in your parish consider traveling to the cathedral or joining a religious community for this liturgy. As a family, sing the Easter Alleluia on the way to Easter Mass and around the family dinner table. The singing of the *Regina Coeli*, which replaces the Angelus, begins on Easter Sunday. The venerable tradition of a blessing of the family

Easter table is recommended and DPPL calls for the festive meal to be blessed with "Easter water, which is brought by the faithful from the Easter Vigil" (DPPL, 150). A blessing for the Easter table is found in *Catholic Household Blessings & Prayers*. Likewise the annual blessing of homes is to be recommended (See DPPL, 152) and can be found in *Catholic Household Blessings & Prayers*.

Devotion to the Divine Mercy in connection with the octave of Easter may be observed (see DPPL, 154) and is found in *Catholic Household Blessings & Prayers*. The *Via Lucis* or the stations of the Resurrection can fill the faithful with "liberation, joy and peace . . . paschal values . . . and is a potential stimulus for the restoration of a 'culture of life,' which is open to the hope and certitude offered by faith, in a society often characterized by a 'culture of death', despair and nihilism" (DPPL, 153).

During the month of May devotion to the Blessed Mother is common and the praying of the Rosary and the Order for Crowning an Image of the Blessed Virgin Mary (May crowning) are popular. The Rogation Days, meaning "to ask," are celebrated three days before the Solemnity of the Ascension (see *Catholic Household Blessings & Prayers*).

The Pentecost Novena, held between the Ascension and Pentecost, honors the tradition of "all . . . joined in continuous prayer, together with several women, including Mary the Mother of Jesus . . . while they awaited being ; 'clothed with the power form on high' (Luke 24, 49)" (DPPL, 155).

The Parish and the Home

Each Sunday of Easter Time members of the Church community renew their baptismal promises. We sing beautiful Glorias and Alleluias along with songs of praise for God's glory and power. It is right that we recognize and sing God's praise but we give God even greater glory when we act like an "Alleluia People." A parish might give households or individual parishioners an "Alleluia," perhaps drawn or written in calligraphy on parchment paper inviting people to display it in a prominent spot. Perhaps they might even replace their crosses of Lent with Alleluias to help remember that it is in our actions that we give God glory and praise. It is another opportune time for parishes to offer concrete ways and places that people may serve those in need in the community, particularly at the local level. Just as the disciples discovered the needs of the widows or those who were neglected, we too find where we are needed especially right around us.

This time of year is a busy time for parishioners who are celebrating Baptisms, Confirmations, and first Eucharist. It is a time for many ordinations, weddings, and graduations. Finding ways to call these moments to the attention of the entire community for prayer and communal blessings helps us mark the joy of Easter Time together.

As we come to the Pentecost celebration marking the end of Easter Time we recognize it as a celebration of how we are Church. Like the ways the disciples in Acts discovered what they were called to do, so we too hear our commissioning to go forth with the power of the Holy Spirit. The psalm response for Pentecost Sunday is "Lord, send out your Spirit and renew the face of the earth" (Psalm 104:30). In the Gospel account from John we hear Jesus give the disciples the Holy Spirit with the instructions to forgive sins. The Spirit comes that we might act.

Mass Texts

◆ CHILDREN'S LITURGY OF THE WORD

With God, nothing is impossible.
For these Fifty days we tell the world
that God did the impossible in the life of Jesus
by raising him from the dead.
The best way to celebrate that miracle
is to believe it so completely that it leaks out
    in all we say and do.
Go hear God's Word, announce the Good News
    of Jesus
and let it teach you how to be the Risen Jesus
    in the world.

◆ DISMISSAL TEXT FOR RCIA

The Easter mysteries reminded us of who
    we want to be:
faithful disciples washed in the Blood of the Lamb
fully incorporated into his Body the Church.
As you continue your journey of preparation,
we rejoice in your commitment
and long for the time when you will share with us
    in the supper of the Lamb.

When you gather with your fellow catechumens
pray for us—as we will pray for you—
that when we share this meal together
we will all be made worthy of the promises
    of Christ.

◆ SEASONAL TEXTS FOR PRAYER OF THE FAITHFUL

Invitation to Prayer:

Even in a season of grace and a time of rejoicing
our need for God does not diminish.

So we turn to you, O Lord, and ask in all humility
For your gracious mercy and your healing love.

Intercessions:

For the needs of the Church, both spiritual and temporal: that many generous hearts respond to God's call and serve God's people in ministry; that those in leadership never compromise their pastoral role and fail to heal and reconcile God's people; and that the resources needed for effective ministry will never be lacking, we pray to the Lord: Risen Savior, hear our prayer.

For those who have embraced the sacred task of leading local and national governments. That they might submit their wills to God and yield to the promptings of God's Spirit as they exercise the power and authority entrusted to them, we pray to the Lord: Risen Savior, hear our prayer.

For the needy and the outcast, the oppressed and the sick, the lonely and the frightened, the unemployed and the homeless, that they might know the power of the Resurrection manifested through the concern and the proactive care of all those who claim Jesus as Lord, we pray to the Lord: Risen Savior, hear our prayer.

For those who have died in war and from disease, through neglect or in loneliness, from old age or much too young, that they might receive an abundance of mercy and live forever in the light of God's kingdom, we pray to the Lord: Risen Savior, hear our prayer.

Concluding Prayer:

Loving Father,
in obedience to you,
Jesus entered the darkness of sin and death
and through your merciful love he broke death's
    hold upon us.
Hear the prayers we offer this day
and from your throne of grace extend your mercy
    toward us.
Through Christ our Lord.
Amen.

April
Month of the Holy Eucharist

MON 21 (#261) white
Monday in the Octave of Easter
SOLEMNITY

The Lectionary for Mass

◆ FIRST READING: A great crowd of Jews gather in Jerusalem for the feast of Pentecost (a day commemorating the giving of the law on Mount Sinai). Sounds of a strong wind and the different languages spoken by the Apostles draw them to where the Apostles are staying (see Acts of the Apostles 2:1–11). Filled with the Holy Spirit, Peter proclaims the Gospel to the crowds: the Jesus whom they crucified has been raised up and exalted. He is the fulfillment of all that was promised under the old covenant.

◆ RESPONSORIAL PSALM 16: Today's response, a song of confidence prayed at a time when sickness and death were life-threatening, is actually cited in the First Reading. It is fulfilled par excellence in Jesus.

◆ GOSPEL: A wide range of emotions and responses to the news of Christ's Resurrection are evident: the simultaneous fear and joy of the women, the panic of the chief priests and elders, their frantic attempt to cover up and explain the empty tomb. What incredible joy the women must have experienced when they saw the Risen Christ and touched him. What they must have felt as they fulfilled the mission: "Go tell my brothers!"

For the sequence see commentary by Paul Turner on page 167. The sequence may be used each day during the Octave of Easter.

The Roman Missal

There is a choice between two Entrance Antiphons for today. In the first, the image of a land flowing with milk and honey is invoked; in the second, the Lord's Resurrection from the dead is mentioned, and therefore our response is to rejoice, since he reigns for all eternity.

The Gloria is sung or said today, as it is every day within the Octave of Easter.

The Collect makes explicit reference to the newly baptized who were initiated at the Easter Vigil as it refers to the "new offspring" given to the Church by God. The prayer goes on to ask that all of us may hold fast to the sacrament (that is, sacramental initiation and consequent life of grace) we have received.

The Prayer over the Offerings asks that the Lord accept our offerings such that, "renewed by confession of your name and by Baptism," we may "attain unending happiness." The prayers of this Mass continue to echo the sacramental initiation that is integral to the understanding of the Easter mystery.

Preface I of Easter is assigned for today, and, as specified at the text for the Preface, the phrase "on this day" is used. If Eucharistic Prayer I, the Roman Canon, is used, the special inserts are used.

The Communion Antiphon proclaims Christ's victory over death, having robbed it of its power. In the Prayer after Communion, we hear the phrase "paschal Sacrament," conveying to us an echo of the Paschal Mystery, Christ's Death and Resurrection, and our participation in that mystery.

The solemn dismissal with the double Alleluia is sung or said today, as it is throughout the Octave of Easter.

TUE 22 (#262) white
Tuesday in the Octave of Easter
SOLEMNITY

The Lectionary for Mass

◆ FIRST READING: Today's First Reading is a continuation of Peter's Pentecost speech. The hearts of many of those who heard Peter's proclamation of Jesus as Lord and Messiah were opened to repentance and the gift of faith. Some three thousand people were baptized.

◆ RESPONSORIAL PSALM 33 is a song of confidence. In his love, the Lord desires that all turn to him in trust. Only in the Lord is their salvation. His goodness fills the earth.

◆ GOSPEL: At the tomb, Mary Magdalene is greeted by the Risen Christ, though she does not recognize him until he calls her by name. She is sent to announce Christ's return to the Father. She becomes the "apostle to the Apostles," the first to announce the Good News of Christ's Resurrection and exaltation.

The Roman Missal

The baptismal imagery continues to take center stage in today's liturgy as the Entrance Antiphon, taken from chapter 15 of Sirach, speaks of drinking of the water of wisdom.

The Gloria is once again sung or said today.

The Collect mentions that God has bestowed on us "paschal remedies," a reference to the Easter sacraments. These sacraments bring us the opportunity to possess "perfect freedom" such that the joy we experience now is destined to reach fulfillment in heaven.

The Prayer over the Offerings brings an eschatological focus as it asks that not only may we not lose the gifts we have received (and in this season we can be reminded of the gift of new life through the sacraments, which keep us under God's protective care), but also that we might "attain the gifts that are eternal."

Preface I of Easter is again assigned for today, and, as specified at the text for the Preface, the phrase "on this day" is used. If Eucharistic Prayer I is prayed, remember to use the special inserts.

The Communion Antiphon echoes one of the options for the

Second Reading for the Mass for Easter Sunday, as it speaks of seeking the things that are above because we have risen with Christ. The Prayer after Communion asks that as we have received "the perfect grace of Baptism," so we may be prepared "for the reward of eternal happiness."

WED 23 (#263) white Wednesday in the Octave of Easter
SOLEMNITY

The Lectionary for Mass

◆ FIRST READING: Peter and John give a gift far greater than alms to the crippled man at the gate of the Temple. Raised up by the hand of Peter in the name of Jesus, he is completely healed.

◆ RESPONSORIAL PSALM 105: This song of thanksgiving is a most appropriate response. For truly, the formerly lame man, now walking and praising God with joy, announces his deeds among the peoples.

◆ GOSPEL: Two of Jesus's disciples, discouraged by the happenings of the previous few days, are desolately leaving Jerusalem. Meeting them along the way and speaking with them about Scripture, Jesus enlivens their hearts. They recognize him in the breaking of the bread.

The Roman Missal

Today's Entrance Antiphon is eschatological in its focus, coming from chapter 25 of Matthew's account of the Gospel, as it expresses the Father's invitation to "receive the kingdom prepared for you / from the foundation of the world. . . . "

The Gloria is once again sung or said today.

The Collect gives voice to the joy we receive as we celebrate "year by year" the solemnity of the Lord's Resurrection, and asks that we may "reach eternal joys" through our celebration of "these present festivities." The phrase "these present

festivities" can be appropriated in a broad sense to include the whole of Easter Time, in addition to specifically pointing to the days of the Octave.

The Prayer over the Offerings asks God to receive "the sacrifice which has redeemed the human race," and to "accomplish in us / salvation of mind and body." The phrasing can remind us of the totality of redemption—mind and body—that has been won for us in the Paschal Mystery, and can also be seen as an echo of the healing power that comes through Jesus's Resurrection, as proclaimed in the First Reading.

Preface I of Easter is again used today, as is the phrase "on this day." If Eucharistic Prayer I is used, the special inserts are also again used.

The Communion Antiphon is taken from the day's Gospel of the Emmaus story. The Prayer after Communion gives voice to the old/new motif as it asks that through the sacrament we may be cleansed from our old ways and transformed into a new creation.

THU 24 (#264) white Thursday in the Octave of Easter
SOLEMNITY

The Lectionary for Mass

◆ FIRST READING: Having drawn a crowd by the miraculous cure of the lame man, Peter addresses them in the Temple. Though Jesus was the servant of the God of Abraham, Isaac, and Jacob, and the "Author of Life," the leaders of his people rejected him, handing him over to death. God raised him from the dead and offers forgiveness and life to all who repent and believe in his name.

◆ RESPONSORIAL PSALM 8 praises and acclaims the name of God and God's goodness to the human creature, whom he crowns with glory and honor. This Psalm is eminently fulfilled in Jesus. His is our destiny as well.

◆ GOSPEL: The two disciples who met Jesus on the road to Emmaus return to Jerusalem and announce the Good News of Christ's Resurrection to the other disciples. As they are speaking, Jesus suddenly stands in their midst. He assures the disciples that he is really alive and speaks to them of the fulfillment of Scripture.

The Roman Missal

The Entrance Antiphon for today is taken from the Book of Wisdom. As we hear about how "wisdom opened mouths that were mute / and gave eloquence to the tongues of infants . . . ," we can think about the wisdom and graces that come through sacramental initiation.

The Gloria is sung or said today, as it is every day within the Octave of Easter.

The Collect makes explicit reference to "those reborn in the font of Baptism," continuing the central place of initiation in the Mass prayers this week. The prayer notes that God has brought many nations to confess his name, and so asks that the baptized "may be one in the faith of their hearts / and the homage of their deeds." This reminds us that one is baptized into a community of faith and into a life that must be lived in union with all the other baptized.

The Prayer over the Offerings states that the sacrificial offerings of this Eucharist are offered for those who have been baptized, and also "in hope of your increased help from heaven." The request for increased help can be understood as not only for the newly baptized, but for all the baptized.

Once again Preface I of Easter is the Preface to be used for today, and the phrase "on this day" is used. If the Roman Canon is used, be sure to use the special inserts.

The Communion Antiphon is clearly baptismal in its theme, as, coming from 1 Peter, it affirms that the chosen people were called out of darkness into God's wonderful light. In the Prayer after Communion, we once again have the celebration of the Eucharist referred to as "this most holy exchange," such that the transformation that has occurred in this offering might give us God's "help in this present life / and ensure for us eternal gladness."

F R I 25 (#265) white Friday in the Octave of Easter SOLEMNITY

The Lectionary for Mass

◆ FIRST READING: Despite their arrest, Peter and John proclaim the Gospel, which draws more believers. Note the emphasis given to the name of Jesus in their witness before their accusers.

◆ RESPONSORIAL PSALM 118: Our response is from the same psalm cited by Peter in the First Reading. We give thanks to the Lord for his goodness, for his wonderful work in establishing the rejected stone (Jesus) as the cornerstone (Lord and Savior).

◆ GOSPEL: The Apostles have returned to their former occupation as fishermen—in this instance, with little success. Jesus gifts them with a miraculous catch of fish, then nourishes them with food for body and spirit. The disciples know, without a doubt, that it is the Lord.

The Roman Missal

Today's Entrance Antiphon continues the week's emphasis on the newly baptized as it uses Red Sea imagery to refer to the ones who have been led (through the waters) in hope while their foes were engulfed by the sea; used in the context of today's liturgy, the reference has a baptismal connotation.

The Gloria is sung or said today.

The Collect reminds us that the Paschal Mystery is the covenant established by God that reconciles us to him, and it goes on to ask that what we celebrate in faith may be expressed in our deeds, thus giving voice to the very purpose of worship—namely, that it might transform us to live out the self-offering of the Paschal Mystery that we commemorate at liturgy.

The Prayer over the Offerings makes another reference about "the solemn exchange brought about by these paschal offerings," an exchange that brings us "from earthly desires / to a longing for the things of heaven."

As with all the days this week, Preface I of Easter is assigned for today, and, as specified at the text for the Preface, the phrase "on this day" is used. If Eucharistic Prayer I, the Roman Canon, is used, the special inserts are used.

The Communion Antiphon echoes the Gospel as Jesus invites his disciples—and us, at this Eucharist—to "Come and eat." The Prayer after Communion prays that God may keep safe those he has saved and redeemed, so that "they may rejoice in his Resurrection." The prayer makes an explicit mention of the Passion of the Lord, a remembrance that is traditional on Fridays, even during Easter Time.

S A T 26 (#266) white Saturday in the Octave of Easter SOLEMNITY

The Lectionary for Mass

◆ FIRST READING: The consternation of the Jewish leaders focuses on the proclamation of the name of Jesus. The disciples are warned to speak it no more, but they only respond that they must—in obedience to God.

◆ RESPONSORIAL PSALM 118: The disciples experience the truth of the psalmist's prayer: their strength is the Lord, who has rescued them from death. They acclaim the work of the Lord.

◆ GOSPEL: This portion of the longer (and probably later) ending of Mark's account of the Gospel summarizes stories that the other accounts tell in more detail: the Lord's appearance to and commission of Mary Magdalene, his appearance to the disciples on the road to Emmaus, and his appearance to the disciples at table. Jesus takes them to task for their stubbornness and lack of faith in refusing to believe the news of his Resurrection. Having seen and believed, they are sent to proclaim the Gospel to the world.

The Roman Missal

The joy of being chosen and being baptized is the theme that underlies the Entrance Antiphon for this Mass.

The Gloria is sung or said today.

The Collect again refers to the initiations that took place at the Easter Vigil as it acknowledges God as the one who gave "increase to the peoples who believe in you." Further explicit mention of initiation is found in the reference to the chosen ones clothed "with blessed immortality," the ones who were "reborn through the Sacrament of Baptism." Thus, Baptism continues to play center stage in the meaning of the Easter Octave, even on this late day.

The Prayer over the Offerings continues the motif of initiation as it refers to "the renewal constantly at work within us," asking for that renewal to "be the cause of our unending joy." That renewal is constantly at work within us, however, through our participation in the liturgy, which is the primary way we share in Christ's Death and Resurrection; thus the prayer includes the petition "that we may always find delight in these paschal mysteries."

Preface I of Easter is to be used today, although today is the last weekday for which it will be exclusively assigned. The phrase "on this day" is again used, as are the special inserts for Eucharistic Prayer I if that prayer is selected.

The Communion Antiphon continues the strong baptismal focus by reminding us that those who have been baptized in Christ "have put on Christ." The use of this phrase from Galatians as a Communion Antiphon can remind us of the close connection between "putting on Christ" in Baptism and the way we "put on Christ" through our union and transformation in him in Communion. This is echoed in the Prayer after Communion, which asks that those renewed by eternal mysteries "may attain in their flesh / the incorruptible glory of the resurrection." Thus we are also reminded that "putting on Christ" has eternal, eschatological effects.

(#43) white

☀ 27 Second Sunday of Easter (or Sunday of Divine Mercy)

About this Sunday

The Sunday of Divine Mercy is a day established by Pope John Paul II as "a perennial invitation to the Christian world, to face with confidence in divine benevolence, the difficulties an trials that humankind will experience in the years to come" (May 23, 2000, the Congregation for Divine Worship and the Discipline of the Sacraments). In a way similar to Passion Sunday (Palm Sunday) or the Fourth Sunday of Easter (Good

Shepherd Sunday), the Second Sunday of Easter bears the additional title of Sunday of Divine Mercy.

This is not a new solemnity or feast, nor does it celebrate a new or separate mystery of redemption, but rather, it leads into the continuing celebration of God's mercy during Easter Time. As the octave day of Easter, the Lectionary readings and prayer texts highlight the mystery of divine compassion that underlies the Church's Easter faith.

The Lectionary for Mass

◆ FIRST READING: We hear a description of the life of the early believers and what a model it offers to us in their devotion to the Apostles' teaching about Jesus, their commitment to their life in common, their fidelity to prayer and the Eucharist. The witness of their lives filled many with awe. No wonder they attracted new believers!

◆ RESPONSORIAL PSALM 118: This psalm of thanksgiving and praise celebrates God's mercy and covenant love. The second stanza can readily be the prayer of those who lost hope at the time of Jesus's arrest and Death (and who were also afraid as we hear in today's account of the Gospel) but experienced deliverance and renewed hope at his Resurrection. Verse 22 was often cited by the early Christians with reference to Jesus's Death and Resurrection. He is the foundation of the life of all believers.

◆ SECOND READING: We hear Peter's prayer of thanksgiving for God's mercy (a link with today's psalm) and the hope and the promise received through the Resurrection of Jesus from the dead. We may fittingly ask ourselves if the joy Peter and these early Christians experienced is ours. Why or why not?

◆ GOSPEL: The opening lines of today's Gospel tell us much about both the disciples and the Risen Jesus. They are behind locked doors

in fear and suddenly the Risen Jesus stands in their midst. Yes, it is really Jesus, but he has changed, his "body" is different now, no longer having the same limitations as before his Death. Although we may associate seeing and believing with the outspoken Thomas, note that the other disciples as well rejoiced when they "saw" the Lord. In particular, it was the sight of his wounds that led them to faith.

Notice that this (Easter evening) is the occasion when the Risen Jesus bestows the Holy Spirit on his disciples. Verses 19–23 are the Gospel for Pentecost Sunday this year, so see the discussion of these verses given there.

The Roman Missal

As the eighth day of the Octave of Easter, this Sunday completes the Easter Octave, and the Missal texts continue to strongly emphasize the meaning and effects of sacramental initiation. Historically, this day was given the name *dominica in albis*—the last day for the neophytes to wear their white baptismal garments. The two options for the Entrance Antiphon reflect this: the first option, from 1 Peter, makes reference to the "newborn infants" who long for "the pure, spiritual milk" that will allow them to "grow to salvation;" the second reminds us of the joy the newly-initiated have received, having been called into the heavenly kingdom.

Keep in mind, given the baptismal character of all of Easter Time, that the Rite for the Blessing and Sprinkling of Water is a good option to take advantage of. The rite may be used as a memorial of Baptism in place of the Penitential Act at the beginning of Mass on Sundays, and parishes and liturgy preparation groups would do well to do this on all the Sundays (and any other major celebrations) during Easter Time. The rite is found in Appendix II at the back of the Missal. The priest and ministers enter as usual, and the priest greets the people as usual. Then, standing at the chair (or perhaps going to the baptismal font), with a vessel containing water to be blessed nearby, he calls the people to prayer and then blesses the water; be sure to use the third option, the prayer during Easter Time. Salt may be blessed and added to the water if that is the custom of the people.

After this, the priest sprinkles himself, the ministers, and the people, ideally moving throughout the church. One of the chants suggested in the Missal or some other appropriate song is sung during the sprinkling. After the sprinkling, the singing ends, and the priest returns to his chair and prays the closing to the rite. After this prayer, the Gloria is sung.

The Collect is replete with the language of initiation: acknowledging that our faith is kindled "in the very recurrence of the paschal feast" (the celebration of the Eucharist), it asks that "all may grasp and rightly understand" the meaning of their initiation, which is spoken in terms of being washed, being reborn, and being redeemed. The reference to grasping and rightly understanding could be understood as the journey of mystagogia, that is, of unpacking the mysteries that were celebrated at the Easter Vigil.

The Prayer over the Offerings asks God to accept our oblations and, in an optional phrase, the oblations "of those you have brought to new birth," referring of course to the neophytes. The prayer goes on to ask that those "renewed by confession of your name and by Baptism" may "attain unending happiness," reminding us again of the promised eschatological fulfillment that is the consequence of being initiated into the mysteries.

Preface I of Easter is assigned for today, although today will be the last Sunday for which it will be the only one to be used; the phrase "on this day" is again the proper phrase to be used among the possible choices. Consider chanting the introductory dialogue and the Preface today, and every Sunday during Easter Time; if this is not the regular practice of your community, this can be a way of powerfully drawing attention to the festivity of the liturgical time, and in particular if this was the practice during Lent, this can be a way of highlighting the continuity of the liturgical times (but be sure to prepare and rehearse your assembly as needed, if your people are not familiar with the responses!). If Eucharistic Prayer I is selected, the proper forms of the "In communion with those" and the "Therefore, Lord, we pray" are still used, as it is the Octave of Easter.

The Prayer after Communion prays that "our reception of this paschal Sacrament" may have an ongoing effect in our life, both in mind and in heart. The phrase "paschal Sacrament" should be understood in a broad sense; while it can refer to the Eucharist itself, it should be seen as encompassing in a wider sense our participation in the totality of the Easter mystery: the Paschal Mystery and the sacraments of initiation, of which the Eucharist is the climax.

If a Solemn Blessing is to be used, it is the Solemn Blessing for Easter Time, found at number 6 in the "Blessings at the End of Mass and Prayers Over the People" section of the Missal immediately following the Order of Mass. Notice how the third section of the blessing continues the baptismal theme of Easter by its specific reference to that sacrament.

Finally, for the last time until Pentecost, the solemn double Alleluia dismissal is used.

Pastoral Reflection

The outpouring love of Jesus, our God in flesh, is unbelievable. Doubt is inevitable and many days we are like Thomas in need of proof and other days we are the voice of hope for another. Dig out the doubt in your life, the place you think cannot be touched and allow God's healing rays of mercy to flood into and touch you. As you are healed, be this instrument of healing to another. Stand in their presence and offer love through your being, not your words. Learn to quietly yet brilliantly shine as Jesus does through his divine mercy. Learn and pray the Divine Mercy chaplet this week and make it a more regular routine.

M O N 28 (#267) white Easter Weekday

Optional Memorials of St. Peter Chanel, Priest and Martyr / red; St. Louis Grignion de Montfort, Priest / white

The Lectionary for Mass

◆ First Reading: After their release from prison, Peter and John address their companions, who join with them in prayer for courage in proclaiming the Gospel and for confirmation of their word through healings, signs, and wonders.

◆ Responsorial Psalm 2 is quoted in the prayer in our First Reading. The disciples experience the rage of the Gentiles as did Jesus. Like Jesus, they also experience deliverance at the hands of their God.

◆ Gospel: Jesus speaks with Nicodemus, a prominent Pharisee and would-be disciple of him, who secretly comes to Jesus at night. Nicodemus is gradually enlightened as to what it means to be born from above, born of the Spirit. At the end of John's account of the Gospel, this same Nicodemus assists with the burial of Jesus (John 19:39).

The Roman Missal

Remember, since we are now outside the Octave, the Gloria is no longer used on weekdays, and the double Alleluia dismissal is discontinued, as are the special inserts for Eucharistic Prayer I.

The Collect for the Easter Weekday links this week to last week's strong emphasis on initiation by referring to participants in this Mass as "we, who have been renewed by paschal remedies." Those who are thus renewed are made new creations—they transcend "the likeness of our earthly parentage." Having thus been made new, the prayer asks that we may reach our final fulfillment in eternity, "transformed in the image of our heavenly maker."

The Prayer over the Offerings gives voice to the joy both of the liturgical time and of the eternal joy that God wants for us, as it recognizes God as the one who has given us cause for gladness and as it asks that "the gifts we bring / may bear fruit in perpetual happiness." The Prayer after Communion for the Easter Weekday recalls the eschatological element in every celebration of the Eucharist, begun here on earth and pointing to fulfillment in the heavenly banquet, as it asks that "those you were pleased to renew by eternal mysteries / may attain in their flesh / the incorruptible glory of the resurrection."

Any one of the five Prefaces of Easter may be used today. While any one of the five is appropriate, perhaps, in light of the Collect's reference to renewal and initiation, and the Gospel's references to being "born from above," either Preface II, with its references to children of the light rising to eternal life, or Preface IV, as it speaks about the old order being destroyed, the renewal of the universe, and life being restored in Christ, would be good choices.

If you are observing the optional Memorial of St. Peter Chanel, only the Collect is proper for the day, and is found in the Proper of Saints in the back of the Missal, at April 28. The other orations may be taken from either the Common of Martyrs: For One Martyr during Easter Time, or from the Common of Pastors: For Missionaries. If the optional Memorial of St. Louis Grignion de Montfort is being celebrated, it is again only the Collect that is proper, although there is a choice from among two options for the Collect; for this memorial, the other orations are found at the Common of Pastors: For One Pastor.

Today's Saints

St. Peter Chanel was a French Marist priest, who was sent to evangelize the southwest Pacific. He brought the Gospel to Polynesia but was martyred when the local king's son sought Baptism. St. Louis de Montfort was a famous preacher in his day. France was then tainted by Jansenism, which mixed Catholicism with Calvinist teachings such as predestination and over-emphasis on human depravity. Louis undid the damage by preaching about the tenderness of God as revealed through the gift to the Church of Mary. His books, *True Devotion to Mary* and *The Secret of Mary*, are still read today.

(#268)   white
TUE 29 Memorial of St. Catherine of Siena, Virgin and Doctor of the Church

The Lectionary for Mass

◆ FIRST READING: The community of believers was completely united in mind and heart, and held all possessions in common. We are introduced to Barnabas, future companion of Paul, who gave the proceeds from the sale of his field to the community. He exemplifies

what it meant to hold all things in common. The Apostles continued their witness to the Risen Christ.

◆ RESPONSORIAL PSALM 93 extols the glorious majesty of God the King. This is also an appropriate response to the proclamation of the Risen Christ: he who was crucified as the King of the Jews is now exalted at the right hand of the Father.

◆ GOSPEL: Jesus teaches Nicodemus about the necessity of being born again, born of the Spirit, born from above. Jesus speaks of himself as the one who has descended from heaven, the Son of Man whose lifting up on the Cross will also be his lifting up in glory.

The Roman Missal

The prayers for this Mass, all proper for the day, are found in the Proper of Saints section of the Missal, at April 29.

The Collect reminds us that St. Catherine was "on fire with divine love / in her contemplation of the Lord's Passion / and her service of your Church." Therefore, we invoke her intercession that, by our participation in the mystery of Christ, we may "ever exult in the revelation of his glory." The Prayer over the Offerings asks that, insofar as we have been instructed by the teaching of St. Catherine, "we may give ever more fervent thanks / to you, the one true God" as we offer this sacrifice commemorating her. The Prayer after Communion calls to mind how the Eucharist unites all members of the Church throughout time, as it acknowledges that the Eucharist has nourished us and conferred eternal life upon us just as it did St. Catherine in her time.

The Preface chosen could appropriately be one of the five Prefaces of Easter, highlighting that we are still in Easter Time. The priest celebrant could also choose one of the two Prefaces of Saints, or the Preface of Holy Virgins and Religious.

Today's Saint

St. Catherine of Siena (1347–1380) was a Dominican tertiary and mystic, the twenty-fourth of twenty-five children. Against family opposition, she dedicated herself to Christ at a very young age. At 16 she withdrew from her family to lead a life of intense prayer. When she emerged, she began to dedicate herself to care of the sick and poor. Her joyful spirit attracted a number of followers. After a series of mystical experiences, Catherine felt compelled to write letters to those in secular and Church authority, which she dictated to her friend, the Dominican Raymond of Capua. Her influence became so great that papal legates consulted her. At this time, the papal residence had moved from Rome to Avignon, France. Catherine begged Gregory XI to return to Rome, which he did in 1377. St. Catherine died in 1380 at the age of 33, leaving behind her writings, *The Dialogue: A Treatise on Divine Providence,* letters, and prayers. She is represented in art holding a lily and wearing the habit of a Dominican tertiary, and is the patron of Europe and Italy. In 1970, Pope Paul VI made her a Doctor of the Church, one of the first women, along with Teresa of Avila, to be so honored.

WED 30 (#269) white
Easter Weekday

Optional Memorial of St. Pius V, Pope / white

The Lectionary for Mass

◆ First Reading: The signs and wonders worked by the Apostles in the name of Jesus draw great crowds. Filled with jealousy, the high priests, and the Sadducees (who deny the Resurrection) arrest the Apostles. They are delivered from prison by an angel of the Lord and are sent to continue their proclamation of the Gospel.

◆ Responsorial Psalm 34: The Lord did indeed hear the cry of his poor Apostles and sent his angel to deliver them. The Apostles themselves have experienced (have "tasted") and "seen" the goodness of the Lord.

◆ Gospel: God's love for the world was so great that he sent his only beloved Son, not to condemn the world, but to give light and life to all who believe.

The Roman Missal

The weekday Collect continues to situate us with the privileged Easter Time by announcing that "we recall year by year the mysteries / by which, through the restoration of its original dignity, / human nature has received the hope of rising again." We can hear echoes of Christ as the new Adam in this prayer. The Prayer over the Offerings, which will be used again on the Fifth Sunday of Easter, again uses the phrase "wonderful exchange," highlighting the important aspect of liturgical theology that it is the very gifts we offer that become the vehicle for our participation in the life of God. That sharing in God's life was begun at Baptism and becomes more and more pervasive through our participation in the Eucharist—the prayer entreats: "as we have come to know your truth, / we may make it ours by a worthy way of life." The Prayer after Communion will also appear again on the Fifth Sunday of Easter; the motif of the old being made new is employed to announce the transformation that is offered to us in the Eucharist: "lead those you have imbued with heavenly mysteries / to pass from former ways to newness of life."

Among the choices of the Easter Prefaces, perhaps Preface II, with its theme of new life in Christ and its explicit mention about "children of light" rising to eternal life, would be a good choice to echo the Gospel. Preface IV, with its mention of "integrity of life" being restored in Christ, could work as well.

For the optional Memorial of St. Pius V, the Collect is the only text proper for the day, and it is found in the Proper of Saints at April 30. The other orations are taken from the Common of Pastors: For a Pope.

Today's Saint

St. Pius V (1504–1572) was a Dominican theologian, elected pope in 1566. His primary task as pope was to implement the reforms of the Council of Trent, which had concluded three years before. During his pontificate, seminaries were reformed, a new Missal was published, and the Catechism and Breviary were also revised. Pius retained his white Dominican habit when he became pope; since that time all the popes have worn white.

May
Month of Our Lady

THU 1 (#270) white
Easter Weekday

Optional Memorial of St. Joseph the Worker (#559) / white

The Lectionary for Mass

◆ First Reading: The high priests and council interrogate the Apostles, who can only respond that it is God whom they must obey. Enraged, the Jewish leaders want to destroy them.

◆ Responsorial Psalm 34: As yesterday, we have Psalm 34 again with its strong confidence in the Lord and his deliverance of the just.

◆ Gospel: The Son is from above, sent by God, to give eternal life to all who believe. Do we "accept his testimony" (John 3:33)?

The Roman Missal

The Collect for the Easter Weekday refers to Christ as "our High Priest" and presents him not only as the one interceding on our behalf, but also as the one who brings salvation through his Paschal sacrifice. Because he is one like us, he can bring us reconciliation; because he is also God, he can free us from our sins. The Prayer over the Offerings speaks of our prayers and sacrificial offerings rising up to God, asking that the effect of that will be our being "conformed to the mysteries of your mighty love." We will use this same prayer again on Monday after the Third Sunday of Easter and on the Sixth Sunday of Easter. The Prayer after Communion, also repeated on those two days, prays that we will experience an increase in "the fruits of this paschal Sacrament" and that our hearts will be strengthened by the saving food of the Eucharist. Thus does the prayer link what we have celebrated in church with observable and practical consequences of living the Christian life every day.

Any one of the five Prefaces of Easter may be used today, although perhaps Preface V, with its theme of Christ as priest and victim and its explicit mention of Christ showing himself as priest, altar, and lamb of sacrifice would resonate well with the Collect.

If you are observing the optional Memorial of St. Joseph the Worker, then all the texts are proper for this Mass and are to be found in the Proper of Saints section of the Missal, at May 1. The Collect takes up the theme of work, asking that "by the example of Saint Joseph and under his patronage / we may complete the works you set us to do / and attain the rewards you promise." The Prayer over the Offerings prays that the gifts we offer at this celebration in commemoration of St. Joseph will become a source of

protection for us. The Preface, proper for the memorial, is the Preface titled "The mission of Saint Joseph" and it is given, both with musical notation and without, along with the other proper texts for today. It is the same Preface used for the Solemnity of St. Joseph on March 19, speaking of him as a "just man" and a "wise and faithful servant." The Prayer after Communion asks that, after the example of St. Joseph, we may cherish "in our hearts the signs of your love" and "ever enjoy the fruit of perpetual peace."

Today's Optional Memorial

Today you may celebrate the optional Memorial of St. Joseph the Worker, a relatively new addition to the calendar. It was introduced by Pope Pius XII in 1955, as an alternative to secular May Day celebrations of the worker, which originated in Communist countries and which did more to promote Communist propaganda than to promote the worker. Pope Pius XII urged workers to look to St. Joseph, the carpenter, and to see the dignity inherent in human labor, which could become a source of holiness.

(#271) white

FRI 2 Memorial of St. Athanasius, Bishop and Doctor of the Church

The Lectionary for Mass

◆ FIRST READING: Gamaliel, a revered teacher of the law, wisely addresses the Sanhedrin: if the witness of the Apostles is of divine origin, then the Sanhedrin will have no power over it. In fact, they may even be fighting God. If it is of human origin, in time it will destroy itself. Though persuaded, the Sanhedrin has the Apostles flogged (as was Jesus). What do we make of their joy that they are found worthy to suffer for the name of Jesus? Would that same joy be ours?

◆ RESPONSORIAL PSALM 27: Our First Reading ends with the Apostles continuing their proclamation of the Gospel in the Temple (the house of God) as well as in their own homes. Thus, today's Responsorial Antiphon: "One thing I seek: to dwell in the house of the Lord." The verses speak confidently of the Lord as one's refuge and salvation.

◆ GOSPEL: The story of the feeding of the multitude is a beautiful illustration that in Jesus, whatever one has is enough for what is needed. Who of us cannot identify with Philip and Andrew? How are we going to do this? If this is all we have, what good is it when so much more is needed? If we could only have the mind of Jesus, take what is at hand, and give thanks. Would we, too, find that it is more than enough?

The Roman Missal

The prayers for this Mass, all proper for the day, are found in the Proper of Saints section of the Missal, at May 2.

The Collect acknowledges St. Athanasius "as an outstanding champion of your Son's divinity" and asks that we may grow in knowledge and love of God because of the saint's teaching and protection. The Prayer over the Offerings notes how St. Athanasius professed "an unblemished faith" and asks that as we commemorate him, so may we witness to the same truth as he did, and thus be brought to salvation. The Prayer after Communion professes the true divinity of Christ, the doctrine St. Athanasius upheld, and petitions that we may be given life and protection through that same divinity of Christ, which we also profess.

The Preface chosen could appropriately be one of the five Prefaces of Easter, highlighting that we are still in Easter Time. The priest celebrant could also choose one of the two Prefaces of Saints, or the Preface of Holy Pastors could also be used.

Today's Saint

St. Athanasius (293/6–373), Bishop of Alexandria and Doctor of the Church, contributed immensely in the areas of doctrine and spirituality. In terms of doctrine, he defended the teaching of the First Council of Nicaea (325 AD) that Jesus was both fully human and fully divine. The Arians, who advocated that Jesus was not divine, unleashed a series of attacks on Athanasius, resulting in his exile not just once, but five times in his life. During one period of exile, he wrote a biography of the renowned hermit and monk, St. Anthony of Egypt. This spiritual classic, *Life of Antony*, continues to be a source of inspiration for people longing to remove worldly distractions that prevent them from mystical union with God. He is also noted for two other writings: *On the Incarnation* and *Discourses Against the Arians*. Many titles have been bestowed upon him, including defender of faith, champion of orthodoxy, mystical theologian, and spiritual master.

SAT 3 (#561) red
Feast of SS. Philip and James, Apostles

The Lectionary for Mass

◆ FIRST READING: Notice that in this our earliest scriptural account of the Resurrection of Jesus, James is specifically named as one to whom the Risen Lord appeared. We can easily become confused in trying to sort out "who's who" in the various appearances named, most of which we find recounted only by Paul. Are the James and the Apostles of verse 7 understood more broadly than the Twelve of verse 5? Paul used the term "Apostles" with reference to himself and others who had not known Jesus before his Resurrection (see 1 Corinthians 15:9). The answer doesn't really matter. What is important is

that it is the experience of the Risen Jesus that gave rise to deep personal faith and became the impetus for the proclamation of the Gospel.

◆ RESPONSORIAL PSALM 19: Today's acclamation is an apt summary of the whole apostolic missionary endeavor, even though the verse itself comes from a psalm in the Old Testament and refers originally to creation as bearing witness to God's glory. The Apostles speak in this same tradition and to the ends of the earth—our own land included—their voice has resounded through the ages.

◆ GOSPEL: It is Philip who is singled out in today's Gospel, depicted here as one whose question to Jesus at the Last Supper not only reveals his own lack of comprehension of Jesus's message, but also leads to further explanation and teaching from Jesus. May we, like Philip, ponder the words of Jesus our Master and take his words to heart.

The Roman Missal

The texts for this Mass are proper and are located in the Proper of Saints section of the Missal, at May 3. The Gloria is sung or said today, since it is a feast.

The Collect notes how we are gladdened by this feast day each year, asking the prayers of the two Apostles that we might be granted a share in Jesus's Passion and Resurrection, and so see God in eternity. The Prayer over the Offerings, a short and direct prayer, simply asks the Lord to receive the offerings we bring on this feast day and, in so doing, to "bestow on us religion pure and undefiled." The Prayer after Communion gives a nod to the Communion of Saints as it observes how together with the Apostles, Philip and James, we contemplate God in his Son and thus "may be worthy to possess eternal life."

The Preface, proper for today, is one of the two Prefaces of the Apostles. Also, in place of the usual final blessing at the end of Mass, the Solemn Blessing for "The Apostles" may be used.

Today's Saints

Two of the chosen Twelve, SS. Philip and James (first century), grace the liturgical calendar today. Although few details are known about St. Philip, Scripture portrays him as one who leads others to Christ. St. Philip introduces his friend Nathaniel to Jesus, and points to Jesus as the source of nourishment in the feeding of the five thousand. He also highlights Jesus as the path to the Father in the Last Supper account. St. James "the Lesser"—not to be confused with St. James "the Greater" (he is honored on July 25)—was gifted with a special appearance of the Risen Christ (see 1 Corinthians 15:7). Throughout history it was believed that he authored the letter of James, but recent biblical scholarship considers this to be unlikely. Both SS. Philip and James died as martyrs, shedding their blood for the sake of the Gospel. They are most likely celebrated together because the Basilica of the Twelve Apostles in Rome is dedicated to them.

Pastoral Reflection

What a promise! We will do greater works than even Jesus did! Is that possible? It seems so. A band of Twelve, mostly unremarkable men, spread the word about Jesus to the ends of the world. SS. James and Philip were two of those people who laid the foundation of the Church that has lasted for over two thousand years. What a promise we have been given, and what greatness we can build upon through the name of Jesus.

The Lectionary for Mass

◆ FIRST READING: On the day of Pentecost, filled with the power of God's Spirit, Peter—and indeed all of the Apostles—stand up and bear witness to Jesus! What a change in these men through the working of God's Spirit! Peter, who earlier had denied knowing Jesus three times out of fear, now, in the power of the Spirit, gives public witness to his Death and Resurrection—events interpreted as part of God's plan and purpose. It is impossible that death would have power over Jesus and God!

◆ RESPONSORIAL PSALM 16: Today's song of confidence is quoted by Peter in today's First Reading and interpreted as fulfilled in Jesus of Nazareth. Death had no power over him. In Jesus, all can see the path to true and everlasting life.

◆ SECOND READING: Peter reminds believers—called sojourners in a land that is not theirs—of the price of their redemption: the blood of Christ, the Lamb of God. Their—and our—faith is centered in him.

◆ GOSPEL: Two of Jesus's disciples, discouraged by the happenings of the previous few days, are desolately leaving Jerusalem. It is Easter evening, and although the women had proclaimed the news of the empty tomb, these disciples, along with others, still did not understand. When an unknown fellow traveler met them along the way and began speaking with them about Scripture, their hearts were enlivened. They recognized the stranger as Jesus when he broke bread with them. Are our own celebrations of the Eucharist occasions for recognizing Jesus in Word and in the breaking of the bread?

The Roman Missal

The Entrance Antiphon speaks of the praise that is offered to God from all the earth, indeed, from all creation; such praise is in keeping with the joy of Easter Time as we continue to proclaim Jesus's Resurrection.

It would be a good idea to again use the Rite for the Blessing and Sprinkling of Water, as discussed for the Second Sunday of Easter. The rite is found in Appendix II at the back of the Missal and replaces the Penitential Act. The Gloria is sung today.

The Collect continues the tone of joy set by the Entrance Antiphon as it describes how God's people have been "renewed in youthfulness of spirit" and rejoice "in the restored glory of our adoption." Such references to youthfulness, restoration, and adoption maintain the imagery of the new life given to us at Baptism that would be recalled in the Rite of Blessing and Sprinkling of Water. The prayer ends by reminding us that such Easter joy goes beyond the present moment—there is a fitting eschatological reference as we ask that "we may look forward in confident hope / to the rejoicing of the day of resurrection." Our present participation in the mystery of Christ's Death and Resurrection cannot be separated from the way that participation points toward its future fulfillment.

The Prayer over the Offerings continues the joyful tone of the texts by describing the Church as "exultant" as we offer these gifts, again asking that the offerings will "bear fruit in perpetual happiness."

Any one of the five Easter Prefaces may be selected for today; if Preface I is chosen, remember that the correct wording is "in this time." Consider chanting the introductory dialogue and the Preface today, and every Sunday during Easter Time, in order to highlight the ongoing festivity of the season.

Three different Communion Antiphons are given for today, corresponding with the Gospel readings for the three cycles of the liturgical year in the Lectionary; since we are in Year A, the first antiphon, highlighting the Emmaus disciples' recognition of Jesus in the breaking of the bread, is the one to use this year. How advantageous this is to have this text placed here, as at this and every Eucharist it is still at that moment (among others) when we recognize the presence of the Lord!

The Prayer after Communion also has an eschatological focus, as it reminds us that our participation in the Paschal Mystery at the Eucharist always looks forward to its fulfillment in "the incorruptible glory of the resurrection."

You might consider using the solemn blessing for Easter Time, found at number 6 in the "Blessings at the End of Mass and Prayers Over the People" section of the Missal immediately following the Order of Mass. Remember that a regular formula for dismissal is used, not the solemn double Alleluia.

Pastoral Reflection

Today's rich Gospel account is full of words that constantly relate to our lives and society today. Disappointment, confusion, frustration, hope for more, and a vision held that does not match the promised gift of God. Open your eyes to see what is present and allow your hearts to burn with a passion to know that the small things mean so much more! Break "bread" with your family and friends, whether this be actual food or breaking open your lives with intentional sharing about the goodness discovered in your day. Share a spoken blessing over your food and with your friends of family. Be intentional. Know the love of Christ in your communion of shared community.

M O N 5 (#273) white
Easter Weekday

The Lectionary for Mass

◆ FIRST READING: Stephen continues the Spirit-filled ministry of Jesus and, like Jesus, encounters opposition and false accusation. Through it all, his countenance was "like the face of an angel" (Acts of the Apostles 6:15), centered in the deep peace that is the gift of the Spirit within.

◆ RESPONSORIAL PSALM 119: Virtually every verse focuses on some aspect of the law and the psalmist's relationship to it. The law, for Israel, was a guide on the way through life, a priceless treasure. In today's verses, the psalmist also prays for deliverance from false accusers, treasuring God's truth above all.

◆ GOSPEL: The crowds pursue Jesus after he so miraculously fed them. Jesus questions them on their motives for seeking him. And what about us: why and what do we seek? Let us hear Jesus's words and seek what endures forever—eternal life.

The Roman Missal

The Collect for today gives voice to the motif of putting off the old self, noting how we have been conformed to the nature of Christ "through the healing paschal remedies." Thus, being remade in this way should result in our living as Christ did. The Paschal Mystery of dying and rising with Christ, and its effects for the way we are supposed to live life, continues to

be present in this Collect, appropriate for Easter Time. The Prayer over the Offerings, heard on the Thursday after the Second Week of Easter, continues the theme of being conformed to the Paschal Mystery, a conformation expressed here as being effected by the rising up of our prayers "together with the sacrificial offerings" which leads to a purification through the graciousness of God. The Prayer after Communion notes how the Resurrection of Christ has restored us to eternal life and asks for an increase of "the fruits of this paschal Sacrament"—particularly, the strengthening of our hearts.

Any one of the five Easter Prefaces may be used today; the readings don't seem to necessarily suggest any one more appropriate than another, although perhaps Preface I, focusing in general on the Paschal Mystery, with its mention that "dying he has destroyed our death, / and by rising, restored our life," would resonate well with the orations.

T U E 6 (#274) white
Easter Weekday

The Lectionary for Mass

◆ FIRST READING: Today's First Reading is the conclusion of Stephen's address to the Sanhedrin, or Jewish council, before whom he is tried. He, however, becomes their accuser. His words challenge us as well. Are we among those who "always oppose the Holy Spirit" (Acts of the Apostles 7:51)? Note his prayer as he dies. Note also the introduction of Saul (Paul) at the end of the reading.

◆ RESPONSORIAL PSALM 31: The response is the words of both Jesus and Stephen as they die. It is a song of trust in God's deliverance.

◆ GOSPEL: The Jews seek signs (miracles) that they might "see and believe" (John 6:30). Jesus invites them to "see" with their minds and

leads them to a deeper faith. The true Bread from heaven is not the manna God provided for the Israelites in the desert, or even the bread with which Jesus fed the multitudes, but Jesus himself, sent to give life to the world. May we too say, "Sir, give us this bread always" (John 6:34). May we know that it is offered to us each day.

The Roman Missal

Today's Collect continues Easter Time's overall emphasis on sacramental initiation with reference to "those reborn of water and the Holy Spirit," as it asks for "an increase of the grace you have bestowed;" this increase is available through the Eucharist, which is the culmination of and renews the life of grace begun at Baptism. The Prayer over the Offerings, recently used this past Sunday, expresses the joy of the Church, a joy that originates in the new life given at Easter and finds fulfillment in the happiness of the Kingdom of God. The Prayer after Communion, also repeated from Sunday, asks that those who have been renewed by eternal mysteries—pointing to how every celebration of the Eucharist is our present participation in the Paschal Mystery—may "attain in their flesh / the incorruptible glory of the resurrection," thus, like the Prayer over the Offerings, reminding us of the eschatological fulfillment that awaits us.

Any one of the five Easter Prefaces may be used today. Perhaps, in light of the First Reading from Acts, which portrays Stephen's death as paralleling Jesus's, we could find in Preface V of Easter, with its mention of Christ our Passover being sacrificed, its reference to the oblation of Christ's Body, and its mention of Christ "commending himself to you for our salvation," an echo of both Jesus and Stephen handing themselves over in death.

W E D 7 (#275) white
Easter Weekday

The Lectionary for Mass

◆ FIRST READING: Stephen's death marks the beginning of a severe persecution of the Jewish Christians spearheaded by Saul. Acting out of his zeal for Judaism and convinced that those who believed Jesus was the Messiah were in error, Saul sets out to destroy this perceived heresy and threat to Judaism. This time of great suffering and dispersion of the disciples nevertheless gives rise to new life and wholeness as the Gospel is proclaimed in new places.

◆ RESPONSORIAL PSALM 66: Today's psalm echoes the joy in the last line of the First Reading. Notice the emphasis on the deeds and works of the Lord, given new meaning in the healings accomplished in the name of Jesus. The God who miraculously led Israel out of Egypt continues to work marvels in their midst.

◆ GOSPEL: "Comings" abound in today's Gospel: that of Jesus into the world, that of the believer to Jesus, and that of the believer to the Father and to eternal life. How strong, how real is our belief in Jesus? Jesus was solely about the will of his Father when he came to earth. Are we?

The Roman Missal

Today's Collect emphasizes God's initiative in saving us, as it points to "those you have endowed with the grace of faith," and it again reminds us to look beyond our present participation in the Paschal Mystery toward our full participation as it asks that God give us "an eternal share in the Resurrection of your Only Begotten Son." The Prayer over the Offerings speaks of the ongoing power of the Paschal Mystery in our life, asking that "the renewal constantly at work within us / may be the cause of our unending joy." We should always remember that the effects of the Lord's Resurrection are ongoing in our lives, especially through the liturgy (in the words of the prayer, "these paschal mysteries"). In the Prayer after Communion we once again hear the felicitous phrase "holy exchange" as we pray that this exchange—this liturgical celebration—"may bring your help in this present life / and ensure for us eternal gladness."

Any one of the five Easter Prefaces may be selected for today; perhaps Preface II, with its theme of new life in Christ, would resonate well with what was said above concerning the orations.

T H U 8 (#276) white
Easter Weekday

The Lectionary for Mass

◆ FIRST READING: Today's account of Philip and the Ethiopian eunuch is a beautiful story of the impact God's Word can have on us if only we are open to it and eager to understand. On hearing Philip's proclamation about Jesus, the eunuch immediately believes, requests, and receives Baptism. The reference to Philip being snatched up evokes other accounts of heavenly translation in Scripture (such as Elijah's; see 2 Kings 2:11). This happening is a witness to the tremendous power of God's Spirit at work in the life of Philip.

◆ RESPONSORIAL PSALM 66: Today's Responsorial Psalm, a call to all the earth to cry out with joy to the Lord, is aptly chosen as a response to a reading about the conversion of the Ethiopian eunuch. As a result of his conversion, the man receives new life (first stanza) and continues on his way rejoicing.

◆ GOSPEL: Faith in Jesus is first of all the result of the Father's initiative in drawing people to his Son, a point beautifully illustrated in today's First Reading. Faith in Jesus leads to eternal life. Within the context of chapter 6 of John's account, having faith in Jesus means recognizing and receiving him as the Bread of eternal life, the Bread that is his very own life given for us.

The Roman Missal

The Collect points to our ongoing celebration of the Fifty days of Easter Time, and the mystery we focus on, as it asks that we experience God's "compassion more readily / during these days when, by your gift, / we have known it more fully." The mention of having been "freed from the darkness of error" can, of course, call to mind the illumination that occurred at Baptism, another theme that runs throughout Easter Time. The Prayer over the Offerings expresses how this "wonderful exchange" makes us partakers of the very life of God (that is in the liturgy the very work of our redemption is accomplished). Being made sharers in the life of God, however, the prayer reminds us that we must "make it ours by a worthy way of life." The Prayer after Communion returns to the old way of life/new way of life motif, asking that we be led to the new way.

Among the Easter Prefaces to be used today, perhaps either II, with its reference to "children of light" or IV, with its statement that "the old order [is] destroyed, / a universe cast down is renewed, / and integrity of life is restored to us in Christ" would continue the themes found in the orations.

F R I 9 (#277) white
Easter Weekday

The Lectionary for Mass

◆ FIRST READING: In this rather long reading, we hear the first of three accounts in Acts of the Apostles regarding Saul's conversion to Jesus. It is important to note that Saul was a deeply religious man prior to this experience on the road to Damascus, zealous for the traditions of his ancestors, and convinced that those who followed the way of Jesus were in error. Notice the interplay of the themes of light and darkness, of blindness and sight, of ignorance and understanding. Notice also the role of hearing, of being led by the hand, and of being healed through the laying on of hands. What openness to God's at times perplexing ways was demanded of both Saul and Ananias!

◆ RESPONSORIAL PSALM 117: Today's Responsorial Psalm is a fitting response to the account of Saul's conversion, for it is exactly what he did for the rest of his life: he went out and proclaimed the Gospel of Jesus to all the world.

◆ GOSPEL: The controversy between Jesus and the Jews continues. How can Jesus give them his flesh to eat and his blood to drink? How can the food he gives be better than the manna God gave to Israel in the desert? Jesus is true bread from heaven. Jesus's very life is nourishment for the world. Jesus's body, given in his sacrificial Death, passed over into glorious new life. Partaking of his Body and Blood, given for believers in every age, is assurance that we share in this glorious new life now and forever.

The Roman Missal

The Collect for today emphasizes new life: since we have "come to know / the grace of the Lord's Resurrection," we pray that we "ourselves rise to newness of life." The prayer reminds us of the agency of the Holy Spirit as it acknowledges that this rising to newness of life will occur "through the love of the Spirit." The Prayer over the Offerings entreats that what we do at this liturgy will become the pattern of our entire lives—that "the oblation of this spiritual sacrifice" may "make of us an eternal offering to you." The Prayer after Communion asks

that since "We have partaken of the gifts of this sacred mystery," that it effects in our life a "growth in charity." The directness of this prayer reminds us that the fruits of the Eucharist must always be made manifest in our love toward one another.

The various references to living in newness of life, and the Gospel's reference to having life because of our feeding on the Bread of Life might make Easter Prefaces I or II likely candidates for use today.

SAT 10 (#278) | white
Easter Weekday

Optional Memorial of St. Damien de Veuster, Priest

The Lectionary for Mass

◆ FIRST READING: After Saul's conversion, the Church experiences a time of peace. The Church was "built up" (Acts of the Apostles 9:31) not only in number, but in conviction and virtue. The Apostles continued to work signs and wonders in the name of Jesus. Today we hear of two such incidents: the paralyzed man Aeneas and the woman disciple, Tabitha, who had fallen sick and died.

◆ RESPONSORIAL PSALM 116: Today's Responsorial Psalm is one of thanksgiving, fittingly prayed by Aeneas, Tabitha, Peter, and all believers, with gratitude for all the good the Lord has done for us.

◆ GOSPEL: Today's Gospel is the conclusion of the sixth chapter of John's account of the Gospel, and we hear verses that might appropriately be titled "the struggle to believe." Those who hear Jesus's words are faced with a decision: Shall we stay with him? Or do we return to our former way of life? What is our response?

The Roman Missal

Baptism continues to take center stage in the Collect for the Easter Weekday as it specifically mentions

"the font of Baptism" and petitions that "those reborn in Christ" be "kept safe" and thus, preserved in "the grace of your blessing." Being preserved and protected are requests that underlie the Prayer over the Offerings as well, a prayer that requests that in accepting our offerings, the Lord may ensure that we never lose what we have received and "attain the gifts that are eternal." The Prayer after Communion also prays for the keeping safe "those whom you have saved by your kindness," so that, having been redeemed in the Passion, we may rejoice in the Resurrection (note the dynamism of the Paschal Mystery that is expressed in this prayer).

In view of the orations for the Easter Weekday Mass, Prefaces I, II or IV, with their references to restoration and new life, would fit in well both with the orations and with the first reading's account from the Acts of the Apostles of the raising up of Tabitha.

If the optional Memorial of St. Damien de Veuster is being observed the Collect is proper and is found in the Proper of Saints section of the Missal, at May 10. It hails St. Damien as "a shining witness of love for the poorest and most abandoned" and therefore asks that "we too may be servants of the most needy and rejected." The Prayer over the Offerings and the Prayer after Communion should be taken from the Common of Pastors: For Missionaries. The Preface may still be one of the Easter Prefaces, if you wish to maintain a strong link to the season, or it may be the Preface I or II or Saints or of Holy Pastors.

Today's Saint

After years of missionary work in the Hawaiian Islands, Damien (1840–1889), a young priest from Belgium, sought to align himself even more with the "crucified" in society. He requested to be stationed on the island of Moloka'i where the lepers and diseased were sent to die. Outraged by the deplorable conditions of the island, he sought to restore a sense of dignity. Within a short period of time, the sick were living in clean houses instead of caves, and upon death they were given a proper burial rather than being dumped into mass graves. Even though leprosy was highly contagious, he chose to remain in close contact with the people. Damien eventually contracted the disease and died from it. He was recently canonized by Pope Benedict XVI on October 11, 2009.

(#49) white

11 Fourth Sunday of Easter
Good Shepherd Sunday

About this Sunday

The Fourth Sunday of Easter is traditionally referred to as *Good Shepherd Sunday*. Hearing the Shepherd's voice, followers recognize and know it is their God. Safe in the knowledge that they cannot be taken from the hand of the Shepherd, those who hear his voice follow as faithful believers willing to go where God calls and sends them. When all the clamor of false voices and seductive distractions threaten to overwhelm, we have only to listen carefully to be led to do the work of the Father. Once again, we are reminded of how loved we are as we hear the echoing words of the psalm: "Know that the Lord is

God; / he made us, his we are; / his people, the flock he tends" (100:3).

The Lectionary for Mass

◆ FIRST READING: We hear Peter's words to the Jews assembled in Jerusalem for the feast of Pentecost, immediately after he and the other disciples had received the powerful outpouring of the Holy Spirit. Their response to the proclamation of Jesus as Lord and Messiah is virtually immediate, as Peter's words "cut [pierced] to the heart." The truth of his words resonated within them, through God's gift of faith. Notice their eagerness to respond: "What are we to do, my brothers?" Hearing his answer, some three thousand people were baptized that day.

◆ RESPONSORIAL PSALM 23: Today's psalm no doubt is chosen in view of the fact that today is *Good Shepherd Sunday*: the Gospel being taken from John 10 each year. Nevertheless, there is a very real way in which Psalm 23 is most apropos today. One way the Lord leads his people is through those who proclaim the Gospel. Can we not think of the waters spoken of in today's psalm as the waters of Baptism? The anointing with oil? Our anointing in Baptism and Confirmation. And the table? Our Eucharist.

◆ SECOND READING: The theme of Jesus as the Shepherd is heard in today's Second Reading as well: he is "shepherd / and guardian" of our souls. The main focus of the text, however, is the witness of what Christ has done for us sheep who have strayed, that we may "follow / in his footsteps." Follow where or what? His example as described in verse 23, and the way he has shown us through death into life.

◆ GOSPEL: Several words and images occur repeatedly in today's Gospel, thus giving emphasis to their importance: "listen," "voice," "gate." Imagine an enclosed area, providing security and protection

for a flock. Jesus is presented as the "sheepgate," through whom we must enter into the fold and follow out if we will find "pasture" (another image from Psalm 23). Jesus is the Shepherd, the one who knows his sheep by name and cares deeply for them, even to the point of laying down his life. He came that we might have life in all its fullness.

The Roman Missal

The Entrance Antiphon continues to set the tone of Easter praise as it proclaims that the "love of the Lord fills the earth." Its reference to the Word of the Lord making the heavens can perhaps bring back to mind the proclamation of the Creation reading in Genesis at the Easter Vigil. The antiphon also reminds us of the life-giving power of God both at the beginning of the world and in the recreation of the world in Jesus's Resurrection.

Continue to use the Rite for the Blessing and Sprinkling of Water, as discussed for the Second Sunday of Easter, or, if you haven't been using it, consider beginning to do so. This rite, found in Appendix II of the Missal, replaces the Penitential Act. The Gloria is sung today.

The Collect refers to God's people as "the humble flock" who ask to "reach / where the brave shepherd has gone before." This, of course, echoes the Gospel reading today, which gives this Fourth Sunday of Easter its popular title of *Good Shepherd Sunday*.

The Prayer over the Offerings, previously used on Saturday within the Octave of Easter, Tuesday after the Second Sunday of Easter, and Wednesday after the Third Sunday of Easter, continues to express our Easter joy by asking that "we may always find delight in these paschal mysteries" and reminds us that the renewal brought about by our participation in Jesus's Death and Resurrection is "constantly at work within us."

While any one of the five Easter Prefaces may be selected for today, certainly Preface III with its reference to Christ as "the Lamb, once slain, who lives for ever," would be appropriate. Continue or begin chanting the introductory dialogue and the Preface today, in order to highlight the ongoing festivity of Easter Time.

The Communion Antiphon continues the Good Shepherd theme as it gives voice to the Good Shepherd as the one who lays down his life for his sheep, willingly dying for his flock.

The Prayer after Communion also employs the shepherd imagery, even mentioning the "eternal pastures," which we hope to settle in. Interestingly, the prayer mentions how we are redeemed "by the Precious Blood of your Son," thus giving a nod to the importance of the shedding of Christ's Blood as the offering of himself and therefore of the importance of regularly offering Holy Communion under both kinds as a sign of our participation in the Paschal Mystery.

You might consider using the solemn blessing for Easter Time, found at number 6 in the "Blessings at the End of Mass and Prayers Over the People" section of the Missal. Remember that a regular formula for dismissal is used, not the solemn double Alleluia.

Pastoral Reflection

Patience is a virtue desired—yet it is also undesirable because one has to wait or follow a path that does not seem to make sense in one's mind. Jesus calls us to follow his plan and a path that leads into him for abundant life. Walk your path without shortcuts accepting the difficulties that came your way. In doing so, accept and learn from the mistakes and difficulties that might come your way. Speak of these moments in detail to God so he hears your voice. When you are able, stop to

answer and be still so you learn to recognize God's voice. Focus on your relationship with God this week through walking mediation—walk alone, slowly, and ask for God and nature to speak to you while you simultaneously share your day and moments of unease with God.

MON 12 (#279) white
Easter Weekday

Optional Memorials of SS. Nereus and Achilleus, Martyrs / red; St. Pancras, Martyr / red

The Lectionary for Mass

◆ FIRST READING: The Gentiles' (non-Jews') acceptance of the Gospel was something the first Christians had not expected. This becomes, in fact, a struggle for them. For example, Gentiles did not observe the Mosaic laws (in this instance, dietary laws are of particular concern). Peter himself did not observe them when he ate with the Gentiles. When confronted by the others, Peter can only respond that he had done as he was instructed in prayer. The subsequent pouring out of God's Spirit was confirmation of his mission's divine origin. Who was he to hinder God!

◆ RESPONSORIAL PSALM 42: All people have an innate thirst or desire for God. Through the words and deeds of Peter in today's First Reading, God's light and fidelity led Cornelius's household to faith (see chapter 10 of Acts of the Apostles). This is true cause for thanksgiving.

◆ GOSPEL: Jesus is the Good Shepherd who risks his own life to protect his flock when he sees the wolf coming to attack them. Jesus, in fact, lays down his life for his flock—as is repeated several times in today's text—even to the point of death. Note the mention of "other" sheep, and the corresponding emphasis on one flock. In contrast to the wolves that scatter the sheep, Jesus came to unite them, desiring

that there be one flock—and so he prays the night before he dies (see John 17).

The Roman Missal

The image of light, so central to the meaning of Baptism and of Resurrection, is used in the Collect for the Easter Weekday as the prayer addresses God as "perfect light of the blessed." The prayer prays for a fulfillment of the life of light and grace begun at Baptism as it asks that we may "rejoice in the full measure of your grace / for ages unending." The Prayer over the Offerings, previously prayed on Monday after the Second Sunday of Easter, on the Third Sunday of Easter, and on Tuesday after the Third Sunday of Easter, continues to speak about the joy of Easter, a joy that will reach fulfillment in "perpetual happiness." The Prayer after Communion, previously heard on the same days as the Prayer over the Offerings, also points us to look forward, in this prayer to attaining in our flesh "the incorruptible glory of the resurrection."

Any one of the five Prefaces of Easter may be used today, although Preface V, with its mention of Christ's bringing "the sacrifices of old to fulfillment" might resonate with the first reading from the Acts of the Apostles.

If you are observing one of the two the optional memorials, either for SS. Nereus and Achilleus or for St. Pancras, in each case only the Collect is proper for the day, and they are found in the Proper of Saints at May 12. The other orations are taken from the Common of Martyrs—For Several Martyrs during Easter Time for SS. Nereus and Achilleus, and For One Martyr during Easter Time for St. Pancras. The Preface may still be one of the Easter Prefaces or one of the two Prefaces of Holy Martyrs.

Today's Saints

The information we have regarding the lives of St. Nereus and St. Achilleus comes from an ancient inscription written in their honor by Pope Damasus I. While serving as second-century Praetorian soldiers, they had a conversion experience resulting in the choice to relinquish their weapons for the Gospel of peace. Because they refused to succumb to idol worship, they were beheaded during the reign of Trajan (98–117).

St. Pancras (+304), a Roman martyr, was a casualty of the Diocletian persecutions. After moving to Rome he converted to Christianity, thus making him a target of the anti-Christian ideology of the reigning emperor. He was beheaded at the age of 14, giving rise to a strong cult of followers. Stemming from St. Pancras' popularity among the faithful, a monastery in Rome and a church in Canterbury were dedicated to him.

TUE 13 (#280) white
Easter Weekday

Optional Memorial of Our Lady of Fatima / white

The Lectionary for Mass

◆ FIRST READING: The number of believers continues to grow not only among the Jews, but among the Gentiles. The disciples recognize this growth as indeed the Lord's work. Barnabas and Saul spend a year in Antioch teaching the first "Christians" as they came to be known, those first followers or disciples of Christ.

◆ RESPONSORIAL PSALM: The verses of today's response are from Psalm 87, a psalm acclaiming Jerusalem (Zion) as the "mother" of those who know the Lord. How fitting, given that Jesus's Death, Resurrection, Ascension, and the pouring out of his Spirit took place there.

The antiphon is from Psalm 117, a song of praise, very appropriate as today's First Reading invites all nations (Gentiles) to praise the Lord.

◆ GOSPEL: The feast of the Dedication (Hanukkah) celebrated the purification of the Temple after its desecration by Gentiles (see 1 Maccabees 4:36–59). The Temple was that sacred place where God dwelt with his people. In today's Gospel, the Jews fail to recognize that Jesus is the very embodiment of God's presence with his people, God's Word in their midst.

The Roman Missal

The Collect for the weekday is very simple and direct: it asks that by "celebrating the mysteries of the Lord's Resurrection, / we may merit to receive the joy of our redemption." The prayer reminds us that if we have died with Christ, then we shall also live with him, and that every Eucharist is a participation in the Paschal Mystery of the Lord's Death and Resurrection. The Prayer over the Offerings, used before, points to the joy of sharing in these Paschal mysteries and of the renewal of life that is "constantly at work within us" as a result of our participation in them; the Prayer after Communion, also previously heard, prays that "this most holy exchange" may bring us not only divine assistance now, but also "eternal gladness" in the future.

Any one of the five Prefaces of Easter may be used today, but perhaps in light of the Gospel reading from John, either Prefaces I, III, or V with their references to Christ as Lamb would be fitting.

For the celebration of the optional Memorial of Our Lady of Fatima, the proper Collect is found at May 13 in the Proper of Saints. The prayer acknowledges Mary to be both Mother of God's Son and our mother; it also echoes the message of Fatima as it asks that we persevere in penance and prayer. The Prayer over the Offerings and the Prayer after Communion for the memorial are taken from the Common of the Blessed Virgin Mary. Although one of the Easter Prefaces may still be used, one of the two Prefaces of the Blessed Virgin Mary may also be chosen; the phrase "on the feast day" may be used in Preface I of the Blessed Virgin Mary.

Today's Optional Memorial

The Blessed Virgin Mary appeared to three shepherd children (Lucía dos Santos and her cousins, Francisco and Jacinta Marto) at Fatima, Portugal, starting on May 13, 1917. World War I was raging at the time, and Our Lady asked the children to say the Rosary every day for world peace. Devotion to the Blessed Virgin Mary under this title (Our Lady of Fatima) became important after World War II at the onset of the Cold War: One of Our Lady's requests was the consecration of Russia to her Immaculate Heart. Francisco and Jacinta (beatified in 2000 by Pope John Paul II) died during the influenza epidemic of 1919, but Lucía became a Carmelite nun and died in 2005 at 91.

WED 14 (#564) red
Feast of St. Matthias, Apostle

The Lectionary for Mass

◆ FIRST READING: After Jesus's Ascension, the men and women who followed him gathered together in prayer. Peter recognized need for a replacement for Judas among the Apostles and cited scriptural evidence in support. The qualifications: the person should have accompanied Jesus during his time on earth, from his baptism until his Ascension. Notice the petition of their prayer: "You show us, Lord" (author's paraphrase) the one. It is the Lord who chooses; the praying assembly must be open and receptive.

◆ RESPONSORIAL PSALM 113: Matthias, counted among the Twelve leaders of God's people, gives new meaning to verse 8 (our antiphon) of this song of praise. Notice the reference to the enthroned Lord in the third stanza, now understood with reference to Jesus.

◆ GOSPEL: The one sent in Jesus's name must first of all be centered (remain, dwell) in Jesus's love. Here is the source of joy, the sustenance needed for bearing fruit. It is Jesus who has chosen that person to be friend, to be messenger, to love as he or she is loved by Jesus.

The Roman Missal

The texts for this Mass, are all proper for the feast today, are located in the Proper of Saints section of the Missal at May 14. The Gloria is sung or said today, since it is a feast.

The Collect identifies Matthias as the one who was "assigned / . . . a place in the college of Apostles." The Prayer over the Offerings asks God both to receive the offerings we present on the Feast of St. Matthias and to strengthen us through them. The Prayer after Communion asks for continued divine gifts upon us as God's family so that, through the intercession of St. Matthias, we may be admitted "to a share in the lot of the Saints in light."

The Preface, proper for today, is one of the two Prefaces of the Apostles. Also, the solemn blessing formula "The Apostles" may be used as the final blessing at the end of Mass today.

Today's Saint

According to the Acts of the Apostles (1:15–26) St. Matthias (first century) was chosen as the successor to Judas. He was selected by the Apostles because he met the following two qualifications: 1) a disciple of Jesus from Jesus's baptism to his Ascension and 2) a witness to Jesus's Resurrection. Historical

details around his apostolic activity are vague, but there is some evidence that he may have preached in Judea and later in Cappadocia near the Caspian Sea. The apocryphal Acts of Andrew and Matthias speak of a mission to evangelize cannibals. Regarding his death, it is said that he was martyred at Colchis or Jerusalem. Legend indicates he was crucified, while artistic representations point to a death by axe or halberd.

THU **15** (#282) white
Easter Weekday

Optional Memorial of St. Isidore / white

The Lectionary for Mass

◆ FIRST READING: The "Apostles"—those sent in the name of Jesus—now number more than twelve! And Paul is prominent among them! These messengers of the Gospel, faithful to their Jewish observances, attend Sabbath services in the synagogue, where the law and the prophets are read. The account of God's saving deeds for Israel of old gives Paul an opportunity to proclaim Jesus as the fulfillment of all that was promised of old.

◆ RESPONSORIAL PSALM 89: The high point of God's goodness toward his people is the sending of Jesus, Messiah and Savior, descendant of David. The verses of today's psalm recount the covenant God made with David, now fulfilled in Jesus.

◆ GOSPEL: The setting of today's Gospel account is the meal Jesus shared with his disciples the night before he died. He has given them an example of what they are to do: wash one another's feet in loving service. As the Father has sent him, so he sends them.

The Roman Missal

The Collect for the Easter Weekday continues to remind us of the effects of Baptism as it acknowledges God as the one who, "through the wonder of rebirth," restores human nature "to yet greater dignity than at its beginnings;" we can recall the early Church's references to Baptism as regeneration. The Prayer over the Offerings reminds us of the transformation that we must be open to in every celebration of the Eucharist as it asks that as our prayers and sacrificial offerings rise up to God, so may we "be conformed to the mysteries of your mighty love." The Prayer after Communion connects the restoration that has come to us in Christ's Resurrection with the ongoing strength we receive from the Eucharist as "the fruits of this paschal Sacrament." Any one of the five Easter Prefaces would seem to be as good a choice as any other today.

If the optional Memorial of St. Isidore is being used today, the Collect, found at May 15 in the Proper of Saints, is the only prayer proper for today. The Prayer over the Offerings and the Prayer after Communion are taken from the Common of Holy Men and Women: For One Saint, and the Preface, if an Easter Preface is not being used, would be either Preface I or II of Saints.

Today's Saint

Today we honor Isidore the Farmer, rather than the Doctor of the Church, Isidore of Seville. Isidore the Farmer was born in Madrid to poor parents who sent him to work for a landowner. He was very devout and married a like-minded woman, Maria, who also became a saint. Isidore attended daily Mass and was often late arriving at the fields, but he managed to get his work done nonetheless. He shared the little he had with the poor. He is the patron of farmers; it is fitting to remember him in the northern hemisphere's agricultural season.

F R I 16 (#283) white
Easter Weekday

The Lectionary for Mass

◆ FIRST READING: Today's First Reading is a continuation of Paul's address to the Jews and Gentile "God-fearing" in the synagogue at Antioch. Drawing upon the history and Scriptures of Israel of old, Paul demonstrated that Jesus is the fulfillment of God's promises. Psalm 2, cited at the end of today's text, is a royal psalm extolling the special relationship God established with the anointed Davidic king, now his Son, a text eminently fulfilled in Jesus.

◆ RESPONSORIAL PSALM 2: God has established his Anointed One and made firm his rule. All kings and rulers of the earth must hear, understand, and respond accordingly.

◆ GOSPEL: This text, which is part of the Last Supper discourse, points to Jesus's Death. In it, Jesus speaks of his return to the Father. This was Jesus's way, and it is ours as well. How comforting it is to know that he will journey with us, taking us to himself.

The Roman Missal

Referring to God as the "author of our freedom and of our salvation," the Collect goes on to note how we have been redeemed "by the shedding of your Son's Blood," thus incorporating verbal imagery that resonates with the fullness of the Eucharistic sign—both Body and Blood. The request in the second part of the prayer that we "may have life through you" sets the context for what we will hear in the Gospel today as Jesus proclaims, "I am the way and the truth and the life." The Prayer over the Offerings reminds us that the gifts we offer in this celebration point to heavenly gifts as the prayer asks that we might "attain the gifts that are eternal." The Prayer after Communion gives voice to the dynamism of the Paschal Mystery as it asks that those who have been "redeemed by the Passion of your Son" may "rejoice in his Resurrection."

Any one of the five Easter Prefaces may be used today, although perhaps using Preface I, II, or IV, with their explicit mention of the life we share in Christ, would provide an echo of the Gospel reading.

S A T 17 (#284) white
Easter Weekday

The Lectionary for Mass

◆ FIRST READING: What conflicting emotions pervade today's reading: the jealousy and vengeance of some of the Jews toward the Apostles in their proclamation of the Gospel, the joyful acceptance of those who believe, and the disciples' joy in the face of persecution. At the heart of it all is the conviction that the call, the command, to proclaim the Gospel comes from the Lord, whose salvation extends to Gentiles as well as Jews, offering eternal life to any who believe.

◆ RESPONSORIAL PSALM 98: This universal offer of salvation is proclaimed in today's psalm. God is king of all nations: God has fulfilled his promises to the Jews and stretched out his loving embrace to people of all nations.

◆ GOSPEL: Today's Gospel focuses on the Father, and more specifically, Jesus's relationship with the Father—a unity so complete, that to see Jesus is to see the Father; to hear Jesus is to hear the Father. The Father works in and through Jesus. Jesus invites his disciples to allow his work to continue in them, through their union with him, and through prayer in his name.

The Roman Missal

The Collect expresses the important point that what we do during liturgy (and what we observe during Easter Time) is supposed to have such a deep effect on our lives that it "may benefit us for eternal life." The Prayer over the Offerings makes a similar connection as it requests that the offering we make at this spiritual sacrifice might "make of us an eternal offering" to God. The Prayer after Communion reminds us that our celebration of the Eucharist perpetuates the Lord's command to do this in his memory, and doing so should have the effect of bringing us "growth in charity."

Any one of the five Easter Prefaces would seem to be equally appropriate for today.

☀ 18 (#52) white
Fifth Sunday of Easter

The Lectionary for Mass

◆ FIRST READING: We hear of complaints among the early Christians, a bit of tension between those of different nationalities. If the basic needs of all are to be met—and the concern here is the daily distribution of food in the community where all things were held in common—the Apostles need assistants. Stephen is among those chosen from men who are reputable, wise, and filled with God's Spirit.

◆ RESPONSORIAL PSALM 33 picks up on the need for food (see the mention of famine in the last line of the last stanza)—a concern in today's First Reading. So, too, the second stanza's concern for "justice and right" is likewise addressed by the Apostles in today's First Reading. Notice also the reference to the "word" (Psalm 33:4) of the Lord in the second stanza—another link with today's First Reading. The Responsorial Psalm is one of thanksgiving for all that God has provided for his people.

◆ SECOND READING: The early Christians loved the image of Jesus as the foundation rock, the cornerstone (Psalm 118:22), a verse cited in today's reading from the First Letter of Peter. Believers are urged to let themselves be as stones joined to Christ, forming a place of praise and worship of the Father. We hear also the language of being called, being chosen—as was Israel of old. In Christ, we have come into the marvelous light of truth and life.

◆ GOSPEL: The theme of a spiritual house is heard again in today's Gospel—only here with reference to eternal dwelling places. Jesus is the way there: both the path by which we arrive and the manner in which we are to travel. Today's Gospel focuses on the Father, and more specifically, Jesus's relationship with the Father—a unity so complete, that to see Jesus is to see the Father; to hear Jesus is to hear the Father speak; the Father works in and through Jesus. Jesus invites his disciples to allow him to continue his work in them, through their union with him and through prayer in his name.

The Roman Missal

In the context of Easter Time, the wonders worked that are proclaimed in the Entrance Antiphon are, of course, the redemption won for us in the saving Death and Resurrection of Jesus, and the life given to us through sacramental initiation. This is the cause for singing a new song to the Lord!

Continue to use the Rite for the Blessing and Sprinkling of Water, as discussed for the Second Sunday of Easter, or, if you haven't been doing it, there's no reason why it cannot be used this week. This rite, found in Appendix II of the Missal, replaces the Penitential Act. The Gloria is sung today.

Even though we are at the Fifth Sunday of Easter, the season is still reverberating with the joy and enthusiasm of the sacramental initiation that occurred at the Easter Vigil: the Collect makes explicit reference to "those you [God] were pleased to make new in Holy Baptism." The prayer goes on to ask that those newly baptized will "bear much fruit / and come to the joys of life eternal." The meaning of Baptism continues to be center-stage in the liturgical theology of Easter Time.

The Prayer over the Offerings, using the important notion of "the wonderful exchange effected in this sacrifice," prays that we might truly come to live the divine life we encounter in the exchange: "that, as we have come to know your truth, / we may make it ours by a worthy way of life."

While any one of the five Easter Prefaces may be selected for today, perhaps an echo of the Gospel might be heard if Preface I, II, or IV were to be used. Continue to chant the introductory dialogue and Preface in order to highlight the ongoing festivity of Easter Time, especially if it is not your practice to do so during Ordinary Time.

The Communion Antiphon is taken from chapter 15 of John's account of the Gospel. It uses the familiar imagery of the vine and the branches, an appropriate image of unity within the Communion Rite.

The Prayer after Communion speaks of the ongoing dynamic quality of a life lived dying and rising in Christ, a dynamism animated by the Eucharistic food, as it asks that God be with us to "lead those you have imbued with heavenly mysteries to pass from former ways to newness of life."

Consider using the Solemn Blessing for Easter Time, found at number 6 in the "Blessings at the End of Mass and Prayers over the People" section of the Missal. Remember that a regular formula for dismissal is used, not the solemn double Alleluia.

Pastoral Reflection

The disciples did not have an iPhone or smart phone, GPS in their sandals, or maps to print from computers and yet they walked. This week be old fashioned and choose a day to let go of technology to get you somewhere where you have never been. It is scary to travel without knowing the path or having a voice telling us when to turn. An experience of being lost makes the importance of learning to trust in God and not be troubled all the more understood.

MON 19 (#285) white
Easter Weekday

The Lectionary for Mass

◆ FIRST READING: Paul and Barnabas have two disparate experiences. On the one hand, the perceived threat to their lives in Iconium causes them to flee from the city. On the other hand, as a result of the miracle performed on the lame man at Lystra, they are hailed as the incarnation of Greek gods. Though mistaken in their conclusion, the people at Lystra were on to something. God had come in human form, but in Jesus of Nazareth. It is his Good News that is proclaimed by the disciples; it is the power of his name that brings healing.

◆ RESPONSORIAL PSALM 115: The words of today's text could well be the response of Paul and Barnabas to their experience in Lystra: Not to us, but to God give glory! In worshipping Zeus, the people bowed down to an idol. All people are called to acknowledge the true God, the creator of heaven and earth.

◆ GOSPEL: The Gospel today stresses the strong connection, almost identification, between loving Jesus and keeping his word or commandment, especially his commandment to love others. Jesus and his Father come to us in and through this love with a power and a presence that is gift and lasting presence.

The Roman Missal

The Collect brings to mind the pilgrim nature of our spiritual journey as people given new life in Christ—in other words, even though we have been made new, we are nonetheless always "on the way"—as it asks that we may have the Lord's "perpetual help" in being "defended from all wickedness" and thus "make our way by means of your heavenly gifts." Perhaps we might hear in this prayer a certain "pep talk" to keep alive the elation we felt at the Easter Vigil and early in Easter Time. The Prayer over the Offerings speaks to how the offering of ourselves in the Eucharist should lead us to be open to be transformed into the likeness of Christ—"conformed to the mysteries of your mighty love." The Prayer after Communion also reminds us of our status as new creations as it affirms God as the one who restores us "to eternal life / in the Resurrection of Christ;" having thus been made new, we must be more receptive to "the fruits of this paschal Sacrament."

Any one of the five Easter Prefaces would work well today; in view of the orations, Preface I or IV might perhaps be considered in particular.

_{T U E} **20** ^{(#286) white}
Easter Weekday

Optional Memorial of St. Bernardine of Siena, Priest / white

The Lectionary for Mass

◆ FIRST READING: The arrival of some Jews who opposed Paul quickly puts an end to the worship he and Barnabas had almost received from the people at Lystra. In fact, Paul is stoned and left for dead. With the support of the disciples, he recovers, and he and Barnabas continue their journey proclaiming the Gospel. Note how they perceive all that happens as part of their following of Jesus. Note, too, their concern that each local community have leaders (presbyters) and that prayer and fasting are important in choosing and installing them.

◆ RESPONSORIAL PSALM 145: The antiphon "Your friends make known, O Lord, the glorious splendor of your kingdom" evokes Jesus's reference to his Apostles as "friends" (John 15:15). And certainly, Paul's and Barnabas's proclamation of the Gospel is a proclamation of God's kingship and kingdom.

◆ GOSPEL: Today's reading is a continuation of Jesus's "farewell discourse" at the Last Supper (see John 13–17). Peace is his farewell gift to his friends. Peace is their lasting inheritance from him. They must stay centered in this peace, not letting troubles or fears disturb it. He is returning to the Father, but he will come back to them and take them to himself (see John 14:3).

The Roman Missal

In the Collect for the Easter Weekday we pray for "constancy in faith and hope" that we may never doubt the promises we have learned from God. The petition is especially apropos in light of the weekday Gospel reading where Jesus exhorts his hearers to not let their hearts be troubled or afraid. Indeed, we

can be reassured at this offering of the sacrifice as the Prayer over the Offerings reminds us that we have cause for "great gladness." One of the reasons for that great gladness can be found in our hope, given voice in the Prayer after Communion, that we may attain in our flesh "the incorruptible glory of the resurrection."

Any one of the five Easter Prefaces may be used today, with perhaps Preface III, describing how Jesus "never ceases to offer himself for us" and how he "defends us and ever pleads our cause before you" providing a nice resonance with the reassurance we hear, and trust we are asked to have, in the words of the Gospel reading for the day.

If the Mass is the optional memorial of St. Bernardine of Siena, only the Collect is proper for the day, as found at May 20 in the Proper of Saints. The Collect, naturally, makes reference to St. Bernardine's "great love for the holy Name of Jesus." The other orations are taken from the Common of Pastors—For Missionaries or from the Common of Holy Men and Women: For Religious. This provides a plethora of choices for the Preface; use one of the Easter Prefaces, or one of the two Prefaces of Saints; or the Preface of Holy Pastors; or the Preface of Holy Virgins and Religious.

Today's Saint

St. Bernardine of Siena (1380–1444), a well-loved Franciscan friar and preacher, emulated the poverty of St. Francis and the intellectual inquisitiveness of St. Bonaventure. He chose to live a simple, austere life devoted to study. People traveled far and near to hear his inspiring words of wisdom even when he was chastising against the abuses of the times: gambling, witchcraft, superstition, and heavy taxation. When preaching, he used creative methods, such as mimicking and acting, to challenge the people to live a life of simplicity and penance. He wrote extensively in the areas of moral and mystical theology as well as Mariology. Other contributions to the Church include fostering a devotion to the Holy Name of Jesus and popularizing the IHS symbol (the Greek abbreviation for the name of Jesus Christ).

WED 21 (#287) white
Easter Weekday

Optional Memorial of St. Christopher Magallanes, Priest, and Companions, Martyrs / red

The Lectionary for Mass

◆ FIRST READING: The early chapters of Acts of the Apostles paint such idyllic pictures of the first Christian community that we tend to forget that internal conflict was a part of their lives as well. Since Jesus and his first followers were Jewish, and Jesus as Messiah was the fulfillment of the promises of old, Gentile believers came as somewhat of a surprise. The question arose: must they become Jews (i.e., be circumcised) to be followers of Jesus? Consultation with the leaders of the community was needed.

◆ RESPONSORIAL PSALM: The house of the Lord, or Temple, is in Jerusalem. Psalm 122 is a pilgrimage psalm, sung by pilgrims as they made their way to the city of Jerusalem where the Temple was located. The first Christians continued their observance of Jewish rituals and went daily to the Temple (see Acts of the Apostles 2:46).

◆ GOSPEL: What does it mean for us to glorify the Father? What kind of fruit glorifies God? Notice that Jesus makes a connection between bearing fruit and becoming disciples in the last line of the Gospel. They had been with him for several years and were still becoming disciples. Why does Jesus speak of discipleship as something they, and we, become?

The Roman Missal

The close connection between Easter and Baptism continues to be highlighted in the weekday Collect as God is addressed as the "restorer and lover of innocence" and as we hear about those who have been "set free from the darkness of unbelief," asking that they "may never stray from the light of your truth." The baptismal imagery of innocence and moving from darkness to light is clear. Baptismal themes can continue to be heard in the Prayer over the Offerings with its reference to "the renewal constantly at work within us." The Prayer after Communion first asks that "this most holy exchange"—this liturgical celebration—may bring us God's help in this life, and then it looks forward to asking for "eternal gladness."

Any one of the five Prefaces of Easter are equally appropriate for today, although if the priest celebrant wished to emphasize the Johannine Gospel theme of the intimate union between Jesus and his followers (the vine and the branches), perhaps either Preface I or Preface III would provide this emphasis most fittingly.

If the optional memorial is being observed, the proper Collect is found at May 21 in the Proper of Saints. The prayer speaks of the fidelity of St. Christopher Magallanes and his companions being faithful "to Christ the King even to the point of martyrdom." The other orations are taken from the Common of Martyrs: For Several Martyrs during Easter Time. The Preface may still be one of the Easter Prefaces or one of the two Prefaces of Holy Martyrs.

Today's Saint

St. Christopher Magallenes (1869–1927), a priest in Mexico, and 24 other companions were martyred for standing up against the anti-Catholic Mexican government of the time. Outraged by attempts on the part of the government to eliminate the Catholic faith (i.e. bans against Baptism and the celebration of Mass), he joined the "Cristero" movement, which pledged an allegiance to Christ and the Church to spread the Good News. The slogan of the Cristero uprising was "Long live Christ the King and the Virgin of Guadalupe!" After years of secretly ministering to Catholics in Mexico, he was imprisoned and executed without a trial. Prior to his death he said, "I am innocent and I die innocent. . . . I ask God that the shedding of my blood serve the peace of our divided Mexico" (quoted in the *BCL Newsletter* from August 2002.

THU 22 (#288) white
Easter Weekday

Optional Memorial of St. Rita of Cascia, Religious /white

The Lectionary for Mass

◆ FIRST READING: Yesterday's reading continues. The solution to the dilemma caused by the Gentiles' reception of the faith and the question of circumcision does not come easy to the Jewish Christian leaders. "Much debate" (Acts of the Apostles 15:7) takes place. We hear the words of Peter and James, who insist that the Gentiles' faith is from God. Salvation comes through grace for all. According to this text from Acts of the Apostles, Gentile believers are asked to observe Jewish dietary laws, avoid idolatry, and refrain from marriage within the prohibited degrees of kinship, but were not required to be circumcised.

◆ RESPONSORIAL PSALM 96, with its exhortation to proclaim God's salvation to all the nations (i.e., Gentiles), is a fitting response to today's First Reading.

◆ GOSPEL: Reflect on how deep is the love that the Father has for

Jesus, how intimate the union between them. That, says Jesus, is the love that he has for each and every one of his disciples, regardless of nationality or ethnic origin. Disciples are to remain (to "live" or "abide," as the Greek verb is sometimes translated) in this love. Jesus also tells us the way to do it: keep his commandments.

The Roman Missal

The weekday Collect contains a richness in describing what God does for us through Baptism: we are sinners, yet are made just; we are pitiable, yet are made blessed. Therefore, we can ask God to "stand by" his works and gifts and, in so doing, give "the courage of perseverance" to "those justified by faith." It is that redeemed people who are made "partakers of the one supreme Godhead," as the Prayer over the Offerings describes, through "the wonderful exchange effected in this sacrifice." Indeed, it is only Baptism that makes true participation in the holy exchange possible (Baptism is the entrance into the Church and the doorway to the Eucharist). Thus, the Prayer after Communion notes that those who have been imbued with these heavenly mysteries are rightly "to pass from former ways to newness of life." Any one of the five Prefaces of Easter might be used equally well today.

For the celebration of the optional memorial of St. Rita of Cascia, use the proper Collect found in the Proper of Saints at May 22. The other orations will have to be taken from the Common of Holy Men and Women: For Religious, and the Preface may be one of the Easter Prefaces, one of the two Prefaces of Saints, or the Preface of Holy Virgins and Religious.

Today's Saint

St. Rita of Cascia (1381–1447) was born to a peasant family in the region of Umbria, Italy. From an early age, she longed to consecrate her life to Christ as a religious, but in obedience to her parents she married instead. Her husband was harsh and sometimes violent, but over the years Rita's unfailing faith and gentleness began to have its effect, and her husband slowly changed. He was stabbed to death in a dispute, and shortly thereafter both Rita's sons died as well. She entered an Augustinian convent, where she remained for forty years. She was especially devoted to the Passion of Christ. It is said that while praying, she received the stigmata of Christ's wounds. The stigmata remained for fifteen years, until her death. Given her life story, it is little wonder that St. Rita is the patron saint of difficult marriages, abuse victims, and lost causes.

F R I 23 (#289) white Easter Weekday

The Lectionary for Mass

◆ FIRST READING: We hear of the contents of the letter sent by the Jewish Christian leaders of the Church in Jerusalem to Gentile believers with word of their decision regarding the question of circumcision. Note their acknowledgment that the troublemakers were self-appointed. Notice their concern that the new Gentile believers not be troubled (recall the Risen Christ's farewell gift of peace). Finally, note their conviction that the decision is not theirs alone, but first and foremost, that of the Holy Spirit.

◆ RESPONSORIAL PSALM 57: Today's Psalm response is one of thanksgiving and praise. This psalm could easily have been the prayer of those first missionaries as they proclaimed God's salvation in Jesus to the Gentile nations.

◆ GOSPEL: Our Gospel reading continues from chapter 15 of John's account of the Gospel, and begins with the commandment disciples are asked to observe. How important it is for believers to remember that we have been chosen by God—faith, mission, vocation is not our own doing; we have been chosen and are loved. Jesus invites us to intimate friendship with himself.

The Roman Missal

The Collect for today first notes how we have been "rightly conformed to the paschal mysteries;" this can remind us of how we have been remade through our participation in the Death and Resurrection of Christ, first through Baptism. Then the prayer goes on to ask that "what we celebrate in joy / may protect and save us with perpetual power," thus pointing to the ongoing effects we hope our participation in liturgy will have. The Prayer over the Offerings points to another aspect of the transformation that must occur in us: as we ask God to accept "the oblation of this spiritual sacrifice," we beg that we will be made into an eternal offering to him. The Prayer after Communion reminds us that the liturgy we just celebrated was something that Christ commanded us to do in memory of him, and so we pray that it "may bring us growth in charity."

Although any one of the five Easter Prefaces would be appropriate for today, perhaps one could find a resonance with today's Gospel reading, where we hear about the love of laying down one's life for one's friends, in Preface III of Easter.

S A T 24 (#290) white Easter Weekday

The Lectionary for Mass

◆ FIRST READING: Perhaps the most striking point in today's reading is Paul's total openness to the direction of the Spirit of God in his ministry of preaching the Gospel (i.e., what to do, where to go). We witness his pastoral concern that there be no stumbling block for believers. Today we meet Timothy, Paul's soon-to-be travelling companion and assistant.

◆ RESPONSORIAL PSALM 100: Our Psalm response once again reaches out to all lands and nations, calling all to know whose we are and to acclaim and serve him joyfully.

◆ GOSPEL: Today's Gospel is a grim message, in the midst of the many upbeat assurances we've heard in recent days: expect persecution and rejection. As Jesus was received, as he was treated, so will his disciples be. As the Father sent Jesus, so Jesus sends the disciples to continue his ministry.

The Roman Missal

Today's Collect, even at this late stage in Easter Time, continues to place Baptism center-stage as it reminds us that God confers on us heavenly life "through the regenerating power of Baptism" (recall that "regeneration" was another way of referring to Baptism in the ancient Church). Eschatological fulfillment is also a major theme in this prayer. It asks that those rendered "capable of immortality" (through Baptism) may indeed "attain the fullness of glory," that is, in heaven. The Prayer over the Offerings also refers to attaining the eternal, as does the Prayer after Communion with its petition that, having been "redeemed by the Passion of your Son," we may "rejoice in his Resurrection."

Of the five Easter Prefaces that can be used today, it is Preface IV of Easter, with its mention of "the old order destroyed" that perhaps provides an echo of the Gospel reading of the day, in which Jesus talks to his disciples about being hated by the world.

☀ **25** (#55) white
Sixth Sunday of Easter

The Lectionary for Mass

◆ FIRST READING: There was a dispersion of the disciples after the death of the deacon Stephen recounted in Acts of the Apostles 7, due to the persecution of Christians spearheaded by Saul. Nevertheless, it was a time of new life for the community as the Gospel was proclaimed in new places where many believed. Today's text focuses on the miraculous deeds wrought by Philip, another one of the deacons named in Acts of the Apostles 6:5 (see last Sunday's reading). The second part of the text highlights the subsequent ministry of Peter and John to the Samaritans, completing the initiation begun by Philip who had baptized the Samaritans in Jesus's name. Through prayer and the laying on of hands, the Samaritans received the Holy Spirit.

◆ RESPONSORIAL PSALM: Today's antiphon (and the first three stanzas of the psalm as well) echoes the joy experienced by the Samaritans as a result of Philip's healing ministry. Were these not "tremendous . . . deeds" of the Lord (first and second stanzas) in their own right? An experience of personal deliverance comparable to the exodus of old (third stanza)? Are they not so in our own lives as well? Let us not neglect to give God the praise that is due (stanza four).

◆ SECOND READING: What a powerful image in today's reading—Christ suffered Death "that he might lead [us] to God"—are we following? Peter instructs us on one way to do that: by "sanctifying"—that is, reverencing Christ as sacred with our hearts. Or, we can also think of it as sanctifying the Christ who dwells in our hearts through our Baptism. Our speech, our conduct, is to be marked by gentleness, reverence, and goodness.

◆ GOSPEL: As in our Second Reading, we encounter once again the powerful image and the reality of Christ dwelling in our hearts, and as Christ is in the Father, so too, are we in him. So, too, is the promised Holy Spirit, the Spirit of Truth, the Advocate on our behalf, who is with us always. These words from John 14 are Jesus's parting words to his disciples—and to us—the night before he died. Can we even begin to grasp the magnitude of this reality?

The Roman Missal

The Entrance Antiphon, taken from Isaiah 48:20, that "The Lord has freed his people," refers to how the Lord has brought freedom from darkness, sin, and death through Jesus's Resurrection and through our sharing in that Paschal Mystery through Baptism. Because of that life and freedom given to us, we should "Proclaim a joyful sound and let it be heard."

Continue to use the Rite for the Blessing and Sprinkling of Water, as discussed for the Second Sunday of Easter. If you haven't been doing it, there's no reason not to use it this week. This rite, found in Appendix II of the Missal, replaces the Penitential Act. The Gloria is sung today.

The Collect situates this celebration within the ongoing festivity of the 50 days of Easter Time as it refers to our celebration "with heartfelt devotion of these days of joy, / which we keep in honor of the risen

Lord." Also, the key connection between liturgy and life is affirmed as we ask "that what we relive in remembrance we may always hold to in what we do."

The Prayer over the Offerings also prays for the liturgical celebration to have an ongoing effect in our lives as it petitions that "we may be conformed to the mysteries of your mighty love." Such transformation, however, is a result of God's grace, not our own efforts alone, as the prayer recognizes our need to be purified by God's graciousness.

Any one of the five Easter Prefaces may be used equally appropriately today. Continue to chant the introductory dialogue and Preface in order to highlight the ongoing festivity of the season, especially if it is not your practice to do so during Ordinary Time.

The Communion Antiphon is taken directly from today's Gospel reading. The Antiphon, along with the readings, signals for us the movement in Easter Time to the approaching time of Pentecost, with its explicit mention of the Paraclete.

The Prayer after Communion affirms both that we have been restored to eternal life "in the Resurrection of Christ," and that we are asking for the "strength of this saving food" to bear fruit in our life. The prayer reminds us that our reception of Holy Communion should always have the effect of increasing our love for one another.

Consider using Solemn Blessing for Easter Time, found at number 6 in the "Blessings at the End of Mass and Prayers Over the People" section of the Missal. Remember that a regular formula for dismissal is used, and not yet the solemn double Alleluia.

Pastoral Reflection

Fairytales are great ways to explore the inexorable depth of God. In your life, who is your Jiminy Cricket, the person helping to guide you through rough situations? God sends gifts, usually in the form of friends, family members, and even strangers. Name with thanksgiving those who have guided and continue to guide you. Choose a specific person in your life to pray for each day this week as you realize that you, too, are the voice of the Advocate (the Spirit)—an offering of strength, wisdom, and peace to someone on your path. Be conscious this week to allow your actions (not your words) to speak loudly as you follow the commandments and teach others in your walk.

(#291)   white

MON 26 Memorial of St. Philip Neri, Priest / white

The Lectionary for Mass

◆ FIRST READING: Continuing from Saturday's reading, we see Paul and his companions embarking for Macedonia (present-day Greece) and arriving at Philippi. Paul seeks out a Jewish community for prayer and encounters Lydia, the "worshiper of God" (which means God-fearing Gentile), the businesswoman and dealer in textiles.

She obviously was a woman of prominence. She and her household, whose hearts were opened to receive the Word, came to faith through the proclamation of Paul.

◆ RESPONSORIAL PSALM 149: Though the word "delight" is not mentioned in today's First Reading, we can imagine the joy that filled Lydia's house, perhaps even with singing and dancing, as they celebrated a festive meal. Even so, how much greater is God's delight in his people.

◆ GOSPEL: In contrast to today's First Reading, which speaks of people coming to the Word, today's Gospel warns against the dangers of falling away in the face of persecution. The Jewish-Christian/Jewish rift was so strong that in time, Jewish Christians were expelled from their synagogues by Jews of good faith and zeal for their ancestral traditions. Be prepared, says Jesus, and stay rooted in the spirit of truth.

The Roman Missal

The prayers for this Mass are all proper for the day and can be found in the Proper of Saints section of the Missal at May 26.

The Collect asks that through the Holy Spirit we may be filled with the same fire as filled the heart of St. Philip Neri; the mention of the Spirit is fortuitous given the approaching feast of Pentecost. The Prayer over the Offerings prays that we may imitate the example of St. Philip by always giving ourselves "cheerfully / for the glory of your name." Thus is a connection made between the giving of ourselves at this offering of the sacrifice and the need to give of ourselves entirely in our whole lives. The Prayer after Communion requests that as we have fed upon the food of the Eucharist ("these heavenly delights") so too may we "always long for that food by which we truly live."

The Preface chosen could appropriately be one of the five Prefaces of Easter, highlighting that we are still in Easter Time, or one of the two Prefaces of Saints, or the Preface of Holy Pastors.

Today's Saint

St. Philip Neri (1515–1595) spent much of his life hearing confessions and providing spiritual direction. He was considered somewhat of a clairvoyant due to his ability to "read" the hearts of people. Fundamental to the counsel he provided was the belief that *non dubitare*, or unreasonable fears, prevent people from living in right relationship with God and others. As a priest ministering in Rome, he offered discourses on Scripture, gradually evolving into afternoons of Scripture study, music, reading the lives of the saints, and personal reflection on the part of both clerics and laypeople. These meetings became known as the "oratory," thus leading to the foundation of the Oratorians, a congregation of diocesan priests bound by the bond of love rather than religious vows and dedicated to the spiritual well-being of souls. One of its most esteemed members was Cardinal John Henry Newman.

T U E 27 (#292) white
Easter Weekday

Optional Memorial of St. Augustine of Canterbury / white

The Lectionary for Mass

◆ FIRST READING: Acts of the Apostles 16:16–21 is omitted by the Lectionary. These verses explain the reason for the imprisonment of Paul and Silas mentioned in today's reading. Paul had healed a demon-possessed slave girl who brought great profit to her owners. Enraged, they had them arrested for creating a disturbance. The high point of the story is not so much the miraculous opening of the prison, as the prisoners remaining in their cell and using the occasion to proclaim the Gospel to the jailer, who on hearing the Word of the Lord, was baptized with all his household. Note the jailer's care of Paul and Silas and his household's rejoicing and celebration at having come to faith.

◆ RESPONSORIAL PSALM 138: Paul and Silas surely witnessed the saving power of the Lord in their experience of imprisonment and their jailer's conversion. It was indeed true cause for rejoicing and gladness.

◆ GOSPEL: Sadness fills the hearts of the Lord's disciples at the thought of his departure, yet he must return to the Father so the Spirit may be sent in his place.

The Roman Missal

The Easter Time weekday Collect prays that "we may in truth receive a share / in the Resurrection of Christ your Son." The Prayer over the Offerings, prays that "we may always find delight in these paschal mysteries." The Prayer after Communion, also a familiar one by now, reminds us of "the holy exchange, / by which [God has] redeemed us."

Any one of the five Prefaces of Easter can be used today. Since in today's Gospel we hear how Jesus will be going to the Father and the disciples will no longer see him, perhaps Preface III of Easter with its reminder that "He never ceases to offer himself for us but defends us and ever pleads our cause before you" would be an apt choice.

If you are celebrating the optional Memorial of St. Augustine of Canterbury, it is the Collect that is proper today, found in the Proper of Saints at May 27; the prayer makes explicit reference to the saint's preaching to the English peoples. The other orations may be taken either from the Common of Pastors: For Missionaries, or from the Mass for a Bishop. For the Preface, use one of the Easter Prefaces, one of the two Prefaces of Saints, or the Preface of Holy Pastors.

Today's Saint

When St. Augustine of Canterbury (+604) joined a group of monks in Rome, little did he know that someday he would become the first Archbishop of Canterbury and hold the title "apostle of the English." At the request of Pope Gregory the Great, St. Augustine led a mission of monks to evangelize Anglo-Saxons in Britain. Although King Ethelbert of Kent had reservations about their arrival, he gave them housing in Canterbury and allowed them to preach. They used relics, heroic stories about the saints, and ancient vessels to inspire faith in the people. Their missionary endeavors proved

to be successful, eventually leading to the Baptism of King Ethelbert and his people. St. Augustine built the first cathedral and school at Canterbury, and later founded the first monastery in close proximity to the cathedral. Within the ecumenical movement he is an icon of unity—a time when Rome and England were of one mind.

W E D 28 (#293) white
Easter Weekday

The Lectionary for Mass

◆ FIRST READING: We hear of Paul's arrival in Athens (verse 15). The Lectionary omits verses 16 to 21 describing his distress at the sight of so many idols in the city and his debating with the local people. Yet Paul's approach is to meet them where they are, so to speak, using their cult of an unknown God as a springboard to proclaim the Good News of Jesus of Nazareth, thus making known the true God whom they had previously not known. He is the one in whom "we live and move and have our being" (Acts 17:28).

◆ RESPONSORIAL PSALM 148 is a song of praise. The heavens and the earth and all who dwell therein are called to praise the Lord. Note how Paul's speech to the Athenians echoes the themes of today's Psalm.

◆ GOSPEL: What is the truth that Jesus speaks of today? Why is it too heavy for the disciples to bear without the Holy Spirit? Today's Gospel leaves us pondering. How can we grasp the reality of the intimate communion of life and knowledge between the Father and the Son, and between the Son and the believer, in and through the Holy Spirit?

The Roman Missal

The Collect today reminds us how every celebration of the Eucharist unites us with the Communion of

Saints: we participate in the fruits of Jesus's Resurrection now, through our liturgical celebration of the mysteries, while the saints already share in the fullness of the Resurrection in the kingdom. In the Prayer over the Offerings we again hear of "the wonderful exchange effected in this sacrifice," which should become the pattern for every aspect of our life; growing in that conformity to the life of Christ is the goal of liturgical celebration. The Prayer after Communion presents the effects of our participating in the "heavenly mysteries" as passing "from former ways to newness of life."

Given the message of farewell that is part of today's Gospel, use of Preface III of Easter, as suggested for yesterday, would again be a fitting choice.

THU 29 (#58) white Solemnity of the Ascension of the Lord
HOLYDAY OF OBLIGATION

About this Solemnity

The distinct celebration of the Ascension of the Lord was unknown in the first three and a half centuries. The chronology of dating the Ascension to Forty days after Lent exists only in the Acts of the Apostles. In the Gospel according to Luke, the Ascension appears to have taken place much earlier, even on Easter Day. The original ending to Mark's account of the Gospel did not include the Ascension at all, and it can only be inferred from Matthew's conclusion. When fourth-century Egeria mentions a celebration Forty days after Easter in Bethlehem, it may have been for the Holy Innocents. But by the fifth century the observance seems to be universally accepted.

In the dioceses where today is celebrated as the Ascension, it is a Holyday of Obligation.

The Lectionary for Mass

◆ FIRST READING: In his introduction to the second volume of his work, Luke begins first of all, as he did in his account of the Gospel, by addressing the man who sponsored his work. Then he proceeds to pick up where the Gospel left off, only with a slightly different chronology concerning Jesus's return to the heavenly realm. In Acts of the Apostles, this takes place after "forty days," that biblically significant number. His point: the Apostles experienced the presence of the Risen Jesus with them over an extended period of time. His parting words to them: wait for the promised Holy Spirit; later described as "power" (the Greek word is *dynamis*). The Holy Spirit is the "power" they will need to be his witnesses, not only to the Jews but to the Gentiles as well.

◆ RESPONSORIAL PSALM 47: Returning to heaven, Jesus is enthroned at the right hand of his heavenly Father. Today's psalm invites all people to break forth in a joyful hymn of praise to our heavenly King.

◆ SECOND READING: Paul's beautiful prayer for the Ephesians makes reference to a startling reality: the same power of God that raised Christ from the dead and seated him at his right hand in heaven, that same power is at work in the lives of each one of us. Do we recognize the surpassing greatness of this power? Do we draw upon it? May the eyes of our hearts be enlightened, may God give us the wisdom to see—and to allow it to work within us.

◆ GOSPEL: Fittingly, in this year of Matthew, we hear his account of Jesus's final words to his disciples (some of whom are still doubting that it is he!). Interestingly, Matthew makes no reference to Jesus's departure or Ascension. His emphasis is, rather, on the presence of Jesus with us always until the end of the age (Matthew 28:20), the last words of the Gospel. The Gospel concludes with an open ending, the sending out of the Eleven to make disciples of all nations.

The Roman Missal

Two sets of Mass formularies are given for the solemnity, one for the Vigil Mass and one for the Mass during the Day. A rubric before the texts for the Vigil Mass explains that where the Solemnity of the Ascension is not observed as a Holyday of Obligation, it is observed on the Seventh Sunday of Easter.

At the Vigil Mass

Reminding us that in the solemnity we acknowledge God's majesty and might over all the kingdoms of the earth, the Entrance Antiphon praises the Lord "who ascends above the highest heavens."

The Collect for the Vigil proclaims that Jesus ascended to the heavens "today," thus, affirming once again the convergence of past, present, and future in liturgical celebration. The prayer goes on to assert a key point about the meaning of the Ascension, as is indicated in both of the Prefaces—namely, that the Ascension is not about Jesus leaving us as much as it is a continuation of sharing in his glorified, risen existence. Thus, the Collect goes on to remind us of his promise and asks that "we may be worthy for him to live with us always on earth, and we with him in heaven."

Remember that the Creed is said today as is the Gloria.

The Prayer over the Offerings reiterates that Christ is our High Priest seated at the right hand of God, appropriate imagery for the Solemnity. Because he intercedes for us, we can dare to ask to "approach with confidence the throne of grace and there obtain your mercy."

The Preface assigned for this Mass is either Preface I or Preface II of the Ascension. Preface I makes explicit that the purpose of Christ's Ascension was "not to distance himself from our lowly state," but rather so that we "might be confident of following where he, our Head and Founder, has gone before." Preface II states the same thing in a slightly different way, noting that the purpose of the Ascension was so that "he might make us sharers in his divinity." As with the Sundays of Easter Time, it would be a good idea to chant the introductory dialogue and Preface today.

If the Roman Canon is used as the Eucharistic Prayer for this celebration, remember that there is a proper form of the *Communicantes* ("In communion with those . . . "); it is found within the prayer itself, on the page that lists the several different forms of the *Communicantes*.

The Communion Antiphon repeats how Christ is seated at God's right hand. The Prayer after Communion bids us to press forward, longing "for the heavenly homeland" as we follow in the Savior's footsteps "to the place where for our sake he entered before us." Thus, does the prayer communicate to us another central theme of the Solemnity, namely, that where Christ has gone, we hope to follow.

There is a special Solemn Blessing specifically for the Ascension of the Lord that can be used for the final blessing at the end of Mass, and it would be good to make use of it. We're not at Pentecost yet, however, so the solemn double Alleluia dismissal is not yet used. Stick with one of the usual dismissal formulae.

At the Mass during the Day

The Entrance Antiphon is directly from the First Reading from the Acts of the Apostles; it refers both to Jesus's Ascension into heaven and the expectation of his return.

There is no reason not to use the Rite for the Blessing and Sprinkling of Water, especially if it has been used on the Sundays throughout Easter Time. Baptism into the Paschal Mystery means immersion in the fullness of the mystery, which includes Christ's ascended glory. The rite is found in Appendix II of the Missal and replaces the Penitential Act. The Gloria is sung today.

The priest celebrant has a choice from among two Collects for today. The first option sets a tone of gladness and joy as it notes that "the Ascension of Christ your Son / is our exaltation" because we, his Body, are "called to follow in hope" where he, our Head, has gone. The reality that liturgy is at its core a celebration of our participation in the mysteries of Christ cannot be stated emphatically enough, and this prayer is yet another example of how this truth is basic to the meaning of liturgical celebration. The second prayer asks that, since we "believe that your Only Begotten Son, our Redeemer, / ascended this day to the heavens," we may be granted to even now dwell in spirit "in heavenly realms." Notice too, the important assertion of "this day," an important reference to the salvific reality being made present in our own time and space.

The Creed is said today.

The Prayer over the Offerings makes use of the important concept of "this most holy exchange," this time asking, in light of the particular solemnity we are celebrating, that through it "we, too, may rise up to the heavenly realms."

See the comments above, at the Vigil Mass, for some thoughts about the two options for the Preface, which are the same for the Mass during the Day, and for the proper insert if Eucharistic Prayer I is used.

The Communion Antiphon, taken from the end of Matthew's Gospel, assures us of the Lord's presence to us "even to the end of the ages."

The Prayer after Communion reminds us that through the liturgy, we can share in heavenly realities even while still here on earth; because of that, we have the hope of being united with the Lord fully one day.

As with the Vigil Mass, it would be good to use the special Solemn Blessing specifically for the Ascension of the Lord as the final blessing at the end of Mass. Since we're not at Pentecost yet, one of the usual dismissal formulae, not the solemn double Alleluia dismissal, is used.

Pastoral Reflection

In letting go of a loved one, the pain is intense. Jesus empowered his friends and left them with a mission. What is your personal mission given by God specifically to you? Pray this week for an answer. Work on writing your personal mission (related to God) that only you can accomplish. In listening and praying, discover new ways to praise God today, be it through music, art, dance, nature, or silent adoration!

THU 29 (#294) white
Easter Weekday

In some dioceses, today is celebrated as an Easter Weekday. The commentaries that follow are regarding this day.

The Lectionary for Mass

◆ FIRST READING: Paul is depicted as an ordinary working man, practicing his trade to make a living. Like the other early Jewish Christians, he continues to attend services in the synagogue and uses this as an occasion to testify to the fact that Jesus is the Christ (Messiah). Meeting with opposition, Paul decides to devote himself totally to the Gentile mission. Note the introduction of Aquila and Priscilla, Jewish Christians who shared Paul's trade. They will come to figure prominently in the ministry of evangelization.

◆ RESPONSORIAL PSALM 98: The Lord's faithfulness to Israel is manifested in the arrival of the promised Messiah, Jesus Christ. His salvation is now made known to all nations (Gentiles) through the missionary activity of the first Jewish Christians.

◆ GOSPEL: We should find comfort in knowing that even Jesus's first disciples had trouble understanding his words! Perhaps part of discipleship is precisely that: to be willing to stand in the mystery, pondering it in our hearts.

Absence, sorrow, and grief are givens. But Jesus gives us his word, the "grief will become joy" in the mystery, in the manner that is his.

F R I 30 (#295) white Easter Weekday

The Lectionary for Mass

◆ FIRST READING: Today's reading, a continuation of yesterday's, contains important information that may be missed if the Ascension was celebrated yesterday. First is the introduction of Aquila and Priscilla, the husband and wife who shared Paul's tent-making trade. Paul stayed and worked with them for a year and a half in Corinth. He continued his ministry of proclaiming the Gospel in the synagogues. Eventually—and here is where today's reading begins—opposition to Paul arises. As was the case with Jesus, the civil authority found nothing with which to charge Paul. Are we surprised that the civil authorities did nothing when the innocent Sosthenes, the synagogue official, is beaten by the Jews, presumably for allowing Paul to teach the Gospel among them? How many, in our own day, are charged unjustly and suffer undeservedly on behalf of the Gospel?

◆ RESPONSORIAL PSALM 47: Our psalm is the same as we had on the Ascension. We are reminded that God is king, more powerful than

any ruler on earth. All will one day be subjected to him.

◆ GOSPEL: In his last discourse to his disciples in John's account of the Gospel, Jesus speaks of the pain and anguish they will experience at his Passion and perhaps at their own as well. It is a life-giving pain, however; that is the nature of the Paschal Mystery.

The Roman Missal

The Missal acknowledges that in some regions the Solemnity of the Ascension, observed on the Seventh Sunday of Easter, has not yet been celebrated, and so it provides a choice for the Collect.

The first Collect is the one to be used if the Ascension was celebrated the day before. It acknowledges that God restores us to eternal life through Christ's Resurrection, and so it asks that we be raised up "to the author of our salvation, / who is seated at your right hand." The prayer then goes on to confess how our Savior will come again in majesty, therefore asking that "those you have given new birth in Baptism / may be clothed with blessed immortality." Notice how the prayer skillfully weaves together various themes we have been hearing throughout Easter Time, incorporating them with the most recent aspect of a focus on Christ's Ascension into glory.

The second Collect is the correct choice for those places where the Solemnity of the Ascension is celebrated on the upcoming Sunday. This prayer more generally asks that what God has promised may be accomplished so that "all your adopted children" (we can hear the language of Baptism here) may attain what has been foretold—eternal life and happiness.

The Prayer over the Offerings, in a somewhat similar theme as the second Collects, begs both that the blessings that have been given by God may not be lost, and that we

may "attain the gifts that are eternal." The Prayer after Communion echoes this petition.

The choices for the Preface today include any one of the five Prefaces of Easter or the two Prefaces of the Ascension. For communities that celebrated the Ascension yesterday, it would be most beneficial to highlight the unique nature of these days as time in between the Ascension and Pentecost by using one of the Ascension Prefaces. For other communities, one of the Easter Prefaces should be used.

S A T 31 (#572) white Feast of the Visitation of the Blessed Virgin Mary

About this Feast

The feast of the Visitation of the Blessed Virgin Mary to Elizabeth originated in the Middle Ages. It was celebrated on various dates until it was assigned this date. It occurs about one month before the celebration of the Solemnity of the Nativity of St. John the Baptist on June 24.

Luke's account of the visitation invites us to engage the tenderness between Mary and Elizabeth. In a tender exchange, Mary and Elizabeth affirm one another's experience of God's presence and action on behalf of his people. As Elizabeth recognized God's presence within Mary, so we are called to help others recognize God's presence with and within them.

What a gift it must have been for these two women to spend time together. Given their miraculous pregnancies and unique experiences of God, they could only turn to each other to ponder and process what was happening. As God brought them together, their companionship during this time must have been a source of mutual comfort, encouragement, and joyful anticipation. Praise be to God for knowing our needs even before we are aware of them, and caring for us through the love and friendship of those around us.

This feast is a good time to bless expectant parents. Announce these blessings well in advance.

The Lectionary for Mass

◆ First Reading (option 1): Two options are given in the Lectionary. A spirit of joy pervades the first from the prophet Zephaniah—both God's joy in Zion (Jerusalem) and Zion's joy in God. Jerusalem's salvation is at hand; the Lord is in her midst. We find these same themes in the feast we celebrate today: the joy of the two women miraculously with child, the joyful movement of John the Baptist in the womb of Elizabeth when he hears Mary's greeting. The Lord is within their midst; the Lord is within Mary.

◆ First Reading (option 2): The behaviors prescribed in Paul's words to the Romans are demonstrably manifest in today's Gospel. What sincere love and mutual affection existed between Mary and Elizabeth, these two humble servants of the Lord! In coming to assist her elderly and pregnant cousin, Mary contributed to the needs of the holy ones, and Elizabeth received her in gracious hospitality. Fervent in spirit, they served the Lord and one another.

◆ Canticle: How both Mary and Elizabeth could fittingly make this prayer from Isaiah their own. How truly God is among them in Mary's unborn child. Both women break forth in praise.

◆ Gospel: As we would expect for today, we hear of the meeting between the pregnant Mary and the pregnant Elizabeth. Each has conceived through the marvelous working of God in her life. Each knows that she is indeed blessed by the Lord and so sings God's praise.

The Roman Missal

The texts for this Mass are all proper for the feast, and are located in the Proper of Saints at May 31. The Gloria is sung or said today, since it is a feast.

The Collect tells of how the Blessed Virgin Mary, while carrying God's Son in her womb, was inspired by God to visit Elizabeth, and then goes on to ask that we may be "faithful to the promptings of the Spirit." When we respond to the promptings of the Spirit, we, along with Mary who also was obedient, magnify God's greatness. (Notice how the prayer presumes the promptings are there; if we do not hear them, it's because we are ignoring them, not because the Spirit is not present to us.) The Prayer over the Offerings parallels the offering we make at this Sacrifice with the offering of charity made by Mary—in the Visitation to Elizabeth, asking that God accept our offering as he was pleased to accept the Blessed Mother's offering. The Prayer after Communion notes how St. John the Baptist leapt for joy in "the hidden presence of Christ," and so, as appropriate for a Communion prayer, asks that we too will rejoice as we receive Eucharistically "in this Sacrament the same ever-living Lord."

The Preface assigned for today is Preface II of the Blessed Virgin Mary, appropriately echoing Mary's Magnificat as heard in today's Gospel reading from Luke. Also, the Solemn Blessing formula titled "The Blessed Virgin Mary" under the grouping "For the Celebration of the Saints" may be used at the end of Mass.

Pastoral Reflection

The power of belief—the power of faith—has the ability to turn the world upside down. Here, Elizabeth, pregnant long after she hoped to be, and Mary, pregnant far sooner than she expected to be, meet and sing the praises of God. Elizabeth

easily could have been resentful and Mary understandably could have hidden herself away, but these women did not respond so negatively. Their faith enabled them to see the wondrous possibilities and rejoice in each other's blessings.

June
Month of the Sacred Heart

1 (#59) white
Seventh Sunday of Easter

Editorial Note: In some dioceses, the Solemnity of the Ascension of the Lord is transferred to the Seventh Sunday of Easter. If this is the case in your diocese, please use the readings and prayer texts from the Ascension. Please see page 206 in this Sourcebook for commentary.

The Lectionary for Mass

◆ First Reading: Obedient to the parting words of the Risen Jesus (see Acts of the Apostles 1:4, the First Reading for the Ascension), the Twelve, the women who had accompanied Jesus from Galilee (see Luke 8:1–3; 23:49), his Mother Mary, and his brothers, gather in prayer waiting for the Holy Spirit to come upon them with power, that they might become witnesses to Jesus.

◆ Responsorial Psalm 27 is a beautiful song of confidence in the Lord, voiced by one who ardently seeks his face. What greater good thing can there be than the gift of God's Holy Spirit dwelling within us? Yes, we see and experience this power even now in our mortal lives. There is no cause for fear with his power at work in our lives.

◆ SECOND READING: The way of the disciple can be no different than the way of the Master and Lord. As Christ suffered in being obedient to the will of the Father, in proclaiming the message of the kingdom, so will his disciples. As Christ was glorified by the Father, so shall we be. Peter exhorts us to rejoice when we suffer for the sake of Christ, for the name of Christ. We are sharing in Christ's suffering; we are endowed with his Spirit.

◆ GOSPEL: Today's Gospel is taken from Jesus's prayer spoken at his last meal with his disciples the night before he died (see all of John 17). In this first part, Jesus prays first for himself, that as he approaches the hour, the time for his passing through death to eternal life, the Father will glorify with him "with the glory [he] had with [the Father] / before the world began." Jesus speaks to the Father concerning the work he has accomplished on the Father's behalf. Jesus prays for his disciples, ourselves among them. Jesus gifts them—and us—with eternal life.

The Roman Missal

If you are in a region that observes the Solemnity of the Ascension today, refer to the comments on page 206 for the celebration of Mass today. What follows is for the Seventh Sunday of Easter.

The Entrance Antiphon, taken from Psalm 27 (26) and used on this Sunday between the Ascension and Pentecost, takes on the connotation of seeking the face of God who has entered into his resurrected-ascended glory.

Continue to use the Rite for the Blessing and Sprinkling of Water, as has been done, it is hoped, on all the Sundays of Easter Time. If this has not been the case, it can nonetheless still be used today if desired. Remember that this rite, found in Appendix II of the Missal, replaces the Penitential Act. The Gloria is sung today.

The Collect acknowledges the paradoxical nature of what we celebrate with the Ascension: that Christ is both with the Father in glory and, at the same time, present among us; the prayer therefore asks that we may indeed "experience, as he promised, until the end of the world, his abiding presence among us." Though the "ascension" and "abiding presence" seem to contradict each other, theologically they are actually different aspects of the same reality.

The Prayer over the Offerings conveys the dynamism of what takes place in liturgical action, as it asks that through the sacrificial offerings we make, "we may pass over to the glory of heaven." Thus are we once again reminded that in every liturgical celebration the work of our redemption is being accomplished.

Although the choice of the Preface may be taken from among the five Easter Prefaces or the two Ascension Prefaces, it would seem to be pastorally advantageous to use one of the two Prefaces of the Ascension. This would highlight the unique segment of Easter Time in which we find ourselves, and also continue to echo themes that have been announced in the Collect and the Prayer over the Offerings. In any event, continue to chant the introductory dialogue and Preface.

The Communion Antiphon, although taken from the same chapter of John's account of the Gospel as that used for the Gospel reading this year, is not from that reading; the antiphon prays for the unity

of Christ's followers, as he and the Father are one.

The Prayer after Communion continues the idea that the celebration of the liturgy accomplishes the work of our salvation. Here, the prayer asks that "what has already come to pass" in Christ as Head of the Church may also "be accomplished in the body of the whole Church."

Use the solemn blessing for Easter Time, found at number 6 in the "Blessings at the End of Mass and Prayers over the People" section of the Missal, and one of the regular formulae for dismissal is used.

Pastoral Reflections

The beauty of a parent-child relationship is seen in today's Gospel. Jesus asks for glory from God so glory may be given back. The love between them is reciprocal and unending for they are one. In general, while admonishment is known by the child from a parent, praise is necessary too as the child knows unabashedly how to adore and idolize their parent. Unleash the child in your heart to play with God and devote your love and admiration to God. Treat today as God's Day—create a card and prepare a gift that you could give to God to share of your deep love.

MON **2** (#297) white
Easter Weekday

Optional Memorial of SS. Marcellinus and Peter, Martyrs / red

The Lectionary for Mass

◆ FIRST READING: Faith is a process of growth, as is evident in today's account of the Ephesian disciples. Coming to faith needs the assistance of others who will proclaim a word and minister a moment of sacred encounter with the Lord.

◆ RESPONSORIAL PSALM 68: Sing to God all nations—God gives a home to the forsaken, a home through faith and the indwelling presence of God in our lives.

◆ GOSPEL: That you might have peace in me, despite the troubles, despite the sense of abandonment and confusion . . . Peace is the gift the Risen Christ desires for all. He was not alone in the time of his anguish and suffering, for the Father was with him. Neither are we alone.

The Roman Missal

These last days of Easter Time have a very unique character to them. The *Universal Norms on the Liturgical Year* and the *General Roman Calendar* tells us, "The weekdays from the Ascension up to and including the Saturday before Pentecost prepare for the coming of the Holy Spirit, the Paraclete" (UNLY, 26). Thus, frequent mention of the Holy Spirit becomes noticeable in the prayers for this week, especially the Collects.

The Easter Time weekday Collect today prays specifically for the power of the Holy Spirit to come to us, that we may keep God's will in mind and "express it in a devout way of life." The Spirit transforms us to live the Christian life. The Prayer over the Offerings, while not explicitly mentioning the Holy Spirit, does pray that "this unblemished sacrifice" might purify us, thus calling to mind the purifying fire of the Spirit, as we ask for "the force of grace from on high" to be imparted to our minds (can we hear reference to the Spirit's gift of Wisdom?).

The Prayer after Communion reiterates a petition that we have made frequently during Easter Time, that, being "imbued with heavenly mysteries," we might "pass from former ways to newness of life." Certainly, it is the Spirit who breathes new life into us.

Although the choice of the Preface may be taken from among the five Easter Prefaces or the two Ascension Prefaces, strongly consider using one of the two Prefaces of the Ascension as a way of highlighting the unique liturgical time in which we find ourselves, in between Ascension and Pentecost in days that pray for the coming of the Spirit.

If you are celebrating the optional memorial of Ss. Marcellinus and Peter, the Collect, found in the Proper of Saints at June 2, is proper today. The other orations are taken from the Common of Martyrs: For Several Martyrs during Easter Time. For the Preface, options include one of the Easter Prefaces, one of the two Prefaces of Saints, one of the two Prefaces of Holy Martyrs, and, of course, one of the Prefaces of the Ascension, which, for reasons noted above, might be preferable.

Today's Saints

Not much is known of these two early martyrs, who died in 304 AD, except that Marcellinus was a priest, Peter was an exorcist, and they were both martyred under Diocletian. While in prison, they managed to convert the jailer and his family. Pope Damasus honored them with an epitaph. They are mentioned in Eucharistic Prayer I.

(#298) red

TUE 3 Memorial of St. Charles Lwanga and Companions, Martyrs / red

Lectionary for Mass

◆ FIRST READING: We hear the first part of what might be called Paul's farewell address as he is en route to Jerusalem for the feast of Pentecost (see verse 16). It is a farewell address in the sense of Paul's parting words in the face of his imminent death, which has been revealed to him by the Holy Spirit. In today's text, Paul testifies to his fidelity to his mission and his eagerness to finish his work and move on to the fullness of life.

◆ RESPONSORIAL PSALM 68: All kingdoms of the earth, Gentiles as well as Jews, are called to acclaim the God of Israel. The God who has cared for his people, fulfilling his promises of old, is a God of salvation. He bears our burdens with us, he "controls the passageways of death"—which are really passageways to life.

◆ GOSPEL: Juxtaposed with Paul's farewell address is that of Jesus in today's Gospel. Jesus testifies to all he has done accomplishing his Father's work. His words are actually part of a prayer to the Father—both a prayer for his own glorification and a prayer for the disciples who will remain on earth.

The Roman Missal

All the orations for today's memorial are proper and are taken from June 3 in the Proper of Saints.

The Entrance Antiphon, taken from the Book of Wisdom, and with its reference to God's chosen being put to the test "as gold in the furnace," recalls the martyrdom faced by St. Charles and his companions, as they were burned on pyres. The Collect uses the familiar imagery of the blood of martyrs being the seed of the Church. The Prayer over the Offerings notes how these martyrs chose death rather than choosing to sin. The Prayer after Communion asks that what helped these martyrs endure torment may "make us, in the face of trials, / steadfast in faith and in charity." Used in the context of the Prayer after Communion, we can recall that it is the Eucharist that nourishes us in that kind of faith and charity, and that the Eucharist is the source of our union with the martyrs who have gone before us.

One of the two Prefaces of Holy Martyrs would be the logical choice for today, although it would not be out of the question to use one of the Easter or Ascension Prefaces.

Today's Saints

St. Charles Lwanga (1865–1886) was a Ugandan catechist who served as a page in the court of King Mwanga

II. King Mwanga felt threatened by the presence of missionaries in his country, and he insisted that Christians renounce their faith. After a massacre of Anglicans in 1885, the head page, Joseph Mukasa, reproached the king, who had him beheaded and arrested his followers. Charles baptized those who were still catechumens, and he and twenty-one others were burnt alive. Although they were not canonized, Paul VI recognized the martyrdom of the Anglican Christians when he canonized Charles and his companions.

W E D 4 (#299) white Easter Weekday

The Lectionary for Mass

◆ FIRST READING: Today's First Reading is Paul's final commission to the leaders of the Church of Ephesus. Note the imagery used: the presbyters or overseers are to be good shepherds who protect their flock. They are to be vigilant on their behalf, they are to help the weak and the poor. Significantly, they are to be built up by the Word of God for the carrying out of their mission. Their affection for Paul is obvious: he is a teacher and a leader who was deeply loved.

◆ RESPONSORIAL PSALM 68: Today's Psalm invites all kingdoms of the earth, all peoples, to praise the Lord. God's power, mentioned in each stanza, is a particular reason for praise. Juxtaposed with today's First Reading, we may think of the power of the Holy Spirit operative in the Church's leaders (Paul included!) as well as the power of God's Word in building them up.

◆ GOSPEL: Just as we are, Father, so may they be . . . such is Jesus's prayer for his disciples. May they be united as one . . . filled with joy . . . consecrated in truth and made holy.

The Roman Missal

The Collect for today, in continuing to include reference to the Holy Spirit, prays for one of the chief gifts of the Spirit, that of unity—specifically, in this prayer, that the Church might be "united in purity of intent." The Prayer over the Offerings relates how the sacrifice we offer was instituted by God's command, and asks that the sacred mysteries we celebrate (namely, the Eucharist) as "our dutiful service" in the present "graciously complete the sanctifying work / by which you are pleased to redeem us." Thus, are we again reminded how all liturgical celebration goes beyond the present moment to bring us along the path of a future fulfillment. The Prayer after Communion asks for an increase of grace, particularly the grace to always be ready to receive so great a gift as "this divine Sacrament." The prayer can remind us that even our hunger for the gift of the Eucharist is itself first a gift from God.

The choices for the Preface today include any one of the five Prefaces of Easter or the two Prefaces of the Ascension. It would seem most beneficial to highlight the unique nature of these days as time in between the Ascension and Pentecost by using one of the Ascension Prefaces.

T H U 5 (#300) red Memorial of St. Boniface, Bishop and Martyr

The Lectionary for Mass

◆ FIRST READING: The Lectionary skips over chapter 21 and much of chapter 22 of Acts of the Apostles. It picks up with Paul in the hands of the Roman cohort in Jerusalem, after having nearly caused a riot when he went into the Temple area. Though perplexed as to what Paul had done, the cohort commander convenes the Jewish leaders trying to get to the truth. Quite cleverly, Paul manages to set the Pharisees

and the Sadducees, two sects within Judaism with opposing views on the Resurrection, against one another. Such an argument ensues that the Roman becomes Paul's rescuer. In the midst of it all are the Lord's words to Paul: "Take courage. For just as you have borne witness to my cause in Jerusalem, so you must also bear witness in Rome" (Acts of the Apostles 23:11).

◆ RESPONSORIAL PSALM 16: This prayer of confidence is most fitting. The word Paul received from the Lord during the night is nothing less than the counsel of the Lord spoken of in the second stanza. Acts of the Apostles presents Paul as having a clear picture of the suffering and death that awaits him in Rome. In light of Christ's Resurrection, he knows that he will enjoy life and joy in God's presence forever.

◆ GOSPEL: Jesus's prayer embraces disciples in every age, including us! Do we grasp the significance of what he says? Of who we are? Note how many times the word "one" occurs. Jesus prays first and foremost for the unity of his followers. How is that unity realized among us today?

The Roman Missal

The only prayer that is proper to the memorial is the Collect, located at June 5 in the Proper of Saints. It asks that St. Boniface be our advocate in holding firmly, particularly through our deeds, to the faith that "he taught with his lips and sealed in his blood." The other orations are taken either from the Common of Martyrs: For One Martyr during Easter Time or the Common Pastors: For Missionaries. As far as the choice for the Preface, either one of the Prefaces of Holy Martyrs or the Preface of Holy Pastors, depending on which set of orations are chosen, would make the most sense, although use of Preface I or II of the Ascension of the Lord could continue to be a possibility as well if desired.

Today's Saint

St. Boniface was an Anglo-Saxon Benedictine monk. He was first sent as a missionary to Frisia, which is in the vicinity of the Netherlands, but he failed because of wars between the local tribes and the Frankish king Charles Martel. Boniface then went to Rome and was commissioned by the pope to evangelize in Germany. He started by chopping down an oak tree dedicated to Thor, and when he was not immediately struck down, the people believed and became Christians. Boniface returned to evangelize the Frisians but was killed by them in 754 AD. He is buried in the cathedral in Fulda.

F R I 6 (#301) white Easter Weekday

Optional Memorial of St. Norbert, Bishop / white

The Lectionary for Mass

◆ FIRST READING: Paul is in Caesarea, having been secretly transported there by the Romans for his protection. They continue to be baffled by the Jews' accusations against him (see Acts of the Apostles 23:12–35). Paul is led before one ruler after another. The heart of the controversy is Paul's proclamation of the Resurrection. Today's reading simply advances both the story and the journey to Rome.

◆ RESPONSORIAL PSALM 103: This Psalm of praise with its mention of the Lord's enthronement is fitting to follow today's First Reading, not only in light of Acts' implicit reference to the Resurrection and Ascension of Christ, but also with reference to the contrast between the thrones of earthly rulers, before whom Paul stands now, and the throne of God, before which

Paul one day, at the conclusion of his earthly journey, shall stand.

◆ GOSPEL: Today's Gospel focuses on Peter's destiny, one which is similar to Paul's in that both will be martyred because of their witness to Jesus. Peter's death, like Jesus's, would glorify God. Peter receives a triple commission to shepherd Jesus's flock (paralleling his earlier threefold denial?). Today's Gospel ends with the command/invitation: "Follow me" (John 21:19). The way of the disciple can be none other than the way of Jesus.

The Roman Missal

The weekday Collect acknowledges God as the one who has "unlocked for us the gates of eternity" through the "glorification of your Christ / and the light of the Holy Spirit." The phrase "light of the Holy Spirit" can call to mind the enlightenment that takes place in Baptism; thus, Easter Time themes of Resurrection, Ascension, and our sharing in those realities through Baptism all come together. The fruits that we ask for in this prayer are deeper devotion and stronger faith. The Prayer over the Offerings also provides an explicit reference to the Holy Spirit; in this prayer, it is to the coming of the Spirit that we await at Pentecost, a coming that will "cleanse our consciences." The Prayer after Communion refers to our Eucharistic celebration as a banquet that, we pray, will bring everlasting life.

Although the choice of the Preface may be taken from among the five Easter Prefaces or the two Ascension Prefaces, consider continuing to give preference to one of the two Prefaces of the Ascension of the Lord on this penultimate Easter Time day of praying for the coming of the Spirit.

If you are celebrating the optional Memorial of St. Norbert, then use the Collect, found in the Proper of Saints at June 6, which is proper for

today. The other orations are taken from the Common of Pastors: For a Bishop, or from the Common of Holy Men and Women: For Religious. For the Preface, options include one of the Easter Prefaces, one of the two Prefaces of Saints, the Preface of Holy Pastors, or, of course, one of the Prefaces of the Ascension of the Lord.

Today's Saint

St. Norbert (1080–1134), a subdeacon and canon in the Rhineland, had a conversion experience similar to St. Paul, in which he was thrown from a horse during a violent thunderstorm. Following this event he had a change of heart. He became increasingly aware of the need to renounce the trappings of the world and to preach reform to the canons. His preaching led him to the valley of Premontre where he laid the framework, along with thirteen disciples, for a reform movement that became known as the Canons Regular of Premontre, the Premonstratensians, or Norbertines. These Norbertines lived together according to the Rule of St. Augustine, wore a simple white habit, and challenged the clergy through preaching and example to recommit themselves to celibacy and simplicity. Although their message was not always well received by the clergy, more and more young men felt called to join the Norbertines. Because of his extraordinary leadership and reforming spirit, St. Norbert was appointed Archbishop of Magdeburg, Germany.

S A T 7 (#302) white Easter Weekday

The Lectionary for Mass

◆ FIRST READING: Today's reading, the conclusion of the Acts of the Apostles, ends on a rather open-ended note. Paul is under house arrest in Rome, awaiting his trial before the emperor. His ministry of proclaiming the Gospel continues unimpeded; his life-situation, perhaps even at its service. Can we, like Paul, see the potential for all things in our lives to work unto good, to be an occasion for speaking—and living—the Gospel message?

◆ RESPONSORIAL PSALM 11: Today's responsorial antiphon echoes the theme of Paul's innocence of the charges against him, his righteousness. Although Paul was in the hands of human courts, it is the judgment of the Most High that ultimately matters. Those who are just and upright will see the face of God.

◆ GOSPEL: We might also think of today's Gospel as having an open ending. Today's reading begins with a typical Petrine comment. When seeing the beloved disciple following them, Peter, having just heard about the nature of his own death, asks Jesus what will happen to the beloved disciple. What good advice Jesus's comment is for us all: never mind; you just follow me—that is more than enough to do! A second main concern of these closing verses of John's account of the Gospel is to verify the authenticity of the witness, the author of the Gospel.

The Roman Missal

Notice how the Missal's designation of "At the Morning Mass" clearly distinguishes this Mass from the Vigil of Pentecost, which will be celebrated later the same day, in the evening.

The Collect, perhaps somewhat curiously, does not specifically mention the Holy Spirit (except in the doxology, of course), but it does convey a sense of completion or coming to a close with its phrase about "we who have celebrated the Paschal festivities,"—throughout these Fifty days. The prayer goes on to ask that we may "hold fast to them in the way that we live our lives," thus affirming the goal of all liturgical

celebration—that what we celebrate in ritual (dying and rising; offering ourselves in union with Christ) may be lived out in daily life. The Prayer over the Offerings does explicitly mention, in a way that connotes a sense of anticipation and excitement, that the Holy Spirit is indeed "coming near," as it asks that the event "prepare our minds for the divine Sacrament, since the Spirit himself is the remission of all sins."

The notion of our being prepared fits well with this point in the liturgy at the Prayer over the Offerings as part of the Preparation of the Gifts; the mention of the remission of sins reminds us of one of the fruits of participation in the Eucharist, namely, forgiveness. The Prayer after Communion uses the old/new motif that we have heard so often throughout Easter Time, as it begs that "as we have been brought from things of the past to new mysteries [both in this Eucharistic celebration and throughout the whole Fifty days of Easter Time, which are coming to a close today], so, with former ways left behind, we may be made new in holiness of mind [the concrete transformation to be brought about through our participation in the mysteries]."

The choices for the Preface today include any one of the five Prefaces of Easter or the two Prefaces of the Ascension, but certainly one of the Prefaces of the Ascension of the Lord could be used to good pastoral advantage at this Mass, the last one for Easter Time this year.

8 (#63) red
Solemnity of Pentecost Sunday

About this Solemnity

The Greek word for Pentecost (*Pentekostē*) means "fiftieth," and in early Christianity it referred to the entire Fifty Days of Easter. The roots of Pentecost can be found in the Jewish festival of Weeks (Shavu'ot), the Fifty-day celebration following Passover (Exodus 23:16). It was a harvest festival in which the first fruits of the harvest were offered to God in gratitude. It eventually became associated with the giving of the Torah on Mount Sinai. Early Christians reinterpreted the Jewish festival as a commemoration of the coming of the Holy Spirit, since Acts records that the Holy Spirit came to the disciples when the festival of Pentecost was fulfilled (see Acts 2:1–11). The celebration of Pentecost may begin on Saturday afternoon or evening with the Vigil. By the end of the fourth century in the West, Pentecost became a time for the initiation of those not baptized at Easter. Thus, a night vigil was added like the Easter Vigil for this purpose. With this early history in mind, this is a most appropriate time to initiate those who were not ready at the Easter Vigil, or (not and) to celebrate the Reception of Baptized Christians into the Full Communion of the Catholic Church (see RCIA, 473).

The Lectionary for Mass

Extended/Shortend Vigil Mass

◆ First Reading (option 1): This story recounts the origin of the many and varied languages spoken by humankind. Such diversity was viewed as both a punishment and a check by the Lord to stop humans from the kind of self-assertion evidenced in their attempt to "make a name" (Genesis 11:4) for themselves through their own efforts. Such misguided and uncontrolled drives could be disastrous. Unable to understand one another because of their diverse languages, the people were dispersed throughout the world. At Pentecost, the disciples' gift of tongues would overcome these barriers and serve the proclamation of the Gospel and the faith of those from far off lands who heard them.

◆ First Reading (option 2): The Jewish festival of Pentecost, Fifty days after Passover, commemorated the giving of the Law on Mount Sinai. Note the reference to Passover ("how I treated the Egyptians" [Exodus 19:4]) at the beginning of the reading. The Israelites, as God's people, have a special relationship with God and accordingly stand out above all other nations on earth. The people acknowledge this and agree to be faithful to God's covenant with them.

◆ First Reading (option 3): The prophet's words at the time of the Babylonian Exile bear witness to the powerful impact the Spirit of the Lord had in his life. Not only are his visions the result of the Spirit's work in his life, the prophet is led to understand that it is the Spirit of the Lord who is the source of all life. It is this same Spirit who will enliven the dry bones of the Israelites. God's people will be raised from the graves of their exile and be restored to life and to homeland.

◆ First Reading (option 4): The prophet looks toward a time when God's Spirit would be poured out upon *all* people. Later in the reading, the phrase "the day of the Lord" (Joel 3:3) is used with reference to the day of judgment, a terrible day marked by signs in the cosmos. This text from Joel is cited by Peter in his speech after the coming of the Spirit upon Pentecost (see Acts 2). A day of judgment has come with the death, Resurrection, and Ascension of Jesus. Cosmic signs of darkness (see Luke 23:44–45) and fire (see Acts 2:3) are evident. Judgment is at hand. All who believe in Jesus will be saved.

◆ Responsorial Psalm 104: This hymn of praise acclaims all the works of God's creation. The verses chosen for today's response focus in particular on the greatness and majesty of the Creator. The responsorial antiphon acknowledges that it is through the life-giving breath of God that all things live (see also the last stanza with its allusion to Genesis 2:7).

◆ Second Reading: Through Baptism, believers have received the Spirit of God, the first-fruit of the new creation. Yet, the life of God is still coming to be realized within us. Until the day of our death, we—and all creation—are in labor pains as this new life comes to birth. The Spirit we have been given works within us and prays within us until all is accomplished.

◆ Gospel: Set within the context of the Jewish Feast of Booths, or Tabernacles (commemorating the time of Israel's desert wanderings after the exodus from Egypt), Jesus speaks of the water he will provide for all who are thirsty in his day—and our own. This living water will arise from within us, from deep within our hearts. It is the water of life of his Spirit. It is the gift to be given after Jesus's glorification through his death and exaltation on the cross.

Mass during the Day

◆ First Reading: Pentecost was one of the three pilgrimage feasts of the Jews, when all who were able came to the Temple in Jerusalem; thus, the presence of so many foreigners in Jerusalem that day. All the disciples were gathered in one place. Acts of the Apostles 1:13–14 identifies these disciples as the Eleven, Mary, the mother of Jesus, the women who journeyed with Jesus from Galilee to Jerusalem (see Luke 8:1–3; 23:49), and his relatives. The cosmic sign of the strong driving wind attracted the crowd. (In Greek, the language in which Acts was originally written, the same word is used for both "wind" and "spirit.") Note also the sign of "fire." The fruit of the Spirit's presence and work is the disciples' ability to proclaim the Gospel in various tongues and be understood by those who heard them.

◆ Responsorial Psalm 104: As at the Vigil Mass, Psalm 104 is used, with the same antiphon. There is some variation in the stanzas. Today's addition in the last stanza voices the desire that both God's glory and God's joy in his creation endure. The psalmist is intent on being pleasing to the Lord and finding joy in him. A beautiful theme for each of our lives!

◆ Second Reading: The contrast between the Spirit and the flesh—and their respective fruits—is emphasized in today's reading. The flesh represents anything that is opposed to God; the Spirit, that which is enlivened by God's power and presence.

Paul's command to live by the Spirit points to the choice we have in the matter. Which fruits are more evident in our lives?

◆ GOSPEL: The setting of today's text is Jesus's last discourse to his disciples, at table with them the night before he died. Jesus promises to send the Spirit, an Advocate on their behalf, the Spirit of truth. Note the intimate workings between the Father, the Son, and the Spirit and how the disciples are drawn into this by the power of the Spirit at work in their lives. On their part, the disciples must receive what the Spirit declares to them and testify on Jesus's behalf.

The Roman Missal

The Missal gives rubrics and texts to be used for the extended celebration of a Pentecost Vigil, and it is hoped that every parish will take advantage of such a celebration for its parishioners. Instructions are even given if a parish wishes to celebrate First Vespers (Evening Prayer I) in common as to how to combine those Vespers with the celebration of Mass. This might be something for communities to consider as a way of highlighting the Liturgy of the Hours as something that is meant to be prayed by every baptized Christian, not just the clergy.

If Evening Prayer I is not to be celebrated communally and Mass is to begin in the usual way, then all is done as usual for the beginning of Mass, including the Kyrie (Lord have mercy), after which the priest prays the Collect of the Mass. This would be an ideal occasion to use the Rite for the Blessing and Sprinkling of Water, found in Appendix II at the back of the Missal, especially if your parish has been doing this on all of the Sundays of Easter Time. Even if you have not been making use of this rite, today is a perfect occasion to do so as it brings together the themes of Paschal Mystery, Easter Time, Baptism, and Holy Spirit, and its use allows the enactment of the ritual to convey the sense of fullness and completion so

appropriate for this solemnity. Remember that this rite takes the place of the Penitential Act. It's important to note, however, that in this extended Vigil, the Collect would be prayed by the priest immediately after the concluding prayer "May almighty God cleanse us of our sins . . . ," not the Gloria, which comes later (see below).

The Collect for this extended Vigil is specified as the "Grant, we pray, almighty God, that the splendor . . . " text, which is the second option for the Collect under the Simple Form of the Vigil Mass (the texts for which follow this first section for the Extended Form). The prayer is replete with imagery appropriate to the Holy Spirit: it speaks of the splendor of God's glory shining forth upon us; it mentions "the bright rays of the Holy Spirit;" it asks that "the light of your light may confirm the hearts of those born again by your grace," thus giving voice to baptismal themes.

After the Collect, an address is given to the people, using the exact words in the Missal or words similar to them. The address asks the people to follow the example of Mary, the Apostles, and disciples who persevered in prayer and who awaited the Spirit as promised by the Lord. We follow that example by listening "with quiet hearts" to the Word of God, meditating "on how many great deeds God in times past did for his people" and praying "that the Holy Spirit, whom the Father sent as the first fruits for those who believe, may bring to perfection his work in the world."

After this follows an extended Liturgy of the Word modeled on the Liturgy of the Word at the Easter Vigil. The Missal refers us to the readings proposed as options in the Lectionary, with a Responsorial Psalm and a prayer corresponding to the reading following each one. (It is possible to have a period of sacred silence in place of any of the

Responsorial Psalms.) The Missal then goes on to give the texts for prayers that correspond to each of the readings and their subsequent psalms. It is then after the fourth reading that the Gloria is sung.

When the Gloria is completed, the priest then prays the Collect in the usual way; this time, the Collect used is the text found as the first one given as the Collect for the Simple Form of the Vigil Mass, the Almighty, ever-living God, who willed the Paschal Mystery . . . . After this, the reading proclaims the Epistle, Romans 8:22–27, and everything continues in the usual way. The texts for the remainder of the Extended Form of the Vigil Mass are taken from the Simple Form of the Vigil Mass, which pages follow in the Missal. Commentary on those texts is provided below.

At the Vigil Mass: Simple Form

If an Extended Form of the Vigil is not being celebrated, then all occurs as usual at Mass; however, there are still proper texts that must be used for the Vigil Mass, distinct from the Mass during the Day.

The Entrance Antiphon, taken from chapter 5 of Romans, relates how the Spirit is the agent of God's love: God's love is "poured into our hearts through the Spirit of God dwelling within us." Of course, as we hear about the Spirit that dwells in us having been "poured into our hearts," we cannot help but think of the pouring of the baptismal waters, when the Spirit first came to us. The baptismal motif is with us during Easter Time in varied ways right up until the end of the season!

As with the extended form of the Vigil Mass, the simple form would be an ideal occasion to use the Rite for the Blessing and Sprinkling of Water, found in Appendix II at the back of the Missal, especially if your parish has been doing this on all of the Sundays of Easter Time. Even if you have not been making use of this rite, consider doing so now. Remember that this rite takes the place of the Penitential Act. The Gloria immediately follows the prayer the priest prays as the conclusion to the Rite for Blessing and Sprinkling of Water.

In the simple form of the Vigil, either one of the two Collects given in the Missal may be used. The second prayer was discussed above, under the extended form. The first option highlights the liturgical time of the Fifty days of celebrating the Paschal Mystery ("Pentecost" referring to the Fifty-day time period of "a week of weeks"), after which it emphasizes a central theme associated with the Holy Spirit, that of unity. Evoking the story of the Tower of Babel from Genesis, the Collect makes explicit reference to "the confusion of many tongues" and therefore presents "heavenly grace" (the Spirit) as the agent for bringing together "into one great confession of your name" that which had been scattered through human pride and sin.

The Prayer over the Offerings begins with a line that sounds like the epiclesis in a Eucharistic Prayer: "Pour out upon these gifts the blessing of your Spirit, we pray, O Lord . . . " How appropriate on a day when we celebrate the coming of the Holy Spirit! The second part of the prayer make the important point that the purpose of invoking the Spirit upon the gifts is so that the Spirit will come upon those who receive those gifts: "so that through them your church may be imbued with such love. . . . "

The Preface assigned for today is the Preface of Pentecost, the text for which (both with and without musical notation) is given along with the texts for the Mass during the Day, two pages further along (this might be a little confusing; the priest celebrant should be sure to check this ahead of time). It reiterates the many themes that both have been running

throughout the season and that coalesce today: there is a baptismal background (" . . . on those you made your adopted children . . . "); there is the sense of fullness and fruition of the Easter mystery (" . . . bringing your Paschal Mystery to completion . . . "); there is the theme of unity, again utilizing the imagery of the Babel narrative (" . . . brought together the many languages of the earth in profession of the one faith . . . "); and there is the ecclesiological dimension (" . . . as the Church came to birth . . . "). Given the festivity of the day, it would be a good idea to sing the introductory dialogue and the Preface, especially if this has been the custom on Sundays throughout Easter Time. Note that if Eucharistic Prayer I, the Roman Canon, is used, there is a proper form of the *Communicantes* (In communion with those), which mentions the traditional image of the Holy Spirit as tongues of fire.

The Communion Antiphon, taken from John 7, announces the Lord's invitation to let anyone who is thirsty "come to me and drink." The verse is appropriate not only in terms of its placement in the Communion Rite, but also because it can remind us of how we can drink of the Spirit, through the Eucharist. The verse can serve to remind us of the importance of offering Communion under both kinds on a regular basis.

The Prayer after Communion notes how the Eucharistic gifts of the Body and Blood of Christ ("the gifts we have consumed") are indeed gifts in the Spirit (since the bread wine were transformed by the power of the Spirit). Having feasted on those gifts touched by the Spirit, we can rightly petition the Lord to make us "always be aflame with the same Spirit" that was poured out on the gifts, the same Spirit also "wondrously poured out" on the Apostles.

A formula for Solemn Blessing is suggested, the formula titled "The Holy Spirit" (number 8 under "Blessings at the End of Mass and Prayers over the People"), and it would be good to use this formula. Since it is Pentecost, the solemn dismissal with the double Alleluia returns for use one last time before Easter Time next year.

Mass during the Day

There is a choice from among two Entrance Antiphons for the Mass during the Day. The second option is the same as the one for the Vigil Mass, and is discussed above. The first option is taken from the Book of Wisdom and relates how the "Spirit of the Lord has filled the whole world." Obviously, the author of Wisdom was not using the phrase in the Christian sense of the Holy Spirit, but the liturgy takes the phrase and places it in the context of the feast we are celebrating.

As with either the extended form or the simple form of the Vigil Mass, the Mass during the Day provides an ideal occasion to use the Rite for the Blessing and Sprinkling of Water, found in Appendix II at the back of the Missal, especially if your parish has been doing this on all of the Sundays of Easter Time, and strong consideration should be given to this. Remember that this rite takes the place of the Penitential Act. The Gloria immediately follows the prayer said by the priest at the end of the Rite.

In the Collect for this Mass, the universality of the gifts of the Spirit is emphasized as we ask God to "sanctify your whole Church in every people and nation." Additionally, we ask that the Spirit who was at work "when the Gospel was first proclaimed" still fills the hearts of believers.

In the Prayer over the Offerings we pray for the Spirit to do something very specific for us in this liturgy: that he "may reveal to us more abundantly the hidden mystery of this sacrifice." In other words, we are asking the Spirit to help us to enter more deeply into the mystery we are celebrating and to help us to understand better the meaning of what we do at this Eucharist. With such insight and understanding, we can be led into all truth—not only in terms of what we do at liturgy, but also in terms of the meaning of all of life.

The text for the Preface, both with and without musical notation, is proper for today and is given right there at the place in the Missal along with the other texts for the Mass during the Day. See above for commentary on the Preface, as well as for notes concerning the proper insert if Eucharistic Prayer I is used.

The Communion Antiphon, taken from chapter 2 of Acts, can remind us of what our spiritual disposition should be as we approach the table of the Eucharist, as we are fed at it, and as we are sent out from it: "They were all filled with the Holy Spirit and spoke of the marvels of God." Although it is not used today, we can be put in mind of the form of dismissal at the end of Mass that states, "Go and announce the Gospel of the Lord," an insight applicable to every Mass whether or not that formula is used.

The Prayer after Communion communicates to us a dynamic quality of the ongoing power of God conveyed through the Eucharist, a heavenly gift bestowed upon the Church; the prayer asks "that the gift of the Holy Spirit poured out upon her may retain all its force." If we are open to such heavenly gifts, then the spiritual food we receive will gain us the "abundance of eternal redemption." The way our Eucharistic celebrations on earth nourish us in our pilgrimage toward the heavenly banquet can never be forgotten.

The formula titled "The Holy Spirit" (number 8 under "Blessings at the End of Mass and Prayers over the People") is suggested for use as the final blessing, and it would be good to do so. Remember that since it is Pentecost, the solemn dismissal with the double Alleluia is used today, one last time before Easter Time next year.

Final Notes about the End of Easter Time

The Missal offers some rubrical instructions concerning the completion of Easter Time. It notes that now (i.e., after the last liturgy on Pentecost Sunday, with the return to Ordinary Time) the Paschal candle is extinguished. The candle now returns to its regular location in the baptistery, and it is to reside there "with due honor" for its use at the celebration of Baptism. If it is the custom that the faithful are either obliged or accustomed to attend Mass on the Monday or Tuesday after Pentecost, then the Mass of Pentecost Sunday may be repeated, or the formularies for a Mass of the Holy Spirit may be used.

Pastoral Reflection

Infused into every part of life to be made manifest in our daily lives, Jesus gives us each a great protector. Because of this we are powerful beings in Christ. Harness this beautiful power and accept your ability to truly make a difference in bold and beautiful ways. Consider downloading from World Library Publications, John Angotti's songs: "I Send you Out" or "Come, Holy Spirit" for both are a true representation to feed your soul about the message necessary to live as an empowered member of the Body of Christ. You are blessed to serve. Serve someone in Christ's name this week.

ORDINARY TIME (DURING SUMMER AND FALL)

The Meaning / The Lectionary for Mass

THERE is nothing "ordinary" about our return to "Ordinary Time." We have just celebrated Fifty days of Easter culminating with the Solemnity of Pentecost. These are not just historical reminisces! We share in the divine life of the Risen Christ through our Baptism. We, too, are gifted and empowered by the Holy Spirit. It is precisely in "ordinary" daily life that these gifts are used and cultivated, until Christ in us comes more and more to full stature, and we are transformed more and more in his likeness.

Few months have as many solemnities and feasts as does June this year! We celebrate the Solemnity of the Most Holy Trinity on the Sunday after Pentecost. Our Lectionary readings draw us into the mystery of our God: Father, Son, and Spirit. As the First Reading points out, our God is a compassionate and gracious God, abounding in kindness and fidelity to us. Jesus showed us this face of God in a most personal way, and we are called now to show that face to one another in love and peace.

On the Solemnity of the Most Holy Body and Blood of Christ, the Lectionary texts focus our attention not only on the ways God nourishes the life of his people, but also on the fact that by sharing in the Eucharistic bread and cup, we become the one Body of Christ in his Church. On the following Friday, we commemorate the Solemnity of the Most Sacred Heart, focusing pre-eminently on the tremendous love that our God has for his people—ourselves included! And, all is God's initiative, God's gift.

The Solemnities of the Nativity of St. John the Baptist and of SS. Peter and Paul focus our attention on their important works of preparing the way for the imminent ministry of Jesus and of the ongoing and far-reaching proclamation of his Gospel. Ordinary everyday life was the locus of their ministries—to which we are now called as well: not only in our own lives, but in the lives of our families, friends, and co-workers.

It is through preparing the way of the Lord and taking his Gospel to heart that we come to know that we are destined for heavenly glory, a glory that we glimpse with the celebration of Jesus's Transfiguration on August 6. We celebrate the heavenly glory that Our Blessed Mother already enjoys on the solemnity of her Assumption into heaven (August 15). We commemorate Mary's nativity (birth) on September 8. The Gospel for this day focuses on Mary as the Mother of Jesus, the child conceived through the power of the Holy Spirit: Emmanuel, God-with-us.

The Feast of the Exaltation of the Holy Cross (September 14) sets before us the Cross of shame, suffering, and death as the means of Jesus's glorification and his passage into risen and eternal life. So it will be for all of us who gaze on it and allow ourselves to be drawn by him through death into the glory of eternal life.

The Archangels (Michael, Gabriel, and Raphael), whose memorial we celebrate on September 29 have important roles in Scripture as messengers of God and protectors of God's chosen ones: Gabriel, in the Book of Daniel and in Luke's account of the Annunciation; Raphael, in the Book of Tobit, and Michael in the Book of Revelation as the leader of the angelic army who defeats the rebellious Satan and his followers. They are among the angelic choirs that stand before God's heavenly throne.

Parables are proclaimed on the twenty-fifth through twenty-eighth Sundays. We are often surprised by what happens in these parables, as they do not unfold as we might think. That is precisely their value! Jesus invites us to a new way of looking at life! One that is in accord with the kingdom of heaven—and not human judgments!

At the beginning of the summer, the First Readings for weekday Eucharists are from the Old Testament and recount the story of God's people from the time of the prophet Elijah to the time of the Babylonian Exile. Next, we hear from the prophets (Amos, Hosea, Isaiah, Micah, Ezekiel, Jeremiah) whose challenges and calls to conversion are as relevant now as they were when they were first uttered. Can we see how that is so?

In the twenty-first through the twenty-fourth week, we hear from the letters of Paul: 2 Thessalonians and 1 Corinthians. Again we find that the basic traits of ordinary people and ordinary life have a timeless commonality. We are called to self-examination.

In weeks twenty-five and twenty six, we ponder the wisdom traditions of Israel: Proverbs, Ecclesiastes, and Job. Proverbs gives wisdom for everyday life while Ecclesiastes and Job ponder life's ultimate meaning. Then, we are back to the letters of Paul: Galatians, Philippians, and Ephesians. Note how Paul shares his own personal experience of faith in the Lord Jesus and what it means for his daily life in these letters.

In the last two weeks of Ordinary Time, as we approach the end of the liturgical year, we read from the Book of Revelation, a prophetic work in which the Christian prophet not only addresses seven Christian communities in Asia Minor with the words of the Lord but also shares his vision of the events of the end-time and the rewards of the just in the heavenly Jerusalem.

For our daily Gospel, we hear from Matthew and Luke respectively. We are contemporary disciples of Jesus, so it is important that we listen closely to his instructions to those first disciples and take them to heart. As people also in need of Jesus's healing touch, we should see ourselves, at least in a figurative sense, in the diseased, the blind, and the lame who come or are brought to Jesus. Slowly ponder these scenes and hear Jesus's healing Word and feel his healing touch. Healing takes place on many levels.

We are not only contemporary disciples of Jesus; we are also his Church, his presence in our world today. The Feast of the Dedication of the Church of St. John Lateran on November 9 speaks not only of this splendid cathedral in Rome, but also of our own reality as Church (see especially the Second Reading for this day). We are the dwelling place of God—such has God made us, so must we become.

And we become who and what we are called to be precisely in the ordinary activities and challenges of daily life. And it is precisely ordinary, everyday life that is addressed by the prophets, the New Testament letters, and the Gospel. This is where we are called to love the Lord our God with all our heart, all our soul, and all our mind. This is where we are called to righteousness. And at the end of time, we must stand before our heavenly Judge and give an account.

The Roman Missal

ORDINARY Time resumes after Easter Time with the Tenth Week in Ordinary Time, starting on the Monday after Pentecost. This year, a large number of Ordinary Time Sundays are replaced. The Solemnity of the Most Holy Trinity on June 15 and the Solemnity of the Most Holy Body and Blood of Christ (*Corpus Christi*) replace the two Sundays after Pentecost, as they always do. However, there are several others: the Solemnity of SS. Peter and Paul, Apostles on June 29 replaces the Thirteenth Sunday in Ordinary Time; the Feast of the Exaltation of the Holy Cross on September 14 replaces the Twenty-Fourth Sunday in Ordinary Time; the Commemoration of All the Faithful Departed on November 2 replaces the Thirty-First Sunday in Ordinary Time; and the Feast of the Dedication of the Lateran Basilica on November 9 replaces the Thirty-Second Sunday in Ordinary Time.

The Roman Missal notes that each Sunday in Ordinary Time has its own proper Collect, Prayer over the Offerings, and Prayer after Communion, as well as Entrance and Communion Antiphons. There are no formularies for ferial weekdays. (Note: since there are no formularies for the Thirty-Fourth Sunday in Ordinary Time, orations for weekday Masses may come from the page with the title "Thirty-Fourth Week in Ordinary Time.")

Continue to explore the rich options in the Missal for weekdays by using the orations not only from the previous Sunday, but from any Sunday in Ordinary Time whose prayers seem to be relevant to the readings or to the life of the worshiping community. Also continue to use the Masses for

Various Needs and Occasions and Votive Masses from time to time, again with an eye toward the spiritual good of the community. There are some rich themes that can serve to powerfully connect the celebration of the Eucharist with the everyday faith life of believers: there are Masses "For the Nation or State" (#21), "For the Preservation of Peace and Justice" (#30), "For Charity" (#40), and "For Giving Thanks to God" (#49). Don't forget to also include "For Ministers of the Church" (#8; particularly if your parish is going through some form of ministry renewal or recruitment, as many do in the fall) and "For Vocations to Holy Orders" (#9).

The Eucharistic Prayers for Masses of Reconciliation should also be used from time to time, and would be appropriate with Masses "For Reconciliation" (#16) and "For the Forgiveness of Sins" (#38), for example.

A return to the simpler greeting of "The Lord be with you," especially on weekdays, might be appropriate. Anything that can be done to distinguish weekday Masses from Sunday ones, making weekdays simpler in order to highlight Sunday Eucharist as the center of our worship with greater festivity, is helpful. This segment of Ordinary Time might be a good opportunity to use a wider selection of originally composed invocations for the Penitential Act. If original invocations are used, be sure they follow the proper format, using the models given in Appendix VI in the Missal as a guide. The invocations are not about us or our unworthiness; rather, they are addressed to Christ and mention something about the mystery of salvation through Christ. Thus, wording such as "For the time we . . . " should be avoided. Also to be avoided is the incorrect addressing of each invocation to one of the Persons of the Blessed Trinity (that is, addressing the first to the Father, the second to the Son, and the third to the Spirit); all invocations are addressed to Christ. Another option is to use the form given at #5 in the Order of Mass, especially at weekday celebrations.

If one is looking to bring a certain liturgical rhythm to the weekdays of Ordinary Time, it might be noted that the Votive Masses for "The Mystery of the Holy Cross" (#4), for "The Most Precious Blood of Our Lord Jesus Christ" (#7) and "The Most Sacred Heart of Jesus" (#8) are appropriate for Fridays. Friday has traditionally been a day to recall the Passion and Death of the Lord. Saturday has been and continues to be a day to commemorate the Blessed Virgin Mary, and eight different sets of Mass formularies for use during Ordinary Time are given under the Common of the Blessed Virgin Mary.

Children's Liturgy of the Word

TEENS can be mentored and trained to lead or assist with the Liturgy of the Word with children, especially as liturgical ministers. For some adult leaders of Children's Liturgy of the Word, this may be a daunting prospect, especially if they have had limited experience with teens and youth. You become a mentor when you help teens recognize that they are an important part of the parish community. You are a mentor when you help young people realize that they have gifts and talents to offer for the glory of God and for the good of others. You are a mentor when you help young people to experience the liturgy as the source and summit of the Christian life.

If you will be working directly with children and teens, check with your parish administrator to see if the parish or diocese requires adults to participate in a specialized training that will safeguard young people's protection. VIRTUS® is a brand name for best-practice programs designed by the National Catholic Risk Retention Group, Inc. to support churches and religious institutions in preventing child sexual abuse. The "Protecting God's Children" program is for the education of employees, volunteers, and parents in parishes, Catholic schools, and diocesan offices. All parish personnel who work with children (paid or volunteer) should be certified through this program or a similar program. These excellent programs will help you to be more aware of what kinds of behavior are inappropriate, and it will help you recognize the signs of abuse. By participating in these programs, you can truly help to prevent child sexual abuse in the Church.

—Written by Latisse A. Heerwig and Karie Ferrell © LTP.

The Saints

DURING this second period of counted time in the Church calendar, we leave behind the intense liturgical focus on specific aspects of salvation history: the "O Antiphons" of Advent are not chanted; the Christmas carols have faded into silent nights; the simple cadences of Lenten hymns of penance once replaced by exuberant Easter anthems and majestic odes to the Holy Spirit are now all carefully filed away by musicians, choirs, and celebrants alike. Throughout the many months of Ordinary Time in Summer and Fall, from the Monday (June 9) following Pentecost Sunday through to the last Saturday (November 29) before the First Sunday of the next Advent, our liturgical celebrations follow the rhythms—the hills, valleys, and plains—of the landscape of the Christian message. We dive into the depths of the Gospel message and appreciate each pearl of wisdom one at a time. All along this pilgrimage the calendar is punctuated by a panoply of saintly guides through salvation history. As each of us seeks the Lord on our voyage through Ordinary Time, the saints are with us through example and prayer just as the stars and constellations directed ancient mariners.

During Ordinary Time in Summer and Fall we rejoice in eight solemnities, only one of which is a Holyday of Obligation this year—the Assumption of the Blessed Virgin Mary (August 15). Four solemnities fall on Sundays: Most Holy Trinity (June 15), Most Holy Body and Blood of Christ (June 22), SS. Peter and Paul (June 29), and Our Lord Jesus Christ, King of the Universe (November 23). The first two great Sunday solemnities are celebrations of two of the different manifestations of the face of God—as Trinity and as the sacramental presence of Christ in his Body and Blood.

Six months before our remembrance of the birth of Christ is the commemoration of the Nativity of St. John the Baptist (June 24). Concerning Christ, St. John the Baptist proclaimed, "He must increase; I must decrease". (John 3:30) Fittingly, in the northern hemisphere, the days begin to get shorter after this celebration, while the days get longer after Christmas. This is one of only three birth celebrations on the liturgical calendar—the Nativity of Christ, the feast of the Nativity of the Virgin Mary (September 8), and this solemnity. The Solemnity of the Most Sacred Heart of Jesus (June 27) (followed by its mirror memorial, the

Immaculate Heart of Mary [June 28]) is an opportune time to reflect on the heart-centered side of our faith. A time to appreciate and grow in the practices of loving mercy and reparation for offenses against the faith and the sacraments.

The tradition of receiving Holy Communion on first Fridays of the month is associated with the devotion to the Sacred Heart. The next stop on our journey is with SS. Peter and Paul (June 29), the great founders of the faith. The twin duties of the Church, to lead and to preach by word and deed, are embodied in the first of the Apostles and in the Father of all Missionaries. While they didn't always agree on everything, they were united in constantly seeking the Lord.

Later in the summer is the Solemnity of the Assumption of the Blessed Virgin Mary (August 15). In all things the Virgin Mary relied on the strength of the Lord and thus was rewarded with being reunited with her Son at the end of her journey. As we near the end of our trek through Ordinary Time, we celebrate all those who travelled this life before us in the double celebration of All Saints (November 1) and its mirror observance, the Commemoration of All the Faithful Departed (November 2). While we believe that in each liturgical ritual throughout the year we are joined in spirit by all the saints and angels, on this day especially we remember all those who rejoice in heaven. This double observance allows us to hold holy the memory of those who are canonized and to pray with and for all our dearly departed loved ones. Books of remembrance, photo montages, multimedia displays are but a few ways to honor these protagonists of our lives.

The last Sunday of the season is reserved for marking Christ's title as King of the Universe (November 23). The political campaigns of the year are mostly ended, the debates of government still wage on, and people everywhere disagree about affairs of state, but today we acknowledge that all of that means nothing unless we look to the face of God and rely on the Lord's strength and dominion over all to bring us home rejoicing. As with every solemnity, but specifically with those that fall on Sunday, there should be a marked difference—a heightened sense of importance—in these celebrations (for example, additional candles at the altar, more festive vestments, and paraments, the use of incense, a sung Gospel, and so on).

There are nine feasts in Ordinary Time in Summer and Fall. Several are dedicated to the first to hear Christ and bring Christ's message to the world: St. Thomas (July 3); St. James (July 25); St. Luke (October 18); and SS. Simon and Jude (October 28). We have already noted the Nativity of the Virgin Mary (September 8). There are three feasts not dedicated to saints: the Transfiguration of the Lord (August 6); the Exaltation of the Cross (September 14), a distinctly appropriate time to highlight again the seeming paradox that death leads to life—torture on the Cross led to joyous life eternal offered to all, and the Dedication of the Lateran Basilica (November 9), focusing on the pope's cathedral church, this feast is a fitting time to preach on how the physical aspects of life (for example, a church building) stand as tangible reminders of deep spiritual realities (for example, the community of believers as the locus of God in our midst).

We also celebrate SS. Michael, Gabriel, and Raphael, Archangels (September 29) as the great celestial messengers of God named in the Bible. Each month and week throughout this season is graced with numerous memorials (both obligatory and optional) in which we remember those who spent their lives constantly seeking the face of God. Some are well known and universally loved—St. Francis of Assisi (October 4), St. Thérèse of the Child Jesus (October 1), and St. Benedict (July 11)—and others are less well known but yet worth learning about—St. Sharbel Makhlūf (July 24), a Lebanese monk of the late 1800s important to the shrinking minority of Christians in the Middle East; St. Peter Julian Eymard (August 2), founder of the Blessed Sacrament Fathers who promoted devotion to the Eucharist as a means to increase charity and apostolic service; and St. Rose Philippine Duchesne (November 18), a religious sister of the early 1800s who worked tirelessly among the Native Americans.

The Liturgy of the Hours

The Hours in the Summer of 2014 for the period of Ordinary Time begin with the Fourteenth Sunday in Ordinary Time, July 6, 2014, Week II of the Psalter. The Solemnity of SS. Peter and Paul, Apostles, June 29, 2014 falls on a Sunday. Consider celebrating Evening Prayer in the context of a gathering for whole community catechesis, on the topic of Baptism, followed by a parish barbecue or picnic.

On the Solemnity of the Assumption of the Blessed Virgin Mary consider holding Evening Prayer. Invite parishioners to bring the bounty of their harvest to be blessed and then shared with a homeless shelter or other agency that provides meals for those living on the margins of society.

The Feast of the Exaltation of the Holy Cross falls on a Sunday in 2014. Here is another opportunity to celebrate Evening Prayer. Perhaps you could invite catechists to gather in the late afternoon for an in-service. Have another group in the parish make dinner and invite their families and the rest of the parish to join them for supper, asking them to bring side dishes and desserts. Follow this time of community building with Evening Prayer.

The Commemoration of All the Faithful Departed (All Souls' Day), November 2 also falls on a Sunday in 2014. Invite parishioners to bring photos of their deceased relatives and friends to Church with them on Sunday, October 26, 2014. Include these photos in your altar of the dead. On November 2, celebrate Evening Prayer and include a time for parishioners to share a brief, but fond remembrance of a loved one. Finally on November 9, the Feast of the Dedication of the Lateran Basilica falls on a Sunday in 2014. During the celebration of the Evening Prayer pray for the intentions of our Holy Father.

Especially beneficial would be the celebration of Sunday Morning Prayer in households or neighborhoods in the domestic Church. This is an excellent way for people to prepare for gathering at their local church for Sunday Eucharist. Also co-workers can gather to pray the hours in the workplace. By using resources such as *Proclaim Praise: Daily Prayer for Parish and Home* (LTP), which includes abbreviated forms of celebrations for Morning Prayer, Evening Prayer, and Night Prayer, and by using seasonal hymns and psalms that could be provided in the parish bulletin, the domestic Church and the folks in the workplace will have the basic material necessary for celebrating the Hours in homes and neighborhoods. In order for the Liturgy of the Hours to fully take root in our parishes, renewed emphasis must be placed upon prayer in households and small groups. Prayer must be recognized for its power and its revolutionary stance of dependence upon the living God. The prayer of the domestic Church should lead to liturgical prayer within the larger community. The liturgy itself is the very living out of our lives, by which we are being transformed into Christ's. The domestic Church is the first place to be Christ for others.

Both GIA and OCP have recently released settings of the Hours for the commuter and people on the go. *My Morning Prayer* and *My Evening Prayer* (Various) are from GIA and *Morning and Evening* (Walker/Freeburg) is from OCP. Simply play the CD or rip the files onto your computer and drag to an iPod or mp3 player. Put on your headphones and pray the Hours while commuting by plane, train, light rail, bus, or on foot.

The Church as tender mother must reach out and embrace this "forgotten stepchild" of the liturgical movement. The Liturgy of the Hours is the communal prayer that will fill people's hunger for devotional and scriptural experiences, it is the prayer that can sustain the lives of many within the faith community, and it is the way the Church has traditionally marked the hours of the day and the seasons of the year with prayer. No one (catechumens, non-Catholics, alienated Catholics) is excluded from participation in the Liturgy of the Hours, and the leadership for the Liturgy of the Hours is not limited to ordained ministers. Therefore, bishops, priests, deacons, pastoral ministers, and the laity must form themselves with an appreciation for the Liturgy of the Hours so that the whole Church can be a visible presence of Christ at prayer.

The Rite of Christian Initiation of Adults

IF your initiation office shuts down for the summer, there may be interested parties who could feel their needs have not been met. They may move to another parish, find another faith tradition, or give up altogether. Even if you decide not to begin a formal inquiry period until later in the summer, keep in touch with those who have expressed interest by sending them regular e-mails with more information on the initiation process, and provide answers to basic questions. Always keep the lines of communication open.

If your program has been operating on a school-year calendar, perhaps this is the time to make the transition to a year-round catechumenate process. Surely, there may be some growing pains, but the benefits will be far greater. Continue dismissals of catechumens throughout the summer season, and offer periods of reflection for them. Even if you need to start by having simpler sessions with a smaller team and a briefer time frame, it is better than not offering the sessions. Ordinary Time provides rich insight into Jesus's life and ministry and the Gospel call to discipleship. It would be a shame to not help the new people unpack it. Like any change, it is important that you communicate it to the entire parish community and the initiation team before it is implemented.

With varying summer schedules, attendance and participation may be sporadic, so consider offering something like an "RCIA barbecue" to help all the participants become better acquainted. Don't forget the nametags.

The Sacraments of Initiation

ONE of the primary liturgical symbols is the assembly. The ritual gesture accompanying the assembly is gathering. During the summer months think about ways to gather those who have celebrated the Sacraments of Initiation over the past year. This will give these families and individuals a sense of satisfaction and pleasure in knowing that they are welcome and wanted—a feeling of belonging and acceptance. Summer is a good time to have a picnic, party, or pot luck to give thanks. Since Eucharist completes initiation, giving thanks would be an appropriate theme. College students home on break, candidates for Confirmation in the upcoming year, confirmandi, and youth group members would be great helpers in organizing the project and entertaining the children. Activities and games could be planned that have something to do with the joyful aspects of initiation such as water balloons, a treasure hunt for the gifts of the Spirit, and a thank-you contest for first communicants, for example, how many people can they name that helped them throughout the year? How many did they thank?

Planning is also a summer task. Take time this summer to review your preparation programs. Survey parents who have been through them to find out what was helpful or not. Talk with the liturgy director to see if there are ways to involve more rituals in the preparation processes. Evaluate

ways you have been able to keep in contact with families and involve them in parish life. Use the summer to recruit catechists and group leaders for sacramental preparation. Look to parents, sponsors, and older teens who were involved in past years' processes. Invite those whom you think might be good preparation ministers.

Fall is a busy time. The gears of school and parish life push us forward. It is a new year. It is crucial that time is taken by the whole staff to come together for preparation and careful scheduling. This is the time to look at the year as a whole. When will all sacramental preparation processes take place? Are there special parish or diocesan events? Is there a parish retreat or renewal program? Are there other rituals or events that will take place on the weekend? In planning everyone needs to be especially conscious of the Sunday assembly. So much of what goes on in various programs impacts the liturgy. The goal here is to keep any given Sunday from being overloaded due to overlapping events, thus disrupting the celebration of Eucharist.

This is also the time for the directors or coordinators of sacramental programs in the parish and school to meet with the liturgy and music directors to prepare and brainstorm ways to incorporate good music and ritual throughout the processes. Be sure liturgists and music directors are familiar with the special catechetical programs being used for preparation. Invite them to help with the ritual aspects in the catechetical materials.

If you are using a liturgical catechetical model for sacrament preparation, set up a workshop for catechists who will lead the session celebrations. Show them how to set up a worship space with a prayer table and/or lectern. Explain the use of different color cloths and banners for each liturgical time. If a classroom is being used, give options for resetting chairs and space so it is appropriate for worship. Invite the liturgy director to give them tips on presiding, proclaiming the Word, and doing liturgical gestures. Have the music director talk about using music from the parish repertoire and suggestions for ways to lead singing during the sessions.

Plan a meeting for parents of young people in the preparation programs. Use the first session to explain the program and process. Give them a calendar and be upfront about expectations. Go through the young person's book and show them the family sections. Conclude the session with a prayer of blessing.

The Rite of Penance

IN many parishes, the Sacrament of Penance is usually celebrated on a Saturday afternoons. Be sure to post the times in the bulletin, on the parish website, and on any signage on the parish campus alerting people as to the location of the Reconciliation Chapel (confessionals).

If Form II of the rite is celebrated in Advent and Lent why not consider scheduling it in Ordinary Time as well? Consider scheduling the celebration around parish or diocesan feast days, before pilgrimages, during retreats, on ember days and during Catholic youth summer camps.

The Pastoral Care of the Sick

CONSIDER beginning a parish nurse program in your parish. Information can be found at www.parishnurses.org/Home_1.aspx. Include nurses, hospice workers, massage therapists, acupuncturists, doctors, and those who work with traditional and non-traditional therapies on your parish team of ministers to the sick and homebound. Schedule a communal Anointing of the Sick during the summer and follow it with an ice-cream social and be sure to have an alternate offering to serve those with special dietary restrictions, for example, lactose intolerance. *Catholic Household Blessings & Prayers* contains prayers for the sick, disabled, and the weary in Part VIII, God's Word in Times of Need. In addition, the prayer for victims of abuse in Part VI Prayers for the Church and the World is an especially poignant prayer for our age.

The Rite of Marriage

THE summer parish calendar will often be filled with a great number of weddings so consider offering the couple the option of celebrating the sacrament at the Vigil Mass of Saturday. When the rite is celebrated on a Sunday or a solemnity only one reading from the *Rite of Marriage* may be used. Since the Church offers the option for the priest to celebrate three Masses on the Commemoration of All the Faithful Departed (All Souls' Day) this would not be a good day to schedule a celebration of the Sacrament of Marriage. The Rite of Marriage may not be celebrated on Holy Days of Obligation such as the Assumption of the Blessed Virgin Mary or All Saints. When celebrating the Rite of Marriage with an ecumenical or interfaith couple, the non-Catholic partner's minister, rabbi, or religious leader may be present and participate in the celebration only with the permission of the local bishop, who frequently delegates this decision to the pastor or parish priest. When many non-Catholics are not present, but large amounts of Christian believers from different ecclesial communions are, consider singing a hymn that is well-known by all present. This practice will automatically create a relaxed and hospitable environment that will encourage all present to participate in the liturgy fully, consciously, and actively.

Be sure to communicate to couples and their bridal parties about appropriate attire for the celebration and the ban on all drugs or alcoholic beverages before or during the wedding liturgy. Make sure the parish has clear policies in place for photographers, and operators of video cameras including a statement that states "flash photography and lights on a video cameras are not allowed during the celebration."

You may also wish to include the bishops' guidelines for the reception of Holy Communion in the worship aid.

Make sure the parish provides ministers of hospitality to assist with parking (if necessary) and directing people to the location of restrooms and assisting the elderly or disabled. The demeanor of the presiding minister (priest or deacon) and their pastoral sensitivity will go a long way in encouraging those present to return to the parish at another time.

Since it is the couple who celebrates the sacrament and the minister who stands as the "official witness," to the sacrament, is important to consider the placement of the couple and their chosen witnesses. Having the couple stand with their backs to the congregation is not a good sign so consider having the couple face the congregation with the minister having his back to the congregation or have the couple and the minister at an angle or both parties facing each other. At the rehearsal the minister or his representative should be sure to address the issue of posture for the celebration and put the couple and members of the wedding party and family at ease and let them know you (the minister) will provide an appropriate cue to alert people when to stand, sit, or kneel. Encourage all to participate fully in the celebration.

The Order of Christian Funerals

THE Sunday Gospel accounts of November offer chilling testimony to the serious side of the future, and they should be taken seriously. November is the time to encourage people to examine their own funeral preparations and make out or review their wills and Advance Health Care Directives. This would be a good time to create parish funeral packets for parishioners and prepare teams to help households, especially of the elderly and infirm fill out these forms. Holding a workshop with representatives from the funeral industry, the local Catholic cemetery, a lawyer, liturgist, pastoral musician, and bereavement minister can be most beneficial. *Now and at the Hour of Our Death* (LTP) is one resource that should be made available to every family in the parish at no cost.

Consider the environment for the Funeral Liturgy and the placement of plants and flowers. Encourage a member of the parish art and environment team to be present to assist the funeral directors and family in the placement of the flowers so they don't hinder access to the altar, ambo, Paschal candle, and coffin. While the OCF allows for the placement of Christian images such as a cross or Bible on the coffin other images may be brought to the church and placed in the vestibule, gathering space, or other appropriate place in the church. These might include photos, stuffed animals, or other treasures that have a significant meaning for the family and friends of the deceased; of course pastoral sensitivity is always encouraged. Many hospice care facilities provide a quilt for those in their final days and it would be appropriate, especially when the cremated remains are present, to cover a small table with the quilt and place the urn and perhaps a photo of the deceased on the table.

Consider putting together a funeral choir in your parish to help inspire full participation in the funeral liturgy. Many communities schedule funerals at the same time when Morning Mass is celebrated. Consider canceling a Morning Mass in the parish on days when funerals are scheduled so that those daily Mass attendees may be present at the funeral. Sometimes members of the Knights of Columbus, Catholic Daughters of the Americas, or representatives from other fraternal organizations or groups from the parish lead the recitation of the Rosary, where this practice is maintained. If the Rosary is prayed publically consider having it end at least 15 minutes before the celebration of the funeral to allow for a time of transition. Funeral homes will usually include a stipend for the use of the church facilities, the presiding minister, and the ministers of music. Every person should be afforded the dignity of a Christian burial and the full complement of the Church's funeral rites so families who may not be able to provide a stipend or gift to the parish or the ministers should never be denied full services. This should be clearly communicated to all ministers including pastoral musicians.

Consider using the setting of the "Song of Farewell" as the concluding song at the Sunday Eucharist during the month of November so that those who attend funerals will be able to participate in a fuller way in this song. Other funeral repertoire could also be used during the month of November at the Sunday liturgy. Especially helpful would be identifying a good musical setting of Psalm 23, "The Lord is My Shepherd" and using it as a Communion song since it is usually the most requested psalm for use at the funeral liturgy.

The Book of Blessings

THE Church provides an order of blessings to be used in various circumstances (Chapter 71) in case you cannot find a blessing for a situation in life that is not addressed in the *Book of Blessings*. The Order for the Blessing of Fathers on Father's Day, June 15, 2014 is found in chapter 56; the Order for Visiting a Cemetery on All Souls' Day (November 2), Memorial Day, or on the Anniversary of Death or Burial is found in Chapter 57. The Order for the Blessing of Food for Thanksgiving Day (Fourth Thursday of November) is found in chapter 58.

September 21, 2014, Catechetical Sunday, would be an appropriate day for the Order for the Blessing of Those Appointed as Catechists (Chapter 4). The Order for the Blessing of Animals

(Chapter 25) would be fitting for the memorial of St. Frances of Assisi on October 4. Mine the riches found in the *Book of Blessings*, which is a treasured reminder to give the God of all creation praise and thanks for all we have, all we do, and all we are. Blessed be God forever, and let the Church say Amen!

The Liturgical Environment

ORDINARY Time has green as its color. Green is the color of living things, but it is an incredibly difficult color to use well. Most green fabrics are only a single shade of green, which is true of hardly anything that is green in the natural world. Leaves, grass, and plants of all sorts have variations of shade and tone as part of what we see as their green color. This variation is part of what makes them look alive, healthy, and flourishing. In choosing fabrics for vestments, and other uses for Ordinary Time, it is best if fabrics can mimic this aspect of natural greens. It will help them to appear less flat and unappealing, and help prevent the quickly dated appearance of many flat greens, which have come into style and just as quickly fallen out. While some fabrics have various tones of green woven or dyed into the fabric, a similar effect can be achieved by using related but different greens in designing liturgical pieces.

Within this counted time, it is worthwhile to attend to landmarks along the way. Feast days, saints' days, and other changes from the norm can be highlighted simply, but to great effect. If the parish has works of art in celebration of particular saints, these can be placed with some plants or other elements to frame them in a location where they will be seen but out of the way of ministers' and the assembly's movement for the feast. Such additions to the environment should always be removed at the close of that celebration. Pay attention to relative solemnity: greater visual emphasis should be made by the additions for solemnities than for feasts, and by those of feasts than for memorials.

The summer is often a good time in a parish's life to catch up on reflection and preparation, which can often seem impossible during the continuous push from Advent to Pentecost. Reviewing what went well, and what you thought could be improved is an important exercise, and the summer

may provide time to plan ahead, construct the new pieces you envisioned, and make improvements for next year. This is part of the ongoing growth we discussed above. It might also be a good time to welcome new members to be part of the preparation of the liturgical environment. It is especially worth asking those who received the Easter sacraments about how the space and its arrangement contributed to their participation in the rite or hindered it. This could even be incorporated into their ongoing mystagogy, if the RCIA team is open to the idea. Reflection on the liturgy with them may also help those who have been responsible for the liturgical environment for a while to see it again with new eyes.

Summer can also be a good time to spare some attention for the exterior spaces of the church. These are also liturgical spaces. Meeting with those responsible for preparing other aspects of the liturgy and the RCIA could facilitate conversations about how the exterior of the church can provide an appropriate environment for these rites. They situate processions with palms and the Eucharist, the conclusion of Holy Thursday and the beginning of the Vigil, they may see rites of welcoming new catechumens or clergy, and they welcome everyone who attends the liturgy all year. The summer may provide the space to reflect, consider, prepare, and implement changes that can help your church be a better home to the whole liturgical life of the parish.

The harvest images of bounty and of reaping are both appropriately highlighted in this last portion of Ordinary Time. The liturgical color remains green, but darker shades might be chosen. The liturgical space might be adorned with plants and other items that bring the fall colors of rich browns, reds, and golds into the liturgical space. Sheaves of wheat and bunches of grapes evoke harvest imagery and connect it to the Eucharistic character of Church.

Many parishes collect food throughout the fall for distribution to those in need. Such collections of food for the poor have been part of the Eucharistic celebration since the beginning of the Church, and it does belong in the liturgy. Our care for the less fortunate ought be part of our coming to the Lamb's feast, and be part of what we go from the table to do. This practice draws on the natural considerations of the preparations for the coming winter, and might be highlighted in the liturgical environment, as long as it doesn't call too much attention away from the primary liturgical spaces.

The feasts of the fall also fit well into this emphasis on harvesting the fruit of the Gospel. The martyrs and the saints can be highlighted as the fruit that grew from the seeds of the Word. Statues or paintings of the saints can be incorporated into the liturgical space along with plants bearing their bounty. The Feast of the Exaltation of the Holy Cross (September 14), calls to mind the many fruits of the seemingly barren tree of the cross. Such temporary additions to the liturgical space should be removed after the feast has passed, so as to allow the season to be the primary emphasis.

The Solemnity of All Saints (November 1) and the Commemoration of All the Faithful Departed (November 2) usher in a month that is often dedicated to thanksgiving and prayer for our beloved dead. Many parishes provide a place where people can inscribe the names of those they remember for the community's prayer. If this is done, the objects by which it is done should be carefully chosen for their beauty. An elegant blank book can be procured at not much cost. Such a book is both more permanent and more beautiful than the three-ring binders one sometimes sees, and lends importance to its ritual use. It also preserves the names from year to year, and allows people to see that their loved ones remain in the community's care. A sturdy lectern or table with some carefully-chosen fabric and a candle or some plants will call attention to this book without dominating the space. It also provides a space for people to spend time with the book, praying for those commended to them.

The final Sunday of the liturgical year is the Solemnity of Our Lord Jesus Christ, King of the Universe. This relatively recent addition to the liturgical year acts as a culmination of the growing eschatological emphasis throughout the fall. Its color is white. After this feast, we once again begin Advent, with its dual preparation for Christ's historical and eschatological Advent, and the cycle begins again.

The Liturgical Music

IN many parish settings, choirs take the summer off, music directors take vacation time, and other staff members and volunteers attend various conferences and workshops. Various guests will be attending liturgies and regular parishoners will be in and out. You will want to take these summer months to revisit old favorites for songs, responses, and Mass settings.

Wedding season runs from summer to fall. The Gloria should be sung at weddings. You may want to think of ways to make it very accessible for those attending parish weddings.

During the weeks of fall, there are many emotional shifts taking place in the liturgy as we move from the harvest and earth motifs, and Jesus's active ministry and teaching, into the more eschatological weeks of the end times. How will the music reflect these shifts? Will you begin learning another Mass setting this fall, or returning to one that your congregation knows already?

If you are introducing new settings and hymns, you'll need to get parts out to cantors and accompanists much earlier in the summer. Most of the publishers provide great mp3s that can be used for rehearsal. If you make your own rehearsal clips, make sure that you have the correct copyrights in place. With today's technology, it is easy to put clips in a shared file online, so that people may import to an electronic device or make a CD if they need to. It is a lot simpler than making dozens of copies like days past.

Visit www.LTP.org/resources for a free PDF of suggested music for this liturgical time.

Liturgical Ministers

COMMUNICATE early with ministers who may be away for all or part of the summer and make sure enough ministers are scheduled for each liturgy. Give those ministers who need a break time off and provide training for new ministers. If you hold a procession on the Solemnity of the Most Holy Body and Blood of Christ (*Corpus Christi*) make sure you create a map for the route the procession will take and ensure someone can monitor traffic along the way (depending on your route a parade permit may be required from your city or local municipality). During the summer hold an ice cream, lemonade, or iced tea social for ministers, volunteers, and parishioners. Consider holding a ministry fair in the fall and announce the event for several weeks in advance. Send letters, provide notices and announcements in the bulletin and on the parish website and at announcement time during

Mass. Remember, however, that the best way to find new ministers is with a personal invitation.

Have parishioners who are currently serving in various ministries share their stories and if you have a sign-up for new ministers be sure to follow up with them in a timely manner. Provide resources for various ministers along with an outline for each ministry including responsibilities and the time commitment required. Recognize peoples' gifts, talents, and time commitment and thank them for their service.

Be prepared with an appropriate blessing or an installation to welcome a new pastor or staff to your parish. Consider scheduling a weekly holy hour on a given night throughout the summer months for parish ministers and follow up with a short time for faith sharing while serving some refreshing beverages or summer produce. Plan to meet with the catechists and schoolteachers in the parish, sometime during the summer months, to explore ways in which liturgy, catechesis, and religious education intersect. Recognize successes and celebrate!

Devotions and Sacramentals

CATHOLICS should call to mind the role of the Trinity in the life of the Church. The *Directory of Popular Piety and the Liturgy* includes an inspiring section on the role of the Holy Trinity (157–160). The Solemnity of the Most Holy Body and Blood of Christ (*Corpus Christi*) may include time for devotions such as Eucharistic adoration and Eucharistic processions (see DPPL, 157–165). *Catholic Household Blessing & Prayers* contains prayers to be used for a holy hour of prayer for life, for vocations, or for peace.

Popular devotions to the Sacred Heart of Jesus include the pious practice of first Fridays of the month, which is rooted in the "great promises" given to St. Margaret Mary Alacoque (1647–1690) that assures those who receive Holy Communion on the first Friday of nine consecutive months will not die without the grace of final repentance, enabling the soul to enter into heaven, thus defeating the negativity of the Jansenists.

Catholic Household Blessings & Prayers contains various prayers for use in the domestic Church and the prayer for victims of abuse, in

Part VI, "Prayers for the Church and the Word," is an especially poignant prayer for our age.

On August 15, the Solemnity of the Assumption of the Blessed Virgin Mary, the Church honors the custom of blessing herbs, plants, seeds, and trees. *Catholic Household Blessings & Prayers* encourages the blessing of the fruits of the harvest on this day.

The Church's teaching about "the existence of the spiritual, non-corporeal beings that Sacred Scripture usually calls 'angels' is a truth of faith. The witness of Scripture is as clear as the unanimity of Tradition" (DPPL, 213).

On October 4, the Memorial of St. Francis of Assisi, households are encouraged to gather together for the blessing of pets.

October 7 is the optional Memorial of Our Lady of the Rosary and it would be a good day to revisit Pope John Paul II's encyclical *Rosarium Virginis Mariae* and mine its treasures. In the encyclical the Holy Father speaks of the use of icons (29), the use of commentary (30), silent prayer (31), and the importance of a Trinitarian structure in all prayer (34).

The noble practice of praying for our beloved dead and knowing that they stand with the great cloud of witnesses, saints named and un-named, around the throne of God gives us great comfort. Devotional customs and practices surrounding *Dia de los Muertos*, the Day of the Dead celebrated on November 2, is a domestic Church practice. Many customs and traditions surrounding the Commemoration of the Faithful Departed are observed in various countries including the flying of kites, *barriletes gigantes*. Kites are flown above graveyards followed by having a traditional dish called *fiambre* (Guatemala). *Finados* (Day of the Dead/*Todos los Santos*) is the day for visiting churches and cemeteries (Brazil); *Araw ng mga*, which is also called *Undos* or *Todos los Santos*, is a national holiday where people clean and decorate graves and they camp out at the cemetery and have a festive celebration with food, drink, singing, and dancing (Philippines); Turamara's headstones are cleaned and repainted, adorned with candles and then the people gather to sing (French Polynesia); the moralistic play, "Don Juan Tenorio" by José Zorilla is where, through God's mercy, the rake Don Juan is dragged out of hell into heaven (Spain); the *Ognissanti* is the day when children are rewarded with presents, sweets, and small toys by the "good souls" if they are well behaved (popular in southern Italy).

Finally in France on the first of November, *La Toussanint et le Jur des Morts,* people visit cemeteries and decorate them with flowers and candles, the graves are blessed with holy water, and food is left at the grave sites. The day is meant to counteract the American importance of Halloween. A new tradition emerged in 2004 when the Archdiocese of Paris, during the Second International Conference on the New Evangelization, with thousands of youth gathered, celebrated what has become to be known as "Holy Wins." It is customary to wear white on this day recalling the passages from the Book of Revelation 7:2–4, 9–14. It is a venerable tradition to visit cemeteries on Memorial Day and on the Commemoration of All the Faithful Departed.

The Parish and the Home

SINCE summer is often a time of vacations or being outside it is a good time to express gratitude for the gifts of the natural world and of God's creation. Offering prayers of gratitude and praise on slips of paper and collecting them at home in a glass jar every time we remember to express ourselves to God is a strong visible reminder of all we have been given. Perhaps over the summer the parish can collect these prayers from community members who bring them forward and offer them in a larger glass jar so they are visible. Since our prayers of praise often lead us to action it could be a good time to examine our parish and home recycling and conservation efforts. Can we start a "Reduce / Reuse / Recycle" effort, walk instead of drive, take a bus, conserve electrical energy, or compost organic materials? The gift of creation from God to humanity will be a sustaining gift to all future generations if we do our part to preserve and protect it. If we already do these things we can explore a deeper issue that threatens the earth such as strip mining, water shortages, or global warming. Teens are especially open to these issues not only because they will inherit this world soon but also they are more attuned to the world of information through the Internet. Let them lead us.

Jesus offers an assortment of parables during the summer weeks about what the Kingdom of God is like. It is like the seeds that have been sown in good and bad places. Where does it pro-

duce what God wants? Where are the weeds? The Kingdom of Heaven is like a mustard seed, yeast in dough, buried treasure, or a net thrown into the sea seeking fish. All these parables invite further reflection and contemplation. These are wonderful teaching tools for children (and even adults). It would be easy to teach about the power of God's Word using the effect of yeast. We can almost see it grow before our very eyes. After baking bread and perhaps even sharing it we can ask children how this might work in life. Where does one small action sometimes yield great results? Teenagers and adults alike might enjoy reading and discussing the book, *The Power of Half: One Family's Decision to Stop Taking and Start Giving Back*, by Kevin Salwen and his 14-year-old daughter Hannah written in 2010. It highlights a story of how reflecting about one's life even as a teenager can have a far-reaching effect.

Summer ends and we begin many routine activities of fall, going back to school; putting the garden to rest; preparing for the coming cold months. Jesus invites disciples to consider the rejection they will face, the cross they will bear. In early September we will celebrate the Feast of the Exaltation of the Holy Cross. The cross is a strong remembrance of Jesus's power over death for us.

More and more during the Gospel accounts of fall, Jesus faces resistance and anger from some of the religious authorities. He continues to teach but they must have ears to hear; they are not always ready to listen. Perhaps that is also our internal reflection question this fall: Are we ready to really hear what Jesus is saying to us knowing it may demand a change of heart, of attitude, or even lifestyle? Many families are affected by the back to school rhythm. These kinds of fall deadlines are an opportunity for each of us to consider what kinds of goals we want to set for ourselves for the remainder of the year. Rather than wait for the ever-present New Year's resolutions we can jumpstart our resolve with several months reflecting on our discipleship.

Forgiveness is a major theme as Jesus tells disciples they must forgive seven times seventy-seven times. Jesus's answer to Peter and the disciples about forgiveness points to the demands of this kind of forgiveness because he knows this is how God forgives us. If we are to be of God then we are to do the same. It might be a good time for us to take a concrete step to mend a broken relationship or reach out to someone with whom we have a difficulty.

The Solemnity of All Saints and the Commemoration of All the Faithful Departed offer an opportunity for members of parish communities to name the holy people who influenced their lives. They might be actual saints but they may also be ordinary people who have shaped us, given witness to the life of a disciple or who have made a positive change in the world around them. We can display their pictures and write their names in our homes or in our parish facilities. We can tell these ordinary stories to the children around us while still encouraging them to read stories of the saints such as their personal namesake or the parish namesake. The parish could host an evening celebration with paper bag lanterns or candles positioned around the parish grounds. Families could bring their lights from home and to write their "saints" on lanterns. Parishioners could walk the journey with the saints outdoors (indoors for bad weather) in silence or singing a litany of the saints along the lighted path. Our prayers make the many Catholic saints, along with those people who have been a witness for us, very present in our midst. Part of our prayer might be to ask for the courage to be a saint for others. Families and parishioners could talk afterward about how they could concretely act to make this happen in their own lives.

If the parish does not have a pastoral care or Befriender ministry, the month of November is a good time to examine that possibility for the future (www.befrienderministry.org). This ministry, which can be overseen by parish staff or team of volunteers, offers a listening presence and compassionate assistance to those who are in need such as having a family member who is ill or has died, struggling with a difficult transition, or experiencing a loss such as a job. This kind of pastoral care is an integral part of the ongoing ministry of community members to one another. Parishes that have developed a pastoral care response have taken active steps to offer a sign of God's loving presence in a concrete way.

As we make our way to the Last Sunday in Ordinary Time and our final feast of Christ the King our readings remind us of the seriousness of the undertaking to be a follower of Christ. It is a time to examine how well we did with our mission this past year, personally and communally. This is a good time for parish leaders, parish council members, and committee members to assess the parish's efforts regarding their mission, vision, or

parish charism. Perhaps the parish can offer a reflective tool using the Sermon on the Mount (Matthew 5:1–12), which we hear again on All Saints along with the passage from Christ the King (Matthew 25:31–46): "When did we see you hungry and feed you, or thirsty and give you a drink . . . ?" These are hard questions for disciples but we have practiced all year. What can we do to be ready to begin anew with another Gospel account? How will Mark's Gospel account (Year B beginning on the First Sunday of Advent) help us further our parish mission? We end one year and get ready for another.

Mass Texts

Summer

◆ Dismissal Text for Children's Liturgy of the Word:

> Even when school is not in session,
> we continue to learn from parents, friends,
>   the books we read, and even television.
> It's important that we never stop learning,
> especially about God and his great love for us.
> We don't take a break from learning about God
> because he is more important than anything else
>   in our lives.
> God speaks to us through the sun and the moon
>   and the stars
>   and through all his creatures.
> And now he will speak to you through his Word
>   and through your teacher.

◆ Dismissal Text for RCIA

> As summer's temperatures fluctuate,
>   sometimes wildly,
>   you are committing to a relationship with Christ
> that won't change with the seasons or grow tepid
>   with time.
> We pray with you that the springtime
>   of your inquiry
> will flourish under the glow of the summer sun
> and yield a lifetime harvest of joyful discipleship.
> May your sharing today deepen your commitment
> and hasten the day when you join us at the table
>   of the Eucharist
> as fully initiated members of our faith community.

◆ SEASONAL TEXTS FOR PRAYER OF THE FAITHFUL

Invitation to Prayer:

The Lord is never far and his love never wanes
just as no season fails to know our needs and
      to witness our affliction.
Let us bring all our petitions to the Lord for
      he is constant in his love
and persistent in his care.

Intercessions:

Without worthy leaders we become "sheep without a shepherd" and easily lose our way. May those charged with the care of souls—lay ministers, deacons, priests, and bishops—recognize the sacredness of their call and serve their people though holy lives of selfless service, we pray: May your love shine down upon us, Lord.

When political leaders seek their own advancement rather than the good of all peace is compromised and the needs of the most vulnerable are ignored. May those entrusted with civil power and authority exercise it wisely and in a spirit of harmony, we pray: May your love shine down upon us, Lord.

When the needs of the most vulnerable are neglected the fabric of a society begins to unravel and the mandate of the Gospel is forgotten. May all among us who suffer and who mourn, who long for relief from the oppression of disease, emotional distress, loneliness, poverty, and every other kind of affliction find comfort and release, especially though the ministry of the Christian community, we pray: May your love shine down upon us, Lord.

If the community we call (insert name of parish) fails to make those who earnestly seek the Lord feel welcome and at home, we are less than what we are called to be. May all we do honor the dignity of the other and foster their growth and their embrace of the faith, we pray: May your love shine down upon us, Lord.

Concluding Prayer:

You made us for yourself,
O Lord, and saved us from ourselves so that
      we might live with you forever.
Hear our prayers, dear God,
so our journey here on earth will help us anticipate
      the glory
we will share when we dwell with you in heaven.
We ask this through Christ our Lord.
Amen.

◆ DISMISSAL TEXTS FOR EXTRAORDINARY MINISTERS OF HOLY COMMUNION

The seasonal joys of summer are often kept
      from those
who suffer from physical or emotional affliction.
What's worse is that those who are in greatest need
are kept from the table that could nourish both
      the body and the soul.
Go to them now and bring the food that
      we have shared
in the forms of Word and Sacrament
and pray with them that their time of pain
      might come to a speedy end.

Fall

◆ DISMISSAL TEXT FOR CHILDREN'S LITURGY OF THE WORD

God uses the seasons to teach us many things and,
      in fall, God tells us about letting go.
As the trees lose their leaves and the world prepares
      for winter's sleep,
we too can focus on those things in us that need
      to change
and the things that need to go away.
In the Holy Scriptures, God speaks to us directly
      telling us who we are
and how we can be more like Jesus.
Go listen now for the kind of change God might
      be asking of you.

◆ DISMISSAL TEXT FOR THE CATECHUMENS

Your journey in the Catechumenate
mirrors the transformation to which the earth
      annually submits.
The new life of spring comes only after autumn's
      yielding and winter's death.
Your own new or recommitted life in Christ
will come after your death in the waters of Baptism.
So learn the lesson of the tress
and accept the pruning and the loss that are
      inevitable in our walk with Christ;
Go to break open his Word and to rejoice that
      new life awaits and fresh growth will come
when we celebrate with Christ the glory
      of his Resurrection.

◆ SEASONAL TEXTS FOR THE PRAYER
OF THE FAITHFUL

Invitation to Prayer:

Nature teaches us to let go, but we cannot lose our need for you, O Lord. And so we come with humble hearts but confident in your love and invoke your mercy, which is constant and unfailing.

Intercessions:

For the Church throughout the world, that it might witness to the truth of the Gospel and call all people to humble submission to your will; and for the leaders of the Church that they might know you well in mind and heart and teach faithfully in word and deed the Truth that is Jesus Christ, let us pray to the Lord: In your mercy, Lord, hear our humble prayer.

For all in public office who bear the responsibility of safeguarding peace and establishing justice, that they might walk on the Way that is Jesus and yield their wills to the will of God, let us pray to the Lord: In your mercy, Lord, hear our humble prayer.

For the needs of the poor throughout the world, for the sick, and those who suffer from oppression and neglect, for members of our families who know the pain of mental illness and the blight of loneliness, that the Life that is Christ will bring them hope, healing, and redemption, let us pray to the Lord: In your mercy, Lord, hear our humble prayer.

For our local community—our pastor, our staff members, and our volunteers, for the families of our parish, the children in our school and religious education program, and for the neighbors who would be with us but for the lack of an invitation, that God may strengthen us, embolden us, and fill us with selfless love so we can go forth as heralds of the Way, the Truth, and the Life that is Jesus the Christ, let us pray to the Lord: In your mercy, Lord, hear our humble prayer.

Concluding Prayer:

Without you, we are powerless, O Lord.
But with you nothing is impossible.
Hear the prayers we offer you today and
    in your mercy grant them,
We ask this through Christ our Lord,
who is the reliable way, the certain truth, and
    the source of life forever and ever. Amen.

June
Month of the Sacred Heart

Except for the days of the First and Thirty-fourth Weeks in Ordinary Time, The Roman Missal *does not provide prayer texts for the weekdays in Ordinary Time. Instead, priest celebrants and those who prepare the liturgy may select from among the prayers provided for the Sundays in Ordinary Time. Your diocesan* Ordo *will provide suggestions. On days celebrated as optional memorials, prayers may be from the Sundays of Ordinary Time, the Proper of Saints, or the Commons. On all Saturdays during Ordinary Time that do not have an obligatory memorial, a memorial to the Blessed Virgin Mary may be celebrated. The prayers may be selected from the Common of the Blessed Virgin Mary. Commentary below is only provided for Sundays, solemnities, feasts, and obligatory memorials.*

MON 9 (#359) green
Weekday (Tenth Week in Ordinary Time)

Optional Memorial of St. Ephrem, Deacon and Doctor of the Church

The Lectionary for Mass

◆ FIRST READING: We hear the ministry of Elijah and the prophets this week. His prophetic word against Ahab is perhaps best understood in light of the verses immediately preceding today's reading, which recount his evil deeds, most prominent of which was his worship of the foreign god Baal at the instigation of his wife Jezebel. Despite the drought that punished the land, God provided for the needs of his prophet.

◆ RESPONSORIAL PSALM 121: God was indeed a help for Elijah and so can be for each one of us. God is ever watchful over us, guarding and

protecting us, until we arrive at life in all its fullness.

◆ GOSPEL: "Blessed are . . ." To be blessed as understood by the Beatitudes is to experience the deep happiness that comes from God alone. The categories singled out as blessed call us to examine our own manner of life. Note that seven of the Beatitudes speak of future reward; two, of present reward. Nine Beatitudes? Yes, our Gospel includes a ninth.

Today's Saint

After serving as head of a cathedral school in Syria, St. Ephrem (306–373), a Doctor of the Church, fled to a cave near Edessa to take up the life of a monk. While devoting himself to an austere life marked by solitude and fasting, he earnestly wrote hundreds of hymns and commentaries on Sacred Scripture. His hymns and discourses on Scripture provided deep insight into the Paschal Mystery of Christ and opposed gnostic tendencies among various sects. At times, he would leave his cave to preach in Edessa. Crowds were attracted to his eloquent preaching; therefore, he became known as "the harp of the holy spirit." Later in life he was ordained a deacon and helped the people of Edessa weather a terrible famine.

TUE 10 (#360) green
Weekday

The Lectionary for Mass

◆ FIRST READING: Today's reading beautifully recounts God's providential care for his prophet, providing food and water for him through the hands of a widow. The widow, alone, without the means for life and with no one to provide for her, is God's chosen instrument to care for his prophet. As she obediently carries out her simple mission, God, in turn, through his prophet, provides for her and for her son.

◆ RESPONSORIAL PSALM 4 confidently expresses trust in God in the midst of affliction. The happiness that comes from God is greater than that found in material provisions (see the last line of the last stanza).

◆ GOSPEL: Jesus compares the presence and ministry of his disciples to salt (which enhances the taste of food) and to light (which is a necessity if we are to see our way in the dark). If salt or light lose their effectiveness, they are worthless. This also applies to the disciples—and we are among them.

WED 11 (#580; Gospel #361) red
Memorial of St. Barnabas, Apostle

The Lectionary for Mass

◆ FIRST READING: Barnabas was a Levite from Cyprus who in the very first days of the Church sold his farm and gave the money to the Apostles. He was involved in the early Christian community from then on, and it is he who first introduces the newly converted Saul to the other Apostles. The context of today's reading is the dispersion of some members of the Jerusalem community after the death of Stephen, the first martyr. Some went to Antioch, where a great number of people received the Good News of the Gospel and believed. As a result, Barnabas is sent there to teach. It is Barnabas who enlists Saul's help and they remained in Antioch for a year. There, the Church heard the voice of the Spirit commissioning Barnabas and Saul for further missionary journeys. With prayer, fasting, and the laying on of hands, they sent them on their way.

◆ RESPONSORIAL PSALM 98: Already in the Old Testament, there is the testimony that all nations—and not just the Jewish people—will receive the revelation of the Lord's saving power. Today's psalm is a case in point. And certainly, the missionary journeys of Barnabas,

Saul, and their companions are further realizations of this word. The Apostles did indeed journey to the ends of the earth—at least as it was known in their day—to proclaim the salvation accomplished by Jesus of Nazareth. For those who received their message, praise and thanksgiving is the only fitting response.

◆ GOSPEL: A key issue in Matthew's account has to do with Jesus's attitude toward the law; in particular, if he ignores it or abolishes it. Subsequent verses in chapter 5 of the Gospel make it perfectly clear: far from abolishing the law, Jesus demands even more than the letter of the law. It is the observance of this "more" that makes one truly a disciple, truly great in the Kingdom of Heaven.

The Roman Missal

All the orations are proper for today, and can be found in the Proper of Saints at June 11. The Collect recognizes the saint for his preaching of the Gospel to the nations, calling him "a man filled with faith and the Holy Spirit." The prayer goes on to ask that the Gospel may continue to "be faithfully proclaimed by word and by deed" even down to our own day. The Prayer over the Offerings asks that the offerings we make will transform us to do that work of spreading the Gospel in the same way St. Barnabas did, "set us on fire" with the same "flame of your love, / by which Saint Barnabas brought the light of the Gospel to the nations." Either Preface I or Preface II of the Apostles is the Preface to be used today. The Prayer after Communion points to the kingdom that is revealed and anticipated in the celebration of the Eucharist, a kingdom we hope to arrive at fully one day, as it asks that "what we celebrate in sacramental signs . . . we may one day behold unveiled."

Today's Saint

Even though St. Barnabas (first century) was not one of the original Twelve Apostles, he was given the title of "apostle" by St. Luke and the early Church fathers, due to his apostolic endeavors on behalf of Christianity. His original name was Joseph, but the Apostles gave him the surname Barnabas, meaning "son of encouragement." Together with St. Paul, he extended the missionary efforts of the Church beyond Jerusalem to Antioch, and after much success moved onto other places throughout Asia Minor. After parting ways with St. Paul over issues regarding circumcision and the Mosaic law, St. Barnabas embarked on further missionary journeys with John and Mark (see Acts of the Apostles 15:36–40). Tradition indicates that St. Barnabas was stoned to death, and his remains were taken to Constantinople where a church stands in his honor.

T H U **12** (#362) green
Weekday

The Lectionary for Mass

◆ FIRST READING: Today's reading actually connects with the first verse of 1 Kings 18, where it is revealed that the Lord's purpose in arranging the meeting between Elijah and Ahab was precisely so that he could send rain upon the earth. Elijah's entreaty to the Lord bears witness to the necessity of perseverance in prayer.

◆ RESPONSORIAL PSALM 65 is a psalm of praise, acclaiming God's goodness in blessing the earth with abundant rains.

◆ GOSPEL: We hear the first examples of Jesus's teaching on the law, where he asks for something more than the letter of the law. Today's Gospel focuses on anger toward another, on speaking offensively to another, on holding grudges. Jesus

prohibits them all and calls for rather strong evidence of amendment: "leave your gift . . . at the altar . . . go first and be reconciled . . . then come and offer your gift" (Matthew 5:24).

F R I **13** (#363) white
Memorial of St. Anthony of Padua, Priest and Doctor of the Church

The Lectionary for Mass

◆ FIRST READING: Elijah is instructed to go to Mt. Horeb (Sinai) where he will experience the presence of God. Although one might expect God to manifest himself with power and might, such as in an earthquake, wind or fire, this was not Elijah's experience. Rather, God manifested his presence to Elijah in "a tiny whispering sound." Are we so attentive? Noteworthy also is the fact that Elijah was fleeing for his life when he went to Mt. Horeb (1 Kings 19:1–10). Yet despite his discouragement, he receives yet another mission from the Lord.

◆ RESPONSORIAL PSALM 27: This beautiful song of confidence is an apt response to the plight of Elijah, whose heart truly longed to see the face of God. Elijah had only God on whom to rely when his life was at stake. And indeed, Elijah "waited" for the Lord on Mt. Horeb. He was not disappointed.

◆ GOSPEL: Jesus asks more of his disciples than the mere letter of the Law. Today's Gospel is concerned with the laws pertaining to adultery and divorce. Jesus prohibits "adultery" in one's heart. Divorce is prohibited except when the Marriage violated the kinship prohibitions in Jewish law (see Leviticus 18:6–18).

The Roman Missal

The proper Collect for the day, found at June 13 in the Proper of Saints section of the Missal, recognizes St. Anthony of Padua "as an outstanding preacher / and an intercessor in their need." The prayer goes on to ask God that, with the saint's assistance, "we may know your help in every trial." (Thus, we can turn to St. Anthony not only when we have lost some item, but when we have lost strength and resolve in the face of struggle and difficulty.) The Prayer over the Offerings and the Prayer after Communion come from either the Common of Pastors: For One Pastor, or from the Common of Doctors of the Church, or from the Common of Holy Men and Women: For Religious. The same variety exists for the choice of the Preface today: Preface I or II of Saints; or the Preface of Holy Pastors; or the Preface of Holy Virgins and Religious.

Today's Saint

St. Anthony of Padua (1195–1231), a member of a noble Portuguese family, joined the Canons Regular of St. Augustine (Augustinians) at a young age, but later joined the Franciscans to engage in missionary work. Although his missionary dreams were halted due to illness, he received public acclaim for his preaching style, which led to the conversion of many and the end of heresy, earning him the title "the Hammer of the Heretics." His writing is extensive, especially in the area of sermons. He was named a Doctor of the Church.

SAT 14 (#364) green Weekday

Optional Memorial of the Blessed Virgin Mary / white

The Lectionary for Mass

◆ First Reading: With symbolic gestures, Elijah designates Elisha as his prophetic successor and in response, Elisha totally renounces his former way of life. Leaving his people, he follows Elijah.

◆ Responsorial Psalm 16: How fittingly this psalm of confidence can be a response to our reading about Elisha whose portion is no longer among his own people or his own possessions but with the Lord.

◆ Gospel: Another example of Jesus asking for more than the law requires . . . not only are we forbidden to swear a false oath, we must not swear at all. Today's Gospel calls us to honesty, integrity, respect in our speech, and mindfulness that these are an area where the Evil One can penetrate.

15 (#164) white Solemnity of the Most Holy Trinity

About this Solemnity

Today's solemnity commemorates the central dogma of Christianity: the Trinity. One of the greatest gifts of the Christian faith is the dogma of the triune God: God is three (tri) in one (une). The Christian God—Father, Son, and Holy Spirit—is relational. How amazing and wonderfully mysterious at the same time!

The Lectionary for Mass

◆ First Reading: Moses experiences the presence of God for a second time on Mt. Sinai. Most important in today's passage is the self-revelation of God in verse 6: "The Lord, a merciful and gracious God, / slow to anger and rich in kindness and fidelity." It is a text that recurs several times in the Old Testament. This is how the Israelites remembered and loved God. It is how God promised to be for them in covenant fidelity.

◆ Canticle: Our response is a hymn of praise from the prophet Daniel, not the Book of Psalms. It is a long hymn, sung by Azariah and his companions from the midst of the fiery furnace where they had been thrown in punishment but stood unharmed (see Daniel 3:1–24). Azariah praises God enthroned in glory in the heavenly Temple but who nevertheless looks into the depths, even into the fiery furnace where Azariah and his companions have been cast.

◆ Second Reading: Relationships within the community of believers are to be characterized by joy, loving concern for others, uprightness, unity, and peace. For such are the characteristics of God, and so must we be, in God's image.

◆ Gospel: We hear Jesus's revelation of God's love for the world, so great that he sent his Son that all might have eternal life through their faith in him. Notice that the word "believe" occurs four times in three verses. Our passage is not about God's revelation, but about human faith. Jesus relates to God as Father, source of life. So is our relationship, our life, through faith.

The Roman Missal

The texts for this solemnity are found after the texts for the Thirty-Fourth Week in Ordinary Time, toward the end of the "Ordinary Time" section of the Missal, and several pages before the "Order of Mass" section begins.

The Gloria is sung or said today.

The Collect expresses for us the meaning of this solemnity not in terms of some dry theological doctrine but rather in terms of the active, dynamic power of the triune

God: the Father sends into the world the Word of truth and the Spirit of sanctification and, in so doing, reveals to the human race his own "wondrous mystery." The prayer affirms that through the Trinity we know the very life of God himself.

The Prayer over the Offerings makes the important liturgical point that as we make the offering of our lives at this liturgy—"this oblation of our service"—its ultimate purpose is that by it we might be made "an eternal offering to you." The prayer expresses how in the liturgy we are swept up into the life of the Trinity so that our entire life might be lived with the same self-emptying, self-giving love as exists between the divine Persons.

The Preface, "The Mystery of the Most Holy Trinity," is proper for today and its text is given along with the other texts for the Mass; there is both a text with and without musical notation. The text reiterates the theological meaning of God being "one God, one Lord: / not in the unity of a single person, / but in a Trinity of one substance, equal in majesty."

The Prayer after Communion also gives voice to the basic statement about the Trinity nonetheless being "undivided Unity."

Since there should be a certain emphasis given to how the life of the Christian should be a reflection of and a participation in the life of the Trinity, perhaps the formula "Go in peace, glorifying the Lord by your life" would be an appropriate choice for the dismissal today.

Pastoral Reflection

The impossibility of fully understanding God is shared today: God as Parent, God as Child, God as Spirit. Knowing God, in all his ways, is vital to living the message that was given. Which aspect of God's nature allows you to speak God's name so others believe? While all natures are vital, our prayer and spirituality is influenced deeply by the Divine nature that makes most sense to us. Uncover your answer and then be bold enough to seek out conversations with faith-filled friends and ask them their thoughts too; in doing so you share the Gospel.

M O N 16   (#365)   green
Weekday (Eleventh Week in Ordinary Time)

The Lectionary for Mass

◆ FIRST READING: The incident in today's First Reading gives apt illustration of the destructive nature of greedy desires, with its effects ranging from bad moods to murder. The land of ancestral heritage was a family's treasure (much as the land of Israel was the treasure of that people). But Ahab could not respect this or honor Nabaoth's response. Jezebel's sarcastic mocking of her husband says much about the nature of their relationship, and her deceitful scheming for the purpose of gaining what she wants at any cost says much about her character. Do we find today's text a mirror for our own society? Our own lives?

◆ RESPONSORIAL PSALM 5: The condemned Nabaoth could well have prayed the words of today's Responsorial antiphon. An innocent man was put to death because of another's greed for possessions. The stanzas of today's psalm give apt commentary on Ahab and Jezebel: wicked, evil, arrogant, bloodthirsty, and deceitful. These the Lord abhors.

◆ GOSPEL: Like deserves like, deemed the law in terms of retaliation for evil, but Jesus radically overturns this: Do not give like for like; rather, absorb the evil and respond in love. Give more than what is asked of you.

T U E 17   (#366)   green
Weekday

The Lectionary for Mass

◆ FIRST READING: Ahab is confronted for his evil deed by Elijah the prophet and his punishment foretold. In addition to the sin recounted in yesterday's reading, today's text makes mention of Ahab's worship of idols, prompted no doubt by his wife Jezebel (see 1 Kings 16:31–32). Nevertheless, at the word of Elijah, prophet of the God of Israel, Ahab "humbled himself" (1 Kings 21:29) by penitential deeds and, accordingly, receives mercy from the Lord.

◆ RESPONSORIAL PSALM 51, a penitential psalm, is a fitting response to the account of Ahab's sin and repentance.

◆ GOSPEL: How easy it is to love those who love us, to show kindness to those who are kind to us. How hard it is to do the opposite. But it is only in so doing, in loving and showing kindness to those who are mean or at least not nice to us, that we show that we are like our heavenly Father who acts in just this manner. The Greek word for perfection, in the last line of today's text, means not so much flawlessness as maturity and wholeness.

W E D 18   (#367)   green
Weekday

The Lectionary for Mass

◆ FIRST READING: The mysterious translation of Elijah going up to heaven, recounted in today's reading, became the basis of the tradition that Elijah had not died and would one day return to earth before the coming of the day of the Lord. The Christian arrangement of the Old Testament ends on this note (see Malachi 3:23–24). We find this same belief mentioned in the

Gospel in relation to John the Baptist and even with reference to Jesus (see Mark 8:28). In today's text, Elisha, successor to Elijah, is empowered with his spirit and his mantle. Notice how the sign of the parting of the waters links not only Elijah and Elisha, but also Moses—all prophets who spoke in the name of the Lord.

◆ RESPONSORIAL PSALM 31: This Psalm, acclaiming God's goodness and deliverance of those who hope in him, fits well with the translation of Elijah, who certainly endured the plottings of others (second stanza) as the narratives of 2 Kings demonstrate. The note of comfort also speaks to Elisha's plight at the parting of his master.

◆ GOSPEL: This proclamation is heard also on Ash Wednesday. While we may associate fasting, almsgiving, and prayer with Lent, they are works that should characterize Christian life at all times. The importance of not making a public display when doing them is stressed repeatedly. We should seek reward from the heavenly Father, not from others.

THU 19 (#368) green
Weekday

Optional Memorial of St. Romuald, Abbot / white

The Lectionary for Mass

◆ FIRST READING: The last chapters of the Book of Sirach, a work reckoned among the Wisdom writings of Israel, extol the praises of Israel's ancestors. Today's text is basically a summary of the Elijah and Elisha narratives in the second book of Kings.

◆ RESPONSORIAL PSALM 97: In today's First Reading, Sirach reckons both Elijah and Elisha as among Israel's just, and today's psalm is a hymn calling all the just to praise the Lord. Another link with today's First Reading is the reference to fire

and mountain, both significant with the reference to Elijah (the fiery chariot and the mountain where he experienced the Lord's presence in the still voice). Both prophets pronounced God's judgment on those to whom they were sent.

◆ GOSPEL: In teaching his disciples about prayer, Jesus teaches them that their heavenly Father so cares for them, that he knows their needs even before they ask—a profound reality. If we look closely at the Lord's Prayer, we see not only the words we are to use in prayer, but the spirit with which we are to approach God: as a trusting child, mindful of God's holiness and reverent before him, aware of our failures and seeking forgiveness, praying for his protection. Forgiveness is given repeated emphasis, especially the forgiveness we are to show to others, for in our prayer we ask God to forgive us just as we forgive others. Today's Gospel calls us to examine how we are doing at forgiving others.

Today's Saint

Aristocratic-born Romuald led a wild life as a young person in tenth-century Italy. This changed at age 20 when he saw his father murder another man. Filled with horror, Romuald fled to a Benedictine monastery to do penance for his father's actions. Even monks found him uncomfortably holy, so he left and wandered throughout Italy, establishing his own monasteries and hermitages along the way. He eventually formed the Order of Camaldoli, a religious group of men who combined the cenobitic tradition of communal living with the eremitical (hermit) life of the Eastern monks. He lived a long life, dying of natural causes in 1027.

FRI 20 (#369) green
Weekday

The Lectionary for Mass

◆ FIRST READING: The narratives concerning the succession of the kings of Judah and Israel depict a tumultuous history, marked by violence and political intrigue, perhaps not unlike, at times, the succession of rulers and governments in our own day. Today's reading focuses on the care taken to protect the young Joash, of the Judean royal family, from the threat on his life made by the wicked queen Athaliah, daughter of Ahab. Athaliah had led many astray by her worship of the foreign god Baal. Joash's succession to the throne inaugurates a period of religious reform through the efforts of the priest Jehoiada.

◆ RESPONSORIAL PSALM 132 acclaims the prominence of Jerusalem (also known as Sion/Zion) as the city where God dwells (because of the temple). The stanzas of today's psalm, however, focus on God's covenant with King David promising that his heir will sit on the throne forever (see 2 Samuel 7). Young King Joash in today's First Reading was a descendant of David.

◆ GOSPEL: "Where is your treasure?" asks Jesus in today's Gospel. "On what is your heart set?" (author's paraphrasing). If we answer honestly, we will discover what we value the most, what we hold most important to us. Does our honest reflection call for any changes?

SAT 21 (#370) white
Memorial of
St. Aloysius Gonzaga,
Religious

The Lectionary for Mass

◆ FIRST READING: After the death of the priest-reformer Jehoiada, King Joash listened to the counsel of the wicked princes of Judah, an act that led to apostasy. Despite the plea of the prophets, the people would not listen. Their evil extended even to the killing of Zechariah, son of Jehoiada, who had called the people to repentance. In punishment for their sins, God allowed the people to be ravaged by the Aramean army.

◆ RESPONSORIAL PSALM 89 celebrates God's fidelity in his promise to David that his dynasty would endure forever. This does not preclude punishment for the people's infidelities (stanzas 3 and 4).

◆ GOSPEL: Serving mammon leads to great anxiety and worry; serving God implies deep trust. The God who so lovingly provides for the seemingly insignificant sparrow will do the same for those who are children of his heavenly Father.

The Roman Missal

The Mass prayers, all of which are proper for the day, can be found at June 21 in the Proper of Saints section of the Missal. The Collect describes St. Aloysius's life as one of penitence joined "to a wonderful innocence of life," applying that to our own journey by asking "that, though we have failed to follow him in innocence, / we may imitate him in penitence." The Prayer over the Offerings again uses the imagery of innocence associated with this saint by asking that "we may take our place at the heavenly banquet, / clothed always in our wedding garment." The banquet imagery is appropriate as we participate in the Liturgy of the Eucharist. The Prayer after Communion announces that we have been fed "with the food of Angels," and goes on to ask that we serve the Lord "in purity of life" and that "we persevere in constant thanksgiving." Although either one of the two Prefaces of Saints could be used today, perhaps the Preface of Holy Virgins and Religious would be a better choice.

Today's Saint

Raised in a wealthy aristocratic family in Italy, St. Aloysius Gonzaga (1568–1591) became aware at the age of 7 that treasures in this lifetime can't satisfy the longings of the heart. Much to the disappointment of his father, Aloysius renounced his inheritance to join the Society of Jesus. His short life as a Jesuit was marked by austere piety, theological study, and service to the sick. Sometimes his piety was a bit severe, so his spiritual director, St. Robert Bellarmine, mentored him in the way of moderation. St. Aloysius's love of study, especially the *Summa Theologica* and the Bible, led to him being declared patron of college students. While ministering to the sick in a Jesuit hospital, he contracted a plague, which led to his death.

(#167)   white

Solemnity of the Most Holy Body and Blood of Christ (*Corpus Christi*)

☀ **22**

About this Solemnity

Today we celebrate *Corpus Christi*, the Solemnity of the Most Holy Body and Blood of Christ. In the Eucharistic feast, the gifts of bread and wine really and truly become the Body, Blood, Soul, and Divinity of Christ. Through this covenant of love, God draws us into his divine life and offers us food for our earthly pilgrimage to continue with the

faith and hope, confident in God's ability to transform our weaknesses and sufferings into life and joy.

The Lectionary for Mass

◆ FIRST READING: Remember . . . do not forget what God has done for you! It's a message repeated throughout the stories of Israel's desert wanderings—and it's a message that we should take to heart as well. When they lacked food, God gave them manna to eat (see Exodus 16:4–35). The manna was but the sign of God's providential care for them made known through the words he spoke to them and the deeds he wrought for them. His word—his commands to them—was the source of their life (see Psalm 119).

◆ RESPONSORIAL PSALM 147: The themes of word and food are continued in this hymn of praise to the Lord for all the manifestations of his providential care. Note the reference to the "best of wheat" in the second stanza. Even more emphasis is given to "word"—occurring twice, in addition to its synonyms: statutes, ordinances. It is through these that God's providential care is made known.

◆ SECOND READING: Chapters 10 and 11 of First Corinthians is the earliest commentary we have on the Church's celebration of the Eucharist. Paul stresses how the Christian community is united as one through its participation in the Body and Blood of Christ. The word "participation" (*koinōía*) is important, signifying a communion not only with the Lord, but with one another. Is that our realization and experience today?

◆ GOSPEL: Jesus speaks of himself as the "living bread"—true manna from heaven—the food that nourishes unto eternal life. The identification of the bread with his own flesh and blood is startling for many of his hearers. And what about those who hear today? Do we realize the great mystery in which we share? Do we recognize what—who—is offered to us in each Eucharist?

The Roman Missal

The texts for today are found immediately following the texts for the Solemnity of the Most Holy Trinity, toward the end of the "Ordinary Time" section of the Missal. You might consider using the Rite for the Blessing and Sprinkling of Water found in Appendix II at the back of the Missal; this might help to reinforce the connection between Baptism and Eucharist, and the Eucharist as the culmination of initiation. The Gloria is sung or said today as is the Creed.

The Collect notes that in the Sacrament of the Eucharist, God has "left us a memorial of your Passion." The prayer goes on to ask that because of our revering of "the sacred mysteries of your Body and Blood," we may "always experience in ourselves / the fruits of your redemption." As this prayer speaks of the fruits of being redeemed, we must always remember that those fruits are expressed in a life of self-emptying love. Therefore, the focus is not so much on a passive contemplation of the Real Presence in the Eucharist, but, as with all liturgical celebration, how our participation in the mystery is a means of being transformed by God to live out the mystery that is being celebrated.

The Prayer over the Offerings reinforces the idea that worship of the Eucharist must be expressed in the practical living out of our lives. This prayer reinforces that one of the chief results of Eucharistic celebration must be unity: as the "one bread" and "one cup" are prayed over at the one altar around which is gathered the one Body of Christ, we see in those signs the mystery of what we are to become—"one body, one spirit in Christ," in the words of Eucharistic Prayer III.

The Preface that is given along with the other formularies for this Mass is Preface II of the Most Holy Eucharist; only the text with music is given, indicating a certain preference for chanting the introductory dialogue and the Preface itself. However, a rubric indicates that Preface I of the Most Holy Eucharist, which can be found along with the texts of other Prefaces further along in the Missal, may also be used.

The Prayer after Communion points to the important but often-overlooked eschatological dimension of the Eucharist, as it reminds us that the reception of the Body and Blood of the Lord in the present age is a foreshadowing of sharing in God's divine life for all eternity.

Noting that it is desirable for a Eucharistic procession to take place after Mass, the Missal gives instructions on how this is to be carried out. The host that will be carried in the procession should be a Host that has been consecrated at this Mass; thus it is made clear how worship of the Eucharist outside Mass is an extension of the grace of the offering of the sacrifice. If such a procession is to take place after Mass, the host to be carried in procession is placed in the monstrance when the Communion of the faithful is over, and that monstrance is set on the altar. The Prayer after Communion is then prayed, but the Concluding Rite is omitted. Instead, the procession forms immediately after the Prayer after Communion. The Missal gives no further rubrics concerning the procession; liturgy preparers should consult the ritual, *Holy Communion and Worship of the Eucharist Outside Mass* for specific instructions. The Missal does note, however, that the procession need not take place immediately after Mass, but may instead follow after a public and lengthy period of adoration coming at the end of Mass.

Pastoral Reflection

How often do you choose to nourish yourself with the physical sustenance of God's unfailing love in the Eucharist? If Sunday Eucharist is your norm, consider going to daily Mass at least once this week. If you are already a daily communicant and do not know the *Anima Christi* prayer, find and then memorize this as part of your prayer to Jesus for the gift offered in Eucharist. The living bread and wine must be part of one's most basic routine so as to live fully in God. Go deep within today and this week, and share with God your understanding of, or struggle with, the true meaning of the Eucharist. As St. Augustine shared, "be what you receive," with God living *in* you, how can this love radiate more fully?

(#371) green

M O N 23 Weekday Twelfth Week in Ordinary Time

The Lectionary for Mass

◆ FIRST READING: At the time of the death of King Solomon, the kingdom of Israel was divided in two. Today's reading recounts the destruction of the northern kingdom at the hands of the Assyrians and the deportation of the Israelite people to Assyria. The prophets interpret this historical event as punishment for Israel's infidelities. Only the southern kingdom remained at this time.

◆ RESPONSORIAL PSALM 60: How truly the words of this psalm of lament could have been spoken by a conquered and exiled people. Both the refrain and the last line are a prayer for God's mercy.

◆ GOSPEL: Today's text speaks directly to the common human tendency to judge others. Jesus's message is clear: as we do to others, so shall it be done to us. What is more, we are called to serious self-examination: What are our wooden beams?

(#586) white

T U E 24 Vigil of the Solemnity of the Nativity of St. John the Baptist

About this Solemnity

John the Baptist was the great prophet and herald of Jesus the Messiah. He prepared the way of the Lord and revealed Jesus to others as both the Messiah and the Lamb of God. St. John exemplifies the Christian life as one who proclaims the Gospel message of healing and repentance while he points out Christ to others and shows them the way to become united with God.

This is an ancient solemnity, reaching back to the fourth century, though the date of the celebration varied in East and West. In the East, the birth of the forerunner was celebrated on the day after Epiphany, January 7, because of the association of that feast with the Baptism of the Lord. In the West, it was celebrated on June 24, in keeping with Luke 1:36, which notes that Elizabeth was six months pregnant at the time of the Annunciation of the Lord.

The Lectionary for Mass

◆ FIRST READING: The prophet Jeremiah was but a youth when he received his prophetic call. In fact, as he himself saw it, he was too young to be about what the Lord asked. Nevertheless, the Lord reassures him: it is the Lord's Word he speaks, not his own. What is more, he will not be alone: the Lord is with him.

◆ RESPONSORIAL PSALM 71: The reference to the mother's womb in our antiphon and in the third stanza are fitting for this solemnity celebrating the birth of John the Baptist, who, as Luke attests, even in his mother's womb bore witness to his Lord. The pleas for deliverance are likewise applicable to John the Baptist who was put to death because of the word he spoke.

◆ SECOND READING: The themes of joy and the working of the Spirit in God's prophets link today's Second Reading with the Gospel announcement of the birth of John the Baptist. Believers in every generation are among those who rejoice because of the salvation that is theirs in Christ.

◆ GOSPEL: The birth of John the Baptist was announced to his elderly father, Zechariah, in a vision as he offered incense in the Temple. As with so many before him, the vision evokes fear, but God's messenger immediately reassures him and speaks of the joy that he and so many others will have because of his son. The messenger speaks of the child's future role: he will be dedicated to God as the Nazirites of old (no wine, strong drink; see Numbers 6) and will be instrumental in the conversion of many in Israel. The Spirit of the Lord will be upon him, even from his mother's womb.

The Roman Missal

Two sets of Mass formularies are given for this Solemnity, "At the Vigil Mass" and "At the Mass during the Day."

At the Vigil Mass

The Entrance Antiphon for this Mass is taken from the angel's announcement to Zechariah in chapter 1 of Luke's Gospel. The Gloria is sung or said today.

The Collect uses the interesting appellation "the Precursor" to refer to St. John, a title somewhat unfamiliar to us but one which certainly defines his role in salvation history. The prayer asks that we may come safely to the One foretold by John.

Remember that the Creed is said at this Mass.

The Prayer over the Offerings once again makes a connection between liturgy and life, petitioning God "that what we celebrate in mystery / we may follow with deeds of devoted service."

The Preface is proper for today, "The Mission of the Precursor," and the text, with and without musical notation, is located among the texts for the Mass during the Day, two pages over from the Vigil Mass texts. The Preface recalls the events associated with St. John the Baptist's life and echo the Scripture passages associated with him: how he was consecrated "for a singular honor / among those born of women;" how "His birth brought great rejoicing;" how he leapt for joy in the womb; how "He alone of all the prophets / pointed out the Lamb of redemption;" how "he baptized the very author of Baptism;" and how he gave witness to Christ by the shedding of his blood.

The Communion Antiphon is taken from the beginning of the Canticle of Zechariah in the first chapter of Luke.

The Prayer after Communion emphasizes the Communion of Saints as it asks that "the prayer of St. John the Baptist / accompany us who have eaten our fill / at this sacrificial feast." There is also a plea for forgiveness through the intercession of the saint: since he was the one to proclaim Jesus as the Lamb who would take away our sins, we ask that "he implore now for us your favor."

An argument could be made that the dismissal formula "Go and announce the Gospel of the Lord" fits in well with today's focus on the life and mission of the Precursor.

(#587) white

24 TUE Solemnity of the Nativity of St. John the Baptist

The Lectionary for Mass

◆ FIRST READING: Several motifs from this "Servant Song" of the prophet Isaiah are particularly apropos for today's solemnity: being called from birth, being "named" by God (see Luke 1:13 and also today's account Gospel), the mission to Israel (Luke 1:17, 68–79; 3:3, 7–12). The text from Isaiah likewise mentions a mission to Gentiles as well, and Luke portrays John as preaching even to the soldiers (Luke 3:14).

◆ RESPONSORIAL PSALM 139: The psalmist acclaims God's knowledge of him, God's plan for him, even from birth. How true this is for him who was the forerunner of Jesus!

◆ SECOND READING: Today's reading provides a brief summary of the Gospel proclamation of Jesus as the promised Davidic Messiah, whose coming was heralded by John the Baptist. Notice that John's proclamation is both to the "sons of the family of Abraham" (Jewish people) and to the "God-fearing," that is, Gentiles who were associated with the synagogue.

◆ GOSPEL: Fittingly, we hear of the birth of John the Baptist. Notice the emotions the event generates among Elizabeth and Zechariah's family and friends: joy, amazement, and even fear and uncertainty as to what it all means. Perhaps these are not so unknown in our own lives in the experiences of God's marvelous deeds. Like John the Baptist, we, too, must grow and become strong in spirit if we are to accomplish the work God has entrusted to us.

The Roman Missal

At the Mass during the Day

The Entrance Antiphon comes from the first chapter of John's account of the Gospel, the Prologue, and specifically introduces the theme of John as the one who came to testify to the light. The imagery, usually associated with the Advent-Christmas time of year, is fitting here as well. The Gloria is sung or said today.

The Collect speaks about the preparatory role of the Baptist as one who was raised up "to make ready a nation fit for Christ the Lord." This prayer prays that we may be directed "into the way of salvation and peace."

Remember that, because it is a solemnity, the Creed is said today.

The Prayer over the Offerings expresses why it is fitting to celebrate the nativity of St. John: it is because he "both foretold the coming of the world's Savior / and pointed him out when he came."

The text for the proper Preface used today is located immediately following the Prayer over the Offerings. See the commentary above under the Vigil Mass.

The Communion Antiphon, like the Communion Antiphon at the Vigil Mass, is taken from the Canticle of Zechariah in Luke.

The Prayer after Communion uses the imagery of the Lamb so closely associated with John the Baptist's announcement of Jesus, and in so doing the prayer gives voice to a rich Eucharistic theology with its phrase "Having feasted at the banquet of the heavenly Lamb. . . ."

As remarked concerning the Vigil Mass, an argument could be made that the dismissal formula "Go and announce the Gospel of the Lord" fits in well with today's focus on the life and mission of St. John the Baptist.

Pastoral Reflection

Most of us celebrate the birth of a baby with gifts, happiness, and support of the family. Do we celebrate other answers to prayers with our friends and neighbors? Do we support families whose members have made radical choices to serve and love others? Our community has a responsibility to celebrate these brave Christians.

(#373) green

25 WED Weekday

The Lectionary for Mass

◆ FIRST READING: The book of the Law of the Lord is found during repairs to the Temple in the reign of King Josiah, a king likened to David (and in stark contrast to his wicked predecessors who abandoned the law of the Lord). The tearing of garments is a penitential gesture, the king's response on hearing the law of the Lord and realizing how far his people had strayed. Josiah assembled all the people, had the book of the law read to them, and led them in ratifying the covenant of the Lord.

◆ RESPONSORIAL PSALM 119 is the longest Psalm in the Bible, all but one of its 176 verses extolling the law of the Lord. The verses chosen for today are a prayer for instruction in the ways of the law that they might be faithfully observed—a fitting response to today's First Reading.

◆ GOSPEL: By their fruits, the goodness or wickedness, the fidelity or infidelity of a person shall be known—as exemplified in today's First Reading. What are our fruits?

(#364) green

26 THU Weekday

The Lectionary for Mass

◆ FIRST READING: The southern kingdom of Judah was conquered by the Babylonians, its Temple destroyed, its treasures and its skilled people deported to Babylon. Only the poor were left in the land.

◆ RESPONSORIAL PSALM 79 is a prayer for deliverance, describing the destruction of the Temple and the siege of the city. The prophets saw this event as punishment for the infidelities of the people.

◆ GOSPEL: The importance of doing the will of the Father—as opposed to only hearing it—is stressed both in the saying of Jesus in the first part of the Gospel and the parable in the second part. Are we hearers or doers? Is our foundation sand or the rock that is Christ?

(#170)   white

FRI 27 Solemnity of the Most Sacred Heart of Jesus

About this Solemnity

Devotion to the Sacred Heart of Jesus became popular in the seventeenth century through St. Mary Margaret Alacoque (1647–1690) [St. Margaret's memorial is October 16], who said that in her visions Christ told her, "Behold the heart that has loved people so, yet is loved so little in return." *Catholic Household Blessings & Prayers* includes a Litany of the Sacred Heart. Pray this. It may also be helpful to have an extended period of prayer in the presence of the Blessed Sacrament or with the parish's image of the Sacred Heart. See Pope John Paul II's prayer, the Litany of the Sacred Heart of Jesus (*Our Sunday Visitor*, 1992) for a deeper understanding of this devotion. Encourage a night vigil until the celebration of the memorial of the Immaculate Heart of Mary the next day, Saturday, June 28.

The Lectionary for Mass

◆ FIRST READING: Already in the Old Testament, the deep love in God's heart for his people is revealed: "the Lord set his heart on you and chose you . . . / the Lord loved you . . . ." Accordingly, God acted on Israel's behalf, delivering them from slavery in Egypt. In love, God made a covenant with them, signifying their special relationship.

As a sign of their love and fidelity, the Israelites are to keep God's commandments.

◆ RESPONSORIAL PSALM 103: The Hebrew word translated in today's antiphon as "kindness" is *ḥesed*, which can also be translated as "covenant love." Today's psalm, a hymn of praise, names several ways God's love is manifest to his people: forgiveness, deliverance, kindness, and compassion. As the last stanza makes clear, God's love is completely gratuitous. It is not something that we have "earned."

◆ SECOND READING: Our call to love one another is rooted in the love we have received from God. We are called to know God, in the sense of a deeply personal experience of God's love. Love is the very nature of God's being, and so it must become ours. God's love for us was given flesh in Jesus of Nazareth, and his love for us made eternal life a reality for us even now. Our salvation, God's love for us—all is God's initiative, God's gift. Our task is now is to remain in this love and to give it expression through our love for one another, loving as God has loved us, freely and unconditionally.

◆ GOSPEL: Jesus gives praise to his heavenly Father for all that has been revealed in love and for the knowledge or relationship with himself and the Father to which he invites us. Note the reference to the "heart" of Jesus. In this context, it is described as "meek and humble." Jesus offers his love in gentleness, as an invitation. Nothing is harshly imposed. But what peace and rest is to be found when we respond to his invitation, when we experience his love.

The Roman Missal

The texts for this Mass are found toward the end of the "Ordinary Time" section of the Missal; they immediately follow the texts for the

Solemnity of the Most Holy Body and Blood of Christ. The Gloria is sung or said today.

There is a choice from among two Collects today. The first one recalls the wonders of Christ's love for us as "we glory in the Heart of your beloved Son." In recalling those wonders, we can ask for "an overflowing measure of grace" from the Heart of Christ, referred to here as "that fount of heavenly gifts." The second Collect speaks more directly about how Christ's Sacred Heart has been wounded by our sins, and so asks that as we pay homage in our devotion, that homage "may also offer worthy reparation."

Remember that the Creed is said today.

The Preface assigned for today is given right along with the other texts for this Mass; both a text with music and one without is provided. The Preface spotlights the image of Christ on the Cross with blood and water flowing from his pierced side. This image is "the wellspring of the Church's Sacraments" that makes it possible so that "all might draw water joyfully from the springs of salvation."

The Prayer after Communion picks up the theme of love, referring to the Eucharist as "this sacrament of charity." Our participation in this Eucharist should transform us, making us "fervent with the fire of holy love" so that we can see (and serve) Christ in our neighbor.

Pastoral Reflection

In times of distress, it may be difficult to feel an easy yoke or a light burden. In these times, Jesus walks very closely with us, offering to share the load, to direct our gaze heavenward, and to strengthen our faith. We admit how desperately we need him, and he responds with abundant love.

(#376, Gospel #573)   white

S A T 28 Memorial of the Immaculate Heart of the Blessed Virgin Mary

About this Memorial

Pope John Paul II raised this celebration to an obligatory memorial. It always takes place on the Saturday following the Second Sunday after Pentecost (Most Holy Body and Blood of Christ/*Corpus Christi*).

The Lectionary for Mass

◆ FIRST READING: Readings earlier in the week described the destruction of Jerusalem and the Temple. Today's text from Lamentations leads us deep into the grief and suffering of the people at that time.

◆ RESPONSORIAL PSALM 74: Why? Why? Why? asks today's Responsorial Psalm in the wake of Jerusalem's destruction. When will you answer and deliver your faithful who are afflicted and poor? God's people could only live with hope in his mercy and trust in his promises.

◆ GOSPEL: Today's Gospel account is proper (Lectionary #573). The text focuses not only on the adventures of the boy Jesus, eager to learn from the teachers of the Word in the Temple, but on the "heart" (Luke 2:51) of Mary, which knew not only pride and love in her Son, but also panic in the face of loss. More than that, there were the enigmatic, inexplicable, and even mysterious things said about and by her Son. That Mary "kept all these things in her heart" (Luke 2:51) is a refrain repeated throughout Luke's account of the birth and childhood of Jesus. Mary is a model for all, not only in terms of keeping the words of Scripture in our hearts (and minds, as Scripture understands the heart) but also the words of our experiences. May our hearts, like Mary's, be pure, that pondering all, we may see the Lord.

The Roman Missal

The location of the texts in the Missal for this memorial can be a little tricky to find; they are given in the Proper of Saints, immediately following May 31, the Feast of the Visitation of the Blessed Virgin Mary. The Collect asks that our lives of faith may parallel that of the Blessed Virgin Mary: as her heart was a fit dwelling place for the Holy Spirit, so too may we be "a worthy temple of your glory." The Prayer over the Offerings asks for God's help and forgiveness as we present our offerings in commemoration of the Blessed Mother of God. Either Preface I or Preface II of the Blessed Virgin Mary may be used today; if Preface I is used, then the phrase "on the feast day" is used. The Prayer after Communion evokes the Marian theme of "fullness of your grace" as it asks that we may experience the continued increase of grace in our own lives.

Pastoral Reflection

We can learn from Mary how to handle struggles as parents, spouses, children, and friends. We may not always understand the others in our lives, no matter how much we love them. Mary "kept all these things in her heart" (Luke 2:51). If we follow her example, we practice patience and calm upon first hearing upsetting news. Then we take time for quiet reflection and prayer. Only then do we act or speak in love and truth.

(#591)   red

29 Solemnity of SS. Peter and Paul, Apostles

About this Solemnity

Today we commemorate SS. Peter and Paul, martyred around the year 64 AD during Nero's persecution following the Great Fire of Rome. Tradition says that Peter fled Rome to avoid arrest and saw Jesus on the road. "Where are you going, Lord," Peter asked. Jesus replied, "I am going to Rome to be crucified again." Peter turned back and was crucified upside down because he felt unworthy to meet his death the same way as Christ. Paul was arrested in Jerusalem and was sent to Rome, where he was placed under house arrest. He was slain by beheading, because as a Roman citizen he could not be subjected to the indignity of crucifixion.

The Lectionary for Mass (Vigil)

◆ FIRST READING: The story of the crippled beggar lying at the gate of the Temple who receives the gift of healing in the name of the Lord Jesus from the hands of Peter and not the alms he expected is the subject of today's First Reading. What better way to give God praise than fully using that which is restored to full health! The man walks and jumps with joy, giving God praise.

♦ RESPONSORIAL PSALM 19 declares the "glory of God" (verse 2) as spoken by creation. In the light of today's First Reading, "their" (see verse 5) refers not to creation, but to the voice of the Apostles.

♦ SECOND READING: Paul speaks to the Galatians of his encounter with the Risen Jesus, a "revelation" that changed his life. Paul turned from persecutor to missionary of the Gospel, sent by the Risen Lord to the Gentiles.

♦ GOSPEL: The Risen Jesus commissions Peter, entrusting to him with the care of the sheep of his flock. Jesus also speaks of how Peter will one day follow him, led by another to death, and ultimately to glory.

The Roman Missal (Vigil)

Through the happenstances of this year's calendar, yet another Sunday in Ordinary Time is replaced by a Solemnity. Two sets of Mass formularies are given for this Solemnity, "At the Vigil Mass" and "At the Mass during the Day."

The Entrance Antiphon for the Vigil Mass highlights for us how both Peter the Apostle and Paul the teacher of the Gentiles have taught the Lord's law. The Gloria is sung or said today.

The Collect continues to honor Peter and Paul together as it affirms that "through them you gave your Church / the foundations of her heavenly office;" the prayer goes on to ask that through them the Church may be assisted on her way to eternal salvation.

Remember that the Creed is said at this Vigil Mass.

The Prayer over the Offerings speaks of hopefulness and encouragement: it tells us that "the more we doubt our own merits, / the more we may rejoice that we are to be saved / by your loving kindness." We offer this Eucharist in union with the Apostles Peter and Paul who themselves, as the Scriptures so clearly tell us, were men who sinned and had their faults and weaknesses.

The Preface is proper for today, and it is found among the prayers for the Mass during the Day, a page turn away from the Vigil prayers. A text is given both with music and without; since it is a solemnity, strongly consider singing the introductory dialogue and the Preface. The Preface mentions in tandem the attributes that are the reasons we commemorate these two Apostles: Peter is "foremost in confessing the faith" and is the one "who established the early Church from the remnant of Israel;" Paul is the faith's "outstanding preacher . . . master and teacher of the Gentiles." Thus is the mission of the Church both within Israel and beyond her to the whole world avowed.

The Communion Antiphon, taken from the Gospel for the Vigil Mass, is the dialogue between the Lord and Simon as the Lord asks Simon if he loves him "more than these" and Simon answers in the affirmative. Placed here, these lines of Scripture might serve to remind us of the question that rightly could be asked of us as we approach Holy Communion: do we love the Lord more than anything else?

The Prayer after Communion entreats that as we have been "enlightened with the teaching of the Apostles," so may we be strengthened by "this heavenly Sacrament."

The Solemn Blessing for Saints Peter and Paul, Apostles (#16 under "Blessings at the End of Mass and Prayers over the People") is suggested, and should be used today. It refers to Peter's "saving confession" and uses the image of the solid rock, and to "the tireless preaching of Saint Paul." It then brings the two together by highlighting "the keys of St. Peter and the words of St. Paul."

The Lectionary for Mass (Day)

♦ FIRST READING: Even in these early days, the persecution of Christians was at times based on political reasons. Was it not that way with Jesus as well? As was the case with Jesus's Death, the persecution of the Apostles takes place at the time of the Passover, the feast of Unleavened Bread. As God delivered Israel of old from slavery in Egypt, so God delivered Peter from the hands of Herod. Peter's following of the angel is but one incident in his following of the Lord Jesus in the ultimate passage from death to life.

♦ RESPONSORIAL PSALM 34 is a song of praise celebrating God's deliverance of his chosen people through the intervention of a heavenly messenger—a most appropriate response for today's First Reading.

♦ SECOND READING: Paul's words reflect his awareness of his imminent death, his "departure" for the heavenly kingdom. In language echoing the ritual sacrifice in the Temple, he speaks of his life's ministry as a sacrificial offering "poured out" (2 Timothy 4:6) and given to God. He also uses the athletic imagery found elsewhere in his writing: the competition, the race, the winner's crown.

♦ GOSPEL: "Who do you say that the Son of Man is?" asks Jesus of his disciples. In today's Gospel we hear Peter's profound confession: "You are the Christ, the Son of the Living God." As Peter confesses Jesus, Jesus commissions Peter: "you are Peter, and upon this rock I will build my Church, and the gates of the netherworld shall not prevail against it."

The Roman Missal (Day)

The Entrance Antiphon foreshadows the readings in that it points to the imprisonment and sufferings that both faced. The Gloria is sung or said today.

The Collect for this Mass during the Day reminds us that the Church's faith came through the Apostles Peter and Paul; it was through them that the Church "received / the beginnings of right religion."

Remember that, because it is a solemnity, the Creed is said today.

The Prayer over the Offerings asks for the powerful intercession of these two Apostles, praying that their prayer may "accompany the sacrificial gift / that we present to your name for consecration." Again we are reminded that every Eucharist is celebrated in communion with all the saints who have gone before us.

The Preface is proper for today; see the commentary for it above, under the Vigil Mass.

The Communion Antiphon recounts Peter's confession of faith from Matthew's account of the Gospel and Jesus's reply to him stating how he will build his Church upon the rock of Peter.

Although the Prayer after Communion does not mention Peter and Paul by name, it does pray that we might persevere "in the breaking of the Bread / and in the teaching of the Apostles"—notice the reference to the Eucharist and to Tradition, without which the Church does not exist—and so live as Church as "one heart and one soul." The unity of the Church founded on the Apostles Peter and Paul is strengthened and nourished through sacrament and through authentic teaching.

As at the Vigil Mass, the Solemn Blessing for SS. Peter and Paul, Apostles (#16 under "Blessings at the End of Mass and Prayers over the People") is suggested for today, and should be used. The blessing mentions Peter's "saving confession" and the image of the solid rock, and Paul's "tireless preaching," also noting "the keys of St. Peter and the words of St. Paul."

Pastoral Reflection

To be as bold as St. Peter requires deep love and a wild passion that cannot be tamed. St. Paul had the same unstoppable and unquenchable desire to boldly proclaim Jesus's love and message. Jesus asks: "Who am I?" What is your answer? If Jesus is friend to you, be a better friend in your listening this week. If Jesus is brother, mend a relationship within your family. If Jesus is redeemer, reconcile a shattered piece of your heart. The nouns we use to describe our knowing of Jesus must then also become verbs to live out that knowing in the world.

(#377)   green

MON 30
Weekday
(Thirteenth Week in Ordinary Time)

Optional Memorial of the First Martyrs of the Holy Roman Church / red

The Lectionary for Mass

◆ FIRST READING: The prophet Amos blasts the people of Israel, so to speak, for their covenant infidelities. Their exploitation of the poor and engaging in cultic prostitution with its consequent idolatry are specifically named.

What a contrast is their behavior with the fidelity of the God who led them out of Egypt. Vivid imagery is used at the end of the reading to describe Israel's ultimate defeat.

◆ RESPONSORIAL PSALM 50: In their infidelity, the people of Israel have literally forgotten the God who was their savior. Their unrighteous behavior bears witness that their pious recitation of the law is only empty words.

◆ GOSPEL: Follow is a key word for discipleship. Today's Gospel touches upon what it means in terms of its practical implications: a certain "homelessness" when following Jesus the itinerant preacher, a new priority of relationship to Jesus, which takes precedence over all others.

July
Month of the Most Precious Blood

(#378)   green

TUE 1
Weekday

Optional Memorial of Blessed Junípero Serra, Priest / white

The Lectionary for Mass

◆ FIRST READING: "Prepare to meet your God, O Israel"—what foreboding words of the Lord are uttered by the prophet Amos. Yet, they are not without reason. The people are reminded of all that God has done for them "more than all the families of the earth." But Israel was not faithful; Israel has not repented; Israel has failed to return to the Lord.

◆ RESPONSORIAL PSALM: The words of today's psalm are spoken by one who knows his need for God, who recognizes that he has been favored by the Lord and relies on God's mercy (ḥesed or covenant love). The psalmist, seeking God's righteousness ("justice," verse 9a), stands in stark contrast with the Israelites addressed by Amos. Notice how the psalmist's words about the evil and arrogant echo Amos's description of the Israelites.

◆ GOSPEL: The mercy of God is likewise manifest in today's Gospel reading as Jesus calms the storm at sea, delivering his terrified disciples from their fear of perishing. Notice that Jesus calls the disciples people of "little faith." This story has much to teach us about of the presence of Jesus in the storms that come up in our lives. May we always remember that he has power over these storms.

Today's Saint

Blessed Junípero Serra (1713–1784) was a Spanish Franciscan friar, best known for founding the string of twenty-one missions that stretch from San Diego to Sonoma, California. Junípero was born in Majorca. At age 16 he entered the Franciscans. After completing his theological studies, he served as professor of philosophy at Majorca before volunteering for the missions in the "New World." Upon arrival, he went to Mexico City to dedicate his mission at the shrine of Our Lady of Guadalupe. Serra founded his first mission at San Diego in 1769, and worked his way up the coast along El Camino Real, making converts as he went. In spite of a leg injury he suffered at the beginning of his ministry, he traveled on foot whenever possible, eventually covering 24,000 miles.

W E D 2 (#379) green Weekday

The Lectionary for Mass

◆ FIRST READING: Israel's cultic sacrifices are empty rituals when justice is lacking in their daily behavior. Seek good, love the good, act justly—this is the call to conversion.

◆ RESPONSORIAL PSALM 50 is not so much a prayer to God as a word from God, an oracle uttered in the Temple precincts, spoken against God's people, who pay only lip service to the covenant, thereby rendering their sacrifices empty rituals.

◆ GOSPEL: Throughout the Gospels, Jesus is portrayed as one who has power over the realm of evil, of all that is opposed to God and God's kingdom. While even his own disciples struggle with the question of his identity, the realm of Satan recognizes him immediately. In today's Gospel, the power of Satan is overcome, and that which is deemed unclean (the swine) is destroyed.

T H U 3 (#593) red Feast of St. Thomas, Apostle

The Lectionary for Mass

◆ FIRST READING: Our unity in Christ abolishes all former distinctions, be they ethnic, racial, or religious. Through our common faith, we are united to Christ and to one another: as brothers and sisters in the family of God, fellow citizens of God's holy city, the household of God, a temple or dwelling place of God. On this feast of St. Thomas, are we aware of how our faith today has been built on the foundation of the Apostles' witness centuries ago?

◆ RESPONSORIAL PSALM 117: Our antiphon, drawn from Mark's account of Jesus's commission of the Apostles, is precisely what Thomas and the other Apostles did for the rest of their lives. As a result, all nations know the Lord's fidelity and loving kindness—true cause for praise.

◆ GOSPEL: Something absolutely unheard of . . . a Resurrection from the dead. Who of us cannot identify with Thomas's doubt? Yet this is the reality that gives our life meaning and our faith hope. Blessed are we who believe without seeing, for one day we shall see him who is our Lord and our God.

The Roman Missal

The texts for this Mass, all proper for the feast today, are located in the Proper of Saints section of the Missal at July 3. The Gloria is sung or said today, since it is a feast.

The Collect points to the Apostle Thomas's acknowledgement of the Lord as read in the Scriptures. The Prayer over the Offerings again refers to St. Thomas's confession, asking that the gifts God has given us—the gifts of faith—be kept safe. The Prayer after Communion again echoes the Gospel as the prayer asks that, in receiving the Sacrament of the Eucharist, "we may recognize

him / with the Apostle Thomas by faith / as our Lord and our God." This recognition of the Lord, however, cannot be a passive gazing; rather, as a result of sacramental Communion, we must go on to "proclaim him by our deeds and by our life."

The Preface, proper for today, is one of the two Prefaces of the Apostles. Also, the Solemn Blessing formula titled "The Apostles" (#17 of the "Blessings at the End of Mass and Prayers over the People") is fittingly used as the final blessing at the end of Mass today.

Today's Saint

Thomas, also called "Didymus" or "the Twin" (John 11:16) was one of the Twelve Apostles. He is remembered for doubting the Resurrection of Christ: "Unless I see the mark of the nails in his hands and put my finger into the nail marks and put my hand into his side, I will not believe." The following week, Thomas was with the Twelve, when Jesus appeared and chided him for his lack of faith: "Have you come to believe because you have seen me? Blessed are those who have not seen and have believed" (John 20:25–29). After seeing the Risen Christ alive, Thomas exclaims "My Lord and my God!" According to tradition, Thomas is the only Apostle who went outside the borders of the Roman Empire to evangelize. Although there is a Gospel account attributed to him, it is not accepted in the canon of Scripture, and is, in fact of gnostic origin. The people of Kerala in South India fervently believe that it was Thomas who evangelized them. He is represented in art with a spear, the instrument of his martyrdom. He is the patron of architects and builders, and of India, where today is a solemnity.

F R I 4 (#381) green
Weekday

Optional Mass for Independence Day / white

The Lectionary for Mass

◆ FIRST READING: Once again we see the emptiness of Israel's religious devotion. Festivals and Sabbaths are but an unwanted pause in their evil doings. The day of God's judgment and punishment is imminent. Today's text ends with warning of an impending famine for the word of God. Israel will have no one to speak in God's name.

◆ RESPONSORIAL PSALM 119: The antiphon comes from the Matthew's account of Jesus's temptation in the desert. One lives by the word of God—and that is precisely what Israel will hunger for, says Amos. Note that each stanza has a different name for the word or law of God.

◆ GOSPEL: It was so very hard for the Jewish officials to be reconciled with Jesus's welcoming and acceptance of everyone, even the despicable tax collectors (who worked for the Roman government and supplemented their own income as well) and sinners. In fact, Jesus not only accepted Matthew the tax collector, he called him to be his disciple.

S A T 5 (#382) green
Weekday

Optional Memorials of St. Anthony Zaccaria, Priest / white; St. Elizabeth of Portugal / white; Blessed Virgin Mary / white

The Lectionary for Mass

◆ FIRST READING: Today's First Reading is a beautiful message from the Lord of all comforts and consolation. Despite the punishment meted out on the wicked, God will one day restore the kingly line of the house of David and the house of Israel. The Lord is ever faithful to his promises.

◆ RESPONSORIAL PSALM 85: Today's antiphon aptly expresses the message of today's First Reading. We are all called to hear his word, to welcome his salvation.

◆ GOSPEL: The image of Jesus as Bridegroom echoes an Old Testament image for God (see Isaiah 54:6). Similarly, the glory of the end time is depicted as a wedding feast (see Revelation 21). When Jesus lived on earth, the divine Bridegroom was one of us and dwelt among us. It was indeed the beginning of a new creation.

Today's Saints

Anthony Mary Zaccaria (1502–1539) was from Cremona, Italy. He was born into a noble family, and dedicated himself to the Lord from a young age. He studied philosophy, went to study medicine at the University of Padua, and practiced for three years before deciding to become a priest. Anthony had already done so much study that he was ordained quickly, in 1528. He founded three religious orders: the Barnabites or Clerics Regular of St. Paul—the first order named for St. Paul—the Angelic Sisters of St. Paul for nuns, and a lay community. The three groups worked together to reform society. Because of the implied criticism of abuses in the Church, Anthony was investigated for heresy twice, but was acquitted both times. In addition to founding the Barnabites, he popularized the forty-hour devotion of exposition of the Eucharist. In 1539, he became ill with a fever, and because his health had been undermined by his penitential practices, he died at the age of 37. Anthony is the patron of his order, the Barnabites, and is represented in art wearing a cassock and with a lily, a cross, or a symbol of the Eucharist. Today the Barnabites can be found in sixteen countries, including Italy, the United States, Brazil, and Afghanistan.

St. Elizabeth of Portugal (1271–1336) was the grandniece of Elizabeth of Hungary and is known by the Spanish version of her name, Isabel. When very young, she was married to the King of Portugal. Elizabeth had been raised to be devout, but at her husband's court, she found much corruption and immorality. In spite of this, she managed to continue her life of prayer, penance, and devotion to the care of the sick. This caused resentment in the court, which Elizabeth bore quietly. After her husband, the king, died, she went to live in a convent of Poor Clares that she had founded, and she took the habit of a Third Order Franciscan. Throughout her life she was well known for her peacemaking skills, most importantly when she prevented a war between Portugal and Castile in 1336. The exertion weakened her health, and she died soon after and is buried at Coimbra. Elizabeth of Portugal is a patron of Franciscan Tertiaries.

☀ 6 (#100) green
Fourteenth Sunday in Ordinary Time

The Lectionary for Mass

◆ FIRST READING: The prophet's words are addressed to a post-exilic Jerusalem. The announcement of the coming of the longed-for Davidic king signaled a new era in her history and the reestablishment of the nation. Note that its boundaries will extend to the ends of the earth! It will be a time of peace not only for Jerusalem but for all nations. Both Matthew and Mark cite this text in their account of Jesus's entry into Jerusalem on Palm Sunday. It is no doubt the reference to the meekness of the coming king that is the basis for its choice as a complement to today's Gospel account.

◆ RESPONSORIAL PSALM 145: This hymn of heartfelt praise and thanksgiving to God our King extols the glory of God's kingdom and the power of his reign. Pay special attention to the second stanza: it is God's self-revelation to Moses on Mt. Sinai (see Exodus 34:6–7). It is the experience of God's fidelity that gives rise to praise and thanksgiving.

◆ SECOND READING: The word "spirit" occurs six times in the space of three verses! All of Romans 8 is a powerful testimony to the work of God's Spirit, bringing us to a new realm of life. We are no longer of the flesh, that is, closed to the action of God's Spirit, and we should not live our daily lives as if we were. We have God's Spirit, bringing eternal life to our own spirits as well as to our bodies!

◆ GOSPEL: Jesus gives praise to his Father for all that he has made known to those who are receptive to his teaching. Does Jesus see himself among the merest children? Meek and humble? It is these who are receptive to God's teaching. It is these who are blessed (see Matthew 5:5). In the second part of today's Gospel, Jesus invites all who are burdened to come and exchange the yokes they are carrying for his yoke. Yes, his will be much lighter, for they will not carry it alone. Yoked to Jesus, they will find peace and rest.

The Roman Missal

The Mass texts for today are found in the "Ordinary Time" section of the Proper of Time. The Gloria is sung or said today.

The Collect points to God's raising up of our fallen world through "the abasement" of his Son. (It is hoped that the hearers at Mass do not mishear the phrase and think that a basement, as in a cellar, is being referred to!) The image is meant to reflect the Paschal Mystery of lowliness leading to glory, which brings "holy joy," as the prayer goes on to ask for "eternal gladness" to be bestowed upon those who have been rescued from slavery to sin (that is, through the Son's act of humble love). The Prayer over the Offerings prays for purification of our lives to occur through the oblation being offered; it reminds us of the concrete changes we must make in our lives if we are going to truly live what we believe, as we pray that participating in this celebration might "day by day bring / our conduct closer to the life of heaven." The Prayer after Communion notes how the food of the Eucharist replenishes us so that "we may gain the prize of salvation / and never cease to praise you." That the Eucharist is nourishment for the journey to heaven must never be forgotten.

Any one of the eight Prefaces of the Sundays in Ordinary Time can be used. In making a choice, note how Preface I, with its mention of Jesus accomplishing "the marvelous deed," or Preface II, with its mention of his humbling himself to be born of the Virgin, could echo the theme of "abasement" (humility) mentioned in the Collect, and the meekness and humility of Christ mentioned in the Gospel for today. Preface IV's reference to experiencing daily the effects of God's care could connect with the notion of "day by day conduct" referred to in the Prayer over the Offerings and also correlate with the notion of the burdened finding rest in the Lord as described in the Gospel. Another possibility would be to use Eucharistic Prayer IV today, with its own proper Preface, because of

its recap of how Jesus proclaimed the Good News of salvation to the poor, freedom to prisoners, and joy to the sorrowful of heart, which would also echo one theme from the Gospel.

Pastoral Reflection

What made you happiest as a child? As you remember, and possibly enact those childhood moments, bring God into them. Today's account of the Gospel also seems to call for a game of hide and seek with a child. In the lightness of God, hide your burdens in God's hands and seek his grace when you are found.

M O N 7 (#383) green Weekday

The Lectionary for Mass

◆ FIRST READING: Today's reading should be seen within the context of the first three chapters of Hosea, who prophesied not only by word, but by action. As instructed by the Lord, he took a harlot for his wife, symbolizing Israel's harlotry through idolatry. As we saw in last Saturday's Gospel, God's covenant relationship with his people was often symbolized in terms of a marriage relationship. In today's text, God promises mercy toward the unfaithful people of Israel and a restoration of their covenant bond.

◆ RESPONSORIAL PSALM 145: God's mercy is extolled in this psalm of praise.

◆ GOSPEL: Two people seek the power of Jesus's touch: an official for his daughter who has just died, and a woman, rendered unclean by her hemorrhage for eighteen years. In contrast with Mark, Matthew gives few details concerning these miracles. The focus is on Jesus, the power of his touch, and the faith of the official and the woman.

T U E 8 (#384) green
Weekday

The Lectionary for Mass

◆ FIRST READING: Today's reading elaborates on the people of Israel's idolatry. They have made a molten calf. The many sacrifices they offer are not pleasing to the Lord. The punishment foretold is a return to Egypt—symbolically understood. Israel was once again deprived of its land and enslaved, so to speak, at the time of the Babylonian Exile.

◆ RESPONSORIAL PSALM 115: Most of today's text addresses the futility of idols, gods that are the creation of human handiwork. These are no match for the power of God. The faithful Israelite will trust not in idols, but in the Lord.

◆ GOSPEL: We see Jesus's power over the realm of Satan and the demons in his cure of the man who was mute. We also hear the opposition of the Pharisees. Perhaps the most touching line in today's Gospel is the depiction of Jesus as one whose heart was moved with compassion for the many people who came to him to hear his word and to be healed. Are we among them? And what is in our heart toward those whom we meet every day?

W E D 9 (#385) green
Weekday

Optional Memorial of Blessed Augustine Zhao Rong, Priest, and Companions, Martyrs / red

The Lectionary for Mass

◆ FIRST READING: Once again, Israel's idolatry is the focus. There is the seeming paradox: the more they were blessed with productivity, the greater their idolatry, building altars to false gods (perhaps to gods of fertility?). They will be punished, however, and their altars destroyed. Hosea calls Israel to the sowing of a new seed, the seed of

righteous, which will produce a harvest of piety.

◆ RESPONSORIAL PSALM: Our antiphon picks up on the last line of the reading. Psalm 105 recounts God's wondrous deeds in Israel's history. Today's verses are from the beginning of the psalm. The remembrance of God's goodness to us in the past should lead to thanksgiving and fidelity.

◆ GOSPEL: Jesus commissions his Twelve Apostles (called disciples here) with the emphasis on their continued learning from him. Their mission first and foremost is to have power over evil spirits and to heal. They are sent to the house of Israel, to those to whom God's promises were first made. (The antagonism toward Samaria seen here and elsewhere in the Gospel dates back to the time of the Babylonian Exile, when those who inhabited this central part of Israel remained in their homeland and intermarried with foreigners who subsequently settled in the land.)

Today's Saints

Between 1648 and 1930, eighty-seven Chinese Catholics and thirty-three Western missionaries, some of whom were Dominicans, Franciscans, Salesians, Jesuits, or Vincentians, were martyred for their ministry or for refusing to renounce their Christian faith. Many of the Chinese converts were killed during the Boxer Rebellion, a xenophobic uprising during which many foreigners were slaughtered by angry peasants. Augustine Zhao Rong was a Chinese diocesan priest who was tortured and killed in 1815, after the Emperor Kia-Kin issued decrees banning Catholicism. Augustine Zhao Rong and the other Chinese martyrs were canonized in 2000 by Pope John Paul II.

T H U 10 (#385) green
Weekday

The Lectionary for Mass

◆ FIRST READING: This reading is, perhaps, one of the most tender images of God in all of the Old Testament: the loving father who gently lifts a child to his cheek, kisses and embraces him or her. Another important motif in today's reading is that of God as healer (see also Exodus 15:26). Healing is a prominent theme for the prophet Hosea. What is noteworthy, is that wherever the word occurs, the mention of conversion, of turning back to God, is found in close proximity.

◆ RESPONSORIAL PSALM 80 is a plea for God's mercy and salvation. God is shepherd of Israel, the powerful Lord of hosts. Israel is the vine planted by God (see also Isaiah 5:1–7) and its king, the "son" established by his right hand.

◆ GOSPEL: Today's text is a continuation of what we heard yesterday: Jesus's instruction to his newly commissioned Apostles (who are also called laborers here). Jesus warns them that not everyone will receive them. Particularly poignant are Jesus's words: "Without cost you have received, without cost you are to give" (Matthew 10:8). Do we see the relevance of that statement for our own lives?

F R I 11 (#387) white
**Memorial of
St. Benedict, Abbot**

The Lectionary for Mass

◆ FIRST READING: The relationship between healing and returning to the Lord is particularly evident in today's reading, in which God's healing brings abundant growth. The reading ends with a call to those who read or hear the prophet's words to receive them wisely.

◆ RESPONSORIAL PSALM 51 is penitential and acknowledges guilt. In the case of Israel in today's First Reading, the sin was idolatry. Confession of sin and the experience of forgiveness leads to praise. Thus, our antiphon.

◆ GOSPEL: Today's text continues from the previous two days. The reading focuses on the persecution and suffering Jesus's Apostles must endure. In the midst of it all, there is the powerful promise: ". . . it will not be you who speak but the Spirit of your Father speaking through you" (Matthew 10:20). Jesus asks his disciples not to worry, but to trust in the providential care of their heavenly Father.

The Roman Missal

The orations, all proper today, are found in the Proper of Saints at July 11. The Collect recognizes St. Benedict as being "an outstanding master in the school of divine service," a nod, of course, to his famous *Rule*. The Prayer over the Offerings asks that we follow Benedict's example in seeking God; the Prayer after Communion prays that, by being attentive to the teaching of St. Benedict, we may serve God's designs and "love one another with fervent charity" as a result of our receiving this sacrament as a "pledge of eternal life." The Preface may be either Preface I or II of Saints or the Preface of Holy Virgins and Religious.

Today's Saint

Saddened by the immoral state of society, St. Benedict of Nursia (480–553/7) left the city to live as a hermit at Subiaco. In time, more and more men were attracted to his charismatic personality as well as to his way of life. He eventually moved a group of monks to Monte Cassino, near Naples, where he completed the final version of his rule, now known as *The Rule of*

Saint Benedict, on the fundamentals of monastic life, including the day-to-day operation of a monastery. The rule asserts that the primary occupation of the monk is to pray the Divine Office in tandem with a vowed life of stability, obedience, and conversion. The whole of the monastic vocation can be summarized in the opening line of his rule, "Listen carefully." St. Benedict is considered the father of Western monasticism.

S A T 12 (#388) green
Weekday

Optional Memorial of the Blessed Virgin Mary / white

The Lectionary for Mass

◆ FIRST READING: Isaiah receives his prophetic call in a vision of the awe-inspiring majesty and glory of God. His experience of God leads him to the awareness of his own sinfulness and his realization that only God can cleanse us of our wickedness. We echo the angelic hymn of praise sung before the heavenly throne at every Mass.

◆ RESPONSORIAL PSALM 93 celebrates God's kingship and proclaims the trustworthiness of all his decrees.

◆ GOSPEL: Once again we hear an excerpt from Matthew's account of Jesus's commissioning of his Apostles. Yesterday we heard of the opposition and persecution that the disciples can expect. Today's reading opens with an explanation why: as it was for the teacher, so it will be for the disciple. Our way can be no other than that of Jesus—nor should it be any other way. The disciple is not to fear (an injunction occurring three times) the opposition, but rather, to fear the loss of life and soul in Gehenna as a result of infidelity.

☀ 13 (#103) green
Fifteenth Sunday in Ordinary Time

The Lectionary for Mass

◆ FIRST READING: The image of rain and snow watering the earth and bringing forth fruit thus accomplishing the purpose for which they were sent by the Lord—is an apt illustration of the life-giving effect God intends his Word to have in the minds and hearts of those who hear it.

◆ RESPONSORIAL PSALM 65: The first two stanzas of today's antiphon celebrate the blessing of the rain and snow that renders the earth abundantly fertile. God's blessings bring joy to the human heart. Today's antiphon is adapted from the parable of the sower and the seed (today's account of the Gospel).

◆ SECOND READING: Creation is likewise the focus of today's Second Reading, in particular, its struggles and labors to become a new creation in the fullness of time, when God's glory—and human glory in him, and indeed, all creation's glory in him—is fully realized (see Revelation 21:1–4). Paul leaves no doubt: all creation will be transformed at the end of time.

◆ GOSPEL: The parable of the sower and the seed is the heart of today's Gospel. The interpretation most likely stems from the time of the evangelist and the early Church. As in today's reading from Isaiah, the seed is the one who receives the Word. The interpretation clearly asserts that growth and fruitfulness are determined by the type of soil that receives the seed. The intervening verses (see Matthew 13:10–17) address the perplexing problem of why not all who heard Jesus believed in him. Matthew can only assert that so it had been foretold in the prophets (see Matthew 13:14–15). In stark contrast to those who do not or cannot hear are the disciples who do see and hear.

The Roman Missal

The Mass texts for today are found in the "Ordinary Time" section of the Proper of Time. The Gloria is sung or said today.

The Collect addresses the living of the Christian life, as it reminds us that God shows the light of truth "to those who go astray," praying that "they may return to the right path." However, we must always remember that we are all among those who could at any time go astray; hence, the prayer goes on to ask that all who "are accounted Christian" may be given "the grace to reject whatever is contrary to the name of Christ." Being converted to the Gospel is an ongoing journey for us all, one that is never complete. The Prayer over the Offerings speaks to the effects of participating in the sacred meal of the Eucharist, noting that the ultimate end of the offerings (of bread and wine) is that of being consumed "by those who believe." Thus, the prayer asks that those offerings "may bring ever greater holiness" to those who consume them. The Prayer after Communion directly picks up on this by its opening reference to the action that has just taken place: "Having consumed these gifts, we pray, O Lord. . . ." Notice how participation in Eucharistic liturgy is highlighted here by the sacred actions of offering and of eating and drinking. It is only participating in the sacred

actions that we can in any way hope that the "saving effects upon us may grow."

Any one of the eight Prefaces of the Sundays in Ordinary Time could rightly be used to equal pastoral advantage today.

Pastoral Reflection

When you are on public display, having to give and provide even when you think you have nothing left to give, what persona do people see? Play with poses and postures that force you to discover balance: tree pose in yoga, walking anything that could be a balance beam, or simply standing on tippy toe! In each moment of attempt at inner balance, consider the peace of Jesus in knowing how to meet the needs of the crowds and provide bites of wisdom. Or, if you are visual, get a spider plant and cut a piece off to create another plant and watch the roots grow. In the container of water, the grace of our soul in Jesus, watch the tender roots become the strength that lasts.

MON **14** (#389) white
Memorial of St. Kateri Tekakwitha, Virgin

The Lectionary for Mass

◆ FIRST READING: Isaiah's words echo those we heard from Amos in the thirteenth week. Israel was correctly doing all the ritual observances as prescribed by the law, but not keeping the precepts regarding wrongdoing and care for the helpless of society (widows and orphans are named here). God does not care for sacrifices when social justice is lacking. In fact, in today's reading, God has had enough (verse 11)!

◆ RESPONSORIAL PSALM 50: Our antiphon of today's psalm reminds us that God's salvation is for the upright. The verses chosen from Psalm 50 reiterate the message heard in today's First Reading: Israel's sacrifices are meaningless.

The people profess God's law with their mouths, but their actions are far from being in accord with it.

◆ GOSPEL: We are still hearing from Matthew 10, Jesus's commission of the Apostles. Today the emphasis is first of all on the opposition Jesus's disciples will encounter, even from their own family members. Yet nothing—no relationship, even that of kinship—can have priority over one's relationship with Jesus. The second part of the text focuses on the blessings to be received by the people to whom the Apostles are sent—if they are receptive to their words.

The Roman Missal

The Collect, the only prayer proper for today, can be found in the Proper of Saints at July 14. It specifically mentions both St. Kateri's Native American heritage and her innocence, praying for the unity of all believers gathered together "from every nation, tribe and tongue." The Prayer over the Offerings and the Prayer after Communion are taken from the Common of Virgins: For One Virgin. Either Preface I or Preface II of Saints would be the appropriate choice for today.

Today's Saint

Kateri Tekakwitha (1656–1680), called the "Lily of the Mohawks," is the first Native American to have been beatified and was recently canonized a saint. The daughter of a Mohawk chief and Christian Algonquin, she vowed to live as a virgin. She eventually decided to convert to Christianity after a few encounters with Jesuit missionaries. Her decision to convert was not received well within her community because Christianity was seen as the religion of the oppressors. St. Kateri was a pious woman who attended daily Mass, fasted twice a week, taught children, and cared for the sick. After she died, a number of miracles and visions were attributed to her intercession. Tekakwitha was canonized in 2012.

TUE 15 (#390) white
Memorial of St. Bonaventure, Bishop and Doctor of the Church

The Lectionary for Mass

◆ FIRST READING: We can all identify with the experience of a trembling heart in the face of a perceived danger, even if our historical situation is not an army encamped opposite us! Today the Lord calls us to courage and faith, just as he called Ahaz and the Judaites. Our faith in God is the source of our strength.

◆ RESPONSORIAL PSALM 48: Today's psalm is a hymn extolling Sion or Jerusalem, the city of the Lord, for it was there that God was believed to be present in his Temple. The third stanza is particularly apropos to the First Reading, with its threat of invading kings.

◆ GOSPEL: The signs and wonders performed by the Lord bring with them a call to those who receive and benefit from them—a call to faith and conversion. Today, Jesus takes those cities to task who were noteworthy for their lack of faith.

The Roman Missal

The Collect proper for today is found in the Proper of Saints at July 15. That Collect recognizes St. Bonaventure's "great learning" and also asks that we may "constantly imitate the ardor of his charity." Both the Prayer over the Offerings and the Prayer after Communion will have to be taken from either the Common of Pastors: For a Bishop, or from the Common of Doctors of the Church. While either Preface I or II or Saints could be used, it would also be fitting to use the Preface of Holy Pastors.

Today's Saint

St. Bonaventure (1221–1274), scholastic theologian and philosopher, was born in Italy and joined the Franciscans in 1243. He studied theology at Paris with his great contemporary, Thomas Aquinas. After teaching for a time, he was chosen Minister General of the Franciscans in 1257, at a time when the order suffered from divisions, which he was able to do much to heal. Later, he was named Cardinal Bishop of Albano. Bonaventure was declared a Doctor of the Church in 1588 by Pope Sixtus V, and is called the "Seraphic Doctor" because his love of God is so evident, even in his philosophical writings. When the Council of Lyons was called to bring the Greek and Latin churches back together, Bonaventure went at the request of Pope Gregory X, but he died before the Council's work was finished, receiving the Sacrament of the Sick from the pope himself. St. Bonaventure is shown in art dressed in a Franciscan habit and wearing a cardinal's hat.

WED 16 (#391) green
Weekday

Optional Memorial of Our Lady of Mount Carmel / white

Today's Optional Memorial

Mount Carmel is part of a mountain range in northern Israel, significant to Christians for its biblical association with the prophet Elijah (see 1 Kings 18). In the twelfth century, the Carmelites were founded at a site reputed to have been Elijah's cave. They soon built a monastery here. The Carmelites honor the Blessed Virgin Mary under the title Our Lady of Mount Carmel. The English Carmelite, St. Simon Stock, is believed to have been given the brown scapular by Our Lady, and those who wear it believe they can be sure of her help at the hour of their death.

The Lectionary for Mass

◆ FIRST READING: God's purposes are accomplished by human means—in this case, the punishment of unfaithful Israel. However, humans must remember that it is God who works through them. Their achievements are not their own accomplishments. In today's reading, God threatens punishment for Assyria for such arrogance.

◆ RESPONSORIAL PSALM 94: In the face of the destruction wrought by Assyria against Israel recounted in today's First Reading, today's psalm brings a word of hope: "the Lord will not abandon his people" (antiphon). The first stanza describes the destruction; the next could well describe Assyria's foolhardiness; and the last two, true wisdom in trusting the Lord's fidelity.

◆ GOSPEL: The wisdom of Jesus's teaching is quite different from what the world esteems as wise. Jesus calls his disciples to a simplicity that renders them open to receive what God would reveal.

THU 17 (#392) green
Weekday

The Lectionary for Mass

◆ FIRST READING: Isaiah speaks of the wisdom of God's ways, a wisdom that must be longed for and sought after. While acknowledging that God's punishment is their just due, the prophet speaks a word of hope and of new life in an age to come.

◆ RESPONSORIAL PSALM 102 is a psalm entreating God's mercy for a desolate Zion (Jerusalem). Israel knew the depth of this anguish at the time of the Babylonian Exile, when its temple was destroyed and its people were captive. The subsequent return to the land and rebuilding of the temple was yet another awe-inspiring experience of God's salvation in Israel's history.

◆ GOSPEL: The words of today's Gospel are tremendous comfort for anyone feeling burdened by his or her situation. Who does not long for the rest (Matthew 11:28)—that restoration and peace—that God alone can give!

F R I 18 (#393) green
Weekday

Optional Memorial of St. Camillus de Lellis, Priest / white

The Lectionary for Mass

◆ FIRST READING: King Hezekiah, a man who was faithful and whole-hearted in the Lord's service, falls mortally ill and prays for God's healing. His prayer is heard, his healing is accomplished through the ministry of God's prophet.

◆ CANTICLE: Today's response, a psalm-like hymn (Isaiah 38:10, 11, 12abcd, 16), is actually a continuation of the First Reading and constitutes Hezekiah's prayer of thanksgiving for his healing and deliverance from death.

◆ GOSPEL: Throughout the Gospel, the Pharisees fault Jesus on what they interpret to be his failure to observe the law. Today is one such incident. In response, Jesus chides them on their failure to recognize the deeper spirit of the law. Jesus makes the weight of his authority clear: the Son of Man is Lord of the Sabbath.

Today's Saint

Laying aside a life of violence and gambling, St. Camillus de Lellis (1550–1614) was ordained a priest and later founded the Order of Clerks Regular Ministers to the Sick (the Camillians), a religious order dedicated to the sick, especially those afflicted with the plague. Whether they were ministering in a hospital or tending to the wounded on the battlefield, the Camillians were easily identified by their black habit with a large red cross on the breast. St. Camillus implemented many innovative approaches to hospital care, including proper ventilation, suitable diets, and isolation of people with infectious diseases. He is also credited with inventing field ambulances and military hospitals. Along with St. John of God, he is patron of hospitals, nurses, and the sick.

S A T 19 (#394) green
Weekday

Optional Memorial of the Blessed Virgin Mary / white

The Lectionary for Mass

◆ FIRST READING: The Lord does not take sins of social injustice lightly. The people of Israel will be punished for their crimes against their neighbors. Their land will be desolate and ruined.

◆ RESPONSORIAL PSALM 10: Perhaps the most striking thing in today's psalm is that both the poor and the wicked are members of God's people. The text is a powerful call to examine our own dealings with others in the light of God's Word.

◆ GOSPEL: The opposition between Jesus and the Pharisees increases to the point where they plot his death. Jesus knows it and quietly withdraws, while still continuing his healing mission to those who would receive him. The text from Isaiah cited by Matthew focuses on the mission of the Servant chosen by God, endowed with his Spirit, who promotes justice and proclaims the God's Good News of salvation even to the Gentiles. Jesus is this servant par excellence.

20 (#106) green
Sixteenth Sunday in Ordinary Time

The Lectionary for Mass

◆ FIRST READING: The words of today's First Reading are actually addressed to God, and acknowledge both his providential care and his justice. Note the words that the author of Wisdom uses with reference to God's justice: "lenience" and "clemency"—as if to say, God bends over, goes the extra mile, for the sake of those he has created and enlivened with his Spirit (see Wisdom 11:24—12:1). We are to learn from God's dealings with us how we are to act toward one another (see Wisdom 12:19).

◆ RESPONSORIAL PSALM 86: The motif of God's forgiveness voiced in Wisdom continues in today's psalm. The third stanza echoes God's self-revelation to Moses on Mount Sinai (see Exodus 34:4–6). Note also the universal orientation of the second stanza: the people of all nations are God's creatures and beneficiaries of his kindness.

◆ SECOND READING: Much of Romans 8 has to do with the presence and work of God's Holy Spirit within us. Today's reading focuses on the Spirit praying within us—especially when we do not know how or what to pray. The message is a profound one: God has planted his Spirit within us that this same Spirit might lead us to him.

◆ GOSPEL: Once again, we hear a story about seeds and growth, and most importantly about the leniency of the householder in allowing both the good seed and the weeds to grow until the time of harvest. Is he lenient toward the weeds? Absolutely not. The concern rather is that the growth of the good seed not be harmed.

The longer form of today's Gospel includes an interpretation of the parable of the good seed and the wheat (verses 36–43) and two additional parables, the mustard seed and the yeast. What powerful effect the tiny mustard seed and yeast grain have—so it is with the Kingdom of Heaven. What powerful effect the seed of the Word, the parable, can have in our lives if we are receptive to its message.

The Roman Missal

The Mass texts for today are located in the "Ordinary Time" section of the Proper of Time. The Gloria is sung or said today.

The Collect, in asking God to "mercifully increase the gifts of your grace," can be seen as setting a tone for hearing the parables in today's Gospel. The Prayer over the Offerings reminds us that Christ's "one perfect sacrifice" completed all prior offerings of the law and asks that our sacrifice, like Abel's, will be made holy; the communal aspect of our worship is highlighted as the prayer gives the reason we ask the sacrifice to be made holy: "so that what each has offered to the honor of your majesty / may benefit the salvation of all." The Prayer after Communion is a prayer used frequently in Easter Time; it asks that we "pass from former ways to newness of life" as a result of our having been "imbued with heavenly mysteries." The passage of the Paschal Mystery focused on so intently during Easter Time is, of course, at the heart of every celebration of the Eucharist.

Any one of the eight Prefaces of the Sundays in Ordinary Time may be selected for today. Preface VIII, with its explicit mention of the Holy Spirit, could provide an echo of today's Second Reading. Using Eucharistic Prayer I, the Roman Canon, with its mention of "Abel the just" could provide a connection with today's Prayer over the Offerings.

Pastoral Reflection

The balance of last week is prime for playing the game of Jenga this week. With steady hands, you choose a piece because you know it can be easily pulled. As adults, our choices require steady balance and knowledge so as to remain rooted as wheat and not strangled by the weeds in life. Our choices, our seeds in life, need to be fine-tuned with God's guidance and our willingness. With conscious hands pulling out the block of wood in Jenga, may your life be held in tender care as the toppling that occurs is God's to own and judge the misguided.

MON 21 (#395) green
Weekday

Optional Memorial of St. Lawrence of Brindisi, Priest and Doctor of the Church / white

The Lectionary for Mass

◆ FIRST READING: God "enters into trial" (Micah 6:2) with his people, bringing serious charges against them. Their infidelities are numerous, despite all the Lord has done for them. They have failed to keep the covenant demands of righteousness and goodness toward others, and humility before God.

◆ RESPONSORIAL PSALM 50 reiterates God's charges against the people of Israel: they hate discipline, the teaching of the law (and they fail to follow its lead). It is the upright who will know God's salvation.

◆ GOSPEL: The theme of judgment continues. The scribes and Pharisees will be condemned. But the entire generation of Jesus's contemporaries—particularly those who witnessed his works yet failed to believe—will also be condemned.

Today's Saint

St. Lawrence of Brindisi (1559–1619), a Capuchin Franciscan in Italy, was an astute Scripture scholar with a comprehensive understanding of ancient and modern languages. His widespread knowledge of Scripture enabled him to be an effective and powerful preacher. He served the Capuchins in several leadership capacities, ranging from provincial of Tuscany and Venice to Minister General (superior) of the entire order. He was declared a Doctor of the Church due to his extensive writings, which are primarily sermons and commentaries.

His writings bear a resemblance to the humanistic approach and optimistic view of humanity, espoused by St. Francis de Sales.

TUE 22 (#396; Gospel #603) white
Memorial of St. Mary Magdalene

◆ FIRST READING: The first words of today's reading are a prayer that God will once again shepherd his repentant people. What beautiful words of comfort in the second part: God is a forgiving God. What a powerful image: He casts all of our sins into the sea; they are no longer remembered.

◆ RESPONSORIAL PSALM 85: With sentiments similar to the thoughts of today's First Reading, the psalmist prays for God's mercy and love, knowing that God is indeed a forgiving God.

◆ GOSPEL: We hear of the appearance of the Risen Christ to Mary Magdalene. She recognizes him only when he calls her by name. The Risen Christ commissions her to be the "apostle to the Apostles."

The Roman Missal

All the orations are proper for today, and can be found in the Proper of Saints at July 22. The Collect hails Mary Magdalene as the one "entrusted . . . before all others / with announcing the great joy of the Resurrection." Therefore, we pray that we may be the same kind of witness, namely, "that through her intercession and example / we may proclaim the living Christ." The Prayer over the Offerings introduces the idea of charity; it points out how the "homage of charity" offered by St. Mary Magdalene "was graciously accepted" by Jesus. We can be reminded how our participation in the Eucharist is supposed to bring about an increase of charity in us. Either Preface I or Preface II of Saints would be the appropriate choice for today. The Prayer after Communion appropriately reminds us of the "persevering love / with which Saint Mary Magdalene / clung resolutely to Christ her Master;" sacramental Communion, itself a clinging to Christ, should also increase in us the love for Christ by which we will cling resolutely to him.

In view of the Collect's recognition of St. Mary Magdalene's role in announcing the Resurrection, it would seem that using the dismissal "Go and announce the Gospel of the Lord" would be appropriate today.

Today's Saint

Mary Magdalene is one of the most misunderstood women of the Bible. She was conflated with several other figures by medieval commentators, including Mary of Bethany (sister of Martha and Lazarus) and the sinful woman who washes Jesus's feet with her hair in Luke's account. The confusion about who she is still exists in the Church's calendar: exactly one week from today we will celebrate St. Martha, sister of a different Mary. What we do know about Mary Magdalene is that Jesus healed her, and that she was the first witness of his Resurrection.

W E D 23 (#397) green **Weekday**

Optional Memorial of St. Bridget, Religious / white

The Lectionary for Mass

◆ FIRST READING: We hear the story of God's call of the prophet Jeremiah. As is common in biblical call stories, the persons called usually set forth objections and reasons why they are unable to fulfill God's call. Jeremiah's objections were his youth and not knowing how to speak. And as is also typical of call stories, there is God's assurance that the person can do the job—and why. Most importantly, the person called will never be alone: God is with them.

◆ RESPONSORIAL PSALM 71 echoes the story of Jeremiah's call (third and fourth stanzas) and prophetic mission—a mission that entailed much suffering, but also the experience of God's deliverance (the first two stanzas). Throughout his life, he relied on the Lord as his teacher and source of strength.

◆ GOSPEL: We hear the first part of the parable of the sower and the seed. The crowds who listened to Jesus on the shore of the Sea of Galilee had only to turn around and see the fields on the hillside for a living illustration of the parable he told. Perhaps the sight of this prompted the imagery he used! What kind of soil are our hearts for the seed of God's Word?

Today's Saint

St. Bridget of Sweden (1303–1373), a wife and mother of eight children, joined a Cistercian monastery after the death of her husband. After a series of visions, she founded the Bridgittine Order—a double monastery for men and women living in separate enclosures dedicated to learning. In another vision, she was instructed to heal the schism of the Avignon papacy by warning Pope Clement VI to return to Rome from Avignon. She was not canonized for her many and varied revelations, but heroic virtue. It is interesting that she shares a feast day with St. John Cassian who founded two monasteries (one for monks and the other for nuns) and was also canonized for a virtuous life beyond reproach.

T H U 24 (#398) green **Weekday**

Optional Memorial of St. Sharbel Makhluf, Priest / white

The Lectionary for Mass

◆ FIRST READING: Today's text touches not only on the mission of the prophet Jeremiah (the first line), but evokes an image we saw in the texts from Hosea: that of Israel as the unfaithful covenant bride of the Lord. The last stanza describes Israel's idolatrous infidelity in terms of forsaking God, the source of living waters, attempting to be sustained on their own.

◆ RESPONSORIAL PSALM 36: Images of God's life-giving waters abound in today's Psalm. The antiphon bids us to remember that God is the source of life.

◆ GOSPEL: Today's Gospel is perplexing. Why is Jesus's teaching so enigmatic? Matthew sees the crowd's failure to understand the fulfillment of the words of the prophet Isaiah: Israel is deaf and blind in its own obstinacy. The disciples are blessed because they see and hear and believe.

Today's Saint

St. Sharbel Makhluf Joseph Zaroun was a Maronite Catholic, born and raised in a small Lebanese mountain village. As a child he led a pious life of prayer and solitude. His favorite book was *The Imitation of Christ* by Thomas à Kempis. When he entered the Monastery of St. Maron at 23, he took the name Sharbel after the second-century martyr of the Antioch Church. He lived an austere life as a hermit, eating only one meal of vegetables each day, sleeping on a pillow of wood, and a duvet filled with dead leaves. His time was devoted to prayer, contemplation, and manual labor. Many came to him for counsel and blessing. He died in 1898 on Christmas Eve.

FRI 25 (#605) red
Feast of St. James, Apostle

The Lectionary for Mass

◆ FIRST READING: Paul's words are aptly chosen for this Apostle who was martyred because of his faith in the Lord Jesus and his proclamation of the Gospel (see Acts of the Apostles 12:2). James, like the other Apostles, was, like each of us, a fragile earthen vessel. Yet, he was sustained by his conviction that he, too, would be raised with Jesus.

◆ RESPONSORIAL PSALM 126 celebrates the deliverance of the Israelites from their exile in Babylon. Notice the marked contrast between the weeping of their exile and the rejoicing of their return to their homeland.

◆ GOSPEL: What mother cannot identify with the mother of James and John, wanting the ultimate best for her son! Jesus's response to her leaves no doubt: glory comes only after drinking the cup of suffering and self-emptying service.

The Roman Missal

The texts for this Mass, all proper for the feast, are located in the Proper of Saints section of the Missal at July 25. The Gloria is sung or said today, since it is a Feast.

The Collect acknowledges the martyrdom of St. James as it notes

that God "consecrated the first fruits of your Apostles / by the blood if Saint James." The Prayer over the Offerings continues this recognition by referring to the saint as "the first among the Apostles / to drink of Christ's chalice of suffering." As the prayer goes on to ask that "we may offer a sacrifice pleasing to you," we cannot help but be challenged to know that such sacrifice involves our willingness to participate in that same chalice of suffering. The Prayer after Communion proclaims that we receive the holy gift of the Eucharist with joy on this feast day.

The Preface, proper for today, is one of the two Prefaces of the Apostles. Also, the Solemn Blessing formula titled "The Apostles," number 17 of the "Blessings at the End of Mass and Prayers over the People," may be used as the final blessing at the end of Mass today.

Today's Saint

The St. James we honor today is the brother of the Apostle John, one of the "sons of thunder" (Mark 3:17) who were privileged witnesses of some of Jesus's greatest signs: the raising of the daughter of Jairus from the dead, the Transfiguration, and the agony in the garden. James was the first Apostle to suffer martyrdom, slain by Herod's orders as described in Acts of the Apostles. According to legend, his remains were carried away by his friends in a rudderless boat, which drifted all the way to Spain. Many centuries later his remains were discovered, and a great cathedral was built over the spot where they were found (*Santiago de Compostela*, which became one of the most popular pilgrimage destinations of the Middle Ages). To this day, hundreds of thousands of pilgrims make their way to that remote corner of Spain to venerate the relics of St. James.

SAT 26 (#400) white
Memorial of SS. Joachim and Anne, Parents of the Blessed Virgin Mary

The Lectionary for Mass

◆ FIRST READING: The word of the Lord spoken by Jeremiah is a stark confrontation of the people of Judah. The presence of God's Temple in Jerusalem had become the basis of presumption and false security. Yes, God dwelt with his people, but this did not mean they could do as they pleased, ignoring the demands of the law, or that they would escape punishment. Note the social nature of the crimes listed and the ever-present sin of idolatry, a result of being incorporated into the culture of their neighbors.

◆ RESPONSORIAL PSALM 84: The mention of God's Temple in today's First Reading prompts the choice of a psalm extolling it as the dwelling of the Lord of Hosts and the desire of God's people.

◆ GOSPEL: Today's parable bids us to take a good look at the field of our lives. Do we know what has been sown there and by whom? Are there good seeds bringing forth grain that nourishes, or are there weeds in our hearts?

The Roman Missal

All the orations are proper for today, and are to be found in the Proper of Saints at July 26. The Collect asks SS. Joachim and Anne to pray that we may attain salvation. The Prayer over the Offerings gives an implicit acknowledgment of the two saints' role in salvation history by asking that "we may merit a share in the same blessing / which you promised to Abraham and his descendants." Either Preface I or Preface II of Saints would be the proper choice for today, with perhaps Preface I being the better choice of the two. The Prayer after Communion reminds us of the divine exchange as it notes that God's Only Begotten Son was "born from among humanity" so that "humanity might be born again from you." The prayer goes on to ask that those who have been fed with the heavenly Bread of the Eucharist might be sanctified "by the spirit of adoption." Thus, the role of SS. Joachim and Anne as parents to the Blessed Virgin Mary continues to be a theme underlying the texts for today.

Today's Saints

The information we have regarding SS. Joachim and Anne, the parents of the Blessed Virgin Mary, comes from an unreliable source known as the Gospel of James. They are portrayed as an old and barren couple who long to bring life into the world. Through an angelic messenger they are told they will bear a child—not just any child, but one who will be revered for all time. A following developed around both of them, but it seems that St. Anne had a stronger following, which continues to flourish, especially in Canada. She is the patron of childless women, expectant mothers, and women in labor.

(#109)   green

27 Seventeenth Sunday in Ordinary Time

The Lectionary for Mass

◆ FIRST READING: We hear the beautiful and humble prayer of King Solomon, son of David, at the be-ginning of his reign. Solomon recognized the limitations his youth and inexperience put on his ability to rule Israel. Accordingly, when God offered him anything for which he might ask, Solomon asked only for wisdom, "an understanding heart"—that he might serve God's people. Solomon's prayer was answered and Solomon's wisdom was without parallel.

◆ RESPONSORIAL PSALM 119 acclaims the wisdom of God as manifest in the law or Word of God and in which the psalmist delights. With but one or two exceptions, each of the psalm's 176 verses makes reference to the law (word, command, etc.). As in today's account of the Gospel, the psalmist finds God's Word, God's law, more precious than earthly riches.

◆ SECOND READING: Paul's words call believers to deep trust in the providential care of God who can and does bring good out of all things for those who love him. The wisdom of God is often enigmatic to human eyes. God's love for us is so great that we are destined to be conformed to Jesus—that is, formed with or like him, called through death (and countless dyings in life) to divine glory. Jesus Christ, risen from the dead, is the firstborn. We are born into this new life after him.

◆ GOSPEL: The shorter form of today's Gospel consists of two parables focusing on the priceless value of the Kingdom of Heaven—all earthly riches are deemed as nothing in comparison! So great is its value, that it is well worth relinquishing all else in order to possess it. Have we? The longer form of the Gospel consists of a third parable pointing to the judgment of the end time and Jesus's question to his disciples about the parables he has taught them. "Do you understand all these things?" he asks. And what would we answer?

The Roman Missal

The Gloria is sung or said today.

The Collect speaks eloquently of God as the firm foundation of our lives; with that foundation, we can "use the good things that pass / in such a way as to hold fast even now / to those that ever endure." The sense of the imminent-yet-not-fully-realized Kingdom of God that underlies this Collect connects well with the Gospel parables today. The Prayer over the Offerings continues to acknowledge the need to progress in the life of the kingdom, which is both here and yet-to-come: we bring our offerings from the abundance of God's gifts (the "already" of the kingdom), and we pray that "these most sacred mysteries may sanctify our present way of life / and lead us to eternal gladness" (growing in grace toward a future fulfillment). The Prayer after Communion highlights the nature of every Eucharistic celebration as anamnesis—the "perpetual memorial of the Passion of your Son."

Any one of the eight Prefaces of the Sundays in Ordinary Time may be selected for today, although perhaps Preface V, with its description of God's sovereignty over creation, or Preface VI, with its reference to how we both "experience the daily effects" of God's care (the kingdom present in our midst) and also "possess the pledge of life eternal" (a recognition of something yet to come), would be apt choices in particular.

The dismissal formula "Go in peace, glorifying the Lord by your life" would reinforce the need for us to live life in a way whereby we grow in the ways of the kingdom.

Pastoral Reflection

Sort through the treasures and trash of your home and recreate the space to allow peaceful space to coexist in your living. Day by day find a space to clear. In each space you choose to clean, look at each item and determine if is necessary or it if is time to give something away. The act is cleansing, meaningful in light of the Gospel, and beneficial to others. The ultimate goal of each Gospel message recently is that our lives are meant to be part of the Kingdom of Heaven which will be sorted through at the end of times.

MON 28 (#401) green
Weekday

The Lectionary for Mass

◆ FIRST READING: How close to himself God had ordained his people to be: they were created to cling to him. However, in their infidelity, they were not what they were created to be. So attests the "parable in sign" performed by the prophet Jeremiah.

◆ CANTICLE: Today's canticle comes from the Book of Deuteronomy, presented as Moses' farewell speech to the children of Israel. His words are an accusation of infidelity. How horrible: to forget the God who gave them birth. God's response will be to forget them, to leave them to themselves. Throughout the book of Deuteronomy, God's Word is clear: obedience leads to blessing; disobedience, to curse.

◆ GOSPEL: Today's Gospel relates two parables, both focusing on very tiny things that have tremendous power for life-giving growth in the right environment (good soil, warm water). So it is with the Kingdom of Heaven (God) in the lives of those who hear and receive God's Word.

TUE 29 (#402; Gospel #607) white
Memorial of St. Martha

The Lectionary for Mass

◆ FIRST READING: The prophet weeps at the sight of Jerusalem and the Temple destroyed at the hands of the Babylonians. The prophets interpreted this historical event as punishment for Israel's sins of infidelity.

◆ RESPONSORIAL PSALM 79 prays for God's mercy and compassion. The appeal is not so much for oneself, though this is the thought of the first stanza, but rather for the glory of God's name (antiphon and second stanza). The psalmist promises praise and thanksgiving through all generations if God heeds his prayer.

◆ GOSPEL: Last Saturday, we heard the parable that is interpreted in today's Gospel. The harvest is the end time judgment, with its subsequent punishment of consuming fire or its heavenly reward of the shining fire of transformation and glorification—as bright as the sun.

The Roman Missal

The proper prayers for this memorial are at July 29 in the Proper of Saints. The Collect gives voice to Martha's hospitality to the Lord and asks that we too may serve Christ faithfully by serving our brothers and sisters. The Prayer over the Offerings reminds us that the offering we make at the Eucharist, and consequently the offering of our lives, must always be an offering of love; it is only that kind of offering that finds favor with God. Either Preface I or Preface II of Saints would be the most appropriate choice for the Preface today. The Prayer after Communion asks that as a result of our reception of Holy Communion we may, like St. Martha, be completely focused on serving the Lord and on growing in sincere love.

Today's Saint

Martha was the sister of Lazarus and Mary, friends of Jesus. She appears to have been a practical-minded woman, for she seems to have organized the dinner in Luke 10:38–42, and she protests when Jesus commands that the stone be rolled from the entrance to her brother's tomb after he'd been dead for three days. At the same time,

however, she is one of the few in the Gospel to profess her faith in Jesus as the Messiah: "Yes, Lord. I have come to believe that you are the Messiah, the Son of God, the one who is coming into the world" (John 11:27). *The Golden Legend* records the tradition that Martha, with her sister, Mary, and brother, Lazarus, fled Judea after the death of Jesus and landed at Marseilles. Martha is supposed to have traveled to Avignon, where she converted many to Christianity. St. Martha is shown in art bearing the tools of a housekeeper—keys or a broom— and is a patron saint of domestic servants, homemakers, cooks, and single laywomen.

WED 30 (#403) green
Weekday

Optional Memorial of St. Peter Chrysologus, Bishop and Doctor of the Church / white

The Lectionary for Mass

◆ FIRST READING: Jeremiah did not find his prophetic vocation an easy path. His writings attest to times of desolation and discouragement such as in today's reading. Jeremiah knows the high of the joy and happiness that God's word brings, as well as the weight of being rejected by those to whom he is sent. Jeremiah himself has need of repentance. God promises Jeremiah deliverance from his oppressors.

◆ RESPONSORIAL PSALM 59: Today's psalm is a prayer for deliverance, describing in detail the psalmist's affliction. Notice the repetition of words related to strength. The psalmist is confident of God's help and sings his praise.

◆ GOSPEL: Two images convey the sense of the immense value of the Kingdom of Heaven (God). Having discovered it, the seeker is willing to relinquish all other possessions in order to obtain it.

Today's Saint

St. Peter Chrysologus (380–450), born in Imola in northeastern Italy, was appointed Archbishop of Ravenna by Emperor Valentinian III. His orthodox approach to the Incarnation and other Church doctrines earned him the support of Pope St. Leo the Great. He was given the title "Chrysologus," meaning "Golden-worded," due to his flair for preaching. This title may have been given to him so that the Western Church would have a preacher equal to St. John "Chrysostom" ("Golden-tongued") of the East. Most of his writings did not survive, but the Church is graced with a number of his sermons. The remaining sermons are written with pastoral sensitivity and optimism, while challenging people to conversion and repentance.

(#404) white
T H U 31
Memorial of St. Ignatius of Loyola, Priest

The Lectionary for Mass

◆ FIRST READING: The parable of God the potter evokes the creation narrative in Genesis 2, where God creates the human creature out of the clay of the earth. Jeremiah warns Israel that God, like the potter, can destroy the vessel and remake it until it is shaped as he intends. The message to Israel is to reform, so that it can become what it was created to be.

◆ RESPONSORIAL PSALM 146: The second stanza of today's Responsorial Psalm picks up on the theme of the human creature as made from the clay of the earth, and it is to this dust that he or she will return at death. The psalm invites us to seek help from the Lord and to put our trust in him.

◆ GOSPEL: Jesus uses the things of everyday life to teach about the kingdom of God. Today, it is the fisherman's net, something used every day by many of Jesus's listeners. Many would have sat on the shore separating their fish—and herein lies the Gospel's important point: the good and the bad will be separated and justly rewarded or punished at the end of time.

The Roman Missal

All the orations, located at July 31 in the Proper of Saints, are proper for this obligatory memorial. The Collect reflects aspects often associated with Ignatian spirituality with its references to the greater glory of God's name and fighting the good fight on earth. The Prayer over the Offerings describes the sacred mysteries we are celebrating as "the fount of all holiness." In view of this, perhaps it would be good to be sure to use Eucharistic Prayer II today, with its mention of the Lord as "the fount of all holiness." Preface I or Preface II of Saints or the Preface of Holy Pastors are all appropriate choices for today's Preface. The Prayer after Communion asks that the "sacrifice of praise" we have offered here on earth may bring us to the joys of eternity where we will "exalt your majesty without end."

Today's Saint

St. Ignatius was the founder and first Father General of the Society of Jesus, or Jesuits, and author of the *Spiritual Exercises.* Born in the Basque region of Spain, he joined the army and was severely wounded in battle. While recovering, he read a life of Christ and lives of the saints, and decided to emulate them. He laid his military equipment before a statue of Mary at the Benedictine abbey of Montserrat, and spent several months in a cave near Manresa. After making a pilgrimage to the Holy Land, he enrolled at the University of Paris, and he gathered six companions who would become the first Jesuits.

August
Month of the Immaculate Heart of Mary

(#405) white
F R I 1
Memorial of St. Alphonsus Liguori, Bishop and Doctor of the Church

The Lectionary for Mass

◆ FIRST READING: Jeremiah is commissioned/sent by the Lord to speak to the people who come to worship in the Temple. They are evil and need to repent. They need to listen to the word of the Lord's messenger. If they refuse, the threatened punishment is the destruction of the Temple and of Jerusalem. On hearing this, the priests and the prophets, the official Temple personnel, laid hold of Jeremiah and sentenced him to death.

◆ RESPONSORIAL PSALM 69: Rejected by his own people, threatened with death, Jeremiah could only turn to the Lord for help and deliverance. The stanzas of today's psalm serve as an apt description of his plight. Jeremiah was a man consumed with zeal for God and his Temple.

◆ GOSPEL: Jesus, the prophet, is rejected by his own people in his hometown. In effect, they say: "Who does he think he is!" (author's paraphrasing). Not only do Jesus's people reject him, they are offended by him. Did his words touch too close to home? How hard it is to recognize and to receive what those closest to us may have to give us.

The Roman Missal

The proper orations for this obligatory memorial are taken from August 1. The Collect points to St. Alphonsus as an example of virtue and it notes his "zeal for souls." The Prayer over the Offerings makes reference to the Holy Spirit, asking God "to enkindle our hearts / with the celestial fire your Spirit," so that we might make a holy offering of ourselves just as St. Alphonsus offered himself. Preface I or Preface II of Saints, or the Common of Holy Pastors, are the choices from which to select the Preface for today. Pointing to the stewardship and preaching of St. Alphonsus, the Prayer after Communion asks that we too, in receiving "this great mystery," may praise God without end.

Today's Saint

Following a successful career as a lawyer, St. Alphonsus Ligouri (1696–1787) lost a legal case that he believed to be a sign from God that he should change his ways and study for the priesthood. At the suggestion of a bishop friend, he founded the Congregation of the Most Holy Redeemer, also known as the Redemptorists, a community of priests dedicated to preaching, hearing confessions, and administering the sacraments. One of his most important contributions to the Church is his prolific writing in the area of moral theology. Also included among his writings are many devotional works on Mary and the saints. He influenced the Church not only through his writings, but also through his leadership as a bishop. Due to his many accomplishments, he was declared a Doctor of the Church and is recognized as one of the greatest moral theologians in Church history.

S A T 2 (#406) green **Weekday**

Optional Memorials of St. Eusebius of Vercelli, Bishop / white; St. Peter Julian Eymard, Priest / white; Blessed Virgin Mary / white

The Lectionary for Mass

◆ First Reading: Jeremiah's words reiterate to the people that he was sent by God and spoke the message with which he was entrusted. If it is not received, if he is rejected and killed, it is they—priests, prophets, and people—who will be guilty of an innocent man's death. In a moment of grace, the people accept Jeremiah's message and mission. He is protected by the son of one of their leaders and preserved from death.

◆ Responsorial Psalm 69: Both the psalm and antiphon are the same as yesterday. We can hear in its words Jeremiah's lament, describing his affliction. We hear as well, in the last stanza, the jubilant cry of praise and thanksgiving in the face of deliverance.

◆ Gospel: The question of Jesus's identity leads to the telling of the story of the death of John the Baptist. Today's Gospel presents a challenge to us: Are we ever like Herod, compromising what we know to be the truth for the sake of our own reputation and esteem?

Today's Saints

St. Eusebius (283–371), the first bishop of Vercelli, spent much of his life trying to settle conflicts between Catholics and Arians. (Arians denied the divinity of Christ.) Because St. Eusebius actively supported the views of the Catholic Church, as expressed in the Nicene Creed, he was severely persecuted by Arian proponents, by means of starvation and exile. It is believed that he contributed to the composition of the Athanasian Creed.

St. Peter Julian Eymard (1811–1868) changed immensely after he had an overwhelming experience of God's love while carrying the Blessed Sacrament during the *Corpus Christi* procession. He decided to leave the Marist order to found the Blessed Sacrament Fathers, a community dedicated to perpetual adoration of the Eucharist. Later, he established a foundation of sisters, known as the Sisters of the Blessed

Sacrament, and a confraternity of laypeople. He believed adoration of the Eucharist was not an end in itself, but a means to evangelization and service.

3 (#112) green **Eighteenth Sunday in Ordinary Time**

The Lectionary for Mass

◆ First Reading: Isaiah's words stem from the time of the Babylonian Exile, a time of distress and anguish for God's people, having lost Temple and homeland. The prophets saw this as punishment for the people's infidelity. Yet it is here in an alien land that God offers such an insistent invitation: "come," "listen," and "heed." In other words, repent and return to the Lord. Drink abundantly of his wisdom and teaching, for in it, you will find life. God will renew his covenant and the promises he made to David their king. All was not lost.

◆ Responsorial Psalm 145: Today's antiphon is adapted from verse 16 of our psalm, a fitting adaptation given the Lord's feeding of his people in both the First Reading and the Gospel. Once again, we find the words of God's self-revelation to Moses in the first stanza of the psalm (see Exodus 34:6). God's provision of food for all creatures is the focus of the second stanza. The third emphasizes God's nearness to those who call upon ("come to"—as in our First Reading) him.

◆ SECOND READING: Paul is only all too familiar with opposition and suffering in his life, especially from those who did not receive his message about Jesus Christ. No matter how great the difficulties experienced, no matter how overwhelming the suffering, Paul is convinced that the love of Christ Jesus the Lord remains with us. Nothing, absolutely nothing, can separate us from that love.

◆ GOSPEL: Jesus's compassion for the hungry and sick crowd mirrors that of God for his people as heard in today's First Reading. With the meager resources at hand, five loaves and two fish, and prayer, Jesus provided food in abundance for the multitude. Matthew's description of the event echoes his account of the Last Supper and our own celebration of the Eucharist.

The Roman Missal

The Mass texts for today are found in the "Ordinary Time" section of the Proper of Time. The Gloria is sung or said today.

The Collect points to how God constantly gives life to his creation: he creates, and he also restores what he creates and keeps safe what he restores. This is the reason we glory in God as our "Creator and guide." The Prayer over the Offerings highlights the theme of offering, which is central to every celebration of the Eucharist, as it petitions and we may be made an eternal offering to God. The Prayer after Communion returns to the theme of protection heard in the Collect, asking that those renewed with the heavenly gifts of the Eucharist might be worthy of eternal redemption.

Of the eight Prefaces of the Sundays in Ordinary Time that could be used today, Preface III echoes the idea of God's protection and restoration as it speaks of God coming to our aid with his divinity. Preface VI speaks about the daily effects of God's care, which perhaps could connect with the feeding miracle in today's Gospel selection from St. Matthew.

Pastoral Reflection

With a new clean home, create your place of prayer—a space you retreat to solely to be nourished in moments of stress, despair, and also a place to give praise. If you cannot create this place indoors, know where to find this outdoors. Once you are fed internally, you can then find ways to live out the multiplication of the loaves and fishes, multiplying the peace of your life as gift to others.

M O N **4** (#407; Gospel #408)   white
Memorial of St. John Vianney, Priest

The Lectionary for Mass

◆ FIRST READING: Jeremiah challenged Hananiah's prophecy of an expeditious end to the Babylonian captivity and denounced him for raising false hopes among the people. Jeremiah, in fact, foretold that the yoke of oppression would increase. As believers we must refrain from offering simplistic solutions and pious aphorisms to people in their need. We are to offer Christ alone as hope for the world.

◆ RESPONSORIAL PSALM 119 emphasizes how the Church celebrates her desire to remain faithful to the Lord in all things. The Church prays that God will continue to maintain her in truth.

◆ GOSPEL: There are several foci in today's Gospel: the motif of Jesus seeking solitude for prayer; the storm at sea; Jesus walking on the sea and his self-revelation: "It is I" (Matthew 14:27), (the *ego eimi* of the Greek translation of Exodus 3:14); Peter's walking on water when he keeps his eyes on Jesus; his faltering when he focuses on the storm instead; his confession that Jesus is the Son of God. The question of who Jesus is cannot be separated from who he is—for us.

The Roman Missal

The Collect for today, located in the Proper of Saints at August 4, rightly describes the "pastoral zeal" of the saint known as the Curé of Ars and petitions "that through his intercession and example / we may in charity win brothers and sisters for Christ." The Prayer over the Offerings and the Prayer after Communion will have to be taken from the Common of Pastors: For One Pastor. While there is nothing to prevent use of Preface I or II of Saints, the Preface of Holy Pastors, in view of St. John Vianney's significance as a parish priest, would seem to be the most appropriate choice this day.

Today's Saint

St. John Mary Vianney (1786–1859) is the patron of parish priests. Although he was not academically astute and had to receive his training privately, he was ordained a priest due to his virtue. He was stationed in a small village, Ars-en-Dombes, in France, where he became a noted catechist, confessor, and spiritual director. Soon, he gained a reputation for working miracles, such as multiplying loaves and physical healings. Consequently, the small village became a place of pilgrimage, attracting over 300 visitors a day, from 1830 to1845, to see the "Cure d'Ars." Special train schedules as well as a special booking office had to be established in the nearby city of Lyons to accommodate the steady stream of visitors.

T U E 5 (#408) green
Weekday

Optional Memorial of the Dedication of the Basilica of St. Mary Major / white

Today's Optional Memorial

Today we celebrate one of Rome's most prestigious churches, the Basilica of St. Mary Major, formerly called Our Lady of the Snows. Among its most prized possessions are relics of the manger in Bethlehem. St. Mary Major sits on the horizon of the seven hills that form Rome, along with three other papal basilicas: St. John Lateran, St. Peter, and St. Paul Outside the Walls.

The Lectionary for Mass

◆ First Reading: To punish Israel for her great guilt, God afflicts her with a painful and incurable wound. All is not lost. In his great mercy, God will restore and rebuild Israel. (Note the use of the prefix "re".) Once again, Israel will have its own king. Once again, Israel shall be God's people.

◆ Responsorial Psalm 102: The theme of restoring and rebuilding is continued in today's psalm. Zion (Jerusalem) is rebuilt when God delivers his people once again.

◆ Gospel: There are several foci in today's Gospel: the motif of Jesus seeking solitude for prayer; the storm at sea; Jesus walking on the sea and his self-revelation: "It is I" (Matthew 14:27), (the *ego eimi* of the Greek translation of Exodus 3:14); Peter's walking on water when he keeps his eyes on Jesus; his faltering when he focuses on the storm instead; his confession that Jesus is the Son of God. The question of who Jesus is cannot be separated from who he is—for us.

W E D 6 (#614) white
Feast of the Transfiguration of the Lord

About this Feast

The Feast of the Transfiguration of the Lord reminds us about the depth of mystery that surrounded Jesus Christ—mystery in the sense that we can never exhaust who he really is or categorize him in any way. Fully human, he may indeed have needed a tent or a place to camp on the mountain, like Peter asked. But just when the Apostles may have been getting really comfortable with their understanding of Jesus as friend and teacher, they catch a glimpse of his heavenly glory, challenging them to remain open to Christ communicating to them who he is as Son of God. We have moments like the Apostles each time we encounter and grapple with a new and challenging image of God in the Scriptures. Remaining humble and open to the revelatory action of God's Word and Spirit is a way to enter ever more deeply into the mystery of who God is for us in Jesus Christ.

The Lectionary for Mass

◆ First Reading: In his night vision, Daniel sees God, the Ancient of Days, enthroned in the heavens. (Notice how Daniel's description has been picked up by artists throughout the centuries!) A second person is introduced, "One like a Son of Man"—like a human being—who is presented before God, honored, glorified, and established as king of all nations. In the Gospel accounts, "Son of Man" is a title used with reference to Jesus.

◆ Responsorial Psalm 97: This psalm celebrating God's kingship is well-chosen in light of Daniel's reference to the "One like a Son of Man" receiving heavenly kingship.

◆ Second Reading: Peter attests to his mountaintop experience when he glimpsed the glory of the transfigured Jesus and heard the Father's voice affirming him. This experience became a guiding light for Peter in all the ways of his discipleship, as he hoped it would be for the community to whom he writes.

◆ Gospel: Jesus takes the chosen three, that inner circle of his disciples, to a mountaintop. There, he is transfigured, literally "changed in form" before them. The description of his clothes evokes those of the Ancient of Days. In other words, the clothing befits the heavenly realm. Moses (the Law) and Elijah (the Prophets), both of whom had significant mountaintop experiences, converse with him. This will be a significant mountaintop experience for the disciples as well, as they hear the voice of the Father instructing them to "listen" to Jesus and to his teaching. Jesus is the "beloved Son" of the Father as well as the "Son of Man," a phrase used with reference to human beings (as in Psalm 8:5) as well as to the exalted figure of the end-time (so Daniel). The evangelists situate the Transfiguration between predictions of Jesus's Passion (note the reference to "rising from the dead"). The glory that God gives is attained only through the way of the Cross.

The Roman Missal

The orations for this feast are all proper for the feast today, and are located in the Proper of Saints section of the Missal at August 6. The Gloria is sung or said today, since it is a feast. (Since the feast is not on a Sunday this year, however, the Creed is not said.)

The Collect places the meaning of the Transfiguration not as some event that took place in the past, but rather as something that serves as an invitation to explore ever more deeply the reality of who God reveals himself to be. Thus, in the

AUGUST

Collect we are enjoined to listen to the voice of God's beloved Son, that is, now, in the present, so that "we may merit to become co-heirs with him." We must recall that all liturgical celebration is about our entrance at the present into the mystery that is being made manifest and present through the ritual actions and the anamnesis of the Church. The Prayer over the Offerings employs imagery of the Transfiguration by referring to the "radiant splendor" of the Son. The Prayer after Communion, which also uses the imagery of radiance and splendor, picks up the theme of transformation: we pray that the "heavenly nourishment" we have received will "transform us into the likeness of your Son. We are reminded that our reception of Holy Communion is never simply a passive reception, but it is always to be an active participation in being transformed into what we receive.

The Preface, "The Mystery of the Transfiguration," is proper for today, and is given in the pages along with the other Mass texts. Music is provided, so perhaps today would be a good day to sing the introductory dialogue and the Preface. This Preface reminds us, as with so many of the mysteries of our faith, that the reality we celebrate about Christ is a reality we are called to also experience—we are all called to be transfigured with Christ, as his Transfiguration shows us "how in the Body of the whole Church is to be fulfilled / what so wonderfully shone forth first in its Head."

Pastoral Reflection

Think about a good yet intense dream you have dreamt that felt so real, every cell and your muscles reacted to the feelings and emotions in the dream. Tap into that imagined power of feeling so boldly alive and then apply that feeling and God's voice to an area where you feel stuck. Listen as God says to you, "rise and

be not afraid." Allow your body to feel the mountaintop moment of joy so as to lift you from the moments in the valley. God empowers you daily to live your life not hidden, but risen in glory through God's saving love.

THU 7 (#410) green
Weekday

Optional Memorials of St. Sixtus II, Pope, and Companions, Martyrs / red; St. Cajetan, Priest / white

The Lectionary for Mass

◆ FIRST READING: God's Word promises not only restoration and rebuilding, it speaks of something new. There will be a New Covenant, written not on tablets of stone but upon the human heart. It will be a covenant marked by forgiveness and the experience of God's intimate love.

◆ RESPONSORIAL PSALM 51 is a penitential psalm, a psalm that acknowledges sinfulness and pleads for God's mercy. The antiphon begs God to create something new: a clean heart, a pure heart, one on which God's Word is inscribed and in which is total love for him. This cannot be accomplished on our own.

◆ GOSPEL: The question concerning Jesus's identity continues. John the Baptist had been beheaded; Elijah had been mysteriously taken up to heaven, thus giving rise to the tradition that he would likewise return before the coming of the Messiah (2 Kings 2:11, Malachi 3:23); Jeremiah was the suffering prophet par excellence. Peter, however, has been gifted with the Father's revelation of Jesus's identity. Note how the title builds on the earlier confession of faith (Tuesday's Gospel): Jesus is the Christ (Messiah), the Son of the living God.

Today's Saints

This third-century pope, St. Sixtus II, was best known for solving the controversy surrounding Baptism performed by heretics. He stated that the validity of Baptism should be based on the recipient's desire to be Christian and not on the errors of the baptizer. This decision restored relations with the African and Eastern Churches. Sixtus was pope for only a year before he and six of his deacons were beheaded by Emperor Valerian.

Today's other saint, Cajetan, is known for establishing the Theatines, a pioneer religious order of the Counter-Reformation, whose mission was to bring clergy back to a life of prayer, Scripture study, preaching, and pastoral care.

FRI 8 (#411) white
Memorial of St. Dominic, Priest

The Lectionary for Mass

◆ FIRST READING: The prophet's words announce good news and promise a day of great rejoicing for the people of Judah. A time of peace is at hand. The "vine of Jacob" (an image for Israel) will be restored. Assyria, the hated enemy, will be destroyed. It was Assyria who had earlier conquered the northern kingdom of Israel and who subsequently made Judah a vassal state. Note the vivid imagery that describes the Assyrian conquest of cities in the second part of the reading.

◆ RESPONSORIAL PSALM: The biblical authors viewed the destruction of the enemies of God's people as the judgment of God. (It was also interpreted as God's judgment and a call for repentance when Israel suffered the ravages of war and destruction.) Today's response is taken from the Book of Deuteronomy. The first two lines of the first stanza refer to Israel's enemies at the time of the settlement of the land (after the Exodus); the next two lines, to God's protection and vindication of his people. Yet Israel was not always faithful to God, and on numerous occasions, was guilty of worshipping other gods (so the second stanza). Israel must learn that YHWH alone is God—a God who judges—and acts—justly.

◆ GOSPEL: Today's text follows immediately upon yesterday's Gospel, where Peter objects to Jesus's teaching about what his Messiahship would mean. Jesus must teach them what it means to think like God: life comes only through death; we save our life only by losing it. In so doing, we will gain all in the kingdom to come.

The Roman Missal

The orations are all to be found at August 8. The Collect not surprisingly underscores Dominic's reputation as an outstanding preacher. The Prayer over the Offerings prays for protection, "through the great power of this sacrifice," for "those who champion the faith"—thus reminding us that we are called to be preachers of the truth, like St. Dominic. The Prayer after Communion again highlights St. Dominic's preaching: since the Church flourished by means of his preaching, we also ask that we might be "helped through his intercession." In view of St. Dominic's life and preaching, the Preface of Holy Pastors would appear to be the most apt choice for today, although Preface I or II of Saints could also be used.

Today's Saint

St. Dominic (1170–1221), a contemporary of St. Francis of Assisi, founded a mendicant order (those who rely on the charity of others) of men, called the Order of Preachers, or Dominicans, to preach against theological error. One of the pressing issues facing the newly established order was the Albigensian heresy, claiming that matter, specifically the body, is evil. Contrary

to this heretical thinking, the Black Friars, as they were commonly known, went from town to town preaching the goodness of the body. In order to preach sound doctrine with clarity, St. Dominic exhorted his sons to engage in rigorous academic study. He eventually started a contemplative female branch of the Dominicans to support the apostolate of the men through prayer.

SAT 9 (#412) green
Weekday

Optional Memorial of St. Teresa Benedicta of the Cross, Virgin and Martyr / red; Blessed Virgin Mary / white

The Lectionary for Mass

◆ FIRST READING: The sovereignty and holiness of God, the wickedness of the faithless, the lament of the faithful, are all found in today's text. God's answer to the longing of the faithful is that "the vision still has its time . . . wait for it" (Habakkuk 2:3). Habakkuk's words offer hope to a suffering people. May it be a word of hope for us in our struggles as well.

◆ RESPONSORIAL PSALM 9: The word of hope continues: God will not forsake those who are faithful. With this realization, we sing God's praise.

◆ GOSPEL: One can never hear of an incident of healing without being deeply touched, and so it is with the miracle in today's Gospel. At the same time, our text has much to say about the faith—or lack thereof—of the disciples.

We see how frustrated Jesus is with them. Today's text calls us to look at our own discipleship. When are we among "the faithless and perverse" (Matthew 17:17)?

Today's Saint

St. Teresa Benedicta of the Cross was born Edith Stein at Breslau in

1891 into an observant Jewish family, but by the time she reached her teens, she had become an atheist. She went on to study philosophy and received her doctorate at Freiburg under the philosopher Edmund Husserl but left her university career to teach at a girls' school when Husserl did not support her further studies. Influenced by her study of Thomism and spirituality, she became a Catholic in 1922. In 1932, she became a lecturer at Munster, but anti-Semitic laws passed by the Nazis forced her to resign, and she entered the Carmel at Cologne in 1933. In an attempt to protect her from the Nazis, she was transferred to a Carmel in the Netherlands, but when the Dutch bishops condemned Nazi racism, the Nazis retaliated by arresting Jewish converts. Edith, along with her sister Rosa, who had also become a Catholic, was deported to Auschwitz and died in the gas chamber on August 9, 1942. She was canonized by Pope John Paul II in 1998.

10 (#115) green
Nineteenth Sunday in Ordinary Time

The Lectionary for Mass

◆ FIRST READING: The prophet Elijah, discouraged by the seeming failure of his prophetic ministry, is actually fleeing for his life when he arrives at Mt. Horeb or Sinai (see 1 Kings 19:1-8). Like Moses and the

Israelites before him, Elijah experiences the presence of God there. God made himself known to Elijah in a "tiny whispering sound," not in the thunder and volcanic activity that Moses experienced (see Exodus 19:16–18). Elijah hid his face when he sensed the presence of God for it was believed that no one could see the face of God and live (Exodus 33:20).

◆ Responsorial Psalm 85: Elijah did indeed see the kindness of the Lord on Mt. Horeb when God reassured him concerning his prophetic mission. Note the virtues associated with the presence of God: kindness, truth, justice, peace. If we read 1 Kings 19 a bit further, we see how God's justice was made known and his kindness manifest (verses 14–18).

◆ Second Reading: Paul writes of the deep anguish and pain that he experiences over the fact that many of his Jewish brothers and sisters have not believed that Jesus was Messiah and Lord. He is the fulfilment of all that was promised to them of old, yet they do not see or understand. What lengths Paul would go to if it would lead them to faith.

◆ Gospel: There are several foci in today's Gospel: the motif of Jesus seeking solitude for prayer; the storm at sea; Jesus walking on the sea and his self-revelation: "It is I" (the *ego eimi* of the Septuagint or Greek translation of Exodus 3:14); Peter's walking on water when he keeps his eyes on Jesus; his faltering when he focuses on the storm instead; his confession that Jesus is the Son of God. The question of who Jesus is, cannot be separated from who he is—for us. Jesus feeds our deepest hungers and delivers us from all that threatens to harm us. All he asks is that we believe in him.

The Roman Missal

The Mass texts for today are found in the "Ordinary Time" section of the Proper of Time. The Gloria is sung or said today.

The Collect gives voice to the relationship we enjoy with God: in bold words, it reminds us that "we dare to call [God] our Father." We can dare to do so precisely because we have been given "the spirit of adoption as your sons and daughters," and so the Collect prays that that spirit of adoption may be brought "to perfection in our hearts." Our relationship with the Father is never complete; it is always capable of being deepened insofar as ongoing conversion—a conversion brought about by repeated immersions in the Paschal Mystery through the liturgy—is a constant task in the life of a Christian. To echo the Gospel, we are constantly being beckoned to come closer to the Lord in faith, doing so with trust. The Prayer over the Offerings recaps that the offerings made at this celebration are to be transformed "into the mystery of our salvation" (and, therefore, we must remember, are the agents to transform us). The Prayer after Communion prays that our communion in the sacrament may "confirm us in the light" of God's truth.

Any one of the eight Prefaces of the Sundays in Ordinary Time are possible choices for today. Perhaps one might see in Preface I, with its description of the chosen people who are called "to proclaim everywhere your mighty works" could be seen as connecting with the Gospel story of being called to trust in Jesus, and the recognition of Jesus's divinity that is proclaimed at the end of the passage.

Pastoral Reflection

Many times challenge courses are used to create a team bond. After challenging someone beyond their desired comfort zone, an individual uncovers a whole new side of trust and belief in themselves and their group. If you ever have a chance to ask for or offer this opportunity, keep this Gospel in mind. If this is not possible, look up footage online of the man who walked a tightrope all the way across Niagara Falls in 2012, for to overcome any challenge, inner balance (prayer) is necessary. Outer balance (trust in or support from others) is vital. And, strength (mind over matter) is paramount. Consider the impossible this week, and allow Jesus's courage to replace your doubt.

MON 11 (#413) white
Memorial of St. Clare, Virgin

The Lectionary for Mass

◆ First Reading: Today's text recounts the inaugural vision of the prophet Ezekiel, a vision that takes place while he is among the exiles in Babylon. The dazzling brightness, the fire, the throne, the splendor are all typical attributes of God elsewhere in Scripture (see, for example, Daniel 7:9–10). Ezekiel's vision is indeed of the glory of the Lord.

◆ Responsorial Psalm 148: The theme of God's glory resounds throughout our Responsorial Psalm as both heaven and earth sing God's praise.

◆ Gospel: Today's Gospel consists of two separate scenes. The first is a prediction of Jesus's Passion and Death, which overwhelms the disciples with grief. Note also the reference to the Resurrection—do they hear this? The second concerns the Temple tax, which all Jewish men were required to pay (see Exodus 30:11–16). Jesus's response can seem enigmatic, yet it demonstrates both his obedience to the law and his concern not to give offense.

The Roman Missal

It is the Collect, found in the Proper of Saints at August 11, that is proper for today, and it speaks of Clare's life of poverty. Consequently, the prayer goes on to ask that we too will follow Christ "in poverty of spirit" and so merit to contemplate God in the heavenly kingdom. The texts for the Prayer over the Offerings and the Prayer after Communion are taken either from the Common of Virgins: For One Virgin, or from the Common of Holy Men and Women: For a Nun. Possible Prefaces are Preface I or II of Saints, or the Preface of Holy Virgins and Religious.

Today's Saint

Inspired by the Lenten sermons of her close friend St. Francis of Assisi, St. Clare of Assisi (1193/4–1253) renounced her wealth to found the Poor Clares, or Minoresses, a community of nuns devoted to a simple, austere life of prayer. She is the patron saint of television, due to a vision she had while lying sick in bed on Christmas Eve, in which she saw the crib and heard the singing just as if she were present in the church. In art, she is often depicted holding a monstrance because she protected Assisi from attackers with the Blessed Sacrament. Her sister St. Agnes eventually joined the Poor Clares.

TUE 12 (#414) green
Weekday

Optional Memorial of St. Jane Frances de Chantal, Religious / white

The Lectionary for Mass

◆ FIRST READING: Today's First Reading is a continuation of Ezekiel's inaugural vision. Its focus is on the prophet's commission. He is commanded to eat the scroll, symbolizing, perhaps, that he must be completely filled with God's word, and that the word he speaks must be of God.

◆ RESPONSORIAL PSALM: Although the word taste in our antiphon means "to experience," it is a most appropriate response for today's First Reading, even in its literal sense. Psalm 119 is a psalm that extols the law of the Lord.

Notice that each stanza contains a synonym for God's law.

◆ GOSPEL: Today's Gospel consists of several separate sayings. The first addresses the perhaps somewhat lost—and certainly difficult—practice of mutual correction. It can only be done in humility and love. The power and authority given to the Church in terms of binding and loosening as community is significant.

Today's Saint

Under the influence of her spiritual director St. Francis de Sales, St. Jane (1572–1641), a wealthy widow and mother from France, founded the Congregation of the Visitation of the Virgin Mary. Unusual in its time, this new community of enclosed nuns welcomed individuals with frailties due to health and age, and who were often refused admittance by other cloistered orders. She was no stranger to pain, from the death of her husband and some of her children, to the death of her dear friend St. Francis, but she transformed her experiences of sorrow into moments of transformation and service to the sick.

WED 13 (#415) green
Weekday

Optional Memorial of SS. Pontian, Pope, and Hippolytus, Priest, Martyrs / red

The Lectionary for Mass

◆ FIRST READING: A reading of the preceding chapter 8 of Ezekiel puts today's text in context. It is there that we find a description of the abominations in the Temple for which the people are punished in today's text. In Ezekiel's vision, those who were faithful to God and not guilty of these abominations were marked on their foreheads with the Hebrew letter "thau" and thus would be spared. The second part of today's reading, from Ezekiel 10, describes the prophet's vision of the departure of the glorious presence of God from the Temple. The vision would be fulfilled when the Temple was destroyed by the Babylonians.

◆ RESPONSORIAL PSALM 113: Our psalm of praise is perhaps best seen in the light of the description of the glory of the Lord in the last part of the first reading. Note the reference to the Lord's glory in the second stanza of the psalm, and the heights from which he looks down upon the earth (second and third stanzas). In addition, we should note that this hymn of praise is a fitting response for those faithful servants of the Lord marked with the "thau" and whose lives were spared.

◆ GOSPEL: Jesus wants the Church, the community of his disciples, to be characterized by forgiveness and reconciliation. Today, he sets forth practices by which this might be accomplished. The first is to speak privately to a brother who has given offense to you. If that doesn't work, enlist the help of one or two others, more if needed. Forgiveness and reconciliation must be sought no matter what. If a brother or sister obstinately refuses to hear, he or she should be expelled from the community lest the whole community be harmed.

Today's Saints

Pontian and Hippolytus (+235) became the target of Emperor Maximinus Thrax who despised Christians, especially their leaders. Pope Pontian and the priest Hippolytus differed in terms of orthodoxy, so much so that they rivaled each other as leaders. Hippolytus did not acknowledge Pontian as the true pope, resulting in a schism in the Roman Church and leading to Hippolytus' reign as the antipope. They eventually reconciled during their exile to Sardinia, known as the island of death, where they died as martyrs due to harsh treatment.

(#416)   red

THU 14 Memorial of St. Maximilian Kolbe, Priest and Martyr

The Lectionary for Mass

◆ FIRST READING: The prophets exercised their ministry not only by the words they spoke, but also by actions. Today we see one such symbolic action in the life of Ezekiel. Its meaning was that still more people were to be exiled to Babylon. The prophets understood this historical event as punishment for Israel's rebellious behavior.

◆ RESPONSORIAL PSALM 78 recounts Israel's history, and the verses chosen for today focus on the people's rebellious deeds in worshipping other gods. The Babylonian Exile and the destruction of Jerusalem were seen as God's punishment. Our antiphon warns: "Do not forget the works of the Lord"— remember and be faithful; remember your past and learn from it.

◆ GOSPEL: There is something inherent in the human mind and heart that wants to know exactly what one must do to fulfill the law or, rather, how much is enough. Today's Gospel deals with the question of forgiveness. How often must one forgive the same offender? As often as it is needed. What is more, the heavenly Father will forgive us in exactly the same manner as we forgive others. It certainly gives us reason to examine how we are doing in this regard.

The Roman Missal

The Collect, the Prayer over the Offerings, and the Prayer after Communion are all proper for today and are taken from August 14. The Collect recognizes the saint for his "zeal for souls and love of neighbor" as well as his Marian devotion. The Prayer over the Offerings asks that through the oblations we present at this celebration, "we may learn / from the example of Saint Maximilian to offer our very lives to you." Indeed, the offering of our lives is the heart of our participation in the Eucharistic celebration. One of the two Prefaces of Holy Martyrs would probably be most appropriate today, although the Preface of Holy Pastors or even one of the two Prefaces of Saints could also be considered. The Prayer after Communion reminds us of our communion with the saints in the Eucharist, as it asks that through the Eucharist "we may be inflamed with the same fire of charity / that Saint Maximilian received from this holy banquet."

Today's Saint

Polish-born Maximilian was a Franciscan friar whose devotion to Mary continues to affect the Church today. He established the Militia of the Immaculata, a Marian apostolate that uses prayer as its main weapon in spiritual battles. His extensive writing on Mary's role as mediatrix and advocate influenced the Second Vatican Council. He was eventually arrested and sent to Auschwitz. He volunteered to die in place of another prisoner and was put in the starvation bunker. Still alive two weeks later, Maximilian was injected with a lethal dose of carbolic acid, dying with a radiant, calm look upon his face.

(#621)   white

THU 14 Vigil of the Solemnity of the Assumption of the Blessed Virgin Mary HOLYDAY OF OBLIGATION

About this Solemnity

This day we celebrate the promise of God expressed fully in the life of Mary, the Holy Mother of God. God invites us to eternal life, to enjoy the glorious new creation of his Son in body, soul, and spirit. Our final hope is the resurrection of our own bodies at the end of time to exist forever in this new order of creation. The Solemnity of the Assumption is our great celebration of this final hope. Mary is a pioneer for us in faith. She was the first among us to accept Jesus Christ into her life. In her bodily Assumption, she is also the first to fully enjoy eternal life at the side of her Risen Son in the glory of heaven. Where she has gone, we hope to follow. We rejoice in the fulfillment of God's promise in her, as we turn to her to guide us to the side of her Risen Son who reigns in heaven.

The Lectionary for Mass

◆ FIRST READING: Today's First Reading recounts David's enthronement of the Ark of the Covenant (the chest containing the tablets of the Law) in the tent he had prepared for it. The Blessed Virgin has traditionally been invoked as the Ark of the New Covenant; thus, the reading from 1 Chronicles is particularly appropriate as we celebrate the heavenly enthronement of her who was the Ark of the Living Lord.

◆ RESPONSORIAL PSALM 132 was sung by Jewish pilgrims as they made their way to the Temple. It recounts David's concern to establish a home for the Ark of the Covenant. Today we celebrate Mary being taken up into the heavenly Temple, enjoying there, with her Risen and Glorified Son, her heavenly rest.

◆ SECOND READING: All of 1 Corinthians 15 deals with the subject of the resurrection of the body. These concluding verses celebrate the victory Jesus has won over death. Assumed into heaven, Mary is clothed with immortality.

◆ GOSPEL: Today's Gospel could seem to put Mary in the background. Far from it. It brings all believers into the foreground with her. The heavenly glory she enjoys will likewise be ours if we hear God's Word and keep it.

The Roman Missal

Two sets of Mass formularies are given for this Solemnity, "At the Vigil Mass" and "At the Mass during the Day."

The Entrance Antiphon for this Mass announces that "Glorious things are spoken of you, O Mary," because she has entered into "eternal triumph with Christ." The Gloria is sung or said today.

The Collect puts forth for us not only the belief concerning the Assumption—that the Blessed Virgin Mary "was crowned this day with surpassing glory," but also the central point that we hope to share that same destiny, that of being exalted on high.

Remember that the Creed is said at this Mass.

The Prayer over the Offerings refers to the sacrifice we are celebrating as a "sacrifice of conciliation and praise."

The Preface is proper for today, "The Glory of Mary Assumed into Heaven," and the text, with and without musical notation, is located among the texts for the Mass during the Day, one page-turn over from the Vigil Mass texts. Consider chanting the Preface and its introductory dialogue today. The Preface reiterates that our liturgy celebrates our (hoped-for) participation in the mystery being commemorated: it describes that the

Virgin Mother of God "was assumed into heaven / as the beginning and image / of your Church's coming to perfection." Thus are we given "a sign of sure hope and comfort." It also gives an easily understandable definition of the dogma as it explains how God "would not allow her / to see the corruption of the tomb / since from her own body she marvelously brought forth . . . the Author of all life."

The Communion Antiphon is suggested by Luke 11:27, the blessing cried out by the woman from the crowd.

The Prayer after Communion prays for freedom "from every threat of harm" as a result of our partaking of the food of the Eucharist.

The Solemn Blessing formula for the Blessed Virgin Mary, number 15 under "Blessings at the End of Mass and Prayers over the People," is suggested for this Mass, and it would be fitting to use it.

(#622)   white

FRI 15 Solemnity of the Assumption of the Blessed Virgin Mary
HOLYDAY OF OBLIGATION

The Lectionary for Mass

◆ FIRST READING: In approaching today's text from Revelation, one must remember that it is part of a vision the author had, thus its highly symbolic language. The description in Revelation 12:1 has given rise to countless artistic representations of the Blessed Virgin. The chapter recounts both the divine deliverance of the woman and her child as well the cosmic battle between good and evil, in which the good, which is of God, triumphs over Satan and the powers of evil, thus inaugurating the Kingdom of God.

◆ RESPONSORIAL PSALM 45 is a royal wedding song, and the Blessed Virgin is traditionally spoken of as

Queen of heaven and earth. Assumed into heaven, Mary has entered into the Father's house, into the palace of the King.

◆ SECOND READING: Paul speaks here of the order or sequence in which the resurrection of the dead will occur. Christ was the first. Today we celebrate the teaching of our Catholic tradition that Mary already enjoys the fullness of resurrected life.

◆ GOSPEL: Today's solemnity celebrates Mary's glorification at the end of her life. The Gospel takes us back to that moment in her life when she responded to God's special call to be the Mother of the Lord. We hear her hymn of praise, now fulfilled in a way we cannot even begin to comprehend.

The Roman Missal

There are two options for the Entrance Antiphon today; the first uses the imagery of the woman with a crown of twelve stars, clothed with the sun and the moon beneath her feet; the second antiphon is an antiphon of rejoicing at the celebration of this feast day.

The Collect reminds us that our final goal is to be sharers in the same glory the Virgin Mary enjoys, and therefore we should always be "attentive to the things that are above."

Remember that, because it is a solemnity, the Creed is said today.

The Prayer over the Offerings asks the Blessed Virgin Mary's intercession that our hearts may constantly long for God. Used at this place in the liturgy, we can make the connection between "longing" and "hungering" for God, a hungering that is ultimately fulfilled only by our participation in the heavenly banquet in the kingdom.

The text for the proper Preface used today is located immediately following the Prayer over the Offerings; see the Vigil Mass above for commentary.

The Communion Antiphon quotes from Mary's Magnificat in Luke's account of the Gospel.

The Prayer after Communion, as do other texts we have seen, prays that, through the intercession of the Blessed Virgin Mary, we will share in the mystery that is being commemorated and be brought "to the glory of the resurrection."

As remarked concerning the Vigil Mass, the Solemn Blessing formula for the Blessed Virgin Mary, number 15 under "Blessings at the End of Mass and Prayers over the People," is suggested for this Mass, and it would be fitting to use it.

Pastoral Reflection

Mary's Song, the Magnificat, would be a good prayer to carry in our pocket, purse, or briefcase. It is a statement of faith for when we want to rejoice or need to rely on God. Pray it after a loved one is kept safe or a difficult obstacle has been overcome. It is a proclamation of trust when we need to call upon God. Pray it in a time of illness, betrayal, or anxiety. Whether we are strong or weak, we can walk with Mary in the footsteps of our ancestors of faith, relying on the Lord.

SAT 16 (#418) green
Weekday

Optional Memorials of St. Stephen of Hungary / white; Blessed Virgin Mary / white

The Lectionary for Mass

◆ FIRST READING: Punishment for sin will not be visited upon generations, as was believed at one time, but only on the one who is guilty of sin. In the prophet's words today, we hear a call to conversion and the Lord's promise of life.

◆ RESPONSORIAL PSALM 51: Today's antiphon attests that a sinner's purified heart is the work of God's grace. Humbly, we pray for this grace.

◆ GOSPEL: We see the gentleness of Jesus, his delight in the simplicity of the children, his eagerness to have them come to him so that he could bless them. Today's Gospel makes them a model for all who would enter the Kingdom of Heaven.

Today's Saint

St. Stephen (967/969/975–1038) christianized the people of Hungary, specifically a pagan group from Asia known as the Magyars. By the time of his coronation as king of Hungary, already a duke, he had established numerous dioceses and monasteries. With the goal of unifying the people, he ended tribal divisions, limited the power of the nobility, and suppressed pagan practices. He had a special love for the needy, so he gave them money often in disguise so people would not recognize him. St. Stephen is also recognized as a saint of the Orthodox Church.

☼ 17 (#118) green
Twentieth Sunday in Ordinary Time

The Lectionary for Mass

◆ FIRST READING: Our reading begins with the first verse of chapter 56, the call to act justly in accord with God's Law. The Lectionary omits verses 2–5, and continues with verse 6. The prophet's words, written shortly after the return from exile in Babylon, point to the inclusion of the Gentiles (those who are not Jewish) as recipients of God's

salvation provided they act justly in covenant fidelity and honor the Sabbath day. It is noteworthy that the return of the Jewish people to their homeland and the rebuilding of their Temple had been decreed by the Gentile, King Cyrus of Persia (see Ezra 1:1–4). God's Word decrees that his house (the Temple) was to be a "house of prayer for all peoples" (Isaiah 56:6).

◆ RESPONSORIAL PSALM 67: Our psalm calls people from all nations to praise the Lord and prays that the message of God's salvation will be made known among them. It is a most fitting response given the mention of Gentiles as well as the Jewish people in relation to the Temple in the First Reading. For the prophet Isaiah, God's guidance of the nations, was particularly evident in the actions of Cyrus, King of Persia (see Isaiah 44:28).

◆ SECOND READING: Again, we hear a bit of Paul's anguish over the failure of many of the Jewish people to believe in Jesus. Today, he focuses on his mission to the Gentiles. Paul's words even suggest that it was because of the Jewish people's rejection of the Gospel that the message was proclaimed to the Gentiles. It is a point that serves his argument well. It is only in the experience of our disobedience and sin that we can know (personally experience) the mercy of God. Paul prays that the Jews will come to faith. God's gifts and call to them—and to each of us as well—is irrevocable, and stem from his great mercy.

◆ GOSPEL: The Canaanite (Gentile) woman in today's Gospel broadens Jesus's understanding of his mission. She has faith in his healing power and is persistent in her request. The encounter leads Jesus to realize that he is sent not only to the lost sheep of the house of Israel but to Gentiles as well. What a marked contrast between the "great . . . faith" of the Canaanite woman in today's Gospel, and Peter's "little faith" in last Sunday's Gospel.

The Roman Missal

The Mass texts for today are found in the "Ordinary Time" section of the Proper of Time. The Gloria is sung or said today.

The Collect speaks to the need to keep God as the highest priority in our lives as it asks that we might love him "in all things and above all things." Ultimately, it is God alone who can fulfill us since what he promises surpasses every human desire. The Prayer over the Offerings reminds us once again that the celebration of the Eucharist is a "glorious exchange"—we offer what God has first given to us, and, in receiving those offerings back, we receive God's very self. The Prayer after Communion expresses how partaking of the Eucharist transforms us now as it conforms us to Christ's image on earth, and then goes on to ask that "we may merit also to be his coheirs in heaven." The transformation begun through sacramental communion reaches its fulfillment in union with Christ in heaven.

Consider using Eucharistic Prayer IV today; use of this prayer means you also must use its proper Preface, not one of the Prefaces of Sundays in Ordinary Time. With its description of how the Lord ". . . proclaimed the good news of salvation [to the poor], / to prisoners, freedom, / and to the sorrowful of heart, joy," and its inclusion at the end of the prayer of "all who seek you with a sincere heart," one might find echoes of the Scripture readings for today that speak about the inclusion of the so-called outsiders.

Pastoral Reflection

Have you ever felt tested beyond your level of patience? It almost appears as if Jesus purposefully does this to the woman so as to prove to his disciples the power of faith. While this may not be the actual case, it is a way to look at any difficult obstacle in your life. What happens when you are told no over and over again, but you need the answer to be yes?

MON 18 (#419) green
Weekday

The Lectionary for Mass

◆ FIRST READING: The prophet performs yet another symbolic action as directed by God. "The delight" of his eyes (Ezekiel 24:15)— his beloved wife—dies, yet he does not perform the customary rites of mourning. His people do not understand why, nor do they understand that they are the delight of God's eyes. They shall die in their sins because of their infidelity.

◆ CANTICLE: Our response is from Deuteronomy 32, the Song of Moses. God is the Mother—the Father who gave birth to Israel, and who took them to himself in covenant love. Their infidelities attest that they have forgotten this.

◆ GOSPEL: What must I do? Like the young man in today's Gospel, we want certainty and assurance; we want to be able to measure ourselves against a norm. And measure himself, he could, but Jesus asks for more. Jesus asks for all. The young man's possessions got in the way of his relationship with Jesus and the Kingdom of Heaven. May it never be so for us.

TUE 19 (#420) green
Weekday

Optional Memorial of St. John Eudes, Priest / white

The Lectionary for Mass

◆ FIRST READING: We are privy to the innermost thoughts of one who has arrogantly considered himself divine and not human. Clearly, he has lost his sense of his own "creatureliness" before God. Death and destruction shall be his punishment.

◆ CANTICLE: Today's verses from Deuteronomy 32 speak not only of Israel's infidelities, but, as in the First Reading, of the arrogance of her foes. Israel's unfaithfulness deserves punishment, but note the twist in the first stanza of our response. God is hesitant to punish the people of Israel at the hands of their enemies, lest these same enemies become arrogant. Indeed they did, and they too would be consumed by God's wrath. The response ends on a note of hope: God will deliver his people.

◆ GOSPEL: Today's text follows up on yesterday's Gospel. Jesus makes it quite clear that riches are a major obstacle to discipleship—a point evident from the young man's response. The saying elicits Peter's boast of having given up all to follow Jesus (unlike the young man), as well as Peter's concern for reward. Jesus promises that the reward for such renunciation will indeed be great.

Today's Saint

St. John Eudes (1601–1680), a successful preacher in France, cared for plague victims on both a physical and spiritual level. In light of the Protestant Reformation, he felt that the academic and spiritual training of priests needed to be strengthened; therefore, he established a society of diocesan priests, the Congregation of Jesus and Mary, commonly called the Eudists. Their sole purpose was directed toward the foundation of new seminaries where future priests would be equipped with the necessary tools to respond pastorally to the turbulent times. He eventually established a religious community of women, the Congregation of Our Lady of Charity of the Refuge, dedicated to the rehabilitation of prostitutes.

W E D (#421) white
20 Memorial of St. Bernard, Abbot and Doctor of the Church

The Lectionary for Mass

◆ FIRST READING: These words addressed to Israel's shepherds are actually addressed to her kings who had the responsibility to shepherd and care for her people as a shepherd cares for his flock. Israel's kings have failed greatly, and we have here a vivid description of bad shepherds. We also have God's promise that he will shepherd his people in their place.

◆ RESPONSORIAL PSALM 23: Today's beautiful psalm of confidence continues the theme of the last line in today's reading, and depicts God doing for Israel all that a good shepherd should do for his flock.

◆ GOSPEL: Yet another image for God is found in today's Gospel: that of a landowner. As parables are wont to do, this one completely overturns what we, like the workers, would think to be just and fair by our reckoning. The landowner is fair as he himself points out. God is extraordinarily generous. What is our response toward others when we see this?

The Roman Missal

All three of the orations are proper for today, found in the Proper of Saints at August 20. The Collect describes St. Bernard with bright and energetic terms such as "zeal for your house," "a light shining and burning in your Church" and asks that "we may be on fire with the same spirit / and walk always as children of the light." Such phrases point to the remarkable influence St. Bernard had on the people of his time. The Prayer over the Offerings continues to extol St. Bernard as a role model as it refers to him as "a man outstanding in word and deed, who strove to bring order and

concord to your Church." Such concord is appropriate in this prayer as it names the sacrament we offer at this celebration as "the Sacrament of unity and peace." We can never forget that unity, concord, and peace must be the fruits that result from Eucharistic celebration. The Prayer after prays that the Eucharist we receive will truly have an effect on our life. Preface I or II of Saints or the Preface of Holy Virgins and Religious would be appropriate choices today.

Today's Saint

St. Bernard (1090–1153) joined the Cistercian abbey at Citeaux, known for its strict and austere way of life. Within a short time he was noticed for his leadership; hence, he was appointed abbot of a new monastery at Clairvaux. His monastic vision at Clairvaux led to the foundation of several monasteries throughout France, Britain, and Ireland. In the solitude he wrote numerous theological and spiritual classics, including his treatise *On Loving God*, 86 sermons on the Song of Songs, and a major work *On Consideration*, a reflection on papal spirituality. St. Bernard had a special devotion to Mary, earning him the titles "Our Lady's faithful chaplain" and "Mary's harper." Bernard was a prolific writer and had a great influence on the Church.

T H U (#422) white
21 Memorial of St. Pius X, Pope

The Lectionary for Mass

◆ FIRST READING: Notice the motivation of God's restorative work among Israel: that the nations might know that the God of Israel is the true God; that his holiness might be revealed. God's restorative work is recreating for Israel a new heart, a new spirit, and a renewed covenant.

◆ RESPONSORIAL PSALM: The antiphon is a verse from today's First

Reading, juxtaposed with penitential Psalm 51. The antiphon speaks a word of promise in answer to the prayer of the psalmist: purification from sin and the gift of a pure heart.

◆ GOSPEL: Throughout the Scriptures, God's covenant with Israel is likened to a marriage bond. Today's parable appropriates this imagery and speaks of future reward as a wedding banquet. The main focus of the parable is on the manner of response to the invitation. It calls us to serious self-examination.

The Roman Missal

Texts for today can be found at August 21. The Collect acknowledges the saint's desire to "restore all things in Christ" as it recognizes his intelligence and great accomplishments. The Prayer over the Offerings reminds us of the reverence with which we must always celebrate the divine mysteries, and the Prayer after Communion asks that "the power of this heavenly table" may make us "constant in the faith." The Preface of Holy Pastors would be a good choice for today since St. Pius X was a pope.

Today's Saint

Known as the pope of the Eucharist, Pius X is remembered for promoting frequent reception of the Eucharist. He did this when Jansenism, a heresy that believed Holy Communion should be reserved for only a select few, was prevalent. Stating that "Holy Communion is the shortest and safest way to heaven," Pius X issued a decree to combat Jansenism, allowing children to receive Holy Communion when they reached the age of reason (age seven), rather than waiting until they were older. Pius X's other accomplishments include reforming the liturgy, encouraging priests to give simple homilies, reintroducing Gregorian chant into services, revising the Roman Breviary, and developing a new catechism.

22 Memorial of the Queenship of the Blessed Virgin Mary

F R I

(#423) white

Today's Memorial

Mary is truly the "Favored One of God." Her relationship with Jesus Christ was like no other, and God filled her life with grace from beginning to end because of her Son. Today we celebrate her at her Son's side in heaven. As Christ reigns in heaven, tradition teaches that God continues to favor the Mother of God, crowning her queen alongside her Son. Even in heaven, her relationship with Jesus Christ fills Mary's life with grace. On this memorial we rejoice in the fullness of hope and promise God shows us in Mary's life. She is Queen of Heaven, as God holds nothing back from her in the glory of heaven. Mary's joy is our hope as she lovingly guides us to join her at the side of her Son in eternity.

The Lectionary for Mass

◆ FIRST READING: There was much that must have seemed dead in the life of God's people exiled in Babylon. Was there any hope for life? Certainly. And it is the Lord who will bring it about, giving flesh to their "dead bones" and enlivening their dead spirits with his own Spirit. God will open their graves and bring his risen and restored people back to their own land.

◆ RESPONSORIAL PSALM 107: Today's psalm calls us to give thanks to the Lord for the marvelous manifestation of his love, as described in our First Reading. The mention of desert evokes the time after the Exodus, but is equally applicable to the experience of exile (in fact, the return to their homeland is described by the prophets in terms of a new exodus). The reference to wasting away fits well with the bones in the First Reading. The Lord continually heard and answered Israel's

cries of distress. His love for them was without end.

◆ GOSPEL: The Pharisees, those strict adherents of the law, set out to test Jesus. The Lectionary omits the incident immediately preceding today's Gospel, in which the Sadducees put Jesus to the test on the question of resurrection. Today's question concerns what is most important in the law. Jesus responds not only in terms of the greatest commandment, but adds another that is just like it.

The Roman Missal

All the orations for this obligatory memorial are proper for today and are located in the Proper of Saints at August 22. The Collect acknowledges the Blessed Virgin Mary as our Mother and our Queen. The Prayer over the Offerings makes explicit the connection between the offering we make and Christ's offering on the Cross, while the Prayer after Communion points to eschatological fulfillment as it asks that through this Eucharist we "may merit to be partakers at your eternal banquet." The Preface is one of the two Prefaces of the Blessed Virgin Mary; if Preface I is used, the correct phrase to use is "on the feast day."

23 Weekday

S A T

(#424) green

Optional Memorial of St. Rose of Lima, Virgin / white; Blessed Virgin Mary

The Lectionary for Mass

◆ FIRST READING: The Lord gifts Ezekiel, prophet in exile, with a vision of the restoration of his glory in the post-exilic restored Temple. What hope this must have brought him.

◆ RESPONSORIAL PSALM 85: Today's response echoes the promise of the First Reading. Looking at the stanzas of the psalm, we see that the antiphon (verse 10) is identified with salvation. How this word must have lifted the hearts of God's exiled people!

◆ GOSPEL: Today's Gospel could be summarized with the adage "Do what they say, not what they do," which, in fact, is almost literally what Jesus says. Indeed, it is a very hard principle to follow when the behavior of the official religious leaders and teachers is less than what it should be. The disciple must be a person of integrity, seeking to serve rather than to be esteemed.

Today's Saint

During St. Rose of Lima's (1586–1617) brief life, people noticed her physical beauty, declaring her *coma una rosa* (like a rose), but the beauty of her soul far surpassed her physical appearance. St. Rose longed to live solely for God so she renounced the institution of marriage by claiming Christ as her spouse. Basing her life upon St. Catherine of Siena, she lived a penitential life, setting up an infirmary in the family home to care for impoverished children and the sick. She gained popularity due to her selfless service to the needy. As the first canonized saint of the Americas, she is the patron of South and Central America, the Philippines, and the West Indies.

(#121) green

☀ **24** **Twenty-first Sunday in Ordinary Time**

The Lectionary for Mass

◆ FIRST READING: The Lord will depose Shebna, the master of David's palace, second in authority after the king, and replace him with a man of his own choosing: Eliakim, the servant of the Lord. The reason for the deposition is not given, but Eliakim is to be as a father to the people. Verse 22 is no doubt the link with today's Gospel, as the motifs of keys and opening and closing—all pointing to authority—recur there.

◆ RESPONSORIAL PSALM 138: Our response is one of thanksgiving. In the context of today's Scriptures, it is for the appointment of Eliakim, his authority in the house of David, and the honor he brings to his family. The Hebrew word translated as "kindness" in the second and last stanzas of today's psalm (and "love" in the antiphon) is *ḥesed* or covenant love. In the context of our liturgy, Eliakim's appointment is but one example of the many manifestations of God's covenant fidelity.

◆ SECOND READING: Today's text follows upon our reading from last Sunday. The lamentable failure of some of the Jews to believe in Jesus and their rejection of those sent in his name—a source of personal anguish for Paul—led to the proclamation of the Gospel to the Gentiles

and their acceptance in faith. God's ways are so mysterious . . . so hard at times to understand and fathom. We must never lose sight of the fact that all things have a place in God's plan and all can ultimately lead to glory.

◆ GOSPEL: The authority over the Church bestowed upon Peter is set in the context of his recognition of Jesus's true identity: "You are the Christ, the Son of the living God"— a revelation given him by the Father. Today's text is one of the two places in Matthew where the word *church* (*ekkēlsía*) occurs, the name Matthew gives to the community of believers. Peter's name (in Greek, *Pétros*) is derived from *pétra* meaning "rock." He is to be a firm foundation for the Church. Juxtaposed with the First Reading, today's text places Peter as second in authority in the Church after Jesus.

The Roman Missal

The Mass texts for today are found in the "Ordinary Time" section of the Proper of Time. The Gloria is sung or said today.

As the Collect asks that we might love what God commands and desire what God promises, it prepares us to hear those commands and promises in the Scripture readings that are about to be proclaimed in the Liturgy of the Word. The Prayer over the Offerings reminds us that we have been gathered by God to become one people "through the one sacrifice offered once for all," and therefore we pray for "the gifts of unity and peace in your Church." The Prayer after Communion asks for completion of the works of God's mercy, thereby implying that those works have begun in our sacramental communion.

Preface I of the Sundays in Ordinary Time describes how we have been summoned "to the glory of being now called / a chosen race, a royal priesthood, a holy nation, a people for your own possession, to

proclaim everywhere your mighty works;" this would certainly pick up on a theme heard in the Prayer over the Offerings. Similarly, so would Preface VIII, which speaks about the people gathered and formed as one, made the Body of Christ, and now manifest as the Church. One of those two Prefaces might be a good choice for today.

Pastoral Reflection

Think back to the time of your Confirmation. Did you have to do a report on the name of the saint you chose? Did you have look up the meaning of your given birth names and the saints possibly connected to each name? Titles and names are identifiable and relational. Look up what your name says about you. If you are a parent, share with your children the story of why you chose their names. Jesus wanted to know what his followers knew of his true identity—once that identity was given Jesus affirmed the blessing and also remained quiet. Our identity in Christ is meant to shine and lead others to God. What do others say about your identity as a Christ follower?

M **25** (#425) green
O
N **Weekday**

Optional Memorials of St. Louis / white; St. Joseph Calasanz, Priest / white

The Lectionary for Mass

◆ FIRST READING: Each of Paul's letters, with the exception of Galatians, begins with a prayer of thanksgiving for the community. From these we learn of the gifts and strengths of the community. In the case of the Thessalonians, these are faith, love, endurance of persecution, and the ability to suffer for the kingdom of God. Recognizing that these strengths are gifts and come from God, Paul prays for an increase of grace and continued growth.

◆ RESPONSORIAL PSALM 96: It is the witness of the Thessalonians' lives that proclaims God's marvelous deeds to the nations: both those in whose midst they live as well as in other churches where Paul preaches. The Thessalonians give testimony to the salvation they have received in the way they live their daily lives.

◆ GOSPEL: All of chapter 23 of Matthew's Gospel is a condemnation of the hypocrisy of the scribes and Pharisees. What a stark contrast between the life-giving silent witness of the Thessalonians in today's First Reading and the death-dealing (at times not so silent) behaviors of the scribes and Pharisees. We glimpse their myopic vision, which has lost sight of the breadth, mercy, and integrity of the Kingdom of Heaven.

Today's Saints

Becoming king of France at the age of 12, St. Louis (1214–1270) imbued French culture with a deep sense of divine justice. Although he enjoyed the finer things in life, including good wine and food, he never lost sight of the poor. It was not uncommon for him to feed the less fortunate from his own table, but he felt this was not enough so he provided homes for them. Even with the many constraints upon his time, he managed to spend several hours a day in prayer. The priest St. Joseph Calazanz (1556–1648) formed a religious order, the Clerks Regular of the Pious School, to set up free schools for the education of poor children. He believed that education would free the young from the dismal life of the slums, basically ending the cycle of poverty, by giving them the necessary skills to build a brighter future. During the plague of 1595 he ministered to the sick with St. Camillus de Lellis.

TUE 26 (#426) green
Weekday

The Lectionary for Mass

◆ FIRST READING: A key issue in the second letter to the Thessalonians has to do with the day of the Lord's coming. Indeed, many in the communities of New Testament times believed that it would be in their own lifetimes. Some, as in our day, even announced the day on which it would come. Don't be caught up in such speculation, advises Paul. Rather, he would say, focus on the Lord and live as you have been taught, receptive to his grace in every word you speak and every deed you do.

◆ RESPONSORIAL PSALM 96: The theme of the Lord's coming is echoed in today's Responsorial Psalm, which celebrates God's kingship over all the earth. For the psalmist, as for the faithful Thessalonians, it will be a day of great joy when all the earth exults.

◆ GOSPEL: In their hypocrisy, the scribes and Pharisees are caught up in externals, thinking that literal observance of the letter of the law renders them righteous. On the contrary, they have observed the letter but not the heartfelt integrity manifest in mercy, fidelity, and right judgment. These are the weightier matters of the law. External observances without these mean nothing.

WED 27 (#427) white
Memorial of St. Monica

The Lectionary for Mass

◆ FIRST READING: Paul stresses the importance of living in an orderly manner, which for him, means that each person carries his/her own weight, working so as not to be a burden to others. This is what Paul has done that he might be a model for them.

◆ RESPONSORIAL PSALM 128: The psalm continues the theme of the importance of work—note the reference to handiwork in the first stanza. The fruits of the work of the one who fears the Lord shall be prosperous.

◆ GOSPEL: We hear Jesus's accusations against the hypocrisy of the scribes and the Pharisees. In their rejection of Jesus, they are as guilty as their ancestors who murdered the prophets.

The Roman Missal

The proper Collect for today, found in the Proper of Saints at August 27, describes St. Monica as one who wept "motherly tears . . . for the conversion of her son Augustine." The Prayer over the Offerings and the Prayer after Communion are taken from the Common of Holy Men and Women: For Holy Women, and either Preface I or Preface II of Saints is the Preface to be used for today.

Today's Saint

St. Monica (332/3–387) knew the pain of disappointment, an unfaithful husband named Patricius who drank too much, and a promiscuous son, St. Augustine of Hippo, who lived an immoral youth. Through patience and love, her husband had a change of heart, choosing to become a Christian. St. Augustine's conversion was a much more difficult task. St. Monica prayed constantly and fasted daily, but nothing seemed to work, so she consulted St. Ambrose, Bishop of Milan, for guidance. Through the intervention of God the two of them managed to lead St. Augustine to the waters of Baptism. St. Monica exemplifies that unconditional love and persistence are portals for God's saving grace.

THU 28 Memorial of St. Augustine, Bishop and Doctor of the Church

(#428) white

The Lectionary for Mass

◆ First Reading: In this beginning of Paul's first letter to the Corinthians, we hear first of Paul's attribution of who the Corinthians already are by virtue of their Baptism: a sanctified (made holy) people who are called to live now as holy people. In the thanksgiving prayer, we have a hint of what the letter will be about: the spiritual gifts possessed by the community. It is for these that Paul gives thanks; it is concerning their proper use that Paul must instruct the community.

◆ Responsorial Psalm 145: Recognition of the Lord's works must lead to praise. In the case of the Corinthians, the "works" with which they should praise the Lord are their spiritual gifts.

◆ Gospel: All of chapters 24 and 25 of Matthew's Gospel contain parables that look to the end times—the coming of the Lord. As a homeowner must be vigilant against thieves, so must the Christian be watchful for the coming of the Lord. Good servants will be rewarded by their masters. Those who are careless and negligent will be punished. Where are we on that scale?

The Roman Missal

The Collect, the Prayer over the Offerings and the Prayer after Communion are all proper for today, located at August 28. In the Collect we pray for the same spirit as that which inspired St. Augustine to thirst for "the sole fount of true wisdom." The Prayer over the Offerings prays that this Eucharist may be for us "the sign of unity / and the bond of charity;" we can recall how that was a major theme of St. Augustine's preaching about the Eucharist. The Prayer after

Communion echoes Augustinian preaching on the Eucharist once again as it asks that "being made members of his Body, / we may become what we have received." The Preface of Holy Pastors would be a most apt choice for today, although either Preface I or II of Saints would be acceptable.

Today's Saint

St. Augustine was born to a pagan father and a devout Christian mother. This wild, unruly young man later became one of Western Christianity's most influential figures. He tried it all—living with a woman, fathering a child out of wedlock, and dabbling in Manichaeism, a heretical belief similar to Gnosticism. Through his mother's prayers and a friendship with Ambrose, he eventually converted to Christianity, was ordained a priest, and then became bishop of Hippo in 396. His prolific writing formulated theories and doctrines on original sin, just war, human will, divine predestination, the Trinity, and Christology.

FRI 29 Memorial of the Passion of St. John the Baptist

(#429; Gospel #634) red

Today's Memorial

For speaking the truth, John the Baptist is imprisoned, and eventually beheaded. The story of his death cries injustice to this day. Yet the courage of John the Baptist to speak the truth to Herod is also inspiring and awesome. How did he find the courage? Did he have a sense of what would be at risk? What might have sustained his spirit in prison? To answer these questions, we could look to the many people, such as political prisoners or victims of religious intolerance or ethnic persecution, who are imprisoned unjustly today for daring to speak the truth. People like Oscar Romero, Edith Stein, and Dietrich

Bonhoeffer are modern-day John the Baptists who continue to remind us of the power of the Holy Spirit that accompanies us even in the most difficult circumstances. Trusting in God's Spirit, we, too, may find the courage to speak and act for God's goodness and truth.

The Lectionary for Mass

◆ First Reading: The first line of today's text can be puzzling, since it is a response to the divisions within the Corinthian community arising from who had baptized its members (see 1 Corinthians 1:10–16). Paul is not interested in that at all. His mission is to preach the Gospel, a message that has the Cross as its heart. For anyone interested in status, in being deemed wise in the ways of the world, in human praise, the Cross is sheer foolishness. Crucifixion was a form of capital punishment for criminals, so cruel that the Romans would not inflict it on one of their own citizens. But through this death, Jesus was raised to life and exalted in glory. Accordingly, for those who have faith, the cross is the power of God.

◆ Responsorial Psalm 33: Praise is the only fitting response in the face of the power and wisdom and goodness of the Lord. The last stanza of today's psalm is particularly fitting in light of today's First Reading.

◆ Gospel: The Gospel text is proper today (Lectionary #634) and it is only fitting that we read the account of John the Baptist's death. What a juxtaposition of reactions to his preaching and proclamation of the truth. Herod feared him and believed that he was a just and holy man. Herodias had a grudge against him because he had said that her marriage to Herod was unlawful. In the end, Herod set aside both truth and the life of John for the sake of saving face. For his disciples, John was a revered teacher. They dare to come forward and ask for his body that they might bury it.

The Roman Missal

The texts for the memorial are to be found in the Proper of Saints at August 29. The Collect reminds us that St. John the Baptist was a forerunner (precursor) of the Lord not only in his birth, but also in his death. We pray in this prayer that "we, too, may fight hard / for the confession" of what God teaches. The Prayer over the Offerings employs imagery and phrases closely associated with the Baptist ("make straight your paths;" "that voice crying in the desert") in the way it asks that the offerings have an effect in our lives. The text for the Preface, "The mission of the Precursor," is given along with the other texts for this Mass, and it is the same Preface as used on the Nativity of St. John the Baptist in June (the text with music can be found there if the Preface is to be sung). The Prayer after Communion prays that we will recognize both what the sacrament signifies and what it effects in us.

SAT 30 (#430) green
Weekday

Optional Memorial of the Blessed Virgin Mary / white

The Lectionary for Mass

◆ First Reading: Are the Corinthians boasting of themselves? Paul's words could be interpreted in this way, especially in light of 1:11–17. Accordingly, he sets out to pastorally put them in their place, recalling their insignificant origins and social status. The power and wisdom of God is found in the very reversal and overturning of human ways of looking at things. Anything they have or are, they have through Christ.

◆ Responsorial Psalm 33: True happiness or blessedness is found in our relationship with God. This

was true of Israel of old with whom God had entered into covenant. It is true for every Christian who lives now in Christ.

Indeed, through the wisdom of the Cross, we have been delivered from death (stanza 2) and gifted with eternal life.

◆ Gospel: This second parable from Matthew 25 deals with the servants' stewardship of what has been entrusted to them by their master. Clearly, the master expected good stewardship manifested in productivity and profit.

Those who proved faithful were rewarded; the "useless" (no productivity, no profit; Matthew 25:30) are punished. Darkness, wailing, and grinding of teeth are all images associated with the punishment of the end time. With what are we entrusted? How will the Lord judge our stewardship?

☀ 31 (#124) green
Twenty-second Sunday in Ordinary time

The Lectionary for Mass

◆ First Reading: Today's plaintive text comes from one of the so-called "confessions" of Jeremiah, in which the prophet, discouraged by the seeming failure of his mission and the personal suffering it has entailed, laments his prophetic call. Have we not all had similar feelings about our "vocations" at one time or another? The strength of God's

power—and Word—at work in the prophet is evident in the image of the "fire" that burns within his heart. The discouraged disciples on the road to Emmaus had a similar experience (see Luke 24:32). So, may it be for us.

◆ Responsorial Psalm 63: Today's antiphon and psalm offer us another vivid image of God's power at work in a person's heart: the intense "thirsting" (antiphon) of the soul for God. For the psalmist, as it would have been for Jeremiah, the thirsting stems from what seems to be "lifeless" and dry. Such experiences are invitations from the Lord, to turn to him, to look upon him, to hold fast to him, to trust that "my soul shall be satisfied" and that he will uphold us. And then, with the psalmist, to give him praise.

◆ Second Reading: Paul exhorts the Romans—and us—to be "living sacrifices" of praise to the Lord, in all that we say and do. How hard it is not to be conformed to the age in which we live, with all the influences of the media and pressures from others. But what a grace and witness it is, if we can be "transformed" according to the will of the Lord.

◆ Gospel: Jesus's words to Peter today stand in stark contrast with what was spoken to him in last Sunday's account of the Gospel where he was acclaimed "blessed"! Today, he is called "Satan"—for the words he speaks to Jesus are not of God, but rather, are a very human way of looking at things. Peter cannot hear or accept the suffering and death (and Resurrection, don't miss it!) that Jesus's mission entails. (It is because of his intense suffering, that Jesus was associated with Jeremiah as in Matthew 16:14, last Sunday's account of the Gospel.) As it was for the Master, so it will—and must—be for the disciple.

The Roman Missal

The Mass texts for today are found in the "Ordinary Time" section of the Proper of Time. The Gloria is sung or said today.

The Collect reminds us of our absolute dependence on God as we turn to him beseeching that he "nurture in us what is good" and keep safe what he has nurtured; thus are we reminded of the constant care God offers us. The Prayer over the Offerings in effect points to the sacramental principle and the efficacy of symbols in liturgical celebration as it asks that this offering may "accomplish in power" "what it celebrates in mystery." The Prayer after Communion calls the Eucharist "the food of charity," thus reminding us that the Eucharist should bear fruit in us by stirring us up to serve God in our neighbor.

In view of today's Gospel in which Jesus predicts his suffering and Death and asks his followers to imitate him in losing their lives, consider using Preface II of the Sundays in Ordinary Time, which refers to the Passion of the Cross, or Preface IV, which mentions his suffering.

Pastoral Reflection

Imagine being in Peter's shoes and the passionate loyalty of a child for their parent. Peter, in disbelief that he could lose his beloved friend and leader, speaks up and is strongly put back into his place as not knowing anything. While Jesus is trying to share his salvific role, it is hard to hear. In your own life be conscious of how you choose to disseminate information to those "beneath you" with love. In responding to situations that shock you, let not your ego get in the way with the words you may choose. In all situations with those in less power than you, choose to build them up so as to give your own life away in a small manner to lift up another.

September
Month of Our Lady of Sorrows

MON 1 (#431) green
Weekday

Optional Mass for Labor Day / white

The Lectionary for Mass

◆ FIRST READING: Paul reflects on his own call and mission. Jesus, the crucified one, is at the center of his proclamation. The death of one executed as a criminal is hardly a demonstration of power and wisdom, at least according to human standards. But the message of Jesus does not stop with the Cross, for the Cross became the locus of the exercise of God's power as Jesus was led through death to a risen and transformed life.

◆ RESPONSORIAL PSALM 119 acclaims the wisdom of God's law, a wisdom that is learned only through openness to—and love of—God's teaching.

◆ GOSPEL: This text from Luke's account is a sort of programmatic statement for the whole of Jesus's ministry and teaching. Empowered by God's spirit, he is sent in particular to those who are poor or imprisoned, physically disabled, or in need of consolation from the Lord. Note that Jesus is in the synagogue in his hometown of Nazareth, and he gets mixed reviews. Jesus, well-versed in the Scriptures, knows that it is often the lot of prophets to be rejected by their own. On this day, those who could not receive his word were so enraged that they tried to kill him. This is a hint of what will happen later in the Gospel.

TUE 2 (#432) green
Weekday

The Lectionary for Mass

◆ FIRST READING: What powerful words: We have received the Spirit from God. What an even more powerful reality for each of us who has been baptized in the name of Jesus the Lord. Throughout this first letter, Paul must help the Corinthians to distinguish between the wisdom of the world or the merely human perspective and the wisdom that is of God or the spiritual perspective. We, like the Corinthians, must live in the reality that is ours in Christ.

◆ RESPONSORIAL PSALM 145 proclaims and praises God's righteousness in all his ways. The first stanza is a repetition of God's self-revelation to Moses in Exodus 34:6–7. The second and third stanzas describe the appropriate response of those who have received the wisdom and spirit of God.

◆ GOSPEL: Today's Gospel reveals the theme of the spirit that is within a person who comes to the fore again in this account of Jesus's healing of the man with an unclean spirit. Jesus's word has power over the evil spirits and is capable of restoring the man to health.

WED 3 (#433) white
Memorial of St. Gregory the Great, Pope and Doctor of the Church

The Lectionary for Mass

◆ FIRST READING: The jealousy and rivalry in the Corinthian community is clear evidence for Paul that they are not yet spiritual people. They still see things "according to the manner of the world" (1 Corinthians 3:3), that is, according to human wisdom. In this instance, the community was divided on the basis of who had baptized them. This means nothing, Paul assures them. What does matter is the reality of what God is doing and making of the community through his human coworkers.

◆ RESPONSORIAL PSALM 33: The blessedness spoken of in today's response is the deep happiness of those who are chosen in God. This prayer of Israel of old is equally applicable to the new people of God in Christ. God looks on his people and knows their ways. We must be faithful to who and what he has called us to be.

◆ GOSPEL: Jesus heals the mother of Peter's wife. Word of his healing activity spread quickly, and many bring their loved ones to him. Jesus must have continued his healing work throughout the night, for at daybreak we see him seeking solitude. In what little solitude he has to commune with God, he comes more and more in touch with his mission to proclaim the Kingdom of God.

The Roman Missal

All the orations, proper for the day, are found in the Proper of Saints at September 3. The Collect points to the way St. Gregory was exemplary in his shepherding role in the Church as pope. The Prayer over the Offerings recalls the forgiveness that comes to us through the Eucharist, since it notes how "through its offering" God has "loosed the offenses of all the world." The Prayer after Communion uses the image of Christ the teacher to ask that those who have been fed with the living bread may learn God's truth, "and express it in works of charity." The appropriate Preface to use for today would be either the Preface of Holy Pastors or Preface I or II of the Saints.

Today's Saint

St. Gregory the Great (540–604) was a mayor, a monk, a pope, and a writer. Unhappy with his life as

mayor of Rome, St. Gregory allocated half of his fortune to the poor and the other half to the foundation of seven monasteries. After joining a monastery in pursuit of a simple life, he was elected to the papacy. As pope, he cared for the poor, implemented the Gregorian reforms to improve Church governance and clerical behavior, promoted the monastic vocation, and renewed the liturgy. His name is associated with Gregorian chant (plainsong) and Eucharistic Prayer II (along with St. Hippolytus). A prolific writer and Doctor of the Church, St. Gregory composed numerous theological texts and is cited 374 times in St. Thomas Aquinas's *Summa Theologiae*.

T
H 4 (#434)   green
U   **Weekday**

The Lectionary for Mass

◆ FIRST READING: In today's First Reading, the Corinthians seem to be priding themselves on the wisdom that is theirs, perhaps on the basis of who had taught them about Christ. To do so is to think in human terms, ascribing importance to one teacher over another. It is not the teacher who is important but the one who is taught and the manner of life that he lived. Paul is quick to differentiate between the wisdom of this age (viewing things from a merely human perspective) and the wisdom that is from God: seeing in the crucified Christ the power and the wisdom of God.

◆ RESPONSORIAL PSALM 24 acclaims God's sovereignty and sets forth what is demanded of the one who seeks to stand in the presence of the Lord.

◆ GOSPEL: Jesus is a man who speaks the Word of God. His message and his authority attract people. Simon must have likewise been attracted by Jesus's Word: he willingly offered his boat to facilitate Jesus's teaching of the crowd, and he obeyed Jesus's command even if at odds with his own experience (they had caught nothing all night). Seeing what Jesus's Word could accomplish, Peter and his companions left all to follow him and work on his behalf.

F
R 5 (#435)   green
I   **Weekday**

The Lectionary for Mass

◆ FIRST READING: Paul speaks of his role and those of the other Apostles and teachers in the community as that of servants and stewards. Both images stress subordination to a master. The image of steward conveys the sense of being entrusted with the master's wealth and possessions and the corresponding responsibility and accountability the position brings. As servants and stewards of Jesus, the Apostles need only to be concerned with their standing before their Lord.

◆ RESPONSORIAL PSALM 37 is the prayer of one who puts his trust in the Lord. In our First Reading, we see Paul doing precisely that, even in the face of the unjust judgments of at least some of the Corinthians.

◆ GOSPEL: It must have been hard for the people of Jesus's day to understand why his disciples seemingly acted so different from those of John the Baptist and the Pharisees. On one occasion when this was questioned, Jesus speaks of himself as a Bridegroom, thus drawing on one image used of God in Biblical tradition (see Isaiah 54:6).

S **6** (#436) green
A **Weekday**
T

Optional Memorial of the Blessed Virgin Mary / white

The Lectionary for Mass

◆ FIRST READING: All of 1 Corinthians 3–4 deals with the community's concern with status, distinction, and self-importance. In today's reading, Paul calls attention to the self-emptying and renunciation that discipleship demands. With perhaps somewhat of a sarcastic tone, Paul contrasts the lowliness of himself and Apollos with the Corinthians' self-exaltation. Don't miss the allusions to Jesus's teaching on blessing persecutors in verse 12. Paul depicts himself as more than a "guide" to the Corinthians, he is their "father" for he has given them life through the Gospel and through his ongoing ministry to them, shows them a father's care.

◆ RESPONSORIAL PSALM 145 is a hymn of praise, as the last stanza, the last verse of the psalm, illustrates. The verses chosen for today highlight some of God's characteristics: his justice and holiness, his attentiveness to those who call upon him, his protection and deliverance of those who love him. As we hear in today's First Reading, Paul worked hard to bring the Corinthian community to the "truth"—of the attitudes and behaviors that should be theirs as believers.

◆ GOSPEL: Too literal, too legal a mindset can block the recognition of the ultimate meaning and significance of the law, and even more, the underlying mercy of God for all his creatures. The person and authority of Jesus has priority over the letter of the law. If exceptions are allowed even in the Old Testament for the man who was king, how much more so for the one who is Son of Man and Lord.

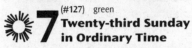

7 (#127) green
Twenty-third Sunday in Ordinary Time

The Lectionary for Mass

◆ FIRST READING: Throughout the Book of Ezekiel, the prophet is addressed as "son of man," (see Ezekiel 33:7) an expression meaning simply, "a human being." Yes, the prophet is one of/from the very people to whom he is sent. What an awesome responsibility is given him: he must speak the word with which he is entrusted or he will be held accountable for the faults of others. If he speaks and the people do not hear and obey, they will be punished but he is not responsible for their failure to heed the call to repentance.

◆ RESPONSORIAL Psalm 95: We are called to hear and obey the word of God—today! The first two stanzas are a call to come joyfully into the presence of the Lord and worship the one who is our Maker and our Shepherd. We are warned against imitating the example of Israel at Massah and Meribah when they grumbled against God because of their lack of faith (see Exodus 17:1–7).

◆ SECOND READING: What it means to hear and obey the Word of God can be summarized concisely: we are to love our neighbors as ourselves. It is not always easy, but it is not an option. Love is demonstrated in action not only when we do good to others, but also when

we refrain from any evil word or action toward them.

◆ GOSPEL: Jesus puts the responsibility to speak words of conversion on each member of the Church. Yes, this prophetic ministry is ours. It is what we are called to do for one another. Note the progression of steps in the instructions of how to go about it: first, try one on one; if that doesn't work, try again with two or three others to help; if that fails, bring the matter to the community as a whole. If that fails, the erring (the hardened) one is to be expelled from the community—done with a view to the welfare of the community. Harsh words? Note that it is done by those gathered in Jesus's name. Note that it is the responsibility of the community. Our Christian life entails serious responsibilities.

The Roman Missal

The Mass texts for today are found in the "Ordinary Time" section of the Proper of Time. The *Gloria* is sung or said today.

The Collect gives a description of those gathered to enact worship: they are redeemed, adopted by God, and are therefore "beloved sons and daughters." We pray that in belonging and in believing in Christ, we "may receive true freedom / and an everlasting inheritance." The Prayer over the Offerings designates two fruits we are hoping for as a result of making the offering this day: that it might allow us to "do fitting homage" to God's "divine majesty," and that it may unite us with one another in mind and heart. The Prayer after Communion acknowledges that the celebration of the Eucharist nourishes us with both "Word and heavenly Sacrament;" we should never forget the inherent unity of the Liturgy of the Word and the Liturgy of the Eucharist, the two parts of the Mass that are so intimately connected that they form one act of worship.

Perhaps Preface VIII of the Sundays in Ordinary Time is the best choice for today. Since its theme is how the Church is united by the unity of the Trinity, and it speaks about how God's people have been gathered together and made the Body of Christ, it would connect well with today's Gospel, which discusses what the life of the Church should be like.

Pastoral Reflection

Consider your pains, the grudges you may hold, gossip that may have ensued, and how reconciliation is needed. The majority of all conflict in our lives and the world comes from an inability to hear the other or be received by another. Both positions cause pain. Read about healthy ways of conflict resolution. Choose one situation in your life to begin with to speak your pain and work toward eventual reconciliation and even forgiveness. Consciously craft a relationship with a prayer partner or partners who can support you, so that you can walk strong in the way of love.

M O N 8 (#636) white Feast of the Nativity of the Blessed Virgin Mary

About this Feast

Exactly nine months after the Solemnity of the Immaculate Conception of the Blessed Virgin Mary (December 8), we come to a feast in honor of Mary's birth. This is one of only three "birthdays" on the liturgical calendar, the other two being the birthdays of Jesus and of John the Baptist (other days recognize a saint's "day of death"). Today we recall the greatness of Mary and her importance in all of salvation history, as we remember her humble and obedient "yes" to give birth to Jesus Christ, the Savior of the World. So on this day we honor the life of this young woman, Mary Immaculate, called to be the Mother

of God and our mother, Queen of heaven and earth.

The Lectionary for Mass

◆ FIRST READING (OPTION 1): What promise is in this word of the Lord spoken to the small and insignificant town of Bethlehem: from it shall come the Davidic heir, the Messiah. This particular passage from the Book of Micah probably stems from the time of the Babylonian Exile when there was no longer a Davidic king on the throne in Jerusalem. Nevertheless, God would not neglect his promise (2 Samuel 7:16). There will once again be an heir on the throne, one who will come from Bethlehem, the city that was home to David before he assumed the throne (1 Samuel 16). His reign shall bring security and peace.

◆ FIRST READING (OPTION 2): God has a plan for each of us. In divine wisdom and providence God can and does work good in and through all things—regardless of how insurmountable and impossible the situation may seem.

◆ RESPONSORIAL PSALM: Today's antiphon is actually from a passage in the prophet Isaiah that promises restoration to the ravaged city of Jerusalem (at the time of the Exile). Truly this promise was cause for joy! The verses chosen are from Psalm 13, a psalm of lament. Actually, only the last verse is used, the verse that acclaims the goodness of God who has heard the prayer of his chosen one.

◆ GOSPEL: We hear Jesus's genealogy as recounted by Matthew, which traces his origins back to King David and even to Abraham. We also hear Matthew's account of the birth of Jesus. When he realized that Mary was with child and knowing that he was not the father, Joseph decided to quietly divorce her according to the Law. (Notice his goodness toward her, not wanting to put her to shame.) The word of the Lord

assures Joseph that the conception of the child is the work of God's Holy Spirit. The one to be born is the fulfillment of God's promise (Isaiah 7:14). The child shall be Emmanuel, God-with-us.

The Roman Missal

The texts for this Mass are all proper for the feast today, and are located in the Proper of Saints section of the Missal at September 8. The Gloria is sung or said today, since it is a feast.

While the Collect acknowledges that today is the Feast of the Nativity of the Blessed Virgin, the prayer also points to the birth of Christ, which is referred to as "the dawning of salvation." There are two options for the Prayer over the Offerings. The first one, in somewhat curious phrasing, asks that the humanity of God's Only Begotten Son come to our aid; it also exalts the Blessed Mother's place in salvation history with its statement that Jesus, at his birth from the Blessed Virgin, "did not diminish but consecrated her integrity." Lastly, the prayer asks that Christ may take away our wicked deeds so that the oblation we offer is acceptable to God. The second option also mentions the humanity of Christ, as it asks that we be "given strength / by the humanity of your Son, / who from her [the Blessed Virgin Mary] was pleased to take flesh." The Prayer after Communion, after noting how the Church has been renewed with these sacred mysteries, now refers to the Nativity of the Blessed Virgin Mary as "the hope and the daybreak of salvation for all the world."

The Preface, proper for today, is one of the two Prefaces of the Blessed Virgin Mary. If Preface I is used, the correct phrase to use is "on the Nativity." Also, the Solemn Blessing formula titled "The Blessed Virgin Mary," number 15 under "Blessings at the End of Mass and

Prayers over the People," is suggested and should be used today. Finally, since Mary is the model disciple who shows us how to follow Christ, perhaps the dismissal formula, "Go in peace, glorifying the Lord by your life" would be appropriate for today.

T U E 9 (#438) white
Memorial of St. Peter Claver, Priest

The Lectionary for Mass

◆ First Reading: Paul's words today will probably not be particularly appealing to lawyers. He clearly teaches that Christians should not be hauling each other into court but should be able to help one another work out difficulties. Paul calls the community not only to be able to absorb injustice in the name of forgiveness, but also to examine their behaviors toward their brothers and sisters in the Lord.

◆ Responsorial Psalm 149: "The Lord takes delight in his people" (antiphon), in those who have come forward to receive Baptism and have been made holy, sacred to God as a result. May they always live to sing his praise.

◆ Gospel: It is interesting to note how many times in the Gospel Jesus goes off by himself to spend time with his heavenly Father in prayer, particularly before important decisions or moments in his life. After prayer, he named his disciples. Through prayer, he knew of his mission to heal and experienced God's power working through him.

The Roman Missal

The Collect affirms St. Peter Claver's ministry to African slaves and echoes his personal vow as "slave of slaves." The prayer asks that we may love our neighbor as St. Peter Claver did, "in deeds and in truth." The Prayer over the Offerings and the Prayer after Communion come from either the Common of Pastors: For One Pastor, or from the Common of Holy Men and Women: For Those Who Practiced Works of Mercy. The Preface of Holy Pastors or Preface I or II of Saints are the options for the Preface today.

Today's Saint

St. Peter Claver (1580/1–1654), a Spanish Jesuit priest, spent his life tending to the needs of African slaves in Columbia, South America. While serving as a missionary, he ministered to the slaves by providing them with food and medicine, washing their wounds, preparing them for Baptism, and witnessing their Marriages. He actively pursued lawyers to plead the cases of imprisoned slaves and prepared criminals for death. Not only did he care for the slaves, but he also preached missions to plantation owners and sailors. The "saint of the slaves," as St. Peter is often called, died after contracting a plague.

W E D 10 (#439) green
Weekday

The Lectionary for Mass

◆ First Reading: Much of 1 Corinthians consists of Paul's answers to questions that had been posed to him by the community. Today is a case in point and deals with the questions of marriage and virginity. We glimpse Paul's belief in an imminent end time (thus, the importance of giving our attention to vigilance and readiness for the coming of the Lord) with no distractions or other concerns. The world as we know it is passing away.

◆ Responsorial Psalm 44 is actually a hymn for a royal wedding. As noted in other commentaries, both Jewish and later, Christian tradition imaged the end of time as a banquet celebrating the wedding of God and his people. We can hear this psalm in that light.

◆ Gospel: Luke's version of the Beatitudes is slightly different from that found in Matthew's account. We see here, for example, his concern for the poor and those who are in need of any kind. These are the ones who are acclaimed as blessed and promised that their needs will one day be met. Correspondingly, those who have great possessions now risk woe and doom if they neglect the needs of others.

T H U 11 (#440) green
Weekday

The Lectionary for Mass

◆ First Reading: The question about meat sacrificed to idols is a non-issue for people in a Western society. However, in ancient Corinth where there were temples to numerous deities in the city, it was a very pressing issue.

Shared meals, which involved the eating of meat that had been sacrificed, were not only religious rituals, but also social events. On the one hand, Paul acknowledges that there is only one God; therefore the idols do not exist. However, if eating the sacrificial meat causes scandal, it is best not to do it. Consideration of the other takes priority. Surely that wisdom is applicable in other circumstances of life as well.

◆ Responsorial Psalm 139 prays for God's guidance. This is most apropos for the decisions the First Reading calls Christians to make. Psalm 139 acclaims God's knowledge of a person: all they are and do.

◆ Gospel: Today's Gospel is a series of sayings that stress loving those who mistreat us, and selfless giving regardless of cost. Above all, believers must be merciful, for this is one of God's main attributes. What we do to others will be done to us.

FRI 12 (#441) green
Weekday

Optional Memorial of the Most Holy Name of Mary / white

The Lectionary for Mass

◆ FIRST READING: Paul's call to Apostleship imposes a strict obligation to preach the Gospel. It is something that he is compelled to do, commanded to do by the Lord, and he must do so without impositions on others (Paul worked as a tentmaker to support himself; see 1 Corinthians 4:10). Paul's unimposing ministry is also evident in his desire to make himself "all things to all" and in his willingness to be a "slave" or "servant" to all (as did Jesus; see Philippians 2:7). The reading concludes with an exhortation to the Corinthians using athletic imagery—something with which the Corinthians would be well-acquainted given their proximity to Delphi and the games that were held there.

◆ RESPONSORIAL PSALM 84: The psalmist speaks of his "pilgrimage" to God's holy Temple and his deep longings for the presence of God. So, too, did Paul see his life's journey as a "race" to an "imperishable crown" in heaven.

◆ GOSPEL: Jesus's words call for clear-sighted vision of one's self, particularly in terms of weakness and sinfulness. How easy it is to focus myopically on the "speck" faults of others and miss the beams in our own eyes!

SAT 13 (#442) white
Memorial of St. John Chrysostom, Bishop and Doctor of the Church

The Lectionary for Mass

◆ FIRST READING: Our sharing in the bread and cup of the Lord makes us one with him and with one another. For the Corinthians, in their time and culture, this meant that they could not partake of the sacrificial meals offered to other deities.

◆ RESPONSORIAL PSALM 116: This Old Testament hymn of praise probably stems from the cult of Israel's Temple worship. Note the references to drinking from a cup, sacrifice, and vows—all in the presence of the Lord and his people.

◆ GOSPEL: Today's Gospel might be considered in two parts. The first is the parable of the tree and its fruit. Like the tree, the human person is known by the fruits of words and actions, which reveal what is in the heart. Those who take Jesus's words into their hearts and give voice to them through their actions are built on a firm foundation. They are not easily shaken by external trials and tribulations.

The Roman Missal

All the orations are again proper for today, found at September 13. The Collect attests both to St. John Chrysostom's famed eloquence and also to his suffering, asking that "we may be strengthened through the example / of his invincible patience." The Prayer over the Offerings points out that St. John teaches us to give ourselves entirely to God in praise; indeed, the total offering of self is the heart of participation in the Eucharist. The Prayer after Communion asks that the mysteries we have received will confirm us in God's love "and enable us to be faithful in confessing your truth." The Preface of Holy Pastors would be an apt choice in light of St. John

Chrysostom's influence as a bishop and preacher; Preface I or II of Saints could also be chosen, however.

Today's Saint

After a short stint as a monk St. John Chrysostom (347–407), whose surname means "golden mouth," returned to Antioch where he was ordained a priest and became a noted preacher. During his free time he wrote commentaries on the Pauline letters as well as the Gospels of Matthew and John. Due to his reputation for preaching and writing, he was appointed Bishop of Constantinople. As bishop he initiated a program of reform that challenged clerical abuses and the extravagant lifestyle of the upper class. His reforms were not always received well, especially on the part of Empress Eudoxia; therefore, he was exiled from the city for a period of time. St. John Chrysostom bears two distinctive titles in the Church: Father of the Church and Doctor of the Church.

14 (#638) red
Feast of the Exaltation of the Holy Cross

About this Feast

God sent his Son into the world so that we might receive life and salvation. Today on the Feast of the Exaltation of the Holy Cross we proclaim the Good News that God transforms suffering and death into new life. Our God is a God of victory who reigns victorious, even over the evil of death. As Christians, today we rejoice in the mystery of the Cross, which brings about our freedom, salvation, and life.

The Lectionary for Mass

◆ FIRST READING: A tired and discouraged Israel let themselves slip into a rebellious attitude toward God and his servant Moses. God punished them through the bites of poisonous serpents. Only then did they acknowledge their sin. God, in his mercy, allowed them to be healed by looking on that which was the source of their death, now raised up at his command.

◆ RESPONSORIAL PSALM 78: The source of difficulties described in the First Reading was precisely that Israel forgot the works of the Lord. The psalmist has learned from their experience and calls on all who hear him to do likewise.

◆ SECOND READING: This early Christian hymn acclaims the self-emptying of Christ, who, relinquishing his heavenly glory, became as one of us that he might show us the way to God—through his obedience, Passion, and Resurrection.

◆ GOSPEL: Jesus's words to Nicodemus recall the incident heard about in today's First Reading. The Greek verb translated as *lifted up* means both "to raise up as on a staff or a cross" and "to exalt." John presents the "lifting up" of Jesus on the Cross as his "lifting up" in glory. Jesus, the crucified and exalted Son of Man has become the source of our salvation and life.

The Roman Missal

Because this Feast of the Lord falls on a Sunday this year, it replaces the Sunday in Ordinary Time. All the texts are taken from September 14 in the Proper of Saints.

The Entrance Antiphon for this Mass is Galatians 6:14, about finding glory in the Cross; it is the same Entrance Antiphon used to begin the Sacred Paschal Triduum at the Mass of the Lord's Supper on Holy Thursday evening. We can be reminded that the Paschal Mystery of the Lord's Death and Resurrection is at the core of every liturgical celebration and indeed the entire liturgical year, and therefore is the focus around which all celebrations revolve. The Gloria is sung or said today.

The Collect speaks of how the human race has been saved by Christ's sacrifice on the Cross, asking that since we know the mystery of the Cross on earth, we "may merit the grace of his redemption in heaven."

The Creed is said at this Mass, since it falls on a Sunday.

The Prayer over the Offerings makes a direct connection between the offering made once by Christ in history and the offering we make today; since the Eucharist makes present for us the salvation won for us in Christ's Death and Resurrection, we can also find in this liturgical celebration forgiveness for our sins.

The Preface is proper for today, "The victory of the glorious Cross," and the text, with and without musical notation, is located right there amid the other texts for the day. This Preface puts forth a very positive theology of the Cross, not focused on Christ's sufferings, but rather on the new life that flows from his sacrifice: "where death arose, / life might again spring forth;" "the evil one, who conquered on a tree, / might likewise on a tree be conquered." There is also the possibility of using Preface I of the Passion of the Lord, the text for which is found immediately following Preface IV of Lent. This text speaks of the power of the Cross, and how

that power reveals "the authority of Christ crucified."

The Communion Antiphon is taken from John 12:32 and gives us the image of Christ lifted up, that is, on the Cross, thus drawing everyone to himself.

The Prayer after Communion speaks of the passage of the Paschal Mystery as it asks that those who have been nourished at the holy banquet may, by the wood of the life-giving Cross, be brought to the glory of the Resurrection. An echo of the Good Friday liturgy can be heard in the phrase "wood of your life-giving Cross." Again, a positive theology of the Cross is espoused, as the wood of the Cross is seen as the instrument of salvation, a salvation we participate in through our sharing in the Eucharistic banquet.

Pastoral Reflection

Do you wear a cross or a crucifix? Consider why or why not. What does each mean to you, as they are different in meaning? In our Catholic faith, the crucified Christ is an image which appears to be a failure to conquer the test of the world. Intently gaze upon Jesus, crucified, on the Cross. What feelings does this provoke? Sit with those emotions. It is hard to comprehend why God chose to come to earth to become a man who would be nailed to a Cross and become our symbol of faith. Teach this difference of understanding to the children in your family or those you know. Finally, choose to wear any piece of religious jewelry with intention and an ability to share fully with others why you wear the sign of our faith.

(#442; Gospel #639) white

MON 15 Memorial of Our Lady of Sorrows (Twenty-fourth Week in Ordinary Time)

Today's Memorial

This is a relatively modern celebration, included on the universal calendar only in 1814. The sorrows of the Blessed Virgin Mary begin with the prophecy of Simeon at the Presentation at the Temple, when he tells her, "Behold, this child is destined for the fall and rise of many in Israel, and to be a sign that will be contradicted (and you yourself a sword will pierce) so that the thoughts of many hearts may be revealed" (Luke 2:34–35). In art, Our Lady of Sorrows has her heart pierced by seven swords, representing the seven sorrows of tradition and the prophecy of Simeon.

The Lectionary for Mass

◆ FIRST READING: Today's reading contains the earliest account of the institution of the Eucharist since Paul's letters predate the Gospel accounts. Notice the context in which Paul relates it: not by way of praise of their celebrations of the Lord's supper. Their behaviors at the meals, which at that time were held in conjunction with the celebrations of the Eucharist, demonstrate that they have failed to understand— and to live—what the Eucharist is all about. Paul calls them to conversation in this regard.

◆ RESPONSORIAL PSALM 40: The antiphon is actually taken from the First Reading, here in the sense of a command: "Proclaim . . . ." The stanzas, verses from Psalm 40, stress that it is not empty rituals that the Lord desires, but, rather, obedient hearts.

◆ GOSPEL: Already in Jesus's infancy, the prophet Simeon foretells the contradiction and opposition that this child would one day endure and the pain and anguish his Mother

would one day suffer. Although it is John's Gospel that tells of the sword that pierced the side of Jesus as he hung on the Cross, it is no doubt this same sword that pierced the heart of Mary as she stood beside him. The thoughts of all hearts are made known in terms of their acceptance or rejection of Jesus.

The Roman Missal

All the orations are proper for today, and can be found in the Proper of Saints at September 15. The Collect draws a direct connection between yesterday's feast and today's memorial as it reminds us that when Christ was "lifted high on the Cross," his Mother was standing close by and sharing his suffering. Thus, we ask that we, with Mary, may also participate in the Passion of Christ so as to share in his Resurrection. Of course, our participation in that Paschal Mystery is effected most completely in the liturgy. The Prayer over the Offerings describes the Blessed Virgin Mary as "a most devoted Mother" who stood by the Cross of Jesus; we can do the same by our fidelity to participation in the Eucharist. Either Preface I or Preface II of the Blessed Virgin Mary is the Preface to be used today, but if Preface I is used, then the phrase "on the feast day" is the correct phrase to use. The Prayer after Communion relates how our participation in "the Sacrament of eternal redemption" is a participation in the Paschal Mystery, including the suffering of Christ.

Although the Missal does not mention it, there is nothing to prevent use of Solemn Blessing number 15, "The Blessed Virgin Mary," at the end of Mass today, particularly if your weekday Mass will see an increased attendance because of a particular devotion to the Blessed Mother under this title.

(#444) red

TUE 16 Memorial of SS. Cornelius, Pope, and Cyprian, Bishop, Martyrs

The Lectionary for Mass

◆ FIRST READING: Paul reminds the Corinthians, at times a community torn apart by factions (1 Corinthians 1:10), that since they have all been baptized in Christ and received the one Spirit, they are all members of the one Body of Christ. Using the analogy of the human body, which has many members each with their own function, Paul shows how the various gifts in the community entrusted to different members each have a particular service in the Church, the one Body of Christ.

◆ RESPONSORIAL PSALM 100: The antiphon highlights one of the images used in this psalm of praise to express the relationship between God and his people: that of a shepherd and his flock. Note that the psalm stresses that all people belong to the Lord. People of every land belong to the one people of God.

◆ GOSPEL: Perhaps it is the mother who is the focus in today's Gospel, rather than the son. She is a widow and now has lost her only son. In the society of her time she would be totally helpless, with no means of financial support. When Jesus saw her, he was moved with pity for her. Raising her dead son to life, he gives him to her. What needs do we have, that the Lord looks on in his mercy? What gifts, in our needs, does the Lord give us?

The Roman Missal

The Collect, the Prayer over the Offerings and the Prayer after Communion are all found at September 16, proper for this obligatory memorial. The Collect hails these two friends as "diligent shepherds" and "valiant Martyrs," and as the prayer asks that we may "spend ourselves without reserve / for the unity of the Church," we can remember that it was for their efforts to preserve that unity that these two saints were martyred. The Prayer over the Offerings connects the Eucharist we offer with the Eucharist offered by SS. Cornelius and Cyprian, as it notes how the Eucharist "gave them courage under persecution" and asks that it will "make us, too, steadfast in all trials." The Preface of Holy Pastors would be a fitting choice today, although one of the Prefaces of Saints could also be used. Since their names are mentioned in Eucharistic Prayer I, perhaps today would be a good day to use the Roman Canon. The Prayer after Communion asks that "through these mysteries which we have received," and by the example of these holy martyrs we might be "strengthened with the fortitude of your Spirit / to bear witness to the truth of the Gospel."

Today's Saints

St. Cornelius (+ 253) and St. Cyprian (+ 258) lived during the persecution by the Emperor Decius. St. Cornelius, the pope, faced the issue of whether or not Christians who renounced their faith during the persecutions should be welcomed back into the Church. With great compassion he publicly declared that these individuals may return to the Church after a period of penance. St. Cyprian, Bishop of Carthage, spent much of his life in hiding due to the persecutions, but this did not stop him from offering pastoral guidance and dispensing wisdom to the people of his diocese. Through letters he urged the people to remain faithful to their Christian call. Both SS. Cornelius and Cyprian shared the same fate—a martyr's death.

W E D 17 (#445) green
Weekday

Optional Memorial of St. Robert Bellarmine, Bishop and Doctor of the Church / white

The Lectionary for Mass

◆ FIRST READING: No matter how great the gifts and talents, it is only the manifestations of love that really matter. Note that love is identified as a spiritual gift, a gift whose source is the Holy Spirit of God. Is there a subtle call to the Corinthians to be like Paul and put aside childish ways so as to live as a mature person in Christ, gifted by the Spirit?

◆ RESPONSORIAL PSALM 33 stresses the unity of God's people and calls them to praise and thanksgiving. As Paul points out so beautifully at the beginning of 1 Corinthians, they are indeed a people the Lord has chosen and made his own.

◆ GOSPEL: Today's Gospel offers an interesting juxtaposition with today's First Reading as Jesus speaks of his contemporaries (those who hear his preaching and who heard John the Baptist) as children; in this instance, children who are not satisfied with what is offered them. Jesus calls his generation to be children of wisdom.

Today's Saint

St. Robert Bellarmine (1542–1621), bishop and Doctor of the Church, was an astute scholar with a knack for diplomatically responding to the controversies of his day. As a Jesuit priest embroiled in the Protestant Reformation, he sensitively communicated through word and writing the Catholic perspective, especially regarding the relationship between Church and state. One of his most important contributions to the Church is a three-volume work, *Disputations on the Controversies of the Christian Faith*, which explained Catholic fundamentals in a non-defensive, systematic way.

St. Robert, a devotee of St. Francis of Assisi, demonstrated heroic virtue by praying for his opponents, living simply, and embracing spiritual discipline.

T H U 18 (#446) green
Weekday

The Lectionary for Mass

◆ FIRST READING: This is the earliest New Testament text on the Resurrection since the writings of Paul predate the Gospel. Some of the appearances Paul names are mentioned only here. Paul, not being among the Apostles at the time of the Resurrection, speaks of himself as being "born" as a Christian "abnormally" (1 Corinthians 15:8), since his encounter was with the Risen Christ on the road to Damascus (Acts of the Apostles 9). Paul's conversion is the work of grace. Anything Paul is or does is the work of grace. Paul's assent to God allows grace to be effective in his life.

◆ RESPONSORIAL PSALM 118: Recognition of the grace we have received should give rise to praise and thanksgiving. The original context of this psalm was deliverance from a serious illness unto death. This deliverance is given new meaning in the light of Jesus's Resurrection from the dead.

◆ GOSPEL: Jesus paints quite a contrast between Simon the righteous Pharisee and the unnamed sinner who washes the feet of his guest with her tears and anoints them with oil. Though Simon invited Jesus to his home for dinner, it is the woman who welcomed and received him into her heart. It is she who received salvation and forgiveness because of her great love.

FRI 19 (#447) green
Weekday

Optional Memorial of St. Januarius, Bishop and Martyr / red

The Lectionary for Mass

◆ FIRST READING: Not everyone among the Corinthians believed Paul's teaching on the resurrection of the dead. Christ's Resurrection from the dead was not the issue, theirs was. For some, perhaps, it was too much, too difficult to believe; for others, who longed to have their souls freed from their physical bodies, it was hardly "Good News." However, Christ's Resurrection is the foundation and proof of our own. The Risen Christ is but the firstfruits of the harvest of the Resurrection.

◆ RESPONSORIAL PSALM 17: In light of Paul's teaching on the Resurrection, today's antiphon could easily be adapted so as to read, "Lord, when your glory appears, so too will ours!" Note also the reference to "waking" in the last line of the psalm in juxtaposition with today's First Reading suggesting the resurrection from the dead. The psalm itself stems from an experience of oppression and is voiced by one who "flee(s) from (his) foes" seeking refuge at God's right hand. Throughout his ministry to the Corinthians, Paul met with opposition to himself and/or to certain aspects of the Gospel message.

◆ GOSPEL: Today's Gospel account focuses on the many women among Jesus's disciples who journey with him from Galilee to Jerusalem, and are present—albeit from a distance—at the Cross. Note that all that is said about Mary Magdalene is that she had been healed of evil spirits and infirmities. She is not to be confused with the sinful women in yesterday's Gospel account.

Today's Saint

St. Januarius (+ 305) was Bishop of Benevento in Italy during the Diocletian persecutions. After suffering the fate of a martyr, being thrown to wild beasts and then beheaded, his relics were transported to Naples, where it is said that a vial of his blood liquefies on three feast days related to his life: today, the day he supposedly prevented an eruption of Mount Vesuvius in 1631 (December 16), and the Saturday before the first Sunday in May, commemorating the transfer of his relics. He is the patron saint of blood banks and Naples, where he is referred to as San Gennaro.

SAT 20 (#448) red
Memorial of Saints Andrew Kim Tae-gŏn, Priest, and Paul Chŏng Ha-sang, and Companions, Martyrs

The Lectionary for Mass

◆ FIRST READING: Who hasn't wondered about what life will be like after death! The Corinthians were no exception. A bit impatiently, perhaps, Paul answers that our resurrected spiritual bodies will be entirely different from what we have now. In fact, we will be the image of the Risen Christ.

◆ RESPONSORIAL PSALM 56 is a prayer of confidence in the experience of God's presence and help, and the conviction of living now in the presence of the Lord.

◆ GOSPEL: Today's Gospel is of the well-known parable of the sower and the seed. The seed, as the interpretation tells us, is the Word of God. The various places the seed falls point to the different types of receptivity God's Word receives in our hearts. Does the Word thrive in our hearts?

The Roman Missal

All the orations for this memorial of the martyrs of Korea are proper for today, and can be found in the Proper of Saints at September 20. The Collect acknowledges the blood of these martyrs as the seed that bears fruit. The Prayer over the Offerings reminds us that in celebrating the Eucharist, we are to offer ourselves, both at the liturgy and in all of life, as it asks that through the intercession of these martyrs "we ourselves may become / a sacrifice acceptable to you for the salvation of all the world." The Prayer after Communion labels the Eucharistic food as "the food of the valiant," thus designating it as the nourishment that strengthens us to cling faithfully to Christ and to "labor in the Church for the salvation of all." Either Preface I or Preface II of Holy Martyrs would be the appropriate choice for today.

Today's Saints

During the eighteenth and nineteenth centuries, approximately eight thousand adherents to the Catholic faith in Korea were martyred, 103 of whom were canonized by Pope John Paul II in 1988. The canonized martyrs were victims of a particularly heinous series of persecutions happening between 1839 and 1867. During this time period, Korea was ruled by an anti-Christian dynasty that did everything possible to eliminate Catholic ideology and influence, including the malicious mass murder of Christian missionaries and their followers. Two of the more notable martyrs are St. Andrew Kim Tae-gŏn (1821–1846), a priest, and St. Paul Chŏng Ha-sang (1794/5–1839), a layman, both of whom were dedicated to the revitalization of the Church in Korea.

(#133)   green

21 Twenty-fifth Sunday in Ordinary Time

The Lectionary for Mass

◆ **First Reading:** Today's reading stems from the time of the Babylonian Exile, a time interpreted by the prophets as punishment for Israel's sins of infidelity. Isaiah's words bring a message of hope to the people. The Lord is near. The Lord is merciful and forgiving. Isaiah's words likewise "command" a response: "Seek the Lord." Forsake your evil ways. Turn to the Lord.

Certainly the ways of the God of the covenant must have been incomprehensible to the people exiled in Babylon in the wake of the destruction of their Temple and the apparent end of the Davidic dynasty. Yet, God's ways can lead to healing, restoration, and life.

◆ **Responsorial Psalm 145:** Our antiphon picks up on the theme of the Lord's nearness to his people (see also the third stanza). Notice the mention of the Lord's mercy in the second stanza, and the ways of the Lord (third stanza). The psalm is one of praise. What other response could there be to a God who is so near and merciful?

◆ **Second Reading:** Paul, writing from prison, faces the possible prospect of his death. He is torn between his desire to live that he might continue to work on behalf of the Gospel and his desire to be fully with

the Lord in heaven, which is why he can call death a gain (see Philippians 1:21). Today's reading skips over two verses in which Paul speaks with assurance that his death is not yet to be for it is of more benefit to them that he lives and labors on behalf of the Gospel (see Philippians 1:25–26). The Lectionary text resumes with verse 27a, an exhortation to the Philippians to live in a manner worthy of the Gospel in which they believe.

◆ **Gospel:** Today's Gospel account images God as landowner. As parables are wont to do, this one completely overturns what we, like the workers, would think to be just and fair by our reckoning. Like the laborers who worked all day, we object. But as we heard in today's First Reading, God's thoughts are not ours. The landowner is being fair as he himself points out. He was not cheating those who worked all day of their due; only being generous to those who were hired last. God is extraordinarily generous. What is our response when we see God acting in generosity and mercy to others? Do we feel cheated?

The Roman Missal

The Mass texts for today are found in the "Ordinary Time" section of the Proper of Time. The Gloria is sung or said today.

The Collect notes how all the commands of God's sacred law are grounded in one foundation: the unity of love of God and love of neighbor. The Prayer over the Offerings prays that we may truly possess what we "profess with devotion and faith;" since the context for this possession is asking God to receive our offerings, then it is the offering of ourselves in union with Christ that we are professing, and it is the offering of ourselves in union with Christ that we pray will become more and more a reality through our participation in the offering

of the Eucharist. The Prayer after Communion also makes an important connection between liturgical celebration and everyday life: it asks that redemption might be ours "both in mystery [liturgical celebration] and in the manner of our life."

Any one of the eight Prefaces of the Sundays in Ordinary Time are appropriate for today. Perhaps Preface VIII, with its emphasis on the Church, could be a way of echoing how Christ has established a whole new order, and how the ways of the kingdom manifest God's wisdom, not the world's, as a way of reinforcing the message of the Gospel. Also, another possibility would be to use Eucharistic Prayer IV today; its recap of salvation history and its announcement that Jesus came to proclaim good news to the poor, freedom to prisoners, and joy to the sorrowful of heart, could also reinforce the values of the kingdom described in the Gospel. (Remember that if you choose this Prayer, you must also use its proper Preface.) In addition, Eucharistic Prayer for Reconciliation II might also be considered for today: its focus on unity, on discord being changed to mutual respect, and on bringing together "brothers and sisters and those of every race and tongue," and on sharing "the unending banquet of unity," could also underscore themes present in today's challenging Gospel parable.

Pastoral Reflection

While today's parable is about Jesus's choice, as God, to love all equally due to his word, the practical application of the actions of the Master seem difficult to swallow in our age. We seek equality, just wages, rights met and honored monetarily because of what we accomplish or how hard or long we work. Similarly, we may struggle with how someone else does not perceivably match our expectations of how to work and yet "get away" with doing little. Know only yourself. Work with integrity with the gifts you have to offer and willingly live up to this each day. We are each expected to offer the fullness of our lives and ability to the situations at hand. In all you do, give only glory to God, and pray to not seek glory for yourself.

MON 22 (#449) green
Weekday

The Lectionary for Mass

◆ FIRST READING: We begin a series of readings from Proverbs, one of the Old Testament Wisdom books, a collection of maxims, not all necessarily religious in tone, and sometimes, but not always, grouped on the basis of similarity in theme. They are attributed to King Solomon, a man whose wisdom was widely acclaimed (see 1 Kings 3). Many of the maxims are similar to those found in the literature of Israel's neighbors. Today's text focuses on behavior toward one's neighbor and exhorts the faithful Israelite to manifest uprightness and humility in all his doings.

◆ RESPONSORIAL PSALM 15: It is the just who shall live in the dwelling place of God. The psalm describes the righteous behavior that is characteristic of such a person.

◆ GOSPEL: "Take care . . . how you hear" (Luke 8:18). In one ear and out the other? Or are we listening with the ear of the heart and shining forth with the light of love for God and others?

TUE 23 (#450) white
Memorial of St. Pius of Pietrelcina, Priest

The Lectionary for Mass

◆ FIRST READING: Once again we see the stark contrast between the ways of the just and the ways of the wicked. One must be directed by the hand of the Lord if one is to live a life pleasing to him.

◆ RESPONSORIAL PSALM 119 acclaims the wisdom of God's law. The psalmist prays for guidance that, faithful to the commands of the law, he will walk in the way of the Lord.

◆ GOSPEL: Hearing and doing the Word of God puts one in a relationship with Jesus closer than the bonds of natural family ties.

The Roman Missal

The Collect, found at September 23, is the prayer that is proper for today. The Collect acknowledges the stigmata that Padre Pio received as it notes that God, "by a singular grace, / gave the Priest Saint Pius a share in the Cross of your Son." Thus do we ask in this prayer to "be united constantly to the sufferings of Christ." The Prayer over the Offerings and the Prayer after Communion come from either the Common of Pastors: For One Pastor, or from the Common of Holy Men and Women: For Religious. Consider using the Preface of Holy Pastors as the Preface for today, although Preface I or II of Saints or the Preface of Holy Virgins and Religious could also be considered.

Today's Saint

Early in life St. "Padre" Pio of Pietrelcina (1887–1968), a Capuchin priest from Italy, demonstrated an unquenchable thirst for God. While praying one day before a crucifix, he received the visible wounds of crucifixion that Christ bore in his Passion and Death, known as the stigmata. After an examination by a doctor, it was determined that there was no natural explanation for the wounds. Along with the stigmata, he experienced other mystical phenomena, including bilocation, the ability to be in two places at the same time, and "reading the hearts" of those who sought counsel and forgiveness in the Sacrament of Reconciliation. These two miraculous gifts enabled him to lead both

the sinner and devout closer to God. Upon his death the stigmata were no longer visible.

WED 24 (#451) green
Weekday

The Lectionary for Mass

◆ FIRST READING: The first saying acknowledges the Lord as a safe refuge and God's word as a sure guide. The second saying is a prayer for integrity and contentment only with what is needed—nothing less, nothing superfluous.

◆ THE RESPONSORIAL PSALM is once again from Psalm 119, focusing on the law. God's Word, God's law, lights our way. It is a priceless treasure. The person with integrity follows it closely.

◆ GOSPEL: The Apostles sent in Jesus's name are empowered by him in their mission of healing and proclamation of the Gospel. He asks for radical trust and contentment with what is offered them by those who receive them.

If rejected, they must testify against those who would not receive them.

THU 25 (#452) green
Weekday

The Lectionary for Mass

◆ FIRST READING: The Book of Ecclesiastes (Qoheleth) opens on the note of the recognizable patterns and indeed transitory nature of human life. It can sound depressing, but its wisdom is that it calls us to focus on the ultimate and most important (eternal) realities in life.

◆ RESPONSORIAL PSALM: The theme of the transitory nature of human life is clearly echoed in the first two stanzas of Psalm 90. A prayer for wisdom about the true meaning of life is voiced in the third stanza, and for prosperity in the fourth. The antiphon speaks of the

Lord as sure refuge for people of every age.

◆ GOSPEL: The question of Jesus's identity pervades the Gospel. In today's text, it is Herod the tetrarch, who is perplexed about him.

FRI 26 (#453) green Weekday

Optional Memorial of SS. Cosmas and Damian, Martyrs / red

The Lectionary for Mass

◆ FIRST READING: All things have their appointed time in God's plan of salvation. There is a peace to be found in this wisdom for sure, especially when we find ourselves discontented with whatever the present time holds. If we are waiting for something, it will come in due time, God's time. If an event in our lives seems untimely, we must trust that in the mystery of God's wisdom, it was the time appointed, even if the reasons are unknown to us. If we can embrace these truths, we will experience the timeless wisdom of God in our hearts.

◆ RESPONSORIAL PSALM 144 is an acclamation of praise, which is repeated in the first stanza of the psalm. With God as his rock, the psalmist can be confident and unafraid in the face of all that life holds. As fleeting as human life is, it is nonetheless watched over by a loving and providential God.

◆ GOSPEL: No doubt the people of Jesus's day had never met anyone quite like him. Who is this? they asked. In today's Gospel—and note the context, prayer—Jesus asks his disciples what people were saying about him. He asks them as well: What do you say? It is Peter who confesses that Jesus is the Christ or the Messiah. Lest his disciples misunderstand the nature of his messiahship, Jesus is quick to tell them that he will suffer and be killed, but also, that he will be raised on the third day.

Today's Saints

SS. Cosmas and Damian (+287?) were brothers, possibly twins, who practiced medicine without accepting money for their services. They are known in the East as the *anargyroi*, meaning "moneyless ones" or "moneyless healers." As vibrant witnesses to the Christian faith, they were arrested during the Diocletian persecutions. When they refused to renounce their faith and engage in idolatrous worship, they were beheaded and cast into the sea. They are patron saints of twins, confectioners, the sightless, and many medical professions (for example, physicians, nurses, and dentists). Their names are included in Eucharistic Prayer I

SAT 27 (#454) white Memorial of St. Vincent de Paul, Priest

The Lectionary for Mass

◆ FIRST READING: Today's First Reading celebrates the joy and hope of the youthful time of life while at the same time reminding the young person that he or she is accountable to God and will be judged accordingly. Most of the reading is a rather dim description of old age with all its limitations, culminating in death. We are dust and unto dust we shall return. These are sober words that call us, whatever our age, to live each day to the fullest, mindful of God's judgment.

◆ RESPONSORIAL PSALM 90: The themes of the transitoriness of human life and the need to live wisely are likewise heard in today's text. We trust in God's help to attain the wisdom for life.

◆ GOSPEL: Jesus keeps telling his disciples what kind of Messiah he will be. Right now they are full of amazement at his mighty deeds; but Jesus says, "Pay attention to what I am telling you" (Luke 9:44): the Passion is coming. But the disciples do not understand; in fact, they are afraid to understand.

The Roman Missal

All the orations are found in the Proper of Saints at September 27. The Collect, not surprisingly, recognizes the saint for his "apostolic virtues" in working for the relief of the poor and, as is sometimes overlooked, for the formation of the clergy. The Prayer over the Offerings describes how St. Vincent imitated "what he celebrated in these divine mysteries;" therefore, we ask that we too may imitate them and become what we receive, that is, "be transformed into an oblation acceptable to you." The Prayer after Communion asks that in being renewed by this heavenly sacrament, we may both be prompted by the example of St. Vincent and be sustained by his prayers. Either the Preface of Holy Pastors or one of the two Prefaces of Saints would be appropriate for today.

Today's Saint

St. Vincent de Paul, a French peasant, was ordained in 1600. As a parish priest in Paris, he founded a home for foundlings because it upset him to see so many babies abandoned by parents unable to care for them. He founded the Daughters of Charity with Louise de Marillac and the Congregation of the Mission (also known either as Vincentians or Lazarists), both dedicated to helping the poor and visiting prisons. Monsieur Vincent, as he was called, became a popular figure in Paris and, in spite of his visits to people such as Cardinal Richelieu, he maintained his simple lifestyle and manner of dress.

(#136)   green

28 Twenty-sixth Sunday in Ordinary Time

The Lectionary for Mass

◆ FIRST READING: The sentiments expressed in today's reading from Ezekiel are of a piece with the complaint of those who had labored all day in last Sunday's account of the Gospel: it's not fair! At issue, is God's forgiveness of the wicked person who repents and punishment of the virtuous who turns to sin. Are God's ways unfair? Or are we projecting our perceptions, our judgments on to God? God is both merciful and just.

◆ RESPONSORIAL PSALM 25: Today's antiphon invokes the God of mercy, prayed by one who no doubt reckons himself among sinners (third stanza) and seeks God's guidance in his life.

◆ SECOND READING: We hear Paul's beautiful exhortation to the Philippians, a community he loved deeply, to grow in love. Notice the repetition of the words "same" and "unity." Such unity demands selflessness on the part of all, a being willing to let go of one's own wishes and interests for the sake of the community. Verses 6–11 are an early Christian hymn that concisely summarizes the Christian mystery: though he was divine, Jesus willingly embraced human likeness and

was obedient to God, even unto a shameful death. Now exalted by God, all creation reverently acknowledges him as Lord.

◆ GOSPEL: Jesus's parable about the two sons, directed to the religious leaders of the people, conveys a powerful lesson—one that illustrates the message of today's First Reading. It is the tax collectors and prostitutes—the sinners who had first said "no" to God—who are entering the Kingdom of Heaven through the "yes" of their repentance, before the professed—and obstinate—religious leaders.

The Roman Missal

The Mass texts for today are found in the "Ordinary Time" section of the Proper of Time. The Gloria is sung or said today.

This Sunday we have the happy occurrence where the theme for the Collect provides a perfect segue into the Liturgy of the Word. We hear in that prayer how God shows his power principally by pardoning and showing mercy. Thus, are we prepared to hear about turning away from sin and choosing the path of life (First Reading) and about how sinners can enter the Kingdom of God (Gospel). The Prayer over the Offerings reminds us that the offering we make is "the wellspring of all blessing." The Prayer after Communion highlights our union with Christ through the Eucharist: we are united in his suffering when we proclaim his Death, so we ask to be "coheirs in glory with Christ."

In choosing the Preface for today, you might consider Preface II of the Sundays in Ordinary Time, with its mention of Christ responding with compassion to "the waywardness that is ours," or Preface IV, with its emphasis on Christ bringing renewal, on his cancelling out our sins, and on his opening the way to eternal life, or Preface VII, as it mentions our disobedience, which has been overturned by Christ's

obedience. Consider also Eucharistic Prayer for Reconciliation I, with its Preface, as another possibility; all of these would echo the theme of the return of the sinner.

Pastoral Reflection

All the knowledge of laws and the "right way" to live and do things, cannot take the place of true conversion of the heart. Is service to the less fortunate part of your life in some way? If not, find a way to work with those deemed as troublesome by society's standards. In working with them, your heart is changed. Expectations and knowledge of God are broadened and compassion grows. As you seek opportunities to serve, educate yourself on the issues that may cause the person to be in their situation. The education necessary, comprehension of Catholic Social Teaching, is vital only if it is then enacted.

(#647)   white

29 M O N Feast of SS. Michael, Gabriel, and Raphael, Archangels

About this Feast

We celebrate the feast of three archangels, SS. Michael, Gabriel, and Raphael, the great heralds of salvation and defenders against the power of evil. St. Michael is guardian and protector of the Church, from its roots in Israel to the Church of today and beyond. In Hebrew, his name means "who is like God." St. Gabriel, whose name means "hero of God," announces that John the Baptist will be born to Elizabeth and Zechariah. He is entrusted with the most important task of revealing to Mary that she will bear the Son of God. Then, there is St. Raphael, whose name is Hebrew for "God has healed." He is named in Tobit 12 as the one standing in the presence of God, and in 1 Enoch (early Jewish writing) as the healer of the earth (10:7).

The Lectionary for Mass

◆ First Reading: (option 1): We share in Daniel's vision of God's heavenly throne. Notice the attributes of the Ancient One (God)—snow white clothing, his throne is flashing fire, he is surrounded by angelic hosts. This latter point no doubt influenced the choice of this reading for today. Similar imagery is found in the book of Ezekiel and in Isaiah 6. Daniel also sees "one like a son of man" who receives glory in the presence of the Ancient of Days. The phrase at its most basic level signifies a human being, but in later Judaism it was used in a titular sense with reference to a specific person and his mission on behalf of Israel.

◆ First Reading (option 2): A description of the heavenly war between Michael and his angels, and the dragon (Devil) and his angels. Defeated in battle, Satan and his angels are cast out of heaven. The text actually looks to the end time final defeat of the powers of evil and the vindication of all who are faithful to the Lamb (Jesus) even to the point of death.

◆ Responsorial Psalm: Our prayer of praise is sung in the presence of the angels, who likewise stand before God's throne with songs of praise. Psalm 138 is a hymn of thanksgiving for help that was received in a time of need.

◆ Gospel: On this feast of the angels, we hear of those ascending and descending on the Son of Man. Throughout Scripture, angels function as heavenly messengers. Again, we meet the title Son of Man, here with reference to Jesus as it is used in the Gospels. Jesus's destiny was to receive glory and dominion through his Passion, Death, and Resurrection.

The Roman Missal

The texts for this Mass, all proper for the feast day, are located in the Proper of Saints section of the Missal at September 29. The Gloria is sung or said today, since it is a feast.

The Collect speaks of the "marvelous order" of creation, which includes the ministry of the angels who both watch over us and defend us on earth, and who minister to God in heaven. The Prayer over the Offerings describes that it is the ministry of angels who bear the gifts we offer into the presence of God's majesty; it is a beautiful reference to how not only these gifts are lifted up, but how our hearts can be lifted up, as we will proclaim shortly in the Preface dialogue. The text for the Preface proper for today is given right there along with the other texts for this Mass; musical notation is provided. The Preface reminds us that when we pay honor to the angels, in fact we are praising God, since their great dignity and splendor shows how great God is. The Prayer after Communion begs that we might "advance boldly along the way of salvation" through both the nourishment of the Eucharist and the protection of the angels.

Pastoral Reflection

Our cultural fascination with angels likely comes from a desire to know that God intervenes on earth. We long to see God's power at work, acting on behalf of his children. Since ancient times, people have shared in this hope. Scripture and tradition reassure us: we can rely upon God's protection and care. Whether angels are truly at our side caring for us, or whether we simply feel the love and guidance of God in an unknown way, we can count on not being alone.

(#456)   white

30 Memorial of St. Jerome, Priest and Doctor of the Church

T U E

The Lectionary for Mass

◆ First Reading: Though not evident from the Lectionary selection of readings, the lament voiced by Job in today's reading comes in response to the affliction of painful boils on his whole body. Job has lost all: children, servants, possessions—even his physical well-being. His wife thinks that all of this must be God's punishment for some sin Job has committed (see Job 2). Job knows he is innocent and is perplexed by his unexplainable suffering.

◆ Responsorial Psalm 88 is the lamenting prayer of one who suffers greatly and describes in vivid detail the nature of the suffering—perhaps here, life-threatening sickness (see the second and third stanzas). The one who prays feels abandoned by God and begs God to hear his prayer.

◆ Gospel: Jesus's journey to Jerusalem—and his Passion and Death—would take firm and resolute determination. There was antagonism between the Samaritans and the Jews stemming from the time of the Babylonian Exile. The issue here, however, is not so much this antagonism but the disciples' desire to seek revenge for the Samaritans' lack of hospitality. Jesus rebukes his disciples for their violent thoughts.

The Roman Missal

All the orations are proper for today, and are located in the Proper of Saints at September 30. The Collect acclaims St. Jerome for his "living and tender love for Sacred Scripture," asking that we "may be ever more fruitfully nourished by your Word." The prayer offers a

---

fitting introduction to the Liturgy of the Word. The Prayer over the Offerings goes on to remind us of how the Word leads to Eucharist: it notes how now that we have meditated on God's Word, we can ask to "more eagerly draw near to offer your majesty the sacrifice of salvation." The Prayer after Communion prays that, having received the holy gifts of the Eucharist, our hearts may be stirred up to be more attentive to sacred teachings (namely, the Scriptures) and so better understand the path we are to follow, thus obtaining everlasting life. How wonderful it is to note how the orations for this day provide a mystagogy on the unity between Word and sacrament! Either the Preface of Holy Pastors or Preface I or Preface II of Saints would be appropriate choices today.

Today's Saint

St. Jerome (345–420) is the patron saint of scholars and librarians. With a great love of learning and books, as a monk and priest he developed a passion for the interpretation of Sacred Scripture. With a comprehensive knowledge of classical languages, St. Jerome produced a Latin text of the entire Bible eventually known as the Vulgate. He wrote numerous commentaries on several books of the Bible, including a highly reputable work on the Gospel according to Matthew. Along with writing, he provided spiritual guidance to wealthy widows and mentored young monks in monastic discipline. St. Jerome joins three other saints (Ambrose, Augustine, and Gregory the Great) as the first Doctors of the Church.

October
Month of the Holy Rosary

(#457)   white

Memorial of St. Thérèse of the Child Jesus, Virgin and Doctor of the Church

WED 1

The Lectionary for Mass

◆ FIRST READING: We hear Job's response to his friend's words to him. Job's friends believed that if a person was good and upright, that person would be blessed and prosperous. Job had suffered great loss; therefore, they reasoned that he must have sinned. Job's response is that God's ways are inexplicable; his wisdom, unfathomable. The marvels of creation demonstrate God's power over all his creation, including Job. The question Job poses to his friend in response is "Who am I to contend with God's ways?"

◆ RESPONSORIAL PSALM 88 is a lament voiced from a situation of desperate need, perhaps even life-threatening illness. The psalmist pleads for life; the dead are no longer able to praise the Lord. The key to endurance is to "wait" (verse 14) upon the Lord (third stanza).

◆ GOSPEL: As Jesus continues his journey to Jerusalem, someone comes up and announces his intended discipleship. Are you willing to be homeless? Jesus asks. Another would-be disciple has a stipulation: first, let me do this before I follow you. Our response must be immediate; the kingdom of God has priority.

The Roman Missal

All the orations are proper for today, as found in the Proper of Saints at October 1. The Collect explicitly mentions the "little way" of St. Thérèse, noting how God's kingdom is open "to those who are humble and to little ones." The Prayer over the Offerings asks that "our dutiful service may find favor" in the sight of God—and by "dutiful service" we can hear both the work of doing the ritual of worship and the work of doing acts of love in the Christian life, which we bring to offer at this Eucharist. The Prayer after Communion prays that the Sacrament we receive will "kindle in us the force of that love with which St. Thérèse dedicated herself" to God; we can be reminded that reception of the Eucharist is never a mere passive reception, but an active pledge to be renewed and revived in living the Christian life. The Preface of Holy Virgins and Religious would seem to be the most appropriate choice for a Preface today, although certainly Preface I or II of Saints could also be used.

Today's Saint

St. Thérèse of Lisieux of the Child Jesus (1873–1897), known as the "Little Flower," was a spiritual athlete, but not in the same way as her contemporaries. Contrary to the spirituality of her time, which favored self-mortification and miraculous phenomena, she approached God through the ordinary experiences of everyday life.

As a Carmelite nun, she coined the phrase the "Little Way," referring to her belief that every act, no matter how small, is an opportunity to meet and praise God. While struggling with the debilitating disease of tuberculosis, she wrote her spiritual autobiography, *The Story of a Soul.* Her autobiography, translated into over fifty languages, has inspired faith in the skeptic and strengthened the soul of the believer. She is patron saint of the missions and a Doctor of the Church.

**T
H
U** **2** (#458, Gospel #650) white
**Memorial of the Holy
Guardian Angels**

About this Memorial

Today we honor the countless un-named angels assigned to guide, guard, and protect us throughout our lives. The belief in angels is supported by their mention in the Book of Psalms and other books of the Old Testament, as well as the Gospel, as in today's passage from Matthew 18:10.

The Lectionary for Mass

◆ FIRST READING: One could certainly question what kind of people Job's three friends were who came to support him in his distress but insisted that he must have done great wrong to receive such afflictions from God. The last part of today's reading speaks of Job's great confidence in God. Job knows that he will be vindicated by God and believes that he shall see God's hand at work.

◆ RESPONSORIAL PSALM 27 picks up on this last theme. The verses chosen today are a prayer of intense need and longing for God.

◆ GOSPEL: The Gospel text draws upon the Jewish tradition that every nation has an angel in heaven. Here, each person has a guardian angel. Most of the text focuses on the child and the necessity of becoming like a child—simple, open, and trusting.

The Roman Missal

Like yesterday, all the orations are proper again for today, and these are found at October 2. The Collect pleads that God will always have the holy angels guard and defend us. The Prayer over the Offerings also asks for the protection of our guardian angels, so that "we may be delivered from present dangers / and brought happily to life eternal." The proper Preface, "God glorified through the Angels," is given right there along with the other texts for

this memorial; it is the same text used for the Feast of SS. Michael, Gabriel, and Raphael the Archangels on September 29 (refer to the text for that day if you wish to have the musical notation to sing the Preface). This Preface describes how the honor we pay to angels results in God being glorified; to venerate the angels is to praise God. The Prayer after Communion reminds us that the nourishment we receive in the Eucharist is nourishment for eternal life; we therefore ask this day that the angels guide us into that life.

**F
R
I** **3** (#459) green
Weekday

The Lectionary for Mass

◆ FIRST READING: God's speech to Job draws upon the mysterious workings of nature as evidenced in both the coming of dawn and the source and depth of the sea. God asks Job: Have you knowledge of these? Of course Job doesn't and is led to the realization of his own insignificance before God.

◆ RESPONSORIAL PSALM 139: The dawn and the sea are mentioned again in the stanzas of today's Psalm, which emphasizes God's scrutiny of every human being and the fact that nothing is hidden from him. From God, there is no escape.

◆ GOSPEL: In this chapter on the mission of the disciples, Jesus speaks of both the reception and the rejection of their message. Acts of power and healing should lead to repentance. Jesus's contemporaries' rejection of the Gospel is far worse than the sins of Tyre and Sidon.

**S
A
T** **4** (#460) white
**Memorial of
St. Francis of Assisi**

The Lectionary for Mass

◆ FIRST READING: Job repents for questioning God's ways. God, in turn, blesses Job in abundance, as our reading describes.

◆ THE RESPONSORIAL PSALM is a prayer for God's blessing and for instruction in God's ways. Psalm 119 celebrates the law of the Lord as a source of wisdom and of life. The psalmist acknowledges that even afflictions can teach us the ways of God.

◆ GOSPEL: Jesus instructs his disciples to rejoice not so much in the acts of power they perform but, rather, in the fact that their names are written in heaven. Jesus's prayer in the second part of the Gospel stresses that the revelation the disciples have received is a gift from the Lord and a source of blessing for them.

The Roman Missal

Once again all the orations are proper for the day; these are found at October 4 in the Proper of Saints. The Collect, as we might expect, gives special recognition to the poverty and humility of St. Francis, praying that by walking in the footsteps of the saint we might also follow Christ. The Prayer over the Offerings observes how St. Francis "ardently embraced" the mystery of the Cross, the mystery that is celebrated in the Eucharist. The Prayer after Communion prays that the holy gifts of the Eucharist may transform us to imitate "the charity and apostolic zeal of Saint Francis" and thus speak God's love everywhere. Preface I or II of Saints would be good choices for today's Preface.

Today's Saint

As the son of a wealthy Assisi merchant, St. Francis (1182–1226) was destined for grand homes, exquisite clothing, and fine food. After a conversion experience he relinquished the trappings of this world to minister to lepers and preach to the spiritually hungry. His home was the earth; his clothing, humility; and his identity, that of an impoverished beggar seeking God. Many young men joined St. Francis in this new way of life, leading to the foundation of the *frati minori* ("lesser brothers"), which eventually became known as the Friars Minor. He is perhaps one of the most popular saints in Church history, due to his love of creation as exampled in his famous "Canticle of the Sun." Pope Pius XI described St. Francis as *alter Christus*, meaning "another Christ."

The Blessing of Animals

Many parishes prepare the blessing of the animals on this day or on the Sunday closest to it. If you will be inviting animals and their caregivers don't forget to place the invitation in the Sunday bulletin in advance and draw attention to it in the announcements. Invite people to donate food, blankets, towels, toys, and money to local no-kill animal shelters. Ten thousand animals are needlessly euthanized every day in the United States because of the lack of space and funding. We are called to help even the smallest of God's creatures.

If parishioners are not able to bring their animals to the blessing of pets, encourage families to bless their beloved pets at home. Here is a prayer they can use from the *Book of Blessings*, chapter 25:

O God,
you have done all things wisely;
in your goodness you have made us
    in your image
and given us care over other
    living things.

Reach out with your right hand
and grant that these animals may
    serve our needs
and that your bounty in
    the resources of this life
may move us to seek more
    confidently
the goal of eternal life.

We ask this through Christ
    our Lord.
Amen.

Someone in the family can make the Sign of the Cross on their pets with holy water taken from the parish church.

(#139)   green

5 Twenty-seventh Sunday in Ordinary Time

The Lectionary for Mass

◆ FIRST READING: As the end of today's reading makes clear, Israel is the vineyard of the Lord (see also today's Responsorial Psalm 80). What more could God have done for his people, given all the signs and wonders he worked for them, all the prophets he sent to them? Nevertheless, they have not listened, they have not borne fruit in fidelity to the covenant. Accordingly, it will be destroyed. This prophetic word was fulfilled with the Assyrian conquest of Judah (the southern kingdom).

◆ RESPONSORIAL PSALM 80: These words were prayed in the wake of a conquest of the kingdom. "Why, O God?" the people cry. They answer their own question in the last stanza of the psalm. They have been unfaithful. The people plead for restoration and protection from God and promise fidelity to him.

◆ SECOND READING: Nothing is more of an obstacle to inner peace than anxiety and worry—about anything and everything. Paul has the perfect solution to the problem:

with prayer and petition, in confidence and thanksgiving, present your needs to God. It goes without saying that God already knows them—but it is good that we sit with them in God's presence. Then, peace can come—the peace that surpasses our human comprehension, logistics, or planning. Its source is God. Paul recommends what we might call "positive" or "noble" thinking as another means to focusing on what comes from God. The goal is to be centered in God's peace.

◆ GOSPEL: Today's Gospel is an illustration of what happens when human thoughts are not true, honorable, just, pure, lovely, and gracious as well as an example of the destructive power of uncontrolled passions and emotions. By killing the son, the tenants would put themselves in a position to acquire the vineyard for themselves, thus they "plotted" the destruction of another for self-serving gain. In the context of these last chapters of Matthew's account, the actions of the tenants toward the servants sent by the landowner, point to the reactions of many to Jesus and the prophets sent before him. As a result, the "tenants" would be punished (as they were when Jerusalem was destroyed by the Romans in 70 AD) and the "vineyard" given to other tenants (the Gentiles who believed the Gospel). Matthew sees the words of Psalm 118:22–23 fulfilled in Jesus, the rejected stone who became the "corner" or foundation stone of God's new people, the Church.

The Roman Missal

The Mass texts for today are found in the "Ordinary Time" section of the Proper of Time. The Gloria is sung or said today.

The Collect recalls that God's love and grace are super-abundant and overflowing; that is the basis for our asking God "to pardon what conscience dreads / and to give what prayer does not dare to ask." God will always surpass our expectations and fill us with life and love, despite our unworthiness. The Prayer over the Offerings recalls that the sacrifice we celebrate today was instituted by divine command, and its purpose is to continue the sanctifying work by which we are redeemed (in the liturgy, the work of our redemption is actually being accomplished). The Prayer after Communion speaks of the important action of transformation: we are to "be transformed into what we consume." (Shades of St. Augustine!)

Any one of the eight Prefaces of the Sundays in Ordinary Time is equally appropriate today.

Pastoral Reflection

Today's Gospel is another strong eschatological passage, speaking of the end times. There are many directions to take today's message, but to keep in line with last week's suggestions to look in Catholic Social Teaching, let us focus concretely on care of the earth. As stewards of the earth, do we care for what God has given, honor the need to keep plants and wildlife present, and produce just fruits that are natural and healthy, not using or buying foods with excess chemicals and genetically modifying foods? Research the many ways to be kind to the earth and choose at least five, that you are not already doing, to start working toward becoming a steward of the physical vineyard given to our care.

**M
O 6 (#461) green
N Weekday**

Optional Memorials of St. Bruno, Priest / white; Blessed Marie Rose Durocher, Virgin / white

The Lectionary for Mass

◆ FIRST READING: The problem facing the Galatians is the presence of Judaizers in their midst—

Christian Jews who insist that the Gentile believers must likewise be circumcised according to the law of Moses. No, Paul emphatically insists. What is more, the Gospel he preaches—including the welcome of Gentiles—is not of human origin; it was something Paul received through a divine revelation.

◆ RESPONSORIAL PSALM 111: The Lord has remembered his covenant and sent deliverance—salvation—to his people. The covenant of old is ratified and brought to fulfillment in Jesus.

◆ GOSPEL: What must I do? Tell me exactly. We all want certitude regarding what we have been asked to do—especially when it is a matter of eternal life. There are several surprising elements in the parable in today's Gospel.

Why did the official religious personnel pass by the man in need? If he were dead, contact with a corpse would have rendered them defiled and therefore unfit for Temple worship. But even more surprising is the way in which the question changes from "Who is my neighbor?" to "Who was neighbor?" Jesus couches the command in a new way: Be a neighbor by showing mercy.

Today's Saints

St. Bruno (1035–1101) longed for a deeper relationship with God, nourished by solitude and austerity; thus, he and six companions built an oratory surrounded by several small hermitages, or cells, in a remote area in the French Alps known as *La Chartreuse*. This marks the beginning of the Carthusian order whose motto is *Stat crux dum volvitur orbis*, Latin for "The cross is steady while the world is turning." Following the *Rule of St. Benedict* in a strict manner, Carthusian monks live an eremitical (reclusive) life, solely seeking the will of God through prayer and manual labor.

Blessed Marie-Rose Durocher (1811–1894) was raised in a large family just outside of Montreal, Quebec. From a young age she expressed the desire to join a religious order, but her poor health stood in the way of this dream. With the approval of the bishop, she founded the Congregation of the Sisters of the Most Holy Names of Jesus and Mary dedicated to the education of the young and poor. Little did she know, the ministry of the sisters would stem beyond Canada to the United States and some developing countries.

**T 7 (#462) white
U Memorial of Our
E Lady of the Rosary**

Today's Memorial

Pope John Paul II called the Rosary "the school of Mary," a special devotion that teaches us about the profoundly close relationship Mary shared with her Son, Jesus Christ. More than this, praying the Rosary invites us into this relationship, nurturing our faith and deepening our understanding of who Jesus Christ was for the world. The Church celebrates Our Lady of the Rosary in order to honor Mary's example and guidance to her Son. May we learn in her school how to open our lives to her Son Jesus, and how to imitate his example of sharing God's love with the world.

The Lectionary for Mass

◆ FIRST READING: Today's First Reading is Paul's account of his conversion experience, his encounter with the Risen Lord on the road to Damascus (though the place is not mentioned here; see Acts 9). Note how Paul describes his zeal for his Jewish traditions—even to the point of trying to eliminate that which he saw as untrue to it (that is, Christianity). Paul sees his call, his vocation, as in God's plan even before his birth. His mission to Gentiles, non-Jews, is integral to his call.

◆ RESPONSORIAL PSALM 139 attests to God's intimate knowledge of every human creature—even before his or her birth. Our antiphon: "Guide me . . ." must have been Paul's prayer particularly after his most unexpected encounter with the Risen Christ. Paul came to recognize that Jesus is indeed the "everlasting way."

◆ GOSPEL: What an interesting study in personalities is set before us today. Both Martha and Mary had great love for Jesus. Martha seems to be the manager of the home; Mary, the quiet one. Martha's (perhaps understandable) reaction: "tell her to help me" (Luke 10:39) reminds us how easy it is to be caught up in anxieties. Mary has chosen the better part: listening to Jesus.

The Roman Missal

All the orations are proper for today, and can be found in the Proper of Saints at October 7. All who pray the Angelus will recognize the text of today's Collect. The prayer recaps the mysteries of faith—the Annunciation, the Incarnation, and the Paschal Mystery—and it asks for the intercession of the Blessed Virgin Mary in bringing us to the glory of sharing in her Son's Resurrection. The Prayer over the Offerings reminds us that we are to be conformed to the offerings we bring—in other words, we are to offer ourselves with Christ and so die and rise with him in this celebration. It is only in that way that we can, in the words of this prayer, "honor the mysteries . . . / as to be made worthy of his promises." Either Preface I or Preface II of the Blessed Virgin Mary is the Preface assigned for today; if Preface I is chosen, use the phrase "on the feast day" where the various options are given in the Preface. The Prayer after Communion again speaks about the way our lives share

in the Paschal Mystery through our participation in this liturgy; liturgy and life intersect.

W E D 8 (#463) green
Weekday

The Lectionary for Mass

◆ FIRST READING: Today's First Reading is a continuation of Paul's account of his conversion experience and its effect on his life. Note how Paul first had "to be" with all that happened. It was some seventeen years after his experience before he consulted the Apostles as a whole in Jerusalem and tells them of his mission to Gentiles. Paul also tells of an incident that demonstrates that even the first Apostles recognized that Jewish dietary laws did not apply to Gentile believers.

◆ RESPONSORIAL PSALM 117: The antiphon is taken from the Gospel commissioning of the Apostles after Christ's Resurrection. "All the world" includes the Gentiles as well as the Jews.

◆ GOSPEL: What a beautiful image. The disciples want to pray in the same manner that they see Jesus praying. The prayer that Jesus teaches them is what we know as the Our Father. God is Father, source of life, provider of our needs, one who loves us so much that we are more important than the wrong that we do, if only we turn to him for forgiveness.

T H U 9 (#464) green
Weekday

Optional Memorials of St. Denis, Bishop, and Companions, Martyrs / red; St. John Leonardi, Priest / white

The Lectionary for Mass

◆ FIRST READING: Paul is completely exasperated with the Galatians. They have let themselves be persuaded by teachers who insist

on full observance of the law by the law (circumcision). It is not by works of the law that one is saved and receives God's spirit, but from faith in the crucified Son of God.

◆ CANTICLE: Today's response is actually taken from the Gospel according to Luke: Zechariah's canticle of praise at the birth of his son John (the Baptist). His words were ultimately realized in Jesus, who fulfilled all that was promised of old and brings salvation to all people, Gentiles as well as Jews.

◆ GOSPEL: Jesus encourages his disciples to be persistent in prayer through the parable of the persistent friend. If human parents demonstrate such watchful care for their children, how much more will the heavenly Father, who gifts all who believe in Jesus with his Holy Spirit.

Today's Saints

In Paris there stands one of the world's oldest churches still in continuous use, the Royal Abbey of St. Denis. Its first stones were laid in the third century. Renowned as the major burial place of the French monarchy, it owes its establishment and subsequent prestige to the presence of the relics of St. Denis, first Bishop of Paris, martyred during the third century. The legend surrounding the saint's life is complex, as three historical figures appear to have been conflated into one legendary figure. He is portrayed as Dionysius, the evangelizer of Gaul; Dionysius the Areopagite, a disciple of Paul; and later as Pseudo-Dionysius the Areopagite, the author of mystical works. Who was the real St. Denis? Historians have not reached a consensus, partly because the stories are too good not to be told. The favorite of the French is about the beheading of Bishop Denis on the hill of Montmartre; he did not lose his head, however, for he picked it up and walked two miles, his lips chanting the psalms, until he reached his chosen burial spot. There his relics have remained ever since. This miracle of cephalophore (picking up your head after being decapitated and walking away) is well attested to in hagiographical accounts and in medieval iconography. Besides being the patron saint of those with headaches, he is the patron of France and of the city of Paris.

St. John Leonardi, founder of Clerks Regular of the Mother of God of Lucca, was born in Tuscany and ordained in 1572. He founded the Confraternity of Christian Doctrine and the College for the Propagation of the Faith, an important part of the Counter-Reformation.

F R I 10 (#465) green Weekday

The Lectionary for Mass

◆ First Reading: Paul demonstrates that God's call to the Gentiles, God's will that all people be saved by faith, is evident even in the Geneseis accounts of Abraham's life. What is more, in his crucifixion—the punishment of death for capital crimes imposed on criminals—Jesus was one whom the law considered cursed. Yet he was raised from the dead by the Faither, thus bringing life to all.

◆ Responsorial Psalm 111: God has remembered his covenant forever. Abraham entered into covenant with God through faith. So will all people of every nation and every age. It is cause for deep thanks.

◆ Gospel: What is the source of Jesus's power over evil? It can only be of God. The two parables at the end of the Gospel remind us that we must be ever watchful of the strength of the Evil One who strives to separate us from God.

S A T 11 (#466) green Weekday

Optional Memorial of the Blessed Virgin Mary / white

The Lectionary for Mass

◆ First Reading: The discussion of the merits of the law versus faith continues. Paul is emphatic: we are justified, that is, put in right relationship with God through faith just as Abraham was; we are children of God through faith. In Christ, all distinctions, Jew, Greek, slave, free are abolished. All are one in Christ.

◆ Responsorial Psalm 105: The salvation accomplished by Jesus is God's remembrance of his covenant in its full realization. Praise and thanksgiving are the only appropriate response. Note the reference to the descendants of Abraham in the last stanza of the psalm—a nice link to today's First reading.

◆ Gospel: Faith in Jesus establishes new relationships, transcending even natural family ties. Note the emphasis not only on hearing the word, but on *doing* it.

☀ 12 (#142) green Twenty-eighth Sunday in Ordinary Time

The Lectionary for Mass

◆ First Reading: The prophet's words lift us in spirit to the heavenly Jerusalem where death is destroyed and the Lord will provide a rich banquet. (Isaiah's "mountain" [see Isaiah 25:6–10a] was Jerusalem where the Temple of the Lord was located.) For a people suffering the duress of war and destruction, Isaiah's words bring a message of hope—and more. The banquet is for all people, not just the Jews—a message that is voiced repeatedly in the prophet. All will be fulfilled on "that" (see Isaiah 25:6–10a) day—the day of the Lord's coming in power.

◆ Responsorial Psalm 23: This psalm's vivid imagery invites us to experience the Lord as our shepherd, leading us to living waters and a table of rich fare. We hear echoes of the First Reading: the banquet, the experience of God's salvation, the saving hand of the Lord that guides and protects. Those who follow God's own will "live in the house of the Lord / for years to come." Juxtaposed with today's other Scriptures, this verse is to be understood not only in terms of this life, but of the age to come.

◆ Second Reading: Paul's words are admirable and much of what he says in his letters witnesses to the truth of the testimony we hear today. The source of his contentment? The strength which comes to him in Christ, and is rooted in him. It is something we should all strive to attain. As in last Sunday's reading, Paul assures them of God's fulfillment of all their needs. Sometimes, this fulfillment comes through the assistance of others, as it did for Paul.

◆ Gospel: God's covenant with Israel is likened to a Marriage bond throughout Scripture (see Isaiah 54:6; Hosea 2:16–22). Today's parable appropriates this imagery and speaks of future reward as a wedding banquet. The main focus of the parable is on the response given to the invitation and the manner in which it is lived out. We are called to serious self-examination. Do we refuse the invitation to the banquet of the kingdom? Put other things first? Come inappropriately attired? Any of these responses can lead to darkness.

The Roman Missal

The Mass texts for today are found in the "Ordinary Time" section of the Proper of Time. The Gloria is sung or said today.

The Collect reminds us that it is only with the help of God's grace that we are able to carry out good works. The Prayer over the Offerings points to the ultimate goal both of the liturgical celebration of the Eucharist and our life as a whole: we pray that as a result of both, "we may pass over to the glory of heaven." The prayer connects with the Scripture readings today insofar as the glory of heaven is described in the First Reading and the Gospel as a rich banquet with choice food and drink and much joy and festivity. The Prayer after Communion asks that we might have some share in that eschatological fullness now by sharing in the divine nature of the Son through our feeding on his Body and Blood at this celebration.

Any one of the eight Prefaces of the Sundays in Ordinary Time could be considered equally appropriate today, although perhaps Preface VI, with its mention that "even now [we] possess the pledge of life eternal," could be understood as connecting with the imagery of the kingdom, which, although it is a promise of fullness yet to come, is also something that has begun in our midst ("For in you we live and move and have our being, and . . . experience the daily effects of your care").

Pastoral Reflection

How do you choose which Mass you "go to" on a weekly basis? Does it simply fit into your schedule, or does your schedule revolve around the communal banquet? When you choose to come to the weekly banquet feast of Christ, how do you dress? Answers to all of the above questions also reflect our changing society. Most people today do not dress up for Mass. Yet if you know you are going to Mass, you have adequate time to prepare your outer garments to, one hopes, match your inner intentions. Be conscious to dress in a manner that states you are choosing to celebrate and honor God and share with those in your family the connection between what one wears and how one is perceived and then possibly rejected or received into a group.

M O N **13** (#467) green **Weekday**

The Lectionary for Mass

◆ FIRST READING: Speaking to Jewish Christians, Paul draws upon their rich Old Testament traditions to elaborate his teaching on freedom. Quoting from Isaiah, he identifies Sarah, Abraham's barren wife who received her child Isaac in her old age, with the heavenly Jerusalem as one who now has countless children from all nations. For the Gentiles to take on the yoke of Jewish practices would be the same as to submit to slavery.

◆ RESPONSORIAL PSALM 113: This hymn of praise exalts the Lord who is over all nations and has mercy on his people in need.

◆ GOSPEL: Jesus speaks to the crowd, drawing upon the heritage of the Old Testament to demonstrate that he is greater than Jonah, who preached repentance to Nineveh, and greater than Solomon, whose reputation for wisdom drew people from far-off lands.

T U E **14** (#468) green **Weekday**

Optional Memorial of St. Callistus I, Pope and Martyr / red

The Lectionary for Mass

◆ FIRST READING: The bottom line of the issue facing the Gentiles is the question of circumcision, the sign of incorporation into Judaism. Is it necessary for Christians? Paul's answer is a resounding "no."

◆ RESPONSORIAL PSALM: We cry out for God's mercy, a word which in Hebrew also can be rendered God's loving kindness. Psalm 119 acclaims the benefits of God's law for the one who lives with fidelity to its teaching.

◆ GOSPEL: Jesus is once again at a meal, sharing table fellowship with his Pharisee host—a strict adherent to the law. Though welcoming his guest, the Pharisee at the same time judges him. Jesus confronts him for his hypocrisy. What matters is not what is on the outside, but what is within, particularly as expressed in loving concern for the poor as evidenced in giving alms.

Today's Saint

Following a life of slavery and hard labor, St. Callistus I (+ 222) was appointed deacon in charge of the Christian cemetery on the Appian Way, now called the catacomb of San Callisto. Recognized for his abounding wisdom and natural bent for leadership, he was eventually elected pope. He had many critics, due to his liberal stance regarding the forgiveness of those who had apostatized during times of persecution. St. Callistus, heeding the commands of Christ, believed the repentant should be forgiven and welcomed back into the Church. Tradition maintains that he began the Ember Days, periods of fasting and abstinence, which are no longer observed among Catholics. He is commemorated as a martyr; he was probably killed during a public disturbance.

(#469) white

Memorial of St. Teresa of Jesus, Virgin and Doctor of the Church

WED 15

The Lectionary for Mass

◆ FIRST READING: Today's reading challenges us to examine whether the works evident in our behaviors in daily life are from the flesh (anything opposed to God) or from the spirit of God. Those who "belong" to Jesus, who have professed faith in him and have received the gift of his Holy Spirit, should have put to death anything in themselves that is not of God.

◆ RESPONSORIAL PSALM 1: Today's verse is from the Gospel according to John. The "following" and "walking" spoken of in this verse and in the psalm refers to a manner of life. We are to live according to the teachings of God's law, for in it, as Psalm 1 proclaims, is our happiness.

◆ GOSPEL: Controversy between Jesus and the scribes and Pharisees pervades the Gospels. While observing the letter of the law, they miss the deeper call to love, to be righteous, and to be open to God's love and mercy. Self-justification is always dangerous.

The Roman Missal

All the orations are proper for this obligatory memorial, and they can be found in the Proper of Saints at October 15. The Collect recognizes St. Teresa's work as a reformer by noting that God raised her up "to show the Church the way to seek perfection." Thus, we pray that we may be nourished by her teaching and be "fired with longing for true holiness." We bring that hunger and longing for holiness and perfection to this and every celebration of the Eucharist. The Prayer over the Offerings asks that our offerings at this celebration will be as pleasing to God as was the "devoted service of St. Teresa." Pointing out that we have been fed with the Bread of Heaven, the Prayer after Communion asks that we "may follow the example of St. Teresa / and rejoice to sing of your mercies for all eternity." It would seem that the Preface of Holy Virgins and Religious would be the most logical choice for the Preface today.

Today's Saint

St. Teresa of Jesus (1515–1582), more commonly known as St. Teresa of Avila, joined the Carmelite Convent of the Incarnation at the age of 21. Disheartened by convent life, in particular, its spiritual laxity, opulent nature, and overly social atmosphere, she began a reform movement that provided the framework for the Discalced Carmelites. Members of this new branch of Carmelites modeled themselves on the poor and crucified Christ, adopting a life of poverty and abstinence. In collaboration with St. John of the Cross, Teresa helped bring this new way of life to the male Carmelite communities. Their reforms met with great resistance, but they moved forward with faith and persistence. Among her many writings, she is well-known for two classics: *The Way of Perfection* and *The Interior Castle*.

(#470) green

Weekday

THU 16

Optional Memorials of St. Hedwig, Religious / white; St. Margaret Mary Alacoque, Virgin / white

The Lectionary for Mass

◆ FIRST READING: The beautiful words of this prayer of praise and thanksgiving call attention to the manifold ways in which the Ephesian community has been blessed by God. They have been chosen by God. They have been destined for adoption as his children through redemption by Jesus his Son. They—and we—have been "lavishly" blessed.

◆ RESPONSORIAL PSALM: The Lord's salvation has been proclaimed to—and experienced by—the Ephesians. Psalm 98 is a hymn of praise for all of God's marvelous deeds. Note the universalism in the third stanza: "all the ends of the earth have seen. . . ." The proclamation of the Gospel to the Gentiles, the Ephesians among them, is the fulfillment of these words of the psalm.

◆ GOSPEL: The rejection that Jesus, like all the prophets before him, experienced at the hands of his own people stands in stark contrast with the faith-filled reception of the Good News by the Gentiles. Woe to those who refuse to believe. Woe to those who are obstacles to the faith of others.

Today's Saints

St. Hedwig married the Duke of greater Poland, with whom she lived a pious life. Together they founded a Cistercian convent, which Hedwig entered when she was widowed.

St. Margaret Mary Alacoque was a French Visitation nun and mystic who promoted devotion to the Sacred Heart of Jesus. In a series of visions, the form of this devotion was revealed: Holy Communion on the first Friday of each month, and the institution of the Solemnity of the Sacred Heart. Margaret Mary was criticized by the other nuns but had the support of the community's confessor, Blessed Claude de la Colombière.

F R I 17 (#471) red

Memorial of St. Ignatius of Antioch, Bishop and Martyr

The Lectionary for Mass

◆ FIRST READING: Chosen to live for the praise of God's glory—that is our raison d'etre according to today's First Reading. What is more, we have been gifted, sealed with God's Holy Spirit, the beginning of our transformation in heavenly glory.

◆ RESPONSORIAL PSALM 33: How blessed, how happy are those whom God has chosen to belong to him! We are among them. Let us rejoice and give thanks and praise.

◆ GOSPEL: We have a virtual mob scene in today's Gospel as people try to get closer to Jesus so as to see and hear him. His message today has several points. First, hypocrisy is like leaven permeating dough and causing it to swell up, only with a not-so-good effect. Secondly, nothing is hidden; all will be made known. Does this call us to conversion and change? Finally, we are worth so much more than the sparrows that God has ever before his eyes—so he also has us.

The Roman Missal

All the orations, found at October 17, are proper for today. The Collect highlights the "glorious passion of St. Ignatius of Antioch." The Prayer over the Offerings contains a wonderful reference to the saint's proclamation before his martyrdom that he was the wheat of Christ, to be ground by the teeth of beasts (a statement that is used as today's Communion Antiphon); the prayer asks that just as St. Ignatius was accepted as the wheat of Christ, so may our oblation be pleasing to God—in other words, may we too be wheat and bread, transformed into an offering acceptable to God

as this gift of bread will be transformed. The Prayer after Communion connects with this thought in asking that the heavenly bread we receive this day renew us "and make us Christians in name and in deed"—the deed perhaps including martyrdom, following the example of St. Ignatius. Given the emphasis on martyrdom in the orations, the most likely choice for the Preface would be one of the Prefaces of Holy Martyrs, although the Preface of Holy Pastors or even one of the two Prefaces of Saints could not be excluded as possibilities.

Today's Saint

St. Ignatius was born in the year 50 and died somewhere between 98 and 117 in Rome. An Apostolic Father and possible disciple of John the Evangelist, he served the community of Antioch as bishop. Living during the anti-Christian reign of the Roman emperor Trajan, he was sentenced to be fed to animals in the Roman Colosseum because he refused to engage in idol worship. His journey to Rome was marked by extensive writing in which he composed seven letters. These letters, directed to various churches, emphasized the humanity and divinity of Christ, the centrality of Eucharist, and the importance of Church unity.

S A T 18 (#661) red

Feast of St. Luke

About this Feast

Today we celebrate the Feast of St. Luke, the evangelist and disciple of the Lord. His account of the Gospel is unique to the other Synoptic Gospel accounts, because it contains the most detail for the Infancy Narratives. Luke furthermore wrote the Acts of the Apostles, which narrates the events of the Apostles and St. Paul during the beginning of the early Church after Jesus's Ascension.

The Lectionary for Mass

◆ FIRST READING: Paul always ends his letters with very personal notes, and today we hear of Luke's loyalty and fidelity in remaining with Paul even though others have deserted him. It is this mention of Luke that results in today's text as the First Reading. We can surmise that it is through the presence of Luke that Paul experienced the strength of the Lord, enabling him to continue his proclamation of the Gospel to the Gentiles.

◆ RESPONSORIAL PSALM 145: Today's responsorial verse calls to mind Jesus's reference to the disciples in John's account as his "friends." Certainly, in writing the Gospel account and Acts of the Apostles, Luke makes known the glorious splendor of God's kingdom. The first two stanzas of today's psalm could well be a description of what a Gospel account "does."

◆ GOSPEL: We hear of Jesus's sending out seventy-two disciples ahead of his own intended visit to various towns and places. Clearly they are to prepare his way. They are to be unencumbered by possessions, realistic about meeting opposition, people of peace, healers of the sick, and proclaimers of God's kingdom.

The Roman Missal

The texts for this Mass, all proper for the feast today, are located in the Proper of Saints section of the Missal at October 18. The Gloria is sung or said today, since it is a feast.

The Collect employs themes typically associated with St. Luke's Gospel: God's love for the poor, and the universality of the Gospel as it goes out to all nations. The Prayer over the Offerings prays that the food of this Eucharist may bring us freedom of heart to serve God, in addition to healing and glory. The Prayer after Communion asks for strength from the Eucharist so that we might continue to be strong "in the faith of the Gospel which Saint Luke proclaimed." The proper Preface designated for today is Preface II of the Apostles.

Today's Saint

Tradition tells us that Luke was a physician and artist who lived in Syria and who wrote at the end of the first century, completing Luke and Acts of the Apostles, a two-volume work, about 80 or 90 AD. He was highly educated, a gifted writer, and a knowledgeable historian as well. He probably knew, and perhaps worked with, St. Paul.

Where would we be without St. Luke? Think how the Church's prayer would be impoverished without Mary's Magnificat, Simeon's canticle of praise on holding Jesus in his arms, and Zechariah's thanksgiving for the birth of John the Baptist. Think how our knowledge and love of the Mother of God would be diminished without Luke's accounts of the infancy of Christ, the Annunciation, the Visitation, the shepherds in the fields at the birth of the Lord, the Presentation and the Finding in the Temple.

(#145) green

19 Twenty-ninth Sunday in Ordinary Time

The Lectionary for Mass

◆ FIRST READING: The Cyrus mentioned in today's First Reading was the Persian king who conquered the Babylonians and allowed the Jewish people to return to their land and rebuild the Temple. Accordingly, Isaiah looks upon him as God's chosen or anointed one regardless of whether he knows Israel's God or not. God's power is at work for his people in and through Cyrus, accomplishing his plan of salvation.

◆ RESPONSORIAL PSALM 96: This psalm of praise acclaims the mighty acts of the Lord; in the context of today's liturgy, specifically those accomplished through Cyrus. Note the reference to the nations or Gentiles in each stanza. The Persians are among them.

◆ SECOND READING: As is typical of the structure of a letter in Paul's time, we have first, the identification of the sender and second, the one to whom it is addressed. Paul begins every letter but one with a prayer of thanksgiving for the community to whom he is writing. The Thessalonians are commended for their faith in action and their endurance in hope. The Gospel Paul proclaimed to them was not merely a matter of notional assent to doctrine, but power at work in daily life.

◆ GOSPEL: The conflict between Jesus and the Jewish religious leaders continues to mount. In today's text, they try to "set up" an opposition between obedience to civil law and covenant fidelity, thus requiring Jesus to make a choice between them. Jesus sees their ruse and affirms the just claims of both: " . . . repay to Caesar what belongs to Caesar and to God what belongs to God."

The Roman Missal

The Mass texts for today are found in the "Ordinary Time" section of the Proper of Time. The Gloria is sung or said today.

The Collect prays that we might always conform our will to God's will, and serve him in sincerity of heart. This petition might in some way be seen as connecting with the Gospel for today, in that discernment of God's will is important in figuring out how we are to live as both citizens of heaven and citizens of the civil society in which we find ourselves. That kind of discernment demands that we constantly seek to purify our actions and our motives, to be focused on the values of the kingdom, and so the Prayer over the Offerings appropriately prays for that purification through our participation in this celebration: that "we may be cleansed by the very mysteries we serve." We need to look at everything through the lens of the Paschal Mystery, celebrated in the Eucharist, in order to properly discern. The Prayer after Communion also assists us in this discernment as it describes how, from our participation in heavenly things (that is, this Eucharist), "we may be helped by what you give in this present age and prepared for the gifts that are eternal."

In choosing a Preface for today, consider how Preface I of the Sundays in Ordinary Time describes for us how we are to live in the world, namely, as a chosen race, a holy nation, and a people belonging to God who proclaim everywhere his mighty works. Also consider using Eucharistic Prayer IV this week, with its own proper Preface; the sweeping résumé of salvation history it gives sets our notions of civil society in its proper perspective before God's majesty.

Pastoral Reflection

Active listening is a skill that is taught to those in counseling and ministerial positions with the purpose being to always fully hear the person speaking and from where they are coming. Jesus was an active listener—knowing he was always being tested, the intention of the questions, and then how to respond so as to answer their question and not fall into their trap. Masterfully Jesus shows us how to listen, receive, and shake off planned verbal attacks with ease. Learn about active listening and find ways to practice and then enact this skill with those who communicate with you.

M O N **20** (#473) green **Weekday**

Optional Memorial of St. Paul of the Cross, Priest / white

The Lectionary for Mass

◆ FIRST READING: Once again, the reality that is now ours in Christ is stressed: eternal life with Christ and immeasurable riches of grace. All is God's initiative in his great love and mercy. Paul speaks of believers as God's handiwork or crafted work, shaped for a particular purpose: that we do the good works God has ordained that we do.

◆ RESPONSORIAL PSALM 100: Again we hear the theme of God's handiwork: "he made us" (Psalm 100:3). The psalm calls people of all lands to be a people of praise in his Temple.

◆ GOSPEL: The situation at the beginning of today's Gospel is sadly too familiar. Jesus's parable touches deeply the truth regarding riches. It is not earthly wealth that ultimately matters, and it certainly cannot be taken with us into the next life. Let us labor, instead, for riches in what matters to God.

Today's Saint

After having a vision of himself clothed in a black habit, St. Paul of the Cross (1694–1775) established the Congregation of the Passion (the Passionists, or Congregation of the Discalced Clerks of the Most Holy Cross and Passion of Our Lord Jesus Christ). The Passionists, a community of priests, were to live a strict monastic life while fostering an intense devotion to the Passion of Christ through preaching and missions. Along with the traditional vows of other religious communities, they took a fourth vow to spread the memory of Christ's Passion. Unique to their habit was a large badge in the shape of a heart, bearing a cross and the words *Jesu XPI Passio*. As they grew in numbers, they engaged in ministry to the sick and dying. Toward the end of his life, St. Paul founded a community of Passionist nuns.

T U E **21** (#474) green **Weekday**

The Lectionary for Mass

◆ FIRST READING: The Ephesians' former status as Gentiles before they knew Christ is highlighted in today's reading. They were seen as completely other by the Jews. But now, through the blood of Christ, the separation, the dividing wall has been demolished. Through the grace of Christ, as a result of God's initiative, all are now one, members of the household of God. How this word, this reality, must have completely overturned their accustomed ways of thinking!

◆ RESPONSORIAL PSALM 85: God has brought a word of peace to people set apart from one another through the salvation that is ours in Christ.

◆ GOSPEL: We are called to watchfulness and vigilance no matter how long into the night we must wait for the Master, for the coming of the Lord. The heavenly reward envisaged in this parable is a banquet served by the Master who becomes servant himself.

W E D **22** (#475) green **Weekday**

Optional Memorial of Blessed John Paul II, Pope / white

The Lectionary for Mass

◆ FIRST READING: We could never attain the knowledge of God's plan for us and for all people on our own. We know only through God's revelation as mediated to us through those chosen for this purpose. Paul was such a one. Do we really grasp the breadth and depth of God's plan for all people? In and through Christ, all are chosen, all are united, all are destined for God.

◆ CANTICLE: Today's text is actually a hymn taken from the prophet Isaiah. Thanksgiving and praise are the only responses we can and must give for the salvation we have received. Let us never cease to do so and to draw God's life-giving water.

◆ GOSPEL: Chapter 12 of Luke contains several parables of vigilance. We hear another one today. Does our Master's (Lord's) delay in returning (to the earth at the end of time) result in our being careless? Perhaps even abusing people and things? We must be prepared to render an account. We know not the time of our Master's coming.

Today's Blessed

In the early years, Catholics and non-Catholics alike were attracted to the athletic man who sneaked out of his villa to ski and reached out to the young at World Youth Days. People of many faiths prayed for him when he was shot in St. Peter's Square and were awed with the mercy he granted his assailant. And none escaped the poignancy of a feeble John Paul II praying at the Western Wall in Israel, leaving a prayer inside the wall. Even a scant follower of the pope knew that the man who forgave his assailant, traveled the world to evangelize, and sought healing in relations with the

Jewish people looked to the Blessed Virgin as a model of faith. To John Paul II, the woman who carried the Savior in her womb, who first gazed on him at birth, and stayed with him by the cross, is the person who can bring followers closest to Christ. In the apostolic exhortation *Ecclesia in America,* he called Mary "the sure path to our meeting with Christ." The pope noted that Our Lady of Guadalupe's meeting with Juan Diego evangelized beyond Mexico and voiced hope that the Mother and Evangelizer of America would guide the Church in America, "so that the new evangelization may yield a splendid flowering of Christian life."

THU 23 (#476) green
Weekday

Optional Memorial of St. John of Capistrano, Priest / white

The Lectionary for Mass

◆ FIRST READING: Today's First Reading is Paul's beautiful prayer for his Ephesian family, which could be prayed for our families as well. Our inner self is where Christ dwells. If only we could grasp at least a bit of the immeasurable love Christ has for us. May the power of his Spirit within us lead us to this realization.

◆ RESPONSORIAL PSALM 33 is a psalm of praise and thanksgiving in recognition of the goodness of the Lord, which fills all the earth. Note the reference to God's plan and design in the third stanza. Happy are we, the people God has chosen as his own.

◆ GOSPEL: There are times, to be sure, when sadly, commitment to the Lord results in division within families. This was a reality in Luke's community and is so still in our own day. Let us pray for our families and for perseverance for those who face opposition in their commitment to the Lord.

Today's Saint

St. John of Capistrano was born in Italy and entered the Franciscans in 1416. He was drawn to the ascetic life and became a follower of St. Bernardine of Siena. After his ordination, John traveled throughout Italy, Germany, Bohemia, Austria, Hungary, Poland, and Russia, preaching penance and establishing numerous communities of Franciscan renewal. When Mohammed II threatened Vienna and Rome, John, then 70, was commissioned by Pope Callistus III to lead a crusade against the invading Turks. Marching at the head of an army of 70,000 Christians, he was victorious in the battle of Belgrade in 1456.

FRI 24 (#477) green
Weekday

Optional Memorial of St. Anthony Mary Claret, Bishop / white

The Lectionary for Mass

◆ FIRST READING: Our call (a word repeated three times), our vocation as Christians, is the subject of today's First Reading. Paul describes in great detail how that call should be lived in the practical details of everyday life. His words challenge and stretch us. It is not easy to follow our crucified Lord in self-giving love.

◆ RESPONSORIAL PSALM 24: Like today's First Reading, our psalm instructs us on the manner of life, the behavior required if we are to stand in God's holy place.

◆ GOSPEL: Jesus chides the crowds who, while being able to interpret the signs of nature, are seemingly unable to discern the sign of the present moment with his presence among them. The saying at the end of the Gospel encourages Jesus's listeners to work out their differences and to seek reconciliation among themselves rather than resort to

law courts, which will only result in punishment.

Today's Saint

St. Anthony Mary Claret, the son of a Spanish weaver, wanted to be a Jesuit, but ill health prevented him from entering that religious order. Instead, he became a secular priest, overseeing a parish in Spain before heading to Catalonia and the Canary Islands as a missionary. He established the Congregation of the Immaculate Heart of Mary (the Claretians), a group of priests and brothers dedicated to seeing the world through the eyes of the poor.

They operate a diverse number of ministries throughout the world. St. Anthony was instrumental in spreading the devotion to the Immaculate Heart of Mary and the Rosary.

SAT 25 (#478) green
Weekday

Optional Memorial of the Blessed Virgin Mary / white

The Lectionary for Mass

◆ FIRST READING: Today's reading begins with reference to the Incarnation, Death, and Resurrection of Christ. It is the risen and glorified Christ who gifts and empowers his Church. A variety of gifts are given, but all for the purpose of building up the Body of Christ in unity and love and maturity—full-growth into the likeness of its head.

◆ RESPONSORIAL PSALM 122: Today's psalm is one originally prayed by pilgrims in the Temple in Jerusalem. Might we not think of it as our own prayer as we make our way to our heavenly home, the Jerusalem on high?

◆ GOSPEL: A tragic incident involving loss of life is reported to Jesus. According to the popular mentality, this was punishment for sin. Jesus warns that a worse fate will come upon those who refuse to take his words to heart and turn from their evil. Perhaps Jesus and our heavenly Father are a bit like the gardener in the parable in the second half of the Gospel: ever patient, always providing opportunities for growth and repentance.

☀ 26 Thirtieth Sunday in Ordinary Time
(#148) green

The Lectionary for Mass

◆ FIRST READING: A very rich wisdom underlies these words of the Lord commanding Israel to show care and concern for the poor and needy, for God, in effect, says to Israel: remember, this was once your lot when you were enslaved in Egypt. Indeed, it was because of God's compassion for Israel when they cried out in their slavery that there was deliverance. So will God hear the cries of the poor in every age and place.

◆ RESPONSORIAL PSALM 18: It is only the one who has experienced his or her own weakness and powerlessness that can truly experience the Lord's strength. Psalm 18 is a beautiful prayer of thanksgiving from one who has known the Lord's saving power and deliverance.

◆ SECOND READING: Today's text follows upon Paul's thanksgiving prayer for the Thessalonians heard in last Sunday's reading. They have been "imitators" of Paul, who strove to imitate the Lord, living according to the model and the teaching

he set forth. In so doing, they have become models for other believers. Can the same be said of us?

◆ GOSPEL: Although the opening line of today's Gospel points to a situation of conflict and challenge, the wisdom of Jesus's answer quickly silences his opponents. *All* of God's teaching; *all* of God's commandments—can be summarized in two ideas: to love God with one's whole being, and also, to love one's neighbor as oneself. Notice that this second commandment is equal to the first.

The Roman Missal

The Mass texts for today are found in the "Ordinary Time" section of the Proper of Time. The Gloria is sung or said today.

Today's Collect asks that we may be made to love what God commands. This reflects the First Reading and the Gospel, where the command is clearly to love our neighbor as we love ourselves. The Prayer over the Offerings bids that what we do in service to God—presumably both within the liturgy (the immediate context for this prayer) and outside of the liturgy (the wider connection with everyday life with which liturgical celebration must always be situated)—may be directed to his glory. The prayer can remind us that we enter into worship not for our own sake, and not to our own ends, but to glorify God and thank God for what he has done. Liturgy ultimately is always about what God has done and is doing, not about what we do. The Prayer after Communion makes an identification between the sacrament and us: it asks that what is within them (that is, the mystery and grace of salvation) may be perfected in us, so "that what we now celebrate in signs / we may one day possess in truth." Thus, are we reminded that the sacramental significations in our liturgies communicate to us the heavenly realities

they signify, which one day we will experience in all their fullness. The liturgical signs participate in the reality and truth of what they signify.

Of the eight Prefaces of the Sundays in Ordinary Time that can possibly be used today, perhaps Preface VIII resonates with the theme of inclusivity and loving one's neighbor that we hear in the readings, as it speaks of scattered children being brought together into the life of the Church. Another strong possibility would be to use Eucharistic Prayer for Reconciliation II, with its own Preface, to highlight the scriptural theme of love of neighbor through its use of phrases such as enemies speaking to one another, adversaries joining hands, people seeking to meet together, hatred being overcome by love, revenge giving way to forgiveness, and discord being changed to mutual respect.

Finally, in view of the call to embody the call to love one's neighbor, perhaps the dismissal formula "Go in peace, glorifying the Lord by your life" would be apropos for today.

Pastoral Reflection

If you are to love your neighbor as yourself, consider some small random act of kindness and do this for another. Pay some portion toward the bill of the person in line behind you. Water your neighbor's grass (probably while doing your own). In small delights, great changes are made to one's frame of mind. Next, consider the questions you ask. Are you seeking to silence a person or to affirm their opinion? In respecting the gifts of the person in your presence, you allow the dignity God places in each person to be honored and therefore learn to love God more in the life created.

M O N 27 (#479) green Weekday

The Lectionary for Mass

◆ FIRST READING: What is expected of us as Christians is clearly spelled out in today's First Reading: imitating God and imitating Christ in daily forgiveness and love, in all of our behaviors. As a result of our Baptism, we are light in the Lord.

◆ RESPONSORIAL PSALM 1: The focus on behavior is heard again in the antiphon. Psalm 1 speaks of the life-giving results of following the Lord's law. In this is true joy.

◆ GOSPEL: A controversy over observance of the Sabbath results when Jesus and a woman, bent over and crippled for eighteen years, are among those who gather for prayer and study of the Scripture in this synagogue service.

Through Jesus's healing touch, the woman is freed from her bondage and is able to stand up straight (a subtle image of resurrection? new life?). Filled with thanksgiving, she glorifies God. The synagogue leader, in contrast, fails to see the power of God at work in their midst.

T U E 28 (#666) red Feast of SS. Simon and Jude, Apostles

About this Feast/Saints

Today we honor two Apostles about whom we know very little. Tradition maintains that St. Simon the Zealot preached missions throughout Persia and Egypt. St. Jude, not to be confused with Judas Iscariot, is the patron of hopeless causes and is called Thaddeus in the Gospel according to Matthew and the Gospel according to Mark. It is believed that he engaged in missionary work in Mesopotamia and Persia. Both Apostles are thought to have been martyred in Persia, and their relics were transferred to St. Peter's Basilica in Rome sometime during the seventh or eighth century.

The Lectionary for Mass

◆ FIRST READING: Our unity in Christ abolishes all former distinctions, ethnic, racial, or religious. Through our common faith, we are united to Christ and to one another: as brothers and sisters in the family of God, fellow citizens of God's holy city, the household of God, a temple or dwelling place of God. On this feast of SS. Simon and Jude, are we aware of how our faith has been built on the foundation of the Apostles' witness centuries ago?

◆ RESPONSORIAL PSALM 19: In its original context, today's psalm speaks of the witness of the heavens to the glory of the Creator God. On this feast of the Apostles, we celebrate the witness of the Apostles who brought the Gospel message throughout all the earth.

◆ GOSPEL: Little is known about the Apostles whose feast we celebrate today. Simon is identified as a Zealot, someone "zealous" to re-establish the nation of Israel and be rid of Roman domination. We might even go so far as to think of him as somewhat of a "revolutionary." Of Jude, we know only that he is the son of James. These and the other Apostles were chosen by Jesus after a night in prayer.

The Roman Missal

The texts for this Mass, all proper for the feast, are in the Proper of Saints at October 28. The Gloria is sung or said today, since it is a feast.

The Collect asks for the intercession of these two saints so that the Church may constantly grow. The Prayer over the Offerings prays that our veneration of the Apostles Simon and Jude may "lead us to worthy celebration of the sacred mysteries." The Prayer after Communion includes a mention of the Holy Spirit, through which we make our prayer that we may remain in God's love in honoring "the glorious passion / of the Apostles Simon and Jude."

The Preface, proper for today, is one of the two Prefaces of the Apostles. Consider using Eucharistic Prayer I, the Roman Canon, today, since SS. Simon and Jude are mentioned in it. Also, the Solemn Blessing formula titled "The Apostles" (in the section "Blessings at the End of Mass" and Prayers over the People) may be used as the final blessing at the end of Mass today.

Today's Saints

Two of the Twelve we remember today: Simon, who was called a Zealot, and Judas, also called Thaddeus. That is the end of the historical record. But the memory of the Church, which might not meet all the requirements of modern historians, does have a deeper record of these two saints. Sometime after Pentecost the two of them went off to spread the Gospel in Persia. There they freed people from the oppression that comes with worshipping idols and confronting magicians and pagan priests. The magicians of the false gods demanded a showdown with the holy Apostles, challenging them like the Egyptian priests challenged Moses and Aaron in the courts of Pharaoh. Many were amazed and came to know the truth of Christ, but the magicians and pagan priests rushed upon the Apostles and killed them.

W E D 29 (#481) green Weekday

The Lectionary for Mass

◆ FIRST READING: The relationship between parents and children, slaves and masters are addressed—again reflecting the social structure of the day. Note the appeal to the commandment of the Lord regarding children and their parents. Fathers, as head of the family, are specifically instructed not to trigger anger in their children but to instruct them in the ways of the Lord. Slaves are to think of themselves as serving

Christ in serving the master and are called to integrity. Masters are to show this same integrity to their slaves and look on them as Christ. Masters must keep in mind that they too are slaves, slaves of Christ.

◆ RESPONSORIAL PSALM 145: The reference to the words of the Lord in today's antiphon echoes not only the text of Scripture cited in the First Reading, but also the reading itself—as the Word of the Lord. The references to the Lord's kingdom likewise fit in with Paul's emphasis that all are servants of the Lord.

◆ GOSPEL: Entering the Kingdom of God demands strength and hard work manifest in faithful adherence to the words and commands of the Lord. Many who are self-assured by virtue of their religious practices may not be as secure in the eyes of the Lord as they are in their own. Similarly, some of those judged most unworthy of the kingdom by self-appointed judges may, in fact, be worthy of a higher place.

T H U 30 (#482) green
Weekday

The Lectionary for Mass

◆ FIRST READING: These concluding words from the letter to the Ephesians call all believers to be ready to combat the powers of evil. The battle is a superhuman one, but believers are to draw strength from the Lord and be appropriately "armed" (see verses 14–17) to stand firm in fidelity. Paul exhorts them to constant prayer, watchfulness, and perseverance.

◆ RESPONSORIAL PSALM 144: Today's psalm is the prayer of one who must engage in battle (the first line), which is all of us, per Paul in the First Reading. God is both refuge and strength in the battle, of which victory is assured.

◆ GOSPEL: Like today's psalmist and like other prophets before him, Jesus knew false accusation and opposition. Herod, in particular, is mentioned in today's text. Jesus senses the imminence of his Death and knows that is inevitable. Yet, in fidelity to the call he has received he must continue on his journey to Jerusalem. In today's text, we hear Jesus use the image of a mother hen that carefully gathers and protects her chicks under her wing to speak of his longing to "gather" Jerusalem's children into the fullness of life and salvation. Though acclaimed initially when he enters Jerusalem as the messenger of salvation (see Luke 19:37–38), he is ultimately rejected and put to death.

F R I 31 (#483) green
Weekday

The Lectionary for Mass

◆ FIRST READING: Paul prays with thanksgiving for his beloved community at Philippi, who has supported, indeed joined with him, in his ministry on behalf of the Gospel. Note the two references to the day of Christ. All of Paul's work, all of Christian life, keeps this day in view. It is the day of the coming of the Lord who will reward his faithful people for their fidelity.

◆ RESPONSORIAL PSALM 111: Like our First Reading, Psalm 111 is a hymn of thanksgiving for all the works of the Lord. Sometimes the works of the Lord are manifested in and through the lives of believers through whom the needs of others are met (see, for example, Philippians 1:6). Paul prays with thanksgiving for his beloved community at Philippi, who has supported, indeed joined with him, in his ministry on behalf of the Gospel.

◆ GOSPEL: Quite often in the Gospel according to Luke, we see Jesus sharing a meal with someone. Such table fellowship pointed to an acceptance of one another and to the mutual bond between the participants. In today's Gospel, the meal—a Sabbath meal and therefore particularly significant—was at the home of a "leading" Pharisee. Perhaps even more important than the meal is the healing that takes place in its context, the restoration of a disabled man to wholeness. And herein lies the potential conflict with the Pharisees. "Is it lawful to cure on the Sabbath or not?" (see also Luke 13:10–17). The law permitted care for animals; for Jesus, it went without saying, that humans were more important (see Luke 10:16).

November
Month of the Holy Souls

S A T 1 (#667) white
Solemnity of All Saints

About this Solemnity

Today we celebrate the Solemnity of All Saints, remembering all the saints known and unknown to us who enjoy the glory of heaven. In today's Gospel account we hear the Beatitudes, which are guidelines for true joy and the attainment of sanctity in our Christian lives. We hear how to live lives of holiness so that we may attain happiness in this life, but even more happiness in the next life as we strive to likewise be numbered among all the saints in heaven.

The roots of this solemnity are deep in our history. As early as the fourth century, a feast in honor of all the martyrs was celebrated in the East, and it had come to Rome by the early seventh century, when, on May 13 in 609 or 610, the Roman Pantheon (the ancient temple dedicated to all the gods) was consecrated *S. Maria ad Martyres*, in honor of Our Lady and all martyrs. The Pantheon is still in regular use as a church today, a wonderful meeting place of cultures and histories, with statues of saints in ancient niches where images of Roman deities formerly stood. All Saints honors the "merits of all the Saints" (Collect), who rejoice in God's presence: the towering figures like Augustine, Francis, Thérèse of the Child Jesus, as well as the humble saints whose names are known to few or none, our own grandparents, friends, and teachers who lived their faith to the fullest. This is a day to celebrate them all.

The Lectionary for Mass

◆ First Reading: John recounts his visions of two groups of people who are gathered in heaven in the presence of the victorious Lamb of God and the enthroned God. The one hundred and forty-four thousand evokes the fullness of the twelve tribes of Israel whose faithfulness is rewarded. The universal scope of salvation is evident with those from every nation, race, and people. All been faithful. All have been victorious, having endured a time of great distress.

◆ Responsorial Psalm 24: Today's antiphon perhaps best describes those of us who are still waiting to come to our heavenly home and be counted among those in the presence of God. The second stanza directs our thoughts to what is required of those who would dwell in the Lord's presence.

◆ Second Reading: These words from John touch on what we already are in the here and now: children of God. John's words also touch on what we have yet to become: something that we cannot begin to fathom other than to know that we shall be like God and we shall see him as he is.

◆ Gospel: We hear the Beatitudes from Matthew's account of the Gospel. Notice that there are nine in today's text, the last one being a reference to those who are persecuted—also a link with today's First Reading. The first and eighth Beatitudes speak of the blessedness or happiness that is enjoyed now by those who are poor in spirit (who know their need for and dependence upon God) or who suffer because of their righteous conduct. It is an inner happiness that God alone can give and it is the realization of life in God's kingdom. The other Beatitudes speak of the heavenly reward that is yet to be realized. Suffering and sorrow are inevitable on the way to the kingdom. Meekness, mercy, integrity, and making peace must all be manifest in the one who would dwell on God's mountain.

The Roman Missal

The Entrance Antiphon for this Mass sets the appropriate tone of festivity and rejoicing as we honor all the saints. The Gloria is sung or said today.

The Collect reminds us of the great cloud of witnesses by which we are surrounded as it tells of how in this one celebration we venerate the merits of all the saints. Thus, we can take comfort in asking for the reconciliation with God "for which we earnestly long" because we can count on the intercession of so many saints.

Remember that the Creed is said or sung at this Mass.

The Prayer over the Offerings reiterates that we live our lives, and offer this Eucharist, in the Communion of Saints, and therefore they celebrate with us. We can experience their solidarity with and concern for us because they are assured of immortality in the Lord.

The Preface, titled "The glory of Jerusalem, our mother," is given, with and without musical notation, right there among the pages for all the other texts for this Mass. The Preface points to Jerusalem as our mother and the heavenly city where our brothers and sisters who have gone before us give God eternal praise. The key point to be emphasized is that we as pilgrims seek to advance to the heavenly Jerusalem as well, and our hope of arriving there is not unfounded since we have the strength and good example of the saints to assist us. This reminds us that the liturgical celebration of All Saints is not only about those faithful upon whom the Church has designated the title of sanctity, but it is also about our call to that same sanctity.

Eucharistic Prayer I, the Roman Canon, with its two listing of saints' names, might be considered an appropriate choice for use at this solemnity.

The Communion Antiphon is taken from the Beatitudes from Matthew's account, and thus the antiphon proclaims for us the virtues of the saints, the virtues we hope to be strengthened in living as a result of our participation in Holy Communion.

The Prayer after Communion reminds us that the holiness of the saints is only possible because it is rooted in God's holiness, God who alone is holy. In addition, although not explicitly so, the image of the heavenly Jerusalem—the eschatological aspect inherent in every Eucharist—is again invoked as the prayer asks that "we may pass from this pilgrim table to the banquet of our heavenly homeland."

The Solemn Blessing formula for All Saints, found in the section of the Missal "Blessings at the End of Mass and Prayers over the People," is suggested for today, and would be well used. Also, in light of the call to sanctity that is given to us all as we strive to imitate and be in communion with the saints, perhaps the dismissal formula "Go in peace, glorifying the Lord by your life" would be the most appropriate form of dismissal for today.

Pastoral Reflection

On this brilliant day when we celebrate the holy men and women who have gone before us in faith, we too are called to be "Beatitude people"—knowing that our home is not here on earth, but beyond. To steep yourself in this holiness, it is good to sit and pray with each Beatitude in depth. Which Beatitude most calls to you? Which one is the hardest to comprehend? Look up a book written by Sr. Macrina Wiederkehr, OSB, *Seasons of the Heart*. Her understanding of each Beatitude in a poetical voice is a great clarion call of personal understanding and a way to live to align ourselves with each aspect of powerful living.

(#668 or #1011–1016)
white / violet / black

2 The Commemoration of All the Faithful Departed (All Souls' Day)

About this Commemoration

All Souls' Day is unique on the liturgical calendar. Neither a solemnity nor a feast, this *commemoration* outranks other feasts and even takes the place of a Sunday in Ordinary Time (should this commemoration fall on a Sunday). Prayer for the dead reaches deep into our human history, and it has been our custom from the earliest days of the Church. The belief that our prayers can be of assistance to the dead is a treasured tenet of our Catholic faith. We profess it every time we recite the Nicene Creed: "I look forward to the resurrection of the dead / and the life of the world to come."

The Lectionary for Mass

Please be aware that the Lectionary provides many options for today's Mass. The commentary below is only one of the many options.

◆ FIRST READING (WISDOM 3:1–9): To all appearances, death can seem the absolute end of life, beyond which there is nothing more, as the first lines of this reading suggest. How far from the truth this is as the first century author of the Book of Wisdom realized. There is hope of immortality and everlasting blessing. What beautiful images for death: God "takes one" to himself (verse 6); God's faithful people "abide with him in love" (verse 9). Note also the references to shining and darting about like sparks (verse 7). This is an image of the transformation that the just will undergo in the age to come, they will be like the angels who are described in similar imagery in the Scriptures.

◆ RESPONSORIAL PSALM 23 is a much loved prayer of confidence whose image of the dark valley represents all our fears and unknowns regarding death. But there is no need to fear, we are led by the Lord to a place of rest and joyful fullness of life in the house of the Lord.

◆ SECOND READING (PHILIPPIANS 3:20–21): God's Word assures us: our weak and lowly bodies will be transformed, conformed with the image of the glorious Risen Christ. Our eyes have yet to see what is in store for us in the age to come!

◆ GOSPEL (JOHN 14:1–6): Jesus's words are spoken to his disciples at the meal the night before he died, so they reflect his awareness of the imminence of his own Death. Perhaps what can speak to us the most on All Souls' Day is the image—again—of Jesus coming to take us to himself at the time of death that we may be with him (verse 3). He is the way to the Father, the way to our heavenly home.

The Roman Missal

Because this Commemoration replaces the Sunday in Ordinary Time, all the texts are taken from November 2 in the Proper of Saints. Any one of the three sets of formularies may be chosen, at the discretion of the priest celebrant or, as appropriate, the parish's liturgy preparation/worship team. All the texts proclaim the centrality of the Paschal Mystery in understanding the meaning of Christian death: because of Jesus's Death and Resurrection, death leads to new life for all those united to Christ. Therefore, because of our faith in the Risen Christ, we can find hope in death. Some of the Mass prayers (the Prayer over the Offerings in formulary set 2; the Prayer after Communion in formulary set 3) explicitly mention Baptism; thus, calling to mind the baptismal symbols used in the funeral Mass (sprinkling with holy water, Paschal candle, white garment). Any one of the five Prefaces for the Dead may be used today, again at the discretion of the priest celebrant or according to the preparations made by a parish committee. Also, the Solemn Blessing formula "In Celebration for the Dead" (number 20 under "Blessings at the End of Mass and Prayers over the People") is suggested and should be used for all Masses today.

Pastoral Reflection

We know not the hour when God will call us home, yet our whole lives are lived waiting to discover what home with God looks like. Today's reading calls us to be conscious of our relationship with God as Father and Jesus as Divine Son. How would you express this to another, especially a child? Imagine you were in your last days wondering if you were going to heaven or fearful of what you have read of hell. How could you both calm yourself and convince another that you know and love God so fully, that you will be remembered fully in God's kingdom? Know this answer and live this answer in all you do.

MON 3 (#485) green
Weekday (Thirty-first Week in Ordinary Time)
Optional Memorial of St. Martin de Porres, Religious / white

The Lectionary for Mass

◆ First Reading: Today's First Reading is Paul's beautiful exhortation to the Philippians, a community much loved by him, to grow in love. Notice the repetition of the words same and unity. Selflessness is called for in attaining this unity—being willing to let go of one's own wishes and interests for the sake of others, for the sake of the community.

◆ Responsorial Psalm 131 is the prayer of a person whose stance toward God and others is humility. As a result, great interior peace has been attained.

◆ Gospel: The theme of selfless love and concern for the needs of others is likewise heard in today's Gospel. We should reach out to those less fortunate who have no means to repay us rather than to those who can and do repay us.

Today's Saint

St. Martin de Porres (1579–1639) had a special love for the marginalized in society; he knew what it was like to feel unaccepted. As the son of an unwed couple (a Spanish knight and a freed slave from Panama), he hardly fit the norm. His father essentially disowned him because he inherited his mother's features, primarily her skin color. Instead of wallowing in his own pain, he chose to become a Dominican brother, focusing on ministry to the "forgotten" in society. St. Martin, called the "father of charity," cared for sick people in the monastery, fed

the needy with food from the monastery, and began a home for abandoned children. He had a close friendship with St. Rose of Lima and is considered the patron saint of racial justice. Include a petition in the Prayer of the Faithful for an end to racial tension and violence.

TUE 4 (#486) white
Memorial of St. Charles Borromeo, Bishop

The Lectionary for Mass

◆ First Reading: Paul incorporates an early Christian hymn into his letter, thereby holding up Christ's self-emptying and humility as an example for the way they should live. Christ humbled himself to a most shameful death.

As a result, God exalted him above all creatures—as Lord.

◆ Responsorial Psalm 22: This hymn of praise is a fitting response to our First Reading, which ends on the note of praise to the Father. See how the psalm echoes themes from the First Reading: the humble exalted, the bowing before the Lord, the Lord's dominion over all.

◆ Gospel: Today's text is a continuation of Gospel passages heard over several days. It begins with a saying looking toward the heavenly banquet. The parable illustrates the relationship between our responses to God's invitation and our participation in the banquet. Are we among those who find excuses not to come? The Master desires that his banquet be filled. Those who are present there may be the ones we least expect or perhaps even shun (blind, outcast, etc.) but who nonetheless responded to God's call.

The Roman Missal

All the orations are proper for this obligatory memorial and are found in the Proper of Saints at November 4. The Collect asks that the Church in our time might be constantly renewed with the same spirit that filled bishop St. Charles Borromeo, thus, identifying the saint as someone noted for reforming the Church in his time. The prayer articulates that the Church is ever in need of being more deeply conformed to the likeness of Christ. The Prayer over the Offerings prays for the specific fruits and good works we are requesting to result from this offering, namely, good fruit and works that embody the same virtues as St. Robert that made him such an attentive pastor. We pray for today's Eucharist to have concrete effect in our lives in the Prayer after Communion also, this time praying for the same determination, "which made St. Charles faithful in ministry / and fervent in charity." The Preface of Holy Pastors could be considered the preferred choice for a Preface today, although Preface I or II of Saints could be used as well.

Today's Saint

St. Charles Borromeo (1538–1584), a doctor of civil and canon law, was a great champion of the Church redefining itself in light of the Protestant Reformation. As Archbishop of Milan, he promulgated the reforms of the Council of Trent, giving special attention to liturgical and clerical renewal. Other significant contributions he made to the Church include the establishment of new seminaries for the education of the clergy, defining a code of moral conduct for clergy, and founding the Oblates of St. Ambrose, a society of diocesan priests, to enforce the reforms of Trent. St. Charles adopted a simple life in which he responded to the needs of the poor and sick by providing monetary and spiritual support.

**W
E
D 5** (#487) green
Weekday

The Lectionary for Mass

◆ FIRST READING: In the first two sentences of our reading, Paul highlights two important realities in our Christian life: first, God working in us; second, the work that we must do. The rest of the reading expounds on what that work is and how it is to be done. Notice the fourfold mention of joy in the last two lines—an important facet of our life in Christ.

◆ RESPONSORIAL PSALM 27: The Lord is our light and our salvation. The Lord enlightens our way to him, showing us what we must do if we would contemplate his glory.

◆ GOSPEL: If we would embrace discipleship, we must first consider the cost. Are we truly willing to put our relationship with the Lord before all other relationships and possessions? That is what it costs.

**T
H
U 6** (#488) green
Weekday

The Lectionary for Mass

◆ FIRST READING: The verses preceding today's reading are important. They establish the context of Paul's words. According to Jewish law, circumcision was the mark of incorporation into the people of God. Repeatedly, throughout all of his letters, Paul, the Pharisee ever so zealous for the covenant of old, emphasizes that now in light of Christ, it is not circumcision but faith in Christ that saves. The last line is particularly powerful. Could we say the same for ourselves?

◆ RESPONSORIAL PSALM 105: The true child of Abraham (last stanza) is one whose boast, whose confidence, whose righteousness is faith in Christ. The response of God's chosen ones, all who have found God through the proclamation about Jesus, can only be praise.

◆ GOSPEL: To sit at table together and share a meal signified the acceptance and welcome of the other person(s). Such was Jesus's attitude toward sinners. The two parables he tells in today's Gospel conveys the joy of the heavenly Father when a sinner, found by Jesus, finds salvation in him.

**F
R
I 7** (#489) green
Weekday

The Lectionary for Mass

◆ FIRST READING: We meet the theme of "imitation" several times in Paul's letters (verse 17). How many of us could invite others to imitate our manner of living as followers of Christ? The other option is to be an enemy of the Gospel message and there were those in Paul's day as well as in our own. Paul reminds the Philippians of their true citizenship in heaven and the coming of our Savior, the Lord Jesus, that they await. At his coming, they—we—will be transformed to conform with his risen and glorified body.

◆ RESPONSORIAL PSALM 122: Originally, today's psalm was sung by pilgrims en route to the Temple in Jerusalem. It is a fitting prayer for us as we make our way to our heavenly homeland.

◆ GOSPEL: Today's Gospel parable of the steward who squandered his master's property stands in stark contrast with the example of Paul who was such a faithful servant of the Gospel with which he was entrusted! Commentators on this parable point out the necessity of understanding Palestinian business practices of the time. The steward was the owner's representative in financial matters and would normally add on his own commission to the debt. Accordingly, by reducing the debts, the steward was foregoing his own commission. In this

was the prudence for which he was commended.

**S
A
T 8** (#490) green
Weekday

Optional Memorial of the Blessed Virgin Mary / white

The Lectionary for Mass

◆ FIRST READING: Paul, in his need, had been the recipient of financial support from the Philippians. He describes their generosity, their almsgiving, as a fragrant sacrifice to the Lord. In between these references to the Philippians' generosity, we have Paul's testimony of what can only be described as a most special gift—the ability to be content in whatever circumstances one finds oneself.

◆ RESPONSORIAL PSALM 112: The last two stanzas of this psalm, which acclaims the generosity of the righteous, is a fitting response to what we heard about regarding the Philippians' generosity.

◆ GOSPEL: How does one "make friends" with "dishonest" wealth (Luke 16:9)? This sounds like a contradiction in terms. But perhaps Jesus calls us through the sayings in today's Gospel to not let wealth become a source of enmity in our relationship with God, but a friend through our good stewardship and sharing with the poor.

(#671)   white

9 Feast of the Dedication of the Lateran Basilica

About this Feast

St. John Lateran is one of the four major basilicas in Rome, with St. Peter, St. Mary Major, and St. Paul Outside the Walls. It is unique among the four since it (not St. Peter's) is the cathedral church of the Bishop of Rome, the pope. "Lateran" was the name of a Roman family whose lands were seized for the Church by the Emperor Constantine, and which then became the site of a great basilica dedicated in honor of John the Baptist. For centuries, the old Lateran palace was the residence of the popes. It was only when the popes returned from the Avignon exile in the 14th century that they took up residence at the Vatican. The basilica now has a triple dedication in honor of St. John the Baptist, St. John the Evangelist, and our Lord. Across the front of the basilica is a Latin inscription that says, "This is the mother and head of all churches in the whole world." It is a reminder of why the dedication of this one church is celebrated by the universal Church: we are one family, one flock, and we are led by one shepherd, the successor of St. Peter.

The Lectionary for Mass

◆ First Reading: Ezekiel's vision of the life-giving waters that flow from the dwelling place of God—what a vision of hope it must have been for the people exiled from their homeland. All creatures flourish in these waters of life whose source is God. Their fruits provide nourishment and healing.

◆ Responsorial Psalm 46: Our antiphon and the second stanza of the psalm echo the theme of the life-giving waters flowing from God's holy Temple. This psalm is one of confidence as it acknowledges God's presence and strength in times that shake us.

◆ Second Reading: What a profound image is given us in this reading, especially in light of the First Reading and psalm. We are God's building. We are God's holy place. God's life-giving water flows in us (see John 7:38).

◆ Gospel: Jesus's body is the true dwelling place of God, the true Temple. "Destroy it," he tells his adversaries, "and it will be raised." His actions, in driving out those who were making God's house a place for their own financial profit challenge us to ask ourselves what is going on in our hearts, since through Baptism, God now dwells in us.

The Roman Missal

For the second week in a row we have a feast that replaces the Sunday in Ordinary Time, so the texts for this Mass are all found in the Proper of Saints section of the Missal, at November 9. The Gloria is sung or said today, since it is a feast.

There is a choice between two options for the Collect today. The first option uses the imagery of living stones to refer to the dwelling place of God, and thus asks for an increase of the spirit of grace in the Church. When the prayer goes on to ask that God's faithful people build up the heavenly Jerusalem by "new growth," it is presumably by a growth in holiness and grace, although certainly growth by the incorporation of new living stones (new members) could also be understood as well. The second option for the Collect uses the imagery of the Church as the Bride of Christ and has a little more of an eschatological focus as it specifically asks that the people of God may be led to attain God's promises in heaven.

Since this feast falls on a Sunday, the Creed is said or sung.

The Prayer over the Offerings, in asking God to accept the offering being made, also asks that those who make that offering may receive "in this place / the power of the Sacraments / and the answer to their prayers." We can note an emphasis intended by inclusion of the phrase "in this place," thus, highlighting the Church both as the living stones and as a people who gather in a sacred space to enact the divine liturgy.

The text for today's proper Preface is given right along with the other texts for this Mass, and it is given both with and without musical notation. The Preface, titled "The mystery of the Church, the Bride of Christ and the Temple of the Spirit," reiterates the imagery of the people as the temple of the Spirit who make the Church resplendent through their living lives acceptable to God. The visible buildings that make up the Church are foreshadows of her heavenly glory.

The Prayer after Communion continues this eschatological theme of foreshadowing by addressing God as the one "who chose to foreshadow for us / the heavenly Jerusalem / through the sign of your Church on earth." Thus, the prayer goes on to ask that by our partaking of the Eucharist, "we may be made the temple of your grace / and may enter the dwelling place of your glory." Indeed, we can be reminded that it is only by celebrating the Eucharist that the Church can be Church; without Eucharist, the Church does not exist.

A Solemn Blessing formula, "For the Dedication of a Church," is suggested as the final blessing, and it would be good to use it today. Given the emphasis in the prayers on the people of God as the living stones of the Church, perhaps the dismissal formula, "Go in peace, glorifying the Lord by your life" should be used today.

Pastoral Reflection

Can you call to mind a place that is sacred to you? Make sure to use this properly and care for this space as it is meant to be. Seek the presence of God at the tabernacle. Offer proper reverence in your bowing for knowing and believing what lies behind those doors. Realize that you too are a holy temple and make sure to not defile your body with negative media, foul language, or unhealthy food. Know that while our sacred space is housed in a structure, all of God's creation is meant to bring forth holiness and call us to find God's image. Care for creation in each choice you make. And when someone or something chips away at the peace of God, speak loudly and clearly: the Church, the tabernacle, and our gift of creation, all need to be protected.

(#491) white
M O N 10 Memorial of St. Leo the Great, Pope and Doctor of the Church (Thirty-second Week in Ordinary Time)

The Lectionary for Mass

◆ FIRST READING: Today's reading is the beginning of Paul's letter to Titus. This letter, like the two addressed to Timothy, stem from a period later than the other Pauline letters. The Church is growing and becoming established, thus the need for designated leaders, presbyters or elders, and bishops as they are called here. The criteria for their selection are set forth. A particular threat at this time was the presence of false teachers (that is, refute "opponents" [Titus 1:9]); thus, the use of terms like "religious truth" (Titus 1:1) and "sound doctrine" (Titus 1:9), which those appointed are to uphold.

◆ RESPONSORIAL PSALM 24: Inherent in true faith is the longing to see God. The second stanza evokes the qualifications of ministers set forth in the First Reading, things that really should characterize all of God's people. Eternal life is the blessing and the reward promised.

◆ GOSPEL: Today's Gospel consists of three sayings: a warning against being a cause of scandal, an exhortation to forgiveness regardless of the number of wrongs, and a teaching on the power of faith. How do the images of the millstone and the mustard seed help us to understand Jesus's message?

The Roman Missal

All the orations are proper for today, as found in the Proper of Saints at November 10. The Collect communicates to us the place of greatness among the successors to the Apostles that Pope St. Leo holds in the life of the Church as the prayer asks the intercession of St. Leo to stand firm in the truth and to "know the protection of lasting peace." Such firmness and protection is assured because God is addressed as the one who never allows the gates of hell to prevail against the Church, founded firmly as it is on apostolic rock. The Prayer over the Offerings prays particularly for those who shepherd the Church, asking that they may be pleasing to God, and also prays that the flock everywhere may prosper. The Prayer after Communion also speaks of governance, noting that it is God who governs the Church he nourishes with the Eucharist; the prayer also asks that under God's direction, "she may enjoy ever greater freedom / and persevere in integrity of religion." Although the Prayer over the Offerings and the Prayer after Communion do not specifically mention Pope St. Leo by name, they certainly reflect the virtues that he lived as pope, and the concerns he faced and addressed in his ministry. Certainly the Preface of Holy Pastors would be perhaps the most appropriate choice for today, although Preface I or II of Saints could also be used.

Today's Saint

As pope and Doctor of the Church, St. Leo the Great (+461) strongly supported the teachings of the Council of Chalcedon, especially on the humanity and divinity of Christ. He advocated papal authority by moving from the traditional approach that the pope is a successor to St. Peter's chair to the pope as St. Peter's heir. Under his leadership, uniformity of pastoral practice was encouraged, liturgical and clerical abuses were corrected, and priests were sent on a mission to extinguish Priscillianism, a heresy that claimed the human body was evil. St. Leo is recognized as a "protector of the people" because he persuaded Attila the Hun to not invade the city of Rome and later prevented the Vandals (East German invaders) from torching the city of Rome and massacring its people.

(#492) white
T U E 11 Memorial of St. Martin of Tours, Bishop

The Lectionary for Mass

◆ FIRST READING: Practical, everyday behavior is the concern of today's First Reading, and all age groups are addressed. Our example in all we do is none other than the incarnate Son of God. It is his coming we await at the end of time.

◆ RESPONSORIAL PSALM 37: Specific behaviors are likewise addressed in today's psalm. We must live as the Lord commands. Our salvation is from him.

◆ GOSPEL: Does it seem like a lot is being asked of servants? We must do all that we have been commanded by the Lord, remembering that we are commanded to love and serve one another. We are only servants.

The Roman Missal

All the orations, found at November 11, are once again proper for the day. The Collect asks that the wonders of God's grace will be renewed in our hearts. The Prayer over the Offerings prays that the spiritual offering of our lives, expressed through the spiritual offering we make through the Eucharistic offerings, will always be the guiding force in our lives, "whether in tribulation or in prosperity." (Commitment to the Eucharistic life is similar to commitment to the nuptial life—in good times and in bad.) The Prayer after Communion expresses how the Eucharist, the "Sacrament of unity," restores us, and, so restored, we ask for perfect harmony with God's will, just as St. Martin submitted himself entirely to God. Use either the Preface of Holy Pastors or Preface I or II of Saints as the Preface today.

Today's Saint

St. Martin of Tours (316–397) was forced by his father, a pagan officer in the Roman army, to join the military. While serving in the military, he had a life-changing event in which he cut his cloak in half to clothe a freezing beggar. Following this encounter he had a vision of Christ wrapped in the cloak. As a result of this experience, St. Martin chose to be baptized and declared himself a soldier of peace for Christ, refusing to participate in any act of violence. He took up the life of

a hermit, thereby introducing monasticism into Gaul. Following his election as bishop of Tours he continued living as a monk, but made numerous trips to visit his people and establish new monasteries. The people of Gaul converted to Christianity due to his example.

(#493)   red

WED 12 Memorial of St. Josaphat, Bishop and Martyr

The Lectionary for Mass

◆ FIRST READING: We might think of the first part of today's reading as an admonition to be good citizens. In the early days of the Church, when Christians were in the minority and perhaps a bit suspect, it was important to stress what a plus Christians were to the society of their day. This meant that Christians really had to be and do that. As Christians, yes, we have committed ourselves to follow Christ's way; but the initiative was entirely his—in kindness, love, and mercy.

◆ RESPONSORIAL PSALM 23 echoes the theme of God's loving kindness and providential care for us. He is our shepherd. Because of his great gift to us in Christ, there is nothing we shall want.

◆ GOSPEL: Lepers were among the outcasts in Israel by virtue of their physical defilement (see Leviticus 13) and the fear of contagion. Thus, they stand at a distance from Jesus. We might think of Jesus's healing acts as another example of the kindness and love of the Lord. It is the leper shunned both because of his physical affliction and where he was from who returns to give thanks.

The Roman Missal

All the orations are proper today, and are taken from November 12. The Collect focuses on the martyrdom of the saint as it asks that "the Spirit that filled St. Josaphat / as he laid down his life for the sheep" be

given to the Church and particularly to all of us, so that we will not be afraid to lay down our lives for others. The Prayer over the Offerings continues the recognition of Josaphat as martyr as it asks that the offerings made at this Mass will "confirm us in the faith / that St. Josaphat professed by the shedding of his blood." The Prayer after Communion asks for the gift of "a spirit of fortitude and peace" as a result of our participation in the Eucharist this day. Strengthened by the Eucharist that way, we pray that we will be able to follow the saint's example, particularly in the way he worked for the unity of the Church. Given the emphasis in the orations today, one of the two Prefaces of Holy Martyrs would seem to be the most logical choice for a Preface; the Preface of Holy Pastors or one of the two Prefaces of Saints could also be considered.

Today's Saint

As a young man, St. Josaphat (1580–1623) was excited about the possibility of the Orthodox metropolitan city of Kiev, comprising Belarussians and Ukrainians, reuniting with the Church of Rome. When he was elected Archbishop of Polotsk, Lithuania, he worked tirelessly to continue the efforts to bring the Orthodox communities of Kiev into full communion with the Catholic Church. Many people were strongly opposed to this reunion; therefore, they established a rival hierarchy and set up groups to defame his name. While preaching in a particularly hostile city, he was murdered. His commitment to ecumenical relations was eventually realized in the Byzantine Rite of Catholicism. St. Josephat, the martyr, is the first Eastern saint to be formally canonized.

THU 13 (#494) white
Memorial of St. Frances Xavier Cabrini, Virgin

The Lectionary for Mass

◆ FIRST READING: Philemon was the owner of the runaway slave Onesimus, who had met and been converted by Paul, while Paul was in prison. Paul sends him back to his owner with a request that the slave be received as lovingly as Paul himself would have been. Paul was a spiritual father to Philemon as well. Paul's selflessness is evident in his promise to cover whatever loss Philemon has incurred because of him.

◆ RESPONSORIAL PSALM 146: The mention of the oppressed and captive in the first stanza is particularly fitting in light of Onesimus's status. Paul, too, is prisoner. Philemon, Onesimus, and Paul all knew God as their help.

◆ GOSPEL: The coming of the kingdom cannot be controlled. It is already present in the person of Jesus and in its continued growth in the lives of believers. We await the coming of the Son of Man at the end of time when God's kingdom will be fully manifest.

The Roman Missal

The Collect is the only proper for today, and it is found at November 13. The prayer describes how the saint was called from Italy to serve the immigrants of America, and then goes on to ask that we might be taught to have the same concern for the stranger and all those in need. The Prayer over the Offerings and the Prayer after Communion are taken from either the Common of Virgins: For One Virgin, or from the Common of Holy Men and Women: For Those Who Practiced Works of Mercy. An appropriate Preface for this celebration would be either the Preface of Holy Virgins and Religious or Preface I or II of Saints.

Today's Saint

Frances Xavier Cabrini was the first American citizen to be canonized. Born in Italy, she studied to be a teacher and wanted to join a religious community but was rejected because of ill health. When the orphanage she managed closed in 1880, Frances and six others took religious vows and founded the institute of the Missionary Sisters of the Sacred Heart of Jesus. Her work brought her to the attention of Leo XIII, who sent her to New York in 1889 to minister to Italian immigrants. St. Frances founded institutions all over the United States of America, as well as in South America and Europe. She died in Chicago in 1917. Visit her shrine in Chicago: http://www.cabrinishrine chicago.com/.

FRI 14 (#495) green
Weekday

The Lectionary for Mass

◆ FIRST READING: There are two foci in today's text: 1) to live by the commandment to love, and 2) to be faithful to the teaching that Jesus Christ is the Word of God incarnate in flesh. False teachers in the community, particularly those with a disdain for material things, including the human body, are a particular threat.

◆ RESPONSORIAL PSALM 119 is the longest Psalm in the Bible. It is a psalm that acclaims the law of the Lord as the source of wisdom and life. The Psalm speaks of the blessedness that is promised as a reward for fidelity.

◆ GOSPEL: Today's First Reading and psalm can be heard as a call to mindfulness. Today's Gospel, on the other hand, is an illustration of inattentiveness and its consequences as evident in the stories of Noah and Lot and their contemporaries. Let us not take God's call, God's commands, and the judgment to come for granted.

SAT 15 (#496) green

Optional Memorials of St. Albert the Great, Bishop and Doctor of the Church / white; Blessed Virgin Mary / white

The Lectionary for Mass

◆ FIRST READING: Fidelity to good works on behalf of others in the community and also (especially?) to strangers is esteemed in today's reading. Are these strangers missionaries? Teachers? Pilgrims? Whomever, their travels are on behalf of the name of the Lord. In helping them, we are "co-workers" (3 John 8) with them. John's words call to mind all those with whom we might be "co-workers" today through our support (ibid.).

◆ RESPONSORIAL PSALM 112: The behaviors described in today's First Reading—and in the stanzas of the psalm as well—are evidence of a fear and reverence for the Lord, especially when we receive others in the name of the Lord. Those who do so will be abundantly blessed.

◆ GOSPEL: Perseverance in prayer is the instruction Jesus's disciples receive in today's Gospel. The parable serves to illustrate the fact that if even a mortal judge yields to the persistent pleas of the widow, the immortal God will certainly respond to the pleas of his chosen ones.

Today's Saint

To the great disappointment of his father, St. Albert the Great (1206–1280), known as "the universal doctor," entered the Dominican order where he was recognized for his acumen. Ahead of his time, he believed that learning did not take place in a vacuum; one must be an interdisciplinary learner. He loved the world of academia, studying everything from the natural sciences to the connection between reason and experience, and more.

As a prestigious teacher, he had the privilege of instructing and mentoring St. Thomas Aquinas, author of the *Summa Theologiae*. Toward the end of his life, he began to experience memory loss and dementia, which led to his gradual demise. He was declared a Doctor of the Church by Pope Pius XI.

(#157)   green

☀ 16 Thirty-third Sunday in Ordinary Time

The Lectionary for Mass

◆ FIRST READING: Today's text from Proverbs extols the priceless value of the "worthy wife" or the valiant woman. Juxtaposing this text with the Gospel allows us to see the woman as an apt illustration of the good and faithful servant who put the talents with which he was entrusted to good use! Not only is she industrious, she faithfully fulfills the Lord's commands regarding care for the poor and the needy. She is the epitome of the biblical wise person: one who fears (reverences) the Lord.

◆ RESPONSORIAL PSALM 128: A fitting complement to our First

Reading, Psalm 128 extols the virtues of the worthy husband. He, too, is one who fears the Lord and observes all his commands. Accordingly, he and all his family shall be blessed.

◆ SECOND READING: Peter's words bid us to be vigilant and ready for the coming Day of the Lord at the end of time. That it will come, we can be sure. When, we have no way of knowing. We are called to be prepared at all times for the coming of the Lord.

◆ GOSPEL: "Come, share your Master's joy!" (Matthew 25:23). This joy-filled invitation awaits those good and faithful servants who recognize the talents, the gifts they have been given and do not fail to develop them. The Master will not tolerate, however, fearful negligence and/or laziness. The parable calls us to examine ourselves in light of the behaviors of the three servants. We will all be called to account on the day of judgment. Is there anything we want to change now?

The Roman Missal

The Mass texts for today are found in the "Ordinary Time" section of the Proper of Time. The Gloria is sung or said today.

The Collect identifies for us where the source of "constant gladness" and "full and lasting happiness" is to be found: it is to be found in serving "with constancy / the author of all that is good." This Collect can serve as a good introduction to one of the points made in the Gospel, that of being sure that we are using all our gifts and resources to serve God well; it is only by doing so that we can hope to share in the fullness of the joy of the kingdom. It can also serve as a reminder about the warning in the Second Reading today: stay alert and sober so we can serve with constancy. The Prayer over the Offerings has an eschatological focus, appropriate for this

penultimate Sunday of the liturgical year, as it asks that what we offer at this Eucharist may "gain us the prize of everlasting happiness." The Prayer after Communion, however, is focused more on the present as it implores that, having partaken of "the gifts of this sacred mystery," we may be given "a growth in charity."

Any one of the eight Prefaces of the Sundays in Ordinary Time are appropriate options for today, but perhaps Preface V might be considered the best choice with its emphasis on God setting humanity "over the whole world in all its wonder;" the text could serve to reinforce the theme of taking responsibility for using the gifts God has given us and building the Kingdom of God as found in the Gospel.

Pastoral Reflection

Matching last week's call to know the oil of your life, go deeper now. Your fuel is the gifts God gave you to spark the world into brilliant colors—however this is seen. Do you have a passion for something that you do not use? Be bold! Step out and use your gifts to help bring forth the Kingdom of God. Be trained as a reader or Extraordinary Minister of Holy Communion. Reach out as a religious education catechist or youth ministry volunteer. Join a choir or new committee that brings you alive so you can bring others to match your joy. Be a steward of the talents given so God may smile with pride at your love and creativity this week.

(#497)   white

M O N 17 Memorial of St. Elizabeth of Hungary, Religious

The Lectionary for Mass

◆ FIRST READING: Today's First Reading comes from the beginning of the Book of Revelation—an apocalyptic writing in the New Testament. The contents of the book are said to have come from a vision given to John. It is a prophetic message—a word from the Lord speaking to the real-life situation of the readers. Seven churches are singled out as the recipients of the message, and we hear the one addressed to the Church at Ephesus today. There is much to be praised in their manner of life as is detailed. They are chided on one account, and it is a most serious charge: they have lost their first love (*agape*), total selflessness and self-emptying toward God and others.

Accordingly, they are called to repentance.

◆ RESPONSORIAL PSALM 1: The antiphon is from the same passage of Revelation as the First Reading. It is the reward promised to the one who repents, "victorious" over the sin of one's fallen ways. The stanzas are from Psalm 1, a Psalm acclaiming the law of the Lord, the joy and prosperity of the one who obeys it.

◆ GOSPEL: The man in today's Gospel might have been blind, but he knew who Jesus was and what he could do. He relentlessly calls out for mercy. He received his sight not only on the physical level, but in the deepest reality of all. He follows Jesus as a disciple.

The Roman Missal

The Collect, found at November 17 in the Proper of Saints, is the prayer that is proper for today. The Collect recognizes St. Elizabeth's ministry to the poor and therefore asks "that we may serve with unfailing charity / the needy and those afflicted." Ministry to the poor is not something that is optional in the Christian life; it is part-and-parcel of what it means to follow Christ. The Prayer over the Offerings and the Prayer after Communion come from the Common of Holy Men and Women: For Those Who Practiced Works of Mercy. For the Preface, use either Preface I of Saints or Preface II of Saints.

Today's Saint

St. Elizabeth of Hungary (1207–1231), the Queen of Hungary and mother of four children, had a special love for the downtrodden. She built a hospital in the basement of her castle, nursed the sick, fed the hungry, and provided life-giving work for the poor. After the death of her husband, she took the habit of a Franciscan tertiary (Third Order Franciscan), devoting herself to a life of simplicity and almsgiving. Along with her selfless service to those in need, she actively pursued God through prayer and spiritual discipline. St. Elizabeth is the patron saint of Franciscan tertiaries, bakers, beggars, brides, the homeless, and charities (among others).

TUE 18 (#498) green Weekday

Optional Memorials of the Dedication of the Basilicas of SS. Peter and Paul, Apostles / white; St. Rose Philippine Duchesne, Virgin / white

The Lectionary for Mass

◆ FIRST READING: The Church in Sardis is not authentic. With the exception of only a few Christians, most there were inwardly dead, even though they appear to be alive. The Church in Laodicea is lukewarm, tepid in spirit. They live under a false security, lacking true self-knowledge. The faithful—and the repentant—are promised the reward of white garments in the age to come, in the presence of the heavenly Father. The reading concludes with the beautiful image of Christ standing at the door and knocking, wishing to be received as guest.

◆ RESPONSORIAL PSALM: The antiphon once again comes from the reading, an image of the reward of the life to come. The stanzas are from Psalm 15 and speak of the behaviors and works that are required of the one who would dwell with God.

◆ GOSPEL: Zacchaeus is certainly an enterprising man—in more ways than one. If we look at our First Reading and Gospel together, we might think of Zacchaeus as opening the door to receive Jesus and salvation. Jesus and Zacchaeus sought out—and found—one another.

The Basilicas

There are four major basilicas in Rome, and each of them has an observance on the Church's universal calendar: St. Mary Major on August 5, St. John Lateran on November 9, and now the Basilicas of St. Peter and St. Paul. It is not so much the church buildings we are honoring, of course, as the saints to whom they are dedicated.

The proper readings for today's memorial focus our attention on the special grace God gave all believers through two imperfect, impetuous, but exceptional men: Peter and Paul.

Today's Saint

Beginning her life as a nun in the Order of the Visitation in France, St. Rose Philippine Duchesne (1769–1852) eventually joined the Society of the Sacred Heart, founded by St. Madeleine Sophie Barat. Due to her missionary zeal, she was sent, along with five other sisters, to St. Louis, Missouri, to care for the poor and educate Native Americans. Under her leadership, the sisters established numerous schools and orphanages. She is remembered for her remarkable work, including evangelization and catechesis with Native Americans, particularly the Potawatomi people. Recognizing her extraordinary ministry, amazing ability to navigate difficulties, and profound spirituality, a contemporary said, "She was the Saint Francis of Assisi of the Society."

W E D 19 (#499) green
Weekday

The Lectionary for Mass

◆ FIRST READING: One characteristic of apocalyptic literature is the use of highly symbolic imagery and vivid descriptions. We see that in today's reading. John is granted a vision of God enthroned in heavenly glory, surrounded by angelic hosts singing his praise.

◆ RESPONSORIAL PSALM 150, a magnificent hymn of praise, concludes the book of psalms. The antiphon is taken from today's reading, our hymn of praise at the Eucharist.

◆ GOSPEL: Jesus makes his way to Jerusalem where a fate of death awaits him. He is the nobleman of the parable—despised by his own people who face imminent destruction. Those servants who are faithful will be rewarded abundantly. Those who are negligent, idle, or fearful will lose what they have.

T H U 20 (#500) green
Weekday

The Lectionary for Mass

◆ FIRST READING: There are two foci in today's First Reading: the sealed scroll in God's hand and the question of who is worthy to open it. Worthy is the Lamb, a designation for Christ that we find not only here in Revelation, but also in the Gospel according to John where Jesus's Death takes place at the very hour that the Passover lambs were sacrificed. Through him, we have been redeemed and become heirs of the Kingdom of God.

◆ RESPONSORIAL PSALM: The antiphon is based on today's First Reading. We are a kingdom of priests, whose call is to the service of God. Psalm 149 is a Psalm of praise, an appropriate response in the face of all God has done for us.

◆ GOSPEL: Jesus weeps for Jerusalem. The people have failed to recognize the presence of the one sent by God or accept his message. Destruction—not peace—awaits them. Jerusalem was destroyed by the Romans in the year 70.

F R I 21 (#501) white
Memorial of the Presentation of the Blessed Virgin Mary

Today's Memorial

According to tradition, Mary spent her life at the Temple from the time she was a little girl. Her parents, Joachim and Anne, presented their young daughter to the Temple for service and study, in thanksgiving for the great gift God had given them through her. Today's memorial celebrates this occasion. It also calls us to think about the ways we prepare and ready ourselves for Jesus Christ in our lives. Mary, conceived in grace, was prepared to carry the Son of God, but her time at the Temple helped form her mind and heart. Likewise, intentionally nurturing our relationship with God builds on the grace God offers each of us. What are some ways you can ready yourself to encounter Jesus Christ today?

The Lectionary for Mass

◆ FIRST READING: A reading of the first seven verses of Revelation 10 gives a helpful context for today's reading. The focus of the verses of our reading is the prophet's reception (eating) of the message on the scroll (analogous to Ezekiel 1). The message is a mixed one, with both pleasant and unpleasant ramifications. The message the prophet must speak is one he has first taken in from the Lord.

◆ RESPONSORIAL PSALM: The theme of the sweetness of God's word is echoed in our antiphon. Psalm 119 acclaims the law of the Lord. The verses chosen for today emphasize the joy that is to be found in adherence to the law of the Lord. Note also the references to "mouth" (eating) in the third and sixth stanzas.

◆ GOSPEL: The first thing Jesus did upon entering Jerusalem, at least as Luke tells it, was to go to the Temple, that most sacred site for Jews, the place where God was invisibly present among his people. Sacrifices were offered regularly. Accordingly, there were numerous sellers of animals for sacrifice and money-changers for the convenience of those travelling at a distance. Profit, however, had superseded service and Jesus drove them out. We also hear in today's text the growing animosity of Jewish religious leaders toward Jesus.

The Roman Missal

The proper Collect is found at November 21 in the Proper of Saints. The prayer asks for the intercession of the Blessed Virgin Mary as we venerate her on this day. The Prayer over the Offerings and the Prayer after Communion are to be taken from the Common of the Blessed Virgin Mary, with the Preface being either Preface I or Preface II of the Blessed Virgin Mary; use "on the feast day" as the choice of phrasing in Preface I.

S A T 22 (#502) red
Memorial of St. Cecilia, Virgin and Martyr

The Lectionary for Mass

◆ FIRST READING: Various people and events from the Old Testament are evoked in today's text, as John continues to describe his visions: the olive trees and lamp stands from the prophet Zechariah; the prophet Elijah and the drought; Moses and the plagues. All of these were witnessed on God's behalf. God's prophets are commonly met with opposition, persecution, and even death as today's reading attests. But that is not the end. God's breath restores their life and calls them to heavenly glory.

◆ RESPONSORIAL PSALM 144: Today's Psalm of confidence uses images of strength to speak of the experience of God's protection and deliverance in a time of war (historical military battles here). The experience leads the psalmist to a hymn of praise.

◆ GOSPEL: The Sadducees were a sect within Judaism who, unlike the Pharisees, did not believe in resurrection. The Sadducees held only to what was revealed in the law of Moses, and resurrection was a later development in understanding. What is most important in today's text is what is said about the nature of our resurrected life: we will be gloriously transformed like the angels.

The Roman Missal

The Collect for the memorial, the only prayer proper for today, is found at November 22. The Collect asks that we might imitate the example of the saint, one of the most famous and revered of the early Roman martyrs. The Prayer over the Offerings and the Prayer after Communion come from either the Common of Martyrs: For a Virgin Martyr, or from the Common of Virgins: For One Virgin. One of the Prefaces of Holy Martyrs would be an apt choice for today, and consider using Eucharistic Prayer I, the Roman Canon, since St. Cecilia's name is mentioned in it.

Today's Saint

According to legend, St. Cecilia (third century) was beheaded because she would not forsake her vow of virginity. She is the patron of musicians, singers, and poets. Her association with music is most likely related to a line from her *Passio* (the oldest historical account of her life), where she is said to have sung "in

her heart to Christ" as the musicians played at her wedding. Upon its foundation in 1584, the Academy of Music in Rome declared her the patron of musicians. St. Cecilia's popularity grew so much that several hymns were written in her honor, and her life is referenced in Chaucer's *The Canterbury Tales.*

(#160)   white

☀ 23 Solemnity of Our Lord Jesus Christ, King of the Universe

About this Solemnity

Today is the Thirty-fourth or Last Sunday in Ordinary Time. Its official name is the Solemnity of Our Lord Jesus Christ the King. This solemnity was established by Pope Pius XI in 1925, an observance celebrating an aspect of Jesus's identity rather than of his life. Conventional understandings of kingship and power are transformed. Rather than calling up images of Jesus Christ dressed in kingly robes, the Gospel proclaims him as king by the sign over his head on the throne of a wooden cross (I.N.R.I.:—*iesus nazarenvs rex ivdaeorvm*—Jesus of Nazareth, King of the Jews). Paradoxically, it is the thief who recognized in Christ the Lord and Messiah.

The Lectionary for Mass

◆ FIRST READING: The shepherd is an image for Israel's king. Sadly, the kings often failed in their God-given charge to care for their people as chapter 34 of Ezekiel vividly describes—and it is well worth reading the chapter as a whole. The words of today's reading are comforting. Israel's kings have failed their people, but God will not. Note that the good shepherd's work is to gather, to reunite, and to heal. The last lines of our reading point to yet another function, that of judgment—as is illustrated in today's Gospel.

◆ RESPONSORIAL PSALM 23 is the beautiful and much-loved prayer of confidence in God our Shepherd. If we follow the way he leads us, we will come to life-giving waters and blessings of abundance. What is more, we will know the joy of dwelling in his house—as is the reward of the sheep in today's Gospel parable.

◆ SECOND READING: Paul looks to the end time with a view to the resurrection of the dead and the full realization of the Kingdom of God. All of chapter 15 of 1 Corinthians treats of the Resurrection—first of Jesus, and subsequently, of ourselves. The end time is harvest time, and Christ is the firstfruit. The end time signals a new creation, beginning with Christ, the new Adam. When all has been accomplished, Christ will hand over the kingdom that he has inaugurated to his Father, the sovereign King over all.

◆ GOSPEL: Jesus's teaching paints a haunting and fearful picture. When, Lord, did we see you hungry, thirsty, a stranger, naked, ill, imprisoned? If only we had known! If only we had recognized you! For those who hear Jesus's teaching, there is no need for excuses at the last judgment. The difference between the sheep and the goats is clearly set forth. Will we be among the sheep who followed the way of our Master?

The Roman Missal

The texts for this Mass are found at the very end of the "Ordinary Time" section of the Missal, immediately following the Mass for The Most Sacred Heart of Jesus, and immediately before the "Order of Mass" section of the Missal.

The Entrance Antiphon is taken from the Book of Revelation, announcing the worthiness of the Lamb who was slain. From the very beginning of this Mass we are reminded that Christ's Kingship lies not in worldly power or authority, but rather in his self-sacrificing love that gives life to others.

You might want to consider using the Rite for the Blessing and Sprinkling of Water today. The rite could serve as a reminder of the kingdom to which we belong, a kingdom into which we have been baptized; we are subjects of the crucified-risen one whose Death and Resurrection we participate in through our Baptism. The rite is found at Appendix II at the back of the Missal.

The Gloria is sung or said today.

The Collect names God as the one whose will it is to restore all things in Christ, the King of the universe; it is therefore the whole of creation that is set free from slavery. The universal sovereignty of Christ as King is thus proclaimed.

The Creed is, of course, said at this Mass, as it is every Sunday.

The Prayer over the Offerings defines the Eucharistic sacrifice we are offering as "the sacrifice / by which the human race is reconciled" to God; because of that, we can pray that the Son "may bestow on all nations / the gifts of unity and peace." To proclaim Christ as King means by definition to participate in the unity and peace his one kingdom will establish.

The Preface is proper for today, "Christ, King of the Universe," and the text, with and without musical notation, is located right along with the other texts for this Mass. Give strong consideration to singing the Preface today if it is not your usual practice. The Preface gives us a rather comprehensive catechesis on the precise meaning of Christ's Kingship. Christ has been anointed Priest and King with the oil of gladness (the Holy Spirit) and has accomplished human redemption "by offering himself on the altar of the Cross." Through this action, all of creation became subject to his rule, and he, in turn, has presented a universal kingdom to his Father. This kingdom, however, is not defined in terms of power or subjection; rather, it is "a kingdom of truth and life, / a kingdom of holiness and grace, / a kingdom of justice, love and peace." (Here is another example where the Preface hands a preacher ready-made jumping-off point for the Homily.)

The Communion Antiphon, taken from Psalm 29 (28), announces the Lord as King forever, blessing his people with peace.

The Prayer after Communion uses the phrase "food of immortality" to describe the Eucharistic food we have just received, a fitting phrase insofar as that heavenly food nourishes us in the ways of Christ's eternal kingdom. Thus do we ask in the prayer that "we may live with him eternally in his heavenly Kingdom," a fitting eschatological focus on this last Sunday of the liturgical year.

Pastoral Reflection

Confirmation students are guided well in the act of "doing service" to "get Confirmed." Once we are confirmed in our faith, the rest of our life is spent choosing to live out the gifts and fruits of the Spirit within us. Part of this absolute need for the Spirit within is to do the tough work of living the Gospel. We are called to live out the corporal and spiritual works of mercy on a daily basis. Make sure you know these works so you can consciously choose to purposefully carry them out in the world. Match up a corporal work of mercy with a volunteer agency in your community. Choose one on the list and actively help. For the rest, be conscious in all you do to allow the actions and love of Christ to be felt in your actions and words.

(#503) red
Memorial of St. Andrew Dũng-Lạc, Priest, and Companions, Martyrs (Thirty-fourth or Last Week in Ordinary Time)

MON **24**

The Lectionary for Mass

◆ FIRST READING: The number one hundred forty-four is the square of 12, the number of the tribes of Israel. We see today a multitude of Israelites, gathered around the Lamb. The name of the Lamb and the name of his Father are written on their foreheads. These one hundred and forty-four thousand are the "first fruits," (Revelation 14:4), the first among the victors from the whole human race who have come to believe in the Lamb and accept his teaching.

◆ RESPONSORIAL PSALM 24: Those gathered around the Lamb are indeed those who longed to see the face of God and lived in such a manner that they might be able to do this. Today's psalm spells out exactly what is expected of the one who would dwell on God's mountain.

◆ GOSPEL: Today's Gospel is the beautiful story of the widow whose offering to the temple treasury came from the very little she had to live on. Needy herself, she freely gave of what she had to God.

The Roman Missal

All the orations are proper for today, and are found in the Proper of Saints at November 24. The Collect recognizes the martyrs St. Andrew Dũng-Lạc and his companions as being faithful to the cross of Christ, "even to the shedding of their blood," and so asks their intercession that we may be God's children "both in name and in truth." The Prayer over the Offerings asks that in accepting the offerings we bring, God will make us faithful "amid the trials of this life." The Prayer after Communion focuses on unity: having been "renewed by the one Bread," we pray that "we may merit by endurance an eternal prize" by abiding as one in God's love. It is the strength that we draw from our unity in the Eucharist and in the Church that gives us the endurance to face the trials of life. It would seem that one of the two Prefaces of Holy Martyrs would be the most appropriate choice of Preface for today, although certainly Preface I or II of Saints could also be chosen.

Today's Saints

St. Andrew Dung-Lac (1785–1839), a Vietnamese priest, in one of one hundred seventeen martyrs canonized in 1988 who died trying to establish and spread the Catholic faith in Vietnam. This effort, which began in 1533 and continued well into the nineteenth century, was fraught with periods of persecution. Although St. Andrew was born into a Buddhist family, he was raised Catholic. His priestly ministry involved evangelization, parish catechesis, and service to the persecuted. Living under a particularly oppressive edict, St. Andrew was killed because he would not renounce his Christian apostolate and succumb to idolatrous ritual.

T U E 25 (#504) green
Weekday

Optional Memorial of St. Catherine of Alexandria, Virgin and Martyr

The Lectionary for Mass

◆ FIRST READING: The harvesting of the earth takes place at the end of time, accomplished by God's heavenly messengers. The first line of today's reading evokes Jesus, Son of Man, coming on the clouds of heaven.

◆ RESPONSORIAL PSALM 96: It is the Lord who comes to judge the earth, to reward and punish its inhabitants. The psalm acclaims God's kingship. All of creation rejoices in his presence.

◆ GOSPEL: There are two foci in today's Gospel: first, the destruction of the Temple, which took place in the year 70 AD; the second, the terrifying signs that will precede the end of time. Luke writes in an apocalyptic tone and points to the judgment that will take place at the end of time.

Today's Saint

St. Catherine of Alexandria (fourth century) lived in Alexandria, Egypt, during the reign of the Roman emperor Maxentius. Legend says that Catherine bravely confronted the emperor about his pagan beliefs.

Maxentius gathered fifty pagan philosophers and challenged her to a debate. Her arguments were so convincing that many of the philosophers converted to Christianity. He then threatened to kill her unless she married him and renounced her faith. She refused and was condemned to death on a spiked wheel, but the wheel fell apart when she touched it. She was then beheaded, and legend says that angels carried her to Mount Sinai. She has been venerated since the tenth century.

W E D 26 (#505) green
Weekday

The Lectionary for Mass

◆ FIRST READING: The reading opens with a description of the afflictions preceding the end time as we heard in yesterday's reading. There is also an account of another vision in which those who were victorious against the beast (devil) are singing the praises of God.

◆ RESPONSORIAL PSALM: The antiphon is taken from the reading: praise of our God. The stanzas are from Psalm 98, likewise a song of praise calling on all creation and all peoples to sing God's praises.

◆ GOSPEL: Today's Gospel speaks of afflictions Jesus's followers will endure—very much a reality in the lives of the early Christians, betrayed by their families and friends, suffering civil persecutions—all because of their belief in Jesus's name. Jesus assures his followers of his presence with them and his protection of them.

T H U 27 (#506) green
Optional Mass for Thanksgiving Day (#943–947) white

The Lectionary for Mass

◆ FIRST READING: Today's reading consists of verses taken from two chapters of the Book of Revelation. Historically—in the sixth century before Christ—Babylon conquered Jerusalem and also led many of its citizens into exile.

God's victory over Babylon is celebrated in today's text. In context of the book of Revelation, Babylon was a code name for Rome, the enemy of God's people at the time of its composition. The Christian prophet is assured that God will ultimately triumph and his praises be sung forever by those who share in his victory. The reading ends with a saying that proclaims the joy and blessedness of those called to

---

the heavenly wedding feast of the Lamb—the ultimate fulfillment of God's covenant with Israel.

◆ RESPONSORIAL PSALM 100 is a hymn of praise sung by those who have entered God's holy dwelling. The antiphon is the last line of the First Reading.

◆ GOSPEL: In an apocalyptic tone, Luke describes the destruction of Jerusalem by the Gentile Romans. God's people must wait until the times are fulfilled. Then, in this unknown time, cosmic signs will anticipate the coming of the Son of Man. These signs must not frighten believers, for it will be the time of their redemption. Victorious in their struggle, they have every reason to stand up straight (a posture of freedom) when facing the judgment at the end.

F R I 28 (#507) green
Weekday

The Lectionary for Mass

◆ FIRST READING: We hear yet another of John's visions. In the first part of today's reading, it is clear that the power of the angel from heaven is stronger than the power of the evil one, who is cast into the abyss until the time is completed. This motif of judgment, punishment, and

reward continues throughout the reading. Next, John sees the souls of the martyrs reigning in glory with Christ. After this, he saw all of those who had died being brought to judgment and accountability at the end time, and rewarded or punished because of their deeds. Finally, John sees the new and transformed heaven and earth, and the glorious heavenly Jerusalem, the bride of the Lamb. She will be presented to her spouse and their joy will have no end.

◆ RESPONSORIAL PSALM: God lives among his people in the heavenly Jerusalem. The verses are from Psalm 83, a song sung by pilgrims on their way to the Temple, the dwelling place of God, in the earthly Jerusalem. The joy of being in God's presence here was but a foretaste of the joys of the age to come.

◆ GOSPEL: The signs Jesus has spoken of should serve as warning to people that the end, the coming of the Kingdom of God in all its fullness is near. Luke's audience, like other Christians of their day, believed that the end-time would be within their lifetimes.

S A T 29 (#508) green
Weekday

Optional Memorial of the Blessed Virgin Mary / white

Morning Mass: The Lectionary for Mass

◆ FIRST READING: We hear John's vision of God's throne in the heavenly Jerusalem. A river of life-giving water flows through the city. The tree of life grows there, fed by the waters of life, bearing healing fruit for all peoples (including the Gentile nations). God's faithful ones will triumph. What a promise of hope for God's people living in a time of darkness and oppression. All will be brought to perfection, life, and light when the Lord comes.

◆ RESPONSORIAL PSALM 95: The antiphon is taken from the end of the First Letter to the Corinthians (see also the end of the book of Revelation). The Aramaic words *Marana tha* are rendered "Lord, come." The stanzas are from Psalm 95, verses of praise and thanksgiving, acclaiming the sovereignty of the Lord, King over all, who is at the same time the loving Shepherd of his people.

◆ GOSPEL: Today's Gospel is a call to wakefulness and watchfulness in daily life, with an ongoing concern for what is most essential: the ultimate realities. We shall one day come before the Son of Man. Let us live so that we may stand before him in uprightness and receive the salvation that he so desires to give us.